Sizonqoba!
Outliving AIDS in Southern Africa

Busani Ngcaweni (ed.)

Sizonqoba! Outliving AIDS in Southern Africa

First Published in 2016 by the
Africa Institute of South Africa
PO Box 630
Pretoria 0001
South Africa

ISBN: 978-0-7983-0499-3

Project Manager: Mmakwena Chipu
Copy-Editing: Empressa
Proofreading: Bangula Educational Services
Cover Design and Layout: Jigsaw Graphic Design
Printing: Kadimah Printers

The Africa Institute of South Africa is a think tank and research organisation, focusing on political, socio-economic, international and development issues in contemporary Africa. The Institute conducts research, publishes books, monographs, occasional papers, policy briefs and a quarterly journal – Africa Insight. The Institute holds regular seminars on issues of topical interest. It is also home to one of the best library and documentation centres world-wide, with materials on every African country.

For more information, contact the Africa Institute of South Africa at
Private Bag X41, Pretoria, South Africa 0001, See more at:
Email publish@hsrc.ac.za; or visit our website at http://www.ai.org.za

Table of Contents

PART II
STRENGTHING THE MULTI-SECTORAL RESPONSE TO HIV AND AIDS
SECTORAL PERSPECTIVES AND EXPERIENCES

PART III
LEVERAGING SOCIAL AGENCY
PERSPECTIVES FROM ACTIVISTS AND PRACTITIONERS

Foreword

Sizonqoba! Outliving AIDS in Southern Africa, ('We will overcome') is a timely and important book as we enter the era of the Sustainable Development Goals and reach for the end of acquired immune deficiency syndrome (AIDS) as a public health threat. This seminal contribution will enrich and enhance global and local responses to HIV. It asks the reader to reflect on the lessons learnt over 30 years of this epidemic, the challenges we must still overcome and the possibility of an AIDS-free world in just a few years.

These stories inspire hope and confidence that South Africa will overcome the world's largest human immune deficiency (HIV) epidemic. *Sizonqoba! Outliving AIDS in Southern Africa,* is a clear, assertive articulation that victory is certain if we leave no one behind. Together, these chapters compel us to see the humanity of all people, recognise their dignity, and appreciate their agency. It challenges evolving systems to deliver health services appropriately, safely, with respect, and without discrimination against those who need them the most.

Sizonqoba! Outliving AIDS in Southern Africa, contains important material on the history of the HIV response in South Africa. This history's myriad storylines are crucial in depicting and explaining the shortcomings in South Africa's early responses to the epidemic. Clearly, understanding this history can benefit current and future generations who will face new and complex global health crises.

These stories also highlight the roles and contributions of people living with HIV, with case studies from the perspective of the AIDS movement's real-life protagonists. The case studies show how those living with, and affected by, HIV claimed their voice and agency, and why the biomedical narrative alone is inadequate in explaining our progress.

The world now looks to South Africa as a leader in bringing HIV services to every person, in every hidden pocket of society. The country has the largest HIV treatment programme in the world, which is saving millions of lives and eliminating the transmission of HIV from mother-to-child. This book highlights major prevention campaigns targeting specific groups, including adolescent girls and students at tertiary education institutions. It also illustrates that, despite excellent treatment and prevention campaigns, the number of new HIV infections in South Africa remains unacceptably high, at about 1000 new infections a day, and approximately three and a half million people living with HIV still lack access to treatment. Stigma and discrimination against vulnerable communities continue.

Poverty, hunger, unemployment, socioeconomic inequality, gender inequality, transactional sex, labour migration, violence, congested informal settlements, as well as ignorance about the spread of HIV, all increase the vulnerability of South Africans to HIV. This book makes a compelling case for a National Health Insurance Plan to expand access to quality health care to all South Africans.

South Africa willingly shares responsibility with international donors by funding more than 80 per cent of its own HIV response. Yet it remains one of the most unequal societies in the world. The twenty-first International AIDS Conference in Durban in July 2016 took place against a backdrop of rising unemployment and inequality. This must be of concern to the people of South Africa and the world. *Sizonqoba! Outliving AIDS in Southern Africa,* underscores the need to strengthen global solidarity while maintaining the momentum to do more with limited domestic resources.

The goal of ending AIDS by 2030 in South Africa is within our reach, and her victory will resonate across every country of the world. We cheered her people on when apartheid was defeated, and we look forward to seeing her end AIDS with the same determination, compassion and respect for human rights.

I congratulate the researchers, authors, editors and publisher for reminding us that South Africa will always be a land of hope, inspiration and unending possibility. *Sizonqoba*!

Michel Sidibé
UNAIDS Executive Director and Under-Secretary-General of the United Nations

Acknowledgements

To begin with, I would like to thank my employer, The Presidency of the Republic of South Africa, for affording me the opportunity to freelance in the demanding world of book writing. Without their tolerance and belief in the significance of documenting history as part of the dual project of building a firm foundation for mastering state craft and to build a heritage, this project would have remained just an idea. In 2009, President Jacob Zuma challenged the public service to do things differently. Many count his 2009 World AIDS (acquired immune deficiency syndrome) Day speech as a decisive policy turn, or a manifestation of the mantra of doing things differently. For my part, the task is easier, balancing a punishing work schedule with the on-going pursuit of intellectual reflections.

A word of appreciation goes to my colleague, Tsakani Chaka, who excellently volunteered her time as an editorial assistant to this project. Without her meticulous attention to detail and co-ordination, this project would probably have taken another year, if not more.

I acknowledge the generous support from the President's Emergency Plan for AIDS Relief (PEPFAR) and Adcock Ingram, which enabled the publication of this edition. Book publishing can be a costly exercise unless there are funders like these two, willing to invest in projects that make humble contributions towards the building of the intellectual archive on the local and international efforts to manage the AIDS epidemic.

To my publisher, Mmakwena Chipu at the Human Sciences Research Council (HSRC), thanks for taking on this project and for remaining calm in spite of many missed deadlines. Even though we argued about some of the peer reviewers' comments, we appreciate all the criticism and suggestions made, knowing full well that without input from peer reviewers we might miss important insights and details whilst chasing publication deadlines.

A special tribute goes to all the individuals and organisations that I have interacted with in the South African National AIDS Council (SANAC) over the past seven years. These are the voices from whose echoes the idea of this edition germinated. Some have contributed chapters to this edition, like my colleagues Dr Nono Simelela, Dr Yogan Pillay, former CEO of the HSRC, Professor Olive Shisana, Professor Helen Rees, Thulani Tshefuta of the South African Youth Council, Nkululeko Nxesi and Mmapaseka 'Steve' Letsike who coordinates civil society within SANAC. My current and former bosses who lead SANAC, Deputy

President Cyril Ramaphosa and former president Kgalema Motlanthe, have inspired this project in many ways by asking penetrating questions, which I believe many chapters in this collection attempt to unpack.

Finally, thank you to my family for their patience whilst I (ab)used family time to work on the manuscript both at home and abroad, where I spent months as Visiting Scholar at Ryerson University working with Professor Anver Saloojee. My supervisor at the University of Johannesburg (UJ), Professor Mary Galvin, now that this project is done, I am sure we can get back to the business of working on the thesis. Professor Tshilidzi Marwala, here is my humble contribution to the scholarly work of UJ's Institute for Pan-African Thought and Conversations.

Dedication

This book is dedicated to the health workers, activists, *oNompilo, amavolontiya*, bureaucrats and all those whose efforts have 'saved' humanity from the perils of HIV, AIDS, TB and other sexually transmitted infections. It is a salute to the local and international development partners who reawakened the spirit of human solidarity, reminding us that, working together, we can do more. Most importantly, this is a tribute to the women of Southern Africa, mothers and grandmothers, who suspended their lives to care for the loved ones affected and infected by the HI Virus.

About the Editor

Busani Ngcaweni is Deputy Director-General in The Presidency and Chief of Staff to the Deputy President. He holds an MSc from Natal University and is pursuing doctoral studies in the Development Studies Department with the University of Johannesburg where he is also a fellow at the Institute for Pan African Thought and Conversations. At the time of completing this book, he was Visiting Scholar at Ryerson University in Toronto. His previous books include *The Future we Chose: Emerging Perspectives on the Centenary of the ANC* (AISA, 2013), *Liberation Diaries: Reflections on 20 Years of Democracy in South Africa* (Jacana Media, 2014), and *Nelson R. Mandela: Decolonial Ethics of Liberation and Servant Leadership* (Africa World Press, 2016) with Professor Sabelo J. Ndlovu-Gatsheni.

About the Contributors

Fareed Abdullah is Chief Executive Officer of the South African National AIDS Council (SANAC). He has served in various positions in government and the development community, contributing to the fight against HIV. Together with his colleagues at SANAC, he has been instrumental in promoting the scale-up of treatment, prevention and human rights programmes for key populations.

Ramneek Ahluwalia is a qualified medical doctor who also has a Master's in Business Administration and a PHD in Public Health. He is currently Director of the Higher Education and Training HIV/ AIDS Programme (HEAIDS), responsible for mitigating the epidemic of HIV and AIDS, TB and STIs and other social and health challenges within all Public Colleges and Universities in South Africa.

Thuthula Balfour-Kaipa is a qualified medical doctor and public health medicine specialist who is currently the Head of Health at the Chamber of Mines of South Africa where she leads the Chamber's TB and HIV screening project.

Hendrieta Bogopane-Zulu is Deputy Minister of the Deparment of Social Development, South Africa. She is currently the Chair of the African Union Specialised Technical Committee on Health, Population and Drug Control.

Imeraan Cassiem, is the Strategic Information Manager for the BroadReach Corporation. He has more than two decades of Public Health sector experience, including a decade of specialised focus on programme implementation and performance monitoring and evaluation at all levels of the system.

Colin Chasi is Head of the Department of Communication and Media Studies at the University of Johannesburg. His interest is in the theory and philosophy of communication, particularly in sense making and decision making, including health and development issues.

Ernest Darkoh is an internationally-known expert in strategic healthcare systems planning, development and large-scale programme implementation, including Botswana's highly-acclaimed Antiretroviral Treatment Programme. He co-founded BroadReach and advises governments across the globe on the development of public and private health programmes as well as international organisations, including the World Bank, the World Health Organization (WHO) and the United Nations Children's Emergency Fund (UNICEF).

Sinead Delany-Moretlwe is a medical doctor with over 15 years' experience in sexual and reproductive health and HIV prevention research. She is currently an Associate Professor and Director of Research at the Wits Reproductive Health Institute.

Nancy Fee is a Senior Policy and Strategic Adviser of the Joint United Nations Programme on HIV and AIDS (UNAIDS) South Africa. She has worked for UNAIDS for the past 20 years (including five years in the Western Pacific), for the World Bank as a HIV technical adviser for South Asia, and as UNAIDS Country Director in Vietnam and Indonesia.

Vanessa Govender is a medical doctor, an occupational health and public health professional who is the owner and director of Masakhane Strategic Health Consulting (Pty) Ltd. Dr Govender is an internationally published author, researcher, editor, speaker and presenter, also at Parliamentary level.

Bernard Katz has over 14 years' experience in Innovation Management, Enterprise Engineering and Business Improvement. He is involved in spearheading the vision for, and management of, BroadReach's data analytic division, developing analytics platforms, tailoring client solutions, integrating data systems and utilising cross-sectoral data.

Mmapaseka 'Steve' Letsike is an activist, feminist, leader, mentor and human rights advocate who is the founding Director of Access Chapter 2. She is a leader and chairperson of the South African National AIDS Council (SANAC) Civil Society Forum and co-chairs SANAC with the Deputy President of the Republic of South Africa, Mr Cyril Ramaphosa.

Amy Maphagela is a current Masters graduate at the University of Johannesburg and a prospective PhD candidate. Her research interests include health communication campaigns, HIV/AIDS as well as communication for social change.

Brad Mears was the Chief Executive Officer of the South African Business Coalition of Health and AIDS (SABCOHA) from 2004 until 2014 where he sought to create an understanding of HIV and AIDS within the business sector and create awareness of available solutions.

Candice Mitchell is currently working as a Strategic Information Analyst for BroadReach Healthcare. Her main focus of research has been to examine the various social, political and economic contexts of infectious diseases in South Africa, with particular emphasis on treatment.

Senzeni Mkhize is a senior manager in the Priorities Programme Directorate, Office of the Premier, KwaZulu-Natal, overseeing the implementation of the province's signature integrated service delivery programme (Operation Sukuma Sakhe), and the Inkululeko Development Projects.

Erasmus Morah is UNAIDS Country Director for South Africa, and previously held several other positions at the UNAIDS headquarters in Geneva and other countries, including Country Director for UNAIDS Kenya and Malawi.

Veni Naidu has extensive senior level experience in social science research, public policies and administration, health system strengthening, strategic planning, business development and marketing. For the past 16 years, her work focused on social and economic development, particularly in areas including the social and economic impact of HIV and AIDS on business, and Operation Sukuma Sakhe – an integrated service delivery model for the province of KwaZulu-Natal.

Fikile Ndlovu currently directs the implementation of Priority Programmes in the Office of the Premier in Kwa-Zulu Natal province, providing strategic leadership on issues of health systems strengthening, poverty reduction, child health, integrated service delivery, climate change and socio-economic development.

Tryphinah Ngwenya is a development practitioner with over 30 years of working experience at district and provincial level. Currently, she is the Director of the HIV and AIDS Directorate in the Office of the Premier, KwaZulu-Natal, and she has been extensively involved in the implementation of Operation Sukuma Sakhe.

Nkululeko Nxesi is currently the Director of Non-profit Organisations (NPO) Governance and Stakeholder relations at the Department of Social Development. Nxesi is also a co-founder and former Executive Director of Community Development Foundation of South Africa (CODEFSA) and a former National Director and Secretary General of National Association of People Living with HIV and AIDS (NAPWA).

Nompumelelo Nzimande is a lecturer and demographer at the School of the Built Environment and Development Studies at the University of KwaZulu-Natal, and is the Academic Coordinator for the discipline of Population Studies within the School. Her key areas of research interest include demography of South Africa and determinants and consequences of different forms of family formation.

Thesla Palanee-Phillips is a medical scientist who specialises in HIV prevention and research in at-risk populations, including young women, and men who have sex with men. She currently serves as a Director of Network Trials at the Wits Reproductive Health and HIV Institute.

Charlotte Pelletan is currently a Ph.D candidate and part of the public policy research programme at the Institute of Political Science of Bordeaux (France). In her Doctoral research, she endeavours to build inclusive access mechanisms to new therapies by re-thinking access to medicines through the reconnection of health systems, architecture of pharmaceutical industry and innovation dynamics.

Yogan Pillay is the Deputy Director-General: HIV & AIDS, TB and MCWH at the Department of Health, South Africa. He is currently overseeing the strengthening of the district health system as well as communicable diseases, non-communicable diseases and nutrition programmes.

Sithembiso Radebe is a civil attorney, motivational speaker, preacher, social and HIV activist, and counsellor on HIV and AIDS-related issues, who has been living with HIV since 2009. She has been practising as an attorney for nine years and worked for Gert Sibande District Municipality. She joined Legal Aid South Africa as a Civil Attorney and is currently a Supervisory Attorney at the Legal Aid Advice Line in Braamfontein.

Pholokgolo Ramothwala is the director and founder of the non-profit organisation, Positive Convention Network – a network for professionals living with HIV – and a public speaker and trainer. His work experience in the field of HIV has always focused on positive living and stigma mitigation for people living with HIV. He has been living openly with HIV for the past 18 years.

Ravikanthi Rapiti, MPH: is currently a Research Associate at the Higher Education and training HIV/TB/STI General Health and Wellness Programme (HEAIDS). She has extensive experience working on public-private partnerships and policy development initiatives in the national and international public health arena. She has designed, implemented and managed large, complex projects. Her cumulative experience has been in the managing of field offices and field-funded projects in Southern Africa and coordinating core-funded activities. She is responsible for designing and supporting the implementation of multi-faceted social and health programmes. She has facilitated collaboration at a multi-sectoral level to capacitate leadership and strengthen governance. Ms Rapiti has strong research skills and has written about M&E concepts being used to provide evidence-based outputs. She has presented widely at International & National Conferences, forums and symposiums across the world relating to HIV and AIDS.

Helen Rees is an internationally renowned researcher and expert in HIV prevention, reproductive health and vaccines. She is the founder and Executive Director of the Wits Reproductive Health and HIV Institute of the University of the Witwatersrand.

Natalie Ridgard is a South Africa Communication and Global Outreach Adviser of UNAIDS. She has extensive research experience in media reporting on HIV in South Africa.

John Sargent is recognised globally as a healthcare solutions thought-leader in market development strategy, health systems analytics and optimisation, and public-private partnerships in emerging markets. John consults governments, multinational companies and donor organisations, and is a co-founder of BroadReach.

Ian Saunderson is currently the Head of Programme (Communication Studies) at the University of Limpopo. During his Doctoral studies, he investigated HIV and AIDS at a South African university.

Palesa Sekhejane is a medical technologist and is currently a research specialist at the Human Sciences Research Council (HSRC). Her current research interests are in health governance, biosciences, innovation and technology.

Sipho Senabe is an Occupational Medical Practitioner who is currently a Chief Director: Macro Policy Analysis at the Department of Public Service and Administration (dpsa). He is a Registrar in Occupational Medicine at the University of the Witwatersrand.

Celicia Serenata is currently a Technical Head for the OPTIMIZE project at the Wits Reproductive Health and HIV Institute. She has a 23-year background in working in the health field, including in the Ministry of Health in South Africa, US Centres for Disease Control and Prevention, (CDC), Medical Research Council and Clinton Health Access Initiative (CHAI).

Geoff Setswe is an Acting Executive Director in the HIV/AIDS, STIs and TB (HAST) research programme. He is a behavioural scientist and has been in the HIV and AIDS field for about 30 years in various capacities and has published widely on the social and behavioural aspects of HIV and AIDS.

Olive Shisana is both a social scientist and a public health specialist currently serving as President and Chief Executive Officer of the Evidence Based Solutions company. She has widely researched and published, including on HIV and AIDS, and her work is read and cited globally.

Nono Simelela is the Social Policy Advisor to Deputy President Cyril Ramaphosa, providing advice on a broad range of social issues including health. Her interest is in women's issues and HIV. She has extensive experience in HIV issues, including the development of the country's first HIV treatment programme.

Jonathan Stadler, an anthropologist with over 20 years of research experience, is the Technical Head of Social Sciences and Senior Researcher at the Wits Reproductive Health and HIV Institute, an institute within the Faculty of Health Sciences at the University of the Witwatersrand.

Tom Zhuwau is a researcher and monitoring and evaluation specialist with broad experience in community and social development, public health, tropical diseases epidemiology, policy development, poverty reduction, integrated service delivery and planning, at both policy and programme levels. He is a National Engagement Manager: Integrated Service Delivery Model, at BroadReach.

Nompumelelo Zungu is a Research Director at the Human Sciences Research Council (HSRC). She has over 17 years' research experience and has extensive experience managing national and international collaborations on HIV and AIDS research. She has expertise in risks involved in sexual behaviour among men and adolescents.

Abbreviations and Acronyms

3TC	lamivudine
ABC	Abstinence, Be faithful and Condomise
ACTG 076	Pediatric AIDS Clinical Trials Group Study
AEOs	Assistant extension officers
AGYW	adolescent girls and young women
AIDC EC	Automotive Industry Development Centre Eastern Cape
AIDS	acquired immune deficiency syndrome
AIDS2000	XIII International AIDS Conference
AIDS2014	2014 global AIDS Conference
ANC	African National Congress
APIME	assess, plan, implement, monitor and evaluate
APIs	active pharmaceutical ingredients
APRM	African Peer Review Mechanism
ART	Antiretroviral treatment
ARV	antiretroviral
AU	African Union
AWA	AIDS Watch Africa
AZT	azidothymidine
BER	Bureau for Economic Research
BME	benefit medical examinations
BRICS	Brazil, Russia, India, China and South Africa
BUSA	Business Unity South Africa
CAB	community advisory boards
CAPRISA	Centre for the Aids Programme of Research in South Africa
CBOs	Community Based Organisations
CCGs	community caregivers
CCM	Global Fund Country Coordinating Mechanism
CCMDD	Central Chronic Medicine Dispensing and Distribution
CCMT	Comprehensive Care, Management and Treatment Plan for HIV and AIDS
CCT	Conditional Cash Transfer
CDC	Centres for Disease Control and Prevention
CDWs	community development workers
CEO	Chief Executive Officer
CHAI	Clinton Health Access Initiative

CHAPS	Centre for HIV and AIDS Prevention Studies
CHGA	Commission on the HIV and AIDS Governance in Africa
CHWs	Community Health Workers
CI	confidence interval
CODEFSA	Community Development Foundation of South Africa
COG	Centre of Government Department
ConCourt	Constitutional Court
COP16	Sixteenth session of the Conference of the Parties
COPC	Community-Oriented Primary Care
CSF	Civil Society Forum
CSO	civil society organisations
CUP	100% condom use policy
DACs	District AIDS Councils
DBSA	Development Bank of Southern Africa
DfID	UK Department for International Development
DHET	Department of Higher Education and Training
DHIS	District Health Information System
DHMIS	District Health Management Information Systems
DIP	District Implementation Plan
DMO	designated medical officer
DMP	disease management programme
DMR	Department of Mineral Resources
DoH	Department of Health
DORA	Division of Revenue Act
DPME	Department of Performance Management and Evaluation
DPME	Department of Planning Monitoring and Evaluation
DPSA	Department of Public Service and Administration
DPSA	Disabled People South Africa
DREAMS	determined, resilient, empowered, AIDS-free, mentored and safe
DST	Department of Science and Technology
DTI	Department of Trade and Industry
DTT	District Task Team
ECD	Early Childhood Development
EFV	Efavirenz/Emtricitabine/Zidovudine
eMTCT	elimination of mother-to-child transmission
ESA	Eastern and Southern Africa
ESKOM	Electricity Supply Commission
FDA	US Food and Drug Administration
FDCs	fixed-dose combination

FTC	Emricitabine
GBV	gender based violence
GDP	gross domestic product
GEAR	Growth, Employment and Redistribution
GEMS	Government Employee Medical Scheme
GERD	Gastroesophageal Reflux Disease
GIPA	greater involvement of people living with HIV
GIZ	German Organisation for International Cooperation
Global Fund	Global Fund to Fight AIDS, Tuberculosis and Malaria
GOVERD	Government expenditure on research and development
GPA	Global AIDS Programme
GPs	general practitioners
GTZ	Organisation for Technical Cooperation
HAART	triple combination therapy
HCT	HIV Counselling and Testing
HEAIDS	Higher Education and Training in HIV and AIDS Programme
HEIs	Higher Education Institutions
HESA	Higher Education South Africa
HIORS	HEAIDS Integrated Online Reporting System
HIV Code	South African Code of Good Practice on HIV and Aids and the World of Work, 2012
HIV	human immunodeficiency virus
HODs	Heads of Department
HPC	Health Policy Committee
HPTN	HIV Prevention Trials Network
HSRC	Human Sciences Research Council
HST	Health Systems Trust
IAT	Institute for Advanced Tooling
IDP	Integrated Development Plan
IDUs	injecting drug users
IESC	International Executive Services Corp
IHPM	Institute for Health and Productivity Management
ILO	International Labour Organisation
IMC	Inter-Ministerial Committee on AIDS
IMC	Integrated Marketing Communications
IP	Intellectual property
IPR	Intellectual Property Rights
IPV	intimate partner violence
ISDM	integrated service delivery models

IT	information technology
JICA	Japanese International Cooperation Agency
KYE/KYR	Know Your Epidemic, Know Your Response
KZN	KwaZulu-Natal
LACs	Local AIDS Councils
LGBTI	lesbian, gay, bisexual, transgender/transsexual and intersexed
LTF	loss to follow up
LTT	Local Task Team
M&E	Monitoring and Evaluation
MAP	World Bank Multi-Country AIDS Programme
MCC	Medicines Control Council
MCP	multiple concurrent sexual partnerships
MDGs	Millennium Development Goals
MECs	Members of the Executive Council
MHSA	Mine Health and Safety Act (Act No. 29 of 1996)
MHSC	Mine Health and Safety Council
MinMEC	Minister and Members of Executive Council
MMC	Medical male circumcision
MOSH	Mining Industry Occupational Safety and Health
MPSA	Minister of Public Service and Administration
MSM	men who have sex with men
MTCT	mother-to-child transmission
MTR	mid-term review
NACOSA	Networking HIV and AIDS Community of South Africa
NACs	National AIDS Councils
NAPWA	National Association of People with AIDS
NASA	National Spending Assessment
NCDs	non-communicable diseases
NDoH	National Department of Health
NEDLAC	National Economic Development and Labour Council
NHI	National Health Insurance
NHLS	National Health Laboratory Service
NIDS	National Indicator Data Set
NIMART	Nurse Initiated and Managed Anti-Retroviral Treatment
NRF	National Research Foundation
NSG	National School of Government
NSI	National System of Innovation
NSP	National Strategic Plan
NUM	National Union of Mineworkers

NVP	nevirapine
OECD	Organisation for Economic Cooperation and Development
OEMs	original equipment manufacturers
OSS	Operation Sukuma Sakhe
OVC	orphans and vulnerable children
PALAMA	Public Administration and Leadership and Management Academy
PCA	Provincial AIDS Council
PCR	polymerase chain reaction
PEP	post-exposure prophylaxis
PEPFAR	The United States President's Emergency Plan for AIDS Relief
PETS-QSDS	Public Sector Expenditure Tracking Survey and Quantity Service Delivery Survey
PFIP	PEPFAR Partnership Framework Implementation Plan
PHC	Primary Healthcare Clinic
PICT	Provider-Initiated Counselling and Testing
PILIR	Policy and Procedure on Incapacity Leave and Ill Health Retirement
PLHIV	people living with HIV
PLWA	people living with AIDS
PMTCT	prevention of mother to child transmission
PPPs	Public-Private Partnerships
PrEP	pre-exposure prophylaxis
PSR	Public Service Regulations
PSVW	Public service volunteer week
PTT	Provincial Task Team
R&D	research and development
RADAR	Rural AIDS and Development Action Research Programme
RCT	randomised controlled trials
RDP	Reconstruction and Development Programme
SAB	South African Breweries
SABCOHA	South African Business Coalition on HIV/AIDS
SABS	South African Bureau of Standards
SADC	Southern African Development Community
SAMI	South African Mining Industry
SAMRC	South African Medical Research Council
SANAC	South African National AIDS Council
SANS	South African National Standard 16001
SCOA	Standard Charter of Accounts
SCPVs	social crime prevention volunteers
SDGs	Sustainable Development Goals

SES	socioeconomic status
SMME	small, medium and micro-sized enterprises
SRCs	sports and recreation coordinators
SRH	sexual and reproductive health
SRL	Socially Responsible Licensing
StatsSA	Statistics South Africa
STDs	sexually transmitted diseases
STIs	sexually transmitted infections
T4P	treatment for prevention
TAC	Treatment Action Campaign
TAF	tenofivir alafenamide fumarate
TB	tuberculosis
TDF	tenofovir disporoxil fumarate
TDF-FTC	tenofovir with emtricitabine
TFV	tenofovir
THP	traditional healthcare provider
THRIP	Technology and Human Resources for Industry Programme
TIA	Technology Innovation Agency
TOPs	termination of pregnancies
Treasury	The National Treasury
TTT	Technical Task Teams
TVET	Technical and Vocational Education and Training
TVETs	Technical Vocational Education and Training Colleges
UNHCR	United Nations High Commissioner for Refugees
UK	United Kingdom
UN	United Nations
UNAIDS	Joint United Nations Programme on HIV/AIDS
UNCRPD	United Nations Convention on the Rights of Persons with Disabilities
UNDP	United Nations Development Programme
UNECA	United Nations Economic Commission for Africa
UNESCO	United Nations Educational, Scientific and Cultural Organization
UNFPA	United Nations Population Fund
UNGASS	United Nations General Assembly on HIV and AIDS
UNICEF	United Nations Children's Fund
UNODC	United Nations Office on Drugs and Crime
US	United States of America
USAID	United States Agency for International Development
UTT	universal test and treat
VCT	voluntary counselling and testing

VMMC	voluntary medical male circumcision
WBPHCOT	Ward-Based Primary health Care Outreach Team
WFP	World Food Programme
WHO	World Health Organization
WSU	Walter Sisulu University
WTT	Ward Task Teams
ZDV	zidovudine

Introduction
Outliving AIDS in the Era of Widening Inequality in Southern Africa

Busani Ngcaweni

Introduction

The story of South Africa is punctuated with tales of hope and triumph of the human spirit over socio-political systems of colonialism and apartheid. The 1994 breakthrough ushered in a vision of a society founded on the values of national unity, non-racialism, non-sexism, democracy and prosperity for all. This new inclusive body-politic was personified by South Africa's founding president, Nelson Mandela, whose revolutionary morality stand as a towering vignette showcasing the society we want and deserve to live in.

As this 'new' story of the democratic order was unfolding, a new existential threat emerged, the ravaging Human Immunodeficiency Virus (HIV) epidemic overwhelming the population and the new democratic government. This would prove to be a tragedy draining the lifeblood of hope from a new nation; made worse by what many perceived to be an idiosyncratic Acquired Immune Deficiency Syndrome (AIDS) denialism and anti-science discourse at the highest leadership levels of the country. Burial businesses boomed. HIV positive people lost their jobs. Stigma ran riot. Children were orphaned, left either with grandmothers or forced to look after younger siblings. Battle lines were drawn between the state and civil society fighting over what ought to have been a humane response to this existential threat. Ultimately the courts prevailed and the government made a sharp policy turn.

This narrative has dramatically shifted over the last decade to become the story of how a nation clawed its way out from under the unbearable weight of death from the disease of AIDS. What is the real story of this monumental transition? Was it due to political change, phenomenal advancements in science, or the development of drugs and diagnostics? Or did the ground-level pressure of the activists, clinicians and the non-governmental organisations (NGOs) – those that battled daily with the virus – eventually break through? Is there another big chapter to come in this narrative? Can we claim to be winning the war with almost 400 000 new HIV infections in the last year alone, and without any decline in the absolute number of new infections between 2010 and 2015?

The aim of this book is to open up this discussion, in the hope that we will better understand the phenomenon of HIV in a country that has faced the fullest might of the disease and yet, after first faltering, has made more progress than any other country in the world in its response to HIV. It aims to reflect the complexity of this narrative and the range of widely differing insights by featuring what is likely the largest number of contributors in a single publication on the subject in South Africa, as well as a full spectrum of specialised areas, ranging from high-end science to personal reflections. This means that the book can be read in any order once the reader has perused the introduction, depending on the subject matter that is of most interest.

The story begins 22 years ago as South Africa emerged from the system of apartheid colonialism characterised by the worst human development indicators for the black majority. The 1994 democratic breakthrough marked a significant turn for those who had suffered for centuries under racial segregation in all facets of social, political and economic life. For its part, the liberation movement, led by the African National Congress (ANC), presented a humanist and inclusive vision of a new society characterised as democratic, non-racial, non-sexist, united and prosperous. By building the biggest international solidarity movement in modern history, the liberation movement successfully mobilised the international community[1] to take a moral stand by isolating the 'skunk' of the world, as Nelson Mandela referred to apartheid South Africa,[2] thereby siding with the poor and the oppressed.

In the coming years, this triumph of the human spirit and international solidary would return to save South Africa from yet another existential threat: the AIDS epidemic. By and large, this AIDS epidemic was present but not making headlines until after the 1994 democratic order.[3]

The significance of the 'emergence' and spread of the AIDS epidemic after 1994 was a backdrop to the poverty and deprivation that was a material reality for the majority of South Africans. These were people who faced the psychological burden of being alienated from the land of their birth and exclusion from the country's body politic and the economy, who also had to deal with the scourge of HIV and AIDS and, at the same time, contend with the broader struggle for socio-economic transformation.

Soon thereafter, historical images of apartheid massacres, the iconography of township life and rural poverty were replaced by images of suffering orphans and funerals. This would proceed to change the tone for a new government engaged in transformative midwifery, giving the country the odious crown of AIDS capital of the world alongside its emergence as the world's newest and most miraculous democracy.

As stated earlier, the HIV epidemic had been a global phenomenon for more than 20 years by 1994, but amid the inequality of South Africa's public health system and the apartheid regime's disregard for the dignity or value of black lives, this biomedical challenge was low down the list of apartheid priorities.[4] Over the years it would morph from a 'disease of homosexuals'[5] into a disease of migrant workers[6] and sex workers. As more records of pregnant women with HIV came to light, it soon became an epidemic facing the general population beyond just the poor.[7]

Had HIV been purely a biomedical issue it may have been a different challenge to confront as the solution would have been largely scientific – engineered in a laboratory. As many chapters in this book demonstrate, it became apparent that it is as much a social and economic issue, the management of which depends on political will and bold leadership. The virus had 'contaminated' our social fabric too, thriving in the threads and weaves of moral judgement, religious and cultural prejudice and the broad fabric of stigma arising from fear, ignorance and the narrow focus on heterosexual transmission.[8]

Elsewhere in the world, in the early 1980s, fear and social disapproval had been fuelled by the pre-existing prejudice against homosexuals, with whom conservative groups around the world had associated the outbreak and globalisation of the virus. Back in Southern Africa, issues such as treatment, transmission by different means and the inequality in intimate relations (that deprived women in the patriarchal world order of their constitutional right to their physical integrity) persisted; while unproductive conspiracy theories about the efficacy of treatment further distracted national attention. The national turnaround – in terms of public policy, partnerships and resource mobilisation – has, in the past decade or so, shifted the country's focus from those early days of crowded cemetery processions to the hope, relief and dignity secured for millions of South Africans by the biggest AIDS response programme in the world.[9]

The staggering scale of the modern AIDS epidemic in South Africa is a physical representation of the inequality and oppression that has existed within the social and political structure of the country for centuries.[10] Faced with the reality of increasing deaths and an estimation of the severity of HIV and AIDS, the South African government had to take another look at their public policies in order to shift the country's focus from crowded cemeteries to hope. The story of the AIDS response in South Africa over the past four years is one of great progress after almost a decade of complex and tragic denialism, which united the world and civil society in a way not seen since the opposition to apartheid.[11]

Shifting AIDS Narratives: From Fear and Death to Life and Hope

The turnaround in the management of the AIDS epidemic in South Africa has moved us, as the metanarrative of this book suggests, from the apartheid paradigm of racial segregation, poverty and social exclusion[12] (pre-1994) to the AIDS epidemic paradigm of fear, stigma and death. Starting about a decade ago, the world's biggest AIDS programme has ushered in a paradigm of life, hope and a future. As we will read in the following chapters, this paradigm of life is a product of collective effort nationally, regionally and internationally. It borrowed from the best traditions of the anti-apartheid struggle: resistance, social mobilisation and unity. It benefited from the best traditions of the anti-apartheid struggle – international solidarity – made up of individuals, governments, communities and organisations, inspired by the idea that life and dignity are a universal human right to be enjoyed by all, irrespective of economic status.

As we celebrate the replacement of the paradigms of oppression and death ('people are dying' as diligently told by Barnett and Whiteside),[13] we are reminded in the chapters of this book that a bigger battle lies ahead. This is the prevention battle. Controlling runaway infection rates, especially among young people, remains a challenge. Some suggest that South Africa's AIDS response has become a victim of its own success. As mortality, morbidity and associated stigma have declined, a sense of complacency has set in. It might even be that, among the middle class in particular, anecdotal trends point to a growing sense of invincibility.

It is for this reason, therefore, that researchers are expending effort and resources studying the social determinants of the epidemic. This is more urgent, given the shifting political economy of HIV infections.

For its part, this book explores this intertextuality of the shifting political economy and the social trends it has produced, which create conditions for the rise in HIV infections. Whereas a decade ago the epidemic was driven by conditions of poverty, deprivation, migrancy and gender-based violence,[14] today it has assumed or added other dimensions including social media, electronic media, reality television and inequality. This challenges prevention strategies to move beyond traditional approaches of above and below the line messaging and condom distribution. To consign HIV to the museum of the history of epidemics, there has to be greater use of social and electronic media, which have created social bubbles where unprotected sex and multiple concurrent partnerships take place.

The book does not necessarily explore this social media phenomenon, save for some of the later chapters that make for interesting reading, although it is worth spending a great deal of time reflecting on various social phenomena that fuel the epidemic. As far as declining knowledge levels are concerned, a study by the Human Sciences Research Council[15] observed that disinvestment in AIDS communications by national government has eroded earlier gains as trends show diminishing knowledge levels among significant sections of the youth population. Add growing gender, inter- and intra-class inequality into the matrix, and the situation deteriorates further. Hence our reference to the shifting political economy of HIV infections with concomitant social trends that reproduced vulnerability to HIV infections.

Prevention: The Next Frontier in AIDS Management

In July 2016, South Africa hosted the biennial International AIDS Conference in Durban. This was the second time that this conference came to South Africa, the first being July 2000. Many chapters in this book document the state of the epidemic and the politics that went with it that year. As many of the conference proceedings and public commentary showed, the 2016 conference took place under significantly altered conditions. The imagery was that of life and hope. There was greater coherence and cooperation between government, civil society, the private sector, international agencies and other role players.

The context in which the HIV and AIDS epidemic continues to expand in countries around the world is one of growing polarisation between rich and poor. This results in the increasing isolation of some segments of the population at a time when others are perversely integrated into the criminal economies of international drug smuggling and the like, and increasing social inequalities that seem to be an integral part of globalisation based on neoliberal economic policies.[16]

Since its very beginning, HIV and AIDS have been subject to uniquely intense scientific controversy and political struggles over the origin of the disease, and the causes of its epidemic spread, in Sub-Saharan Africa.[17] Throughout this decade, the prevailing narrative on the links between socioeconomic status and HIV portrays poor individuals and households as being more vulnerable to HIV infection,[18] and least able to cope with the ensuing impacts of AIDS-related disease and death.

HIV continues to be a major global public health issue, having claimed more than 35 million lives thus far. According to the World Health Organization (WHO), there were approximately 36.7 (34.0–39.8) million people living with HIV at the end of 2015 with 2.1 (1.8–2.4) million people becoming newly infected with HIV in 2015 globally.[19]

The epidemiology of HIV and AIDS in Africa is fundamentally different from that of the rest of the world.[20] Africa is one of the most important global public health issues of our time, perhaps in the history of mankind, and AIDS is one of the top causes of death on the continent.[21] Globally, Africa is the poorest continent with by far the most serious AIDS epidemic, but it is in Southern Africa where socio-economic, gender inequalities and population mobility are most extreme. This is where AIDS is hyperendemic (one-third of all people living with HIV reside in southern Africa).[22]

Sub-Saharan Africa contains about 10 per cent of the world's population, yet, in 2001, accounted for over two-thirds of 40 million people living with HIV; had 68 per cent of the incidence of HIV infections and 77 per cent of AIDS deaths; and accounted for more than 90 per cent of AIDS orphans and children infected with HIV.[23] In 2007, an estimated 1.7 million adults and children in this region became newly infected, while 1.6 million died of AIDS.[24] To date Sub-Saharan Africa remains the most affected region in the world and is home to almost 67 per cent of all people living with HIV (an estimated 22.5 million).[25]

South Africa is home to the largest concentration of people living with HIV anywhere in the world.[26] The AIDS epidemic has had many negative implications for South African society, which stem from the illness and eventual death resulting from HIV and AIDS.[27] When AIDS first emerged few could know how the epidemic would evolve, and fewer still could describe with any certainty the best way of combating it.[28] The estimated overall HIV prevalence rate at the time of writing was approximately 11.2 per cent of the total South African population. Furthermore, the total number of people living with HIV was estimated at approximately 6.9 million in 2015. For people aged 15–49 years, an estimated 16.6 per cent of the population is HIV positive.[29]

Globally, adolescent girls and young women aged 15–24 years are particularly at high risk of being infected with HIV.[30] According to UNAIDS, an estimated 20 per cent of adolescent girls and young women (AGYW) in the world, compared with 14 per cent of adolescent boys and young men, were newly infected with HIV in 2015.[31] Furthermore, in Sub-Saharan Africa, 25 per cent of AGYW, compared to 12 per cent of adolescent boys and young men, were newly infected in the same year.

The HIV epidemic was a silent one until the end of apartheid in 1994, but cases in the general population began to increase, with 7.4 per cent of pregnant women reported to be HIV positive and an estimated 1 500 people reported to be infected every 24 hours.[32] The racial and gender picture changed: there were more black African women and men living with HIV, compared to other racial groups.[33] Although the epidemic in South Africa is generalised, there are specific groups that have HIV prevalence above the national average, and which are classified as key populations with higher risk of HIV exposure. These groups are: black African females aged 20–34 years (HIV prevalence of 31.6 per cent), people co-habiting (30.9%), black African males aged 25–49 years (25.7%), disabled persons 15 years and older (16.7%), high-risk alcohol drinkers 15 years and older (14.3%), and recreational drug users (12.7%).[34]

Table 1 HIV prevalence of persons aged two years and older by age group, sex and race, South Africa, 2002, 2005, 2008 and 2012.

	2002		2005		2008		2012	
AGE	N	HIV+%	N	HIV+%	N	HIV+%	N	HIV+%
Total	8428	11.4	15 847	10.8	14 222	10.9	27 860	12.6
Children (2-14)	2348	5.6	3815	3.3	3414	2.5	7154	2.4
Youth (15-24)	2099	9.3	4120	10.3	3617	8.7	5890	7.1
Adult (>25	3981	15.5	7912	15.6	7191	16.8	14 816	19.9
SEX								
Male	3772	9.5	6342	8.2	5938	7.9	12171	10.4
Female	4656	12.8	9509	13.3	8284	13.6	15079	15.4
RACE								
African	5056	12.9	9950	13.3	8702	13.6	17 603	15.8
White	701	6.2	1173	0.6	1327	0.3	1722	1.2
Coloured	1775	6.1	3382	1.9	3067	1.7	5305	3.4
Indian/Asian	896	1.6	1319	1.6	1102	0.3	2567	1.5

Source: For Age, Shisana et al. (2014); for sex and race, authors' calculation based on the 2012 population-based survey on HIV conducted by the HSRC.[35]

Note: N=sample size

The trend analysis shows that HIV prevalence varied according to age groups. Among children aged 2–14 years, the prevalence declined significantly, from 5.6 per cent in 2002[36] to 2.5 per cent in 2008,[37] and remained at that level in 2012.[38] The youth HIV prevalence, however, declined from 9.3 per cent in 2002 to 7.1 per cent in 2012. In contrast, the prevalence in adults over 25 continued on an upward trend, rising from 16.8 per cent in 2008 to 19.9 per cent in 2012.

According to the trend analysis above, HIV affects females more severely than males, with the prevalence among males on a downward trend during the period 2002–2008; however, between 2008 and 2012 the prevalence for males increased, again presumably because of increased access to treatment. For similar reasons, the prevalence among females was stagnant until the period between 2008 and 2012, when it rose by nearly two percentage points. The gender difference observed in HIV prevalence is probably due to multiple factors, including: the biological make-up of women, which makes them more susceptible to HIV infection;[39] gender-based violence, including rape;[40] intergenerational sex with older men who do not use condoms;[41] and transactional sex.[42]

To date we are still combating this epidemic, and for South Africa to really meet the targets that have been set it will be necessary to examine the underlying factors that contribute to the ever-growing prevalence of HIV and AIDS in the populace. Many scholars have written about the underlying causes or drivers of the HIV and AIDS epidemic. It is in the spaces of poverty, racism, gender inequality and sexual oppression that the HIV epidemic continues today – in large part unencumbered by formal public health and education programmes, let alone by the advances in treatment that might otherwise convince us that the emergency has passed.[43]

In the year 2000, South Africa had already encountered a well-established AIDS epidemic with an estimated 4.2 million people living with HIV. Only a few thousand patients were on anti-retroviral therapy (almost entirely in the private sector or clinical trial sites) and treatment in pregnancy was only available in the Western Cape, resulting in an estimated 1000 deaths per day nationally.

Sixteen years on and South Africa has the largest treatment programme in the world with 3.4 million people living with HIV (PLHIV) on treatment, and a transmission in pregnancy down to 1.5 per cent compared to a background rate of 30 per cent in the absence of treatment in pregnancy. The success of treatment has led to an increase in life expectancy from 56 years in 2006 to 61 years 2015, and a more than 50 per cent decline in HIV-related mortality. Survival on treatment has led to the paradoxical effect of increasing HIV prevalence and the absolute number of people living with HIV, which stood at 7 million people at the time of writing (2016).

Recognition of the epidemic in parts of Africa, and of the potential for it to spread internationally, came in the mid-1980s, and led to the first global response: the creation by WHO of the Special (later the Global) Programme on AIDS. While tremendous progress has been made on the treatment front, the high volume of new HIV infections poses the biggest challenge to bringing the epidemic under control. According to the Joint United Nations Programme on HIV and AIDS (UNAIDS) Prevention Gap Report released at the International AIDS Conference in Durban in 2016, South Africa had 380 000 new infections in 2015. Incidence is declining slowly since the peak of the epidemic in the middle of the last decade and, given the growth of the population, the absolute numbers of new infections have not declined since 2010. There is an increasing feminisation of HIV incidence, especially in the age groups 15–19 and 20–24 where the rate is up to seven times higher in women than their male peers.

In 2012, HIV prevalence in women aged 30–34 was estimated at 36 per cent compared to 25.6 per cent for males of the same age group – using prevalence levels adjusted for antiretroviral treatment (ART). For females between 20 and 24 years, prevalence levels stood at 17.4 per cent compared to 5.1 per cent for males in the same age group.

This picture has changed over the past three years, as we now see another trend of increasing infection rates among young people. A Human Sciences Research Council (HSRC) report[44] attributes this to deficiencies in communications: South Africa has not had a single massive national communications campaign and prevention strategy since at least 2010, when the Khomanani Campaign scaled down. As a result, the HSRC reports, knowledge levels have significantly declined among young people.

South Africa launched a revised AIDS plan on 1 December 2011 for the period of 2012–2016. This strategic plan recognised the need to consolidate the gains made in curbing mother-to-child transmission and to provide treatment to people with viral loads of 350. The plan moved us to new frontiers where we needed to confront rising infection rates among the most productive members of our population – those in their late-twenties and mid-thirties. It reminded us that AIDS is not just a pandemic affecting the poor and the marginalised. Necessarily, the plan emphasised prevention as the most potent weapon in the fight against AIDS. Consequently, safe sex messages must change, given the multi-class nature of the audience as well as complex social determinants driving the pandemic.

This approach to targeted interventions is best exemplified by the March 2016 launch of the National Sex Worker HIV Plan by Deputy President Cyril Ramaphosa, in his role as Chairperson of the South African National AIDS Council (SANAC). In the same month, the biggest tuberculosis (TB) testing and treatment campaign was launched, targeting people who reside in mining communities where TB infection rates are generally high.

Another significant contribution of the current National Strategic Plan (NSP) (2012–2016) is that it balances the call for biomedical interventions with the need to expand the frontiers of understanding social determinants – the social context within which the epidemic thrives. The next NSP, currently under discussion within SANAC, is likely to bring us full circle by emphasising the central role of HIV prevention through addressing the social and structural drivers of the epidemic, mobilising the country for behaviour change to reduce HIV risk, and expanding bio-medical prevention interventions such as Treatment as Prevention (TasP) and Pre-exposure Prophylaxis (PrEP).

We should read this within the context of the already documented evidence that social media plays a role in the spread of HIV and other sexually transmitted infections (STIs) in cities like London, as it facilitates speed dating and increase the casualisation of sex. Condoms are not always available in these speed dating and casual sex circumstances.[45]

How the Book is Organised

This 30-chapter book is arranged in four parts that vary in tone and presentation style. Through this mixture of academic papers, reflective pieces and policy statements, the reader will engage with perspectives that speak to the common metanarrative: that significant progress has been made in southern Africa to eliminate and reduce the burden of AIDS. Through evidence-based, organisational and personal accounts, one gets a sense that all social partners and stakeholders believe that *sizonqoba* (we shall overcome), through targeted interventions, political will and collective effort. To the extent that today's headlines are punctuated with tales of hope and triumph over adversity, the trends do suggest that it is possible to outlive AIDS in Southern Africa in, at least, another generation or two.

Parts I and II feature evidence-based accounts of the dynamics of HIV infections and of the efficacy of the AIDS response. Parts III and IV are constituted of essays and public statements from practitioners, activists, leaders and prominent people, whose direct involvement over the years have contributed to the arrest of runaway infection rates and unresponsive public policy responses. These activities and public figures helped to raise funds for prevention, treatment, care and support programmes. Importantly, they shaped or redirected public policy.

The non-academic Parts III and IV were included here in order to enrich the metanarrative of hope and triumph emanating from the preceding evidence-based sections. Further, they are included in this edition in order to bring the dynamism, balance and inclusion typical of the Southern African AIDS response, which has seen civil society activists, government, business, labour and experts participate as equal partners through institutions like South Africa's National AIDS Council, and which has produced NSPs as national blue prints for HIV, AIDS, TB and STI prevention and treatment.

Part I opens with a chapter by Simelela, Pillay and Serenata, which sets the tone for the book by chronicling the South African posture towards HIV since the late Mandela's administration. This chapter is significant in many ways, including the fact that it is penned by people who have first-hand experience of the evolution of public policy towards HIV and AIDS as they worked as bureaucrats in the Health Department at the time. In fact, all three authors continue to play a central role in the current programme. Through this chapter, we gain insights into the inner workings of government, the health ministry, and local and international interlocutors who played a role in lifting the AIDS epidemic onto a national agenda. The chapter has had to be carefully edited in order to include all the important – and somewhat previously unknown – information without necessarily unduly declassifying sensitive Cabinet information.

Chapter two, by Shisana, Zungu and Evans outlines the historical and socio-cultural aspects of HIV, drawing extensively from previous surveys conducted by various researchers. The two delve into the complex question of what drives the epidemic in South Africa, touching on both biological and social factors. That is, the risks associated with genital inflammation, especially among black women in Southern Africa, malnutrition (which compromises the immune system), as well as socio-cultural factors, such as the migrant labour system (which extracted men from their families to live in single-sex hostels in the Transvaal); the prevalence of multiple concurrent sexual partners; and poverty, which reduces the capacity of women to negotiate safe sex. This chapter is significant for the discussion of the historical and socio-economic realities of apartheid South Africa which made the ground fertile for the spread of HIV, for example, the migrant labour system. We do well to recall that, in northern KwaZulu-Natal for instance, the rapid spread of AIDS was associated with returning migrants.

Setswe and Zungu problematise the relationship between evidenced-based research and public policy in chapter three, showing that most of the achievements made in the anti-AIDS programmes can be attributed to the ground-breaking work of biomedical and social researchers. They cite many examples, the most recent and compelling being the introduction of medical male circumcision (MMC) by government as a public-policy response to the AIDS epidemic. This was a direct result of biomedical research that showed that uncircumcised men have a greater chance of contracting HIV compared to those who have been circumcised. This is another unique feature of the South African response, which is now being replicated in other parts of the world.

Chapter four, by Stadler, Rees, Delany-Moretlwe and Palanee-Phillips, is a significant contribution to this book in that it outlines the history of clinical trials in South Africa, in part for the scientific breakthroughs in HIV prevention, but more so as a sign of how the epidemic drove South African researchers into research and innovation at breath-taking speed and with great audacity. The introduction of MMC as a prevention method (that Setswe and Zungu discuss in their chapter) is but one of many innovations owing its origins to the work of clinical trial researchers.

Building further on the theme of research and innovation, Sekhejane and Pelletan in chapter five discuss the political economy of innovation in healthcare systems and biomedical technologies. They make the case that local innovation efforts require adequate support in order to promote home-grown scientific solutions and thus reduce dependence on the west.

In chapter six, Saunderson shares insights from his fieldwork in the province of the Eastern Cape. From this chapter we enter the world of culture and how it influences vulnerability to HIV infections, especially among women in a patriarchal society. It is distinct in that through it, we take a journey with the researcher who, from the reader's point of view, swaps roles and becomes a subject.

As one of the biggest employing organisations, government plays an important role in the management of HIV among its employees. As a sub-sector of SANAC, government is expected to implement its own prevention, treatment, care and support programmes. The limitation of some of these programmes has been inadequate coordination and reporting. Senabe, in chapter seven, discusses strides made by government towards becoming a responsible and responsive employer committed to reducing the burden of HIV and AIDS within its rank and file.

Chapter eight, by Nzimande, draws on statistical data to demonstrate the extent of demographic changes in South Africa occasioned by the AIDS epidemic. With mortality rates decreasing (thus pushing up prevalence levels as people with HIV live longer and fewer die), demographics have changed compared to the time when mortality rates were high, resulting in higher levels of child-headed households as well as households with children living with their grandparents. In turn, children in such circumstances become vulnerable to abuse and HIV infection. Nzimande concludes her chapter by asserting that the future may not be as gloomy as once predicted, provided that prevention and treatment efforts bear fruit to prove her argument that the AIDS epidemic has shown the resilient nature of the South African population.

In chapter nine, Chasi draws on critical theory and contemporary public discourses to outline how dominant knowledge systems have undermined African agency and created sub-texts that blur the true experiences of black people's interaction with the burden of HIV and AIDS. He argues that HIV and AIDS is not taboo in black communities, as many have asserted. Chasi argues that it is important to work against colonial discourses that deny the legitimacy of blacks in speaking out about their existential concerns and pain. As demonstrated in his study, one way of doing this is to explore, record and research hidden black scripts of living in the times of HIV and aspirations of outliving AIDS in black communities.

Chapter ten, by Ahluwalia, outlines what is fast becoming a best practice model of targeted intervention. The target audience of the First Things First programme discussed here are students who face varying degrees of vulnerability perpetuated by poverty and inequality. This chapter is important because evidence continues to warn that students, especially those at technical and vocational training colleges, are somewhere near the epicentre of the epidemic due to their socio-economic and living conditions. Insights from the First Things First programme are taken further in chapter 14, by Ahluwalia and Rapiti, presenting a case study of an HIV testing and counselling campaign among young people.

Most of the advances being made in treatment, care and prevention programmes are facilitated by the ever-increasing use of data and information management systems, which help with targeted monitoring and evaluation. In this connection, chapter 11 by Katz, Sargent, Darkou, Cassiem and Mitchell presents valuable insights, using KwaZulu-Natal as a case in point. The provincial case study is important because of successes from its integrated service delivery model, otherwise known as Operation Sukuma Sakhe. International organisations, like UNAIDS, have singled out this programme as one of the best approaches to fight HIV while addressing social determinants such as poverty, service delivery, gender-based violence and access to quality education. This chapter can be read together with chapter 16 – by Zhuwau, Ndlovu, Naidu, Ngwenya and Mkhize – which attributes these successes to the effective use of community participation through the Ward-based War Rooms that bring together government, civil society, traditional leaders and community to champion community development.

As stated above, among the social drivers of infections among girls and young women are poverty and inequality, which provide conditions for intergenerational sex and abuse. This has created the phenomenon of sugar daddies – another dimension of the debate about the shifting political economy of HIV infections explored in this introductory chapter. Amy Maphagela elaborates on the sugar daddy syndrome in chapter 12, building a case for why prevention programmes should focus on girls and young women, using education and economic empowerment as the most potent weapons.

Insights from Zungu's chapter thirteen are compelling in that they demonstrate a transition from the notion of AIDS as a death sentence to HIV as a chronic disease that can be managed. Read with chapter eight by Nzimande, this chapter builds on the narrative of resilience and hope, which has come to characterise AIDS in Southern Africa, another important contribution to the book's metanarrative of triumph: *sizonqoba*!

Part II of the book consists of five chapters by Morah, Ridgard and Fee (chapter 15); Zhuwau, Ndlovu, Naidu, Ngwenya and Mkhize (chapter 16); Balfour-Kaipa, Govender and Baloyi (chapter 17); Mears (chapter 18); and Abdullah (chapter 19). These are located within the sub-theme of strengthening the multi-sectoral response to HIV, AIDS and TB. They range from case studies of international solidarity (chapters 15 and 19) to private-sector programmes (chapters 17 and 18) and community ownership of the response (chapter 16).

In essence, these chapters demonstrate that the tale of HIV, AIDS and TB management in Southern Africa is incomplete without the story of the social pact forged by communities, development partners, civil society, business and organised labour to fight the epidemic. Working through formal networks and structures like SANAC, these social partners continue to craft the mosaic of unity against the virus that once threatened their communities.

This is the most defining feature of South Africa's response to the pandemic. Chapter 17 also details recent developments that flow out of the signing of the Southern African Development Community (SADC) Declaration on TB in the Mining Industry in August 2012, a development which added impetus to the regional response to TB, HIV and silicosis. It is important to note that the mining industry is now taking responsibility for extending treatment to former employees and their families throughout southern Africa.

The five chapters of Part III are an important contribution to this edition in that they are written by practitioners and activists with first-hand (and non-academic/researcher) experience of living with HIV and working with HIV-positive people. They advance the notion of agency and inclusion as determinants of victory in the fight against HIV and AIDS. Bogopane-Zulu, in chapter 20, discusses the inter-sectionality of HIV, AIDS and disability in South Africa, a subject grossly under-studied in Southern Africa. This is followed by Mmapaseka 'Steve' Letsike's contribution, which delves into the governance politics of SANAC and the role of civil society in that regard.

The captivating instalment by long-time AIDS activist, Ramothwala, adds an important dimension to this book as he presents first-hand narration of the less known, but prevailing, practice of widow sex cleansing in the regions where it is practiced: in some communities in Limpopo the surviving spouse of the late HIV-positive person is expected to have unprotected sex as part of the cleansing process, which obviously adds to the spread of HIV infection. Still on matters of cultural practices, Nxesi (in chapter 23) problematises the controversial issue of the transition and intersection of traditional and medical circumcision. This is controversial in that MMC has been widely accepted in the province of KwaZulu-Natal – where it is championed by King Goodwill Zwelithini – but it has nearly divided communities in the Eastern Cape where traditional circumcision is preferred. These divisions impact on uptake of MMC and incense those who want to preserve tradition against the encroaching Western practice. There are also unintended consequences of victimisation and stigma, with young boys who went through MMC being compelled to return to the mountain for their 'real' circumcision.

Sithembiso Radebe provides a personal account of being an HIV-positive woman surviving stigma in a patriarchal society. Again, as we see in many other contributions in this edition, Radebe's article sums up the feeling of many people in southern Africa: that HIV and AIDS can no longer prevent people from achieving their dreams, challenges of poverty, unemployment and inequality notwithstanding. Now working as a supervisory attorney at the Legal Aid Advice Line in Johannesburg, her story is a testimony to the idea of outliving AIDS; a counter-narrative to perceptions of HIV as a contagious death sentence which manufactures stigma.

Still on the subject of stigma established in the preceding chapters, chapter 24 sustains the *sizonqoba!* metanarrative of this book. Through the voice of Sithembiso Radebe, we are taken on a journey of a young, educated woman undergoing the trials and tribulations of learning about her HIV status, battling stigma at home, among peers and in the community, and the struggle to establish an identity and meaning in life. In the end, she tells a story of triumph and finding a greater purpose. The chapter further adds value to this edition in that, using observations and first-hand experiences at community-level, it complements evidence on socio-cultural drivers of HIV discussed in other chapters in the book, for example, chapters two, six and nine.

As already indicated, Part IV contains selected speeches by leaders and prominent members of society. We include them partly because, without such bold leadership South Africa and the region might still be gripped by the 'AIDS scare' which terrified many families and communities at the turn of the twenty-first century. These leaders and activists paved the way for HIV to move from a life-threatening disease into a manageable chronic illness which, according to an insurance-contracted nurse who came to draw blood samples at the office at the time of writing this introduction, 'is better than cancer, because through lifestyle and care, it can be managed for decades. The trouble with cancer is that you do treatment today and it reappears tomorrow even if you change your lifestyle.'

A disclaimer is in order here: these old speeches are not the only expressions of hope and policy direction that South Africa, in particular, has experienced. But a choice had to be made of 10 from what we call memorable speeches or statements that changed the face of HIV in the past 16 years. It is important to note that permission to publish these speeches was granted subject to them not being altered other than to modify the format for alignment with the layout and formatting of the book. Readers should engage the content with this disclaimer in mind.

We start with former president Nelson Mandela's closing address at the 13th International AIDS Conference in Durban in July 2000. Many observers believe, had it not been for Madiba's steadfastness on the matter, and his open challenge to his successor's passive stance towards the AIDS epidemic, South Africa's response would not have evolved to where it is today. In short, Madiba's speech gave much-needed impetus from a towering moral authority, who himself had experienced HIV in his family, with his son succumbing to an AIDS-related illness.

With permission from Nkosi's Haven, a Johannesburg-based NGO that assists children infected or affected by HIV, we republish an address by Nkosi Johnson delivered at the same July 2000 AIDS Conference in Durban. This is, arguably, an address that placed treatment on the global agenda and, most certainly, at the doorstep of public policy in South Africa. The speech continues to echo in the boardrooms where policy and funding decisions are taken, in the NGOs and orphanages where vulnerable children are given shelter and protection, and in conferences where best practices are shared. Some commentators even suggested that from that conference onwards, Nkosi Johnson became the face of the struggle against HIV in southern Africa.

The 2001 United Nations (UN) General Assembly Special Session on HIV and AIDS speech by former Botswana President, Festus Mogae, who now provides regional leadership through the platform of Champions for an AIDS-Free Generation, is also reprinted here to add weight to the story of the region taking responsibility for the AIDS epidemic. This was at a time when the South African government was still bickering with civil society on matters of treatment and care for HIV-positive people.

A year later, the then Secretary-General of the United Nations, Kofi Annan, gave a very important 2002 World AIDS Day Message. By this time, the AIDS agenda was firmly entrenched in the work of the UN to a point of establishing a dedicated programme – UNAIDS. The global community was mobilised. The United States President's Emergency Plan for AIDS Relief (PEPFAR), the Global Fund and other funding organisations would later be formed (see chapter 19 by Fareed Abdullah) to mobilise funding to fight the epidemic. South Africa would then become the biggest recipient of support from the Global Fund, especially for the life-saving treatment. Again, we argue, had it not been for the bold leadership by Kofi Annan, many of the gains acknowledged in this book – and many others – could have been a dream deferred.

It is now a fact of history that President Jacob Zuma's 2009 World AIDS Day speech is regarded as the most decisive policy statement since the debates about HIV and AIDS amplified in post-apartheid South Africa. Significantly, the President announced new treatment guidelines and protocols, such as treating at CD4 count of 350 – up from 200. This meant more people could access treatment before they got too sick. HIV-positive patients who had TB could now be treated irrespective of their CD4 count. Also announced was the extension of treatment to pregnant mothers, irrespective of their CD4 count, and the expansion of prevention of mother-to-child transmission (PMTCT). See chapters one, three, seven and ten for details of how the national HIV response changed on 1 December 2009. As a consequence, South Africa today is regarded as a country with the most ambitious HIV response in the world, especially from the point of view of expanding life-prolonging treatment. In this connection, the July 2016 AIDS conference in Durban was expected to be a celebration of this milestone, compared to the wrangling and politicking that characterised the 2000 conference.

The script of international solidary against the AIDS epidemic is incomplete without the storylines emphasising the role played by eminent celebrities like Sir Elton John. As we can read from his 2012[46] address to the International AIDS Conference, Elton John's name features prominently among public personalities who have used their popularity as a force for social change, influencing behaviour change for millions of audiences worldwide, and many governments have made significant policy changes as a result of his championing humanist approach to the scourge of AIDS.

A short 2015 World AIDS Day statement by Judge Edwin Cameron is significant in many ways, not least for its striking contrast to his 2000 address to the International AIDS Conference in Durban, where civil society was at odds with government. Fareed Abdullah introduces chapter 19 by quoting extensively from that 2000 address. Reading the new text, it is clear that the narrative of hope and triumph echoes across society and comes from people of different stations in life, including those in the judiciary, like Judge Cameron.

Conclusion

The message carried in many of the chapters of this collection is clear: social partners in Southern Africa should intensify efforts to turn the tide against HIV, AIDS and TB. They should move beyond biomedical science and investigate the social science, that is, real-life experiences that increase vulnerability to HIV infection. They should ask and seek answers to questions like why infection rates increase even among the most educated and upwardly mobile people. What social pressures affect the middle class to the extent that they readily exhibit risky sexual tendencies, much like the least educated and marginalised population groups that are exposed due to sexual violence, poverty and inter-generational sex? Is it some false sense of invincibility that 'this won't happen to me', or 'surely this banker can't be HIV positive', or 'let us just enjoy sex unencumbered by intermediaries like condoms'? Social and behavioural scientists need to study this phenomenon in order to realign national strategies in response to what statistics tell us about incidence and prevalence trends.

Evidence-based studies are urgently required to develop a thorough understanding and response to challenges presented by the growing use of social media. Deeper insights into the dynamic use and misuse of social and electronic media will help policy makers and stakeholders turn tables, affecting positive behaviour change through the same platforms that are currently used to promote risky lifestyles, as Action AIDS has argued.[47]

Zero infections remain our goal. An AIDS-free generation is possible. Bold steps need to be taken, however, by individuals, organisations, communities and stakeholders to spread the message – and to live by it – that safe sex is the way to go; and knowing one's status is a prerequisite for unprotected sex, in addition to faithfulness.

This book is presented as an unflinching, but hopeful, discussion on the history, mythology, challenges and innovations that have marked South Africa's journey with a biological phenomenon that reaches profoundly into all aspects of personal social interaction and national life. This discussion also illustrates our resilience and the coalitions we can build and sustain in responding to the profound challenges that our society faces.

Notes and References

1 Säve-Söderbergh, B., and Peltola, P., 2013. The Scandinavian anti-apartheid movement: International solidarity in action. In Ngcaweni, B. (Ed.), *The future we chose: Emerging perspectives on the centenary of the ANC*, Africa Institute.

2 Nelson Mandela addressing a concert at Wembley Stadium, London on 16 April 1990. Available at http://www.mandela.gov.za/mandela_speeches/1990/900416_wembley.htm [Accessed 22 August 2016].

3 Shisana, O., Meyiwa, T., Nkondo, M., Zungu, N., Chitiga-Mabugu, M., Simbayi, L. and Nyamnjoh, F., 2014. South Africa's response to the HIV and AIDS epidemics. In Meyiwa, T, Nkondo, M., Chitiga-Mabugu, M., Sithole, M. and Nyamnjoh, F. (eds) *State of the Nation: South Africa 1994–2014: a twenty-year review*. Pretoria: HSRC Press.

4 For more details on the evolution of the AIDS epidemic in South Africa, see Chapters 1 and 2 in this book; also Shisana, O., & Zungu-Dirwayi, N. 2003. Government's

changing responses to HIV/AIDS. In Everatt, D. and Maphai, V. (eds.) *Development Update: The (real) State of the Nation: South Africa After 1990, Vol. 4*. .Johannesburg: Interfund; and Shisana, O., Meyiwa, T., Nkondo, M., Zungu, N., Chitiga-Mabugu, M., Simbayi, L. and Nyamnjoh, F., 2014. South Africa's response to the HIV and AIDS epidemics. In Meyiwa, T, Nkondo, M., Chitiga-Mabugu, M., Sithole, M. and Nyamnjoh, F. (eds) *State of the Nation: South Africa 1994–2014: A twenty-year review*. Pretoria: HSRC Press.

5 Sember, R., 2009. Sexuality research in South Africa: The policy context. In Reddy V, Sandfort, T., and Rispel, L. (Eds). *From social silence to social science: Same-sex sexuality, HIV and AIDS and gender in South Africa*. Cape Town: HSRC Press. Another useful study on a similar subject is: Herek, G.M. and Capitanio, J.P., 1999. AIDS Stigma and Sexual Prejudice. *American Behavioral Scientist*, 42(7).

6 Caldwell, J.C., Anarfi, J.K., Caldwell, P., 1997. Mobility, migration, sex, STDs and AIDS: An essay on sub-Saharan Africa with other parallels. In Herdt, G. (Ed.) *Sexual cultures and migration in the era of AIDS: Anthropological and demographic perspectives*. Oxford: Oxford University Press.

7 Shisana, O. and Simbayi, L. 2002. *Nelson Mandela/HSRC study of HIV/AIDS: South African national HIV prevalence, behavioural risks and mass media: Household survey 2002: Executive Summary*. Pretoria: HSRC Press.

8 Shisana, O., Meyiwa, T., Nkondo, M., Zungu, N., Chitiga-Mabugu, M., Simbayi, L. and Nyamnjoh, F., 2014. South Africa's response to the HIV and AIDS epidemics. In Meyiwa, T, Nkondo, M., Chitiga-Mabugu, M., Sithole, M. and Nyamnjoh, F. (eds) *State of the Nation: South Africa 1994–2014: A twenty-year review*. Pretoria: HSRC Press.

9 South African National AIDS Council. March 2016. *Enhanced Progress Report of the South African National Strategic Plan on HIV STIs and TB: 2012–2016*, pp. 72–73. Available at http://sanac.org.za/2016/07/05/enhanced-progress-report-of-the-south-african-national-strategic-plan-on-hiv-stis-and-tb-2012-2016/ [Accessed 17 August 2016].

10 Fassin, D., 2008. The embodied past. From paranoid style to politics of memory in South Africa. *Social Anthropology*, 16(3).

11 Simelela, N.P. and Venter, W.D.F., 2014. History of HIV in SA: A brief history of South Africa's response to AIDS. *The South African Medical Journal*, 104(3).

12 Ngcaweni, B. (Ed.) 2014. *Liberation diaries: Reflections on 20 years of democracy in South Africa*. Johannesburg: Jacana Media.

13 Barnett, T., Whiteside, A., 2002. *AIDS in the twenty-first century: Disease and globalisation*. New York: Palgrave Macmillan.

14 See Chapter 2 of this edition for more details; and Ngcaweni, B., n.d. An exploration of the socio-economic barriers to marital unions and HIV incidence correlates: A policy poser for South Africa. In Mpofu, B. and Ndlovu-Gatsheni, S.J. (Eds). *Rethinking development, inequality and poverty in Sub-Saharan Africa after the 2008 global financial crisis*, Berhahn Books (forthcoming, 2017).

15 Shisana, O., Rehle, T., Simbayi L.C., Zuma, K., Jooste, S., Zungu, N., Labadarios, D., Onoya, D. et al. (2014) South African National HIV Prevalence, Incidence and Behaviour Survey, 2012. Cape Town: HSRC Press.

16 Castells, M., 1998. *End of Millennium*. Blackwell, Oxford.

17 Parkhurst, J.O., Hunsmann, M., 2015. *Review of African political economy: Breaking out of silos-the need for critical paradigm reflection in HIV prevention*. Available at http://www.tandfonline.com/doi/abs/10.1080/03056244.2015.1064373?src=recsys&journalCode=crea20 [Accessed 17 August 2016].

18 Gillespie, S., 2008. Poverty, food insecurity, HIV vulnerability, and the impacts of AIDS in Sub Saharan Africa. *IDS Bulletin*, 39, no. 5.

19 World Health Organization. 2016. HIV/AIDS fact sheet. Available at http://www.who.int/mediacentre/factsheets/fs360/en/ [Accessed 1 September 2016].

20 De Cock, K.M., Mbori-Ngacha, D. and Marum, E., 2002. AIDS in Africa: Shadow on the Continent. Public health and HIV/AIDS in Africa in the 21st century. *The Lancet*, 360.

21 Medwiser. 2013. AIDS in Africa. Available at http://www.medwiser.org/hiv-aids/around-the-world/aids-in-africa/ [Accessed 1 September 2016].

22 Gillespie, S., 2008. Poverty, food insecurity, HIV vulnerability, and the impacts of AIDS in Sub Saharan Africa. *IDS Bulletin*, 39, no. 5.

23 UNAIDS, 2001. *AIDS epidemic update*: December 2001. Geneva: UNAIDS.

24 Mbonu, N.C., Van den Borne, B. and De Vries, N. 2009. Stigma of people with HIV and AIDS in Sub-Saharan Africa: A Literature Review. *Journal of Tropical Medicine*, 2009.

25 Joint United Nations Programme on AIDS. 2004 Report on the Global AIDS Epidemic. Available at http://files.unaids.org/en/media/unaids/contentassets/documents/unaidspublication/2004/GAR2004_en.pdf [Accessed 17 August 2016].

26 Simelela, N.P. and Venter, W.D.F., 2014. History of HIV in SA: A brief history of South Africa's response to AIDS. *The South African Medical Journal*, 104(3).

27 Gow, J. and Desmond, C., 2010. *The Impact of the AIDS Epidemic on South Africa's Children*. UNICEF Innocenti Research Centre. Available at https://www.unicef-irc.org/publications/pdf/aids_book/chapter4_gow.pdf [Accessed 17 August 2016].

28 UNAIDS, 2001. *AIDS epidemic update: December 2001*. Geneva: UNAIDS.

29 STATSSA, 2015. Mid-year population estimates. Available at www.statssa.gov.za [Accessed 18 August 2016].

30 Shisana, O., Rehle, T., Simbayi L.C., Zuma, K., Jooste, S., Zungu, N., Labadarios, D., Onoya, D. et al. (2014) South African National HIV Prevalence, Incidence and Behaviour Survey, 2012. Cape Town: HSRC Press.

31 UNAIDS, 2016. *Global AIDS updated*. UNAIDS: Switzerland.

32 Shisana, O. and Zungu, D.N., 2003. Government's changing responses to HIV/AIDS. In Evaratte, D. and Maphia, V. (Eds). *The real state of the nation: South Africa after 1990*. Johannesburg: Interfund Development Update.

33 Shisana, O. and Simbayi, L. 2002. *Nelson Mandela/HSRC study of HIV/AIDS: South African national HIV prevalence, behavioural risks and mass media: Household survey 2002: Executive Summary*. Pretoria: HSRC Press.

34 HSRC, 2014. South African National HIV prevalence, Incidence and Behaviour Survey, 2012. HSRC Press. Cape Town

35 Shisana, O., Meyiwa, T., Nkondo, M., Zungu, N., Chitiga-Mabugu, M., Simbayi, L. and Nyamnjoh, F., 2014. South Africa's response to the HIV and AIDS epidemics. In Meyiwa, T, Nkondo, M., Chitiga-Mabugu, M., Sithole, M. and Nyamnjoh, F. (eds) *State of the Nation: South Africa 1994–2014: A twenty-year review*. Pretoria: HSRC Press

36 Shisana, O. and Simbayi, L. 2002. *Nelson Mandela/HSRC study of HIV/AIDS: South African national HIV prevalence, behavioural risks and mass media: Household survey 2002: Executive Summary*. Pretoria: HSRC Press.

37 Shisana, O., Rehle, T., Simbayi L.C., Zuma, K., Jooste, S., Zungu, N., Labadarios, D., Onoya, D. et al. (2014) South African National HIV Prevalence, Incidence and Behaviour Survey, 2012. Cape Town: HSRC Press.

38 Shisana, Zungu and Simbayi, 2014.

39 Gray, R.H., Li, X., Kigozi, G., Serwadda, D., Brahmbhatt, H., Wabwire-Mangen, F., Nalugoda, F., Kiddugavu, M., Sewankambo, N., Quinn, T.C., Reynolds, S.J. and Wawer, M.J. 2005. Increased risk of incident HIV during pregnancy in Rakai, Uganda: A prospective study. *Lancet*, 366(9492), pp. 1182–1188.

40 Jewkes, R.K., Dunkle, K., Nduna, M. and Shai, N., 2010. Intimate partner violence, relationship power inequality, and incidence of HIV infection in young women in South Africa: A cohort study. *Lancet*, 376(9734), pp. 41–48.

41 Anderson, K.G., Beutel, A.M. and Maughan-Brown, B., 2007. HIV perception and first sexual intercourse among youth in Cape Town, South Africa. *International Family Planning Perspective*, 33(3), pp. 98–105.

42 Dunkle, K.L., Jewkes, R.K., Brown, H.C., Gray, G.E., McIntyre, J.A. and Harlow, S.D., 2004. Transactional sex among women in Soweto, South Africa: Prevalence and risk factors associated with HIV infection. *Social Science and Medicine*, 59(8), pp. 1581–1592.

43 Richard, P., 2002. The Global HIV/AIDS pandemic, structural inequalities, and the politics of international health. *American Journal of Public Health*, 92(3).

44 *Ibid.*

45 Please see 20 May 2011 *Daily Mail* article titled *Social networking linked to rise in STDs: How health experts blame Facebook for making it easier to find casual sex*. Available at http://www.dailymail.co.uk/news/article-1388719/Social-networking-linked-STD-rise-Facebook-blamed-making-casual-sex-easier.html [Accessed 22 August 2016]; also see 27 April 2016 reports of a similar nature from *The Star* of Canada titled Is *social media fanning passions and helping boost STI rates?* Available at https://www.thestar.com/news/canada/2016/04/27/alberta-says-hook-ups-arranged-on-social-media-a-big-factor-in-sti-spike.html [Accessed 22 August 2016].

46 Elton John also gave a significant speech at the 2016 International AIDS Conference in Durban demonstrating consistency of leadership on his part and, more generally, the work of his Foundation.

47 Bevilacqua, L. 2015. Social Media: An Opportunity for HIV Prevention. Available at http://actionaids.org/blog/social-media-opportunity-hiv-prevention [Accessed 18 October 2016].

PART I

BALANCING THE BIOMEDICAL AND SOCIAL DETERMINANTS

THE DYNAMISM OF THE AIDS RESPONSE IN SOUTHERN AFRICA

Chapter 1

The South African Response to the HIV Epidemic

A Historical Overview

Nono Simelela, Yogan Pillay and Celicia Serenata

Introduction

The human immunodeficiency virus (HIV) epidemic continues to occupy centre stage in global health discourse due to the devastating impact it has had on many developing countries, as well as some developed countries. In Sub-Saharan Africa, South Africa remains at the epicentre of the epidemic, with 6.8 million people estimated to be HIV-positive. The country now has the largest antiretroviral treatment programme in the world, which is no mean feat given the troubled history that caused a significant amount of anguish and controversy during the early part of the response to the epidemic.

Much has been written by a wide range of commentators across the world and in South Africa, but not much has come from government officials who were in the eye of the storm. This chapter provides a glimpse behind the scenes where the hard work of developing and writing the various policy documents that informed discussions by the leadership was done. The story began shortly after the drama with Virodene and Sarafina had subsided,[1] and trust had been restored between government and civil society.

The launch of the Partnership Against AIDS by then Deputy President, Mr Thabo Mbeki, on 9 October 1998, marked a fresh start in rebuilding the social contract on how the country was going to tackle the epidemic. The speech conveyed a sense of urgency and concern for the future of the country in the face of what was then a complex and challenging disease. Deputy President Mbeki noted that:

> Many of us have grieved for orphans left behind with no one to fend for them. We have experienced AIDS in the groans of wasting lives. We have carried it in small and big coffins to many graveyards. At times we did not know that we were burying AIDS victims. At other times we knew, but chose to remain silent.

These were sobering words given the exponential rise in HIV prevalence among pregnant women receiving care in public health clinics across the country. Like many other countries across the world, South Africa had already established a surveillance system which revealed that antenatal HIV prevalence had risen dramatically from 0.7 per cent in 1990 to 22.8 per cent in 1998 (Figure 1). Knowing what transpired post this announcement by Deputy President Mbeki in 1998, and the era of AIDS denialism under his presidency, this was an ironic twist in the story of the HIV response.

Figure 1 Antenatal HIV Prevalence Rate, 1990-2013 (Department of Health)

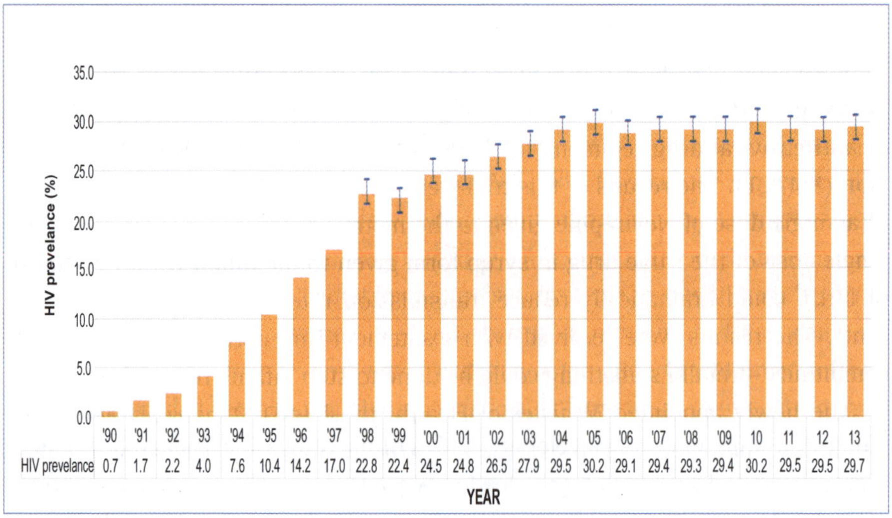

	'90	'91	'92	'93	'94	'95	'96	'97	'98	'99	'00	'01	'02	'03	'04	'05	'06	'07	'08	'09	10	11	12	13
HIV prevelance	0.7	1.7	2.2	4.0	7.6	10.4	14.2	17.0	22.8	22.4	24.5	24.8	26.5	27.9	29.5	30.2	29.1	29.4	29.3	29.4	30.2	29.5	29.5	29.7

Source: Department of Health

In the late 1990s, South Africa's response was limited to HIV prevention programmes with a significant focus on awareness campaigns, condom distribution, behaviour change communication and syndromic management of sexually transmitted infections. The rise in antenatal HIV prevalence was accompanied by rising infant mortality due to mother-to-child HIV transmission during pregnancy, labour and delivery. Evidence of transmission through breast-feeding represented a challenge, particularly because of the progress the country had made in the promotion of breastfeeding to enhance infant health outcomes. Many of the developed countries, such as the United States (US) were already seeing dramatic decreases in HIV transmission from mother to child, as reported by the Pediatric AIDS Clinical Trials Group Study (ACTG 076) in 1994, which showed a 67 per cent reduction in perinatal HIV transmission through the use of prenatal, intrapartum and neonatal Zidovudine. Where developed countries could report rates as low as 1 per cent, developing countries were still struggling to get to grips with transmission rates of up to 40 per cent in the absence of any interventions.[2]

Given the disproportionately high burden of disease borne by developing countries and the fact that there was very limited access to antiretroviral therapy at the time, a plethora of research studies focussing on identifying solutions for perinatal transmission were undertaken. Many of the studies were designed to investigate shorter, more feasible and affordable regimens for resource limited settings. By the late 1990s and early 2000 several trials on the use of Nevirapine were being carried out across Africa, notably the SAINT[3] trial, the ACTG 316 trial,[4] HIVNET 012 and HIVNET 023, and DART.

Enrolment started in 1997 for the HIVNET 012 trial conducted in Uganda. This was a randomised control trial to evaluate the efficacy of two short courses of antiretroviral drug regimens for the prevention of mother-to-child transmission (PMTCT). The results of this trial were released in 1999. A simple regimen of a single dose of Nevirapine given to the mother at the onset of labour, and a single dose of the same drug in syrup form given to the infant within 72 hours of birth, could dramatically reduce transmission rates (by as much as 67 per cent). The results were received with excitement and optimism by the global community – finally something could be done to stop infants from dying.

The newly appointed Minister of Health, the late Dr Tshabalala Msimang, announced that one of her first tasks was to lead a high-level delegation of policy makers, programme managers and civil society to Uganda. The aim of this visit was to learn how this small country with limited resources and with one of the highest mortality rates in Africa, had achieved this phenomenal outcome. The announcement generated a sense of hope and optimism that was palpable in the country.

The South African delegation received a warm welcome and the visit was extensive, informative and inspiring. Despite the sense of pain and loss that was evident among many of the health providers, one was struck by the dignity, warmth and determination which permeated the lively discussions during the visit.

This was an empowering lesson for South Africa and upon the return of the delegation, the HIV Directorate was given the responsibility of convening a wide range of relevant stakeholders to examine how what was learnt from the visit could be applied in a local context. The task ahead did not seem as daunting as it could have been, because some of the local researchers were already engaged in this work.

Most importantly, the World Health Organization (WHO) had already included Nevirapine in the Model Essential Drug List in December 1999 for PMTCT, and the subsequent registration of Nevirapine paediatric syrup in South Africa would allow for its use in the country. The clinical trials highlighted earlier provided the evidence for the introduction of a PMTCT demonstration project in the public sector following a decision by the Health Minister and Members of the Executive Council (MinMEC) in August 2000.

As programme managers and technocrats in the National Department of Health's HIV programme, our task was to understand the issues and put together a credible programme based on the best available knowledge and evidence. This we did as we prepared to roll out the new policy.

Concerns about drug toxicity started to surface in the discussions of the MinMEC even though these were not entirely 'unknown'. Some of the issues of concern were being addressed in the trials and through post-marketing surveillance, as required by regulatory institutions such as the Medicines Control Council (MCC) in South Africa, the US's Federal Drug Authorities (FDA) and similar bodies in other developed countries. Nevirapine had already been registered for use in adults. Despite this evidence, reluctance to move forward with implementation solidified. Somewhere between the visit to Uganda and the eve of what we all believed was the beginning of a new era for the country, and for women living with HIV in particular, momentum was slowed down by these persistant concerns about drug safety, drug resistance and the unknown long-term effects of antiretrovirals.

It is not easy to pinpoint the seminal event that took us from the optimism of the study tour to Uganda to the debilitating legal arguments in the Constitutional Court (ConCourt) – but that is where we found ourselves; instead of being in the antenatal clinics, providing guidance to health workers who were to ensure that all HIV positive pregnant women received the life-saving medicine for their unborn infants.

As concerns about drug toxicity started taking centre stage in the policy-development space, more evidence to counter these came to the fore. Firstly, the results from the HIVNET study showing significant reductions in rates of transmission were confirmed and accepted by the international scientific community. Secondly, the MCC, whilst highlighting a number of administrative mishaps during the study conducted in Uganda, was not considering deregistering Nevirapine. Thirdly, Boeringer Ingelheim, the pharmaceutical company which manufactured Nevirapine, announced a donation of the drug to South Africa. Furthermore, positive results from the SAINT trials conducted in KwaZulu-Natal were reported during the International AIDS Conference held in Durban in 2000, with the Western Cape Province having already started pilots for PMTCT. The rational question the world was asking was: what was the South African government waiting for? Why was there no urgency to roll out this critical programme to those who desperately needed it? This was a legitimate question and one that officials had no credible response to. In the final instance, pressure from activists across the globe yielded a disappointingly timid response. South Africa would proceed cautiously to establish two pilot sites per province to conduct further operational research on Nevirapine. With sufficient evidence already in the public domain from parts of Africa and South Africa specifically, this decision baffled the world and was viewed as a delay tactic. The activists lost faith and patience, and turned to the highest court in the land to seek relief. The Treatment Action Campaign (TAC) case against the State has been well documented, as was the court's ruling against the government.[5] Whilst what played out in the courts was profound for the entire country, what never caught anybody's attention were the officials who were at the centre of this painful drama. For each one of the people in the programme, the court case took a huge emotional and psychological toll. On many occasions people were attacked and their integrity questioned. Some of the most surreal moments remain too painful to revisit. As qualified and well-trained specialists in the very field under contestation, we grappled with balancing the ethical and logical approach we knew the programme needed to take and the responsibility we had to discharge our responsibility as public servants. To sit night after night, day after day preparing submissions to buttress the arguments the legal experts were trying to make on behalf of the government was painful.

The only way to keep going was to focus on the goal, to remain committed to the inevitable moment we knew had to come. At some point a decision to implement an evidence-based and scientifically sound programme was going to be made. We just did not know how long this would take. Often the strain felt like one was running a marathon for which one was ill-prepared. The worst part was not knowing whether this was a half-marathon or an ultra-marathon. Each one of us had a choice to walk away, but as a team we were committed to staying the course. The most fulfilling part, is knowing that we played a role in what has now turned into a success story for the country.

As a team and members of the HIV community in South Africa, we knew back then as we do today that *Sizonqoba* (we will overcome!).

Despite the way in which it was introduced, crossing the PMTCT bridge was a huge and critical milestone in many ways. Even though the intervention was 'prophylactic' and classified as a prevention intervention, the programme opened up the space for discussions on antiretroviral treatment in a real and tangible way. Although this may not have been obvious – or clearly stated – the natural and logical question we had to confront was: once we had infants born HIV-free, what was to happen to them when their mothers inevitably succumbed to HIV-infection? How could we not keep the mothers alive knowing that evidence showed that keeping mothers alive increased survival chances for their infants?

The early phase of the response to the epidemic was challenging and complex in a number of ways. First, the country was facing a huge, virtually 'unknown' epidemic on a scale which had never been seen before. Although HIV infection was not 'new' – the US and many other developed countries already had guidelines and treatment was available – the numbers involved were much smaller than what we faced in South and Southern Africa. Secondly, the epidemiology of HIV transmission was also different: epidemics in the North were largely confined to so-called 'key populations' – men who have sex with men, people who inject drugs, and minorities or a concentrated epidemic – whereas ours was, and continues to be, classified as a generalised epidemic.

In South Africa HIV was largely transmitted heterosexually, and the numbers exploded shortly after we entered our new democracy in 1994, as reflected in Figure 1. The fact that this epidemic had almost everything to do with 'sex', meant that we had to deal with sex and sexuality in a society largely unused to speaking openly about such issues, which were considered to be private and personal.

Although relations between government and civil society had been strong during the pre-1994 period, the contestation about the causality of HIV, the slow pace of implementation of evidence-based interventions and the ConCourt PMTCT event fractured these bonds, making policy development processes a battleground instead of a platform for robust debates on how to tackle this new 'enemy'. All these factors impacted heavily on the development of policy in the country – at a time when we needed the best scientists working hand-in-glove with technocrats to quickly translate the evidence into a practical, rational and sustainable programme – each constituency ensconced in their particular corner, passionately defending their respective views. Nobody was willing to concede, there was no appetite to find a common position. The media hype and international outcry made a rational debate between the constituencies impossible. Swords were drawn and war had been declared.

Those of us tasked with developing a plan for the country often felt as if we lived in two different worlds, In her analysis of power relationships between various actors in the debates and the role and legitimacy of the state in determining policy, Schneider[6] captures this dual world eloquently. She points out that even as the political and scientific arguments took centre stage, the condom distribution programme was allocated more resources to expand the prevention programme. The PMTCT programme expanded – and quite unexpectedly – with Cabinet approval. The provision of post-exposure prophylaxis for survivors of sexual assault became part of the policy response. This last intervention made for a significant and monumental shift forward in the provision of comprehensive care for survivors of sexual assault. It provided further impetus to the HIV programme, enabling the country to take a step forward towards a comprehensive response.

Most importantly, technocrats in the Department of Health understood that new information and evidence was emerging every day. We were acutely aware of the reality we faced. The whole world was looking for a sustainable solution to this devastating epidemic, and we had to be able to differentiate between scientific evidence and emotive pseudoscience, as well as traditional claims of a cure. We also knew that whatever we presented had to be of the highest standard; we could not make mistakes that could cost lives, nor could we commit state resources to a dubious, unsustainable programme. Striking that balance meant engaging with scientists and establishing trusting relationships – they had to concede gaps in knowledge where these were apparent and we had to commit to provide unferreted support for the evolving research agenda. We could not afford any more lost time, the deaths had to be stopped. Very often we were between a rock and a hard place, but we did not have the luxury of reflecting on personal costs, which for most of us were immeasurable. Every death counted – for those affected our debates were a luxury they could ill afford. We understood that then, as we do today.

The development of the antiretroviral treatment (ART) Plan is often presented as a single big moment toward the end of 2003 when Cabinet adopted the policy. In reality, the history of South Africa's changed HIV response was a four-year process that began mid-1999. The time to develop the new 2000-2005 National Strategic Plan (NSP) on HIV/AIDS and sexually transmitted diseases (STIs), was rapidly catching up with the team. At the time, Dr Tshabalala-Msimang had only held the position of Minister of Health for a few months, but already there were strong indications of her support for alternative cures for HIV with garlic, lemons, beetroot and a host of other non-scientific interventions on her strange menu.

The challenge in mid-1999 was how to write treatment into the NSP while at the same time getting the document approved by the Minister, and ultimately Cabinet. After all the consultations and inputs, it came down to a small team to write, refine and finalise the document. After much deliberation and debate, we agreed on the following language related to HIV treatment (in Goal 7 of the NSP): 'Improve treatment, care and support for people living with and affected by HIV/AIDS' by developing 'guidelines for the treatment of HIV/AIDS patients in health facilities and the community' – broad enough to not be too threatening to the doubters, but also vague enough to allow for the next steps in the process of initiating patients on treatment for HIV.

Getting the NSP approved was a major victory. There was a brief period where everyone worked well in collaboration – government, civil society, and business. This was also the time when the South African National AIDS Council (SANAC) was established. It was supposed to be a body that would bring together relevant stakeholders to serve advisory functions in a more structured way than had been the case before, but in reality the Minister ensured that she selected members that were 'friendly' to the Department of Health, and who would not challenge government views. As such, SANAC was not effective and it served as a forum to "rubber-stamp" the Minister's priorities. Despite the prevailing climate of cooperation, support from the donor community, and the language in the NSP, we needed to move forward and find a way to make ART a reality in South Africa.

Mid-2000, the first step was to engage with Médecins Sans Frontières in South Africa to conduct a study on the cost-effectiveness of models for antiretroviral therapy (with financial support from the United States Agency for International Development (USAID)). The main elements of this study were to look at the costs of treatment, the therapeutic benefits and costs of treatment options, and how ART would likely impact on transmission rates.

The role of business

The path to ART in South Africa was certainly not limited to the role of the usual actors we think of – the Department of Health, the TAC – but what is often overlooked is the role that business played. The establishment of the National Economic Development and Labour Council (NEDLAC) in the mid-1990s was critical in creating a forum for business and government to discuss common goals, and HIV was certainly a major focus on the health front. With the 2000-2005 NSP, the first major player to step up to the plate was Pfizer. In late 2000 Pfizer met with the Department of Health to establish the Diflucan donation programme. Diflucan is a drug for the treatment of two major HIV opportunistic infections – cryptococcal meningitis and oesophageal candidiasis. Important components of this programme were the training of health workers, and the development of a training manual, which covered a broad spectrum of HIV management topics, and also addressed the issue of increasing the knowledge base of health workers on HIV management.

The pharmaceutical industry and research bodies further accelerated the move to introducing ART to the public in 2004 by funding various studies on ART usage, as well as on Nevirapine for the PMTCT.

The study report[7] clearly laid out the rationale for introducing ART: averting the projected 500 000 deaths due to HIV by 2003, and the reduction in life expectancy to 36 years by 2010. With more than 4 million people living with HIV in 2000, the need for intervention was clearly evident. A spectrum of approaches were recommended:

- Scaling up palliative and home-based care;
- Treatment of opportunistic infections; and
- Antiretroviral therapy.

The first two strategies were uncontroversial, and were implemented through the public health system. The third option would prove much harder to implement. Apart from the political apathy around ART, there was also the high cost of treatment. In 2000, ART cost between US$10 000 and US$15 000 per annum in the US and Europe, but could be around 80 per cent cheaper if generics were used. Accessing these cheaper drugs would require major changes, though, to the mechanisms used to purchase medicines (for example consideration of using compulsory licencing), and the costs were still considered high when the other associated costs were taken into account (laboratory infrastructure, training of health staff and infrastructure improvements). Though the cost-effectiveness of ART was not under dispute from most of the decision-makers, especially in the National Treasury, the initial financial investment was considerable. This made it easy for those not in favour of ART in the public sector to argue against its provision and often the argument the Minister and others expressed was: if you cannot give ART to everyone, then no one should get it – an equity-based justification – which was a difficult argument to win given the new democratic dispensation.

Against this backdrop, the next major development was a document on policy recommendations for safely and effectively using antiretroviral therapy in South Africa. This document, developed through consensus in 2001, provided the broad framework for what would be needed to implement ART in the public sector, and was a precursor to the plan developed in 2003. This plan called for an investment in health infrastructure; ensuring a continuum of care; sound communication and advocacy around the benefits of ART; and good monitoring and evaluation of programme implementation, including measuring clinical efficacy, cost-effectiveness, and safety. Again, the major issue was that of affordability. The annual estimates for ART implementation, at a cost of between US$350 and US$600 per patient per annum, increased from around R3.7 billion in 2001 to R12.5 billion in 2010.

These developments also paved the way for the introduction of more (limited) treatment interventions, such as the provision of ART for survivors of sexual assault in 2002. By 2003 the stage was set for the most significant development in the path to ART implementation and scale-up in South Africa: the establishment of the Joint Health-Treasury Task Team (the Joint Task Team). The Joint Task Team was established through cooperation between the two departments with the view that its primary function was the development of a clear proposal for introducing ART in South Africa. After months of hard work, countless arguments, and dealing with (sometimes) obstructionist views, the Joint Task Team presented its findings to Cabinet in August 2003. The report from the Joint Task Team provided the rationale for implementing a full suite of prevention, care and treatment interventions focused on both the 40 million HIV-negative people, as well as the 4.7 million HIV-positive persons. For the HIV-negative population, the Joint Task Team proposed scaling up information, education and communication around safe sexual behaviour, post-exposure prophylaxis for survivors of sexual assault, effective management of STIs, and scaling up voluntary HIV counselling and testing. For HIV-positive people, the call was for a continuum of care (which included nutritional support as well as infant feeding for HIV-positive mothers), scaling up PMTCT, and providing ART in a 'phased and progressive manner'. This required significant investment in the necessary prerequisites for success, for example, infrastructure, training, logistical systems, and laboratory support. The Joint Task Team report aimed to make recommendations in line with the relevant WHO guidelines (e.g. ART eligibility at CD4 level below 200, confirmatory HIV testing, clinical assessment, and counselling on adherence). It provided three scenarios for ART coverage: 20 per cent, 50 per cent and 100 per cent, with the 2003 costs for ART only ranging from under R100 million to R700 million, rising to between R2 billion and R15 billion by 2010. The full cost of treatment would be even higher – around R21 billion by 2010.

Though daunting, the projected benefits in life years gained were impressive: from five million life years gained under a 20 per cent coverage scenario, to over nine million life years gained in a 100 per cent coverage scenario. The choice that the country needed to make was clear: ART implementation was needed immediately. Cabinet, confronted with this report, clearly had to agree and approved the report in its meeting on 8 August 2003:

> Cabinet decided that the Department of Health should, as matter of urgency, develop a detailed operational plan on an antiretroviral treatment programme. The Department will be assisted in this work by South African experts as well as specialists from the Clinton Foundation AIDS Initiative

> who have not only offered to contribute to this effort; but have also been of great assistance in commenting on the work done thus far.[8]

What may not be well known was the instrumental role of an external entity, the Clinton Foundation, in bringing about change. The Clinton HIV/AIDS Initiative (CHAI),[9] following a meeting between former President Mbeki and former US President Clinton, sent a team of people to South Africa in July 2003 to work alongside officials of the Department of Health, particularly in the HIV/AIDS and Health Economic Directorates, to assist with the Joint Task Team report, and the subsequent planning process. CHAI was ideally placed to provide this support, having provided similar assistance to other countries, and brought with it some of the top US HIV clinicians involved in the implementation of ART programmes in the US and elsewhere. Alongside prominent clinicians, a team of young CHAI associates paired up with officials from the Department of Health in the fields of procurement, planning, financing and others. As early as 20 August 2003 – a mere two weeks after the Cabinet approval of the Joint Task Team report – plans were made for Department of Health and CHAI staff to visit facilities in all provinces to review the infrastructure of proposed facilities for ART implementation.

Visits to provinces probed the readiness of public health facilities identified by the provinces for ART implementation by examining the physical facilities, management information systems, clinical services, human resources, laboratory and diagnostic services, pharmacy staff and infrastructure – including commodity security, care and support services, transportation systems, data management systems, quality assurance, and community resources (e.g. support groups).

To complement the efforts of the Department of Health and CHAI, the Minister appointed a new task team to oversee the development of the plan. At this point the Minister was already de-emphasising the ART component of the plan, with the press release announcing the establishment of the task team referring to the "task team charged with examining treatment options to supplement comprehensive care for HIV/AIDS in the public sector".

There were not only several members on the task team from the Department of Health, but also external members from the South African Medical Council, the South African Nursing Council, the Health Professions Council of South Africa, the National Institute for Communicable Diseases, the South African Military Health Services, and the WHO. Despite this, the bulk of the work was conducted by the team from the Department of Health and CHAI.

The planning process was intense. Daily meetings, which often ran to the early hours of the morning, were held to draw up outlines, create assessment tools for facility visits, and engage with provinces to develop province-specific plans. Often

'I can only reflect on the ART plan writing and can honestly say that despite being in South Africa for only a brief period, it was the most challenging, most sleep deprived, but also most inspiring and energising period in my career to date because of the true teamwork and great synergy. The sense of common purpose was powerful and uplifting within the crisis around us'.

Dr Eugene Kroon, clinician and member of the CHAI support team

the team spent the whole day and evening working on a particular item, only to be told that the quality was inadequate, or there were gaps in the information. This, of course, meant even longer working hours for the team. This was a team sustained not only by coffee and sugar, but also the belief that what they were working on was worth the momentary sacrifice to our personal lives.

The task was daunting: to develop a comprehensive plan to expand HIV/AIDS care and treatment. This meant addressing key issues of care and treatment, including HIV testing, integration with existing programmes on PMTCT and tuberculosis (TB), nutrition, testing algorithms and treatment options, clinical monitoring, and patient adherence and follow-up. Focus was also placed on the support services and systems that needed to be in place to make treatment successful, including facility accreditation, training of staff, safe and reliable drug storage, patient information systems, drug procurement and distribution, and laboratory monitoring.

Draft after draft was produced, scrutinised, rejected, and amended, until slowly, but surely, an outline that would be acceptable to Cabinet developed. This included a detailed operational plan (a week-by-week Gantt chart), which was eventually titled the *Comprehensive Care, Management and Treatment (CCMT) Plan for HIV and AIDS*.

The Minister played an active role in the final stages, insisting on diminishing the treatment component of the plan and strengthening the sections on nutrition and the use of traditional medicine. As officials, it often seemed as though we were engaged in a battle of wills, and weeks of back and forth debate drained us all – physically and mentally. What sustained us was the approval of the Joint Health-Treasury Task Team Report, the 8 August 2003 Cabinet statement, and the behind-the-scenes support from the TAC, AIDS Law Project, and a large number of HIV clinicians.

Despite the support, the constant changes requested by the Minister had the Task Team wondering if the plan would ever be approved and implemented. The plan was finally submitted for discussion by Cabinet on 19 November 2003 – two months later than the original mid-September that had been requested. We fully expected further delays in adoption and implementation should the Minister convince the Cabinet that more work was needed on the plan. When Cabinet approved the plan and gave the Department the mandate to move forward with implementation, the Task Team was astounded. Four years of struggle and fighting (with the Minister, the TAC, NAPWA and so many more), with eventual collaboration (following the ConCourt case, mended), had finally borne fruit. When we wrote the NSP in 1999, we were hopeful, but we were never fully convinced we would be able to implement ART until the next NSP that could hopefully be more ambitious. The elation of the Task Team was, however, to be short-lived.

The drama did not, as expected, end after submission to the Cabinet on 19 November 2003. The next challenge would be to prepare for the implementation of the plan starting 1 April 2004. Buoyed by the success of the plan's approval, the willingness of provinces and external stakeholders to support the process, the additional funding from the National Treasury, and the confluence of the ART Plan with the start of the United States President's Emergency Plan for AIDS Relief (PEPFAR) programme in South Africa, we knew we had the financial resources, and the necessary intellectual capacity, to make this a success.

The next step was the accreditation process to determine which health facilities were ready to offer treatment. The tool for this was included in the plan, and it needed to be implemented by teams of officials from the national Department of Health, along with provincial counterparts, by visiting health facilities and signing off on their readiness. The Minister pressured provinces to only nominate two facilities per province, which would eventually scale up to one per district, with wider scale-up after that. Though some could argue that this was based on concerns about quality as well as issues like capacity and financial resources, for those close to the situation, the only purpose appeared to be to create further delays. To their credit, the provinces generally paid little attention to this, and though there were not that many facilities ready on 1 April 2004, the notion of two facilities per province had quickly been abandoned. Bureaucracy was, surprisingly, of assistance in the accreditation process. The Minister wanted regular updates on which facilities were being accredited, but since it could take some time for documents to reach the national Department, and the Minister had a busy travel schedule, it often meant that by the time she saw a list, the accreditation process was completed.

The beginning of the 2004/5 financial year (1 April 2004), and the official commencement of the ART programme, was one of the most joyous times for all government officials involved in this process. It was incredibly rewarding to know that lives would be saved through our efforts and perseverance. With the assistance of the US government's PEPFAR programme, we had the financial resources, and additional human resources, to assist with implementation of the

ART programme. Despite the optimism, though, the rollout of the programme was slow. Much of this slow pace was attributable to lack of leadership, weak management and institutions, and lack of adequate human resources at the facility level – essentially a weak public health delivery system. The programme scaled up, but slowly, until 2008.

When President Mbeki was recalled in 2008, the newly appointed President Kgalema Motlanthe appointed Barbara Hogan as the Minister of Health. One of her first public announcements was that HIV caused AIDS – ending the period of denialism in South Africa. In a meeting hosted by the Department of Health to strengthen the PMTCT programme, she called on all partners to work with the Department of Health to prevent infants from becoming infected – a process called the A-Plan.[10] She also co-led a process to reform the health system, which was facilitated by the Development Bank of Southern Africa. This process led to the crafting of what was called a Health Roadmap that included a list of recommendations – the 10-Point Plan – and which was the basis of the new five-year strategy for the Department of Health.

The Health Roadmap noted that even though there had been achievements since 1994, health outcomes in South Africa were worse than in 1990. For example, using 2005 data, life expectancy was at 45 years, maternal mortality was 400/100 000 and infant mortality was 69/1000 live births. Compared to countries with similar levels of development, South African outcomes were far worse. Life expectancy trends for both males and females were what one would expect if South Africa was at war. In fact, the country was at war – with HIV and AIDS as the enemy. The Health Roadmap noted that deaths associated with HIV and AIDS rose from three per cent in 1995 to 46 per cent in 2005. In addition, TB rates had increased and were amongst the highest in the world. It was clear, therefore, that unless South Africa dealt with the twin epidemics with significant seriousness, health outcomes and social and economic development would not improve.

Key issues in the 10-Point Plan related to HIV programming included:

- Develop appropriate messaging for communication campaign by Minister and Presidency (with other key stakeholders), with particular focus on ensuring that the entire society addresses HIV/AIDS and TB as society's problem.
- Develop a strategic focus on child and maternal health:
  - Address constraints to districts reaching required PMTCT uptake; and
  - Ensure maternal health systems are optimised, for example PMTCT and ART.

In addition, in August 2009 the Lancet published a series on South Africa with six series of comments and six papers drafted by South African academics. In their comment on the various papers the editors[11] noted:

> Not since the first democratic elections in 1994 has there been so much hope and expectation for a better health system, with improved health outcomes for all, in South Africa. The country is at an important crossroads. The new government under President Jacob Zuma has inherited a massive task to improve health and health care for about 49 million South Africans, and to provide a lead and example for other countries in sub-Saharan Africa. The challenges are great. Morale of doctors and other health workers is at an all-time low. Strikes are threatening to damage an already stretched public health system. And health outcomes are widely disproportionate to spending, which was sizeable during the years of relative economic stability.

In their advice to the Minister, Abdool Karim et al.[12] provided steps to be taken to deal with the twin epidemics of TB and HIV. These authors provide four steps to control TB, four steps to avert new HIV infections and four steps to strengthen HIV treatment.

The national elections in April 2009 ushered in a new vision for HIV. South Africans voted the African National Congress back into power with President Jacob Zuma as the head of state. President Zuma, in turn, appointed a new Cabinet, with Dr Aaron Motsoaledi, a medical doctor and former MEC from Limpopo, as the new Minister of Health. Before his appointment, Minister Motsoaledi's views on HIV were not generally known, but it soon became apparent that his view, like Barbara Hogan who he replaced, differed significantly from that of former President Mbeki as well as the former Minister of Health, Dr Manto Tshabalala-Msimang.

Armed with the 10-Point Plan, and soon after taking office, the new Minister met with AIDS activists and declared that he believed that HIV caused AIDS and that improving access to ART was fundamental to the AIDS response. His views on the need to rapidly scale up access to ART were also conveyed to managers in the national Department of Health. His instruction to the Deputy Director-General responsible for the HIV programme was to remove all barriers to rapid scale-up of the ART programme. These barriers included: the onerous requirements for a hospital to provide ARVs, which included only doctors initiating patients on first-line treatment; availability of a nutritionist or dietician as well as a psychologist or social worker to provide counselling; and infrastructure requirements which included a separate clinic – called ARV clinics – with dedicated staff. These requirements were discussed with our international partners, including the WHO, and approved for implementation – despite the acknowledgement that many of the required resources were not immediately available in many public hospitals.

These requirements meant that very few facilities were able to initiate patients on ARVs given the large number of patients that required treatment. At this time the WHO guidelines were to initiate patients with CD4 less than and equal to 200 cells on treatment. Whilst ART was only provided at hospitals, treatment for tuberculosis was available at primary health care facilities (clinics and community health centres), and professional nurses could give treatment.

The number of patients on ART rose slowly from 2003. By 2008 a cumulative total of 488 000 HIV-positive patients were initiated on ART at CD4 <200 cells. Minister Motsoaledi, with the support of President Zuma and Deputy Minister Kgalema Motlanthe, initiated a series of interventions to strengthen and accelerate the delivery of HIV services. The first set of changes to the ART programme included:

- The relaxation of the facility accreditation process which assessed facility readiness to provide ARVs;
- The decision to decentralise ARV initiation from hospitals to primary health care facilities;
- The decision to task shift – training of nurses to initiate patients on ART (Nurse Initiated and Managed Anti-Retroviral Treatment (NIMART) trained nurses); and
- To train lay counsellors to provide voluntary counselling and testing services.

In 2009, only 250 nurses were trained to initiate patients on ARVs. By March 2011, more than 10 500 nurses had been trained and began to initiate patients on treatment at primary health care facilities in the public sector.

The second major change was the decision – announced by President Zuma in December 2009 (World AIDS Day), to become effective in April 2010 – that South Africa would change the ART eligibility criteria from CD4 <200 to CD4 <350, in line with the latest WHO guidelines. In addition, the President announced that patients co-infected with TB and pregnant women would be initiated on ART without CD4 or staging criteria being applicable, and that TB and HIV-positive patients would be treated in an integrated fashion – under one roof.[13] These changes were hailed globally, but at the same event the Executive Director of UNAIDS, Michel Sidibé, challenged South Africa to use its purchasing power to obtain ARVs at lower prices, noting that the country was still paying far too much. More could be done if the cost of treatment could be lowered.

To initiate large numbers of patients on ARVs, and challenged by the Executive Director of UNAIDS, the country changed its procurement practices with assistance from CHAI and WHO, using international benchmark prices as the base price that the country was prepared to pay suppliers. This resulted in the cost of ARVs being reduced by 53 per cent and saved the country a massive R4.7 billion on the tender for the two years 2011-2012, which was announced in December 2010. These financial gains assisted the initiation of more than 3.2 million people on ARVs – the largest programme in the world – by August 2015.

As soon as suppliers could provide large quantities of the fixed-dose combination (FDCs) – which would reduce the pill burden on patients – and the Medicines Control Council registered the drugs, the Minister of Health announced that FDCs – or one pill once a day – would be available from April 2013 to patients on first-line ARVs. This news was greeted with much enthusiasm by patients who previously had to contend with taking three or four tablets twice or three times a day. Besides decreasing the pill burden on patients and improving adherence, the FDC was also procured by the Department of Health at significantly lower cost.

According to South Africa's 2013 report on the MDGs, in 2005 an estimated 13.9 per cent of those eligible for ARVs were on treatment. By 2009 this percentage had increased to 41.6 per cent, and was 72.5 per cent by 2011. Bekker and others estimated that ART coverage had actually reached 84 per cent by the end of 2010.[14] This means that the 2008/09 interventions to rapidly improve ART coverage had worked.

In January 2015 the country changed its ART eligibility in line with the 2014 WHO guidelines, from eligibility at CD4 <350 cells to CD4 <500 cells, which would further expand access.

In order to initiate patients on treatment, people needed to know their HIV status. In April 2010, led by President Zuma, the country initiated a national testing campaign with the aim of testing 15 million people in 15 months. This target was exceeded and has led to an increase in the number of people testing for HIV each year. In 2009, two million people were tested annually; due to the campaign, as well as the move from voluntary counselling and testing to provider initiated testing, this increased to over nine million people being tested annually by 2013/14.

The plan to align fully with WHO guidelines – starting with all those that test HIV positive on ART, regardless of CD4 levels – is another major steps in the development of progressive ART programmes that can provide the best possible access to those in need.

Changes to the HIV prevention programme, apart from those to the PMTCT and HIV counselling and testing (HCT) programmes, were a significant increase in the number of male and female condoms procured and distributed for free by the Department of Health; as well as the introduction of a medical male circumcision (MMC) programme. Independently conducted surveys by the Medical Research Council showed that mother-to-child transmission of HIV reduced from eight per cent in 2008 to 2.6 per cent in 2012. Data from the National Health Laboratory Service (NHLS) shows that the transmission at six weeks postpartum had decreased to 1.5 per cent by 2014.

It is well known that consistent use of condoms prevents HIV transmission (and other STIs), as well as unwanted and unplanned pregnancies. The number of male condoms distributed by the Department of Health increased from 288 million in 2008 to over 500 million in 2012. This increased even further to 750 million in 2015. Distribution of condoms, however, needs to be accompanied by better targeting as well as information about both correct and consistent use. Similarly, the number of males that were circumcised has also increased significantly since the voluntary MMC programme was introduced in 2010. Cumulatively, more than two million MMCs were performed in the past five years.

HIV has had a major impact on health outcomes, as shown at the beginning of this section. The interventions introduced since 2009 have, however, had a significant impact on health outcomes. The Medical Research Council's Burden of Disease Unit estimates that life expectancy increased from 57.1 years in 2009 to 62.2 years in 2013.[15] Similarly, under-five mortality decreased from 57/1000 live births to 41/1000, and maternal mortality decreased from 287/100 000 in 2008 to 197/100 000 in 2011. These declines have also been noted, together with the decrease in the contribution of HIV to under-five mortality.[16]

Despite these achievements, HIV is still a major cause of morbidity and mortality with an unacceptably high number of new infections. Estimates from modelling suggest that HIV is associated with 12.8 per cent of under-five deaths and that there are more than 1 740 new HIV infections in girls and young women between the ages of 15 and 24 years every week.[17]

Estimates of health outcomes as reflected above indicate that the country did not reach its Millennium Development Goals of 38/100 000 for maternal mortality and 20/1000 live births for under-five mortality. In addition, the country (at the time of writing) is still far off the 2030 National Development Plan target of 70 years life expectancy.

As the country develops plans to implement the Sustainable Development Goals, there is still much work to be done to end AIDS. As part of the Investment Cases for TB and HIV completed during 2015, modelling exercises showed that

South Africa could reach the global targets by 2020 for HIV and TB with the adoption of the 90-90-90 targets.[18] This implies testing the most vulnerable for HIV and TB (or those with HIV and TB, but who do not know their status; or those that know their status, but are not on treatment), putting those with these diseases on treatment, ensuring that the HIV-positive patients on treatment are virally suppressed and TB patients are successfully treated. This can be done with existing knowledge, diagnostics and medication. To reach targets that are lower, however, new diagnostics and treatment regimens will be needed after 2020 – but this means that these new technologies need to be in an advanced development stage now.

The latest WHO treatment guidelines, released on 1 December 2015, requests countries to consider new guidelines on the use of ARVs to prevent HIV infection and for treatment. South Africa has to seriously consider the use of ARVs to prevent new HIV infections (pre-exposure prophylaxis or PrEP) and universal test and treat (UTT). This implies offering ARVs as prevention to people who consider themselves at high risk for HIV acquisition as well as treatment upon diagnosis for all HIV infected patients, irrespective of CD4 count or staging. Offering all HIV-positive patients treatment potentially means increasing the number on treatment from 3.2 million to 6.8 million (the estimated number of people infected with HIV in the country). In addition, it means offering large numbers of people PrEP, starting with the most at risk, including HIV-negative sex workers, men who have sex with men, as well as young women at risk.

Even as South Africa contemplates putting large numbers of HIV-positive patients on treatment, the importance of ensuring that those who are on treatment are virally suppressed cannot be over-emphasised. This means the provision of adherence support to large numbers of people. Equally, the importance of prevention of HIV acquisition also needs to be prioritised. The use of PrEP should be considered as part of comprehensive and combination prevention, and not as a silver bullet. This means making use of all of the existing biomedical technologies as well more emphasis on the structural drivers of the HIV epidemic.

Finally, this chapter provides an insiders' view of the path travelled from denialism to a country with the world's largest HIV treatment programme. It also reveals at a micro-level how the policy-making process unfolded – in the context of contestation between a false ideology and science. This final quote from a member of the Joint Task Team sums it up well.

At the time, this period felt like a long and gruelling struggle, with what often felt like painfully slow progress. Yet, in retrospect, the pace of this progress was actually quite extraordinary – moving in the space of five years from a fragmentary and limited strategy that was confined almost wholly to prevention, to commencing the implementation of an integrated treatment and prevention programme of unprecedented scope and scale.

The unique circumstances of this period posed extraordinary challenges for policy development and planning processes. It can be argued that, at times, a relatively small group of public officials found themselves mediating and navigating uncomfortably between the complex, denialist-inspired reluctance to engage with effective action in some parts of Government, and the 'all or nothing', rights-based insistence on all-encompassing action by the advocacy community. This was profoundly challenging. The legitimate, democratically elected government of the day appeared deeply reluctant to accept uncontroversial scientific evidence on HIV and effective strategies to combat it. At the same time, highly effective advocacy groups were able to promote an exceptionally ambitious and untested policy agenda, at times without being exposed to legitimate questioning and scrutiny (on such matters as cost, feasibility, targeting etc.). The intellectual blight of HIV denialism paradoxically strengthened the ability of the treatment advocates to argue for a 'maximalist' strategy that might – in more 'normal' policy-making circumstances – have stood little chance of being adopted in full.

Overall, the great lesson of this period is that implementing and scaling up large and complex intervention programmes is hard. It always takes longer than we want; it doesn't go smoothly; and parts of the system struggle to achieve what seems simple to others. That is the nature of implementation. Advocates suffer from acute optimism bias. Slow progress and poor uptake are portrayed as being due to a lack of commitment, rather than to the inherent challenges of asking an under-resourced and under-skilled delivery system to improve its performance massively. It will always be like that, and to fail to accept this reality – and therefore to plan effectively to overcome it – represents a lack of professionalism, not a triumph of idealism.[19]

Notes and References

1 For more on these, see http://www.politicsweb.co.za/news-and-analysis/the-virodene-affair-i and http://www.nytimes.com/1996/10/08/world/south-africa-scandal-over-sarafina-spotlights-corruption-in-the-anc.html?_r=0 [Accessed 18 February 2016].

2 See for example, Fowler, M.G., Lampe, M.A., Jamieson, D.J., Kourtis, A.P. and Rogers, M.F., 2007. Reducing the risk of mother-to-child human immunodeficiency virus transmission: Past successes, current progress and challenges, and future directions. *American Journal of Obstetrics and Gynaecology*, 197(3), Supplement, pp. S3–S9 and Paintsil, E. and Andiman, W.A., 2009. Update on successes and challenges regarding mother-to-child transmission of HIV. *Current opinion in pediatrics*, 2009, 21(1), pp.94-101, doi:10.1097/MOP.0b013e32831ec353.

3 South African Intrapartum Nevirapine Trial.

4 US AIDS Clinical Trials Group.

5 Budlender, G., 2001. South African court rules on the state's obligation to prevent mother-to-child transmission of HIV. Available at http://www.saflii.org/za/journals/LDD/2001/2.pdf [Accessed 18 February 2016].

6 Schneider, H., 2002. On the fault-line: the politics of AIDS policy in contemporary South Africa. *African Studies*, 61(1). Available at http://home.sandiego.edu/~jmwilliams/ps195yspring2004aidsinafrica3.pdf. [Accessed 18 February 2016].

7 Kasper, T., Hilderbrand, K., Tshabane, N., et al., 2002. Antiretroviral therapy in primary health care centers in a South African township. XIV International AIDS Conference, Barcelona, 7-12 July. Abstract MoOrB1095. Kleinert, S. and Horton, R., 2009. South Africa's health: departing for a better future? The Lancet. Published online: 25 August 2009. Available at http://www.thelancet.com/journals/lancet/article/PIIS0140-6736%2809%2961306-4/fulltext [Accessed 28 December 2015].

8 Government Communications, 2003.

9 Now known as the Clinton Health Access Initiative.

10 Barron, P., Pillay, Y., Doherty, T., Sherman, G., et al., 2012. Eliminating mother-to-child HIV transmission in South Africa. *Bulletin of the World Health Organization*, 91, pp.0-74. doi: 10.2471/BLT.12.106807. Available at http://www.who.int/bulletin/volumes/91/1/12-106807/en/ [Accessed 28 December 2015].

11 Kleinert, S. and Horton,R., 2009.

12 Abdool Karim, S.S., Churchyard, G.J., Abdool Karim, Q. and Lawn, S.D., 2009. HIV infection and tuberculosis in South Africa: an urgent need to escalate the public health response. The Lancet. Published Online: 25 August 2009. Available at http://www.thelancet.com/journals/lancet/article/PIIS0140-6736%2809%2960916-8/fulltext [Accessed 28 December 2015].

13 Zuma, J. 2009. Address by President Jacob Zuma on the occasion of World AIDS Day Pretoria Showgrounds, 1 December 2009. Available at http://sbeta.iol.co.za/news/politics/zuma-s-full-speech-on-world-aids-day-466376 [Accessed 28 December 2015]

14 Bekker, L-G., Venter, F., Cohen, K., Goemaere, E., et al., 2014. Provision of antiretroviral therapy in South Africa: The nuts and bolts. *Antiviral Therapy*, 19 Suppl 3, pp.105-116, DOI: 10.3851/IMP2905.

15 Dorrington, R., Bradshaw D., Laubscher, R., Nannan, N., 2014. Rapid Mortality Surveillance Report 2013, Medical Research Council, Pretoria.

16 Byass P., et al., 2015. A Successful Failure: Missing the MDG4 Target for Under-Five Mortality in South Africa. *PLoS Med,* 12(12).

17 Johnson, 2015. Personal communication.

18 UNAIDS, 2014. 90,90,90: An ambitious treatment target to help end the AIDS epidemic. UNAIDS, Geneva. Available at http://www.unaids.org/sites/default/files/media_asset/90-90-90_en_0.pdf [Accessed 28 December 2015]; Stop TB Partnership. 2015. The Paradigm Shift, 2016-2020: The Global Plan to end TB. Available at http://www.stoptb.org/assets/documents/global/plan/GlobalPlanToEndTB_TheParadigmShift_2016-2020_StopTBPartnership.pdf [Accessed 28 December 2015].

19 These are comments from Martin Hensher, Health Economist, Member of the Health and Treasury Joint Task Team, personal communication, 27 January 2016.

Chapter 2

Historical, Social and Cultural Aspects of HIV

A Missing Link in HIV Prevention

Olive Shisana, Nompumelelo Zungu and Meredith Evans

Introduction

Africans are disproportionally affected by the human immunodeficiency virus (HIV), and black women in particular are at high risk of being infected with HIV.[1] Over the past two and a half decades, from 1990 to 2015, South Africa's HIV and acquired immune deficiency syndrome (AIDS) epidemic grew from under one per cent to slightly more than 12 per cent of the population, or an estimated 6.8 million people.[2] In South Africa, AIDS was initially associated with gay men, persons receiving unsafe blood transfusions, and haemopheliacs, with the first cases of the epidemic identified in the 1980s among men who have sex with men.[3] During the early 1990s, the HIV epidemic spread quickly throughout the general population through heterosexual interactions as well as mother-to-child transmission, with pregnant women and children bearing the brunt of the disease. The epidemic grew rapidly in the black African population, particularly among those who lived in informal settlements, where poverty is rife.[4] The HIV epidemic became generalised and grew exponentially from around 1990. In 2012, new infections were still rising at the rate of 369 000 per year[5] and HIV/AIDS-related mortality was estimated at 43.3 per cent of all deaths in 2011.[6]

A re-analysis of South African mortality data reported to the United Nations revealed that 94 per cent of all the HIV/AIDS-related deaths between 1996 and 2006 were misclassified and not counted as HIV/AIDS-related deaths. Conditions such as tuberculosis, other respiratory infections, intestinal infectious diseases, parasitic diseases, meningitis, other infectious conditions, digestive disorders and ill-defined ailments were excluded from HIV/AIDS-related mortality statistics.[7] The epidemic continued to disproportionally affect key populations, such as young black women aged 20 to 34 and men aged 25 to 49, men who have sex with men, drug users and sex workers.[8] The rate of new HIV infections in young adult African women aged 20 to 34 was found to be extremely high at 4.5 per cent in 2012.[9] Furthermore, the epidemic was clustered in 28 districts (out of 52), where the HIV prevalence was higher than 15 per cent.[10]

This chapter focuses on HIV transmission among the black population, particularly black women who are disproportionately affected by HIV. It aims to unpack the interaction of historical and current migratory labour practices and the consequent disintegration of families, coupled with the loss of protective cultural practices, in the spread of HIV. The chapter explores the role of migratory labour practices, urbanisation and the disintegration of families; changes in the political landscape; poverty and related issues of informal settlements, unemployment, and age-disparate transactional sex (colloquially referred to as 'sugar daddies' or 'blessers' and 'sugar mummies'); and, lastly, changes in social norms among youth in the spread of HIV.

Method

This chapter includes a combined approach of a review of the literature and a quantitative analysis of data from the 2012 South African National HIV Prevalence, Incidence and Behaviour Survey; and interpretative analyses of observed changes in social structures, practices and norms.

The literature review included peer-reviewed journal articles, and reports in the public domain using key word searches in search engines, including PubMed, African Journals Online, Google Scholar and Google, among others. Emphasis was placed on literature published over the past 24 years on the historical, social and cultural aspects of HIV in South Africa. Key searches included: migratory labour practices, urbanisation, poverty, informal settlement, unemployment, age-disparate transactional sex, and new communication technology as they relate to HIV.

Primary data from the 2012 national population-based household survey, conducted by the Human Sciences Research Council (HSRC), was analysed using Stata version 14.0. The study population included persons of all ages living in selected households and hotels, excluding residents of institutions, with a sample size of 20 706 adults aged 15 years or older. Further details on the methodology used for the population-based survey can be found in the report published by the HSRC.[11] Using this data, we conducted bivariate analyses to assess the relationships between HIV prevalence and variables used to measure poverty. This analysis considered the association between different measures of poverty and HIV stratified by gender. Measures of poverty include: monthly income relative to national average, perceived socio-economic status, educational levels, location of residence (living in an informal settlement area), and employment status. Confidence intervals (95 per cent) were computed around each estimated

HIV prevalence to allow for comparison by gender and across different socio-economic groups.

Setting the Context

Although the country has various programmes aimed at HIV prevention, treatment and care, in recent years there have been great successes made on the treatment front. The country has made significant progress in increasing the number of people on antiretroviral treatment (ART) and saving the lives of people living with HIV (PLHIV). By 2012, the country had expanded the ART programme to more than three million people, and it has also reduced mother-to-child transmission of HIV due to the expansion of the prevention of mother-to-child transmission (PMTCT) programme. The PMTCT programme is a combination of ART for all pregnant women living with HIV, antenatal services and appropriate infant feeding practices.

Access to ART was enabled by a strong domestic and international political commitment to finance the programme, robust civil society activism and the dedication of health workers, as well as by the people of this country who sought to be tested and enrolled into treatment programmes. Evidence suggests that ART has benefits beyond saving lives in that it also reduces new HIV infections by reducing viral load.[12]

Although the roll-out of ART increased survival among PLHIV, the expansion of treatment and prevention services for PLHIV simultaneously increased pressures on the capacity of the public health care system. Public health care facilities were faced with the challenges of drug and staff shortages and overdemand. Nevertheless, efforts were made to improve health care for PLHIV through the public health care system, most recently through the South African government announcement in May 2016 that ART would be provided free for all PLHIV, regardless of CD4 count.[13]

Despite the impressive expansion of ART in South Africa, more than 1000 new infections continue to occur daily.[14] It is estimated that in 2012, 24 per cent of new infections occurred among young women aged 15 to 24 years, and 63 per cent among adult men and women aged 25 years and older.[15] While strides have been made in preventing new HIV infections in South Africa, particularly for the youth, the same cannot be said for adults. HIV incidence declined by 60 per cent among young people in the period between 2002 and 2008.[16] Unfortunately, HIV incidence has remained relatively stable among adults.

New HIV infections continue to be driven by biological, social and structural factors. Research and intervention programmes, in South Africa and globally, have prioritised biomedical initiatives (such as ART) and individual behaviour change (such as the ABCs of Abstinence, Be Faithful, Condomise) and have focused less on the social determinants of HIV.[17] Although much has been done to prevent HIV infections, the prevalence and incidence remain stubbornly high, prompting researchers to look closer at the structural and historical factors that are underlying the spread of HIV in South Africa.

Until recently, there has not been a conscious focus on the historical context in which HIV is spread.[18] This is despite scholars such as Campbell[19] and Hunter[20] making significant contributions towards shifting the focus to include the historical social context that allowed HIV to thrive in South Africa. Earlier contributions included the high-risk situation model advanced by Zwi and Cabral.[21] Although this model is not widely referenced for understanding why HIV spread so quickly in South Africa, it is a useful framework for understanding risk and how social conditions contribute to high-risk situations that fuel the spread of HIV. The high-risk situation framework is useful 'to describe the range of social, economic and political forces that place groups at particularly high risk of HIV infection'.[22]

These scholars suggested that several features from a variety of settings characterise what they termed high-risk situations. Citing the work of Wilson et al.,[23] they identified several core factors that create high-risk situations: impoverishment, disenfranchisement of certain marginalised groups, rapid urbanisation, transactional sex, powerlessness of women to negotiate safe sex, widespread population movements and displacements of people, social disruption, and wars, especially counter-insurgency wars.[24] Many of these characteristics of high-risk situations are still present in the South African landscape today and continue to be drivers in the spread of HIV.[25] We unpack some of these factors below, with a focus on how they have contributed to the current spread of HIV.

Migratory Labour Practices, Urbanisation and the Disintegration of Families

The industrialisation of South Africa – which began in the late 19th century and continued throughout the colonial and apartheid eras and persists to the present day – led to a dramatic increase of internal migration from rural to urban areas, particularly of black male mine workers. Morrell[26] points out that colonialism and urbanisation destroyed the material base of African economies and challenged masculinities that were constructed and shaped by traditions where men were powerful and superior. The new economic landscape forced African men to migrate to the exploitative workplace.[27] In the majority of cases, men worked in gold mines and, until the 1980s, the goldmines remained the main employer in

South Africa.[28] By the 1990s, however, the levels of employment began to decline and vast numbers of both men and women joined the ranks of the unemployed.[29] Various studies report that masculinities and manhood are threatened and suffer when men are not able to provide for themselves and their dependents.[30] It has been suggested that this leads to an increase in the propensity to risk.[31]

The migrant labour system led to weakening of many social structures such as that of the family.[32] Mobility can facilitate multiple and concurrent sexual relationships caused by unstable and transient conditions; furthermore, for partners who are forcibly separated, there may be a tacit understanding between them – and to some extent, society – that they can seek sex outside their marital union or primary partnership, which increases the risk of HIV infections.[33] The migration of young men and women to urban areas for work opportunities leaves rural areas underdeveloped, perpetuating a cycle of migration that, in turn, increases the dependency of older women who often remain in rural areas looking after homesteads.[34]

Beyond the labour migration that had an impact on the disintegration of black families,[35] legislation under apartheid that regulated residence in urban areas through influx control also resulted in the separation of families.[36] With the Group Areas Act (No. 41 of 1950), which segregated business and residential sections of urban areas, black Africans who had been able to migrate and find residence in urban areas were once again dislocated by forced removals. This time they were moved from their residences close to the towns to high-density dwellings in smaller areas of land in the peri-urban areas.[37] The first wave of dislocation that was enforced by apartheid laws was followed by another wave – in the late 1980s to the early 1990s – that saw informal settlements mushrooming near cities all over South Africa.[38]

The apartheid-built townships consisted of different-sized dwellings.[39] Some of the houses had four rooms while others were smaller, with only two rooms, prompting South Africans to refer to them as 'match boxes' or '*veza nyawo*' (meaning that when sleeping, their feet would protrude outside because the house was too small to accommodate the whole body). To enforce the temporary nature of black Africans in urban areas, the apartheid government built single-sex hostels in the same urban communities where families lived.[40] The construction of hostels and the small houses that were not designed to accommodate families contributed to the separation and disintegration of black African families.[41] Migration to the cities in search of work continued, however, and increasing numbers of shacks were erected in the back yards of formal township homes to accommodate extended families and migrants who were moving to urban areas in search of jobs, mostly in the mines and the construction industry.[42]

This situation was not sustainable, either economically or socially.[43] The resulting high density of the township premises created its own social challenges and strained relationships between tenants and landlords.[44] In the late 1980s, social and political formations such as Sofasonke (we are in it together) led to defiance campaigns to occupy vacant municipal or government-owned land around the townships.[45] The late 1980s campaign was called '*Phumula Mqashi*' (a Zulu term meaning 'tenants, liberate yourselves' from backyard rentals). Early attempts to occupy vacant municipal or government land were met with resistance from the state.[46] Violent clashes between the residents and the police became commonplace, with the municipal police instructed to demolish the shacks as soon as they were erected. The changing political landscape, marred by violence and the intensification of resistance, meant that the state could not sustain its demolition campaign, especially as these areas had now become theatres of struggle against apartheid laws. In many cases, this struggle was joined by various human rights organisations in solidarity. The phenomenon of erecting shacks around the country continues to this day, even as the democratic government tries to contain it and to build houses for the homeless as rapidly as possible,[47] creating a fertile environment for the spread of HIV.

In the 1990s, while some township residents may have considered the occupation of land as a victory for the poor, informal settlements had no infrastructure, such as paved streets, electricity, water or toilets. The living conditions in these informal settlements were inhumane at best, and criminal at worst.[48] Other social ills emerged, including crime, and illegal water and electricity connections. The use of the open veld as toilets, and poor sanitation, meant that outbreaks of cholera were always a threat.[49] Informal settlements tend to lock people in a cycle of poverty with high levels of health issues, including HIV that is now a feature of these areas. Unfortunately, there is little hope that this situation will be eradicated soon, despite the efforts of the African National Congress (ANC) government which has tried to tackle the problem by providing free housing for some who cannot afford it.[50] The number of people on the Reconstruction and Development Programme (RDP) housing waiting list has grown annually, soaring past 2.3 million at the last census.[51] In 2014 an estimated 1.6 million households lived in informal settlements in South Africa,[52] an area that has the highest HIV prevalence.[53]

In the post-apartheid era, unequal wealth re-distribution policies contributed to poverty and dislocation. Thus, a historical cycle of dislocation prevails, affecting mainly young African men and women who are already vulnerable to HIV infection.[54] Morrell and Richter[55] and Wilson[56] pointed to the role of apartheid laws that restricted movement in displacing and depriving black men of fatherhood, and have explored how this has negatively influenced the construction of fatherhood and African masculinity. The disintegration of families and dislocation of people also led to high rates of alcohol abuse,[57] which is an important determinant of HIV risk.[58] Alcohol consumption, combined with multiple sexual partners and casual sex, helped create a ripe environment for the spread of HIV. In the first half of the 20th century the introduction of municipal-run beer halls in South Africa was met by opposition and tension, because they were seen as disrupting families.[59] Shebeens (informal home-based taverns) and beer halls, however, later became a feature of township and hostel culture in black urban areas. Under apartheid, alcohol became a form of escapism for African men living under extremely dehumanising and stressful conditions. Alcoholism among African men was promoted by unethical labour practices that included paying workers with alcohol under the 'tot' or 'dop' systems.[60] Excessive use of alcohol or binge drinking remains high among Africans[61] and, increasingly, research has linked alcohol consumption to masculinity as a symbolic marker of gender difference.[62]

A local study among mineworkers and women living in HIV hotspots, found that participants who did not use alcohol had a significantly lower risk of HIV infection than those who did.[63] The use and abuse of mind-altering substances are associated with an increased risk of HIV infection resulting from unprotected sex associated with being intoxicated.[64] A growing body of empirical evidence associates substance use and HIV infection.[65]

Although there were no 'official' wars in South Africa, the transition from apartheid to democracy was characterised by high levels of political violence perpetrated by the state against the black population.[66] This violence led to a high number of people being displaced and finding themselves driven from their homes to informal settlements in urban black townships.[67]

State-sponsored violence increasingly began to manifest in domestic environments throughout apartheid.[68] Although domestic violence has always been gendered, its prevalence, nature and expression intensified.[69] Gender violence, including sexual violence, continues to play a significant role in the spread of HIV. During apartheid, sexual violence was used as a political weapon, which is typical in situations of war or in conflict zones.[70] In post-apartheid South Africa, sexual violence has also been used as a political weapon, for example sexual violence against women belonging to the opposing political parties in KwaZulu-Natal.[71] Interestingly, as the province with the highest HIV-prevalence in South Africa today, KwaZulu-Natal experienced the highest levels of political violence during apartheid, which resulted in scores of deaths and dislocation of the population, especially women and children.[72] According to Marks, violence became a response to a 'crisis in the gendered ordering in African society'.[73]

Post-apartheid South Africa has seen an increase in gender violence.[74] Some scholars propose that this increase in gender violence can be attributed to an increase in reporting of incidents of the raping of women and children in the newly democratic state.[75] Others argue that violence against women and children has become more prevalent, pervasive and extreme.[76] It has been argued that the escalation of gender violence is underpinned by exaggerated expressions of African masculinity that reflect attempts to compensate for feeling 'less than a man', and loss of control linked to the global economic downturn, unemployment and deepening of poverty in the 1990s.[77] Sexual violence, gender-based violence and gender oppression have, to some extent, contributed to the increase in HIV infections in high-risk situations.[78]

Changes in the Political Landscape

Most contemporary societies are male dominated, with patriarchy prevailing and women suffering.[79] The end of apartheid ushered in hope for a new era of freedom for all, including for women. The women's mantra for liberation was to end the triple oppression where women were discriminated against because of their gender, race and belonging to a lower socio-economic class. In the new South Africa, policies were established to promote gender equality and equal representation of women in all spheres of life. Based on the 2015 Human Development Report, South Africa has made progress in gender equality. For example, there is a high proportion (40.7%) of seats occupied by women in Parliament, and a high proportion of women have achieved secondary education (75.9%). Despite this notable progress, however, South Africa ranks 83 out of 188 countries based on the gender inequality index (UNDP). One of the contributing factors of this poor gender equality ranking is the low labour participation rate of women compared to men (44.5% vs 60.5%). Moreover, more women than men are unskilled labourers; consequently, women earn less than their male counterparts.[80] This has a detrimental impact on the socio-economic status of women and is the reason why women are largely unemployed and are often locked in a cycle of poverty.

Unemployment does not only affect how masculinities are constructed; it perpetuates high levels of poverty, reduces marital rates and leads to increasingly higher levels of social inequalities.[81] Historically, the unemployment of traditional breadwinners has led to women moving to cities in search of employment.[82] Arriving in the city, many women are trapped into human trafficking whereby they are promised jobs, but are not offered real employment and soon find themselves forced into commercial sex work.[83] Dislocated, with no social support, and in a state of anonymity,[84] some enter into a cycle of transactional sex for survival.[85] In transactional sexual relationships, the power imbalance makes negotiating safer sex near impossible,[86] creating fertile ground for the spread of HIV and other sexually transmitted infections (STIs).

Research has shown that women living in poverty who engage in transactional sex for survival are at increased risk of HIV.[87] Also, with no long-term sexual partners, the rate of serial short-term monogamous relationships tends to increase. Within this context of changing gender relations and poverty, South Africa has also seen a decrease in the rates of marriage as well as an increase in the ages of couples entering into marriage.[88] Being unmarried and marrying at a later age has been linked to high HIV rates.[89]

The high turnover of sexual partners that is endemic in transactional sex[90] is a feature of disintegrated societies that are at high risk. This is currently a major factor in the spread of HIV.[91] Transactional sex and multiple concurrent partnerships have been discussed extensively in literature and it has been shown that multiple concurrent partnerships remain a norm, and are associated with notions of 'normative' masculinity.[92] In high-risk situations where poverty is rife, men may have a large pool of sexual partners who are willing to engage in transactional sex, which broadens their choice of sexual partners and increases the risk of being infected with HIV.[93]

The end of apartheid promised racial equality and freedom from racial oppression. Unfortunately, at the time of writing, this had not yet been fully realised for African women or men. Access to quality health care and education was still largely determined by race, despite the fact that racial discriminatory laws were abolished in 1996.[94] Using Statistic South Africa data, Mabela[95] showed that enrollment in medical aid schemes (private health care insurance) was still determined by race and gender. Medical aid scheme membership rates remained at more than seven times higher among whites than black Africans. Over 70 per cent of white men and women belonged to a medical aid compared to only a little over nine per cent of black men and women, which meant that black men and women were extremely unlikely to access private health care.[96] Consequently, black Africans had to endure long waiting service lines, queuing for assistance in public health facilities. It was encouraging that the White Paper on National Health Insurance promised to end inequality in access to health care by ensuring universal health coverage with quality health services, through a better resourced and integrated public health care system.[97]

Access to quality education remains a challenge in South Africa today. Whites and a few black middle class members can afford to enroll their children in independent, well-resourced private schools where the pass rate is high, while a majority of African students have to attend poorly resourced public schools.[98] Lack of access to good quality health care and education perpetuates socio-economic inequalities for young Africans, a phenomenon which has been linked to HIV risk. Many parts of impoverished Africa have seen an increase in the numbers of older men colloquially referred to as 'sugar daddies' or 'blessers', who offer money and gifts in exchange for sex with younger women.[99] On average, about one third of young women in South Africa are involved in age-disparate sexual relationships with men at least five years older than them.[100] Older men's preference for younger partners may be associated with an element of hegemonic masculinity that seeks to subjugate women and control sexual decisions.[101] Younger women are more vulnerable to power dynamics than older, independent women. Indeed, some men use culture and patriarchy to justify subordination and exploitation of younger women.[102] Transactional age-disparate relationships are legitimised, to some extent, by the transactional nature of love relationships in general.[103] In conditions of poverty coupled with inequalities of gender and age, transactional relationships are, however, an HIV risk and endanger the health of young women.[104]

While the transactional sexual behaviour studied was mostly between young women and older men, some younger men reported engaging in this kind of sex for economic reasons with older, mostly married or widowed women, known colloquially as 'sugar mummies'.[105] In South Africa, it is estimated that only 0.7 per cent of young men are involved with older women,[106] and the infrequency of the practice may explain why there is a paucity of research on the subject. A recent qualitative study by Phaswana-Mafuya, Shisana, Davids et al.,[107] found, however, that South Africans are more accepting of the practice of 'sugar mummies'. Furthermore, the assumption that the risk of HIV infection for young men involved with older women is low[108] remains untested, given that older women have a relatively high HIV incidence and HIV prevalence compared to young women.[109]

Research on age-disparate sex tended to focus predominantly on younger women's vulnerability in relation to their older male partners.[110] There is, however, an increase in the call for research that focuses on younger men who have sex with older women, and also with younger men who have sex with older men. Indeed, evidence abounds that has shown the existence of power dynamics and exploitation of younger boys by older men in same-sex relationships.[111] Greater access to resources enables older men and women to exercise power and gives them the negotiating instruments that can be exchanged with partners for sex.[112]

Transactional relationships are motivated by many factors; however, in most cases poverty is the key driver.

Among black Africans, the relationship between poverty and HIV is gendered. A recent article showed that low socio-economic status (SES) was strongly associated with being HIV-positive among black women aged 20 to 34 and was marginally significant among black men aged 25 to 49.[113]

The end of apartheid, and the ushering in of a new democratic dispensation, gave black woman the hope that belonging to a low rank of the socio-economic ladder would become something of the past. This has also, however, not been fully realised. For this to become a reality, massive numbers of jobs need to be created. Unfortunately, the economy that was growing at more than five per cent per annum between 2005 and 2007[114] declined in growth to a snail's pace of under 0.6 per cent in 2014.[115] The stagnation of the economy, partly due to the global financial crisis of 2008 and reduction of jobs in the mining sector as a major source of employment,[116] makes it difficult to absorb those who are unemployed, the overwhelming majority of whom are black and young.[117]

Even though affirmative action legislation and policies were introduced to improve the chances of black African men and women obtaining a share of the economic pie, this, to a large extent, has not materialised. Data released by the Commission on Employment Equity and the Department of Labour showed that the majority of senior positions within the private sector were still occupied by white men, despite the enactment of laws on affirmative action supported by policies, advocacy, publication of the annual reports on this subject and other provisions for improving gender equality in employment.[118] As long as black Africans, African women in particular, remain at the bottom of the economic ladder, they are likely to remain at risk of contracting HIV due to the socio-economic factors that continue to drive new infections in South Africa.

Poverty and HIV

While high-risk situations exacerbated by poverty may vary, they are often characterised by 'situations where there is diminished concern about health, increased risk taking, and reduced social concern about casual sexual relationships',[119] and lack of social cohesion.[120] This is characteristic of most urban informal settlements in South Africa where poverty and HIV are widespread.[121] Evidence pointing to an association between poor living conditions found in informal settlements and the risk of HIV and AIDS abounds.[122]

The association between poverty and HIV has been studied for the last decade,[123] and is often confounded by gender dynamics.[124] The directionality of the relationship is difficult to establish because it is not feasible to conduct randomised controlled trials of poverty, and hence the norm is to assess associations between poverty and HIV while controlling for a number of co-variates. A review of the literature on the relationship between poverty and wealth concluded that the risk of exposure to HIV is no different for the poor compared to the wealthy.[125] Since the publication of this study in 2007, more studies have, however, shown a strong and positive association between poverty and HIV. Poverty can be measured in terms of objective economic indicators,[126] through self-perception, or with a composite index of socio-economic indicators (education, employment and income).[127] To further our understanding of the gendered nature of the relationship between poverty and HIV, we present findings from the national population-based survey in the section below.

Using income as a measure of poverty, in poor households women, compared to men, tended to have a high prevalence of HIV; whereas in middle income households, both men and women had rather similar levels of HIV. In high income households, the situation was reversed, where men had higher HIV prevalence compared to their female counterparts, even though the differences were not statistically significant (Figure 1).

Figure 1 Relationship between Poverty and HIV in South Africa, 2012

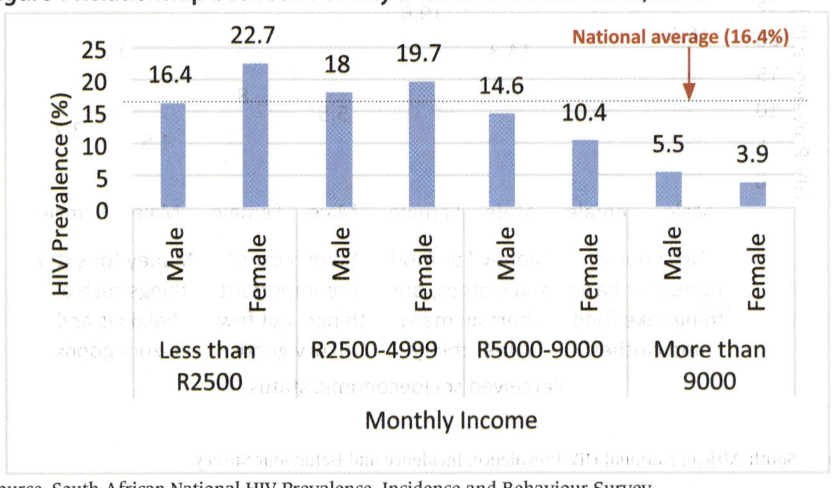

Source: South African National HIV Prevalence, Incidence and Behaviour Survey.

Women living in poor households may engage in high risk behaviours for survival, whereas men living in high income households may use their financial resources to engage in risky sexual behaviours.[128] Being without an income means individuals have to depend on others for financial support. In doing so, the individual may lose control over issues such as taking protective measures against HIV, leading to sex without a condom or engaging in sex when they are unwilling to do so.

The results suggest that HIV risk depends on how men and women perceive their location on the socio-economic ladder. Women who reported to be living in poor households, where they were short of basic necessities, were at increased risk of contracting HIV, but if they perceived themselves to be living in comfort, their risk was low. The situation was the same for men, but they had a lower HIV prevalence compared to their female counterparts. There were no significant differences in HIV prevalence between men and women who perceived themselves to be economically well resourced. This finding needs to be further investigated to determine the reasons for differences in the observed relationships between HIV and both objective and perceived measures of socio-economic status in men (Figure 2).

Figure 2 HIV Prevalence by Sex and Perceived Household Socio-economic Status, South Africa 2012

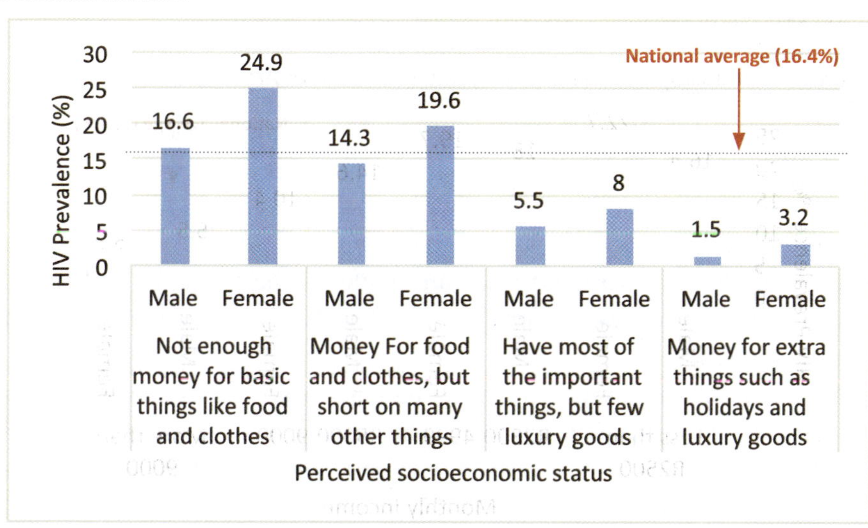

Source: South African National HIV Prevalence, Incidence and Behaviour Survey.

As noted above, living in informal settlements exposes one to risks of HIV. Data shows consistently that HIV is more prevalent in informal settlements than in formal dwelling areas.[129] Data also shows that female residents of urban and rural informal areas had a high HIV prevalence (one in three were HIV positive) that was above the national average, and significantly higher than the HIV prevalence of men living in informal areas (Figure 3).

Figure 3 HIV Prevalence by Sex Locality Type, 2012

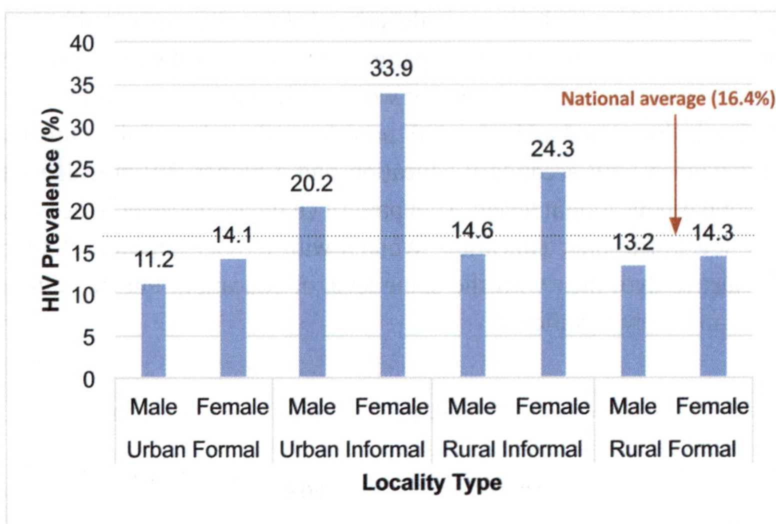

Source: **South African National HIV Prevalence, Incidence and Behaviour Survey.**

By contrast, female residents of urban and rural formal areas had insignificantly higher levels of HIV than males living in similar areas. Overall, living in informal areas was associated with high HIV prevalence, especially for women, whereas living in formal areas was associated with low HIV prevalence. As noted before, the conditions in these areas are fertile for the spread of all kinds of diseases due to overcrowding and poor, or no, sanitation,[130] and the standard of living is very low.

Living in informal settlement areas presents major social challenges that degrade the residents in that these informal structures are often overcrowded, with households in very close proximity to one another.[131] There are also high rates of mobility, which reflect historical labour migratory patterns from rural to urban areas.[132] The environment is also conducive to violence in general, and sexual violence in particular.[133] It is therefore not surprising that these areas have higher HIV prevalence than formal neighbourhoods.[134] Unless assisted by the state through the provision of free formal housing, such as through the RDP, people living in informal settlements are often trapped in poverty and have limited means for relocating to formal housing and better social conditions.

Education is an important determinant of HIV status. Those with higher education are more likely to obtain gainful employment and have access to HIV prevention information. They also have the means to use the information to prevent themselves from becoming infected with HIV.[135] Figure 4 shows the association between HIV prevalence and educational status disaggregated by gender. Overall, the more educated the participants were, the lower their HIV prevalence. Examining data by gender showed that women who had no education, or only a primary level education, had higher HIV prevalence than their male counterparts. Similarly, women with secondary education had a higher HIV prevalence than men of similar educational levels. This pattern changes, however, when considering the level of tertiary education. Women with tertiary education had lower HIV prevalence than men with the same level of education, but this difference was not statistically significant.

Figure 4 HIV Prevalence by Sex and Education Status, South Africa 2012

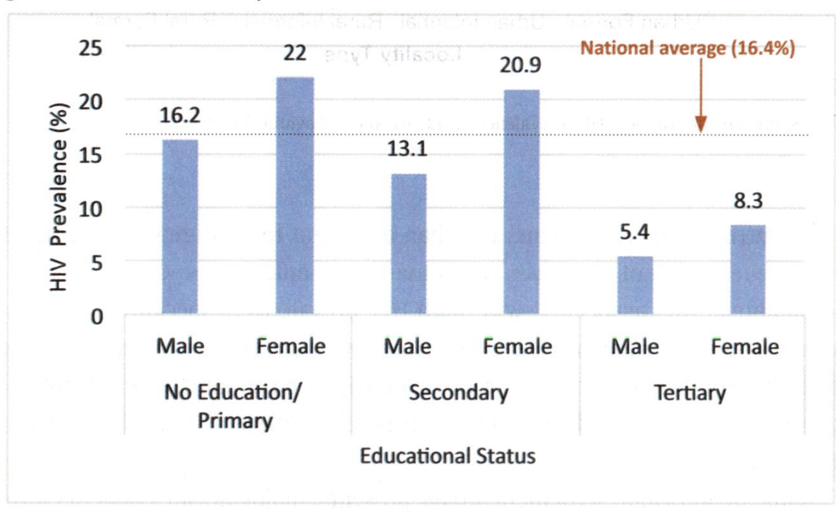

Source: **South African National HIV Prevalence, Incidence and Behaviour Survey.**

These results generally support the hypothesis that poverty is related to HIV. Although poverty increases vulnerability to HIV, this relationship is also determined by gender. The poorer the person, the higher the likelihood of being HIV positive. Poverty is a consequence of unfavourable situations such as migration, unemployment, lack of education and underdeveloped skills necessary to earn a living. Conditions associated with poverty and the struggle for basic needs may supersede concerns about general health and HIV prevention, in particular.

There are many instances in South Africa that show that when individuals are desperate to survive, they become vulnerable to the risk of HIV, and that this is normally fuelled by frequent occurrence of sexual networking, gender-based violence and survival sex.

Change in Social Norms among the Youth

The transition to democracy led to what has been referred to as the 'liberalisation of sexuality'.[136] Within an African context the spread of HIV/AIDS is often attributed to the corruption of traditional culture by modernity, and the desertion – by the youth – of their culture and what has been referred to as ancestral ways.[137] In recent history we have seen a rise in casualisation and commercialisation of sex, often driven by social media. As discussed in detail earlier, the facilitation of transactional sex through 'sugar daddy finder' websites and 'blesser finder' social media pages point to rapidly changing sexual norms in South Africa.

Culture is understood to be a set of shared practices, values and norms that inform social interaction and prescribe what is accepted by a particular community.[138] Culture is often informed by historical experiences that shape worldviews. There have been vast changes in cultural norms and values that regulate sexuality and reproductive lives in South Africa, linked to previously discussed historical factors.

Changes in social norms, particularly through migration and the disintegration of families, led to men being absolved from the responsibility and accountability for unplanned or premarital pregnancies.[139] The rejection of culturally enforced sanctions, such as *intlawulo* (damage reparation) and *isondlo* (maintenance), meant that women were increasingly becoming responsible for their children being pregnant. Previously, men who impregnated single unmarried women were required to 'pay for damages', because of the belief that it would be difficult for the woman to find a partner to marry.[140] With limited financial resources, young men were careful to take responsibility for prevention of pregnancy and would engage in non-penetrative sex, such as thigh sex, as a socially accepted alternative to penetrative sex.[141] This is one of the practices that would have contributed to the prevention of HIV. Changes in social norms and the increasing rejection of *intlawulo* and *isondlo* have, however, been accompanied by an increase in unplanned pregnancies through premarital penetrative sex, as well as increases in sexually transmitted infections and the practice of multiple sexual partnerships.[142] Left to raise children without any support or maintenance, women are caught in a cycle of poverty that continues to impact future generations and increase the risk of HIV spread.

The Internet is now widely available through computers, tablets, laptops and smart phones, particularly for young people. This means porn and transactional sex 'sugar daddy' and 'blesser finder' websites are increasingly accessible. Although there is an increasing recognition of the influence of social media on sexual behaviour and risk, HIV prevention programmes and those responsible for implementation have not capitilised on this medium for delivering prevention messages.

Conclusion

The aim of this chapter was to unpack the complex relationship pertaining among several social and economic variables. These are historical migratory labour practices and the resulting disintegration of families, which happened concomitantly with the loss of protective cultural values and practices, as well as poverty, all of which ultimately continue to create a fertile ground for the spread of HIV in South Africa. Using literature and quantitative data as well as interpretation of observed societal practices, we recommend policy and programmatic changes aimed at reducing new HIV infections.

Migratory labour practices continue to occur, even though movement is not restricted today. Unemployment remains a major challenge and is an underlying factor driving risky sexual behaviour, especially among young women. There is a need to create work opportunities through the support of entrepreneurship to create local employment in order to reduce the number of people who leave their homes and seek jobs in major cities. Where people still migrate from rural to urban areas, or from small towns to major cities, public and private sectors need to develop policies that enable spouses to relocate with their family whenever there is a need for transfer to other work areas. Keeping families together will reduce the HIV infection risk associated with multiple sexual partnerships.

Eradication of informal settlements was expected to have been achieved by 2014, if the Breaking New Ground housing policy had been implemented as designed. As long as massive economic inequalities continue to exist in South Africa, vulnerability to HIV infection will remain. Some may argue that the only focus should be on proven biomedical interventions in order to reduce new HIV infections, such as massive roll out of ART, introduction of Pre-Exposure Prophylaxis and medical male circumcision. Changing the social environment that gives rise to risky sexual behaviours (such as improving the socio-economic conditions of women, reducing overcrowding, improving the educational levels of women and reducing violence against women, which is common in informal settlements) is however necessary for a sustainable solution to the HIV epidemic.

The disintegration of the African family has been to the detriment of our country. There is a need to build and strengthen the African family, however defined. Randomised controlled trials of programmes to strengthen families are required to provide evidence that can be used across different family settings, similar to those developed by the University of Iowa.[143] The phenomenon of 'sugar mummies', and 'sugar daddies' or 'blessers', constitutes an increasingly popular practice with significant risk for young women and young men as a result of age, gender and economic power imbalances. Future research should continue to assess the impact of these social practices on HIV risk to all the parties involved, while refraining from moralising or stigmatising the behaviour. More studies are needed to develop interventions to increase self-efficacy in sexual decision making to ensure an equitable power balance in sexual relationships.

Figure 5 HIV Prevalence by Sex and Employment Status, South Africa, 2012

Source: South African National HIV Prevalence, Incidence and Behaviour Survey.[144]

Acknowledgements

This data collected as part of the 2012 South African National HIV Survey was made possible through the dedication of fieldworkers and research staff of the HSRC and partners, as well as through the contributions of study participants. The authors thank Professor Dan Ncayiyane for his helpful comments and suggestions on previous versions of this chapter.

Notes and References

1 UNAIDS, 2014. The Gap Report. Geneva: UNAIDS. Available at http://www.unaids.org/sites/default/files/media_asset/UNAIDS_Gap_report_en.pdf. [Accessed 08 June 2015].

2 UNAIDS, 2015. Focus on location and population. Geneva: UNAIDS. Available at http://www.unaids.org/sites/default/files/media_asset/WAD2015_report_en_part01.pdf. [Accessed 08 June 2015].

3 Anderson, R., Prozesky, O.W., Eftychis, H.A., Van der Merwe, M.F., Swanevelder, C. and Simson, I.W., 1983. Immunological abnormalities in South African homosexual men. *South African Medical Journal*, (64), pp.119-122; Ras, G.J., Simson, I.W., Anderson, R., Prozesky, O.W. and Hamersma, T., 1983. Acquired immunodeficiency syndrome. A report of 2 South African cases. *South African Medical Journal/Suid-Afrikaanse Tydskrif Vir Geneeskunde*, 64(4), pp.140-142.

4 Shisana, O. and Simbayi, L.C., 2002. Nelson Mandela/HSRC study of HIV/AIDS: South African national HIV prevalence, behavioural risks and mass media: Household survey 2002. Cape Town: HSRC Press.

5 Shisana, O., Rehle, T., Simbayi, L.C., Zuma, K., Jooste, S., Pillay-Van Wyk, V. and SABSSM III Implementation Team, 2009. *South African national HIV prevalence, incidence, behaviour and communication survey, 2008: A turning tide among teenagers?* Cape Town: HSRC Press.

6 Mayosi, B.M., Lawn, J.E., Van Niekerk, A., Bradshaw, D., Karim, S.S.A., Coovadia, H.M. and Lancet South Africa team, 2012. Health in South Africa: Changes and challenges since 2009. *The Lancet*, 380(9858), pp.2029-2043.

7 Birnbaum, J.K., Murray, C.J. and Lozano, R., 2011. Exposing misclassified HIV/AIDS deaths in South Africa. *Bulletin of the World Health Organization*, 89(4), pp.278-285.

8 Shisana, O., Zungu, N., Evans, M., Risher, K., Rehle, T. and Celentano, D., 2015b. The case for expanding the definition of 'key populations' to include high-risk groups in the general population to improve targeted HIV prevention efforts. *SAMJ: South African Medical Journal*, 105(8), pp.664-669; Shisana, O., Rehle, T., Simbayi L.C., Zuma, K., Jooste, S., Zungu N., Labadarios, D., Onoya, D. et al., 2014. South African National HIV Prevalence, Incidence and Behaviour Survey, 2012. Cape Town, HSRC Press; Cloete, A., Simbayi, L.C., Rehle, T., Jooste, S., Mabaso, M., Townsend, L., Ntsepe, Y., Louw, L., Naidoo, D., Duda, T., Naidoo, P. and Marang Project team, 2014. The South African Marang Men's Project Report. Cape Town: HSRC Press.

9 Shisana et al., 2014.

10 Wabiri, N., Shisana, O., Zuma, K. and Freeman, J., 2016. Assessing the spatial nonstationarity in relationship between local patterns of HIV infections and the covariates in South Africa: A Geographically Weighted Regression Analysis. *Spatial and Spatio-temporal Epidemiology*, 16, pp.88-99.

11 Shisana et al., 2009.

12 Cohen, M.S., Chen, Y.Q., McCauley, M., et al., 2011. Prevention of HIV-1 infection with early antiretroviral therapy. *N Engl J Med*, 365(6), pp.493-505.

13 Motsoaledi, A., 2016. Debate on the health budget vote National Assembly, 10 May 2016. Cape Town.

14 Shisana et al., 2014.

15 Shisana, O., 2014. AIDS: The story behind the numbers. The Sunday Independent, 6 April 2014.

16 Rehle, T.M., Hallett, T.B., Shisana, O., Pillay-van Wyk, V., Zuma, K., Carrara, H. and Jooste, S., 2010. A decline in new HIV infections in South Africa: Estimating HIV incidence from three national HIV surveys in 2002, 2005 and 2008. *PloS one*, 5(6), p. e11094.

17 Zwi, A.B. and Cabral, A.J., 1991. Identifying 'high risk situations' for preventing AIDS. *British Medical Journal*, 303(14), pp.1527-1529.

18 Shisana, O., 2014.

19 Campbell, C., 2003. Letting them die: Why HIV/AIDS intervention programmes fail. Oxford: The International African Institute and Double Storey Books, Juta Company.

20 Hunter, M., 2005. Cultural politics & masculinities: Multiple-partners in historical perspective in KwaZulu-Natal. *Culture, health sexuality & African sexualities. An international Journal for Research, Intervention & Care*, 7(4), pp.389-403; Hunter, M., 2007. The changing political economy of sex in South Africa: The significance of unemployment and inequalities to the scale of the AIDS pandemic. *Social Science & Medicine*, 64, pp.689-700.

21 Zwi, and Cabral, 1991, pp.1527-1529.

22 Ibid.

23 Wilson, D., Sibanda, B., Mboyi, L., Msimanga, S. and Dube, G., 1990. A pilot study for an HIV prevention programme among commercial sex workers in Bulawayo, Zimbabwe. *Social Science & Medicine*, 31(5), pp.609-618.

24 Zwi and Cabral, 1991, pp.1527-1529.

25 UNAIDS, 2015.

26 Morrell, R., 2001b. From boys to gentlemen. Settler masculinity in colonial Natal 1880-1920. Pretoria: UNISA Press.

27 Morrell, R., 2001a. The times of change: Men and masculinity in South Africa. In Morrell, R. (ed.), Changing men in Southern Africa. pp.3-37. Pietermaritzburg: University of Natal Press.

28 Hunter, M., 2006. Fathers without amandla: Zulu-speaking men and fatherhood. In Morrell, R. (ed.), Baba: Men and fatherhood in South Africa. pp.99-117. Cape Town: HSRC Press; Sharp, J., 1994. A world turned upside down: Households and differentiation in a South African Bantustan in the 1980's. *African Studies*, 53(1), pp.71-88; Shefer, T., Crawford, M., Strebel, A., Simbayi, L. C., Dwadwa-Henda, N., Cloete, A. and Kalichman, S., 2008. Gender, power and resistance to change among two communities in the Western Cape. *Feminism Psychology*, 18, pp.157-182.

29 Hunter, 2006, pp.99-117.

30 Barker, G. and Ricardo, C., 2005. Young men and the construction of masculinity in sub-Saharan Africa: Implications for HIV/AIDS, conflict and violence. Social development papers: Conflict prevention & reconstruction. Washington DC: The World Bank; Mfecane, S. 2010. Exploring masculinities in the context of ARV use: A study of men living with HIV in a South African village (Unpublished doctoral thesis). University of Witwatersrand, Johannesburg.

31 Jewkes, R. K., Dunkle, K., Nduna, M. and Shai, N., 2010. Intimate partner violence, relationship power inequity, and incidence of HIV infection in young women in South Africa: A cohort study. T*he Lancet*, 376(9734), pp.41-48.

32 Ramphele, M., 1993. A bed called Home: Life in the migrant hostels of Cape Town. Cape Town: Edinburg University Press; Ramphele, M., 2000. Teach me how to be a man. An exploration of the definition of masculinity. In V. Das, A. Kleinman, M. Ramphele, and P. Reynolds (eds.), Violence and Subjectivity, pp. 102–119. Los Angeles, California: University of California Press; Shisana, O., Risher, K., Celentano, D.D., Zungu, N., Rehle, T., Ngcaweni, B. and Evans, M.G., 2015a. Does marital status matter in an HIV hyperendemic country? Findings from the 2012 South African National HIV Prevalence, Incidence and Behaviour Survey. *AIDS care*, pp.1-8; Shisana, et al., 2015b, pp.664–669.

33 Hunter, M., 2005, pp.389-403; Lurie, M., Williams, B., Zuma, K., Mkanya Mwamburi, D., Garnett, G., Sweat, M. and Karim, S. 2000. Who infects whom? HIV-1 concordance and discordance among migrants and non-migrant couples in South Africa. *AIDS Care*, 17, pp.2245-2252; Zuma, K., Gouws, E., Williams, B. and Lurie, M., 2003. Risk factors for HIV infection among women in Carletonville, South Africa: Migration, demography and sexually transmitted diseases. *International Journal of STD & AIDS*, 14, pp.814-817; Shisana et al, 2015a, pp.1–8.

34 Hunter, M., 2006, pp.99-117 ; Hunter, M., 2007, pp.689-700; Zungu, N., n.d. Social representations of AIDS and narratives of risk among Xhosa men. University of Cape Town.

35 Zwi and Cabral, 1991, pp.1527-1529.

36 Hunter, M., 2002. The materiality of everyday sex: Thinking beyond 'prostitution'. *African Studies*, 61(1), pp.99-120; Jewkes, R., 2009. HIV and women. In P. Rohleder, L. Swartz, S.C. Kalichman and L.C. Simbayi (eds.), HIV/AIDS in South Africa 25 years on: Psychosocial perspectives, pp.89-104. New York: Springer.

37 Morrell, R., 2001b. From boys to gentlemen. Settler masculinity in colonial Natal 1880-1920. Pretoria: UNISA Press; Zwi and Cabral, 1991, pp.1527-1529; Mears, R. 2007. Historical development of informal township settlements in Johannesburg since 1886. Paper presented at the Economic History Society of Southern Africa, Conference, 10-12 September 2007; Mears, R., 2011. Historical development of informal township settlements in Johannesburg since 1886. Indaba Hotel, Fourways, Johannesburg and at ERSA Research Workshop, 2-4 November 2011, Kopanong, Johannesburg.

38 Oakes, D., 1989. Readers Digest Illustrated History of South Africa: The Real Story. Cape Town: The Readers Digest Association South Africa (Pty) Ltd.

39 Ibid.

40 Hocking, A., 1973. Oppenheimer and Son. McGraw-Hill: Johannesburg; Van Onselen, C., 1982. Studies in the Social and Economic History of the Witwatersrand 1886–1914. Vol 1: New Babylon, Vol 2: New Nineveh. Longman: London; Johannesburg: Ravan.

41 Oakes, D., 1989.

42 Bonner, P. and Segal, L., 1998. Soweto: A History. Cape Town: Maskew Longman.; Huchzermeyer, M. and Karam, A. (eds.), 2006. Informal Settlements: A Perpetual Challenge? Cape Town: UCT Press.

43 Mels, A., Castellano, D., Braadbaart, O., Veenstra, S., Disktra, I., Meulmen, B., Singels, A. and Wilsenach, J.A., 2009. Sanitation services for the informal settlements of Cape Town, South Africa. Desalination, 248, pp.330-337.

44 Ambert, C., 2006. An HIV and Aids Lens for Informal Settlement Policy and Practice in South Africa. In Huchzermeyer, M. and Karam, A. (eds.), Informal Settlements: A Perpetual Challenges? Cape Town: University of Cape Town Press.

45 French, J.K., 1983. James Mpanza and the Sofasonke party in the development of local politics in Soweto. M. A Dissertation submitted to the Faculty of Arts, University of the Witwatersrand, Johannesburg for the Degree of Master of Arts; French, K., 2007. Father of Soweto. Cape Town: Viva Books, South Africa; SA History. 2013. Available at http://www.sahistory.org.za/topic/james-sofasonke-mpanza-and-johannesburg%E2%80%99s-squatter-movement-1938-1947#sthash.3VYPyqIm.dpuf. [Accessed 28 December 2015].

46 French, K., 2007; Stadler, A.W., 1979. Birds in the Cornfield: Squatter Movements in Johannesburg, 1944-1947, *Journal of Southern African Studies*, 6(1), Special Issue on Urban Social History. (Oct.1979), pp.93-123.

47 Misselhorn, M., 2008. Position paper on informal settlements upgrading. Prepared as a draft for the strategy for the second economy for the office of South African Presidency. Project Preparation Trust of KwaZulu-Natal: Urban LandMark.

48 Ambert, 2006; Mels, A. et al., 2009, pp.330-337.

49 Mels, A., et al., 2009, pp.330-337.

50 Misselhorn, 2008.

51 Murray, R., 2008. Informal settlements "give rural poor a foothold" in urban centres. Available at http://www.bdlive.co.za/national/2014/01/28/informal-settlements-give-rural-poor-a-foothold-in-urban-centres. [Accessed 28 December 2015].

52 Ibid.

53 Shisana, O., Peltzer, K., Zungu-Dirwayi, M. and Louw, J., 2005. The Health of our Educators: A focus on HIV/AIDS in South African public schools. Cape Town: HSRC Press.

54 Campbell, C., 2003. Letting them die: Why HIV/AIDS intervention programmes fail. Oxford: The International African Institute and Double Storey Books, Juta Company; Hunter, 2005, pp.389-403; Shisana, O., Rehle, T., Simbayi, L. C., Parker, W., Zuma, K. and Bhana, A., 2005. South African national HIV prevalence, HIV incidence, behaviour and communication survey, 2005. Cape Town: HSRC Press.

55 Morrell, R. and Richter, L., 2004. The fatherhood Project: Confronting issues of masculinity and sexuality. *Agenda,* 62(21), pp.36-44; Morrell, R. and Richter, L. 2006. Introduction: Baba, men and fatherhood in South Africa. In L. Richter and R. Morrell (eds.), Baba, men and fatherhood in South Africa, pp.1-12. Cape Town: HSRC Press.

56 Wilson, F., 2006. On being a father and poor in southern Africa today. In L. Richter and R. Morrell (eds.), Baba: Men and fatherhood in South Africa, pp.26-37. Cape Town: HSRC Press.

57 Campbell, C., 2003.

58 Shisana et al., 2005; Kalichman, S. C., Ntseane, D., Nthomang, K., Segwabe, M., Phorano, O. and Simbayi, L. C., 2007a. Recent multiple sexual partners and HIV transmission risks among people living with HIV/AIDS in Botswana. *Sexual Transmission Infection*, 83(5), pp.371-375; Kalichman, S. C., Simbayi, L. C., Jooste, S., Vermaak, R.

and Cain, D., 2008a. Sensation seeking, alcohol use, prediction of HIV transmission risk: A prospective study of sexually transmitted infection clinic patients, Cape Town, South Africa. *Addictive behaviour*, 33, pp.1630-1633; Kalichman, S. C., Simbayi, L. C., Vermaak, R., Jooste, S. and Cain, D., 2008b. HIV/AIDS risks among men and women who drink at informal alcohol serving establishments (shebeens) in Cape Town, South Africa. Prevention Science, 9, pp.55-62; Kiene, S. M., Simbayi, L. C., Abrams, A., Cloete, A., Tennen, H. and Fisher, J. D., 2008. High rates of unprotected sex occurring among HIV-positive individuals in a daily diary study in South Africa: The role of alcohol use. *Journal of Acquired Immune Deficiency Syndrome*, 49(2), pp.219-226; Morojele, N. K., Kachieng, M. A., Mokoko, E., Nkoko, M. A., Parry, C.H.D., Nkowane, A.M. and Saxena, S., 2006. Alcohol use and sexual behaviour among risky drinkers and bar and shebeen patrons in Gauteng province, South Africa. *Social Science & Medicine*, 62, pp.217-227, Norman, P., Armitage, C. J. and Quigley, C., 2007. The theory of planned behavior and binge drinking: Assessing the impact of binge drinker prototypes. *Addictive Behaviors*, 32, pp.1753-1768.

59 Zungu, n.d.

60 Campbell, 2003; Jewkes, pp.89-104.

61 Shisana et al., 2005.

62 Peacock, D., Redpath, J., Evans, K., Daub, A. and Greig, A., 2008. A literature review on men, gender and health in South Africa. Johannesburg: Sisonke Gender Justice.

63 Johnson, L. and Budlender, D., 2002. HIV risk factors: A review of the demographic, socio-economic, biomedical and behavioural determinants of HIV prevalence in South Africa. Care Monograph 8, Centre for Actuarial Studies Research. Cape Town: University of Cape Town.

64 Zwi and Cabral, 1991, pp.1527-1529.

65 Ashley, J. W., Levine, B. and Needle, R., 2006. Summary of the proceedings of meeting in alcohol, HIV risk behaviours, and transmission in Africa: Developing programmes for the United States President's Emergency Plan for AIDS Relief (PEPFAR). *African Journal of Drug & Alcohol Studies*, 5, pp.192-200; Fisher, J. C., Bang, H. and Kapiga, S. H., 2007. The association between HIV infection and alcohol use: A systemic review and meta-analysis of African studies. *Sexually Transmitted Diseases*, 34, pp.856-863; Kalichman, S C., Simbayi, L C., Kaufman, M., Cain, D. and Jooste, S., 2007b. Alcohol use and sexual risk for HIV/AIDS in sub-Saharan Africa: Systematic review of empirical findings. *Prevention Science*, 8, pp.141-151; Raj, A., Reed, E., Santana, M.C., Walley, A.Y., Welles, C., Hosburg, C.R. and Silverman, J.G., 2009. The associations of binge alcohol use with HIV/STI risk and diagnosis among heterosexual African American men. *Drug & Alcohol Dependence*, 101, pp.101-106.

66 Jewkes, 2009, pp.89-104; Marks, S., 2002. An epidemic waiting to happen? The spread of HIV/AIDS in South Africa, a social and historical perspective. *Africa Studies*, 6(1), pp.13-26; Manganyi, C. and Du Toit, A., 1990. Political violence and the struggle in South Africa. London: Macmillan.

67 Hunter, S., 2003. Who cares? AIDS in Africa. New York: Palgrave Macmillan; Marks, 2002, pp.13-26.

68 Marks, 2002, pp.13-26.

69 Abrahams, N., Jewkes, R., Laubsher, R. and Hoffman, M., 2004. Sexual violence against intimate partner in Cape Town: Prevalence and risk factors reported by men.

Bulletin of World Health Organization, 82, pp.330-337; Abrahams, N., Jewkes, R., Laubsher, R. and Hoffman, M. 2006. Intimate partner violence: Prevalence and risk factors for men in Cape Town, South Africa. *Violence & Victims*, 21(2), pp.247-264; Fisher, J. C., Bang, H. and Kapiga, S. H., 2007. The association between HIV infection and alcohol use: A systemic review and meta-analysis of African studies. *Sexually Transmitted Diseases*, 34, pp.856-863; Jewkes, K.R., Levin, J B. and Penn-Kekana, L.A., 2003. Gender inequalities, intimate partner violence and HIV preventive practices: Findings of a South African cross-sectional study. *Social Science & Medicine,* 56, pp.125-134; Vetten, L. and Bhana, K., 2001. Violence vengeance and gender: A preliminary investigation into the links between HIV/AIDS and violence against women in South Africa. Johannesburg: The Centre for the Study of Violence & Reconciliation.

70 Harvard School of Public Health. 2006. HIV/AIDS and gender-based violence literature review. Program on International Health and Human Rights. Available at www. Hsph.harvard.edu/pihhr [Accessed 10 June 2010]; Jewkes, R., Penn-Kekana, L., Levine, J., Tatsaka, M. and Schrieber, M., 2001. Prevalence of emotional, physical, and sexual abuse of women in three South African provinces. *South African Medical Journal*, 91(5), pp.421-428; Matthews, S., Abrahams, N., Martin, L., Vetten, L., Van der Merwe, L. and Jewkes, R., 2004. 'Every six hours a woman is killed by her intimate partner': A national study of female homicide in South Africa, gender and health research group. Tygerberg: Medical Research Council; Swart, L. A., Seedat, M., Stevens, G. and Ricardo, I., 2002. Violence in adolescents' romantic relationships: Findings from a survey amongst school-going youth in a South African community. *Journal of Adolescence,* 25 (4), pp.385-395.

71 Hunter, 2006.

72 Hunter, 2003; Marks, 2002, pp.13-26.

73 Marks, 2002, p.20.

74 Leclerc-Madlala, S., 2002. On the virgin cleansing myth: Gendered bodies, AIDS and ethno medicine. *African Journal of Psychology*, 23(1), 15-20; Varga, C. and Makubalo, L., 1996. Sexual non-negotiation. *Agenda*, 28, pp.31-38; Wood, K., Maforah, F. and Jewkes, R., 1998. He forced me to love him: Putting violence on the adolescent sexual health agenda. Social Science & Medicine, 47, pp.233-242; Wood, K. and Jewkes, R. 2001. Dangerous love: Reflections on violence among Xhosa township youth. In R. Morrell (ed.), *Changing men in Southern Africa*, pp.317-336. Pietermaritzburg: University of Natal Press.

75 Johnson, L. and Budlender, D., 2002. HIV risk factors: A review of the demographic, socio-economic, biomedical and behavioural determinants of HIV prevalence in South Africa. Care Monograph 8, Centre for Actuarial Studies Research. Cape Town: University of Cape Town; Posel, D., 2005a. The scandal of manhood: 'Baby rape' and politicization of sexual violence in post-apartheid South Africa. *Culture, Health & Sexuality*, 7(3), pp.239-252; Posel, D. 2005b. 'Baby rape': Unmaking secrets of sexual violence in post-apartheid South Africa. In G. Reid and L. Walker (eds.), Men behaving differently, pp.125-153. Cape Town: Double Storey Books; Walker, L. 2005. Men behaving differently: South African men since 1994. *Culture, Health & Sexuality*, 7(3), pp.225-238.

76 Marks, 2002, pp.13-26; Xaba, T., 2001. Masculinity and its malcontents: The confrontation between struggle masculinity 'and post-struggle masculinity' (1990-1997). In

R. Morrell (ed.), Changing men in Southern Africa, pp.105-124. Pietermaritzburg: University of Natal.

77 Jewkes, 2009, pp.89-104; Posel, D., 2004. Getting the nation talking about sex: Reflection on the discursive constitution of sexuality in South Africa since 1994. *Agenda*, 62, pp.53-63; Ramphele, 2000, pp.102-119; Xaba, 2001, pp.105-124.

78 Ambe, D., Karth, V., Khumalo, B., McNab, E., Peacock, D. and Redpath, J., 2007. South African country report: Progress on commitments made at the 2004 United Nations Commission on the Status of Women on implementing recommendations aimed at involving men and boys in achieving gender equality. Cape Town: Sisonke Gender Justice & The National Office on the Status of Women; Andersson, N., Ho-Foster, A., Matthis, J., Marokoane, N., Mashiane, V., Mhatre, S. and Sonnekus, H. 2004. National cross sectional study of views on sexual violence and risk of HIV infection and AIDS among South African school pupils. *British Medical Journal*, 329(7472), pp.952-954; Morrell, R. 2001a. The times of change: Men and masculinity in South Africa. In R. Morrell (ed.), Changing men in Southern Africa. pp.3-37. Pietermaritzburg: University of Natal Press; Zwi and Cabral, 1991, pp.1527-1529.

79 Zungu, n.d.

80 Statistics South Africa, 2013. Gender Gaps in South Africa. Available at http://www.statssa.gov.za/wp-content/uploads/2013/11/Fieldworker-AugSept-2013.pdf.

81 Hunter, 2006, pp.99-117; Shisana et al., 2015a, pp.1-8; Shisana et al., 2015b, pp.664-669.

82 Hunter, 2006, pp.99-117.

83 Campbell, C., 2000. Selling sex in the time of AIDS: The psycho-social context of condom use by sex workers in a Southern African mine. *Social Science & Medicine*, 50, pp.479-494; Campbell, 2003; Hunter, 2006, pp.99-117.

84 Zwi and Cabral, 1991, pp.1527-1529.

85 Campbell, 2000, pp.479-494; Campbell, 2003.

86 Campbell, C., 2001. Going underground and going after women: Masculinity and HIV transmission amongst black workers on the gold mines. In R. Morrell (ed.), Changing men in Southern Africa (pp., 275-286). New York: Zed Books; Gould, C. and Fick, N., 2008. Selling sex in Cape Town. Sex work and human trafficking in a South African city. Cape Town: SWEAT/ISS; Leggett, T., 2008. Drug, sex work, and HIV in three South African cities. South African health information. Available at http:www.sahealthinfo.org/admodule/drugs/htm [Accessed 10 August 2010].

87 Dunkle, K.L., Jewkes, R.K., Brown, H.C., Gray, G.E., McIntyre, J.A. and Harlow, S.D., 2004. Transactional sex among women in Soweto, South Africa: Prevalence and risk factors associated with HIV infection. *Social Science & Medicine*, 59(8), pp.1581-1592.

88 Shisana et al., 2015, pp.664-669.

89 Ibid.

90 Zwi and Cabral, 1991, pp.1527-1529.

91 Halperin, D.T. and Epstein, H., 2007. Why is HIV prevalence so severe in Southern Africa? The role of multiple concurrent partnerships and lack of male circumcision: Implications of AIDS prevention. *The Southern African Journal of HIV Medicine*, 8(1), pp.19-25; Leclerc-Madlala, S., Simbayi, L.C. and Cloete, A. 2009. The sociocultural aspects of HIV/AIDS in South Africa. In P. Rohleder, L. Swartz, S.C. Kalichman, and

L.C. Simbayi (eds.), HIV/AIDS in South Africa 25 years on: Psychosocial perspectives. pp.13-26. New York: Springer; Mah, T.L. and Halperin, D.T., 2008. Concurrent sexual partnerships and the HIV epidemic in Africa: Evidence to move forward. *AIDS and Behaviour*, 14(1), pp.11-16.

92 Leclerc-Madlala et al,. 2009, pp.13-26; Mfecane, S., 2008. Living with HIV as a man: Implications for masculinity. Masculinities in crisis: Volume II. *Psychology in Society*, 36, pp.45-59; Pettifor, A.E., Measham, D.M., Rees, H.V. and Padian, N.S. 2004a, Sexual power and HIV risk in South Africa. *Emerging Infectious Disease*, 10(11), pp.1996-2004; Pettifor, A. E., Rees, H., Stefenson, A., Hlogwa-Madikizela, L., MacPhail, C. and Vermaak, K., 2004b. HIV and sexual behaviour among young South Africans: A national survey of 15-24 years olds. Pretoria: National Department of Health.

93 Shisana, O., Zungu-Dirwayi, N., Toefy, Y., Simbayi, L. C., Malik, S. and Zuma, K., 2004. Marital status and risk of HIV infection in South Africa: original article. *South African Medical Journal*, 94(7), p.537.

94 Fleisch, B., 2008. Primary education in crisis: Why South African schoolchildren underachieve in reading and mathematics. Cape Town: Juta and Company Ltd; Mabela, T. 2013. Gender Gap in South Africa. *The Field Worker*, 4(2), August/September. Statistics South Africa.

95 Mabela, 2013.

96 Ibid.

97 Shisana, O., 2014. AIDS: The story behind the numbers. The Sunday Independent, 6 April 2014; Department of Health, 2015. National Health Insurance White paper, South Africa Policy Paper. Available at http://www.gov.za/documents/national-health-insurance-south-africa-policy-paper [Accessed 2016-05-10].

98 Fleisch, B., 2008. Primary education in crisis: Why South African schoolchildren underachieve in reading and mathematics. Cape Town: Juta and Company Ltd.

99 Harrison, A., 2005. Young people and HIV/AIDS in South Africa: Prevalence of infection, risk factors and social context. In S. S. Abdool Karim, and Q. Abdool Karim (eds), HIV/AIDS in South Africa, (pp.305-328). Cape Town: Cambridge Press; Kuate-Defo, B. 2004. Young people`s relationships with sugar daddies and sugar mummies: What do we know and what do we need to know? *African Journal of Reproductive Health*, 8(2), pp.13-37; Leclerc-Madlala, S., 2003. Transactional sex and the pursuit of modernity. *Social Dynamics*, 29(2), pp.231-233; Leclerc-Madlala, S., 2005. Popular responses to HIV/AIDS and policy. *Journal of Southern Africa Studies*, 31(4), pp.519-533; Masvawure, T., 2009, April 15-18. 'I just need to be flashy on campus': Transactional sex at the University of Zimbabwe. Paper presented at the VII Conference of the International Association for the Study of Sexuality, Culture and Society, Hanoi, Vietnam; Paulin, M., 2007. Sex, money and premarital partnership in Southern Malawi. *Social Science & Medicine*, 6(5), pp.2383-2393.

100 Mercer, C.H., Copas, A.J., Sonnenberg, P., Johnson, A.M., McManus, S., Erens, B. and Cassell, J. A., 2009. Who has sex with whom? Characteristics of heterosexual partnerships reported in a national probability survey and implications for STI risk. *International Journal of Epidemiology*, 38, pp.206-214; Shisana et al., 2009; Shisana, O., Zungu, N. and Simbayi L., 2014. South Africa's response to the HIV and AIDS epidemics. In T. Meyiwa, M. Nkondo, M. Chutiga-Mabungu, M. Sithole and Francis

Nyamnjoh (eds.). State of the Nation: South Africa 1994–2014: A twenty-year review of freedom and democracy, pp.347-378. HSRC Press: Cape Town.

101 Lindegger, G. and Quayle, M., 2009. Masculinity and HIV/AIDS. In P. Rohleder, L. Swartz, S.C. Kalichman, and L.C. Simbayi (eds.), HIV/AIDS in South Africa 25 years on: Psychosocial perspectives. pp.41-54. New York: Springer.

102 Airhihenbuwa, C. O., 2007. Healing our differences: The crisis of global health and the politics of identity. USA: Rowman & Littlefield Publishers; Niang, C., 1996. Integrating Laobe women into AIDS prevention strategies. In S. Zeidenstein, and K. Moore (eds.), Learning About Sexuality: A Practical Beginning, pp.210-222. New York: The Population Council & The International Women's Health Coalition.

103 Hunter, 2005, pp.389-403.

104 Harrison, 2005, pp.305-328; Jewkes, R. and Morrell, R., 2012. Sexuality and the limits of agency among South African teenage women: Theorising femininities and their connections to HIV risk practices. *Social Science & Medicine*, 74, pp.1729-1737; Leclerc-Madlala, 2003, pp.231-233; Leclerc-Madlala, 2005, pp.519-533.

105 Chatterji, M., Murray, M., London, D. and Anglewicz, P., 2005. The factors influencing transactional sex among young men and women in 12 sub-Saharan African countries. The policy project. Washington: USAID; Mataure, P., McFarland, W., Fritz, K., Kim, A., Woelk, G., Ray, S. and Rutherland, G., 2002. Alcohol use and high-risk sexual behaviour among adolescents and young adults in Harare, Zimbabwe. *AIDS & Behaviour*, 6, pp.211-219.

106 Shisana et al., 2009.

107 Phaswana-Mafuya, N., Shisana, O. , Davids, D., Tabane, C., Mbelle, M., Matseke, G., Banyini, M. and Kekana, Q., 2014. Perceptions of sugar mommy practices in South Africa. *Journal of Psychology in Africa*, 24 (3): pp.257–263.

108 Hallett, T.B., Lewis, J.J.C., Lopman, B.A., Nyamukapa, C.A, Mushati, P., Wambe, M. and Gregson, S., 2007b. Age at first sex and HIV infection in rural Zimbabwe. *Studies in Family Planning*, 38(1), pp.1-10; Shisana et al., 2005.

109 Shisana et al., 2014, pp.347-378.

110 Hallett, T.B., Gregson, S., Lewis, J.J.C., Lopman, B.A. and Garnett, G.P., 2007a. Behaviour change in generalized HIV epidemics: Impact of reducing cross-generational sex and delaying age at sexual debut. *Sexually Transmitted Infections*, 83(1), pp.150-154; Hallett et al., 2007b, pp.1-10; Leclerc-Madlala, S., 2007. Intergenerational relationships in the context of HIV prevention in Southern Africa. Paper presented at the SAT/SAfAIDS regional HIV prevention meeting. Livingstone, Zambia; Leclerc-Madlala, S., 2008. Age-disparate and intergenerational sex in southern Africa: The dynamics of hyper-vulnerability. AIDS, 22(4), pp.17-25; Longfield, K., Glick, A., Waithaka, M. and Berman, J., 2004. Relationships between older men and younger women: Implications for STIs/HIV in Kenya. *Studies in Family Planning*, 35(2), pp.125-134.

111 Friedman, M.S., Marshal, M.P., Stall, R., Cheong, J. and Wright, E.R., 2008. Gay-related development, early abuse and adult health outcomes among gay males. *AIDS and Behavior*, 12(6), pp.891-902.

112 Niehaus, I., 2005. Masculine domination in sexual violence: Interpreting accounts of three cases of rape in Southern African Lowveld. In G.W. Reid, and L. Walker (eds.), Men behaving differently, pp.65-87. Cape Town: Double Story Books.

113 Shisana et al., 2015a, pp.1-8.

114 Bhorat, H., Hirsch, A., Kanbur, R. and Ncube, M., 2014. Economic policy in South Africa–past, present and future (No. 180150).
115 Trading Economics. 2016. South Africa GDP Growth Rate. Available at http://www.tradingeconomics.com/south-africa/gdp-growth.
116 Bhorat et al., 2014.
117 Statistics South Africa. 2016. Quarterly labour survey. Available at http://www.statssa.gov.za/?p=7281.
118 Commission on Employment Equity report 2014–2015 annual report. Available at http://www.labour.gov.za/DOL/downloads/documents/annual-reports/employment-equity/2014-2015/15thceeannualreport2015_part3.pdf [Accessed 10 May 2016].
119 Zwi, and Cabral, 1991, p.1527.
120 Marks, 2002, pp. 13–26; Whiteside, A. and Sunter, C., 2000. AIDS: The challenge for South Africa. Cape Town: Human & Rousseau.
121 Pettifor et al., 2004a, 2004b; Shisana et al., 2005; Shisana et al., 2009.
122 See Hunter, 2005, 2007; Shisana et al. 2005; Shisana et al., 2009; Shisana et al., 2014; and Shisana, O., et al., 2014. *South African National HIV Prevalence, Incidence and Behaviour Survey*, 2012. Cape Town: HSRC Press.
123 Krueger, L.E., Wood, R.W., Diehr, P.H. and Maxwell, C.L., 1990. Poverty and HIV seropositivity: the poor are more likely to be infected. *Aids*, 4(8), pp.811-814.
124 Gillespie, S., Kadiyala, S. and Greener, R., 2007. Is poverty or wealth driving HIV transmission? *Aids*, 21, pp.S5-S16; Shisana, O., Rice, K., Zungu, N. and Zuma, K., 2010. Gender and poverty in South Africa in the era of HIV/AIDS: A quantitative study. *Journal of Women's Health*, 19(1), pp.39-46. doi:10.1089/jwh.2008.1200.
125 Gillespie et al., 2007, pp.S5-S16.
126 Krueger et al., 1990, pp.811-814; Statistics South Africa. 2014. Poverty Trends in South Africa: An examination of absolute poverty between 2006 and 2011, Pretoria. Report no.: 03-10-06 80pp ISBN 978-0-621-41873-6
127 Howe, L.D., Galobardes, B., Matijasevich, A., Gordon, D., Johnston, D., Onwujekwe, O., Patel, R., Webb, E.A., Lawlor, D.A. and Hargreaves, J.R., 2012. Measuring socio-economic position for epidemiological studies in low-and middle-income countries: a methods of measurement in epidemiology paper. *International journal of epidemiology*, dys037.
128 See also Shisana, O., Zungu-Dirwayi, N., Toefy, Y., Simbayi, L. C., Malik, S. and Zuma, K. (2004). Marital status and risk of HIV infections in South Africa. *South African Medical Journal*, 94(7), pp.537-543.
129 Shisana and Simbayi, 2002; Connolly, C., Colvin, M., Shisana, O. and Stoker, D., 2003. Epidemiology of HIV in South Africa-results of a national, community-based survey. *South African Medical Journal*, 94(9), p.776; Simbayi, L.C., Chauveau, J. and Shisana, O., 2004. Behavioural responses of South African youth to the HIV/AIDS epidemic: a nationwide survey. *AIDS care*, 16(5), pp.605-618.
130 Zwi, and Cabral, 1991, pp.1527-1529; Ambert, 2006; Ambert, C., Jassey, K. and Thomas, L., 2007. HIV/AIDS and Urban Development Issues in Sub-Saharan Africa: Beyond Sex and Medicines: Why Getting the Basics Right is Part of the Response! Sweden: Swedish Sida.
131 Housing Development Agency. 2012. Western Cape: Informal settlements status. Cape Town: HAD.

132 Turok, I. and Borel-Saladin, J., 2015. The theory and reality of urban slums: pathways-out-of-poverty or cul-de-sacs? Draft REDI3x3 working paper. Available at http://www.econ3x3.org/article/informal-settlements-poverty-traps-or-ladders-work#sthash.dVTmkL19.dpuf [Accessed 12 May 2016]; Turok, I. 2015. Informal settlements: poverty traps or ladders to work? Available at http://www.econ3x3.org/sites/default/files/articles/Turok%202015%20Informal%20settlements%20FINAL_0.pdf [Accessed 12 May 2016].

133 Meth, P., 2016. Informal Housing, Gender, Crime and Violence: The Role of Design in Urban South Africa. *Br J Criminol* (2016), doi: 10.1093/bjc/azv125, First published online: January 11, 2016. Available at http://m.bjc.oxfordjournals.org/content/early/2016/01/10/bjc.azv125.full

134 Ambert, 2006; Ambert et al., 2007.

135 Gillespie et al., 2007, pp.S5 S16.

136 Walker, L., 2005. Men behaving differently: South African men since 1994. *Culture, Health & Sexuality*, 7(3), pp.225-238.

137 Marks, 2002, pp.13-26; Posel, 2004, pp.53-63; Zungu, n.d.

138 Lehman, D. R, Chiu, C. and Schaller, M., 2004. Psychology and Culture. *Annual Review of Psychology*, 55, pp.689-714

139 Hunter, 2007, pp.689-700; Delius, P. and Glaser. C., 2002. Sexual socialisation in South Africa: A historical perspective. *African Studies*, 61(1), pp.27-54.

140 Zembe, Y., 2013. Sexual risk taking and HIV vulnerability among young women in post-apartheid South Africa. Unpublished doctoral thesis. Karolinska Institutet, Sweden. Available at https://openarchive.ki.se/xmlui/handle/10616/41772

141 Hunter, 2007, pp.27-54.

142 Hunter, 2002, pp.99-120; Zembe, 2013.

143 University of Iowa, 2011. Strengthening Families Program. Available at http://www.strengtheningfamiliesprogram.org/docs/StrengthFPsamhsa.pdf.

144 South African National HIV Prevalence, Incidence and Behaviour Survey, 2012, Cape Town: HSRC Press.

Chapter 3

The Nexus between AIDS Research Evidence and Policymaking in South Africa

Geoffrey Setswe and Nompumelelo Zungu

Introduction

In the first two post-apartheid decades, the human immunodeficiency virus (HIV) and acquired immune deficiency syndrome (AIDS) pandemics have, without a doubt, been South Africa's most devastating challenge. AIDS became a test case of the post-apartheid government and society's ability and capacity to deal effectively with a disease that remained embedded in a complex socio-economic context. In this chapter we explore the intricacy of these changes by discussing the nexus between AIDS research evidence and policymaking in South Africa, and the obstacles and barriers to evidence-based policymaking. The chapter also outlines how biomedical, behavioural and structural HIV research was translated into policies and programmes in the country.

Background

It is not within the scope of this chapter to engage in a detailed discussion of the role of politics in the connection between AIDS research evidence and policymaking in South Africa.[1] It is, however, important to acknowledge the significant role that politics has played in the way that evidence was translated into policies, and how HIV and AIDS have been managed by the post-apartheid government.[2]

The South African post-apartheid government became associated with denialism under the Mbeki administration.[3] Post-apartheid controversies include the promotion of non-evidence-based prevention interventions, such as funding the Sarafina III AIDS play and the drug Virodene.[4] The most controversial was the promotion of dietary-based 'cures', such as garlic, beetroot and lemons, as treatment for AIDS.[5] Finally, there was the denialism related to the cause of AIDS,[6] including the questioning of 'the reliability of the HIV tests'.[7]

Today the South African response and policies are evidence-based and the government focusses on up-scaling existing evidence-based interventions, such as condom promotion, voluntary HIV counselling and testing (HCT) and antiretroviral (ART) treatment.[8] There is also support for research into new technologies, and the government is implementing new interventions, such as post-exposure prophylaxis (PEP) for both survivors of sexual assault and occupational exposure, as well as medical male circumcision.[9] While progress has been made to bridge the gap between evidence and policymaking in South African, it is important to acknowledge that the country's HIV and AIDS response was not always informed by evidence. In many cases the push for the use of evidence-based research in policymaking sparked political drama, heated debates and, in some instances, resulted in court cases.[10]

Within the South African landscape, it is not possible to talk about HIV, AIDS, and the nexus between AIDS research evidence and policymaking, without reflecting on the role certain organisations representing people living with HIV (PLHIV) – namely, the Treatment Action Campaign (TAC), the National Association of People with AIDS (NAPWA) and recently the Positives Convention – have played in lobbying for policies that are informed by evidence. These organisations, particularly the TAC, have played an important role in shaping the fight against HIV and AIDS, and advocating for policies that are evidence-based and pro-people living with HIV and AIDS.[11] They have become campaigners for human rights and watchdogs of the South African government, not only in the implementation of HIV and AIDS interventions, but also that of evidence-based policies.[12]

Despite the vast amount of HIV and AIDS research conducted in South Africa, researchers working with civil society have had to lobby hard for policymakers to use the evidence for policymaking and to save lives. The previous lack of political will and delays in implementing prevention of mother-to-child transmission (PMTCT) and, later, failure to roll out universal access to antiretroviral treatment,[13] are reported to have caused the deaths of 333 000 people in the country.[14] It was the efforts of activists that forced the government to use research evidence to change policy and increase access to AIDS treatment.

Activists in South Africa have on several occasions used constitutional law to achieve HIV and AIDS rights. These include:

- Winning the Constitutional Court case in 2002, which forced the South African government to provide Nevirapine to pregnant women in order to prevent mother-to-child HIV infection;[15]
- Involvement in a case in 2004 for access to the implementation plan for the ARV roll out (also known as the Operational Plan on Comprehensive Treatment Care and Support);[16]
- Involvement in a 2006–2007 case for access to ARV treatment for prisoners at Westville prison in KwaZulu-Natal province;[17]

- On an ongoing basis, challenging the profiteering by multi-national pharmaceutical companies, notably GSK, Boehringer Ingelheim[18] and Merck Sharp & Dohme;[19] and
- Defending the Medicines Act against individuals such as Matthias Rath, a wealthy German industrialist, who denounced ARV treatment, but marketed his own vitamin pills instead as therapy for HIV and AIDS.[20]

The barriers and delays in translation and implementation of research evidence to policy are not unique to South Africa. Globally there is a challenge to link science to policies, and this frequently results in national priorities and policies that are not evidence-based.[21] The lack of scientific evidence in policymaking can, to some extent, be attributed to the complicated nature of translating scientific (and other forms of) evidence into policy.[22]

Several problems characterise the relationship between AIDS researchers and policymakers. In many cases mutual scepticism and differences exist between the two.[23] At times the relationship is combative, with policymakers convinced that the aim of researchers is to embarrass the state, while researchers believe that policymakers want to suppress research evidence instead of acting on it. In many cases, within the nexus of the translation of evidence into policy, and in particular where evidence is ignored, activism is often adopted to force the state to act. In South Africa, activism – led mostly by the TAC – entered the scene during the controversy linked to the former president, Thabo Mbeki, who called into question the cause of AIDS.[24] TAC was supported by a multidisciplinary team that included HIV and AIDS activists from all walks of life, people living with HIV and AIDS, and professionals.[25] TAC members worked intensively on the ground to mobilise the community. Instruments used to force the government to change its AIDS policy included protest marches to parliament and sit-ins at government offices.[26]

Another challenge is that not all researchers and scientists conduct ethical research that is geared toward a greater good. South African examples of unethical research include an unofficial trial on AIDS patients using a freezing solution (dimethylformamide).[27] Other scientists have been involved in misinformation campaigns. Among those targeted by the TAC was the misinformation promoted by dissident Matthias Rath, the German doctor who supported the then Minister of Health, Manto Tshabalala-Msimang, in the promotion and use of vitamins and micronutrient supplements as a treatment for AIDS in the country.[28] Indeed, Mbeki's position on AIDS was largely supported by Tshabalala-Msimang[29] and a group of scientists who raised questions about the safety and toxicity of azidothymidine (AZT),[30] and the role of poverty and poor nutrition in the progression from HIV to AIDS.[31]

As leaders of the government, President Mbeki and Minister of Health Tshabalala-Msimang, refused to provide scientifically tested antiretroviral drugs for people living with AIDS.[32] Instead, working with certain "dissident" researchers, they promoted untested nutritional and traditional herbal-based treatment alternatives for AIDS.[33] At the time, South Africa became known for promoting untested treatment options that were predominantly based on healthy eating[34] and the use of traditional herbal medicines, such as *ubhejane*.[35] In the resulting vacuum, the TAC drove the treatment agenda in South Africa and became the 'custodian of the citizen's national and human rights to health'.[36]

In many cases, as witnessed within the HIV and AIDS sector, pharmaceutical industry profits came into play, threatening the implementation and translation of evidence into policies through exorbitant prices for life-saving technologies. The fight to access treatment has not been limited to the South African government only: in 2003, the TAC and their supporters took the Minister of Health and the pharmaceutical companies to court, charging them with the deaths of 600 HIV-positive people a day due to them not having access to AIDS treatment.[37] They also lodged complaints against pharmaceutical companies for not licensing the production of affordable generics locally, a fight which intensified as government joined in the latter part of 2003. This made ARVs affordable, enabling the government to roll out a universal treatment programme.[38]

These gains and the push to increase the number of people on ARVs have continued. For example, during the 2010/2011 financial year when the Department of Health achieved a significant reduction in the price of antiretroviral medicines and they were able to award a tender for the supply of antiretroviral medicines to the value of R4.2 billion over two years, which resulted in savings of R4.4 billion (53%) when compared with previous tender prices.[39] The lower prices of ARVs enabled the Department of Health to re-allocate more resources towards enrolling more people on antiretroviral treatment (ART) with its existing budget.[40]

Policymakers may also delay translating evidence into policy because they believe it is their duty to protect the interest of their citizens by gathering as much evidence as possible before acting.[41] This too, to a great extent, was informed by the distrust that exists between policymakers and researchers.[42] For example, in South Africa the myths and confusion about the cause of AIDS was driven, to some extent, by the debate about the toxicity of AIDS treatment and the belief that pharmaceutical companies were using Africans as guinea pigs to experiment with toxic and lethal medicines.[43]

The challenges outlined above are things of the past and South Africa has made great strides towards an evidence-based response and policies. It has been suggested that significant change in policy and direction in the South African HIV/AIDS response can be attributed to the implementation of the 2007-2011 National Strategic Plan (NSP)[44] and, more recently, the 2012-2016 NSP for HIV/AIDS, sexually transmitted infections (STIs), and also tuberculosis (TB).[45]

Nexus between AIDS Research Evidence and Policymaking

Recent policies and guidelines in South Africa have mostly responded to new evidence and the situation on the ground. Major changes in the approach to the HIV epidemic were guided by the NSP of 2012-2016.[46] At a political and policy level, there was a renewed vision to reduce new infections and eliminate HIV (Towards Zero Infections), not only in South Africa, but globally. The Joint United Nations Programme on HIV and AIDS (UNAIDS) 2016-2021 strategy set 10 ambitious targets to end the AIDS epidemic by 2030.[47] South Africa also adopted the 90-90-90 strategy (90 per cent of people living with HIV knowing their HIV status, 90 per cent of those living with HIV accessing treatment, 90 per cent of people on treatment having supressed viral loads), aimed at fast-tracking the fight against AIDS.[48] Under the leadership of President Zuma, Minister of Health, Dr Aaron Motsoaledi, and the South African National AIDS Council (SANAC) led by the Deputy President, Cyril Ramaphosa, the government has shown the highest level of political commitment to the principle of universal access to treatment, improving healthcare and respecting human rights.[49]

Although there are frameworks that illustrate the nexus between research, policy and practice it is important to note that this relationship is never as simplistic as it is often portrayed and as illustrated in Figure 1. Figure 1 is a simple framework, where it is assumed that good evidence-based research on HIV/AIDS issues will be translated into good HIV/AIDS policies by policymakers. This framework also assumes that if good policies are implemented using good or best practice guidelines, then HIV incidence and prevalence, mother-to-child transmission (MTCT), morbidity and mortality from AIDS-related diseases will be reduced.

Figure 1 Framework on research-policy-implementation in HIV and AIDS

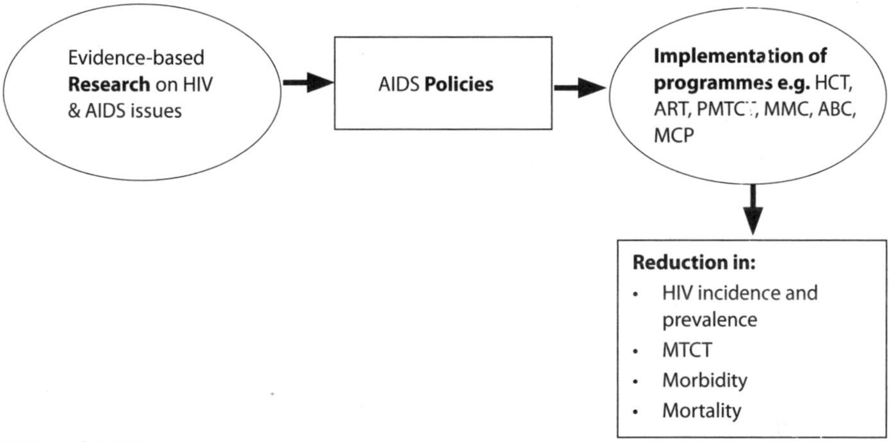

Evidence-based **Research** on HIV & AIDS issues → AIDS **Policies** → **Implementation of programmes e.g.** HCT, ART, PMTCT, MMC, ABC, MCP

↓

Reduction in:

- HIV incidence and prevalence
- MTCT
- Morbidity
- Mortality

HIV and AIDS

Source: Setswe[50]

Translation of Biomedical HIV Research into Policies

Although HIV infections are driven largely by behavioural and structural factors, the focus and investments have been mostly on biomedical interventions. Biomedical interventions are those HIV prevention interventions that are implemented by medical and clinical practitioners such ART, PMTCT, medical male circumcision (MMC), microbicides, vaccines and male and female condoms. Although biomedical interventions have been popular compared to behavioural interventions, their implementation and roll-out, and later the push towards scale-up, has required intense lobbying. This was done by activists, researchers, non-governmental organisations (NGOs), community based organisations (CBOs), United Nations (UN) agencies and local and international donors to push many governments to implement, increase access and, lastly, to translate into policy the research evidence that showed that interventions such as ART, PMTCT and MMC do work. In the history of HIV and AIDS globally, the majority of tensions experienced have been around the provision of ART and translating emerging evidence into new guidelines and policy for countries most affected – like South Africa.

It is estimated that ART has saved 1.3 million lives in South Africa since 1995.[51] Research on ART has continued to grow, leading not only to better treatment regimens, but also better guidelines relating to when people should be initiated on treatment.[52] The World Health Organization (WHO) guidelines to initiate treatment changed from a CD4 cell count below 350, to a CD4 cell count below 500, with an opportunistic infection.

Recently, there were suggestions that people who test HIV positive should be immediately initiated into treatment.[53] This evidence has revolutionised the response and the fight against HIV, and while these advances are celebrated, it has also meant that treating those living with HIV and AIDS remains a moving target with many countries struggling not only to keep up with evidence, but to translate that evidence into domestic policy. South Africa has announced that, in September 2016, it will remove CD4 count as an eligibility criterion for ARV treatment.[54] This means that it will be adopting the test and treat approach, which is in line with the 2015 WHO guidelines. This shift in targets represents progress; nevertheless there are concerns that this will have huge financial implications for countries like South Africa with its high burden of HIV and AIDS that is coupled with TB, and a rising epidemic of non-communicable diseases (NCDs).

Translation of ART Research and Treatment as Prevention into Policies

Evidence shows that providing ART to a patient with AIDS reduces mortality and morbidity by 60 to 80 per cent.[55] In South Africa, AIDS deaths declined from 320 000 in 2010 to 140 000 in 2014, a situation largly attributed to the provision of ART.[56] ART reduces the viral load in the blood, as well as in genital secretions (for both men and women), and the drugs can be detected in semen and vaginal and cervical secretions. This information strongly suggests that ART may make HIV-infected people less contagious,[57] hence the push to test and treat, as this would reduce infections that are often spread after a recent infection when the viral load is high and the person is most infectious.[58] In fact, a landmark clinical trial in 2011 showed that people with HIV who began taking anti-HIV medications early (before their immune systems were significantly weakened), experienced a 96 per cent reduction in their risk of transmitting HIV to their sexual partners.[59]

This evidence is supported by findings among HIV-serodiscordant couples. For example, HIV Prevention Trials Network (HPTN) 052 – a Phase III, two-arm, multi-site, randomised trial to determine the effectiveness of two treatment strategies in preventing the sexual transmission of HIV in serodiscordant couples – found that early use of ART, or treatment for prevention (T4P), by an HIV-infected individual reduces heterosexual transmission to an uninfected partner by 96 per cent.[60]

Using this research evidence, the WHO recommended a policy to provide triple therapy for HIV positive patients with CD4 <350 and later CD4 <500, with an opportunistic infection. This was possible as AIDS advocacy groups fought to get dramatic reductions in the price of ARVs which were later offered for free at public health services.[61] In recent years we have seen a dramatic reduction in the cost of ARVs and many countries have lobbied hard, not only for reduced prices, but also for the use of generics, which are cheaper. Today, access to ARVs is free through the public health system in South Africa and, according to UNAIDS, coverage increased from 25 per cent in 2011 to more than 45 per cent in 2014. An estimated 3.3 million people were reported to be on ART by June 2015.[62] Globally, positive strides have been made in the provision of ART. Recently released figures show that an estimated 15.8 million people were on ART by June 2015.[63]

Treatment as Prevention for People with HIV

As already stated earlier, treating people with HIV lowers the amount of virus in their body and can dramatically reduce their risk of transmitting HIV to others, underscoring the importance of HIV testing and access to medical care and treatment. This evidence has led to research that explored the possibility of using treatment as prevention in the general population.[64] It should be noted that using treatment as prevention is not a new idea, however, until recently the application of this evidence has mainly been limited to its use as a PEP, for instance, for PMTCT, emergency cases such as rape incidents, and needle stick injuries. In all these cases, ARVs were used after exposure to reduce chances of transmission, while the new proposed approach would use ARVs before exposure to HIV.

With Pre-exposure Prophylaxis (PrEP), HIV-negative individuals take a daily dose of ART to reduce their chances of acquiring HIV. When used consistently, PrEP reduces the risk of HIV infection among adult men and women at very high risk for HIV infection through sex or injecting drug use.[65] Studies to evaluate the use of the drug TDF (tenofovir disoproxil fumarate), alone or in combination with FTC (emtricitabine), have shown that the level of protection is strongly related to the level of adherence to the daily regimen. In time, PrEP will play an important role in HIV prevention, and work is ongoing to determine how to successfully implement PrEP programmes in an efficient and cost-effective manner.[66] South Africa indicated that it was exploring the use of PrEP and there were several ongoing trials investigating the use of PrEP among key populations and adolescents.[67] In a recent development, the Ministry of Health has announced that it will provide PrEP to sex workers in 10 sex worker programmes from June 2016. There were also plans to provide PrEP to vulnerable young women; however, this will be informed by evidence from demonstration projects.[68] This effort will also be supported by the publication of guidelines for safe use of PrEP in Southern Africa.[69] In the general population, evidence from KwaZulu-Natal showed the preventative effects of increased treatment coverage at community and household levels.[70]

Translation of Prevention of Mother to Child Transmission (PMTCT) of HIV

As illustrated above, antiretroviral medications used to treat HIV are also used to prevent it. Administering antiretroviral medications to HIV-infected pregnant women and their new-born babies significantly reduces the risk of HIV transmission to infants during pregnancy, labour and delivery, as well as during breastfeeding.[71] Research evidence has shown that starting short courses of ARV drugs in late pregnancy or during labour reduces the risk of in-utero and peripartum HIV transmission by up to 92 per cent. Regimens recommended by WHO[72] include Zidovudine (ZDV) and/or in combination with Lamivudine (3TC), and Nevirapine (NVP). A regimen of ZDV given from 28 weeks of pregnancy, plus single-dose NVP during labour and single-dose NVP and one-week ZDV for the infant is highly efficacious. Alternative regimens based on ZDV alone, short-course ZDV plus 3TC, or single-dose NVP alone, are also recommended.[73]

Over 100 countries implementing national PMTCT programmes have developed PMTCT policies and strategies emanating from this WHO recommendation. In practice, 15 countries, including South Africa and Botswana, were able to provide more than 80 per cent of HIV positive pregnant women with ARVs to prevent transmission to their babies. More than half (53 per cent) of pregnant women in poorer countries who needed services for PMTCT, received them by 2009.[74] Approximately 1.2 million HIV infections among infants have been averted since the mid-1990s.[75] In line with the guidelines from the United Nations Children's Fund (UNICEF),[76] the South African government implemented policies to increase universal access to free antiretroviral therapy for HIV-positive pregnant mothers and their infants. The changes in guidelines were aimed at targeting all pregnant women who were HIV infected, all infants born to mothers who were HIV-positive, all persons who had CD4 of less or equal to 350 CD cells/mm3, and all persons with TB who were co-infected with HIV.[77]

The changes in the PMTCT guidelines led to HIV infection in new-born babies declining from eight per cent in 2008 to 2.7 per cent in 2011.[78] The last two HSRC surveys reveal that the HIV infection in new-born babies almost halved from 3.3 per cent in 2008 to 1.7 per cent in 2012.[79] According to the Minister of Health, mother-to-child transmission of HIV reduced from 70 000 babies in 2004 to less than 7 000 in 2015.[80] The impressive declines were also attributed to the excellent coverage and quality of the PMTCT programme.[81] Although there has been progress in reducing HIV transmitted from mother-to-child, it is estimated that globally about 220 000 children still acquire HIV each year and only 30 per cent of children living with HIV are receiving ART.[82]

Translation of VMMC Evidence into Policy

UNAIDS has recommended voluntary medical male circumcision (VMMC) as a priority programme in countries like South Africa with high HIV prevalence and low rates of male circumcision. Scientific evidence gathered from 1986 suggested that male circumcision should be recognised as an efficacious intervention for HIV prevention.[83] VMMC is considered as 'a high-impact, one-time procedure that reduces HIV acquisition risk by approximately 60 per cent'.[84] At a WHO-UNAIDS[85] policy meeting, policy recommendations for implementing MMC programmes were made.

Policymakers and politicians asked their National AIDS Commissions to interrogate the evidence and advise on policy. The WHO moved quickly to interpret the evidence and make policy recommendations on how to implement MMC policy. Figure 2 shows the nexus between research evidence, policymaking and implementation of MMC programmes.

UNAIDS estimated that by the end of 2014 more than nine million men had undergone VMMC in 14 priority countries in Eastern and Southern Africa.[86] The South African government introduced its medical male circumcision policy and programme in 2010, with the target of reaching 80 per cent of HIV negative men aged 15-49 by 2015, or 4.5 million men, as recommended by the 2012-2016 NSP.[87] Although male circumcision rates increased from 38.2 per cent in 2002 and 40.6 per cent in 2008 to 45.5 per cent in 2012,[88] MMC rates are still low. According to the UNAIDS[89] the primary preventative effect of male circumcision is for female-to-male sexual transmission. Like ART there is, however, evidence to suggest that high coverage can create a protective effect for entire communities. It is therefore hoped that the VMMC programme will be scaled up by creating more demand for the services in South Africa. Data from the Centre for HIV and AIDS Prevention Studies (CHAPS) suggests that the expansion of the programme and creating demand is possible in South Africa.[90]

Figure 2 Translation of MMC evidence into policy and programmes

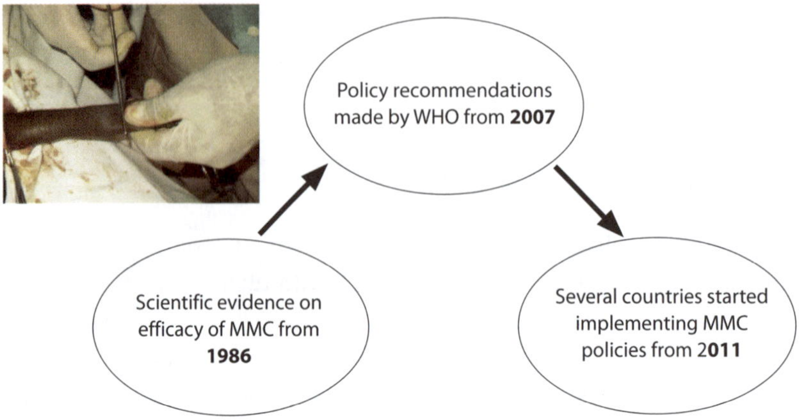

Source: WHO/UNAIDS

Translation of evidence on male and female condoms

Evidence from family planning programmes over many years makes it abundantly clear that the male condom is a safe and relatively effective method. It was initially used for preventing unwanted pregnancies and STIs, but is now also used for HIV prevention. A meta-analysis by UNAIDS[91] shows that male condom use is 90 per cent effective in preventing HIV transmission, if used correctly and consistently. Based on laboratory and clinical evidence, the US Food and Drug Administration (FDA) approved the female condom as 94-97 per cent effective in reducing the risk of HIV infection, if used correctly and consistently.[92] Research has shown that increasing the availability of condoms is associated with significant reductions in HIV risk.[93] According to UNAIDS,[94] condoms have averted an estimated 50 million new HIV infections since the onset of the HIV epidemic.

The 100 per cent condom use policy (CUP) aims to reduce sexual transmission of HIV and STIs among sex workers, their clients and the public at large by assuring that condoms are used in 100 per cent of entertainment establishments in a large geographic area, 100 per cent of the time by 100 per cent of the people involved in high-risk sexual relations.[95] In South Africa, increased condom use has contributed to reductions in HIV incidence[96] and the government has set high targets to annually distribute 1 billion male condoms (50 male condoms per adult male per year) and 25 million female condoms, by 2016.[97]

Although condoms are effective, reports of 'condom fatigue' and declines in condom use at last sex have been observed in South Africa and Sub-Saharan Africa.[98] There are also growing concerns that condoms have been 'deprioritised' in many countries and donor support for condoms has not increased. For example, it has been stated that globally 'the United States President's Emergency Plan for AIDS Relief (PEPFAR) and the Global Fund to Fight AIDS, Tuberculosis and Malaria (Global Fund) are spending less than 1 per cent of their resources on condoms'.[99] However, within the South African context it is important to note that PEPFAR does not fund the procurement of condoms as the South African government uses its own budget for this purpose. [100]

Translation of Research on STI Screening and Treatment

STIs increase an individual's risk of acquiring and transmitting HIV, and STI treatment may reduce HIV viral load. Therefore, STI screening and treatment may reduce the risk of HIV transmission.[101]

Research also continues on the development and assessment of topical gels that could potentially be applied to the vagina or rectum to interrupt transmission during sex. While additional research is needed, promising results from one South African study in 2010 suggest that a topical gel using antiretroviral drugs may ultimately prove to be an effective female-controlled strategy for HIV prevention.[102]

Translation of Behavioural HIV Prevention Interventions

Individual, small-group, and community interventions for people who are at high risk of HIV infection can reduce risk behaviours and can play an important role in many comprehensive HIV prevention strategies.[103] When these programmes are delivered by health care providers, peers, and others, they have been shown to significantly reduce risk behaviours among people who have been diagnosed with HIV to help ensure they do not transmit the virus to others. Again, partner services can reduce the spread of HIV by confidentially identifying and notifying partners who may have been unknowingly exposed to HIV, providing them with HIV testing and linking them to prevention and care services.[104]

Translation of ABC Research into Policies and Programmes

There is mixed evidence on whether ABC (Abstinence, Be faithful and Condomise) works. In the United States early abstinence-only interventions have failed. For an example, an evaluation of four abstinence only education programmes showed that youth enrolled in the programmes were no more likely than those not in the programmes to delay sexual initiation, to have fewer sexual partners, or to abstain entirely from sex.[105] On the other hand, Jemmott, Jemmott and Fong[106] have suggested that they have clear evidence that abstinence education works and they argue that their data could change the conversation about young people and sex. In the 2010 abstinence-only study,[107] researchers followed sixth and seventh graders in separate groups. In one, the focus was abstinence; in the other, they taught contraception and safe sex. Half the students learning about safe sex were having sex, while only a third in the group focused on abstinence were engaged in sex. These findings provide some evidence that an abstinence programme could work. However, this evidence has to be tested in different contexts to be able to conclude that abstinence-only programmes work universally.

Indeed, some researchers[108] credit the success to the Ugandan government's promotion of 'ABC behaviours' to abstinence, and fidelity, in particular. Many African countries say their HIV prevention policy is based on ABC. Research in Malawi provides additional evidence that poor women's protective strategies in response to the threat of AIDS have been overlooked by many AIDS prevention programmes.[109]

Translation of Evidence on Multiple Concurrent Sexual Partnerships (MCP) as Drivers of HIV Infection into Policy

There is mixed evidence on whether MCP are the drivers of the HIV epidemic in Africa and South Africa. Mah and Halperin[110] argue that there is evidence that concurrent sexual partnerships are the drivers of the HIV epidemics in Africa. Lurie and Rosenthal,[111] and Sawers and Stillwagon,[112] however, rebut the evidence that concurrency is driving Africa AIDS epidemics by indicating that the evidence was not conclusive. They also show that concurrent sexual partnerships do not explain the HIV epidemics in Africa through a systematic review of evidence.

Despite the mixed evidence, the Ministers of Health in Africa signed the Maseru Declaration (2006), which recommended a policy on reducing the number of partners in the Southern African Development Community (SADC). SADC countries have been slow in implementing this policy, even though NGOs supported reducing the number of sexual partners.

Translation of HIV Counselling and Testing (HCT) Research Evidence into Policies

Our research assumption is that testing increases health-seeking behaviours, equips those who test HIV negative with ways of ensuring that they do not get HIV; and creates a quick and easy entry point to accessing wellness and treatment services for those who test HIV positive. In reality, there is conflicting evidence on whether HCT increases health-seeking behaviours. A meta-analysis of 11 studies on the impact of counselling and testing for PLHIV found a 68 per cent reduction in high risk sexual behaviours with partners not already HIV positive (95% CI: 59% – 76%). Findings for men and women were very similar. While examining a pool of 27 studies, however, a meta-analysis found no significant impact of 'counselling and testing' bundle on behaviour relative to the untested.[113]

The 2001 policy on HCT in South Africa was replaced with a new policy which included HCT and Provider-Initiated Counselling and Testing (PICT). The President of South Africa tested publicly to show political will and support for the campaign. He launched a campaign in all provinces in April 2010 with a goal of testing 15 million people by June 2011. More than 12 million HIV tests were done by June 2011.[114] According to the Minister of Health, the HCT Campaign tested 18 million South Africans for HIV within a period of 18 months, and 10 million South Africans continue to be tested annually.[115]

Translation of Structural HIV Prevention Research into Policies and Programmes

Structural HIV prevention interventions are relevant to HIV because they address social and economic inequalities, HIV risk behaviours and HIV-related stigma and discrimination. These factors exacerbate marginalisation and vulnerability to HIV infection.[116]

South Africa implements three types of structural or social protection programmes emanating from research. These include HIV-sensitive, HIV-related and comprehensive social protection programmes. HIV-sensitive social protection programmes focus exclusively on PLHIV and those affected by HIV. These include the provision of free HIV services, cash refunds to encourage people to access services and, to encourage adherence, free food and nutritional supplements for PLHIV on HIV or tuberculosis treatment.

HIV-related social protection programmes are designed for the general public and tend to address HIV. These include social-protection programmes targeting community health workers who face the burden of providing HIV-related care and services in the community.

Comprehensive social-protection programmes address a range of measures for policy and programming, such as legal reforms to protect the rights of PLHIV, women and key populations; economic empowerment programmes and referrals; and linkages to maximise the impact of funding across sectors.[117]

Research by Cluver, Boyes, Orkin, Pantelic, Molwela and Sherr[118] shows reductions in HIV incidence of 51 per cent and 71 per cent respectively in transactional sex and age-disparate sex among adolescent girls, which are attributable to the child grants in South Africa, denoting the role of social grants in HIV prevention.

Conclusion

This chapter indicates that South Africa has done very well in producing large amounts of HIV research evidence and in translating HIV research evidence into policies. The government remains committed to up-scaling existing evidence-based interventions, such as condom promotion, and also supports research into new technologies and implementation of newer interventions, such as PEP for both survivors of sexual assault and occupational exposure, as well as MMC.

The examples provided clearly show a link between research evidence and policy development and/or implementation. However, the Global HIV Prevention Working Group[119] warned that there is no 'magic bullet' for HIV prevention. It is not obvious that where research evidence exists, it was always used to develop policies for HIV prevention. We have more tools to effectively prevent HIV than ever before. Since there is no single strategy that provides complete protection, or is right for all individuals, a combination of methods is needed to help reduce HIV transmission.

Despite the good work of translating mountains of research evidence into policies in the past 10 years or so, there is still no cure for HIV and AIDS. More than 35 million people are infected with HIV, more than 20 million people have died from this epidemic and AIDS has turned out to be the world's worst epidemic. The disappointing news on HIV and AIDS research was the failure of tenofovir microbicide research in the Vaginal and Oral Interventions to Control the Epidemic (VOICE) study, while the surprising news was that countries were implementing policies where there was weak, or no, evidence of efficacy, such as the HCT policy.

South Africa has made remarkable advances in obtaining research evidence of HIV prevention, interventions that work with MMC, PMTCT and ART being the best examples. HIV is being halted in its tracks in many African countries, including South Africa, through the implementation of evidence-based policies. South Africa is among the countries which have recorded the most progress. The paper illustrated the benefits of having policymakers that are able to translate evidence into policy and implement programmes that are effective in the fight against the epidemic. While challenges remain, it is clear that partnerships formed early in the onset of the epidemic are yielding results in the country.

Notes and References

1 Nattrass, N., 2005. AIDS Policy in Post-Apartheid South Africa. Draft: July 2005. Available at http://www.yale-university.net/macmillan/apartheid/apartheid_part1/nattrass.pdf. [Accessed 03 December 2015]; Shisana, O. and Zungu-Dirwayi, N., 2003. Government's changing responses to HIV/AIDS. In Everatt, D. and Maphai, V. (eds.), *The real state of the Nation*, 4(3), pp.165-187. Johannesburg: Interfund Development Update; Zungu N., 2013. Social representations of AIDS and narratives of risk among Xhosa men. Doctoral Thesis, University of Cape Town.

2 Campbell, C., 2003. Letting them die: Why HIV/AIDS intervention programmes fail. Oxford: The International African Institute & Double Storey Books, Juta Company; Fassin, D., 2007. When bodies remember: Experiences and politics of AIDS in South Africa. California series in public anthropology. Translated by A. Jacob and G. Varro. Berkeley, Los Angeles and London: University of California Press; Gevisser, M., 2008. The dream deferred. Cape Town: Jonathan Ball Publishers; Nattrass, N., 2012. The AIDS conspiracy: Science fights back. New York: Columbia University Press; Posel, D., Kahn, K. and Walker, L., 2007. Living with death in a time of AIDS: A rural South African case study. *Scandinavian Journal of Public Health*, 69, pp.138-146; Shisana and Zungu-Dirwayi, 2003.

3 Fassin, 2007; Gevisser, 2008; Leclerc-Madlala, S. 2005a. Popular responses to HIV/AIDS and policy. *Journal of Southern Africa Studies*, 31(4), pp.519-533; Nattrass, 2012; Nattrass, N. and Kalichman, S., 2010. The politics and psychology of AIDS denialism. In Rohleder, P., Swartz, L., Kalichman, S.C. and Simbayi, L.C. (eds.), HIV/AIDS in South Africa 25 years on: Psychosocial perspectives, pp.123-134. New York: Springer; Robins, S., 2008. From revolution to rights in South Africa: Social movements NGOs and popular politics after apartheid. Pietermaritzburg: University of KwaZulu-Natal Press.

4 Nattrass, N., 2004. The moral economy of AIDS in Southern Africa. Cambridge Africa collection. Cambridge: Cambridge University Press; Posel, D. 2008. AIDS. In Shepherd, N. and Robin, S. (eds.), New South African Keywords, pp.13-24. Johannesburg: Jacana Media; Thornton, R., 2008. Unimagined community: Sex, networks and AIDS in South Africa and Uganda. Berkeley, CA: University of California Press; Shisana and Zungu-Dirwayi, 2003; Zungu, 2013.

5 Nattrass, 2012; Posel, 2008, pp.13-24; Shisana and Zungu-Dirwayi, 2003.

6 Gevisser, 2008; Nattrass, 2007. Mortal combat: AIDS denialism and the struggle for anti-retrovirals in South Africa. Scottsville: University of KwaZulu-Natal Press; Nattrass and Kalichman, 2010.

7 Mbeki, T., 2000. Speech of the President of South Africa at the opening session of the 13th International AIDS Conference. Durban, South Africa; Mbeki, T., 2001. Address of the President of South Africa, at the Third African Renaissance Festival. Held in Durban on the 31st of March 2001.

8 Shisana, O., Zungu, N. and Simbayi, L., 2014. South Africa's response to the HIV and AIDS epidemics. In Meyiwa, T., Nkondo, M., Chutiga-Mabugu, M., Sithole, M. and

Nyamnjoh, F. (eds.), State of the Nation: South Africa 1994-2014: A twenty-year review of freedom and democracy, pp.347-378. Cape Town: HSRC Press.

9 Ibid.

10 Strydom, W.F., Funkel, N., Nienaber, S., Nortje, K. and Steyn, M., 2010. Evidence-based policymaking: a review. S. Afr. j. sci. 106, pp.5-6. Available at http://www.scielo.org.za/scielo.php?pid=S0038-23532010000300010&script=sci_arttext. [Accessed 4 August 2016].

11 Mbali, M., 2013. South African AIDS activism and global health politics. Political & International Studies Collection. DOI: 10. 1057/9781137312167; Pithouse, K., 2004. 'Look forward, look back, and look around you': Young South African women on the path of HIV/AIDS activism. *Agenda*, 60, pp.22-26; Zungu, 2013.

12 Geffen, N., 2010. Debunking delusions: The inside story of the Treatment Action Campaign. Auckland Park: Jacana Media.

13 Robins, S., 2004. Long live Zackie, long live AIDS activism: Science and citizenship, governance after apartheid. *Journal of Southern Africa*, 30(3), pp.651–672; Robins, S., 2006. From 'rights' to 'rituals': AIDS activism in South Africa. *American Anthropologist*, 108(2), pp.312-323.

14 Chigwedere, P., Seage, G. R ., Gruskin, S. J. D. and Lee, T., 2008. Estimating the lost benefits of antiretroviral drug use in South Africa. *AIDS Journal of Acquired Immune Deficiency Syndromes*, 49(4) pp.410-415.

15 Mbali, 2013; Shisana and Zungu-Dirwayi, 2003; Shisana et al., 2014, pp.347-378.

16 Treatment Action Campaign, 2004. Constitution of TAC. Cape Town: TAC.

17 Hassim, A., 2006. 'The 'Five Star Prison Hotel'? The right of access to ARV treatment for HIV positive prisoners in South Africa. *International Journal on Prisoner Health*, 3.

18 AIDS Law Project, 2003.

19 Treatment Action Campaign. 2008. The wrongs of Matthias Rath. Available at www.tac.org.za/community/rath. [Accessed 4 August 2016].

20 Ibid.

21 Strydom et al., 2010.

22 Hanney, S.R., Gonzalez-Block, M.A., Buxton, M.J. and Kogan, M., 2003. The utilisation of health research in policymaking: Concepts, examples and methods of assessment. *Health Res Policy Syst.* 1(2); Bowen, S. and Zwi, A.B., 2005. Pathways to evidence-informed policy and practice: A framework for action. *Policy Forum* 2:e166. Available at http://www.plosmedicine.org/ [Accessed 4 August 2016]; Mubyasi, G.M. and Gonzalez-Block, M.A., 2005. Research influence on antimalarial drug policy change in Tanzania: Case study of replacing chloroquine with sulfadoxine-pyrimethamine as the first-line drug. *Malar J.* 2005, 4, p.51; Shung-King, M., 2006. The ebb and flow of child health policy development in South Africa: Three case studies reflecting the role of the Children's Institute at the University of Cape Town in shaping child health policy in South Africa. Cape Town: Children's Institute, University of Cape Town, 2006, p.44.

23 Choi, B.C.K., Pang, T., Lin, V., Puska, P et al., 2005. Can scientists and policy makers work together? *J Epidemiol Community Health*, 59, pp.632-637.

24 Gevisser, 2008; Mbeki, 2000; Mbeki, 2001; Nattrass, 2007; Natrass and Kalichman, 2010, pp.123-134.

25 Baker, H. D., 2005. Negotiating power and profitability of HIV/ AIDS in South Africa. Unpublished M. A. thesis. Brown University, US; Cameron, E., 2005. Witness to AIDS. Cape Town: Tafelberg; Zungu, 2013.
26 Colvin, C.J., 2012. True believers or modern believers: HIV sciences and the work of the Dr Rath Foundation. In Levine, S. (ed.), Medicine and the politics of knowledge, pp.33-53. Pretoria: HSRC Press.
27 Shisana and Zungu-Dirwayi, 2003.
28 Colvin, 2012, pp.33-53; Cullinan, K. and Thom, A. (eds.), 2009. The virus, vitamins and vegetables: The South African HIV/AIDS mystery. Auckland Park: Jacana Media; Zungu, 2013.
29 Chiasson, R., 2000. The World AIDS Conference in Durban, South Africa – science, politics and health. The world HIV report, division of infectious disease and AIDS service, John Hopkins University. Available at http:www.hopkins-aids.edu/piblications/report/sept000_1.html. [Accessed 5 December 2006.]; Colvin, 2012, pp. 33–53; Geffen, N., 2006. Echoes of Lysenko: State sponsored pseudo-science in South Africa. Centre for Social Science Research Working Papers: University of Cape Town; Zungu, 2013.
30 Nattrass, 2005; Susser, I., 2009. AIDS, sex and culture: Global politics and survival in Southern Africa. Hoboken, New Jersey: Wiley-Blackwell.
31 Mbali, M., 2004. AIDS discourse and South African State: Government denialism and post-apartheid AIDS policymaking. *Transformation*, 54, pp.104-122.
32 Colvin, pp. 33-53; UNAIDS. 2003. HIV, AIDS and the reappearance of an old myth: Background brief. Available at http://www.unaids.org/special/ [Accessed 20 January 2005]; UNAIDS, 2004. Women and HIV/AIDS: Confronting the crisis. A joint report of the UNAIDS, UNFPA, UNIFEM. Available at www.un.org/ [Accessed 20 January 2005]; Robins, 2008; Shisana and Zungu-Dirwayi, 2003.
33 Zungu, 2013.
34 Colvin, 2012, pp.33-53; Nattrass, 2004; Natrass, 2007; Ncayiyana, D., 2007. HIV/ AIDS, TB and nutrition. *South African Medical Journal*, 97(10), p.893; Zungu, 2013.
35 Levine, S., 2012. Testing knowledge: Legitimacy, healing and medicine in South Africa. In S. Levine (ed.), Medicine and the politics of knowledge, pp.55-76. Pretoria: HSRC Press; Ndaki, K., 2009. Traditional alternatives? In Cullinan, K. and Thom, A. (eds.), The virus, vitamins and vegetables: The South African HIV/ AIDS mystery, pp.143-156. South Africa: Jacana Media; Shisana and Zungu-Dirwayi, 2003.
36 Baker, 2005: pp.50.
37 Baker, 2005; Zungu, 2013.
38 Colvin, 2012, pp.33-53; Mbali, 2004, pp.104-122; Mbali, 2013; Zungu, 2013.
39 Republic of South Africa Global AIDS Response Progress Report, 2012. Available at http://www.unaids.org/en/dataanalysis/knowyourresponse/countryprogressreports/2012countries/ce_ZA_Narrative_Report.pdf [Accessed 27 April 2013].
40 Ibid.
41 Nattrass, 2005.
42 Choi et al., 2005, pp. 632-637.
43 Colvin, 2012, pp. 33-53; Geffen, 2006; Robins, 2008.
44 Department of Health, 2007. The HIV, AIDS and STIs national strategic plan for South Africa, 2007-2011. Pretoria: National Department of Health.

45 SANAC, 2011. The HIV & AIDS and STI Strategic Plan for South Africa 2007-2011. Pretoria: South African National AIDS Council; Shisana and Zungu-Dirwayi, 2003.
46 Shisana and Zungu-Dirwayi, 2003.
47 UNAIDS, 2015. Focus on location and population. Geneva: UNAIDS.
48 UNAIDS, 2014. HIV and social protection: Guidance note. Geneva: UNAIDS.
49 Republic of South Africa Global AIDS Response Progress Report, 2012; Shisana et al., 2014, pp.347-378.
50 Setswe, G., 2010. Translation of HIV prevention research into policy and practice. Keynote presentation at the 11th International Congress of Behavioral Medicine. Washington DC.
51 UNAIDS, 2015.
52 WHO, 2015
53 Ibid.
54 Motsoaledi, A., 2016. Debate on the health budget vote National Assembly, 10 May 2016. Cape Town.
55 Rodger, A.J., Lodwick, R., Schechter, M., Deeks et al., 2013. Mortality in well controlled HIV in the continuous antiretroviral therapy arms of the SMART and ESPRIT trials compared with the general population. *AIDS*, 27(6), pp.973-979. doi: 10.1097/QAD.0b013e32835cae9c.
56 Motsoaledi, 2016.
57 Rodger et al., 2013.
58 UNAIDS, 2015.
59 Cohen, M.S., Chen, Y.Q., McCauley, M., et al., 2011. Prevention of HIV-1 infection with early antiretroviral therapy. The HPTN 052 Study Team. *N Engl J Med,* 2011. DOI:10.1056/nejmoa1105243.
60 Rodger et al., 2013.
61 Building Political Momentum Towards Universal Access PMTCT High-Level Global Partners Forum 2007. Sandton Sun Hotel, Johannesburg, South Africa 26-27 November 2007. Available at: http://www.who.int/hiv/mtct/MTCT_GPFConceptNoteNov07.pdf [Accessed 24 June 2016].
62 UNAIDS, 2015.
63 Ibid.
64 Tanser, F., Bärnighausen, T., Grapsa, E., Zaidi, J. and Newell, M.L., 2013. High coverage of ART associated with decline in risk of HIV acquisition in rural KwaZulu-Natal, South Africa. Science 339(6122), pp.966-997; Vandormael, A., Newell, M.L., Barnighausen, T. and Tanser, F., 2014. Use of antiretroviral therapy in households and risk of HIV acquisition in rural KwaZulu-Natal, South Africa, 2004-12: A prospective cohort study. *Lancet Glob Health*, 2:e, pp.209-215.
65 Bekker, L-G., Rebe, K. and Venter, F., 2016. Southern African guidelines on the safe use of pre-exposure prophylaxis in persons at risk of acquiring HIV-1 infection. *S Afr J HIV Med.*, 17(1), Art. #455, 11 pages. Available at http://dx.doi.org/10.4102/sajhivmed.v17i1.455. [Accessed 4 August 2016].
66 Centers for Disease Control and Prevention. 2015. Proven HIV prevention methods. July 2015. Centers for Disease Control and Prevention: Atlanta GA.
67 UNAIDS, 2015.
68 Motsoaledi, 2016.

69 Bekker et al., 2016.

70 Tanser et al., 2013, pp.966-971; Vandormael et al., 2014, pp.209-215.

71 Perinatal HIV Guidelines Working Group, 2009.

72 WHO, 2012. World Health Organization. Technical update on treatment optimization: Use of efavirenz during pregnancy: A public health perspective. 2012. Available at http://www.who.int/hiv/pub/treatment2/efavirenz/en/ [Accessed 22 June 2016].

73 PMTCT High-Level Global Partners Forum, 2007.

74 Ibid.

75 UNAIDS, 2015.

76 UNICEF, 2010.

77 Know Your Epidemic, Know Your Response Report, 2011. HSRC and SANAC. Pretoria

78 SAPMTCT Impact Study 2012; also see RSA 2013.

79 Shisana, O., Simbayi, L.C., Rehle, T., Zungu, N.P. et al., 2009. South African national HIV prevalence, incidence, behaviour and communication survey, 2010: the health of our children. Cape Town: HSRC Press; Shisana, O., Rehle, T., Simbayi, L.C., Zuma, K. et al., 2009. South African national HIV prevalence, incidence, behaviour and communication survey, 2008: turning the tide among teenagers? Cape Town: HSRC Press. Shisana, O, Rehle, T, Simbayi LC, Zuma, K. et al., 2014. South African National HIV Prevalence, Incidence and Behaviour Survey, 2012. Cape Town: HSRC Press.

80 Motsoaledi, 2016.

81 Shisana et al., 2014, pp.347-378.

82 UNAIDS, 2015.

83 Auvert, B., Taljaard, D., Lagarde, E., Sobngwi-Tambekou, J. et al., 2005. Randomized, controlled intervention trial of male circumcision for reduction of HIV infection risk: The ANRS 1265 Trial. *PLoS Med* 2: e298. doi:10.1371/ journal.pmed.0020298; Byakika-Tusiime, J., 2008. Circumcision and HIV infection: assessment of causality. *AIDS Behaviour*, 12(6), pp.835-841; Gray, R.H., Kigozi, G., Serwadda, D., Makumbi, F. et al., 2007. Male circumcision for HIV prevention in men in Rakai, Uganda: A randomised trial. *Lancet*, 369, pp.657-666; Gray, R., Kigozi, G., Kong, X., Ssempiija, V. et al., 2012. The effectiveness of male circumcision for HIV prevention and effects on risk behaviours in a post-trial follow-up study. *AIDS*, 26, pp.609-615; Maughan-Brown, B., Venkataramani, A.S., Nattrass, N., Seekings, J. and Whiteside, A.W., 2011. A cut above the rest: Traditional male circumcision and HIV risk among Xhosa men in Cape Town, South Africa. *J Acquir Immune Defic Syndr*, 58(5), pp.499-505; Weiss, Hanksin, and Dickson, 2009. Male circumcision and risk of HIV infection in women: a systematic review and meta-analysis. *Lancet Infect Dis*, 9(11), pp.669-677. doi: 10.1016/S1473-3099(09)70235-X.

84 UNAIDS, 2015, p.50.

85 WHO/UNAIDS, 2007. Technical Consultation Male Circumcision and HIV Prevention: Research Implications for Policy and Programming. Montreux, 6-8 March 2007.

86 UNAIDS, 2015.

87 SANAC, 2011.

88 See Shisana, O, Rehle, T, Simbayi LC, Zuma, K. et al., 2014; Zungu, N. P., Simbayi, L. C., Mabaso, M., Evans, M., Zuma, K., Ncitakalo, N. and Sifunda, S., 2016. HIV risk perception and behavior among medically and traditionally circumcised males in South Africa. *BMC Public Health*, 16(1):357 DOI:10.1186/s12889-016-3024-y;

Connolly, C., Simbayi, L.C., Shanmugam, R. and Mqeketo, A., 2008. Male circumcision and its relationship to HIV infection in South Africa: Results from a national survey in 2002. *South African Medical Journal*, 98(10), pp.789-794.

89 UNAIDS, 2015.

90 Ibid.

91 UNAIDS, 2004.

92 Hearst, 2004.

93 Cohen, D.A., Farley, T.A., Bedimo-Etame, J.R., Scribner, R. et al., 1999. Implementation of condom social marketing in Louisiana, 1993 to 1996. *Am J Public Health*, 89, pp.204-208

94 UNAIDS, 2015.

95 Setswe, 2010.

96 Johnson, L.F., Hallett, T.B., Rehle, T.M. and Dorrington, R.E., 2012. The effect of changes in condom usage and antiretroviral treatment coverage on human immunodeficiency virus incidence in South Africa: a model-based analysis. *Journal of the Royal Society Interface*, 9, pp.1544-1554.

97 UNAIDS, 2015.

98 Ibid.

99 Ibid, p. 59.

100 UNAIDS, 2015.

101 Dunne EF, Whitehead S, Sternberg M., Thepamnuay, S. et al., [Accessed4 August 2016]. Suppressive acyclovir therapy reduces HIV cervicovaginal shedding in HIV- and HSV-2-infected women, Chiang Rai, Thailand. *Journal of Acquired Immune Deficiency Syndromes*, 49, pp.77-83.

102 Karim, Q.A., Karim, S.S., Frohlich, J.A., Grobler, A. C. et al., 2010. The CAPRISA 004 Trial Group. Effectiveness and safety of tenofovir gel, an antiretroviral microbicide, for the prevention of HIV infection in women. Science 3: 329(5996), pp.1168-1174.

103 Centers for Disease Control and Prevention (CDC). 2006. Evolution of HIV/AIDS prevention programs – United States, 1981-2006. *MMWR* 55:597–603.

104 Hogben, M., McNally, T., McPheeters, M. and Hutchinson, A.B., 2007. The effectiveness of HIV partner counselling and referral services in increasing identification of HIV-positive individuals: a systematic review. *Am J Prev Med* 33(2 Suppl):S89-100.15

105 Trenholm, C. et al., 2007. *Impacts of Four Title V, Section* 510 *Abstinence Education Programs Final Report*. Princeton, NJ: Mathematic Policy Research, submitted to U.S. Dept. Health & Human Services, Assistant Secretary for Planning and Evaluation; Kirby, D., 2002. Do Abstinence Only Programs Delay the Initiation of Sex Among Young People and Reduce Teen Pregnancy? Washington DC: National Campaign to Prevent Teen Pregnancy.

106 Jemmott, J., Jemmott, L. and Fong, G., 2010. Efficacy of a theory-based abstinence-only intervention over 24 months. *Archives of Pediatric Adolescent Medicine*, 164(2), pp.152-159.

107 *Archives of Pediatrics and Adolescent Medicine* in 2010.

108 Murphy, E. M., Greene, M. E., Mihailovic, A. and Olupot-Olupot , P., 2006. Was the "ABC" Approach (Abstinence, Being Faithful, Using Condoms) Responsible for Uganda's Decline in HIV? PLOS Published: September 12, 2006. Available at http://dx.doi.org/10.1371/journal.pmed.0030379. [Accessed 4 August 2016].

109 Watkins, S., 2004. Navigating the AIDS Epidemic in Rural Malawi. *Popul Dev Rev,* 4, pp.673-705.
110 Mah, T. L. and Halperin, D. T., 2008. Concurrent sexual partnerships and the HIV epidemic in Africa: Evidence to move forward. *AIDS and Behaviour*, 14(1), pp.11-16.
111 Lurie, M. N., and Rosenthal, S., 2009. Concurrent partnerships as a driver of the HIV epidemic in sub-Saharan Africa? The evidence is limited. *AIDS Behaviour*, 14, pp.17-24.
112 Sawers, L. and Stillwaggon, E., 2010. Concurrent sexual partnerships do not explain the HIV epidemics in Africa: a systematic review of the evidence. *J Int AIDS Soc* (13), pp.13-34. doi: 10.1186/1758-2652-13-34.
113 Marks, G., Crepaz, N., Walton Senterfitt, J. and Janssen, R.S., 2005. Meta-analysis of high-risk sexual behavior in persons aware and unaware they are infected with HIV in the United States: Implications for HIV prevention programs. *J Acquir Immune Defic Syndr*, 39(4), pp.446-453; Weinhardt, L.S., Carey, M.P., Johnson, B.T. and Bickham, N.L.,1999. Effects of HIV counselling and testing on sexual risk behavior: A meta-analytic review of published research, 1985-1997. *Am J Public Health*, 89(9), pp.1397-1405.
114 SANAC. 2011. The HIV & AIDS and STI Strategic Plan for South Africa 2007–2011. Pretoria: South African National AIDS Council.
115 Motsoaledi, 2016.
116 UNAIDS, 2014.
117 Ibid.
118 Cluver, L., Boyes, M., Orkin, M., Pantelic, M., Molwela, T. and Sherr, L., 2013. Child-focused state cash transfers and adolescent risk of HIV infection in South Africa: A propensity score-matched case-control study. *Lancet Global Health* 2013, 1, e362–370.
119 Global HIV Prevention Working Group, 2008.

Chapter 4

Women, HIV and Clinical Trials in South Africa

Jonathan Stadler, Helen Rees, Sinead Delany-Moretlwe and Thesla Palanee-Phillips

Introduction

South Africa has a mixed record in achieving the 2002 Millennium Development Goals, particularly those aimed at improving women's reproductive and maternal health, and reducing the burden of morbidity and mortality from the human immunodeficiency virus (HIV) and acquired immune deficiency syndrome (AIDS). Between 1998 and 2007, maternal deaths increased fourfold;[1] the delay, until 2002, in rolling out prevention of mother-to-child transmission (PMTCT) resulted in thousands of preventable child deaths from HIV;[2] and political inaction in the provision of lifesaving antiretroviral treatment (ART) resulted in 330 000 avoidable deaths.[3] An estimated 6.4 million people are currently infected with HIV in South Africa and this will severely affect the country for decades to come.[4]

More recently, however, significant achievements have been accomplished. South Africa has the largest ART programme worldwide, mother-to-child transmission of HIV has been reduced, and medical male circumcision programmes to reduce infection amongst men are being scaled up.

A critical concern that is yet to be resolved is the persistently high HIV incidence amongst adolescent girls and young women aged 15 to 24 years. Women in this age category represent almost a quarter of all new infections in South Africa.[5] Consequently, there is an urgent need for programmes to address HIV infections in this particular demographic.

In this chapter we map a history of interventions that have sought to address women's vulnerabilities. We focus our attention on clinical trials of female-controlled options to prevent HIV acquisition and discuss their progress, considering the dynamic political, social and epidemiological context.

Our analysis is ordered according to distinct stages that reflect shifting trends in the field of HIV prevention.

1. From the early to late 1990s, HIV prevalence increased dramatically. During this era, characterised by AIDS denial and political inaction, HIV prevention was limited to behavioural interventions and methods that were largely 'male controlled'.

2. By the early 2000s, interest in 'female-controlled' methods were gaining ground, and amid political ambivalence, public mistrust and scepticism, several large randomised controlled trials (RCT) took place in Sub-Saharan Africa.
3. The late 2000s witnessed a revolution in HIV prevention: after suffering setbacks from numerous unsuccessful clinical trials for women, the field was reinvigorated by solid evidence of the effectiveness of antiretrovirals (ARV) based compounds to manage HIV. Concerns about the potential benefit for young women and adolescent girls emerged from trials that were, however, unable to demonstrate effectiveness due to low adherence.
4. This has led, in the current setting, of an exploration of the social contexts of young women and adolescent girls' lives, and a realisation of the critical importance of approaches that combine biomedical interventions with those that address the structural drivers of HIV. We conclude the discussion by looking forward to current and future clinical trials and new technologies.

Early Responses to a New Epidemic

In the early to late 1980s, HIV in South Africa was limited to a small number of haemophiliacs, gay men and foreign mine workers. In 1990, antenatal prevalence was 0.7 per cent, yet by 2004 this had risen to 29.5 per cent.[6] Understanding the dramatic and unrelenting increase in infections during this period requires exploring the social transformations that took place and how these shaped public health responses to the spread of HIV.

The first democratic election in South Africa ushered in a period of heightened optimism. As racially-defined geopolitical boundaries were dissolved, sexual identities were freed up and liberalised.[7] A new constitution prohibited discrimination on the basis of sexual preference; the state legalised the termination of pregnancy and considered decriminalising sex work.[8] On the eve of political liberation, however, AIDS was an epidemic 'waiting to happen'. It was rooted in colonial and apartheid political economies[9] that traced the fault lines of political, social and economic exclusion of the vast majority of South African citizens.[10] In the post-apartheid setting, groups of poor women became increasingly vulnerable due to material inequalities, the erosion of marriage and oscillating migration between rural and urban informal settlements.[11]

The initial response to the AIDS epidemic was characterised by inaction and confusion. The South African government under Nelson Mandela, committed to ensuring a peaceful transition to democracy, was unable to engage with the looming threat that AIDS posed. In 2000, the President at the time, Thabo Mbeki, adopted an adversarial position against mainstream scientific and orthodox theories of HIV, effectively delaying a coherent response to the epidemic.[12]

Surrounded by secrecy and stigma, and no public sector access to treatment, there was widespread resistance to HIV testing, despite appeals to individuals to know their status. In the mining town of Carletonville, not a single respondent out of 2 500 accepted the invitation for a free and anonymous HIV test.[13] Fears of HIV testing were widespread,[14] underscored by the – occasionally violent – persecution of people suspected of being HIV positive. In 1998, community members stoned Gugu Dlamini to death for publicly disclosing her HIV status.[15] Not surprisingly, rates of HIV disclosure were extremely low across the country. The 2001 study of 726 HIV positive patients found that 92 per cent had not informed anyone of their status.[16]

It is in this challenging context that HIV prevention efforts were mobilised. Awareness campaigns, which used images of death, generated fear and stigma. The main thrust of the message was to generate behaviour change by encouraging abstinence, urging people to 'be faithful', and to use condoms – a strategy commonly known as 'ABC'. Yet these efforts yielded uneven results.[17] Of seven behavioural interventions tested in randomised clinical trials, none had any effect on HIV outcomes.[18] While targeted at changing individual behaviours, HIV prevention campaigns often discounted local cultural constructs of the disease,[19] as well as structural drivers, such as socio-economic inequalities, that shape the epidemic.[20]

Public health programmes also faced pervasive mistrust, due in part to the colonial legacy of complicity with segregationist laws, but also due to more recent disclosures of the role of medical practitioners in apartheid atrocities.[21] When Wouter Basson, a cardiologist and head of South Africa's secret chemical and biological warfare programme (Project Coast) during the apartheid era, was tried for murder in the South African Supreme Court, revelations of gruesome atrocities lent credence to the idea that HIV was manufactured and purposefully spread.[22]

Community rumours endorsed these views, alleging that HIV diagnostic and prevention technologies spread HIV,[23] and that a cure for AIDS was known but withheld.[24] Popular speculation of AIDS conspiracies were fuelled by scandals, such as the 1998 Virodene trial, a substance lauded by the Cabinet as a miracle AIDS cure, but exposed by the Medicines Control Council as an industrial solvent with dangerous side effects.[25] Senior scientists were lambasted by President Mbeki in ANC Today as being controlled by the pharmaceutical industry, as was retired President Mandela when he tried to raise the issue of treatment within ANC structures. It is under these unforgiving circumstances that scientists, researchers and activists sought to develop new ways of combatting the epidemic amongst women.

Female Empowerment and Microbicides

Condoms (male and female) are highly efficacious in preventing transmission of HIV, but are often applied inconsistently and selectively depending on particular circumstances.[26] Usually preferred in short-term relationships, condoms are incompatible with the sentiments of trust and fertility desired in longer-term partnerships.[27] Monetary reward also mediates condom use, for instance with sex workers[28] and in other transactional relationships.[29] Condoms are associated with reduced sexual pleasure, distrust, and perceived 'blockage' and infertility.[30] Moreover, intimate partner power dynamics can undermine individual agency to demand condom use.[31] Recognising the limitations of condoms as a HIV prevention method, alternative methods that did not require male partner initiation became a high priority. Included in these technologies were the female condom, the diaphragm, and vaginally applied microbicides.

The female condom was launched in 1984, as 'a new technology which offered the promise ... of enabling women to take care of themselves in sexual terms, and thus to empower themselves in this context'.[32] Fashioned from polyurethane, a lighter, more sensitive and robust material than latex, the female condom resembles an oversized male condom, open at one end and closed at the other with a ring to fit in the cervix. In 1991, the United States (US) Food and Drug Administration (FDA) approved the female condom for distribution, and by 2009 the Joint United Nations Programme on HIV and AIDS (UNAIDS), the World Health Organization (WHO) and the United Nations Population Fund (UNFPA) endorsed its effectiveness.[33] The device was regarded as broadly acceptable and feasible by female users, but not by their male partners.[34] The product was more than 10 times as expensive as a male condom, and while social marketing campaigns were successful in some countries (Zimbabwe), the technology failed to gain traction amongst policymakers. To try and reduce costs, a study amongst sex workers in South Africa reported that 83 per cent of those interviewed would consider washing and reusing the female condom. The same study demonstrated that re-use was feasible, safe and that the condom was robust enough for re-use.[35] Despite this compelling data, the WHO failed to endorse re-use as a strategy to increase access to the female condom; and in spite of its potential as an empowering technology for women, the female condom has not enjoyed much success as a prevention method, possibly due to its perceived unacceptability amongst policymakers.[36] Other repurposed barrier methods, such as the diaphragm, have enjoyed even less success as HIV prevention methods. A multi-site trial assessed the efficacy of the diaphragm in preventing HIV infection, but found no additional protective effect with use.[37]

The idea of a microbicide first surfaced in the early 1990s. Observing increasing rates of infection amongst Southern African heterosexual women, Zena Stein proposed microbicides as a female-controlled technology that could empower women to prevent HIV infection.[38] Microbicides are topical applications of chemical agents in the form of vaginal gels, rings, film, creams and sponges, which contain an active drug to prevent infection. The distinct advantage of microbicides is their potential to be used in a clandestine manner, without the need for male partner approval.

The steady growth of the microbicide field was accomplished by linking microbicides to the goal of female empowerment. Unlike research driven by pharmaceutical interests, microbicide research became a movement 'by women and for women'[39] and international advocates established networks of scientists and researchers, attracting donor funds for research and development. By 2009, 12 Phase 2 and Phase 3 clinical trials of microbicides had been completed, involving more than 31 000 women.[40]

The early trials of experimental microbicides to prevent HIV were, however, largely unsuccessful. One of the first trials (from 1996 to 2000) tested Nonoxynol 9, a registered and widely used spermicide, and had unforeseen outcomes: the trial enrolled sex workers, and those who used the gel more than three to five times per day were almost twice as much at risk of acquiring HIV than those on the placebo.[41] These results seriously impaired the microbicide field[42] and researchers sought to acquire safer anti-HIV agents. Hope for an effective and safe microbicide came in the form of polyanions or viral entry inhibitors, such as Carraguard, PRO-2000 and Cellulose Sulphate.[43]

The results of these trials were, however, also disappointing. Although fewer HIV infections were recorded for the Carraguard arm than the placebo, the difference was not significant enough to establish efficacy;[44] and virtually at the same time, the Cellulose Sulphate trial was closed due to safety concerns.[45] Again, these results impacted negatively on public perceptions of microbicides.

Much hope was invested in PRO-2000, which had displayed marginal efficacy in a 'proof of concept' trial,[46] and further testing in a large Phase 3 trial was planned. The Microbicide Development Program launched the MDP301 trial, aiming to assess the safety and efficacy of PRO-2000/5 in five countries in Africa, with three trial sites in South Africa. Over 15 000 women were screened, while more than 9000 eventually joined and completed the trial. Commencing in 2005, the trial lasted four years, and showed that although it was safe to use, PRO-2000 vaginal gel was ineffective in preventing HIV acquisition; no difference in HIV infections was observed between the active drug arms and the placebo arms.[47]

While discouraging, important lessons were learnt about recruiting, enrolling and maintaining large cohorts of healthy female participants, especially given the unsupportive environment for clinical research. At this time, the South African government was, at best, indifferent – and occasionally hostile – toward biomedical research. Reiterating ideas of the harmful and exploitative nature of trials, former president Mbeki stated: 'Our people are being used as guinea pigs and conned into using dangerous and toxic drugs'.[48] In 2007, following the closure of the Cellulose Sulphate trial, then National Health Minister, Manto Tshabalala-Msimang, declared that all microbicide trials would be suspended to determine whether unethical conduct was taking place.[49] In KwaZulu-Natal, Peggy Nkoyeni, former political head of health in that province, led her own local enquiry into alleged misconduct in microbicide trials.

These events provided fertile ground for the popular media's portrayals of HIV clinical trials as inherently exploitative and intentionally harmful.[50] Media headlines sensationalised the outcomes of trials, as in the wake of the closure of the Cellulose Sulphate trial in 2007: 'Hundreds of women in South Africa, Benin, Nigeria, Uganda and India, who are being used as human guinea pigs in the US-funded research on HIV prevention, are feared to have contracted the virus during the course of the trials'.[51] Consequently, distrust of biomedical research was highly prevalent and accounts of malicious medical researchers pervaded discussions of HIV and AIDS and prevention.[52]

Although detractors claimed to represent women's views, those women who participated in clinical trials rejected the label 'guinea pigs', offering very different accounts of their experiences. Instead of tales of exploitation and harm, women's narratives of MDP301 portrayed the trial as a hopeful enterprise that helped them gain control over HIV. They referred to what they had gained from understanding their health, and the security of regular HIV testing, counselling, and access to care.[53]

Furthermore, although vaginal microbicides were 'foreign technologies', women valued the effect that they had on enhancing sexual pleasure and intimacy, and believed the gels cleansed their bodies. Acquiring local meanings and assimilation into cultural notions of pollution and cleansing, microbicide gels became acceptable from a local point of view.[54]

Medical research on microbicides was also firmly linked to a strong activist network. Established in 1998 and based in Washington, Nairobi and Johannesburg, the Global Campaign for Microbicides promoted the development of ideas, political buy-in, and civil society engagement. It stressed the involvement of both scientists and women's health activists from the beginning of the development process, and promoted the participation of community members in clinic trial sites.

Researchers invested significant time and resources in community engagement structures and activities in a way that has been unique to HIV prevention. In a similar way to the struggle that had, decades previously, been led by AIDS activists in the US,[55] microbicide research was framed by a human rights ideal that highlighted the needs of participants and the local community.

Creating awareness and collective participation in clinical trials at the local level required innovative and creative strategies to explain the rationale for scientific research methods and designs, and to manage the expectations of those people desperately seeking solutions.[56] Researchers forged relationships with Community Based Organisations (CBOs), and community advisory boards (CABs) were established to provide guidance and advise researchers. Regular educational and awareness activities took place, aiming to enhance research literacy. Community radio stations were particularly useful in communicating and educating the public about clinical trials and participants' rights.[57]

In summary, although facing an accumulated history of perception of medical research as harmful and exploitative, researchers led trials that engaged local communities and in which participants viewed their role as important in controlling the epidemic, and for their improved personal health. While these early trials were not successful in identifying an effective product to prevent HIV, they provided the foundation for future studies as the search to find methods to prevent HIV amongst women continued.

Antiretrovirals and the New HIV Prevention Technologies

While researchers experienced frustration in finding an effective method to prevent HIV amongst women, successful results emerged from trials of medical male circumcision (MMC) in preventing female to male transmission. Three trials reported that MMC could reduce sexual transmission from women to men by 60 per cent (32% to 76%; 95% confidence interval (CI)) and had the potential, over time, to reduce infection in both directions by 37 per cent.[58]

At the same time, the treatment landscape changed significantly. First announced in 2004, public access to ARVs finally became available in the late 2000s. This ushered in a new era of optimism: the period 2009 to 2012 witnessed increases in life expectancy from 56 to 61 years, improved access to PMTCT, and decreases of 25 per cent in infant deaths.[59]

Despite the advances in expanding access to prevention and treatment services, the most recent population-based data showed a significant increase in overall HIV prevalence from 10.9 per cent in 2008 to 12.6 per cent in 2012.[60] This increase is partially explained by prolonged survival associated with expanded access to ART, but there remains worrying evidence of on-going risk and consequent sexual transmission of HIV in those aged 15 years and over.[61] Young women continue to be disproportionately affected by the HIV epidemic. Among those aged 15 to 24 years, HIV incidence is four-fold higher in women than in men (2.5% vs. 0.6%).[62]

Adolescent girls and young women's high vulnerability to HIV is due to many factors. Adolescence is a period of rapid physical, neurodevelopmental and social growth, during which young people have limited access to reproductive and sexual health services. A range of individual-level behavioural factors contributes to the increased vulnerability to HIV, including younger age at sexual debut,[63] older partner(s),[64] concurrent sexual partners,[65] lack of consistent condom use,[66] physical and sexual violence,[67] and alcohol use.[68]

Structural factors, such as poverty, gender inequality and high exposures to violence, limited economic options, and the low social power of young people, also contribute to their high risk.[69] In particular, gender inequalities and violence form a significant backdrop to the HIV epidemic in women in Eastern and Southern Africa,[70,71] with studies in South Africa and Uganda demonstrating the link between intimate partner violence (IPV) and the risk of HIV acquisition.[72] These structural and behavioural factors give shape to young women and adolescent girls' vulnerability to HIV. As we discuss below, the same factors also have implications for this demographics' adoption of prevention options.

Pre-exposure prophylaxis (PrEP), including topical gels, daily oral tablets or potentially longer-acting rings and injectables, represent promising female-controlled methods of biomedical HIV prevention. As we noted earlier, first-generation vaginal microbicides showed no preventive effect in six efficacy trials.[73] Compounds with direct anti-HIV activity offered a more promising option.

Trials involving men who have sex with men (MSM) provided strong evidence of the effectiveness of oral ARVs as PrEP. Four placebo-controlled trials in MSM, injection drug users, and heterosexual serodiscordant couples in Eastern and Southern Africa showed that daily oral PrEP with tenofovir (TFV) alone or co-formulated with emtricitabine (TDF-FTC) resulted in a 44 to 75 per cent reduction in HIV incidence.[74,75] These results allowed the registration of Truvada® for PrEP use by high-risk individuals: In 2012 by the US Food and Drug Agency; and in November 2015, by the South African Medicines Control Council.

Clinical trials that tested the same drugs with HIV negative heterosexual women were, however, less conclusive. Between 2010 and 2015 four major trials of oral and topical PrEP were undertaken in Sub-Saharan Africa with variable results.

In 2010, CAPRISA 004, a Phase 2B trial (of pericoital intravaginal TFV one per cent gel), provided proof-of-concept that topical PrEP could safely reduce the risk of HIV acquisition by 39 per cent (CI 0.06 0.60, p=0.017).[76] Importantly, greater coverage of sex acts was associated with higher effectiveness.

Hopeful that these results would be confirmed and TFV one per cent gel would be licensed, the FACTS 001 licensure trial was launched in October 2011. This trial enrolled 2059 women in nine sites across South Africa, and was completed in August 2014. In this larger cohort of women drawn from diverse populations across the country, no overall difference in effectiveness was shown between the intervention and placebo group (IRR 1.0, 95% CI 0.7-1.4),[77] and although the majority of women used the gel more than 50 per cent of the time, their usage was insufficient to provide protection. There was a similar trend suggesting some effectiveness among women who used the product consistently, but since the overall study found no protection from TDF gel, the prospects for the development of topical peri-coital PrEP amongst women were diminished.

Two other studies explored topical and oral PrEP. The VOICE and FEM-PrEP studies enrolled women from Eastern and Southern Africa. The VOICE trial assessed daily treatment with oral tenofivir disoproxil fumarate (TDF), oral TDF-FTC, or TFV one per cent vaginal gel as pre-exposure prophylaxis against HIV infection amongst 5029 women in South Africa, Zimbabwe and Uganda. In September 2011, the oral TDF arm was discontinued due to futility, and in November of the same year the TFV gel arm was also stopped for the same reasons. The final results of the trial found that none of the products tested were effective in preventing HIV acquisition.[78] FEM-PrEP, conducted amongst women in Kenya, South Africa, and Tanzania, also tested daily oral TDF-FTC against a placebo. The study was halted in April 2011 due to the lack of efficacy.[79] Overall, adherence was too low in either trial to observe efficacy, with TFV detected in less than 30 per cent of plasma samples.[80]

In the aftermath of trials that failed to demonstrate effectiveness, harsh criticism was expressed toward women who were accused of 'lying' to the trial coordinators about their adherence. Indeed, in an analysis undertaken after the VOICE trial, blood tests to detect drug levels showed that 50 to 58 per cent of women who participated in the trial had no detectable level of the drug in their blood. The popular press challenged women's motivations for taking part in the trial, accusing them of doing so purely for the money. Theirs were 'elaborate deceptions'.[81]

A closer look at women's lives reveals that, while the stipends women receive to reimburse transport and other costs were important incentives for participation, this could not explain their behaviour. Instead, an in-depth understanding of women's everyday lives, their circumstances and what the clinical trial meant to them showed that remaining in the trial was more important than adhering to the product. Trial participation not only offered women access to good health care, but also generated hope for an end to HIV and optimism for a more meaningful and promising future.[82] Moreover, participation in clinical trials and the ability to be adherent are often shaped by women's personal experiences of using experimental HIV prevention methods, the dynamics of intimate partnerships, and the particular social and economic settings.

Research in clinical trial settings highlighted the uncertainty and ambivalence about using ARVs for the purpose of prevention,[83] as well as concerns about side effects and anticipated stigma. Several studies identified HIV-related stigma as a barrier to PrEP use.[84] In Kenya and Thailand, participants in oral PrEP trials reported experiencing stigma which resulted in their concealment of product use, and subsequent lower adherence.[85] In VOICE, topical and oral PrEP was associated with HIV illness by participants, their male partners and community members. Concerned that they would be mistakenly identified as HIV positive, participants concealed study products; and unintentional disclosure occasionally led to relationship conflicts resulting in early trial termination.[86] PrEP use was also associated with promiscuity, creating suspicion amongst male partners.[87] Understanding the dynamics of intimate partnerships is critical to the analysis of variable adherence in clinical trials.

Male partners' influence over sexual decision making and prevention choices can limit women's decisions.[88] Although envisaged as clandestine, women feel compelled to disclose use of HIV prevention methods to their partners, partly due to fears of accidental discovery, but also out of respect for male authority. While men could be supportive, depending on the dynamics of the relationship,[89] women also encountered resistance to their decisions to use prevention.

In the MDP301 trial, male partners were perceived as authoritarian, controlling and suspicious and were often perpetrators of IPV.[90] Fear of violence influenced women's decisions to disclose trial participation and gel use, but attempted concealment of gel use led to additional strain on relationships. In the same trial in Tanzania, women disclosed their gel use to partners only after they had decided to participate in the trial. They narrated numerous tactics to avoid angry or violent responses from their partners, and concealed gel use if their partners resisted.[91] In CAPRISA 004, a third of women expressed fear of disclosing gel use and trial participation.[92] Non-disclosure of gel use was associated with greater difficulty to use the gel. In contrast, disclosure of gel use to partners was associated with modest (14 per cent) increases in adherence.[93] In VOICE, male partners' support and comprehension of the trial and the products being tested, had a significant influence on women's use of PrEP.[94]

Trial data also suggests that while many women can successfully negotiate the use of these products, some experience difficulties integrating PrEP use into their daily lives.[95] Their personal circumstances often constrain their ability to participate fully in clinical trials, unable to juggle their commitments to sustaining their households and meeting the trial requirements.[96]

Data from trials suggest that PrEP use could potentially improve communication and sexual relationships with intimate partners and that women endorse the idea of female-controlled HIV prevention technologies as empowerment. There is still, however, a very clear need to understand how women will incorporate new HIV prevention technologies, like PrEP, into their everyday sexual lives outside of the supportive environment of a trial, particularly when these products are introduced into settings where gender-based violence and stigma are extremely high.[97] There is growing recognition of the ways in which fear of violence, rejection or stigmatisation may have a profoundly negative influence on women's ability to incorporate HIV prevention into their relationships.[98]

These results have had significant implications for the field, raising questions about the feasibility of topical and oral PrEP for young women. While efficacy against HIV for oral PrEP is as high as 80 to 92 per cent, this only occurs with high adherence.[99] In other words, PrEP works, but only when it is taken. Moreover, these findings complimented a growing body of research that underscores the need for biomedical approaches to be combined with interventions that address structural drivers of HIV infection.

Combining Biotechnologies with Structural Interventions

In September 2015, WHO announced that tenofovir-based oral pre-exposure prophylaxis should be offered to those at substantial risk of HIV infection. This recommendation was based on a systematic review to determine PrEP effectiveness for populations at substantial HIV risk. It identified 18 studies across a range of populations and settings, and found that PrEP was effective in reducing HIV risk across gender, PrEP regimen, dosing, and mode of acquisition, and that increased adherence was associated with a demonstrable increase in PrEP effectiveness.[100]

The cumulative data from clinical trials strongly suggests that supportive interventions that address the social and structural factors which influence adherence to biomedical HIV prevention are urgently needed. While these data illustrate the potential that gender inequalities, gender-based violence and stigma may have for PrEP uptake and adherence, we need to be careful not to over-generalise findings from trials. The motivations for participation in placebo-controlled trials with a product of uncertain efficacy are complex, and are also likely to have influenced adherence.[101] Recent data from open-label PrEP studies in MSM suggest that uptake and adherence to open-label products of proven efficacy may be higher than in trials;[102] and less is known about open-label delivery of oral PrEP for women at risk for HIV, violence and stigma in Eastern and Southern Africa.

PrEP is being introduced into contexts where background levels of violence in partnerships are very high. In most parts of the African continent, an estimated 37 per cent of sexually active women will experience physical and/or sexual violence from a partner or other man. Gender-based violence (GBV) and inequality are closely linked with HIV risk, as shown by a recent study, which found that violence, or the threat of violence, can limit HIV prevention behaviours.[103] Given that partner violence and gender inequitable relationships are strongly associated with HIV acquisition,[104] as well as other adverse health outcomes, it is important to assess the potential for integrating health sector responses to GBV into HIV prevention programmes. Such service-based interventions have a moderate impact at best, so efforts to find other social and legal tools to reduce GBV remain critical.

The challenge and opportunity for future PrEP introduction, therefore, is to develop ways to identify women at greatest risk of social harm and/or non-adherence, and along with effective referral, identify ways to support women's empowerment, reduce their risk of violence and stigma, and increase their ability to introduce and consistently use PrEP in their relationships.[105]

Conclusion

Despite its relatively short duration, the history of clinical trials to prevent HIV amongst women is complex and dynamic. The field of study has been in constant flux, responding to changes in policy, epidemiological trends, new technological innovations and trial results. Most recently, the ASPIRE (Microbicides Trial Network) and Ring (International Partnership for Microbicides) trial of a sustained release cervical ring containing dapivirine reported that the incidence of HIV infection was lower in the dapivirine group by 27 per cent than the placebo group (95 per cent CI). Notably, the higher rates of protection (56 per cent; 95

per cent CI) observed amongst older women in contrast to women 21 years and younger, were attributed to lower adherence in the younger age group.[106]

The recent findings that PrEP can be highly effective in preventing HIV acquisition have brought hope to a field that has experienced many disappointments. Yet, many issues regarding its suitability for specific populations remain and need to be resolved. Understanding the multi-faceted reasons for non-adherence to PrEP in all its formulations remains a key question for prevention technology development for adolescent girls and young women. Learning more about patterns of use once a product such as the dapivirine ring is known to be partially effective needs more research, as does understanding whether alternative long-acting technologies, such as ARV containing injectables, will be more acceptable. The field has understood that technology must be integrated into women's daily lives, and that social and structural drivers of HIV risk must also be addressed.

Notes and References

1 Garenne, M., McCaa, R. and Nacro, K., 2011. Maternal mortality in South Africa: An update from the 2007 community survey. *J Popul Res*, 8, pp.89-101.

2 Chopra, M., Daviaud, E., Pattinson, R., Fonn, S. and Lawn, J., 2009. Saving the lives of South Africa's mothers, babies and children: Can the health system deliver? *Lancet*, 374, pp.835-846.

3 Chigwedere, P., Seage III, G. R., Gruskin, S., Lee, T. H. & Essex, M. 2008. Estimating the lost benefits of antiretroviral drug use in South Africa. *J Acquir Immune Defic Syndr*, 49, 410-415.

4 Simelela, N., Venter, W. D., Pillay, Y. and Barron, P., 2015. A political and social history of HIV in South Africa. *Curr HIV/AIDS Rep*, 12, pp.256-261.

5 Shisana, O., Rehle, T., Simbayi L.C., Zuma, K., Jooste, S., Zungu N., Labadarios, D. and Onoya, D., 2014. South African National HIV prevalence, incidence and behaviour survey, 2012. Cape Town: HSRC Press.

6 Simelela, Venter, Pillay and Barron 2015, pp.256-261.

7 Donham, D., 1998. Freeing South Africa: The 'modernization' of male-male sexuality in Soweto. *Cultural Anthropology*, 13, pp.3-21.

8 Wojcicki, J., 1999. Race, class and sex: The Politics of the decriminalisation of sex work. *Agenda*, 42, pp.94-105.

9 Marks, S., 2002. An epidemic waiting to happen? The spread of HIV/AIDS in South Africa in social and historical perspective. *African Studies*, 61, pp.13-26.

10 Fassin, D., 2007. When bodies remember: Experiences and politics of AIDS in South Africa. SF: University of California Press.

11 Hunter, M., 2007. The changing political economy of sex in South Africa: The significance of unemployment and inequalities to the scale of the AIDS pandemic. *Social Science & Medicine*, 64, pp.689-700.

12 Fassin, D. and Schneider, H., 2003. The politics of AIDS in South Africa: beyond the controversies. *British Medical Journal*, 326, pp.495-497.

13 Mkaya-Mwamburi, Qwana, E., Williams, B. and Lurie, M., 2001. HIV status in South Africa: Who wants to know and why? Johannesburg: Centre for Scientific and Industrial Research.
14 Niehaus, I. and Jonsson, G., 2005. Dr. Wouter Basson, Americans and wild beasts: Men's conspiracy theories of HIV/AIDS in the South African Lowveld. *Medical Anthropology*, 24, pp.177-206.
15 *Sunday Times*, South Africa, December 27, 1998.
16 Pawinski, R. and Lalloo, U., 2001. Community attitudes to HIV/AIDS. *SAMJ*, 91, p.448.
17 Campbell, C., 2003. Letting them die: Why HIV/AIDS prevention programmes fail. Oxford, James Currey.
18 Padian, N. S., Mccoyb, S. I., Balkus, J. E. and Wasserheitd, J. N., 2010. Weighing the gold in the gold standard. Challenges in HIV prevention research. *AIDS*, 24, pp.621 635.
19 Heald, S., n.d. It's never as easy as ABC: Understandings of AIDS in Botswana. AIDS in Context 2001, Johannesburg.
20 Auerbach, J.D., Parkhurst, J.O. and Caceres, C.F., 2011. Addressing social drivers of HIV/AIDS for the long-term response: Conceptual and methodological considerations. *Glob Public Health*, 6 Suppl 3, pp.S293-309.
21 Fassin, D. and Schneider, H. 2003. The politics of AIDS in South Africa: Beyond the controversies. *British Medical Journal*, 326, pp.495-497.
22 Niehaus and Jonsson 2005, pp.177-206.
23 McNeill, F. G., 2009. Condoms cause AIDS: Poison, prevention and denial in Venda, South Africa. *African Affairs*, 108, pp.353-370.
24 Stadler, J., 2003. Rumour, gossip and blame: Implications for HIV/AIDS prevention in the South African lowveld. *AIDS Education and Prevention*, 15, pp.357-368.
25 Mbali, M., 2003. HIV/AIDS policy-making in post-apartheid South Africa. In Daniel, J., Habib, A. and Southall, R. (eds). *State of the Nation: South Africa 2003-2004*. Cape Town: HSRC Press.
26 Hearst, N. and Chen, S., 2004. Condom promotion for AIDS prevention in the developing world: Is it working? *Studies in family planning*, 35, pp.39-47.
27 MacPhail, C. and Campbell, C., 2001. 'I think condoms are good but, aai, I hate those things': Condom use among adolescents and young people in a South African township. *Social Science and Medicine*, 52, pp.1613-1627.
28 Stadler, J. and Delany, S., 2006. The healthy brothel: Sex workers' perceptions and experiences of clinical services in Hillbrow, South Africa. *Culture, Health and Sexuality*, 8, pp.451-464.
29 Hunter, M. 2002. The materiality of everyday sex: thinking beyond 'prostitution'. *African Studies*, 61, pp.99-120.
30 Stadler, J. and Saethre, E., 2011. Blockage and flow: Intimate experiences of condoms and microbicides in a South African clinical trial. *Culture, health & sexuality*, 13, pp.31-44.
31 Pettifor, A.E., Measham, D.M., Rees, H.V. and Padian, N.S. 2004a. Sexual power and HIV risk, South Africa. *Emerg Infect Dis*, 10, pp.1996-2004.
32 Kaler, A., 2004. The female condom in North America: Selling the technology of 'empowerment'. *Journal of Gender Studies*, p.13.

33 Peters, A.J., Scharf, M.M., Van Driel, F.T. and Jansen, W.H., 2010. Where does public funding for HIV prevention go to? The case of condoms versus microbicides and vaccines. *Globalization and Health*, p.6.

34 Beksinska, M., Rees, V., Mcintyre, J. and Wilkinson, D., 2001. The acceptability of the female condom in different groups of women in South Africa: A multi-centered study to inform the national female condom introductory strategy. *South African Medical Journal*, 91, pp.672-678.

35 Pettifor, A., Beksinska, M., Rees, H., Mqoqi, N. and Dickson-Theti, K. 2001. The acceptability of reuse of the female condom among urban South African women. *Journal of Urban Health*, 78, pp.647-657.

36 Peters, A., van Driel, F. and Jansen, W. 2014. Acceptability of the female condom by sub-Saharan African women: A literature review. *Afr J Reprod Health*, 18, pp.34-44.

37 Padian, N., 2007. Straten A van der, Ramjee G, Chipato T, de Bruyn G, Blanchard K, Shiboski S, Montgomery E, Fancher H, Cheng H: Diaphragm and lubricant gel for prevention of HIV acquisition in southern African women: A randomised controlled trial. *Lancet*, 370(9583), pp.251-261.

38 Stein, Z., 1990. HIV Prevention: The need for methods women can use. *American Journal of Public Health*, 80, pp.460-462.

39 Karim, Q.A., Humphries, H. and Stein, Z., 2012. Empowering women in human immunodeficiency virus prevention. *Best Pract Res Clin Obstet Gynaecol*, 26, pp.487-493.

40 Padian, N. S., Mccoyb, S. I., Balkus, J. E. and Wasserheitd, J. N., 2010. Weighing the gold in the gold standard: Challenges in HIV prevention research. *AIDS*, 24, pp.621-635.

41 Van Damme, L., Corneli, A., Ahmed, K., Agot, K., Lombaard, J., Kapiga, S., Malahleha, M., Owino, F., Manongi, R., Onyango, J., Temu, L., Monedi, M. C., Mak'oketch, P., Makanda, M., Reblin, I., Makatu, S. E., Saylor, L., Kiernan, H., Kirkendale, S., Wong, C., Grant, R., Kashuba, A., Nanda, K., Mandala, J., Fransen, K., Deese, J., Crucitti, T., Mastro, T.D. and Taylor, D., 2012. Preexposure Prophylaxis for HIV Infection among African Women. *New England Journal of Medicine*, 367, pp.411-422.

42 Ramjee, G., Govinden, R., Morar, N.S. and Mbewu, A., 2007. South Africa's experience of the closure of the cellulose sulphate microbicide trial. *PLoS Med*, 4, e235.

43 Lederman, M.M., Offord, R.E. and Hartley, O., 2006. Microbicides and other topical strategies to prevent vaginal transmission of HIV. *Nature Reviews Immunology*, 6, pp.371-382.

44 Skoler-Karpoff, S., Ramjee, G., Ahmed, K., Altini, L., Plagianos, M. G., Friedland, B., Govender, S., De Kock, A., Cassim, N. and Palanee, T., 2008. Efficacy of Carraguard for prevention of HIV infection in women in South Africa: A randomised, double-blind, placebo-controlled trial. *The Lancet*, 372, pp.1977-1987.

45 Van Damme et al., 2012, pp.411-422.

46 Karim, S.S.A., Richardson, B.A., Ramjee, G., Hoffman, I.F., Chirenje, Z.M., Taha, T., Kapina, M., Maslankowski, L., Coletti, M.A. and Profy, A., 2011. Safety and effectiveness of BufferGel and 0.5% PRO2000 gel for the prevention of HIV infection in women. *AIDS* (London, England), 25, p.957.

47 McCormack, S., Ramjee, G., Kamali, A., Rees, H., Crook, A.M., Gafos, M., Jentsch, U., Pool, R., Chisembele, M. and Kapiga, S., 2010. PRO2000 vaginal gel for prevention of

HIV-1 infection (Microbicides Development Programme 301): A phase 3, randomised, double-blind, parallel-group trial. *The Lancet*, 376, pp.1329-1337.

48 Hoad, N., 2005. Thabo Mbeki's AIDS blues: The Intellectual, the Archive and the Pandemic. *Public Culture*, 17, pp.101-127.

49 Ramjee et al., 2007.

50 Cooper, S., Anafi, P., Sun, C., Naidoo, N., Reddy, P. and Buchanan, D., 2009. Content analysis of local newspaper coverage of the microbicide trials in South Africa. *International Quarterly of Community Health Education*, 29, pp.105-121.

51 Cited in Ramjee et al., 2007, p.1169.

52 Saethre, E. and Stadler, J., 2013. Malicious whites, greedy women, and virtuous volunteers: Negotiating social relations through clinical trial narratives in South Africa. *Medical Anthropology Quarterly*, 27, pp.103-120.

53 MacPhail, C., Delany-Moretlwe, S. and Mayaud, P., 2012. 'It's not about money, it's about my health': Determinants of participation and adherence among women in an HIV-HSV2 prevention trial in Johannesburg, South Africa. *Patient preference and adherence*, 6, p.579; Stadler, J.J., Delany, S. and Mntambo, M., 2008. Women's perceptions and experiences of HIV prevention trials in Soweto, South Africa. *Social Science & Medicine*, 66, pp.189-200.

54 Montgomery, C.M., Gafos, M., Lees, S., Morar, N.S., Mweemba, O., Ssali, A., Stadler, J., Pool, R. and Team, M.D.P., 2010. Re-framing microbicide acceptability: Findings from the MDP301 trial. *Cult Health Sex*, 12, pp.649-662; Stadler, J. and Saethre, E. 2012. Off label. *AIDS Review*, 2012, University of Pretoria, Centre for the Study of AIDS.

55 Lowy, I., 2000. Trustworthy knowledge and desperate patients: Clinical tests for new drugs from cancer to AIDS. In Lock, M., Young, A. and Cambrosio, A. (eds). Living and working with the new medical technologies: Intersections of inquiry. Cambridge: Cambridge University Press.

56 Delany-Moretlwe, S., Stadler, J., Mayaud, P. and Rees, H. 2011. Investing in the future: Lessons learnt from communicating the results of HSV/HIV intervention trials in South Africa. *Health Research Policy and Systems*, 9, S8.

57 Medeossi, B.J., Stadler, J. and Delany-Moretlwe, S. 2014. 'I heard about this study on the radio': Using community radio to strengthen Good Participatory Practice in HIV prevention trials. *BMC Public Health*, 14:876; DOI: 10.1186/1471-2458-14-876.

58 Williams, B.G., Lloyd-Smith, J.O., Gouws, E., Hankins, C., Getz, W.M., Hargrove, J., De Zoysa, I., Dye, C. and Auvert, B., 2006. The potential impact of male circumcision on HIV in Sub-Saharan Africa. *PLoS Med*, 3, e262.

59 Simelela, N., Venter, W. D., Pillay, Y. and Barron, P., 2015. A political and social history of HIV in South Africa. *Curr HIV/AIDS* Rep, 12, pp.256-61.

60 Shisana et al. 2014.

61 Ibid.

62 Ibid.

63 Pettifor, A.E., Van der Straten, A., Dunbar, M.S., Shiboski, S.C. and Padian, N.S. 2004b. Early age of first sex: A risk factor for HIV infection among women in Zimbabwe. *AIDS*, 18, pp.1435-1442.

64 Hallett, T.B., Gregson, S., Lewis, J.J., Lopman, B.A. and Garnett, G.P., 2007. Behaviour change in generalised HIV epidemics: Impact of reducing cross-generational sex

and delaying age at sexual debut. *Sex Transm Infect*, 83 Suppl 1, i50-54; Pettifor, A., O'brien, K., Macphail, C., Miller, W.C. and Rees, H., 2009. Early coital debut and associated HIV risk factors among young women and men in South Africa. *Int Perspect Sex Reprod Health*, 35, pp.82-90.

65 Halperin, D.T. and Epstein, H., 2004. Concurrent sexual partnerships help to explain Africa's high HIV prevalence: Implications for prevention. Lancet, 364, pp.4-6; Mah, T.L. and Halperin, D.T., 2010. Concurrent sexual partnerships and the HIV epidemics in Africa: Evidence to move forward. *AIDS Behav*, 14, pp.11-16; discussion pp.34-37.

66 Reddy, S., James, S., Sewpaul, R., Koopman, F., Funani, N., Sifunda, S., Josie, J., Masuka, P., Kambaran, N. and Omardien, R., 2010. *Umthente Uhlaba Usamila – The South African Youth Risk Behaviour Survey* 2008. Cape Town: South African Medical Research Council.

67 Jewkes, R., Dunkle, K., Nduna, M. and Shai, N., 2010. Intimate partner violence, relationship power inequity, and incidence of HIV infection in young women in South Africa: A cohort study. Lancet, 376, pp.41-48; Jewkes, R.K., Levin, J.B. and Penn-Kekana, L.A., 2003. Gender inequalities, intimate partner violence and HIV preventive practices: Findings of a South African cross-sectional study. *Soc Sci Med*, 56, pp.125-134.

68 Fisher, J.C., Bang, H. and Kapiga, S.H., 2007. The association between HIV infection and alcohol use: A systematic review and meta-analysis of African studies. *Sex Transm Dis*, 34, pp. 856-863.

69 Gupta, G.R., Parkhurst, J.O., Ogden, J.A., Aggleton, P. and Mahal, A., 2008. Structural approaches to HIV prevention. *Lancet*, 372, pp.764-775.

70 World Health Organisation, 2005. *WHO multi-country study on women's health and domestic violence against women: summary report of initial results on prevalence, health outcomes and women's responses*, Geneva, World Health Organization.

71 Devries, K.M., Mak, J.Y., Garcia-Moreno, C., Petzold, M., Child, J.C., Falder, G., Lim, S., Bacchus, L.J., Engell, R.E., Rosenfeld, L., Pallitto, C., Vos, T., Abrahams, N. and Watts, C.H., 2013. Global health. The global prevalence of intimate partner violence against women. *Science*, 340, pp.1527-1528;

72 Dunkle, K., Jewkes, R., Brown, H., Gray, G., Mcintryre, J. and Harlow, S., 2004. Gender-based violence, relationship power, and risk of HIV infection in women attending antenatal clinics in South Africa. *The Lancet*, 363, pp.1415-1421; Lary, H., Maman, S., Katebalila, M. and Mbwambo, J., 2004. Exploring the association between HIV and violence: Young people's experiences with infidelity, violence and forced sex in Dar es Salaam, Tanzania. *International Family Planning Perspectives*, pp.200-206; Maman, S., Mbwambo, J.K., Hogan, N.M., Kilonzo, G.P., Campbell, J.C., Weiss, E. and Sweat, M.D., 2002. HIV-positive women report more lifetime partner violence: Findings from a voluntary counseling and testing clinic in Dar es Salaam, Tanzania. *American Journal of Public Health*, 92, pp.1331-1337.

73 Friend, D. R. and Kiser, P. F., 2013. Assessment of topical microbicides to prevent HIV-1 transmission: concepts, testing, lessons learned. *Antiviral Res*, 99, pp.391-400; Obiero et al., 2012.

74 Obiero, J., Mwethera, P. G. & Wiysonge, C. S. 2012. Topical microbicides for prevention of sexually transmitted infections. *Cochrane Database Syst Rev*, 6, CD007961

75 Baeten, J.M., Donnell, D., Ndase, P., Mugo, N.R., Campbell, J.D., Wangisi, J., Tappero, J.W., Bukusi, E.A., Cohen, C.R., Katabira, E., Ronald, A., Tumwesigye, E., Were, E., Fife, K.H., Kiarie, J., Farquhar, C., John-Stewart, G., Kakia, A., Odoyo, J., Mucunguzi, A., Nakku-Joloba, E., Twesigye, R., Ngure, K., Apaka, C., Tamooh, H., Gabona, F., Mujugira, A., Panteleeff, D., Thomas, K.K., Kidoguchi, L., Krows, M., Revall, J., Morrison, S., Haugen, H., Emmanuel-Ogier, M., Ondrejcek, L., Coombs, R.W., Frenkel, L., Hendrix, C., Bumpus, N.N., Bangsberg, D., Haberer, J.E., Stevens, W.S., Lingappa, J.R. and Celum, C., 2012. Antiretroviral Prophylaxis for HIV Prevention in Heterosexual Men and Women. *New England Journal of Medicine*, 367, pp.399-410.

76 Abdool Karim, Q., Abdool Karim, S.S., Frohlich, J.A., Grobler, A.C., Baxter, C., Mansoor, L.E., Kharsany, A.B., Sibeko, S., Mlisana, K.P., Omar, Z., Gengiah, T.N., Maarschalk, S., Arulappan, N., Mlotshwa, M., Morris, L. and Taylor, D., 2010. Effectiveness and safety of tenofovir gel, an antiretroviral microbicide, for the prevention of HIV infection in women. *Science*, 329, pp.1168-1174.

77 Rees, H., Delaney-Moretlwe, S., Baron, D., Lombard, C., Gray, G., Myer, L., Panchia, R., Schwartz, J. and Doncel, G., 2015. *Facts 001 phase iii trial of pericoital tenofovir 1% gel for hiv prevention in women*. Conference on Retroviruses and Opportunistic Infections (CROI). Seattle, WA, USA. Abstract 26LB.

78 Marrazzo, J.M., Ramjee, G., Richardson, B.A., Gomez, K., Mgodi, N., Nair, G., Palanee, T., Nakabiito, C., Van der Straten, A., Noguchi, L., Hendrix, C.W., Dai, J.Y., Ganesh, S., Mkhize, B., Taljaard, M., Parikh, U.M., Piper, J., Mâsse, B., Grossman, C., Rooney, J., Schwartz, J.L., Watts, H., Marzinke, M.A., Hillier, S.L., Mcgowan, I.M. and Chirenje, Z.M., 2015. Tenofovir-Based Preexposure Prophylaxis for HIV Infection among African Women. *New England Journal of Medicine*, 372, pp.509-518.

79 Van Damme et al., 2012, pp. 411–422.

80 Marrazzo et al., 2015, pp.509-518; Van Damme et al., 2012, pp.411-422.

81 McNeill, 2009, pp.353-370; *New York Times*, 4 February, 2015.

82 Stadler, J., Scorgie, F., Van der Straten, A. and Saethre, E. In press. Adherence and the lie in a HIV Prevention Clinical Trial. *Medical Anthropology*.

83 Van der Straten, A., Stadler, J., Luecke, E., Laborde, N., Hartmann, M., Montgomery, E.T. and Team, V.-C.S., 2014a. Perspectives on use of oral and vaginal antiretrovirals for HIV prevention: The VOICE-C qualitative study in Johannesburg, South Africa. *Journal of the International AIDS Society*, p.17.

84 Ambia, J. and Agot, K., 2013. Barriers and facilitators of adherence in user-dependent HIV prevention trials, a systematic review. *International STD Research & Reviews*, 1, pp.12-29.

85 Tangmunkongvorakul, A., Chariyalertsak, S., Amico, K. R., Saokhieo, P., Wannalak, V., Sangangamsakun, T., Goicochea, P. and Grant, R., 2013. Facilitators and barriers to medication adherence in an HIV prevention study among men who have sex with men in the iPrEx study in Chiang Mai, Thailand. *AIDS Care*, 25, pp.961-7.

86 Van der Straten et al., 2014a, p.17.

87 Hartmann, M., Montgomery, E., Stadler, J., Laborde, N., Magazi, B., Mathebula, F. and Van der Straten, A., 2015. Negotiating the use of female-initiated HIV prevention methods in a context of gender-based violence: The narrative of rape. *Cult Health Sex*, pp.1-14.

88 Montgomery, C.M., Lees, S., Stadler, J., Morar, N.S., Ssali, A., Mwanza, B., Mntambo, M., Phillip, J., Watts, C. and Pool, R., 2008. The role of partnership dynamics in determining the acceptability of condoms and microbicides. *AIDS Care*, 20, pp.733-40.

89 Venables, E. and Stadler, J., 2012. 'The study has taught me to be supportive of her': Empowering women and involving men in microbicide research. *Culture, Health & Sexuality*, 14, pp.181-194.

90 Stadler, J., Delany-Moretlwe, S., Palanee, T. and Rees, H., 2014. Hidden harms: Women's narratives of intimate partner violence in a microbicide trial, South Africa. *Soc Sci Med*, 110, pp.49-55.

91 Lees, S,. 2014. Emergent HIV technology: Urban Tanzanian women's narratives of medical research, microbicides and sexuality. *Cult Health Sex*, pp.1-16.

92 Succop, S.M., Macqueen, K.M., Van Loggerenberg, F., Majola, N., Karim, Q.A. and Karim, S.S.A,. 2014. Trial participation disclosure and gel use behavior in the CAPRISA 004 tenofovir gel trial. *AIDS care*, 26, pp.1521-1525.

93 Mngadi, K.T., Maarschalk, S., Grobler, A.C., Mansoor, L.E., Frohlich, J.A., Madlala, B., Ngcobo, N., Karim, S.S.A. and Karim, Q.A., 2014. Disclosure of microbicide gel use to sexual partners: Influence on adherence in the Caprisa 004 trial. *AIDS and Behavio*r, 18, pp.849-854.

94 Montgomery, E., Van der Straten, A., Stadler, J., Hartmann, M., Magazi, B., Mathebula, F., Laborde, N. and Soto-Torres, L., 2014. Male partner influence on women's HIV prevention trial participation and use of pre-exposure prophylaxis: The importance of "Understanding". *AIDS and Behavio*r, pp.1-10.

95 MacPhail, C., Terris-Prestholt, F., Kumaranayake, L., Ngoako, P., Watts, C. and Rees, H., 2009. Managing men: Women's dilemmas about overt and covert use of barrier methods for HIV prevention. Culture, *Health & Sexuality*, 11, pp.485-497.

96 Magazi, B., Stadler, J., Delany-Moretlwe, S., Montgomery, E., Mathebula, F., Hartmann, M. and Van der Straten, A., 2014. Influences on visit retention in clinical trials: Insights from qualitative research during the VOICE trial in Johannesburg, South Africa. B*MC women's health*, 14, pp.1-8.

97 Lees, S., 2014. Emergent HIV technology: Urban Tanzanian women's narratives of medical research, microbicides and sexuality. *Cult Health Sex*, pp.1-16.

98 Barr, L., Andrasik, M.P., Rappoport, C.M., Jessica, Vogel, A.D., Rossi, L.A. and Alio, A., 2014. Gendered Violence, HIV Acquisition, and Clinical/Behavioral Researc. *Journal of Health Disparities Research and Practice*, 7, pp.77-89; Okal, J., Stadler, J., Ombidi, W., Jao, I., Luchters, S., Temmerman, M. and Chersich, M. F., 2008. Secrecy, disclosure and accidental discovery: Perspectives of diaphragm users in Mombasa, Kenya. *Culture, Health and Sexuality*, 10, pp. 13-26; Stadler et al., 2014, pp. 49-55; Tolley, E., Eng, E., Kohli, R., Bentley, M., Mehendale, S., Bunce, A. and Severy, L., 2006. Examining the context of microbicide acceptability among married women and men in India. *Culture, Health & Sexuality*, 8, pp.351-369.

99 Baeten et al., 2012, pp.399-410.

100 WHO, 2015.

101 Amico, K.R., Mansoor, L.E., Corneli, A., Torjesen, K. and Van der Straten, A., 2013. Adherence support approaches in biomedical HIV prevention trials: Experiences, insights and future directions from four multisite prevention trials. *AIDS Behav*, 17, pp.2143-2155; Van der Straten, A., Stadler, J., Montgomery, E., Hartmann, M.,

Magazi, B., Mathebula, F., Schwartz, K., Laborde, N. and Soto-Torres, L., 2014b. Women's experiences with oral and vaginal pre-exposure prophylaxis: The VOICE-C qualitative study in Johannesburg, South Africa. *PLoS One*, 9, e89118; Ware, N.C., Wyatt, M.A., Haberer, J.E., Baeten, J.M., Kintu, A., Psaros, C., Safren, S., Tumwesigye, E., Celum, C.L. and Bangsberg, D.R., 2012. What's love got to do with it? Explaining adherence to oral antiretroviral pre-exposure prophylaxis for HIV-serodiscordant couples. *J Acquir Immune Defic Syndr*, 59, pp.463-468.

102 Grant, R.M., Anderson, P.L., Mcmahan, V., Liu, A., Amico, K.R., Mehrotra, M., Hosek, S., Mosquera, C., Casapia, M., Montoya, O., Buchbinder, S., Veloso, V.G., Mayer, K., Chariyalertsak, S., Bekker, L.G., Kallas, E.G., Schechter, M., Guanira, J., Bushman, L., Burns, D.N., Rooney, J.F. and Glidden, D.V., 2014. Uptake of pre-exposure prophylaxis, sexual practices, and HIV incidence in men and transgender women who have sex with men: a cohort study. *Lancet Infect Dis*, 14, pp.820-829.

103 Jewkes, R. 2010. HIV/AIDS. Gender inequities must be addressed in HIV prevention. *Science*, 329, pp.145-147.

104 Jewkes et al., 2010, pp.41-48.

105 Jones, A., Cremin, I., Abdullah, F., Idoko, J., Cherutich, P., Kilonzo, N., Rees, H., Hallett, T., O'reilly, K., Koechlin, F., Schwartlander, B., De Zalduondo, B., Kim, S., Jay, J., Huh, J., Piot, P. and Dybul, M., 2014. Transformation of HIV from pandemic to low-endemic levels: a public health approach to combination prevention. *Lancet*, 384, 272-9.

106 Baeten et al., 2012, pp.399-410.

Chapter 5

HIV and AIDS Triumphs and Struggles

Developmental Gap for Biomedical Sciences and Healthcare Systems Innovation in South Africa

Palesa Sekhejane and Charlotte Pelletan

Introduction

The advent of human immunodeficiency virus (HIV) and acquired immune deficiency syndrome (AIDS) in Africa, and the period of its early discovery, reigned like the biblical chariots of fire on judgement day. HIV and AIDS were introduced in a fashion that emphatically suggested the punitive results of sexual immorality, creating mounting fear and tension. Despite the limping healthcare systems and infrastructure, there has been a general improvement in social attitudes and perceptions towards HIV and AIDS. Another dimension in HIV and AIDS is the existing gap for research and development (R&D) for innovative therapeutics, such as vaccine or sophisticated medicines.

> Spaces are segmented and still. Everyone sticks to one's place. And if one moves, one might lose its life, as a contagion or as a punishment (translated from French '*Espace découpé, immobile, figé. Chacun est arrimé à sa place. Et s'il bouge, il y va de sa vie, contagion ou punition*'.[1]

Since the nineteenth century, plagues, for instance tuberculosis, were combatted through a wide range of spatial segmentation, such as quarantines, urban planning and racial differentiation. The history of epidemics is, before all, a history of segregation. The narratives surrounding Africa as we have come to know them, are densely linked with the continent being burdened, dark and problematic to the rest of the world. The links to these troubled aspects extend widely, between the geography and disease, climate and moral economy, and many others. In South Africa the interlinked dimensions of unemployment and inequality, reduced marital rates and sequential progression to one person-headed households, and the rising migration between rural areas and urban areas, greatly exacerbated the transmission of the HIV.[2] A study conducted by Schatz et al.[3] is one of the works that capture the realities of women who live in the rural areas of

South Africa, showing how the burden of illness presents heterogonous barriers to manage a household, leaving them helpless and vulnerable.

That said, the pandemic affected levels of economic prosperity for Sub-Saharan Africa (SSA) countries as it led to the gradual erosion of economic activities. The burden of HIV infections and AIDS-related deaths placed insurmountable pressure on a number of institutions, particularly those in the already frail healthcare systems. Economic prosperity also dwindled due to a plethora of factors, such as volatile governance, illiteracy, loss of human life through HIV and AIDS-related illnesses, unavailability and inaccessibility of medicines, and inequalities. In the study conducted by Museru, Toerien, Gossel, et al.,[4] the evidence suggested that economic aid has contributed to the growth of SSA countries between 1992 and 2011, especially before the economic meltdown crisis (1992-2007). Nevertheless, they show that although foreign aid has had a positive impact on growth once potential endogeneity has been accounted for, aid effectiveness may have been neutralised by volatility in public investment. All in all, HIV and AIDS mismanagement has been symptomatic of a history of inequalities and of the perpetuation of unsound governance: 'a sorry tale of missed opportunities, inadequate analysis, bureaucratic failure and political mismanagement'.[5]

In South Africa, the HIV and AIDS epidemic has 'embodied the past',[6] in that it highlighted the persistence of racism, inequalities and prejudices in the post-apartheid era. The AIDS epidemic in South Africa has been represented as a punishment for sexual immorality,[7] while the role of socio-economic factors, such as poverty and the failure of healthcare systems in the spread of the epidemic, has been denied for a long time. In the words of Michel Sidibé:

> Thirty years into the HIV epidemic we still have major discrimination and stigma related to HIV, as well as laws and law enforcement that drive people away from HIV services (...). This will only change if we make major investments in programmes to reduce such stigma and increase access to justice for those affected by HIV.[8]

Based on the rich historical experiences widely recorded by scientists from various backgrounds, such as anthropologists, economists and social scientists, the HIV and AIDS pandemic, in a similar way to Ebola, can be seen as a double-edged sword. Nations most affected by the pandemic were presented with an epoch during which they could have taken the bulls by the horns, as it were, to become invested in the development of innovative solutions towards curbing the pandemic. One of the opportunities that should have been taken advantage of, was the study of biomedical sciences and technologies, specifically the development of instrumentation. Unfortunately, even at the conceptual level, understanding of the role of biomedical sciences and technologies in society remains an issue that needs to be grappled with in order to derive inclusive AIDS policies. The amount that South Africa invests in R&D is below one per cent of the gross domestic product (GDP). This figure suggests that more needs to be done in order to invigorate R&D and increase expenditure to a tangible investment amount.

The aim of this chapter is to acknowledge that while there are success stories about saving lives and innovating healthcare systems, there are also great opportunities for the development of home-grown biomedical technologies to boost troubled healthcare systems. The struggle against HIV and AIDS has partly been shaped by the quest for sophisticated and adapted treatments in a context where several aspects of HIV treatment remain largely dependent on the intervention and innovation agenda of the west for funding, licensing of patented components, and standards that are mostly set according to the guidelines of western countries. These aspects are likely to undermine the flexibility of local scientists.

The focus on biomedical technology and innovation in South Africa casts a new light on the history of HIV and AIDS by highlighting a 'behind the scenes' struggle to formulate local treatments and break the dependence on a maladapted therapeutic portfolio. The possibilities of developing biomedical research in South Africa are at the core of this article as we assume it is the next step towards sanitary, economic and social independence of the continent.

HIV and AIDS as an 'Economic Disaster'

Pollock[9] asks, 'Why do we assume that knowledge has to flow just one way – that the only place knowledge can be made is in the global north? Is it possible to imagine a world in which knowledge-making is more democratically and equitably distributed?' Nevertheless, all the initiatives led by the government and small and medium companies in efforts to trigger local biomedical research – that were flourishing in 2008 – have already failed.[10]

The failure of the national biopharmaceutical sector led to a new period of suspicion about multinational originator companies who determine the global research agenda by promoting expensive patented products, and in the process neglect entire therapeutic areas (for example, paediatric HIV formulas). This creates what amounts to an economic disaster as the South African state becomes dependent on the available HIV-related treatments, without local alternatives and innovation and serves the interests of importers.

As a consequence, AIDS economists underline the epidemic's impact on the South African economy through sectoral analyses.[11] These discussions lead to criticism of a hidden sovereignty at two levels. On the one hand, in order to keep its internal sovereignty, the State must ensure that the socio-economic rights of individuals are met. This, according to various authors, means ensuring not only access to basic social services and dignity, but also to value-added employment by relocating knowledge making within the territory.[12]

On the other hand, the failure of the biopharmaceutical industry in South Africa relates to the issue of dependence, and puts into question the state's external sovereignty, that is to say its ability to be considered a critical player in the global economy. South Africa imports 95 per cent of active pharmaceutical ingredients (APIs) and 65 per cent of its demand for pharmaceuticals.[13] South Africa's dependence on the importers of API stems from three main issues.[14] First, the social and environmental costs of pharmaceutical infrastructure could be high, as the high levels of pollution due to APIs in India and China show. Secondly, there is no manufacturing capacity in South Africa due to disinvestment. Eventually, this disinvestment leads to the undesirable consequence of the national manufacturers being crowded out by national tenders that prioritise increasing supplies of foreign, low-cost, antiretroviral generic drugs. Unfortunately this situation results in a massive technology gap due to the acceleration of pharmaceutical innovation which the south does not seem able to absorb.[15] Finally, the inability to adopt these new technologies or advances is not disconnected from public health, but, on the contrary, has a significant impact on it, as the study by Kudlinski et al concludes: 'While millions of AIDS sufferers in developing countries have benefitted from low-cost generic medicines, so far the dissemination of modern pharmaceutical technologies has benefitted just a few countries, first and foremost India and China and to a much lesser extent Brazil and South Africa', all BRICS (Brazil, Russia, India, China and South Africa) countries except for Russia.[16]

The situation of economic destruction as characterised by the complete dependence on imports of the HIV-related innovation market, presents a striking paradox since antiretroviral medicines are the only segment of the pharmaceutical market in South Africa that appears to be the best, and which attracts national and foreign, public and private investment. Given that there have, since the early 2000s, been many political initiatives in favour of pharmaceutical innovation (National Biotechnology Strategy, 2001; National Research and Development Strategy, 2002; National Research Foundation (NRF); the South African HIV and AIDS Research Platform; Industrial Policy Action Plan), the current situation is surprisingly unfavourable as the aforementioned strategies demonstrate the gap due to a disconnection between strategies and industrial revolution to support these initiatives.

Various policies counter the government's will to effectively manage biopharmaceutical innovation in South Africa (for example, the Publicly Financed Research Act of 2008). In these various policies and initiatives, a broader perspective of innovation is considered than the one described in the Intellectual Property Act 1978, article 25.1: 'any new invention which involves an inventive step and which is capable of being used or applied in trade or industry or agriculture'. The Department of Science and Technology (DST) underlines the social value of innovation through the notion of inclusive innovation.[17]

All of these policies and plans are presented as tools to achieve a National System of Innovation (NSI)[18] which consists of 'a solid foundation for organising the country's collective efforts in science and technology in a much more integrated and holistic fashion'.[19] Essentially, the NSI approach serves to understand how technological innovation operates, that is, as the result of several interactions and knowledge flows between the stakeholders involved in public health. As Callon[20] explains, owing to the notion of technical-economic networks, these flows are articulated around three main poles: scientific, technical and market. All in all, in a budget-constrained environment, the South African policy aims to reconnect the stakeholders in order to enhance existing research activities by favouring synergies and circulation of innovation flows from the experts to the patients. That way, innovation is not conceived as an 'individual adventure but as a collective work which amounts to networking activities'.[21]

If policies increasingly emphasise the government's role in pharmaceutical innovation, what then explains the continuous failure of the biomedical technology sector in South Africa? Before our demonstration of an explanation, it is important to understand the persistent gaps between stakeholders that make the implementation of a NSI difficult. Our analysis points out three types of disconnections:

- The government itself has no clear transectoral strategy to enhance indigenous innovation. What we conclude from our qualitative data is that policies are not produced in synergy between state departments, and are sometimes even contradictory. For example, tender designations by the Department of Trade and Industry (DTI) are meant to encourage procurement from local manufacturers instead of privileging low cost imports, but the Department of Health (DoH), which manages the tenders, informally refuses to comply with this policy. HIV and AIDS is presented as a mere health problem and so is managed almost exclusively by the DoH (from the development of the Essential Drug List to controlling tenders), which administers rationale-based procurement rather than developing long-term investment strategies on biotechnological research.

- The HIV-related innovation market constantly mutates, resulting in a gradual mismatch between supply and demand. R&D expenditure on tuberculosis, HIV and AIDS and malaria decreased from R2 053 billion in 2010 and 2011 to R2 007 billion in 2011 and 2012,[22] that is to say a one per cent drop in gross domestic expenditures on R&D GERD growth in two years. Arguments from the private sector underscore the gradual disinvestment of multinational companies from HIV and AIDS research as a result of the supply of the bulk of the treatments at a very low price by the public sector. The overall (even if slight) decrease of the business expenditure ratio in R&D for HIV and AIDS, calls for the increase of public investment, as the HSRC reports: 'Government expenditure on R&D (GOVERD) in current Rand value was R1.011 billion in 2010/11 and R1.236 billion in 2011/12, an increase of R225 million'.[23]
- State-business relations reveal that there is no organisational division of work between universities, companies and public research agencies. The story of the Ketlaphela project (which emanates from the DTI) shows how complicated it is to create public-private partnerships and to find common interests. This situation puts a question mark on the whole South African healthcare system and calls for a reform of innovation financing, procurement dynamics, private and public sectors relations.

Demonstration

Methodology

Our analysis is based on statistical and qualitative data (semi-directive interviews). We resort to three main storylines: the Ketlaphela project, Strategic Health Innovation Partnerships and the Centre for the Aids Programme of Research in South Africa (CAPRISA). These biomedical research projects are publicly-led programmes that involve heterogeneous stakeholders, and they epitomise the complex processes of innovation-making that continuously links different stakeholders and diverging interests. The aim of the chapter is not to describe and exhaustively list the failures of the local biotechnological sector,[24] but to highlight the paradoxes between South Africa's first-world innovation capacities and the difficulty of disseminating them in society so that people have access to them and can benefit from this.

Theoretical framework and public policy discourse

South African state departments resort to the NSI to promote their policy objectives for economic development in the country. The 1996 White Paper on Science and Technology introduced the notion of a 'national system of innovation' into

South Africa's policy objectives. This document, acknowledged as the basis of government policy for science and technology, defines the NSI as 'a means by which a country seeks to create, acquire, diffuse and put into practice new knowledge that will help that country and its people achieve their individual and collective goals'.[25] Ever since, the DTI together with the DST, claim that the country would enter a '*knowledge based economy*, with *internationally competitive* South African industries'.[26]

In order to shift from a public discourse to an analytical perspective, this official definition has to be linked to more accurate descriptions of NSI. Basically, Lundvall forged the concept of NSI in order to link technical and institutional change. As a result, the NSI has been described as the 'elements and relationships which interact in the production, diffusion and use of new, and economically useful knowledge [sic]...'[27] Niosi suggests a more concrete definition of NSI: a 'system of interacting private and public firms (either large or small), universities, and government agencies aiming at the production of science and technology within national borders'.[28]

Nevertheless, the empirical use of the NSI has proved that the concept is too complex to implement. We take a closer look at two critical aspects that the NSI theory originally promoted.[29] The application of the NSI as a policy tool may have distorted the original scope of the theory. By pinpointing this fact, we would like to remind the reader of two significant elements that could shed light on the ambiguities of the South African NSI model.

- First, the NSI was not meant to align developing countries to a western economic development style through a high added-value economy. On the contrary, 'the concept was intended to help develop an alternative analytical framework to standard economics and to criticise its neglect of dynamic processes related to innovation and learning when analysing economic growth and economic development'.[30] All in all, the idea was to confront national economic policy strategies and standard economics. The theory can be regarded as a reaction to simplistic ideas of competition which dismiss non-price competitiveness in favour of national nominal wage reductions or devaluations of the national currency.
- Secondly, in order to more deeply explore this idea of alternative models, the concept of NSI was used to emphasise the key role of the state in the technological infrastructure of countries.[31] This idea had already been evoked a century before by List in *Das Nationale System der Politischen Ökonomie*. The author 'puts emphasis on industrial development through technological innovation, as a means to accomplish enduring economic well-being'.[32] The NSI ought not to be a standardisation of national trajectories, but rather an

original way of dealing with nationally specific factors that include the epidemiological profiles, and the sociological profiles together with industrial and academic capacities of the country.

As a result, the NSI is not a tool to force and artificially create interactions. It is neither a mere alignment to dominant economic ideology, nor a way of reificating innovation – which has to be understood as a process and not only a patent.

Our use of the NSI will be limited. We will merely use it as an operational tool to grasp the dynamics between main groups of stakeholders gathered into pools:[33] the scientific pool, which includes the academics, the public or private research agencies and the internal laboratories of companies; the technical pool, which gathers engineers and biomedical researchers; and the market pool, which eventually designates the world of patients, doctors, and so forth.

This way, we will follow the DTI's focus on networks and interactions. The DTI report, *Technology Trends: A review of technologies and policies*, states that 'a possible mechanism for the development of sector based support can be the creation of THRIP (Technology and Human Resources for Industry Programme) type programmes'.[34] Nevertheless, we will use a more flexible vision of the sector thanks to the pools that do not limit the theory to the study of formal institutions. In order to assess the NSI in South Africa, we will use two simple variables:

- On the one hand, we will focus on the networks' alignment.[35] It designates the extent to which the stakeholders have to resort to intermediaries within the network to implement the activities. The alignment is not necessarily weak because the stakeholders can be substituted and contacted independently. On the contrary, as stakeholders in the network, the more people collaborate and the more they need each other, the more aligned the network becomes.
- On the other hand, the notion of coordination will help us understand the depth and the intensity of interactions.

PARADOX 1: South Africa is at the core of HIV and AIDS-related international research, but leads neither the global nor the local agenda.

South Africa has an ambiguous role in the global value chain. An examination of the networks in the biopharmaceutical sector in South Africa reveals that the international activities in South Africa involve only one segment of the R&D process, and do not resort to local knowledge and expertise (weak alignment). As a result, the international activities are poorly connected to local activities, and do not assist implementation of real innovation networks as they are supposed to do.

We would like to broach two striking illustrations of the phenomenon. On the one hand, South Africa presents a conducive environment for R&D due to its financial resources and public incentives, and its epidemiological profile together with infrastructural capacity. This means that the country is ideal for international clinical trials, but local industry and health are not enhanced by these activities.

On the other hand, the country is at the centre of the so-called technology transfer of international learning processes, but it turns out that these trendy initiatives perpetuate the gap between international and local elites.

A. Fragmented innovation networks and research extroversion

> The bottom line as I see it is that all of the pharmaceutical companies are mostly interested in manufacturing, have their license from elsewhere and selling them. (A researcher previously involved in CAPRISA.)

South Africa has been acknowledged as a clinical-trials paradise by many multinational investors in the world. There are currently 1 848 trials registered in South Africa,[36] an increase from 1 305 in 2012. Historically, there have been numerous clinical trials in South Africa which account for three per cent of the global market. The continuous increase of clinical trials in South Africa has become a profitable market for the pharmaceutical companies as well as for the contract research organisations. Most of the applied research conducted in South Africa does not derive from local basic research, but from foreign research.

Local biotechnological companies benefit from low venture capital, a shortage of high-skilled scientists, a tax burden and so forth.[37] They build 'hybrid business models'[38] based on the provision of a service or a product element to generate revenue and help fund innovative activities. In other words they sell contract services to – most of the time – multinational companies.

The services provided consist of clinical trials that are completely isolated from the local research and development activities from two points of view. The first of these is that most of the clinical trials undertaken in South Africa in 2015 tackled diseases that did not fit health priorities in South Africa. As a matter of fact, 72 clinical trials were dedicated to HIV and AIDS or AIDS-related diseases out of 1 848 trials. The second is that these trials do not fulfil the requirements of local innovation-led industry, since the trials are the only segment of the innovation process that takes place in South Africa. The basic research is often conducted in western countries, and most of the manufacturing activities in less regulated environments, such as India. The uncertainty of this situation is that these clinical trials do not lead to the injection of venture capital in the South African market.

In spite of big investments in clinical trials, private financing for biotechnology remains limited in South Africa. Lack of venture capital in South Africa stems from risk aversion, a lack of understanding of what biotechnological research in South Africa is, what it stands for and what the opportunities are. Early stage research remains weak and, as a consequence, the focus of pharmaceutical R&D in South Africa is in the area of clinical trials, and not discovery.[39]

The value of clinical trials for South African R&D dynamics is all the more questionable since the innovative value of these activities are not always proven. The regulations in terms of paragraph (e) of definition of 'research and development' in Section 11D (1) of the Income Tax Act, 1962, on criteria for clinical trials in respect of deduction for research and development, betrays a real concern:

> The following activities do not qualify as research and development in respect of clinical trials being carried on for the purposes of section 11D of the Act:
> (a) a phase IV clinical trial, as defined in Appendix F to the Guidelines other than a clinical trial conducted for the purpose of developing new indications, developing new methods of administration or developing new combinations of pharmaceutical products; (b) post-marketing research; (c) cost-effectiveness research; (d) an activity undertaken solely for the purpose of compliance with regulatory requirements; (e) a product familiarisation programme...

This paragraph shows how the South African clinical trial paradise might be a shelter for companies in search of tax deductions – the new regulations allow for clinical trials and multi-sourced pharmaceutical product development (generics) to qualify for a 150 per cent tax deduction– or easy compliance with high-level standards since South Africa is compliant with the International Conference on Harmonisation good clinical practice guidelines.

B. Technology transfer, technical assistance or gap skills perpetuation?

NSI theories pinpoint learning as a key process to enable innovation. The South African Medical Research Council (SAMRC) released the Socially Responsible Licensing (SRL) guidelines for technology transfer offices 'so as to ensure that licensing practices were meant to encourage dissemination of know-how'.[40] Thanks to three examples taken from heterogeneous situations, we will see that so-called technology transfer dynamics were not conducive to building capacity in South Africa.

Our first example tackles the intra-company transfer phenomenon. Occasionally multinational companies can transfer an employee in a key position to South Africa. In terms of the Skills Development Amendment Act 2008, Proclamation on transfer of skills development legislation, effective 1 November 2009, it is compulsory that this decision be part of a skills transfer plan that trains a South African citizen and enables him or her to assume the relevant job position as soon as possible. Our experience shows that – most of the time – these skills transfer initiatives merely amount to the transfer of high-skilled personnel from head offices abroad to subsidiary companies in South Africa. The Chief Executive Officer (CEO) of an Indian company explained that his firm was very involved in technology transfer. Given the high turnover of Indian national employees in the company, together with the significantly constrained number of fixed South African staff in the South African office (we identified three of them), and the division of work activities where almost all of the South African staff were involved in packaging activities, we could not agree that this foreign industry presence in South Africa really meant 'technology transfer', or even 'development of local industry'.

> 'It was obvious that there isn't a great deal of interest in investing in innovative research and in developing new drugs in South Africa. It's mostly buying into existing grounds and selling them'.[41]

Furthermore, it appears in the second example that the role South Africa plays in the global value chain may increasingly be undermined by the disintegration of the 'traditional' division of work for the South African drugs public procurement.

> 'No small product for Big Pharma'.[42]

The gradual withdrawal of large pharmaceutical companies from South Africa (37 plants closed down in South Africa over the past 17 years from date of writing)[43] and the local production of pharmaceuticals did not make a big impact on local innovation since clinical trials would certainly be maintained. Rather, it deprived state departments and foreign generic producers of useful middlemen for transactions between the state and industry. These interactions usually took place in the context of the introduction of innovative drugs to the public market at a low cost. An employee of a multinational corporation explained that in order to introduce their patented and unaffordable drug into the public sector, they resorted to a third party: a foreign generic manufacturer that produced a generic version of the product which would be sold to the public market. According to the interviewee, that kind of commercial agreement enabled generic manufacturers to benefit from companies' technical expertise. The gradual flight of pharmaceutical companies from the country together with the costs constraints leads to the weakening of that kind of technology transfer.

> Given the difficult economic climate, the capital flows in South Africa fluctuate significantly and are clearly dependent on foreign agendas. The CAPRISA's Tenofovir gel project is the third example. Here is the opinion of a role player regarding the perennity of international partnerships based on Technology Transfer.
>
> ... I see it ... [CAPRISA] as a partnership. And in fact when things were looking good, there was actually a meeting and then there was a press conference with the US ambassador and the South African Department of Science and Technology (DST). We were talking about the partnership and for clinical research certainly South Africans were in charge so to speak. But as I say for the part of development there's not a lot of interest. I will say this: when things were looking good for the Tenofovir gel there was a fair amount of money invested in planning to build a plant and other aspects of getting it to market.[44]

PARADOX 2: Local basic research is competitive and significant but opportunities to develop are scarce.

Now it is important to shift to another aspect of innovation making in South Africa: the development of local innovation. The South African biopharmaceutical environment's golden age of 2008-2009 was characterised by the development of biomedical small and medium enterprises. Al Bader et al[45] presented the 2001 National Biotechnology Strategy as the key driver of the South African biomedical sector. The DST's key measure, the Regional Innovation Centers (they have been called BRICs) of 2002 had, however, already been replaced by the Technology Innovation Agency (TIA) in 2008. Its role was 'to support the development and commercialisation of competitive technology-based services and products'.[46]

The South Africa government, through involvement with innovation policies, agreed that an appropriate policy framework was at the core of scientific and technological development. The TIA's mission was '... to support and enable technology innovation... to achieve socio-economic benefits and enhance South

Africa's global competitiveness'.[47] This mission was not only a matter of institutional and financial assistance directly to stakeholders, but also to the rules that governed the interaction amongst the different stakeholders.[48] Ramazan Uctu and Hassan Essop[49] added an important remark: 'such hierarchies and programmes must consider stakeholder needs since any government intervention in the biotech industry is likely to fail if stakeholders are ignored'.

According to the 2008 National Biotechnology Audit,[50] there were 78 active biotechnology companies, of which 38 were core biotechnology companies (the other ones were services companies). Why, 15 years after the National Biotechnology Strategy, had there been no emergence of a biomedical sector? Why were promising research centres, such as iThemba, failing? The gaps that need to be tackled are those between local innovation capacities and their failure to develop commercially, and between biomedical research as a continuous participative process and as a product. This issue is illustrated by two public private partnerships: CAPRISA and Ketlaphela.

> There are lots of very good clinical investigators in South Africa ... and CAPRISA does a lot of work, really good clinical research but they just do not have the pharmaceutical development, they don't have the aspect of it and I don't see really strong one elsewhere. (A previous staff member of CAPRISA.)

Most of the stories on public partnership R&D projects show that the problems – and sometimes the failure of the project – are tightly linked to the reluctance of companies to manage the development and commercialisation of products. This reluctance stems from the fact that the public-private projects do not support highly profitable products, but focus mostly on essential medicines that will enter the public markets at low prices. The problem is how to bring basic research to the point of commercialisation of a concrete product when the partnerships, as well as the product development, are too difficult to be led by the public sector.

Initially, public-private partnerships were considered as the best 'win-win' solutions to the commercialisation gap. Two critical projects were launched in the period between 2005 and 2015, and the same story emerges: private partners withdraw from projects once they have been assessed by the companies' headquarters abroad.

CAPRISA conducted a clinical trial to prove whether the preventative use of a Tenofovir gel could give evidence of a lower transmission rate. Cipla South Africa was recruited as partner for eventual commercialisation by the TIA under a public-private partnership. Unfortunately, the drug did not prove to be efficient enough for commercialisation, but that is beside the point. A critical role-player in CAPRISA explained that 'even before the FACTS study didn't bear fruit, Cipla South Africa was taken over by Cipla India and Cipla India really did not show interest in investing in this project'.

The first aspect of the public-private partnership weakness obviously stemmed from the fact that multinational companies do not have an interest in risky investments on the local market. This idea is reinforced by the fact that those projects launched by the public sector do not always conform to market realities. The Ketlaphela project, 'the state company' targeting the national production of APIs, shows how reluctant companies are to become involved in projects of that nature. The story will be told according to the three different attempts to create partnerships with the private sector.

The Lonza story

The first attempt was a partnership with the company, Lonza. This collaboration was announced by the state at a press conference in Cape Town in 2013. Two weeks later, Lonza withdrew from the project.

The first reason why the company withdrew confirms our first point: multinational companies do not have interest in investing in local R&D. Lonza had invested in many projects like Ketlaphela, and was losing the confidence of its shareholders and traditional market in India.

The second reason was that the product was already not competitive. Ketlaphela was meant to produce Efavirenz and Emtricitabine and Zidovudine (EFV). The pre-feasibility tests showed that in 2010, EFV was worth US$1 000 per kg, but it dropped to around US$125 per kg, which meant that Lonza was no longer interested in working on the project.

The search for a replacement

The second attempt consisted of a tender to find a replacement partner. The DTI received responses from four companies (two national, two foreign). In spite of the very good bids, the price of APIs was then so low that the government would have had to guarantee the new partner a permanent subsidy.

Finding niche products, specialising South Africa

At this point, the project reached a turning point which has been the third attempt: since Ketlaphela was not able to compete with India anymore, the DTI chose to develop niche products. The new Ketlaphela project targeted lower quantities of a more innovative drug. The shift from tenofivir disoporoxil fumarate (TDF) to a 20 mg a day dosage of tenofivir alafenamide fumarate (TAF) corresponded with a strategy directly based on scientific evidence. The reduction of the antiretroviral (ARV) dosage meant that Ketlaphela not only moved in a new direction, but was also innovative. The new partners are not yet known.

The Ketlaphela project has been described by some people as a residual symbol of South Africa's fantasy about its domestic capacities. Others emphasise that it was a first step towards a knowledge-based economy. All in all, what we would like to underline is that, from a commercial point of view, the public sector does not always raise relevant projects. Multinational companies are not willing to invest in costly projects that could be nothing more than symbolic initiatives.

The Mismatch between the Public Incentives and the Economic Reality

The failure of the local biotechnology sector, primarily led by strong innovation policies, seems to be linked to the public sector's inability to understand the logic of the market. The lack of venture capital, long-term planning and of intellectual property (IP) incentives (the legislation is based on the US Bayh-Doyle Act, in which universities and research institutions are granted ownership of inventions developed with government funds, in an attempt to promote technology transfer), makes it imperative to find efficient synergy of interest between the stakeholders. The predominance of the public sector in biotechnology projects in South Africa is likely to be an issue if it does not include a real partnership with a shared interest.

In 2003, Biovac was a public-private partnership that was meant to produce quality vaccines in South Africa. A technology transfer agreement was concluded with two other national institutes, but the R30 million investment was not enough, according to a role-player we interviewed. Other technology transfers have been attempted with other vaccine suppliers, such as Sanofi Pasteur, Pfizer, Glaxo and MSD. Almost all of them gave up, saying that Biovac was not ready to absorb that kind of technology. Biovac's contract with government expires in 2016. Fortunately, a new public-private partnership with Pfizer has been concluded, saving Biovac from bankruptcy. Some pharmaceutical companies are heavily reliant on the state, as this staff member of a multinational company put it, 'We know that without the State's subsidies it will not survive'.

Investing in public-private partnerships to enable development, production and commercialisation of medicines seems less and less interesting for multinational companies. Our insights into Strategic Health Innovation Partnership

Projects dedicated to HIV show that not only are pluri-disciplinary interactions complex, but the selection of a private collaborator is also very difficult.

Most of the stakeholders are academics, but some private companies are selected and subcontracted for their specific competencies, such as expertise on antibodies. It creates a heterogeneous environment where different tasks, different ways of seeing co-exist and need to be coordinated constantly. You cannot force people to work together. For example, two genomics projects have been funded as one: it gave birth to so many conflicts that it failed.[51]

Contracts between Strategic Health Innovation Partnerships (SHIP) and private companies are compliant with the Intellectual Property Rights (IPR) from the Publicly Financed Research and Development Act, 2008. Patents can be shared or licensed for companies, and in that case the conditions to secure the contract include making the final product available and affordable to ensure access. Nevertheless, SAMRC is not in charge of commercialisation since it is too expensive, and no plan has been formulated concerning this. It is understood that the IPR Act also governs the conditions to license a product. It seems that some private entities are likely to be reluctant to work with the public sector under the terms prescribed by the Act.

The core issue lies in the academic culture clash with the private sector. 'As in many emerging countries, the interface between academia and private sectors in South Africa is often problematic and generates several barriers to entrepreneurial activity'.[52]

The relationship between universities and industry seems to be problematic since universities wish to retain their independence,[53] while some academics maintain that they are not immediate sources of innovation and do not contribute enough to a broader national development.[54] Difficult and protracted IP negotiations are also problematic, with one interviewee commenting, 'I would say that the South African IP policy of universities is more than 100 years old. It just does not favour entrepreneurship'.[55]

Finally, we noticed that the South African innovation strategy was mainly focused on the commercialisation of publicly generated innovation. It did not appear to be a relevant strategy in a resource-constrained context where the public sector requires private entities to develop the biomedical sector. A review of innovation in South Africa by the Organisation for Economic Cooperation and Development (OECD)[56] stated that 'a major gap in current innovation policy is the lack of comprehensive support to innovation in SMEs'.

Recommendations

Develop entrepreneurial universities

The core of this analysis is to emphasise the key-role of partnerships in innovation dynamics in South Africa. The situation characterised by significant gaps between key players calls for the renewal of partnerships through the implementation of strong technology hubs in South Africa. We have already mentioned that the DST launched a range of initiatives and, among them, some incubators – eGoli Bio (Johannesburg) and Acorn Technologies (Cape Town). The first one specialised in neutraceuticals, and the latter was recently amalgated into Cape Biotech. During the 2000s, emphasis has been strongly placed on the role of small and medium enterprises for R&D (see, for example, Lindile 2008[57]) through DST policies and multi-partnerships projects. For instance, the Silicon Cape Initiatives, a private sector community movement, has promoted start-up companies as a key pillar to 'attract and bring together local and foreign investors to foster the creation and growth of world-class global IP start-up companies in an environment that competes with other similar hubs around the world'.[58]

Nevertheless, no significant success has been reported from these SMEs-centered initiatives, due to a range of issues already pinpointed by this chapter. As a matter of fact, the actual configuration of innovation flows in South Africa leads to looking towards the universities as the real epicentre of local innovation. HIV-related research is increasingly led by 'public money' investments in international research projects, governmental initiatives, nongovernmental research or universities. Since these public initiatives try to expand their activities and are broadly supported by national and international donors and universities, they really are a compulsory interlocutor for any stakeholder.

That is why successful innovation hubs are more likely to involve universities to drive innovation agendas, according to an 'entrepreneurial university model' which consists of placing innovation and enterprise at the core of the organisation, through strong mechanisms of communication and learning processes between heterogeneous players and mindsets.

Reform the Intellectual Property mechanisms

As we tried to demonstrate in this chapter, innovation has to be understood from an interactionist point of view. Kline and Rosenberg[59] describe an innovation as a medley of multiple players, places and non-hierarchisation of the innovative activities. They explain that 'inventions, when taken upstream, are substantially rough and primitive, and their performance indicators have nothing to do with what they will be later'. They hint that the patent is only one small indicator of innovation and is not enough. According to Kline and Rosenberg's definition of innovation, the patent system seems inadequate to enhance local innovation, which is mostly incremental (improvement of pre-existing innovation rather than radical invention, or *ex nihilo* innovation), because it stands for a monopoly that prevents other scientists from accessing critical knowledge. Furthermore, patenting mechanisms do not take into account incremental innovation, and if they do so, it is called 'evergreening', which is when a patent is renewed for an insignificant financial investment in R&D. The prominent role of universities in AIDS-related research could be the key to an efficient national system of innovation which requires a new patenting model to enable public research organisations not only to drive the innovation agenda, but also to control the patent system which is said to block innovation flow. In effect, too broad a protection on basic inventions can discourage follow-on inventors as access to essential technology can be refused under patenting conditions. This concern is all the more pertinent for biotechnology[60] since genetic material or testing might be inaccessible due to patents. As a result, in respect of diffusion and competition issues, the patenting system also blocks the diffusion of information and threatens R&D activities more than it incentivises it in South Africa.

This issue has to be taken into account for itself since it pinpoints other concerns than 'evergreening' and access to medicines. In effect, intellectual property entails the containment of ideas for twenty years (and sometimes even more) that could be used for other radical inventions or cumulative ones. According to this point of view, a patent does not seem favourable to that kind of incremental innovation, which is elaborated through broad participative processes within the scientific community. We saw that the role of government in an increasingly 'public' research area (HIV and AIDS) is likely to be critical in the modelling of a new patent model. Governments should – and South Africa is beginning to do this – explore ways to encourage alternative means of disseminating knowledge in order to improve the diffusion of patented inventions that could be used, for example, in follow-on research.

The 2008 Act, even if it has represented a clear disincentive for SMEs,[61] can also be read as a first step towards the remote control of the innovation agenda. By patenting public research, government aims at expanding its control area in spite of that of the industry (most of the time, big pharmaceuticals buy intellectual property from start-up innovators). The patent system is likely to shift from an appropriation tool towards a pool where the roles of players are adjusted by the state through licenses. The case of the Tenofovir antiretroviral medicine, which has been transferred from companies to organisations to project groups (CAPRISA) to foundations (Desmond Tutu Foundation), shows the importance of spreading innovation. This trajectory has led to a gradual improvement of the HIV preventative gel through what we call 'follow-on innovation'.

Conclusion

We assert that scientific and technical creation cannot exist without several interactions between various stakeholders from the worlds of science, market and technique that bring a discovery to a social reality. If the South African biomedical sector continuously launches highly symbolical research initiatives, and has known biomedical success stories, the objective of this chapter was to highlight the mismatch between funding, innovation and technology development in South Africa for yielding responsive healthcare systems. Indeed, after two decades of civil society's efforts to make treatments a universal right against the industry's vision of a medicine as a product, it is more and more difficult to connect policies, stakeholders and research projects to build efficient research and development networks.

> More than the development of new products in firms, innovation is the creation of new arrangements among the institutional spheres that foster the conditions for innovation.[62]

Notes and References

1 Foucault, M., 1975. Surveiller et punir: Naissance de la prison Collection. Paris: Gallimard.

2 Hunter, M., 2007. The changing political economy of sex in South Africa: The significance of unemployment and inequalities to the scale of the AIDS pandemic. *Social Science & Medicine*, 64, pp.689-700.

3 Schatz, E. et al. 2011. Female-headed Households Contending with HIV/AIDS-related Hardship in Rural South Africa. Health & Place, 17(2).

4 Museru, M., Toerin, F. & Gossel, S. 2014. The Impact of Aid and Public Investmnet on EConomic Growth in Sub-Saharan Africa. *World Development.* 55, pp.138-147.

5 Nattrass, N., 2004. The Moral Economy of AIDS in South Africa. Cambridge: Cambridge University Press.

6 Fassin, D., 2006. Quand les corps se souviennent. Expériences et politiques du sida en Afrique du Sud Collection. Recherches Éditeur: La Découverte.

7 Campbell, J.C., 2005. Family care in HIV/AIDS: Exploring lived experience. *Journal of Marriage and Family*, 67(2), pp.530-531.

8 Michel Sidibe, UNAIDS Executive Director, August, 2011.

9 Pollock, A., 2015. Places of pharmaceutical knowledge-making: Global health, postcolonial science, and hope in South African drug discovery. *Social Studies of Science*, 44(6), pp.848-873.

10 Al Bader, S., Frew, S.E, Essajee, I., Liu, Y.L. et al., 2009. Small but tenacious: South Africa's health biotech sector, *Nature Biotechnology*, 27.

11 Channing, A. and Lewis, J.D., 2001. The HIV/AIDS pandemic in South Africa: Sectoral impacts and unemployment. *Journal of International Development*, 13(4), pp.27-49; Nattrass, N., 2003; Campbell, J.C.I., Baty, M.L., Ghandour, R.M., Stockman, J.K. et al., 2008. The intersection of intimate partner violence against women and HIV/AIDS: A review. *Int J Inj Contr Saf Promot.*, 15(4), pp.221-231. doi: 10.1080/17457300802423224.

12 Liebenberg, S., 2010. Socio-economic rights under a transformative Constitution. Cape Town: Juta.

13 DTI economic database. Available at http:// tradestats.thedti.gov.za/ [Accessed 4 August 2016].

14 Kudlinski A., 2013. Harmonizing national policies for healthcare, pharmaceutical industry and intellectual property: The South African experience. In Abbott, F., Correa, C. and Drahos, P. (eds.), Emerging markets and the world patent order: The forces of change. Cheltenham, UK ; Northampton, MA, USA: Edward Elgar

15 Kudlinski, 2013.

16 Ibid.

17 Utz, M.A. and Dahlman, C., 2007. Promoting inclusive innovation. In Dutz, M.A. (ed.), Unleashing India's innovation: Toward sustainable and inclusive growth. World Bank.

18 Lundvall, B.-Å., 1985. Product innovation and user–producer interaction. Aalborg: Aalborg University Press.

19 Manzini E., 2012. Social innovation and design. DESIS Network Department of Industrial Design, Arts, Communication and Fashion – Politecnico of Milano, Via Durando 38/a 20158, Milano; Callon, M., 1991. Techno-economic networks and irreversibility. In Law, J. (ed.) *A sociology of monsters: Essays on power, technology and domination*. London: Routledge.

20 Callon, 1991.

21 Callon, M., 1999. Actor-network theory – The market test. In Hassard, J. and Law, J. (eds.), Actor-network theory and after. Oxford: Blackwell Publishers.

22 DST research and development survey 2010-2011, issued on March 2015.

23 See National Survey of Research and Experimental Development: Main Analysis Report 2012/13. HSRC, Pretoria.

24 Muchie, M., 2003. Rethinking Africa's development through the National Innovation System. In: Muchie, M., Gammeltoft, P. and Lundvall, B.-A. (eds.), Putting Africa first: The making of an African innovation system. Aalborg: Aalborg University Press; Motari, M., Quach, U., Thorsteinsdóttir, H., Martin, D.K. et al., 2004. *Nat. Biotechnol.*, 22 (Suppl.) (2004), pp.37-41 (see NACI Report, 2007 on public incentives issues).

25 See The 1996 White Paper on Science and Technology by the Department of Arts, Culture, Science and Technology, Pretoria.

26 The Technology and Human Resources for Industry (THRIP) programme, partnership financed by the dti and managed by the National Research Foundation (NRF).

27 Lundvall, B.-Å., 1992. User-producer relationship, national systems of innovation and internationalization. In Lundvall, B-Å. (ed.). National systems of innovation. Towards a theory of innovation and interactive learning. London: Pinter, pp.45-67.

28 Niosi, J., Saviotti P., Bertrand B. and Crow M. 1993. National Systems of Innovation: In search of a workable concept. *Technology in Society*, 15(2), pp.207-227.

29 Lundvall, B.-Å., 2004. 'Introduction' to Freeman, C. Technological infrastructure and international competitiveness. *Industrial and Corporate Change*, 13(3), pp.531-539.

30 Lundvall, 2004.

31 Freeman, C., 1991. Networks of innovators: A synthesis of research issues. *Research Policy*, 20, pp.499-514.

32 Manzini, 2012.

33 Callon, 1999.

34 Etzkowitz, H. and Leydesdorff, L., 1995. The triple helix: University–Industry–Government relations: A laboratory for knowledge-based economic development. *EASST Review*, 14, pp.14-19.

35 Callon, 1999.

36 Clinical Trial Register Data.

37 Al Bader et al., 2009.

38 Ibid.

39 Kingdon, A.K., 2008. South African economic policy under democracy. Oxford: Oxford University Press.

40 SRL guide, SAMRC, Coordinators: Rabogajane Busang and Rosemary Wolson, 2013.

41 Role-player at CAPRISA project, interview conducted in 2015.

42 An employee of a multinational company, interview conducted in 2015.

43 Andre Kudlinski, Department of Trade and Industry (Feb 2013): The SA Pharmaceutical Sector: Presentation at the Chemical Industry Education and Training Authority (CHIETA) colloquium.

44 A CAPRISA role-player, interview conducted in 2015.

45 Al Bader, S., Frew, S.E, Essajee, I., Liu, Y.L. et al., 2009. Small but tenacious: South Africa's health biotech sector, *Nature Biotechnology*, 27.

46 TIA website, http://www.tia.org.za/ [Accessed 4 August 2016].

47 Technology Innovation Agency, 2012.

48 Hartwich, F., Alexaki, A. and Baptista, R., 2007. Innovation systems governance in Bolivia: Lessons for agricultural innovation policies. IFPRI Discussion Paper 00732, pp.1-80.

49 Uctu, R. and Essop, H., 2012. The role of the South African Government in developing the biotechnology industry – from Biotechnology Regional Innovation Centres to the Technology Innovation Agency. Working Papers 19/2012, Stellenbosch University, Department of Economics.

50 DST, 2008. Available at http://www.dst.gov.za/publications-policies/strategies-reports/strategies-reports [Accessed 4 August 2016].

51 A staff member of Strategic Health Innovation Partnerships, SAMRC.

52 Al Bader et al., 2009.

53 UNAIDS employee, interview conducted in 2015.

54 Muchie, 2003.

55 Al Bader et al., 2009.

56 OECD Reviews of Innovation Policy: South Africa, 2007, OECD, Paris.

57 Ndabeni, L.L., 2008. The contribution of business incubators and technology stations to small enterprise development in South Africa. *Development Southern Africa*, 25(3), pp.259-268.

58 Please see http://www.siliconcape.com/.

59 Kline, S. and Rosenber, G., 1986. An overview of innovation. In: Landau, R. and Rosenberg, N. (eds.). The positive sum strategy: Harnessing technology for economic growth. Washington, DC: National Academy Press, pp.275-305.

60 Bar-Shalom, A. and Cook-Deegan, R.M., 2002. Patents and innovation in cancer therapeutics: Lessons from CellPro. *The Milbank Quarterly*, 80, pp.637-676. London: Routledge.

61 Al Bader et al., 2009.

62 Etzkowitz, H. and Klofsten, M., 2005. The innovating region: Towards a theory of knowledge based regional development. *R&D Management*, 35, pp.243-255; Bar-Shalom and Cook-Deegan, 2002, pp.637-676.

Chapter 6

Lived Experiences from HIV and AIDS Research in the Eastern Cape

The Intersection of Culture and Gender

Ian Saunderson

Introduction

This chapter shares some of my work in the field of the human immunodeficiency virus (HIV) and acquired immune deficiency syndrome (AIDS) research at Walter Sisulu University (WSU), Eastern Cape, during the period 2002 to 2014. During this time I lectured at WSU for a period of 12 years, prior to my appointment at the University of Limpopo in 2015. The narrative includes a humble, lived-experience HIV and AIDS train-the-trainer workshop held in 2002, classroom experiences and subsequent reflexivity promoting healthy sexual behaviour, working on a PhD (2006–2013), and then a further study (2013–2014) which dealt with manifested beliefs on HIV and AIDS through language expression.

This chapter attempts to show how perceptions regarding HIV and AIDS have changed during this period, and indicates how positive conceptual shifts have occurred in the minds of students and staff regarding HIV and AIDS prevention. This discussion is thus a retrospective analysis and should be rèad in this context.

The research orientation is qualitative and reflective. First, the journey begins with early encounters and varies from constructions taken from field notes, workshops and experiences from the classroom. Secondly, interpretative understandings stemming from my PhD study follow, and I examine two key themes from the thesis, inclusive of culture and gender perceptions. The data which resulted in these themes was collected over a period of two years, with two cohorts, consisting of 20 one-hour interviews with key role players in HIV and AIDS at the WSU, as well as 20 one-hour interviews with students enrolled at a postgraduate centre of the Engineering Faculty at the Institute for Advanced Tooling (IAT).

The data is presented in a manner which discusses some of the comments made by research informants whilst summarising their overall opinions on issues. The last study is on language and nomenclature of HIV and AIDS. This study was conducted a few years later, and dealt with manifested beliefs on HIV and AIDS through language expression. In this study, 20 interviews were again conducted with key role players at WSU about HIV and AIDS, specifically aimed at interpreting the beliefs behind popular language phrases which were commonly used to describe HIV and AIDS at the institution.

The findings from all three studies are compared in the discussion and conclusion, which highlights how perceptions have changed over the years at WSU. The discussion will argue that conceptual changes are largely culturally driven, in a constantly contested way. They encompass all aspects of everyday life, manifesting through contextual factors, such as gender perceptions, cultural rites and the perceptions surrounding them, and the bio-medical and traditional beliefs dichotomy surrounding health and well-being.

The chapter first discusses key literature related to culture and gender, as well as the methodological orientation. This is followed by an examination of these themes through analysis of data within the timeframes discussed above (early years, the PhD and the nomenclature study). The last section, the discussion and conclusion, weaves all of the strands together into a tapestry which shows how perceptions of these themes have changed at the WSU during the period of 2002 to 2014.

Key Literature and Methodological Orientation

Culture and health

To discuss HIV and AIDS within a cultural context one may begin by interrogating the concept of culture. If we were to examine texts such as those by Kuper,[1] Robins[2] and Saugestad,[3] various definitions of culture emerge. Kuper[4] explains that terms such as culture are 'romanticised' in a South African setting. My experience of this occurred while interviewing research informants, who would often use the term 'in our culture' to explain their own beliefs, and were comfortable using this terminology. This is also reported in research conducted by Van der Vliet,[5] Tutani and Rankin,[6] and Chuene.[7] The use of the term 'culture' should also be viewed in the context of how the term 'health' is used.

The African Religion Health Assets Programme[8] maintains that in many cultures the understanding of the term 'health' encompasses far more than it does with the standard bio-medical view; i.e. that it involves 'a far richer description, one that encompasses the spiritual elements of health that the bio-medical model tends to ignore, and one that is linguistically embedded in a non-Cartesian unity of subject and object, of religion and health'. Evidence suggests that approximately 80 per cent of people in the Eastern Cape depend on traditional healers for guidance on health-related issues,[9] which indicates a far deeper understanding of health than the mere bio-medical.

Following an interpretative approach, Kahn and Kelly[10] state that 'being Xhosa means subscribing to a general culture of social practice, and a culture of health and healing'. Various authors[11] suggest that heterogeneity in terms of identity should be a concern when conducting research within isiXhosa-speaking research populations. In this way, Chuene[12] highlighted that there are great differences between elderly people and urbanised youth in relation to perceptions surrounding health and HIV and AIDS. For instance, Duku[13] stated: 'African identity is neither exclusively a matter of tradition and culture, nor exclusively a matter of modernity and citizenship', but as Mamdani's[14] approach (on the face of it) suggests, a 'melting pot of multiple identities'.[15] Faced with the concept of bio-medicine, Kahn and Kelly[16] further describe conceptualisations of health amongst the Xhosa as '... a pluralistic system and draw on both cultural worlds in an adjunctive way without a single core set of principles'.

Determination of cultural beliefs related to the causes of HIV and AIDS could help us understand existing belief systems that shape the basis of acceptance or non-acceptance of advocated preventative behaviour. HIV and AIDS prevention models of the past did not take into account 'African belief systems',[17] and consequently have not been successful.[18] Van Dyk[19] stated that 'people can experience the world in a unique and very specific way that is different from the way Westerners experience it'. She then continues:

> HIV and AIDS education and prevention programmes have mostly been based on Western principles, and no attempt has been made to understand and integrate the diverse cultural and belief systems of Africa into such programmes. Might this not be one of the reasons why HIV and AIDS education systems failed so dismally in Africa...?

It is one of the aims of this study to establish to what extent attention needs to be given to local perceptions of HIV and AIDS when considering social issues surrounding HIV. I acknowledge that it can be argued that recognising and working through local accounts is important when dealing with issues of the disease, and that terms such as 'cure' should be understood contextually. I also entirely agree with Wreford[20] that treating HIV and AIDS requires bio-medical intervention, and that the two systems, localised health care and bio-medical health care, can work together. In terms of witchcraft, an explanation of HIV provided by Ashforth[21] pertains to a practice called *idliso*, or poisoning: the belief that an evil source could poison a person upon whom they wish ill-health. The characteristics of such poisoning are allegedly similar to those of HIV, and include 'respiratory infections, the long absence of symptoms and inevitable death for infected people'.

These symptoms 'have led people to interpret HIV and AIDS as idliso, and therefore as witchcraft'.[22] What is thus required is the critical understanding of the role that cultural beliefs play in defining health and illness, and a critical engagement with these beliefs in terms of future prevention efforts.

Gender and sexual behaviour

Sexual behaviour is gendered, entailing 'socio-culturally constructed behaviours',[23] which manifest in all world-view interpretations of sexuality,[24] and are clearly not unique to isiXhosa-speaking research informants. These behaviours have a direct bearing on HIV-prevalence, since it is argued that a lack of agency causes women to be more susceptible to contracting HIV.[25] Some authors are of the opinion that the beliefs of isiXhosa-speaking males regarding gender roles are formed at circumcision schools,[26] and also that the role of circumcision schools has changed.[27]

Some authors describe it as a patriarchal society.[28] Others state that violence against women is prevalent,[29] and the study of gender in this context therefore specifically relates to sexual agency and the extent to which this may have a bearing in relation to HIV and AIDS.

Mis-conceptualisations surrounding Xhosa gender and the construction of HIV and AIDS have been discussed by authors such as Delius and Glaser.[30] In their work on polygamy, they make it clear that views held by many South African researchers on HIV and AIDS in respect of the interrelatedness between promiscuity and polygamy are 'simplistic'. They opposed two basic arguments: one, that historical polygamy creates an expectation of multiple sexual partnerships for men; and two, that historical polygamy therefore 'contained male sexual urges'.

The core claim behind Delius and Glaser's argument was that in the Xhosa context, marriage was not about sex, but entailed issues such as offspring, *lobola*[31] and the organisation of labour duties. Their paper further argues that 'a great deal of sex took place outside of marriage'.[32] Sex outside marriage and the way in which gender roles are viewed, inclusive of sexuality, is a determining factor of HIV and AIDS infection given the significance of infection rates in multiple sexual partnerships.

Methodology – 'Lived Experience'

This chapter uses an interpretative approach in all three sections of the analysis (early years, PhD and nomenclature study). Interpretative research aims to focus on 'lived experience' and is concerned with the viewpoint of research participants. Denzin[33] states that 'the focus of interpretative research is on those life experiences that radically alter and shape the meanings persons give to themselves and their experiences'. Denzin's approach, which he termed interpretative interactionism, rests on three core conceptions: interaction, problematic interaction and interpretative interactionism.[34]

What Denzin termed 'the problematic' – epiphanies in peoples personal lives at the moment when they made sense of intense personal problems – signifies for this study a problem arising from sexual relations and dealing with HIV and AIDS infection, which in turn relates to how power-relationships are perceived within a specific cultural setting. Denzin later states that interpretivism is ideal for investigation into 'personal troubles' and societal influences that may shape perceptions and understandings of such problems.[35] My concern is to understand how the 'problematic' of HIV and AIDS is perceived and how it is dealt with by those affected within a particular cultural context.

In this study I frequently employ the 'I', as with first person writing. Where necessary, third person writing is also employed. I felt it was important that I should not 'erase' myself from the study as I am aware of the influence that I am likely to have exerted on my research respondents.[36] This approach also allowed for insider-outsider views to be contextualised.[37]

The early years: 2002–2005

My first encounter with HIV and AIDS in the research environment was when the Vice Chancellor responded to the call to action made to WSU that we, as academics, include HIV and AIDS education within our curriculum, as it was identified nationally as an area of concern. In 2002 I was asked, on behalf of the department in which I lectured, to attend a workshop hosted by another South African university, partially funded by United States Global (USG) donors through PEPFAR (President's Emergency Plan for AIDS Relief). The focus was primarily on: the epidemiology of HIV and AIDS, perceived causes of HIV and AIDS and gender. It was clear that they wanted to address some of the beliefs surrounding the origin of HIV and AIDS.

Discussions on gender sparked an opportunity for open talk on issues of sexuality, a conversation which was deemed by some as 'against cultural principles'. At this stage, condom usage and abstinence were presented as the major methods of combatting the disease, but it had not yet evolved into what was later to become known as the ABC programme. The message to the lecturers was this: to start some discussion around the topic with students, to create general awareness and, from an institutional point of view, to create policies and best practises.

As a lecturer at the time, I could initiate some discussion in the classroom context. What I encountered was far more sophisticated than what was portrayed at the workshop: students had moved past simplistic beliefs, such as same-sex orientations being the cause of HIV and AIDS, and had already progressed to discussions surrounding behavioural aspects, such as the 'alcohol argument'. It was explained to me that alcohol usage lowers inhibitions, leading to situations where students do not make sensible decisions, such as avoiding unprotected sex. I found the students' ability to discuss traditional beliefs and agency particularly insightful, and I had no doubt that they understood many of the social issues of HIV and AIDS proliferation. What was always in question was whether they adhered to prescribed, or what they called 'cultural', beliefs.

These are only some of the ideas that shaped my thinking around HIV and AIDS issues at the time, and which eventually led to my PhD study. Whilst the PhD saw the emergence of many themes, only issues concerning perceived causes of HIV and AIDS are discussed here: the bio-medical, supernatural, stigma and agency, as well as gender, specifically gender roles and the circumcised male.

Doctoral Studies: 2006–2013

Cultural beliefs and HIV and AIDS: bio-medical, supernatural, stigma and agency

In this section I intend to explore some of the central understandings of my research informants regarding the causes of HIV and AIDS. The key finding from this section was that, albeit a highly debated area, research informants expressed contested views related to both traditional beliefs and bio-medicine, and talked about the need for sensitivity towards cultural beliefs. The common understanding was, however, that the underlying cause of AIDS was viral. As for 'physical health', when asking about HIV as a cause for ill-health, it was also described as 'viral' (38 and 40 responses). In general it was clear that both students and key role players accepted a bio-medical explanation of the disease.

Example 1 (IAT student)[38]

> When you say HIV and AIDS for me it is like a virus that is circulating in South Africa. I think it is more in the young people, but I won't say it is not in the adults, but I think it is the virus that is more in the young people. I think the young people get it by having unprotected sex, I think that is the virus that is being caused by that, or any other contact with blood with other people that has the virus.

From the interviews conducted, no impression was gained that a misconception existed about the causality of HIV as understood from a bio-medical perspective. In the example, the student respondent clearly spoke about unprotected sex causing the virus, which was a frequently occurring phrase in other interviews. One should, however, be careful of assuming that this interpretation cannot coexist with other understandings of health, as Wreford[39] highlights from the experience of a traditional healer who explained how traditional medicines strengthened immune systems 'against the virus'. The conclusion that can be drawn here is that the reference to 'viral transmission' does not allow for the conclusion that research informants did and do not also subscribe to traditional beliefs surrounding health, since the term 'virus' also found itself into traditional health discourse. Research informants also subscribed to the coexistence of traditional and bio-medical understandings. One of the research informants, a medically qualified health promoter, contrasted his position with that of traditional medicine.

Example 2 (Key role players)[40]

> I am a health promoter and at the same time I'm a health provider because we also prescribe medicines [medical] and we are educating students about health so it's health promotion. That's why I am saying they are both together, culturally even with HIV and AIDS also they say that they can cure it with traditional medicine. They give you something that promotes diarrhoea and vomiting...

In the same manner, whilst discussing the process of treating students that have been diagnosed as HIV positive, one of the key role players highlighted the question of when it would be relevant to introduce a HIV positive student to ARVs. Of importance here is the fact that the research informant presented it as a logical and foregone conclusion that a person would receive ARVs under certain conditions if under the care of WSU HIV and AIDS key role players. Generally students and key role players distanced themselves from suggestions that witchcraft was associated with HIV infection, but frequently research informants referred to it.

This is to say: they referred to it more in relation to the spiritual side, but always, notably, informants would preface such discussion with a phrase such as 'they say', so that in this, or a similar way, they (the informants) always distanced themselves from these beliefs.

Example 3 (IAT students)[41]

> Not actually the Sangomas, but the witchcraft they can do it. One of my other family members is a nurse in a hospital and she believes that they can actually put AIDS into you. She can describe it to you as saying the one you can get from sexual intercourse and the other you die immediately. She firmly believes that because the witchcraft is very strong especially with the Xhosas because they can take you away but leave the body that represents you.

The student in Example 3 was explaining beliefs held by one of her 'other family members', a nurse, who is reported to believe that witchcraft is seen to be a cause of HIV and AIDS. Whilst the majority of informants referred to belief regarding witchcraft, none of them gave the impression that they actually believed in this themselves. It was always an aunt, a brother or a sister who was said to hold such beliefs. It is always someone else who experienced it (cf. above: 'She firmly believes...').

Interestingly, Wreford[42] refers to a similar incident involving an HIV positive nurse. The nurse, from Cape Town, was said to have travelled to the Eastern Cape to consult with a traditional healthcare provider (THP) about her HIV positive diagnosis. Wreford questioned why a bio-medically trained person would resort to witchcraft, and in the process described experiences reported by both Stein[43] and Ashforth,[44] where research informants related witchcraft to stigma.

Added to the issues of stigma and agency described above, another question that emerged was why students would resort to references to witchcraft when discussing 'respect for the culture'. My understanding was that it would be 'disrespectful' not to refer to 'cultural' explanations of the disease as well, as is also seen in Wood's[45] description of the term 'respect' (*hlonipha*). It appears important for students to be respectful to the beliefs of 'others' (ancestors, the elderly, and the distinctly rural), and to refer to these beliefs in a respectful manner, to the extent that the uninformed might actually misconstrue their true core beliefs as being the same as those of the 'others'.

A nurse maintained that he did not believe that witchcraft could cause HIV and AIDS, although he continually had to make me aware of the fact that he had to respect the 'culture' when referring to it. The impression was gained that research informants rejected cultural explanations of the causes of HIV and AIDS, and that they opted for a biomedical explanation. It seemed acceptable to discuss views with an outsider in an interview setting where ideas suggesting witchcraft and HIV and AIDS were opposed.

Gender: The transition to masculinity

This study did not set out to explore rites of passage or initiation in themselves. During the course of interviews it became apparent, however, that the initiation process was important in terms of understandings of gender and sexual behaviour and was therefore of consequence for HIV and AIDS prevention.

Example 4 (Key role players)[46]

> ... the *amakanghata*, the people who are doing the classes, three weeks ... believe me a boy that goes into the initiation ceremony comes out a much more worse person than what they were, they are taught to be arrogant, they are taught to be disrespectful, taught to assert themselves as men, so it is all negative things that they are taught about how to treat women. I see it as a place where they could be told to use a condom and why...

A female lecturer and HIV and AIDS activist described the situation in Example 4. Her view was broadly supported by my respondents, and all research informants described men who had just completed circumcision school as behaving differently to those who had not. On examining the data from the cohort of IAT students, the general description of 'boys being more arrogant' emerged clearly from the responses (17 and 20), and *all* responses from this cohort confirmed the necessity for women to 'be submissive' in a male-dominated environment. In the examination of the data from the cohort, IAT students, the majority of research respondents showed an understanding that culture was not fixed (16 and 20), and typically provided responses such as the following.

Example 5 (IAT Students)[47]

> This thing starts as you get one guy trying it and his friend will try it and it then ends up being a cultural thing, like most of the Xhosa things that they are doing, like for example, having to control your wife. Another example of being cultural is that now they are using brandy and not *mkomboti* (beer) at their cultural ceremonies, but nowadays if you only have *mkomboti* at your ceremony the people won't come because you don't have brandy. This brandy thing is now like a cultural thing... though it is not.

In this example the research informant explains how various practises become 'cultural' once people begin to engage in particular behaviours. It is notable that the element of 'to control your wife', was seen as such an example by this research informant. In this way the research informant is informing us that particular gendered constructions are seen as 'part of the Xhosa culture, though it is not'. In the examination of the data from the key role players cohort, the majority of the research respondents showed an understanding that culture is socially constructed (17 and 20), and typically provided responses such as the one that follows.

Example 6 (Key role players)[18]

No, I think because you want to make them aware that some of these things that we are sticking to we are doing because we say it's our culture and it also encourages HIV and AIDS. Sexual violence as a form of respect is a practice really because most of the time it has nothing to do with the culture. It is something that is created by people.

The research informant revealingly notes: 'we say it's our culture and it also encourages HIV and AIDS'. Of importance, and far more evident in the second cohort, was the fact that research informants displayed a deeper understanding of the connection between cultural constructions of masculinity and its effects on the HIV and AIDS prevalence rate. Research informants reflected a wider pattern across both examined cohorts, questioning how far the term 'culture' could be used as justification for anything: the first, by insisting that cultures change over time; and the second by explicitly claiming that one cannot defend oppression by referring back to culture. This profound critical scepticism towards cultural practice, and the claims of tradition, brings us back to terms such as 'invented tradition', and the realisation of research informants that people, not 'culture', are responsible for changing behaviour.

During one of the interviews in the key role players cohort, an HIV and AIDS counsellor described what she termed 'isiqwati'. When this topic was brought up in subsequent interviews, research informants (16 and 18) recognised it in some form, but they mostly rejected the idea that woman should succumb to it based on a 'cultural' argument.

Example 7 (Key role players)[49]

> I don't know in isiXhosa it is called *isiqwati*... there is something that you must take out ... if you had a steady girlfriend before the ceremony you are not supposed to sleep with that girlfriend of yours... once you sleep with that one it means that definitely your relationship is going to break. So for your relationship to work you must sleep with someone else so that you can take out that isiqwati to that person... so you go to your real girlfriend... That I think can also exacerbate the spread of HIV.

This description refers to a belief that men who have just completed initiation must have sex with a woman. The woman must not be romantically involved with the man at the time (such as a girlfriend). Following this, the man must then return to his girlfriend, and the relationship will last as a result of the above act. All of the research informants were of the opinion that this act is expected to be 'flesh on flesh', but also stated that in some cases the nature of the sex did not matter. The reasoning behind this practice, they explained, was that 'a man carries evil following initiation, and the evil has to be 'dumped' (disposed of). The 'evil' is said to be 'bestowed upon' or transferred to the female in question.

As illustrated by Example 7, it can be seen that some of the research informants recognise the fact that the decision to engage in risky sexual behaviour should not be tied to local beliefs, and was understood to be 'a choice of your own'. Whilst most of the research informants from the IAT students cohort referred to 'sex after the initiation process' (15 and 20) in some form, students were more aware of the social impact it has upon women, and the likelihood that women would respond in a 'positive' manner. We should be reminded that this cohort consists only of young men of a certain age.

Example 8 (IAT students)[50]

> ... the young girls if you are coming from the initiation schools they think that you are just the guy so if they were to proposed to one of the girls to sleep with him she will say yes just because you are the man coming from the initiation school, knowing that he is doing this to cleanse himself...

Whilst it was found that these research informants related to the description, they often distanced themselves from this practice when they described it to me, often framing such beliefs using phrases like 'they believe that...' Bell[51] highlights how 'ritual and belief are intertwined and yet separable, since it is conceivable that one might accept beliefs but not rituals associated with them'.

The research informants were also quick to remind me that the practice was 'not cultural'. The distinction between what constitutes the 'ritual' would be the notion of the initiation ritual itself, whilst the notion of acceptance of manhood, and the required 'training', becomes what Bell refers to as 'logically prior ideas'. We must, however, recognise the fact that these respondents demonstrate that they don't simply think of ritual as 'thoughtless action'.[52]

In many ways the above statements summarise several issues discussed in this section surrounding initiation. While it is clear that these research respondents made the point that associated beliefs surrounding initiation are 'not cultural', they clearly did recognise that it was through initiation that a masculine identity emerges. This creates the impression that, given the background where females have been described as 'submissive', some males believe that having endured hardship in the bush during their initiation, they were entitled to become a decision maker, or a patriarch. This would include issues surrounding sexual decision making, which under certain circumstances could be conducive to the spread of HIV and AIDS.

The fact that the majority of the research informants always distanced themselves from whatever they were describing, thus creating an 'us' and 'them' dichotomy, could be partially attributed to flux and change in beliefs, the recognition that these beliefs are socially constructed, as well as social distancing and stigma that occurs as a result of HIV and AIDS. What emerged from the above section was the clear attempt to oppose claims that masculine domination can be justified on cultural grounds. The lesson for intervention would be that there is already a strong critical, reflexive consideration of 'culture' – at least amongst students – in this context.

Breaking barriers

The realisation of the need for strategies to overcome cultural beliefs that may foster the spread of HIV and AIDS, clearly emerged. Many local strategies were found during the course of this research, and some women expressed the need to be empowered.

Example 9 (Key role players)[53]

They need to be empowered. They need really to be motivated and stand up and say 'NO' and stick to their rights. Some of them really don't want to but a man is forceful a man traditionally has a right to say whatever...

It was clear that in some instances patriarchal masculine identities seemed to prevail. It was also established that these might have an effect on risk behaviour, but in some instances males realised the need for females to be more empowered against male behaviour. A strategy of 'men preaching to men' emerged, with its origins in the belief that women are subservient and therefore men would not listen to prevention strategies presented by them. There are some fundamental flaws in this argument, in that it presents a chauvinist approach to HIV and AIDS education: it suggests that only men can teach other men about gender discrimination and HIV and AIDS. Some of these programmes have, however, been rather successful, such as a strategy of involving men in HIV education in the East London Xhosa community, run by the Ikhwezi Wellness Centre in East London – who also ran the 'Other half Project: Involving men in HIV and AIDS programming'. According to the programme, 'the process seeks to empower women by involving men, which ultimately strives for males to become role models, not only in respecting the rights of females but also in carrying the burden of shared responsibility'.

Language and Nomenclature: 2013 – 2014

Language, how it is used as well as interpreted, is significant when dealing with HIV and AIDS. It is also interlinked with cultural beliefs and highlights how students reason through the choice of their words with regard to the spread of HIV and AIDS and preventative measures. The aim of this study was thus to examine popular language phrases and associated beliefs identified as barriers in the fight against HIV and AIDS by key role-players at WSU. It looked at the perceptions of these key role-players with regard to HIV and AIDS prevention. The emerged themes from the data discussed here relate to perceived causes of HIV and AIDS and gender.

The key finding of the study was that cultural beliefs, play a strong role in WSU students' perceptions surrounding HIV and AIDS. Students did not show opposition to cultural beliefs due to cultural constructions of respect, but they had highly individualised understandings of the disease which reflected mostly bio-medical beliefs and associated behaviour with regards to HIV and AIDS prevention. Their duality of belief structures sometimes caused internal conflict, which had an effect on their ability to use preventative measures successfully. The major themes related to gender-agency issues, perceptions surrounding nutrition and general well-being, as well as the insensitivity of the ABC approach to localised beliefs.

In relation to gender, the impression was created that circumcision was a rite of passage, although views regarding the associated rights related to sexual agency as a result of the circumcision were varied. Students described beliefs as 'they believe', thereby engaging in a form of social distancing, and furthermore, also engaged in what Hobsbawm and Ranger[54] referred to as 'invented tradition'. Invented tradition 'includes both traditions, actually invented, constructed and formally instituted and those emerging in a less easily traceable manner within a brief and dateable period – a matter of a few years perhaps – and establishing themselves with great rapidity'.

This was clear when students expressed rather heterogeneous beliefs related to condom use and gender, although they all stated that their beliefs were related to 'their culture', but that they believed that condoms could prevent contracting HIV, yet not everyone practised safe sex. Furthermore, notions of respect also had similarities with the text of Wood[55], whereby the necessity of not expressing sexual agency was included as a sign of respect.

The finding is indicative that uncertainty exists about what the true beliefs in relation to gender are, and that the beliefs expressed, or referred to in many cases, seem to be personally constructed rather than those of a particular collective. Such heterogeneous beliefs have implications for sexual agency and preventative efforts. A method advocating social debate, as opposed to a one-sided message, such as the ABC approach, would therefore be more appropriate. Social debate surrounding this element would have to be encouraged and, through the use of bio-medical practitioners and indigenous health practitioners, students would have to be encouraged to ensure that their general health is well looked after.

Overall, this study provided some evidence that the subscription to cultural beliefs is related to language expression concerning cultural constructions of the disease. The question of addressing the disease could be neither purely cultural nor bio-medical, since students' beliefs lie somewhere between adherence to bio-medical medicine and cultural constructions of the disease.

Discussion

Of importance here is the shift in the manner in which HIV and AIDS have been addressed culturally and socially. We can see that in the early years the focus of the approach was on behavioural change, with an emphasis on merely passing on information as opposed to truly understanding how people located HIV and AIDS socially and culturally. As was evident from the above, in the early years of these studies research informants had clearly moved beyond information-reception, while the government was still passing on information and dealing with how to position themselves within the cultural and social debate.

During the later years of this study we can see that not only behavioural issues, but issues of culture, human rights, gender empowerment, education, protest and mobilisation are on the national agenda, and that the focus has shifted from behavioural change to social change. There has been a clear realisation that merely passing on information is inadequate, and that the subsequent social and cultural issues underlying the proliferation of HIV and AIDS need to be addressed, not only by government, but by the recipients of government communication themselves.

Conclusion

In the early years, institutions were not adequately equipped to deal with this 'new disease'. The fact that academics, such as myself, were 'trained' to address simplistic misconceptions about the disease, while the students themselves were clearly far beyond this stage – and had already begun debating behavioural aspects amongst themselves – makes this evident. Although constantly contested, students had moved past beliefs that were not bio-medical, and for it to be addressed in the way we had been instructed, was clearly insufficient. The success story comes from the realisation by institutions, such as WSU, that the argument is largely a cultural one. It was recognised that it was necessary to move away from simplistic one-sided messages, such as the ABC approach and 'garlic and onion' constructions of a cure, as advocated by the former Minister of Health, Manto Tshabalala-Msimang. In 2004 she stated that 'it was her intention to wean our people from antiretrovirals and present a diet of lemon, garlic, onion and olive oil as an alternative means of treatment'.[56] The newly emerged approach is debate-driven, juxtaposing traditional and bio-medical ideas, ranging from peer-intervention programmes, men-teaching-men and curriculum innovation strategies.

Research into contextual factors allows for sensitivities around localised issues to be determined that might not have been visible following other conventional approaches. A concern to understand the 'cultural meanings that shape and construct sexual experience', and the examination of 'structural forces that impinge upon sexual life',[57] expose the social forces and social determinants of sexual agency, and place the researcher in the middle of social debates that have an important effect on how HIV and AIDS proliferates in society.

The emerging key to social change and addressing the pandemic of HIV and AIDS lies with social debate and consensus on what constitutes knowledge, beliefs and safe practices in an approach that is not prescriptive, but combines all the social forces impacting upon the proliferation of the disease. The approach encourages the public statement of views for the purposes of debate, which could result in a society advocating healthy sexuality. This can best be achieved through culturally sensitive, social prevention programmes that foster social debate in a peer approach, at all levels of society.

The shift is thus from being perceived as 'doing the right' thing to 'let's put together policies to deal with it' through active classroom engagement and agency, even while cultural beliefs always lurk in the background, with differing perceptions on all aspects about how it plays out on the ground – what people say 'culture' says, what pure culturists believe and how actual behaviour manifests. What you have is a cesspit of dangers, too many for any researcher or health promoter from any orientation to safely navigate – from promoting local knowledge to the necessity to address imagined cultural practices. It boils down to what people do to ensure that they do not contract the disease, and ultimately safety lies in personal strategies that can only be built through fostering local awareness and putting a condom in the hand of every person. Whether it is worn, is a determinant mix of risk taking and risk acceptance negotiation. There is no correct path or universal truth, rather a convergence of circumstances, which we as HIV and AIDS researchers and activists create.

Notes and References

1 Kuper, A., 2003. The return of the native. *Current Anthropology*, 44(3), p.390.

2 Robins, S., 2001. Whose culture, whose survival? In Barnard, E. and Kenrick, J. (eds.). Africa's Indigenous Peoples: 'First Peoples' or 'Marginalized Minorities'? University of Edinburgh: Centre for African Studies, p.239.

3 Saugestad, S., 2001. Contested Images: 'First Peoples' or 'Marginalised Minorities' in Africa? In Barnard, E. and Kenrick, J. (eds.). Africa's Indigenous Peoples: 'First Peoples' or 'Marginalized Minorities'? University of Edinburgh: Centre for African Studies, p.203.

4 Kuper, 2003, p.390.

5 Van der Vliet, V., 1991. Traditional husbands, modern wives? Constructing marriages in a South African township. In Spiegel, A. and McAllister, P.A. (eds.). Tradition and transition in Southern Africa: Festschrift for Phillip and Iona Mayer. Johannesburg: Witwatersrand University Press, p.236.

6 Tutani, L. and Rankin, J., 2000. 'Let's talk about sex baby' while condoms explode in our faces and social practises and beliefs are re-stored. Paper presented at 7th International Conference, SAAMFT, Cape Town, p.8.

7 Chuene, M.M., 2006. Belief systems of Xhosa-speaking people on HIV and AIDS. MA: Mini-dissertation, Department of Social Work, University of Johannesburg, p.130.

8 ARHAP (African Religion Health Assets Programme), 2006. ARHAP Literature Review: Working in a bounded field of unknowing. UCT and WITS ARHAP Resource Centre: Unpublished, p.15.

9 Mulaudzi, F.M., 2001. Synergy between indigenous knowledge systems, modern health care systems and scientific research – a vision for the 21st century. *Health* SA Gesondheid, 6(4), p.7.

10 Kahn, M.S. and Kelly, K.J., 2001. Cultural tensions in psychiatric nursing: Managing the interface between Western mental health care and Xhosa traditional healing in South Africa. *Transcultural Psychiatry,* 38(1), p.47.

11 Venter, D., 2004. What is Sociology that Religionists should be Mindful of it? In Chidester, D., Tayob, A. and Weisse, W. (eds.), Religion, politics, and identity in a changing South Africa. Munster: Verlag, p.202; Chuene, 2006; Duku, N.S., 2007. Outsider from within: Reflections of my fieldwork journey in a native and foreign Eastern Cape school governance context. *Education as Change*, 11(2), p.4.

12 Chuene, 2006, p.13.

13 Duku, 2007, p.4.

14 Mamdani, M., 1996. Citizen and subject. Princeton, NJ: Princeton University Press.

15 Nyamnjoh, F.B., 2002. Might and right: Chieftaincy and democracy in Cameroon and Botswana. Paper prepared for CODESRIA's 10th General Assembly on 'Africa in the New Millennium', Kampala, Uganda. Available at http: and and www.codesria.org and Archives and ga10 and Abstracts%20GA%2015 and colonialism_Nyamnj [Accessed 19 May 2003].

16 Kahn, M.S. and Kelly, K.J., 2001, p. 47.

17 Airhihenbuwa, C.O. and De Witt Webster, J., 2004. Culture and African contexts of HIV and AIDS prevention, care and support. *Journal of Social Aspects of HIV and AIDS Research Alliance*, 1(1), p.6.

18 Setswe, G., 2007. Abstinence and faithfulness programmes for prevention of HIV and AIDS among young people: What are the current debates? *SA Journal of Family Practise*, 49(8), p.5.

19 Van Dyk, A.C., 2008. (4th ed.). HIV and AIDS care and counselling: a multidisciplinary approach. Cape Town:Pearson, p.201.

20 Wreford, J., 2005. Missing each other: Problems and potential for collaborative efforts between biomedicine and traditional healers in South Africa in the time of AIDS. *Social Dynamics*, 31(2), p.55.

21 Ashforth, A., 2002. An epidemic of witchcraft? The implications of AIDS for the post-apartheid state. *African Studies*, 61(1), p.121.

22 Ibid.

23 Ragnarsson, A., Onya, H.E., Thorson, A., Ekström, A.M. and Aarø, L.E., 2008. Young males' gendered sexuality in the era of HIV and AIDS in Limpopo Province, South Africa. *Qualitative Health Research*, 18(6), p.740.

24 Pollis, C.A., 1985. Value judgements and world views in sexuality education. *Family Relations*, 34(2), p.286.

25 Ampofu, A.A., Beoku-Betts, J., Njambi, W.N. and Osirim, M., 2004. Women's and gender studies in English-speaking Sub-Saharan Africa: A review of research in the social sciences. *Gender and Society*, 18(6), p.692.

26 Stinson, K., 2008. Male circumcision in South Africa: How does it relate to public health? Available at http: and and www.africanvoices.co.za and culture [Accessed 4 September 2008], p.2.

27 Vincent, L., 2008. 'Boys will be boys: Traditional Xhosa male circumcision, HIV and sexual socialisation in contemporary South Africa. *Culture, Health and Sexuality*, 10(5), p.431.

28 Müller, J.C. and Pienaar, S., 2004. Stories about care: women in a historically disadvantaged community infected or affected by HIV and AIDS. *Theological Studies*, 60(3), p.1029; Motshekga, A. 2010. Florence Matomela Memorial Lecture. 'The importance of the 1956 Women's March' by Ms Angie Motshekga, Minister of Basic Education and President of the ANC Women's League, Walter Sisulu University, 8 August 2010.

29 Peltzer, K. and Pengpid, S. 2008. Sexual Abuse, violence and HIV risk among adolescents in South Africa. *Gender and Behaviour*, 6(1), p.1466.

30 Delius, P. and Glaser, C., 2004. The myths of polygamy: A history of extra-marital and multi-partnership sex in South Africa. *South African Historical Journal*, 50, p.84.

31 *lobola*: Bridewealth (similar to *dowry*, India). Reddi (2007, p.511) described it as 'a feature of African culture and usually consists of a large payment to the bride's family by the groom, traditionally, of cattle, but in modern times, of money or other items of value.' Mtuzi (1990, p.30) highlights, in a South African context, the term remains in the vernacular, due to the fact that there is no accurate translation.

32 Delius and Glaser, 2004, p.84.

33 Denzin, N.K., 2002. Interpretive interactionism, Applied Social Research methods series, 2 (16). Thousand Oaks: Sage:, p.ix.

34 Denzin, 2002, p.32.

35 Ibid., p.3.

36 cf. Clifford, J. and Marcus, G.E. (eds.), 2005. Writing culture: The poetics and politics of ethnography, 25th Anniversary Edition. California: University of California Press.

37 cf. Geertz, C., 1973. The interpretation of cultures: Selected essays. New York: Basic Books.

38 Student: IAT, Xhosa, 26, Male, interview by author, East London, College Street, 2007.

39 Wreford, 2005 , p.64.

40 HIV and AIDS co-ordinator: male nurse, Xhosa, 41, Male, interview by author, East London, Potsdam, 2006.

41 Student: 3rd year, ND, Mech Eng, Xhosa, 22, Male, interview by author, East London, Chiselhurst, 2007.

42 Wreford, 2005 , p.73.

43 Stein, J., 2003. HIV and AIDS Stigma: The latest dirty secret. CSSR Working Paper 46, CSSR, Cape Town: University of Cape Town.

44 Ashforth, 2002, pp.121-143.

45 Wood, L.A., 2009. What kind of respect is this? Shifting the mindset of teachers regarding cultural perspectives on HIV and AIDS. *Action Research*, 7(4), p.412.

46 IAT Employee: Xhosa, 24, Female, interviewed by author, East London, College Street, 2006.

47 Student: 3rd year, ND: Mech Eng, Xhosa, 23, Male, interviewed by author, East London, Chiselhurst, 2007.

48 Residence Officer: Xhosa, 48, Male, interviewed by author, East London, Potsdam, 2006.

49 HIV and AIDS co-ordinator: Xhosa, 44, Female, interviewed by author, East London, Potsdam, 2006.

50 Student: IAT, Xhosa, 26, Male, interviewed by author, East London, College Street, 2007.

51 Bell, C., 1992. Ritual theory, ritual practice. Oxford: Oxford University Press, p.18.

52 Ibid.

53 HIV and AIDS worker: Xhosa, 26, Female, interviewed by author, East London, College Street, 2006.

54 Hobsbawm, E. and Ranger, T., 1983. The invention of tradition. Cambridge: Cambridge University Press, p.1.

55 Wood, 2009, p.412.

56 Myburgh, A., 2005. Mbeki on AIDS. The Oxford Forum. [Online:]. Available at http: and and homepage.mac.com and zoe.flood and oforum and issue_01_2005 and of_01_2005_p2427.htm [Accessed 9 July 2009].

57 Parker, R. G., 2001. Sexuality, Culture, and Power in HIV and AIDS research. *Annual Review of Anthropology*, 30, p.173.

Chapter 7

Mainstreaming HIV and AIDS Response into the Public Service in South Africa

Sipho Senabe

Introduction

The developmental outcome of South Africa's Department of Public Service and Administration (DPSA) is that of delivering an efficient, effective and development oriented Public Service.[1] In the context of the human immunodeficiency virus (HIV) and acquired immune deficiency syndrome (AIDS) response, this means management of HIV and AIDS as a development challenge.[2] The Minister of Public Service and Administration determines norms and standards for HIV and AIDS, and tuberculosis (TB) management, in the Public Service as provided for by the Public Service Act, Public Service Regulations, and the HIV/AIDS and TB Management Policy for the Public Service.[3] There are other determinations, in the form of Employee Health and Wellness Policies,[4] which provide for HIV and AIDS management[5] related Health and Productivity Management;[6] Safety Health Environment Risk and Quality management;[7] and Wellness management.[8] These have additional provisions for the internal HIV and AIDS mainstreaming and specific integration with TB, occupational health and safety and wellness management programmes for the benefit of public servants as employees, and persons other than the employees, in the work environment. The external mainstreaming of HIV and AIDS for the benefit of the recipients of Public Services rendered by government departments is provided for by the HIV/ AIDS and TB Management Policy for the Public Service. The concept of mainstreaming is basically about management of HIV and AIDS as a development issue. The last two South African HIV and AIDS, and sexually transmitted infections [STI] National Strategic Plans (NSPs)[9, 10] incrementally pronounced themselves on HIV and AIDS mainstreaming; and the DPSA has been involved in advocacy, capacity development, policy development and implementation tools, including a monitoring and evaluation framework based on the Southern African Development Community's (SADC) indicators on HIV and AIDS mainstreaming into development. DPSA has also been the focal department on HIV and AIDS mainstreaming at the SADC HIV and AIDS focal point forum, at the African Union (AU) level reporting using the African Peer Review Mechanism (APRM), and at the United Nations

Development Programme (UNDP) level on development of continental guidelines and projects on HIV and AIDS mainstreaming.

Historical Context of Mainstreaming-Maseru Declaration

The DPSA is a Centre of Government Department (COG) that is responsible for the mainstreaming of HIV and AIDS into development efforts. The following is an historical policy account of how this matter was managed and continues to be implemented in South Africa. Most of the work began during the implementation of the HIV and AIDS NSP 2000–2006.

During this period, the political economy of the epidemic was that it was a generalised epidemic and it had reached a stage where people were dying of HIV and AIDS-related diseases, and there was concern about the possible impact of this on sectors of the economy that were labour-intensive, such as mining, agriculture, construction and manufacturing. There were also concerns on the possible impact on human resources for essential public services. With limited access to treatment, the focus was on creating awareness and promotion of the use of condoms and reduction of multiple concurrent partners.[11]

In 2003 the SADC member states signed the Maseru Declaration,[12] which is the regional economic development community's policy position on how to manage the HIV and AIDS epidemic and its possible impact on health and development. Equally important were the inadvertent ways in which development could contribute to the spread of the epidemic.

What was significant about the Maseru Declaration was that it contained affirmation by the SADC leaders of the proposition that the

> HIV and AIDS pandemic is reversing developmental gains made in the past decades and is posing the greatest threat to sustainable development of the region due to loss of the most productive individuals in all sectors of our economies, decline in scarce resources from production to care and support of the HIV and AIDS infected and affected persons, as well as mitigating the effects on various sectors, and resulting in an increase in the number of orphans and disruption of family structures.[13]

Furthermore, the SADC leaders and signatories of the Maseru Declaration recognised that the principal contributory factors to the spread of HIV and AIDS are extreme poverty, ignorance and negative attitudes and practices. It was also acknowledged that 'the general underdevelopment and unfavourable international economic environment, as reflected in the high indebtedness of some of the SADC Member States, limited access to international markets and declining official development assistance, further aggravate the pandemic'[14]

The Maseru Declaration, among others, provided for a mainstreamed response to HIV and AIDS. SADC adopted the same definition of HIV and AIDS Mainstreaming to be used by all 15 member states of the Joint United Nations Programme on HIV and AIDS (UNAIDS). This shared definition of HIV and AIDS mainstreaming is:

> Mainstreaming HIV and AIDS is a process that enables development actors to address the causes and effects of HIV and AIDS in an effective and sustained manner, both through their usual work and within their workplace.[15]

In addition, the Maseru Declaration called for acceleration of development and, while mitigating the impact of HIV and AIDS, factoring HIV and AIDS into our own Regional Integration Process and focal intervention areas (trade liberalisation, infrastructure development, food security, social and human development).

At the time of the Maseru Declaration, the reaction to HIV and AIDS in Southern Africa was largely a health response, and coordination of this was led by the Department of Health. The focus was mainly on raising awareness, management of the causal relationship between HIV and AIDS, and appropriate policy positions on this.

Coordination of HIV and AIDS from DOH to DPSA

In 2004, a year after the Maseru Declaration, the coordination of the HIV and AIDS programmes within government was transferred to DPSA as a COG.[16] The DPSA commenced work advocating the mainstreaming of HIV and AIDS, and ensured there was national consensus on the definition, as well as technical competencies to develop and implement the policies.

In September 2006, a directorate responsible for HIV and AIDS mainstreaming was appointed. The scope of this directorate was, among others, to guide government on HIV and AIDS mainstreaming beyond that of the narrow focus on HIV and AIDS in the work place/human resource management response. This was at the time when the NSP Plan 2000–2006 was under review and the scope of HIV and AIDS mainstreaming was expanded beyond municipalities to include all three spheres of government.

In April 2007, South Africa sent a delegation to Livingstone in Zambia to train government officials on HIV and AIDS mainstreaming, and to ensure that there was capacity development among all 15 member states of the SADC on the same UNDP Curriculum on HIV and AIDS mainstreaming. South Africa's delegation included the DPSA's newly appointed Dr Sipho Senabe as Director for HIV and AIDS. The outcome of this training was for each country to draw up a capacity development rollout programme when their delegates returned home.

DPSA Commitment to HIV and AIDS Mainstreaming

Upon their return, the South African delegation compiled a report for the then Minister for Public Service and Administration (MPSA) Ms Geraldine Fraser Moleketi, who appointed the Director HIV and AIDS, Dr Sipho Senabe, as the focal point on HIV and AIDS and communicated such to the SADC and the South African National AIDS Council (SANAC). SADC then confirmed this through the Department of Foreign Affairs. Furthermore, the MPSA affirmed South Africa's commitment to HIV and AIDS mainstreaming and, in particular, the capacity development programme.

The position of the DPSA on the public sector response to HIV and AIDS as part of implementation of the NSP 2007–2011 was a commitment to develop the Employee Health and Wellness Strategic Framework for the Public Service by the end of the 2007–2008 financial year, and also to develop four related policies by the end of the 2008–2009 financial year.[17] The DPSA was also to serve on, and be represented in, SANAC's Technical Task Team on HIV prevention, as well as providing the HIV and AIDS mainstreaming focal point at SADC. A further commitment was for the Minister of Public Service and Administration to be the focal point at the AU on the regular tabling of the APRM which reports on, amongst other issues, the social governance of HIV and AIDS. This was the first commitment made by the DPSA to the SANAC Plenary of 7 September 2007 after the launch – in April 2007 – of the NSP 2007-2011.

An initial 400 people, mainly public servants with a few members of public sector trade unions, were trained by University of Pretoria in the financial year 2008/2009, using financial resources from the DPSA and the German Development Agency (GTZ). At the end of the financial year of 2007/2008, true to the commitments made at the 2007 SANAC Plenary to implement NSP 2007–2011, the DPSA had developed and launched the Employee Health and Wellness Strategic Framework for the Public Service. It had also successfully developed the HIV/AIDS and TB Management Policy for the Public Service. This was the first of such policies to integrate HIV and AIDS and TB in the country. This policy, among others, provided for the mainstreaming of HIV and AIDS. The responsibility for HIV and AIDS mainstreaming was placed on a senior manager who, according to the earlier Public Service Regulations,[18] was responsible for the HIV and AIDS response of each national and provincial department.

At this stage the work of HIV and AIDS thus had both political and diplomatic support. The Capacity Development programme was conducted in partnership with the University of Pretoria as the institution appointed in South Africa to institutionalise the HIV and AIDS Mainstreaming Capacity Development. All other 15 member states of SADC had to appoint a training institution to assist with the institutionalisation of this HIV and AIDS mainstreaming training. The next institution that DPSA had to capacitate was the predecessor of the National School of Government (NSG), then called the Public Administration and Leadership and Management Academy (PALAMA). PALAMA and other higher education institutions (HEI) were to continue with the training beyond the scope of the University of Pretoria, which was itself trained by the SADC together with other training institutions of all 15 member states.

DPSA's contribution to the international relations work of the HIV and AIDS response was through the successive APRM reports to the AU, the regular reports to the SADC on HIV and AIDS mainstreaming, and through participation in the country's delegations to the United Nations General Assembly on HIV and AIDS (UNGASS) – in support of the head of the delegation, Dr Mantombazana Tshabalala-Msimang, as Minister of Health and head of South Africa's delegation in 2008; and Mr Kgalema Motlanthe, as Deputy President and Head of Delegation in 2011 to the United Nations (UN) High Level Meeting on HIV and AIDS.

On HIV and AIDS in the Workplace

The first response to this work was a departmental guide provided by the DPSA to national and provincial departments as early as 2001. The guidance provided was aligned with the 2001 International Labour Organisation (ILO) Code of Good Practice on management of HIV and AIDS of 2001.[19] This ILO code was itself preceded by the Department of Labour's Code which was adopted as part of the Employment Equity Act No 55 of 1998. The DPSA's guide was thus aligned with both the Department of Labour and the ILO guides on HIV and AIDS. These guides emphasised the need to respond to HIV and AIDS among employees based on the understanding of the HIV dynamics in the communities from which they came. The understanding of the causes and effects of the epidemic was thus always emphasised. This resonated with the concept of HIV and AIDS mainstreaming developed by the UNDP earlier in 1985, and validated by the Maseru Declaration in 2003.

The major achievements of the public service in managing HIV and AIDS are: the Public Service Regulations PSR 2001 (as amended); the HIV/AIDS and TB Management Policy for the Public Service; the Policy and Procedure on Management of Ill Health and Retirement (PILIR); the Government Employee Medical Scheme (GEMS); and the Guidelines on Compensation for Occupational Diseases in the Public Service.

Applicable Public Service Regulations

The Public Service Regulations (PSRs) are norms and standards, from the MPSA, for accounting officers in national and provincial departments to implement specific public administration related interventions that will ensure efficiency, effectiveness and development oriented public service. The PSRs specifically instructs the accounting officer – the Cardinal norm in Part IV of the PSRs[20] – to ensure that there is a department specific policy on HIV and AIDS developed in consultation with labour and management. The regulations also provide for the appointment of a senior manager, a departmental HIV and AIDS committee, an implementation plan, a budget, and monitoring and evaluation of the departmental HIV and AIDS response.

In 2012, these regulations were amended to specifically provide for HIV and AIDS mainstreaming. Later on they were further amended to provide for both employees and citizens/clients of the departments, as well as two categories of beneficiaries who receive services through the two dimensions of internal and external mainstreaming, respectively.

These regulations are similar to the Technical Assistance Guidelines of the Department of Labour[21] which are meant for all employers, including the public service as an employer. These guidelines are applicable to all national, provincial and municipal departments as employers. They are the legal response to the ILO Recommendation 100 of 2010 on HIV and AIDS in the world of work.[22]

HIV/AIDS and TB Management Policy for the Public Service

This policy was the first to integrate HIV/AIDS and TB in South Africa. Among other items, the policy provides for the management of HIV and AIDS in the work place, and the benefit of clients of government departments. Legally, this is in the form of a determination which makes the relevant head of department accountable for its implementation and consistency with the PSR.

The policy provides for the appointment by the head of department of a senior manager who is responsible for capacity development, development of operational plans, and budget allocation of the mainstreamed response of the department. Beyond the traditional HIV Counselling and Testing (HCT) is the promotion of equality, protection of labour rights of HIV infected employees, and treatment support for the employees and their dependants. The policy provides for the departmental response for the benefit of the clients and stakeholders of the department.

The performance on this policy is that 90 per cent of government departments were implementing this policy as at 30 March 2013.[23] The emphasis has, however, been on the workplace response more than the external mainstreaming for the clients of the departments. While some departments, like the Department of Health, have done well with the antirctroviral (ARV) programme for the community, there has not been the appropriate internal mainstreaming for the benefit of health workers. The department is currently correcting this to ensure the necessary balance between the internal and external mainstreaming dimensions. Other departments, like Basic Education, have the necessary balance in HIV and AIDS mainstreaming dimension for the benefit of both learners and educators, and support staff.

To ensure a structural balance between the HIV and AIDS mainstreaming guidelines, the DPSA amended Programme One functions to include the human resources units for internal mainstreaming and the transversal programmes, now called change management, responsible for external mainstreaming function.

Systems Monitoring Tool

Before implementation of the HIV/AIDS and TB Management Policy for the Public Service, a system monitoring tool was developed for departmental self-assessment of elements that will ensure implementation. These include management commitment, planning, implementation management system, and a review system.

Each department is supposed to annually assess its implementation readiness status, and to continually improve this before they develop implementation plans for the next financial year.

The DPSA Dummy Operational Plans

The DPSA also prepared 'dummy operational plans' to guide each department in the development of their operational plan which must be costed, and budgets allocated, for each financial year. This document borrows extensively from the World Bank Operational planning templates. The National Treasury was also consulted to ensure the document complies with features of the Annual Performance Plans. The department specific operational plans have been deliberately crafted to ensure that the departments' implementation is at the lowest level of the ward – local and district municipal levels – in addition to the national and provincial levels of implementation and in line with the integrated service delivery model called *Operation Sukuma Sakhe Model*, as agreed in previous SANAC Plenary meetings and SANAC special council meeting called *Lekgotla*.

To ensure accountability in terms of both the budget allocation and expenditure, the DPSA agreed with the National Treasury to amend the Standard Charter of Accounts (SCOA) so that each department is compelled to report on the expenditure on HIV and AIDS operational plans for each financial year.

The DPSA, as a focal department at SADC, developed the monitoring and evaluation framework on HIV and AIDS mainstreaming. This framework has indicators for the 14 outcomes of South Africa's national development as determined by the Department of Performance Management and Evaluation (DPME). The departments were consulted on the use of these indicators which were also fashioned on the SADC HIV and AIDS Mainstreaming Guidelines developed in consultation with all 15 member states of the SADC during the period of 2012 and 2013. The relevant departments were consulted on the monitoring and evaluation framework and departments are supported in implementation based on the relevant indicators. Evaluation of the impact of HIV and AIDS mainstreaming will be informed by the monitoring and evaluation indicators which were only developed at SADC level during 2012 and 2013 and within the public service during the 2014 and 2015 period.

Government Employee Medical Scheme (GEMS)

GEMS was established as a structural benefit and part of conditions of service and social security framework for government employees. GEMS has a developmental and progressive approach when it comes to HIV and AIDS related benefits. Workers in the lowest levels of employment (levels 1–5) have a special subsidy dispensation of full HIV and AIDS treatment benefits, even if they cannot afford to be on a medical aid.

There has been significant achievement progress in this area of GEMS work as the first two years of the HIV and AIDS, STI and TB NSP 2012–2016 implementation showed an increase in the proportion of GEMS members on antiretroviral treatment (ART) and members who are being prepared to take treatment Pre-ART. By 2014 an estimate of 85–91 per cent of those who were HIV positive were accessing treatment.[24] This is significant as the achievement is closer to the envisaged 90 per cent national target agreed at the SANAC *Lekgotla* and plenary meeting after the consensus reached in the Melbourne International HIV and AID Conference held in 2014. Those that were entering the treatment programme had increased from September 2012 when the HCT Campaign was launched by the Deputy President. The proportion of those on treatment with controlled viral load over time of treatment, reached 80 per cent in the first two years of implementation of the NSP 2012–2016. The proportion of those on treatment with improved immune status also increased. The average CD4 count increased from below 200 to about 450 for 50 per cent of those who accessed treatment through GEMS.[25]

There were 118 890 members registered on the GEMS HIV and AIDS disease management programme (DMP) in July 2015, a slight increase of 1.07 per cent compared to June 2015. The total HIV prevalence on GEMS was 6.8 per cent[26]

In July 2015, 87.5 per cent of the DMP membership was on ART, and 7.5 per cent was on pre-ART, i.e. those who had undergone the HIV counselling and testing and were being prepared to take their ART. This 87.5 per cent achievement approximates the 90 per cent target the DPSA committed to achieve in the recent South African National AIDS Council *Lekgotla*, which was chaired by the Deputy President, Mr Cyril Ramaphosa in June 2015.[27]

The DMP is gender sensitive and developmental as evidenced by the June 2015 statistics which showed that 5 457 members accessed the Prevention of Mother-to-Child Transmission (PMTCT) programme. This means 5 457 newborns were born without the HIV virus in their blood and immune system. Equally encouraging are the 301 GEMS members who accessed Post Exposure Prophylaxis (PEP) in June 2015.[28]

These results are a reflection of the policy implementation support provided by DPSA to national and provincial departments through policy support workshops conducted in the last financial year. In these workshops complaints about GEMS were around other benefits, and not on its HIV and IDS DMP. This is because GEMS DMP has a progressive factor of deliberate HIV and AIDS DMP subsidy for the lowest categories of employment (levels 1-5). This is unique to GEMS, as no other medical aid scheme has been able to match this.

The DPSA initiated engagement with the Institute for Health and Productivity Management (IHPM), the medical schemes and administrators of medical schemes funding government employees, to assess to what extent those who are on treatment are also productive at work.

The DPSAs Contribution to HIV Prevention

During 2009 and 2010, the DPSA advocated for the assessment of the HIV and AIDS epidemic using the 'Know Your Epidemic, Know Your Response' (KYE/KYR) approach of UNAIDS.[29] The proposition of this approach to HIV and AIDS response was that if a country knows its epidemic and the fact that the HIV epidemic is heterogeneous – as it occurs differently in different districts and provinces – it can respond more precisely with targeted interventions relevant for each district and province, according to the identified drivers of the epidemic. The DPSA also championed the analysis of the National Spending Assessment (NASA) with support from the World Bank. This work also tracked the HIV and AIDS communication surveys conducted over the years until 2010. These analyses were used extensively to inform the NSP 2012–2016.[30]

The DPSA also facilitated further analyses called the Public Sector Expenditure Tracking Survey and the related Quantity Service Delivery Survey (PETS-QSDS) first in KwaZulu-Natal, and then in Gauteng.[31] This was to assess the flow of financial resources from disbursement to service delivery facilities levels. Areas of wastage were identified and recommendations made on how to improve the service delivery arrangements. This work was done with the two provinces and national treasury.

At the time of writing, the DPSA had recently concluded work supported by the United States Agency for International Development (USAID) to pilot the use of spatially-based KYE/KYR situational and gap analysis tools to inform district combination HIV prevention strategies.[32] This pilot was conducted in Ehlanzeni District in Mpumalanga and will be used to amend the existing guidelines on HIV and AIDS mainstreaming that guide all departments to mainstream their response and integrate their efforts with those of the departments at a ward, local and district levels of implementation.

International Relations

The DPSA is a focal department at SADC on HIV and AIDS mainstreaming. In fulfilling this role, the DPSA has lead several projects based on agreements at the SADC Level. These include the capacity development of HIV and AIDS mainstreaming, and the development of the continent's Guidelines on integration of HIV and AIDS Gender into Major Capital Projects.[33] This work was done in partnership with the UNDP, Department of Environmental Affairs, and the Development Bank of Southern Africa (DBSA). Other projects in this regard include the mainstreaming of HIV and AIDS into the Major Transport Corridor (North South Corridor), which involved the mainstreaming of HIV and four border pilot sites in partnership with ILO and various civil society organisations. This project targeted women in transport corridors and aimed at reducing their vulnerability through economic empowerment interventions, and policy dialogue on economic development with the economic cluster of departments.

The MPSA has developed and delivered several APRM reports to the AU. Delivered in his role as a focal person at the AU forum, these APRM reports include presenting accounts of the social governance of HIV and AIDS.[34]

The DPSA has technical support from the Japanese International Cooperation Agency (JICA) which followed the Presidential Minute signed by then Acting President Motlanthe. This came as an instruction to the MPSA to sign the first Memorandum of Understanding (MOU) with JICA on HIV and AIDS monitoring and evaluation. This partnership yielded the capacity development projects on monitoring and evaluation of HIV and AIDS, and the development of the HIV and AIDS monitoring and evaluation framework. This work specifically entails the deployment of two JICA officials on HIV and AIDS mainstreaming to DPSA. These officials also support the monitoring and evaluation capacity development of five other SADC countries: Zimbabwe, Lesotho, Namibia, Botswana and Swaziland.

The DPSA also represented South Africa at the United Nations Economic Commission for Africa (UNECA) regional office in Addis Ababa, Ethiopia, to account for the implementation of the AIDS Governance in Africa framework as determined by the Commission on the HIV and AIDS Governance in Africa (CHGA).[35] This work is based on the current scholarship in HIV and AIDS policy and governance and is the culmination of a unique consultation of CHGA Commissioners with a wide constituency in Africa and beyond. The findings and recommendations not only embody deep analytical insights derived from the CHGA's own research, but also reflect the views of the more than 1 000 Africans – including senior policymakers, advocacy groups, nongovernmental organisations, community-based organisations, people living with HIV and AIDS (PLHIV), research organisations and UN agencies – who took part in the consultation process. The insights gathered from CHGA framework will also be used to update the current guidelines on HIV and AIDS. The DPSA is the focal department on the UNAIDS Evaluations Technical Task Team in Geneva, as nominated by the Department of Planning, Monitoring and Evaluation in the Presidency. The evaluation of the South African response, especially the developmental indicators of life expectancy, maternal mortality rate, infant mortality rate and under-5-mortality rate, revealed some of the achievements that have been shared with the UNAIDS Evaluations Technical Task Team.

Conclusion

The DPSA, as a COG, developed norms and standards in the form of the Public Service Regulations (2001 as amended), the HIV/AIDS and TB Management Policy for the Public Service 2009, and the Guidelines on HIV and AIDS mainstreaming in the Public Service 2012. These legally mandated policy instruments were aligned with the requirements of the NSP 2012–2016 and the Department of Labour's Technical Assistance Guidelines, the ILO's Convention 200 of 2010, and the SADC HIV&AIDS Mainstreaming Framework.

Ninety per cent of government departments were implementing the HIV/AIDS and TB Management Policy for the Public Service by June 2015. The quality of this implementation is continuously being improved with amendments to the regulations, policy implementation tools and accountability tools.

There was significant improvement on the health of public servants accessing ARVs (85–90%). This was as a result of progressive provisions of the GEMS HIV and AIDS DMPs that kept public servants and their dependants alive. There is a need to increase the capacity of government to measure thc productivity associated with this positive development, and to adequately account for this as part of the efficiency and effectiveness of the public service.

The DPSA coordinates government's mainstreamed response through the governance forum on HIV and AIDS mainstreaming. This is where both HIV and AIDS, and internal and external mainstreaming issues, are addressed. This structure will be rearticulated in the DPSA's HIV and AIDS Mainstreaming Guidelines.

Notes and References

1 Republic of South Africa Presidency 2014 *Medium Term Strategic Framework* (MTSF) 2014–2019. Pretoria, Government Printers.

2 Southern African Development Community (SADC), 2003. *Maseru Declaration on the Fight Against HIV & AIDS in SADC Region*. 4 July 2003. Kingdom of Lesotho.

3 Republic of South Africa 2001, *Public Service Regulations*, Pretoria: as amended; Department of Public Service and Administration. 2008.

4 Department of Public Service and Administration 2008 *Employee Health and Wellness Strategic Framework for the Public Service*; Pretoria

5 Department of Public Service and Administration. 2009. *HIV & AIDS and TB Management Policy for the Public Service*, Pretoria.

6 Department of Public Service and Administration. 2009. *Health and Productivity Management Policy for the Public Service.*

7 Department of Public Service and Administration. 2009. *Safety Health Environment Risk and Quality Management Policy for the Public Service Pretoria.*

8 Department of Public Service and Administration. 2009. *Wellness Management Policy for the Public Service Pretoria.*

9 South African National AIDS Council 2007, National Strategic Plan for 2007-2011, Pretoria.

10 South African National AIDS Council 2011, National Strategic Plan for 2012-2016, Pretoria.
11 Department of Public Service and Administration 2008 *Employee Health and Wellness Strategic Framework for the Public Service*; Pretoria.
12 Southern African Development Community (SADC) 2006; *Expert Think Tank Meeting On HIV Prevention In High-Prevalence Countries in Southern Africa Report*, Maseru, Lesotho.
13 Southern African Development Community (SADC) 2003; *Maseru declaration on the fight Against HIV and AIDS in the SADC*, Maseru, Lesotho.
14 Ibid.
15 Ibid.
16 South African National AIDS Council 2011, National Strategic Plan for STI, HIV and AIDS 2012-2016, Pretoria.
17 Department of Public Service and Administration 2007, *Commitment to Implementation of the NSP Presentation to SANAC Plenary*, Pretoria.
18 Republic of South Africa 2001, *Public Service Regulations*, Pretoria: as amended; Department of Public Service and Administration. 2008.
19 Department of Labour, 2012. *Technical Assistance Guidelines on the HIV&AIDS Management*, Pretoria.
20 Republic of South Africa 2001, *Public Service Regulations*, Pretoria: as amended; Department of Public Service and Administration. 2008.
21 International Labour Organisation (ILO) *Recommendation 100 of 2010 on HIV in the workplace*, Geneva Switzerland.
22 Department of Labour, 2012. *Technical Assistance Guidelines on the HIV&AIDS Management*, Pretoria.
23 Department of Public Service and Administration. 2009. *HIV & AIDS and TB Management Policy for the Public Service*, Pretoria.
24 Department of Public Service and Administration Annual Report 2012–2013, Pretoria p51.
25 Department of Public Service and Administration 2015 *Report to the Office of Public Service Commission on HIV&AIDS Disease management in the Public Service*, Pretoria
26 Department of Public Service and Administration Annual Report 2012–2013, Pretoria p51.
27 South African National AIDS Council 2010, *Know Your Epidemic, Know Your Response Report*, Pretoria.
28 Ibid.
29 Department of Public Service and Administration; World Bank 2013 *Public Sector Expenditure Tracking Survey and Quantity Service Delivery Survey (PETS-QSDS)* Pretoria.
30 United States Agency for International development 2015 *Know Your response, Know Your Response, Know Your Capacity- Guidelines to Department*, Pretoria.
31 United Nations Development Programme (UNDP) International Labour Organisation/ African Development Bank, Guidelines on Integration of HIV&AIDS and Gender into Major Capital Projects.
32 Department of Public Service and Administration 2013; Second Report on the Implementation of the Africa Peer Review Mechanism, Pretoria.
33 United National Economic Commission for Africa (UNECA), 2008, *Commission on Economic Governance and HIV&AIDS in Africa*, Addis Ababa.

Chapter 8

South Africa's Demographic Dynamics in the Era of HIV and AIDS

Nompumelelo Nzimande

Introduction

Demographic research has shown that the impact of an epidemic on the population was felt differently during various phases of its epidemiologic stages. From the onset, the human immunodeficiency virus (HIV) and acquired immune deficiency syndrome (AIDS) were expected to have a long-term effect on the South African population. The immediate impact was on morbidity and mortality of the infected population. Later, the impact was felt on population size and age structure - given higher infection rates in reproductive ages. It is well documented that the impact of HIV and AIDS is far worse in 'Southern Africa than it is in Central and Eastern Africa, where it first began'.[1] The past two decades have advanced our understanding of the epidemic. This chapter explores the impact of these advancements on the size and age-sex-structure of the South African population.

Data and Methods

This chapter uses three population censuses conducted in South Africa (i.e. 1996, 2001 and 2011). The age and sex structure analysed are those provided in the *Census In Brief* reports, in which census results are published.[2] The reported census counts were not altered, except for the 1996 census count where unspecified age was extrapolated according to the observed age distribution in 1996. Although the age structure presented is directly that from the census, some caution needs to be exercised when reviewing the age structure (particularly the very young age groups) as there may be inconsistencies.[3] Several reports from Statistics South Africa (StatsSA) that shed light on mortality and age-sex structure of the South African population at different periods, were also utilised.

The Effect of HIV and AIDS on the Size of the Population

It is impossible to ignore the impact of HIV and AIDS on population size and age structure. Earlier studies suggested that HIV and AIDS would wipe out significant parts of the infected populations in Sub-Saharan Africa and compromise the well-being of future generations.[4] Figure 1 shows the United Nation (UN) estimation of the South African population and the actual population count from census years as presented by StatsSA.

The UN projections conducted until 2020 suggest that without HIV and AIDS, the population of South Africa was expected to continue growing exponentially such that the expected population in 2011 was about 55 million. The projections further show the expected population taking the influence of HIV and AIDS in account, and arrived at an estimated figure of about 48.5 million.[5] This indicates that HIV and AIDS was expected to account for a difference of 6.5 million persons in the South African population. The actual count of the South African population in 2011 was about 51.8 million,[6] with a growth rate of 1.4 per cent since 2011. Although this growth rate is a reduction from that observed between 1996 and 2001 (at two per cent), the size of the South African population continues to grow steadily, and was estimated to be 54.9 million at midyear in 2015.[7]

While UN projections are to be treated with caution, the projected population (with HIV and AIDS) in 2011 is not too far from the actual size observed from the census count amid a period of higher migration. This suggests that HIV and AIDS may have had an effect on the size of the South African population through increased mortality. Moreover, this is confirmed by causes of death reports that list HIV and AIDS as one of the leading causes of death in South Africa.[8]

Figure 1 South Africa population size from different sources

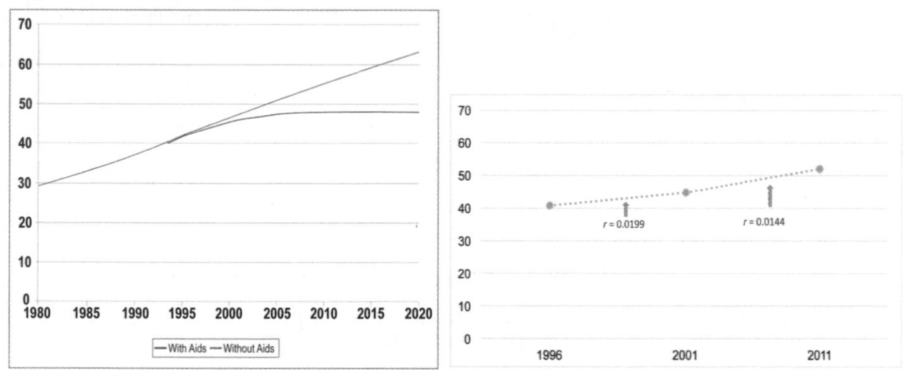

Source (panel 1): United Nations, *World Population Prospects*: The 2004 Revision (CD-ROM Edition—Extended Dataset), 2005

Source (panel 2): StatsSA, *Census 2011 in Brief*, Report No. 03-01-41

The continuous increase in the South African population – as indicated by the mid-year estimates – is an indication that South Africa was in a stage of recovery with regards to the impact of HIV and AIDS. This follows drastic increases in mortality since the 1990s, mostly due to the epidemic.[9] The recovery is also observed in increased life expectancy at birth from 2006, and which was estimated at 56 years in 2010 – an indicator that further demonstrates that South Africa was recovering from a period of high mortality impact of HIV and AIDS.[10] Given this, it is therefore less likely to observe a population growth trajectory of zero population growth post 2005 as projected by the UN in Figure 1. Instead, the population of South Africa is likely to continue increasing in size.

Mortality and HIV and AIDS

South Africa's mortality trajectory has been largely influenced by HIV and AIDS. After continuous improvements in mortality until the early 1980s, South Africa saw a reversal in mortality gains during the era of HIV and AIDS.[11] Figure 2 shows both an era of increasing mortality from 1997 until a peak at above 600 000 annual deaths in 2006, and an era of mortality decline that commenced thereafter. Due to the impact of the epidemic in South Africa in the 1990s and early 2000s, very few studies anticipated that South Africa would soon recover from the period of high mortality.[12]

Figure 2 Mortality trend in South Africa

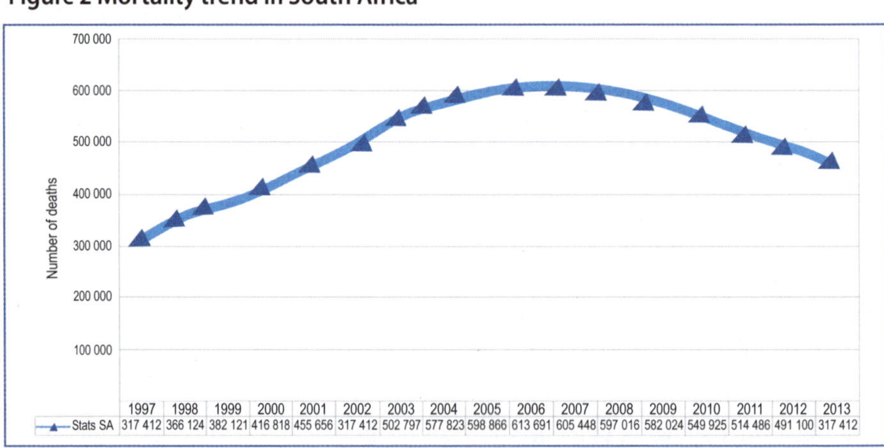

	1997	1998	1999	2000	2001	2002	2003	2004	2005	2006	2007	2008	2009	2010	2011	2012	2013
Stats SA	317 412	366 124	382 121	416 818	455 656	317 412	502 797	577 823	598 866	613 691	605 448	597 016	582 024	549 925	514 486	491 100	317 412

Source: (StatsSA 2014) – Mortality and causes of death in South Africa: Findings from death notification

The StatsSA report (2014)[13] also shows varying mortality by sex as indicated in Figure 3. A reversal in the decline in the median age at death is shown. This decline was observed until 2004, when median age declined from 52 years in 1997 to about 43 years in 2004.[14] This shows that mortality increase was indeed concentrated in the younger population, and resulted in higher premature mortality. In turn this prompted studies that explored the social and economic impact of the epidemic.

Figure 3 Median ages at death by sex and year

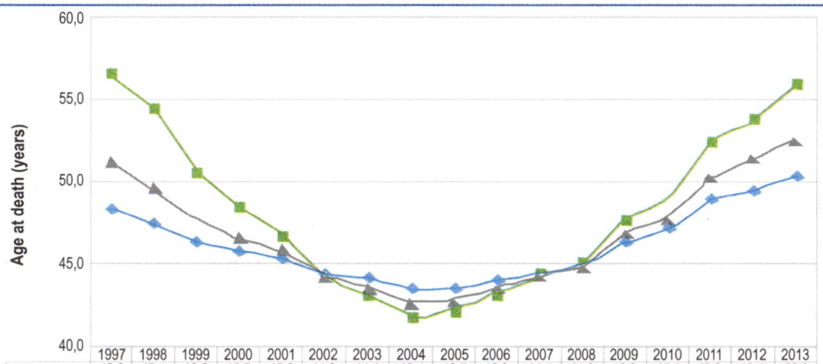

Age at death (years)

	1997	1998	1999	2000	2001	2002	2003	2004	2005	2006	2007	2008	2009	2010	2011	2012	2013
Males	48,3	47,4	46,3	45,7	45,3	44,3	44,1	43,4	43,5	43,9	44,4	44,8	46,3	47,1	48,9	49,4	50,3
Females	56,6	54,4	50,5	48,4	46,7	44,1	43,1	41,7	42,1	43,2	44,2	44,9	47,7	48,9	52,4	53,8	55,9
Total	51,3	49,7	47,8	46,5	45,7	44,2	43,6	42,6	42,8	43,5	44,3	44,8	46,8	47,8	50,3	51,1	52,5

Year of death

Source: StatsSA

Early in the etiology of the epidemic HIV and AIDS: the pandemic impacted the sexes differently.[15] Statistics show that females in reproductive ages were more affected by the epidemic than males, and this impact could be felt through higher female mortality and a reduced fertility in infected women.[16] Figure 3 shows this more clearly. The median age at death for females was higher between 1997 and 2002 – as expected in a normal population. There was, however, a cross-over in mortality for males and females between 2002 and 2007, where the impact of HIV and AIDS was mostly felt through an increase in mortality of females of reproductive ages.[17] The switch in male/female median age at death after 2008 corresponds with improvements in mortality after that period, as shown in Figure 2 – thus showing evidence of recovery in HIV and AIDS related mortality in South Africa.

Impact of HIV and AIDS on Age-sex Structure

The age structure of population is a representation of past fertility, mortality and migration. It is also a framework that determines the likely size and structure of future population. Figure 4 depicts the age-sex structure of South Africa in 2020 as projected by the UN (figure on left).[18] The figure on the right presents the age-sex structure of South Africa at three census counts: 1996, 2001 and 2011. In the 'with AIDS' pyramid, the UN shows the projected effect of HIV and AIDS on the South African population. In summary, the projection suggests that HIV and AIDS would be felt through a reduction in population in all age groups, but more so in age groups above 25 years. Females were expected to have higher reductions in population size. This is in line with studies that show that mortality due to HIV and AIDS is highest among the adult population in reproductive ages and particularly amongst women.[19]

Figure 4 South Africa population

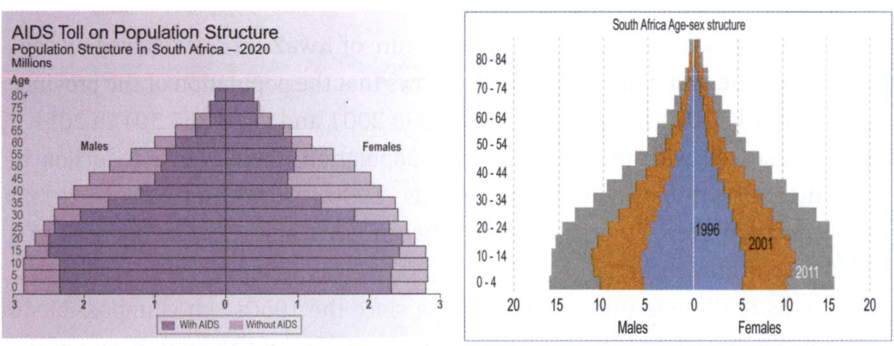

Source: own analysis from various UN and Stats SA sources

The age structure on the right in Figure 4 shows a different age structure in 2011 what was projected for 2020. Granted, there is a nine year difference between the two points of comparison; however, the observed age structure in 2011 shows a reduced impact of HIV and AIDS mortality than earlier predicted. Although one may argue that increased migration may have an effect such that migrant population compensated for the high mortality in reproductive ages (as observed in the UN projection), such an argument may not hold for one reason: the literature shows that although female migration is on the increase, male migration remains higher.[20] As a result, even with higher migration, the reduced population count of females in reproductive ages should still be visible. Therefore, the population pyramid on the right suggests that HIV and AIDS programmes were effective in reducing mortality, which otherwise would have been more keenly felt on women of reproductive age.

The Case of KwaZulu-Natal

Despite differences in the estimated levels of HIV prevalence, the results of the 2012 survey by the Human Sciences Research Council (HSRC) on HIV prevalence, incidence and behaviour[21] and the projections based on pregnant women attending antenatal clinics,[22] confirmed that there were provincial differentials in the prevalence of HIV and AIDS. The KwaZulu-Natal province recorded the highest prevalence of the epidemic, while the Western Cape had the lowest prevalence levels. The ranking of provincial prevalence (outside of the upper and lower bound) varies between these two studies, is understandable since a survey and a clinic-based estimation tend to capture slightly different samples. This section will discuss the impact of HIV and AIDS on the age structure of KwaZulu-Natal, the province with the highest prevalence.

Figure 5 presents the size and age structure of KwaZulu-Natal based on census counts. The first panel of the figure shows that the population of the province grew from 8 417 021 in 1996 to 9 426 018 in 2001 and to 10 267 301 in 2011.[23] Just as observed with the South African population, there was a reduction in population growth between the two periods (1996 to 2001 and 2001 to 2011). The population grew by one per cent between 2001 and 2011 as opposed to a two per cent growth between 1996 and 2001. This is mostly attributable to a continuous fertility decline in South Africa since the 1960s.[24] It is impossible to rule out the impact of HIV and AIDS in the reduction of the growth rate of the population of KwaZulu-Natal given the HIV-related mortality in the province.[25] As such, it remains unclear whether the switch in the provincial population size observed between 2001 and 2011 – where KwaZulu-Natal lost its rank as the most populous province in South Africa to Gauteng – is a result of high HIV-mortality during this period, increased migration out of the province, or high migration into Gauteng.

Panel 2 in Figure 5 shows age-specific population changes in the province between 1996 and 2011. Due to scepticism on the age structure of the census of younger ages (as previously indicated), less will be said regarding changes in the population below 15 years of age. The figure, however, shows that the population grew in size for each age group above the age of 15, with the highest growth observed between the ages of 20 and 29 years. This is likely to be the result of previous fertility, since these age-groups are a product of higher fertility during the early 1990s. Marginal growth was observed for ages between 35 and 54

Figure 5 KwaZulu-Natal population count and age stucture

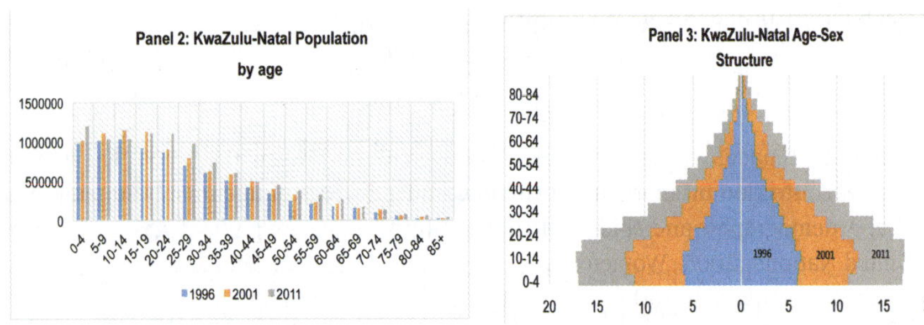

Source: Calculations from *Census in Brief* 1996, 2001 and 2011 (StatsSA 1998, StatsSA 2003, StatsSA 2012)

years. This was also observed in a provincial study that compared Census 2001 and the Community Survey of 2007.[27] This may result both from higher mortality due to HIV and AIDS of this cohort in the early 2000s (as observed in Figure 2), or emigration. Panel 3 also shows this reduction in population size between the ages of 35 and 54 for both males and females.

Conclusion

HIV and AIDS have changed the course of population growth and age-sex structure of South Africa, particularly in areas most affected by the epidemic. The effect was most felt between 2002 and 2008, when HIV-related mortality was high – more so for females. There is evidence that the catastrophic impact of HIV and AIDS on population change is slowing down. Mortality decline that resumed in 2008 showed signs that the South African population was recovering from the impact of the epidemic. This has resulted in a reversal of the anticipated devastating impact of earlier projections. The future may thus not be as gloomy as once predicted – provided that prevention and treatment efforts continue. Ultimately, HIV and AIDS have shown the resilient nature of the population.

Notes and References

1 Merli, M. and Palloni, A., 2004. The HIV and AIDS epidemic, kin relations, living arrangements and the elderly in South Africa. CDE Working Papers. Unites States of America: University of Wisconsin.

2 StatsSA, 1998. Census in brief: The people of South Africa population census 1996, 03-01-11 (1996) Pretoria, South Africa: Statistics South Africa; StatsSA, 2003. Census in brief: Census 2001 in brief, 03-02-03 (2001) Pretoria, South Africa: Statistics South Africa; StatsSA, 2012. Census in brief. Census 2011 in brief, 03-01-41. Pretoria, South Africa: Statistics South Africa.

3 Udjo, E.O., 2005. An evaluation of age-sex distributions of South Africa's population within the context of HIV and AIDS. *Development Southern Africa*, 22(3), pp.319-345.

4 Nicoll, A., Timaeus, I., Kigadye, R.M., Walraven, G. and Killewo, J., 1994. The impact of HIV-1 infection on mortality in children under 5 years of age in sub-Saharan Africa: A demographic and epidemiological analysis. *AIDS*, 8, pp.995-1005.

5 United Nations, 2005. Women joining migration streams in unprecedented numbers and proportions. New York: UN Department of Public Information.

6 StatsSA, 2012. Census in Brief: Census 2011 in Brief, 03-01-41. Pretoria: Statistics South Africa.

7 StatsSA, 2015a. Mid-year population estimates. Pretoria: Statistics South Africa.

8 StatsSA, 2014. Mortality and causes of death in South Africa 2013: Findings from death notification, P0309.3 Pretoria: Statistics South Africa.

9 Reniers, G., 2011. Adult mortality trends in Africa. *International Handbook of Adult Mortality*. Netherlands, Springer.

10 StatsSA, 2015b. Population Dynamics in South Africa, 03-01-07. Pretoria: Statistics South Africa.

11 StatsSA, 2014.

12 Palloni, A., 1996. Formal dynamics of populations with HIV and AIDS. Meeting of the Population Association of America, New Orleans.

13 StatsSA, 2014.

14 Ibid.

15 Ibid.

16 Zaba, B., 1994. The demographic impact of AIDS: Some stable population simulation results. Centre for Population Studies, London School of Hygiene and Tropical Medicine.

17 Camlin, C., Garenne, M and Moultire, T.A., 2004. Fertility trends and patterns in a rural area of South Africa in the context of HIV and AIDS. *African Journal of Reproductive Health*, 8(2), pp.38-54.

18 StatsSA, 2014.
19 United Nations, 2005.
20 Dorrington, R., Johnson, L.F., Bradshaw, D. and Daniel, T., 2006. The demographic impact of HIV and AIDS in South Africa: National and provincial indicators for 2006. Cape Town: Centre for Actuarial Research, South African Medical Research Council and Actuarial Society of South Africa.
21 United Nations, 2005.
22 Shisana, O., Labadarios, D., Simbayi, L.D., Onoya, D. et al., 2014. South African national HIV prevalence, incidence and behaviour survey, 2012. Cape Town: HSRC Press.
23 Dorrington et al., 2006.
24 StatsSA 1998; StatsSA 2003; StatsSA 2012.
25 Moultrie, T. A. and Timaeus, I. M., 2003. The South Africa fertility decline: Evidence from two censuses and a demographic and health survey. *Population Studies*, 57(3), pp.265-289.
26 Dorrington et al., 2006.
27 Doctor, H., 2010. Population and development indicators of KwaZulu-Natal. In Nzimande, N. (ed.), State of the population of KwaZulu-Natal: Demographic profile and development indicators. KwaZulu-Natal: Department of Social Development.

Chapter 9

Can HIV and AIDS Communication Theory make Rhodes Fall?

Colin Chasi

Introduction

Even after the formal end of colonial and apartheid rule, black South Africans generally live amid direct, structural and cultural violence. To wit, and unsurprisingly, a significant number of South African black lives are widely characterised by pain. Considering this, I offer an autoethnographic note of what Scott[1] calls the 'hidden script' on dying of acquired immune deficiency syndrome (AIDS), before presenting autoethnographic notes on writing black human immunodeficiency virus (HIV) and AIDS communication theory. I speak not only of a marginalised body of theory, but also of my struggle to overcome resistance to the granting of recognition to black existential concerns and experiences. Deliberate or otherwise, by asserting the sufficiency of western knowledge schema to describe, explain and direct black experience, resistance to African theorising works to stymie and hold the emergence of new black HIV and AIDS communication theory.

Violence 'after' Colonial and Apartheid Oppression

Pervasive patterns of violence characterise economically disadvantaged black southern societies in the wake of the formal collapse of colonial and apartheid oppression. This is to say that in these societies, violence persists in patterns of direct, indirect and structural violence which are culturally normalised. These are societies that demonstrate the horrid realisation that, as Galtung[2] puts it, 'Cultural violence makes direct and structural violence look and even feel right – or at least not wrong'.

That violence was central to colonial and apartheid rule is unsurprising. After all, the founding violence of colonial and apartheid rule was the absolute acceptance of arbitrary and violent racial and other differences as means and modes for systematic dispossession and political distributions of goods and harms. The violence of this is apparent once one recognises that it occurs whenever something is taken away forcibly and illegally from someone without their consent. Here, arbitrariness manifests as

> … violence with the distinctive feature of committing acts of destruction that, in their starkness, scale, and "knock-out" effects, have the peculiar characteristic of concealing human suffering, burying it in an infinite circle centered, so to speak, everywhere. This is, then, the arbitrariness that accomplishes its own work and validates itself through its own sovereignty, and thereby permits power to be exercised as a right to kill and invests Africa with deaths at once at the heart of every age and above time.[3]

The order of things that emerges after the formal end of colonial and apartheid misanthropic rule is that of direct and structural violence which are arbitrarily, or culturally, made to appear normal. The work of violent colonial and apartheid cultures is to divest individuals of responsibility for black lives by constructing myths of separate development that put forward accounts of white superiority and black inferiority. Without necessarily intending to scholars who uncritically privilege western scholarship and schema function as legitimators and amplifiers of bodies of knowledge that function as botched mirrors through which Africans meant to know themselves as distorted beings because they are not westerners. An inherent and perverse feature of this literature is how it unquestioningly assumes to know Africans and what their needs are. In other words, this literature denies that Africans have the choice and freedom to either bring unexpected light to things, or to be tremendous mysteries, 'being, by reason of [the human's] privileged ontological status as creator, maintainer and destroyer of worlds… in this fundamental way that is beyond our intention, human…".[4]

The problem, then, is not so much that there is a distant past historical process of colonisation which has entrenched inequities. It is that, as Bandile Mdlalose[5] argues with reference to the indigenous social rights movement, *baseMjondolo*, indigenous experiences and voices are often subjected to what mediating white and western elites construct and communicate. In Bandile's view, which has many critics, all too often white and western opinions and readings are published and authenticated in ways that silence the black and indigenous peoples that these same experts claim to represent. The rejection and degradation that is implied by this, is but one feature of what has been called 'black pain'.

Black Pain

Whereas in healthy societies cultures distort realities so that people can live[6] in ways that altruistically enable individuals to be the most that they can be,[7] under colonial and apartheid norms cultures were established to make the black person know her or his place. This is, of course, another way to say that colonial and apartheid regimes are violent. What this does not say is that when subjected to violence, all people feel pain and in the context of this argument possessed black South Africans feel pain.

Often, in the misguided and Manichean guise of protecting 'their own', racists deny that blacks feel pain when violence is inflicted upon them. They deny that blacks feel pain when separated unjustly from associating with other humans or when denied access to the same education, work and remuneration as others. Something of this idea is evident in Nixon's[8] account of how the racist apartheid government spent billions to convince the rest of the world that apartheid was good for blacks. For our purposes, what matters is not an exhaustive examination of how racists attempt to silence and generally deny black facts and experiences. What counts is to know that material, symbolic, cultural and other forms of violence, hurts blacks.

Fanon's[9] analysis was that black pain can be seen in the violence with which blacks use rage to overcome feelings associated with being made to feel insignificant. Fassin's[10] interpretation – with palpable implications for how communication on HIV and AIDS was to prove challenging in South Africa – is that black pain from violence orchestrated under colonial and apartheid arrangements and their legacies built up a large reservoir of painful memories and suspicion, particularly against 'anyone making any claims to authority'.

Gevisser[11] writes that, apparently concerned to address the black pain of being bearers of inordinate poverty and carriers of horrid stereotypes as oversexed vectors of disease, Thabo Mbeki (as President of South Africa), always mentioned safer-sex campaigns when he talked about HIV and AIDS. He seemingly also sought to point out the role of other factors in ways that lessoned the significance of orthodox medical narratives which presented sexual intercourse as the cause of the epidemic. Mbeki's[12] concern for black pain could be seen in how he reportedly felt that communicating a view that did not perpetuate black stereotypes was worthwhile, even if it may have had unintended consequences.

As the mass student movements of 2015 in South Africa have shown, there is a need to present theory that recognises and values black existence, experiences, pain and hopes. Those who have resisted this have been identified by our students as custodians, curators and perpetrators of cultures of violence. Their stout defence of scholarship has, as usual, been pinned to violent cultures that fundamentally refuse to account for differing human experiences and perspectives through the misuse of claims that they 'protect standards'.

Hidden Black Scripts on HIV and AIDS

Even from the most well-meaning of people, much has been made of the idea that Africans do not speak of HIV and AIDS. I have problematised this view elsewhere[13] by demonstrating that there is ample empirical evidence that Africans know and speak about HIV and AIDS. A problem appears here, as in many instances, that the observational and conceptual lens used by scholars is not able to recognise and give value, not only to who and what Africans are, but also to how and why Africans do what they do. This problem is, no doubt, allied with the fact that blacks have occupied historically subordinate roles which have driven them to hide, or place in the background, scripts that reveal their actual experiences. Scott,[14] therefore, reasons that uncovering and analysing hidden scripts of oppressed blacks carries 'the portent of political breakthroughs. The first step in understanding such moments is to place the tone and mood experienced by those who are speaking defiantly for the first time near the centre of our analysis.'

To speak of the black pain and anguish that are experienced in the midst of HIV and AIDS, I will retell a hidden conversation I had, stringing in quotes and citations that the reader can tie to extant reading. The point will not just be to say 1) that what was said in the conversation is only valuable when read as reflective of what western scholars have written; the point will also not be to merely show 2) that humanities scholarship of good potential reverberates in many places and spaces; also 3) to indicate through an economical method lines of deep conceptual insight into human existence that have been explored elsewhere, by others; and 4) to do all this while serving the purpose of furthering recognition and valuing of African experiences as the starting point for guiding action that bears on African needs.

To be sure, I am after doing something different from merely sounding African experience against western theory. I am critical, in fact, of how the African scholarship, including on HIV and AIDS communication, of those who have defended received theory has not asked who received theory speaks for. They have refused to accept that there is anything unique and worth learning in the experiences of others in ways that sacrifice ethicality itself. In the words of Jacques Derrida,[15] they have thereby forsaken their 'obligations to other others'. Work that goes beyond attempts of writers such as Fassin,[16] Steinberg[17] and McGregor[18] to explain black experiences to others is needed if we are to obtain powerful black first-person experiences that are written for purposes of meeting black needs. I offer here a descriptive analysis of a 'black conversation' on HIV and AIDS. It serves to set the scene for later presentation of a summary view of my black HIV and AIDS communication theory.

Beyond the above, the point is to make insightful breakthroughs by speaking of a hidden black conversation on HIV and AIDS. These breakthroughs will relate to reflecting how black people experience pain and anguish in the face of the structural and cultural violence of our times. Even though my own experience is of being involved regularly in such conversations, it is of significance that conversations such as the one that I will present are not foregrounded in the literature on HIV and AIDS communication. This also means it is reasonable to take it that these scripts are hidden, that is, subjected to image management so that they are not part of the open record and interactions that Scott[19] calls the 'public transcript', and which 'is not positively misleading, [but] is unlikely to tell the whole story about power relations. [As it] is frequently in the interest of both parties to tacitly conspire in misrepresentation.'

Autoethnography

At the risk of being accused of setting myself up as a paragon of goodness, I want to say something about how my own journey to writing on HIV and AIDS has been an attempt to do so while taking seriously the experiences of those I know. Presentation of such first-person accounts has the benefit of grounding the abstract discussion of cultural and other violence, and of black pain, in a complex lived flux of experiences.

In writing this, I follow the advice of Ellis[20] to boldly own up to my subjective situation. This is in order to make available for discussion what is to be gained by investing in revealing the subjectivities of the researcher. The simple fact is that, as Ellis anticipated, my autoethnographic move is to contaminate abstract conceptualisation with everyday life experiences of a researcher whose work is reflexive. The stuff of real life will challenge readers to think about how they theorise and assess research on HIV and AIDS communication and, hopefully, also how they practice such communication. Even though the authors do not justify their writing with reference to autoethnography, the book *The Instant of My Death/Demeure: Fiction and Testimony*,[21] is an excellent example of the kinds of insight that can be drawn from simultaneously narrating and re-theorising a single encounter.

A Hidden Script Conversation about AIDS-death

Outside the public transcripts of the dominant scholarship that powerfully projects western schema, my experience is that HIV and AIDS are not topics that are far from everyday hidden conversations. In hidden conversations people talk about it to express varied interests, experiences and existential fears. I will share an illustrative conversation I had with two immigrant, black, blue-collar workmen, with whom I shared a number of days of manual labour.

The workmen spoke of what they would do if they found that they had AIDS. The older of the two, a determined and extremely hard working man, said he would go back to his home country to die. He figured his family would let him die quietly. In his view, having AIDS would mean having to stop really living. He said taking antiretroviral medication would be to get life as a kind of gift and he would not take it.

I replied saying I understood, in the manner of the sceptics,[22] that life is characterised by unrest and frustrations so that to live is, as the colloquialisms go, to 'keep on moving on' when the 'going gets tough'. I also pointed out that the language of survival threatens to simplistically reduce discussion of human living to a matter of only meeting practical-functional needs when we know that people love and other less tangible things. In other words, I argued that people do not live by bread alone!

It was my contention that his view, which appeared to suggest that bodily illness would direct his life, did not appear to recognise that individuals do have agency to co-create the world and to choose the meanings of what happens in the world. So I put it to him that whatever illness one may have, it was possible to have a joy-filled life.

The older workman's counter-argument was curious. Having lived amidst the HIV and AIDS epidemic, poverty and death, he said, he had long decided against trying to live fully. So he said he had constrained himself to the barest of relations with family and friends. In trying to live with the barest of relations with others, he claimed to have conned himself into really seeing that 'with respect to this disaster called life, we die too late'.[23]

The younger workman, who was carefree in manner, interjected. His unexpectedly harsh view was that in the event he acquired AIDS, he would not go back to his home country. He would not want anyone there to be burdened by his suffering and, in fact, he wanted to die as soon as possible without suffering a long illness. Before death he would, however, try to do everything in his power to send as much money as possible to the family he had left in his home country. He added that even though he sent them money whenever he could, it had been eight years since he last saw them. Clearly all impressions of him as carefree were shallow and uninformed by the hardships and determination that characterised his life.

It pained me that I knew he had left home as a 15-year-old and had not yet managed to earn enough to go back, even for a brief visit. Further, I knew that he had recently separated from his girlfriend.

She had lost a child in early labour. When she was in hospital he asked me to visit her and pass on some money and food. I had done this and added a little money of my own to help her get some much needed treatment. He told me he could not visit because he needed to work to pay for her stay in hospital. In fact, I know that during that time he did not sleep, working with barely a moment of rest to earn enough to ensure that they could 'make it'. So, I was initially surprised to hear he had broken up with her. Mutual acquaintances told me, though, that the stress of losing the child and the frustration that he did not earn enough money had affected him so badly that he could not find it in him to continue the relationship with his girlfriend.

I asked the younger man why he did not talk of taking antiretroviral medication.

He replied by asking me what the point would be, and what life was it that he had, anyway. He said that he had very little money and had given up trying to make it work with women. He queried what was left of life when there was real hunger and sex was so complexly wrapped in risks and fears about death. His view was that 'one should die proudly when it is no longer possible to live proudly'.[24]

There was a long silence in which the two men and I worked quietly, as though each of us was alone. Finally, the silence was broken when, in a long soliloquy, the young man spoke of thinking a great deal about how so much pain and harm filled his life. He said he would even turn to crime to become a dignified person of means.[25]

The older of the workmen restarted the conversation by saying that he would try very hard to never know if he was HIV-positive or not. He said that the hardships of his life were too much already for him to cope with news of being HIV-positive. Steinberg's[26] biography of Sizwe, a man in the Lusikisiki district of South Africa's Eastern Cape who knew of HIV and AIDS, but refused to get tested, can be read as a story about men, who, like this man, are reluctant to be tested for HIV and AIDS – even when they suspect they may have the virus – men who could refuse to take medical treatment because that would speak of death.

At the time of writing, the older of the two workmen had married and his wife had given birth to a child, of whom he was very proud. I do not know if he had tested for HIV. The younger of the two men had later on turned, I was told by reliable sources, to crime. Perhaps he saw crime as a path to gaining respect and dignity. For him, it seemed, life was war. This is war: 'life for some, for others, the cruelty of assassination.'[27]

What is certain is that in the time I shared with the two men I found nothing that could serve as a useful mechanism with which to innovatively solve the problems of their, and my own, humanity. I could not find plans by which to execute communication to ensure that none of us would have to face HIV and AIDS; the matter was such that 'plans for mankind and collaboration between men in those tasks which increase the sum total of humanity are new problems, which demand true inventions.'[28] My finest resolve was to dignify myself and them by not making positive regard conditional, and by making the work-based relationship I had with them the most productive and rewarding possible. In this way I tried to open all doors of possibility by recognising, and so not unhelpfully questioning, the maturity of each of us to forget cause and make decisions from the depths of our singularities.[29]

If the matter had been that these men were simply ignorant about HIV and AIDS, I could certainly have informed them about it, but only in a very limited number of instances did I find anything that required information to which I was privileged. Basics that inform the need to abstain, be faithful and use a condom were commonly given to us.

The matters under discussion involve what it means to live and eventually to die. They were about how to make it so that the life one lives would be evidence of highest resolves as regards the greatest good. I am not sure what role our conversation had in the lives of all involved.

The hidden transcript presented above revealed multiple, layered and contradictory experiences of the black pain experienced by two men who chose, in freedom, amid violently constraining circumstances. They convincingly showed that HIV and AIDS raises painful existential issues and begs difficult existential questions, and that these will be answered differently by different people from their unique biographical positions. These issues and questions should be addressed by scholars, but, as I will point out in the next section, there is much resistance to this. Black scripts are not just hidden, they are also often suppressed.

Autoethnographic Notes on the Struggle for Black HIV and AIDS Communication Theory

There is a need to present theory that accounts for the kinds of violence, pain and existential fears that characterise everyday African lives. I have tried to act upon this realisation. For this reason my 2010 philosophical and poetic book on AIDS started with the following autobiographical observation:

> Not yet middle-aged, I witness the scourge of HIV and AIDS as a man who has lived beyond the life expectancy of the girls, women, boys and men he grew up with. I write to find words to voice questions that affirm and challenge who we are, that speak of this wretched time in ways that humanise and so dignify us.[30]

I was trying to philosophically and poetically elaborate a human-centric or existential approach that theorises the inalienable freedom by which African people can act amidst suffering. It was my strong conviction that this form of conceptual intervention was needed where people have been too often, and for too long, historically marginalised. So I lamented how, 'to coin an unfortunate pun, the *communication* of HIV and AIDS in its most bitter harshness evidences the success of this epoch in mythologizing real questions of life and death as merely requiring appropriate information. [So that it] becomes strange to recall that sex is the ultimate language of life, the eternal reply to death'.[31]

In a Kantian emphasis, I charged that individuals need to have courage to live by their convictions. 'The guardians who would supervise others towards the ABCs may regard this as overly optimistic and even dangerous...', but for 'the better cause of democracy, health and development, human dignity is accorded to human beings in the understanding that each individual is a creator and a destroyer of worlds ... The risk is to follow the proud tide of democracy and to not thereby seek to tame the wild dogs of freedom with lame words of simplest ABCs'.[32]

The point I was making is worth re-explaining as follows: Sontag[33] was right: 'no "we" should be taken for granted when the subject is looking at other people's pain.' A similar and profound realisation – of how limited and violent human communication is – led Kierkegaard to see that one cannot communicate directly to another about existential matters, that is about matters that are demonstrably about how life and death should be faced. Since we live lives that are fundamentally separate or parallel, Kierkegaard[34] saw that direct communication about existential matters is not sufficient to vitally direct how an individual chooses in freedom how his or her life is lived and died. My basic, but still strangely often challenged, point was that HIV and AIDS raises painful questions relating to life, sex and death that are fundamentally existential.

Journal reviewers have often said that what is required to address HIV and AIDS is known. So they have: 1) shown exasperation at the fact that I have attempted to present something different; 2) contested the references to existential theory and to western theorists to present an African position; or 3) simply demanded that I focus on testing available theory. These reviewers have thus denied that: 1) while there is no new theory on African HIV and AIDS communication, extant practices of communicating about HIV and AIDS continue unchallenged even though their weakness are demonstrated by the fact that millions have turned away from its prescripts, as evidenced by how so many have been and are infected, and affected, by HIV; 2) The reviewers have thus, for example, protected a western way of knowing Africans that refuses to countenance that Africans develop cultures in the face of questions regarding the possibility of death; and 3) Indeed, the upshot is that these reviewers have insisted that the way to carry out legitimated research is to work with narrowly identified western schema.

Being committed to sharing insights that honour marginalised experiences, I have continued to smash holes through the resistance by finding unprotected spaces in which the foundations of a quintessentially African theory of communication on HIV and AIDS can be presented. My 2014 book, *HIV and AIDS Communication in South Africa: Are you human?*[35] expands the foundations and horizons of my theorising by working towards a re-appraisal of theory on the African moral theory of *ubuntu* in order to etch out a reading that is consistent with everyday experiences of what is good and possible.

Elsewhere, it has turned out that sceptical reviewers are quite keen to recommend materials for publication that question the power and moral standing of African leaders. They have thus been willing to publish work such as: 'Role models in politicians will disappoint you: Cautionary notes on AIDS leadership in post-apartheid South Africa'[36] which questions the idea that the communication of politicians is a panacea by which the HIV and AIDS behaviours of multitudes can be directed. What they have failed to pick out in these instances, or what they have tolerated, is that the arguments made have been couched in humanocentric or existential assumptions about people not being easily directed, particularly when it comes to existential concerns that speak of how life, pain, sex and death should be faced.

I am sad that it requires guile to write and publish foundational truths about black existence and pain. These truths must include insights found in hidden black conversations.

Conclusion

From founding father Kierkegaard, to Jean-Paul Sartre, to the father of black existential thought, Lewis Gordon, existential scholars have recognised that life is a struggle filled with anguish, angst and dread that people experience as they thrive to become all they can be, before inevitable death. Life is so filled with violence and other sources of hardships that sceptics such as David Benatar[37] claim that it is better to never have been born. Certainly, since colonial times, African life has been filled with violence and brutish death. In contemporary times the burden of HIV and AIDS is inordinately borne by Africans who could legitimately play on Sartre's words by saying: Hell is African! In part, they can say this because they experience hell in how scholars deny and play down their experiences of violence, pain and marginalisation.

It is important to work against colonial discourses that deny the legitimacy of blacks speaking out about their existential concerns and pain. As demonstrated in this brief discussion of one set of black experiences, one way of doing this is to explore, record and research hidden black scripts on HIV and AIDS.

When will we be able to speak of human communication as a process that is tied to the complex and whole lives we live? When will communication stop being seen as something that is targeted at us? Until when shall we speak of communication as though it has, for us, a genealogy that is not our own? When we begin to address communication as a process that is meaningful within the context of our pain and strivings, it will become possible to establish the kinds of new society that enable us to become the most we can be.

Written in the context of student protests against western education that does not speak of their needs, this chapter has offered a case for a black existential theory of communication on HIV and AIDS that ensures that black experiences are recognised and addressed in shaping responses and actions. Indeed, it is time to move away from western conceptual schema and to build black theory of HIV and AIDS communication. Failing this, the often unsaid threat is that people will turn further away from humanities and social science scholarship for viable descriptions and explanations that guide action.

Notes and References

1 Scott, J.C., 1990. Domination and the arts of resistance: Hidden transcripts. New Haven: Yale University Press.

2 Galtung, J., 1990. Cultural violence. *Journal of Peace Research*. 273, p.291.

3 Mbembe, A., 2001. On the postcolony. Berkeley: University of California, p.13.

4 Christians, C.G. and Traber, M., 1997. Communication ethics and universal values. Thousand Oaks: Sage Publications, p.13.

5 Mdlalose, B., 2014. The Rise and Fall of Abahlali baseMjondolo, a South African Social Movement: *Politikon*, 41(3), pp.345-353.

6 Becker, E., 1973. The denial of death. London: The Free Press.

7 Tomasello, M., 2009. Why we cooperate. London: MIT Press.

8 Nixon, R., 2015. Selling apartheid: South Africa's global propaganda war. London: Pluto Press.
9 Fanon, F., 1986. Black skin, white masks. London: Pluto Press, p.35.
10 Fassin, D., 2007. *When bodies remember: Experience and politics of AIDS in South Africa*. London: University of California Press, p.20.
11 Gevisser, M., 2009. A legacy of liberation: Thabo Mbeki and the future of the South African dream. New York: Palgrave MacMillan, p.285.
12 Ibid.
13 Chasi, C., 2013. Communication and expressing, not speaking, on AIDS. *Critical Arts: A Journal of Media Studies*, 27(3), pp.386-402.
14 Scott 1990, p.203.
15 Derrida, J., 1995. The gift of death. London: University of Chicago Press, p.69.
16 Fassin, 2007.
17 Steinberg, J., 2009. Three letter plague: A young man's journey through a great epidemic. London: Vintage.
18 McGregor, L., 2005. Khabzela. Johannesburg: Jacana Media.
19 Scott, 1990, p.2.
20 Ellis, C., 2004. The ethnographic I: A methodological novel about autoethnography. Oxford: AltaMira, p.89.
21 Blanchot, M., Rottenberg, E. and Derrida, J., 2000. The instant of my death. Stanford: Stanford University Press.
22 Benatar, D., 2004. Life, death and meaning: Key philosophical readings on the big questions. Lanham, Md.: Rowman and Littlefield Publishers, p.73.
23 Blanchot et al., 2000, p.4.
24 Nietzsche, F.W., 2007. Twilight of the idols: With the antichrist; and Ecce homo. Ware: Wordsworth Editions, p.67.
25 Nietzsche, 2007, p.72.
26 Steinberg, 2009, pp.325-326.
27 Blanchot et al., 2000, p.7.
28 Fanon, F., 1963. The wretched of the earth. New York: Grove Press, pp.312-313.
29 Rogers, C.R. and Stevens, B., 1967. Person to person: The problem of being human: A new trend in psychology. Walnut Creek: Real People Press, p.52.
30 Chasi, C., 2010. Hard words: On HIV and AIDS communication. Johannesburg: Real African Publishers, p.1.
31 Ibid., p.12.
32 Ibid., p.70.
33 Sontag, S., 2003. Regarding the pain of others. London: Penguin, p.7.
34 Kierkegaard, S., 1968. Kierkegaard's concluding unscientific postscript. Princeton: Princeton University Press, for American Scandinavian Foundation, pp.246-247.
35 Chasi, C., 2014. *Communication on HIV and AIDS: Are you human?* London: Palgrave.
36 Chasi, C., 2012. Role models in politicians will disappoint you: Cautionary notes on AIDS leadership in post-apartheid South Africa. *Communicatio: South African Journal of Communication Theory*, 38(3), pp.312-328.
37 Benatar, 2004.

Chapter 10

Improving the HIV Landscape among Young Students in South Africa

Reflections on the First Things First Best Practice Model

Ramneek Ahluwalia

Introduction

South Africa has made great efforts in prevention and treatment to curb the human immunodeficiency virus (HIV) epidemic,[1] but HIV prevalence still remains high.[2] Young people between the ages of 15 and 24 years comprise the group with the highest rate of new infections and account for half of new HIV infections annually.[3] In 2012, the Joint United Nations Programme on HIV and AIDs (UNAIDS) reported that youth were at the centre of preventing the progression of the HIV and acquired immune deficiency syndrome (AIDS) pandemics.[4] It is in this light that the Higher Education and Training in HIV and AIDS (HEAIDS) has adopted the First Things First Programme – that emphasises that the first priority of every young South African is to look after their health, which includes knowing their HIV status and knowledge of other micro-epidemics among our population.

The vision of the programme is to build a culture among the youth to test for HIV, and to screen and educate themselves in order to detect the virus early.[5] In this way, the programme contributes to the reduction of infections[6] and to the UNAIDS target of 90-90-90.[7] The goal is to help end the AIDS epidemic by ensuring that 90 per cent of all people living with HIV know their HIV status; and that 90 per cent of those who are diagnosed with HIV receive antiretroviral therapy in accordance with South Africa's National Strategic Plan (NSP) on HIV and AIDS, TB and STIs 2012–2016.[8] This will in turn enable 90 per cent of people living with HIV to attain viral suppression, and brings us closer to achieving the goal of zero new HIV infections by 2020. Service provision is in the form of a free comprehensive health and screening service with appropriate treatment, care and support provided to all 429 campuses country-wide.

Encouraged by political commitment, the HIV programmes have become strategic by focusing on the coordination of resources and addressing those that form part of the key population. This has led to an increase in the number of people on antiretroviral treatment (ART), resulting in a decrease in AIDS mortality and an increase in life expectancy.[9] Within the higher education sector, Dr Blade Nzimande, the Minister of Higher Education and Training, launched the Higher Education HIV, TB and STIs Policy and Strategic Framework in December 2012, which was aligned with the National Development Plan, the Millennium Development Goals, the NSP for HIV and AIDs, TB and STIs (2012-2016) and the White Paper for Post-School Education and Training. The aim of this document, compiled by HEAIDS, is to support a national programme to develop the HIV, Tuberculosis (TB) and sexually transmitted infections (STI), and general Health and Wellness mitigation initiatives, across all South African Public Higher Education Institutions (HEIs) and Technical and Vocational Education and Training (TVET) Colleges. With this vision, the Deputy Minister of the DHET, Mr Mduduzi Manana, with support from the Minister of Health, Dr Aaron Matsoaledi, and all the Vice Chancellors and College Principals, launched the HEAIDS First Things First Programme across the nation.

Worldwide, HEAIDS is a unique programme, with all universities, colleges and training centres (including post-school knowledge worker sectors) combining together as one force to change the landscape of the epidemic. This makes First Things First a powerful youth voice, with over two million youth identifying with the programme and therefore endorsing the programme as their own as it addresses their needs.

Nevertheless, effective HIV prevention efforts for young people aged between the ages of 15 and 24 have been dogged with challenges. Such challenges include access to quality, youth-friendly HIV and sexual and reproductive education, and sexual and reproductive health (SRH) services.[10] Young South African students face multiple risks including HIV, STI and TB infection, chronic conditions driven by poor lifestyles, cancers, unwanted pregnancies and substance abuse habits.[11] The epidemic in South Africa is generalised. However, there are specific groups that have HIV prevalence above the national average.[12] Of greater concern is that, amongst the adolescent population, the estimated HIV prevalence among females between the ages of 15 and 19 was eight times that of their male counterparts.[13] According to the UNAIDS figures published in 2013, South Africa was one of the countries where risky sexual behaviours, such as an increase in the number of sexual partners.[14] An additional driver of the epidemic was gender-based violence, which increases the risk of HIV infection. UNAIDS reported that, in South Africa, women – especially those aged between 15 and 26 years – who had experienced gender-based or intimate partner violence were 50 per cent more likely to contract HIV than women who had not experienced violence were noted.[15]

The HIV Prevalence and Related Factors, Higher Education Sector Study, South Africa (2008-2009), found that 65 per cent of students were sexually active and reported using condoms in their most recent sexual encounter, and 54 per cent of students had never had an HIV test.[16] The study found that fear of stigma and rejection, and a lack of understanding about living positively with HIV, contributed to the low levels of HIV testing. Students feared the outcome of testing and delayed testing.[17]

Almost a third of young women in South Africa fall pregnant before 20 years of age, and the majority of these pregnancies are unplanned, indicating that there is limited access to family planning.[18] Research has shown that a third of all students attending a tertiary institution had been pregnant, or had made someone else pregnant.[19] Only a quarter of these pregnancies were planned and approximately a fifth of students had decided to end the pregnancy prematurely.[20]

According to the Global status report on alcohol and health (2011)[21] the hazardous and harmful use of alcohol is a major global contributing factor to death, disease and injury: to the drinker through health impacts, such as alcohol dependence, liver cirrhosis, cancers and injuries; and to others through the dangerous actions of intoxicated people, such as drinking and driving and violence, or through the impact of drinking on foetal and child development.[22] Research has indicated that alcohol and substance use is associated indirectly with HIV transmission via risky sexual behaviour, such as sex with multiple partners and unprotected sex.[23]

Evidence also shows that six per cent of all male students and staff report having had sexual relations with men. This is a vulnerable group with HIV prevalence being reported at 4.1 per cent, which is more than twice the HIV prevalence of heterosexual men (1.7 per cent). Additional evidence suggests high levels of risk-taking behaviour among men who have sex with men. Unprotected anal and oral sex with partners whose HIV status was unknown was reported by a number of respondents when speaking about their own experiences. Further, there is a low rate of use of condoms in oral and anal sex, avoidance of being tested for HIV and not wanting to know the status of the sexual partner.[24]

STIs are also high amongst young people[25] and strengthening the capacity to provide for the prevention, treatment, care and support for students is included in the HEAIDS mandate in the form of STI education, screening and referral. HEAIDS research undertaken at TVETs indicate that although students had a high knowledge around STI transmission, this knowledge did not translate in how students conducted their personal lives to reduce their risk of acquiring STIs as indicated by their negative views toward condom use. Additional research evidence from the same study indicated that 29 per cent reported lifetime testing for TB and 21 per cent of those participants who had ever been tested for TB were found to have the disease. Knowledge that TB can be cured was significantly lower (86%) among students that participated in the research[26]. It is in lieu of this research evidence that the First Things First model includes screening of TB and related ailments.

Evidence reported by the World Health Organization (WHO) shows that male circumcision reduces the risk of heterosexually acquired HIV infection in men by approximately 60 per cent and is an important HIV prevention intervention.[27] Research has found that one-third of male students were uncircumcised and that there was a positive attitude toward medical male circumcision.[28] HEAIDS recognised that bringing medical male circumcision services to young men attending institutions in the post-schooling sector was imperative and served to contribute to the HIV prevention efforts. What is being done in South Africa about this, for youth and/or in Health Education?

HEAIDS' primary focus is to address the various risks that young South African students face, which include HIV, STI and TB infection, lifestyle issues, cancers, unwanted pregnancies and substance abuse habits. It aims to support the higher education sector in delivering competent, healthy graduates into society, thereby protecting one of South Africa's most precious investments.

The purpose of addressing the post-schooling sector is to ensure that the teaching and learning, research and innovation, and community engagement is adequately accomplished, as HIV is one of the core programmes at HEAIDS. The HEAIDS First Things First Programme supports institutions in responding to the pandemic through their core functions of teaching and learning; research and innovation; and community engagement. This programme protects the investment made by South Africa in the post-school sector and is a USAID funded programme.

The programme is rooted in a concept of the responsibility of HEIs to address the HIV pandemic on a human rights basis on at least five fronts:

- Developing HIV prevention programmes for students and staff, and facilities for the treatment, care and support of students and staff living with HIV;
- Providing a comprehensive HIV and AIDS programme in the workplace that caters to the needs of staff;
- Educating and equipping students to make a contribution to the national HIV and AIDS response in their future career fields;
- Conducting research that will strengthen society's ability to resist and overcome the pandemic; and

- Providing HIV and AIDS services to related communities through outreach projects and practical training programmes.

The aim of this chapter is to describe the HEAIDS First Things First Model and provide an overarching portrayal of the achievements attained.

First Things First Model

The HEAIDS First Things First Programme established itself as a flagship programme which saw much success from 2011 to 2015 in terms of the up-take by the number of young people who accessed the services provided. This programme was implemented in both the TVET college sector and at HEIs. Designed to address the prevention focus of the NSP on HIV, STIs and TB during the period of 2012-2016,[29] the programme also encourages health-seeking behaviour and quality life enhancement in young people through regular testing, screening of major aliments including HIV, TB and STIs, cancers and cardio-vascular risk factors, among others. The HEAIDS First Things First Model is driven by compartmental projects that include the Men's Health and Empowerment Programme; Women's Health and Empowerment Programme; Alcohol and Drug Abuse Prevention Programme; LGBTI Programme; HIV and AIDS Curriculum Development and Research; and the Future Beats Youth Development and HIV Prevention through Campus Radio and Social Media.

Figure 1 First Things First Model

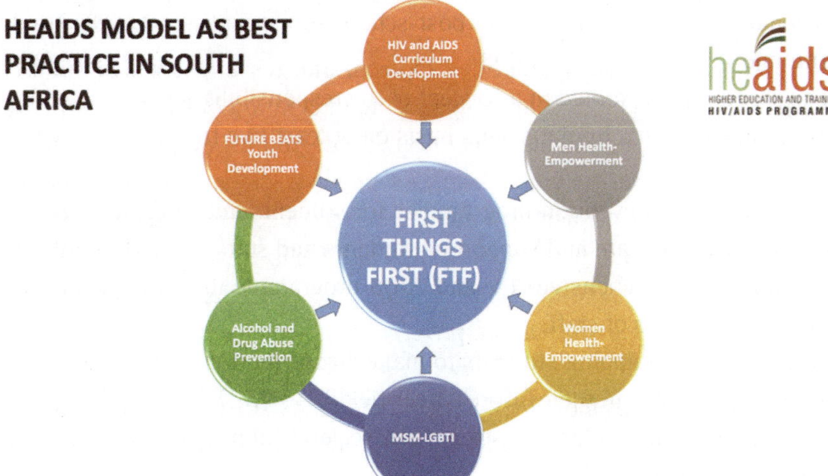

Source: HEAIDS best practice model developed by HEAIDS[30]

The model's premise is that the first priority of every South African is to take care of oneself, that is, improving outcomes in: youth development; graduate competencies; return on investment; comprehensive health and wellness methodology; informed competent next generation labour; and increasing post-school education enrolment. The interwoven links of each component of the model provides direct services of basic health – including HIV testing, screening of other dual epidemics of TB, STIs and other components – with proper treatment, care and support to students at no cost to the institution or the student. The Men's Health and Empowerment Programme targets male students and staff, and addresses the risks associated with issues around men, male violence free zones, medical male circumcision, multiple and concurrent partners, STIs, cancer and wellness screening amongst men, and sexual behaviour practices.

The Women Health and Empowerment Programme is an advocacy, mass media and mobilisation programme that addresses gender inequalities by encouraging young women to draw on their inner strength, power, and self-confidence to know themselves and what they stand for – and so to guide their life decisions. Issues of rape, sexual violence, dual protection, breast and cervical cancers and STI screening, contraception and transactional sex, are other components that are also dealt with in the programme.

The Alcohol and Drug Abuse Prevention Programme involves risk screening and brief interventions including service provision via internet, health clinics, trained professionals and lay counsellors. The LGBTI Programme aims to promote an enabling environment and access to appropriate health and wellness care and prevention services and destigmatisation for men who have sex with men (MSM) and lesbian, gay, bisexual, transgender/transsexual and intersexed (LGBTI) persons.

The HIV and AIDS curriculum development and research aims to build the capacity of the academic staff and support the integration of HIV and AIDS and related issues into the curricula. The Future Beats Youth Development and HIV prevention programme, delivered through Campus Radio and Social Media, is a pilot project aimed at establishing a radio and social media programme at university radio stations in South Africa with the objective to create greater awareness concerning HIV and AIDS and related issues, for example, human rights and social justice, social transformation, poverty, youth unemployment, alcohol and drug abuse.

All of these programmes jointly encourage all youth from every sphere to participate in First Things First and test early, thus supporting the broader vision to build a culture where youth screen and become educated in order to detect the virus early. In this way, the programme contributes to the reduction of infections

and to the UNAIDS target of 90-90-90. The goal is to help end the AIDS epidemic by ensuring that 90 per cent of all people living with HIV know their HIV status, and to ensure that those who are diagnosed with HIV receive antiretroviral therapy. This will in turn enable 90 per cent of people living with HIV to attain viral suppression. This occurs when the viral load of an HIV positive person becomes undetectable and decreases the chances of spreading the virus.
The First Things First Programme facilitates access to the following services:

- HIV education, screening and referral;
- TB education, screening and referral;
- STI education, screening and referral;
- Hypertension/diabetes/cardiovascular risk factors education, screening and referrals;
- Cancer education, screening and referral;
- Family planning education and awareness and/or provision of contraceptives;
- Condom promotion programme; and
- Medical Male circumcision.

The HEAIDS First Things First Programme initially targeted HIV testing of first year students. Over time the programme has broadened to include general health testing, screening and proper referral for treatment care and support; and is inclusive of all students.

First Things First: Our Story

The noticeable success of the model has been attributed to the increase of HIV testing, which was provided under the auspices of the wellness programme through which young South Africans become concerned about their health, with a resultant destigmatisation of HIV and the creation of demand for basic health services. Service provision is in the form of health screening activations, or camps, that take place at various campuses. In 2011, HEAIDS provided various services through 23 camps, the number of which has increased annually since inception. In 2015 alone, the programme supported service provision through 708 medical camps at campuses throughout the country. The creation of increased demand for these services to students has produced several success stories, including those of the testing of 300 000 students and staff for HIV, TB and STIs, and general health and wellness screenings.

HEAIDS crossed another landmark by testing 174 026 students and staff for HIV, TB and STI and general health and wellness screenings (including cardio-vascular risk factors, several cancers, and other deliverables like circumcision and contraception) within the first six months of 2015. Due to the launch of the national HIV Counselling and Testing (HCT) campaign, more South Africans have become aware of their HIV status. In 2012, 44 per cent of adults were tested for HIV and were aware of their status.[31] HEAIDS has contributed to the increase in the national HCT. Each year, the targets for testing young people increases by 25 per cent of the number that were tested the previous year.

Table 1 HIV Testing conducted at medical camps at higher education institutes

Year	2011	2012	2013	2014	2015
Number of HIV Tests	22 093	66 497	41 373	97 174	174 026

Source: HEAIDS Annual Review Report, 2014 & 2015[32]

The First Things First Programme accounts for 96 per cent of the total HIV testing, TB and STIs, and other general health and wellness interventions, conducted through campus activations across all universities and colleges. The Higher Education Campus Service remains challenged with a total staff component of only approximately 100 health care workers (in 72 university campuses, but with almost all TVET and other university campuses without such basic health services), attending to close to two million students, which can only account for four per cent of the HIV, TB and STI and other general health and wellness interventions (4 000 HIV tests). This makes the First Things First Programme a viable intervention as it has introduced a wellness programme that has contributed to providing the required support – in so far as human resources and capacity allows – to reach the UNAIDS 90-90-90 goal of which the first 90 per cent relates to the testing for the disease.

The First Things First Programme provided 25 per cent of first time testers, an opportunity to know their status and receive the appropriate care and support required thereafter. As much as repeat testing is critical – especially for young students, particularly those with multiple partnerships and those that engage in transactional sex and abuse drugs and alcohol – the prime goal remains to test the first timers, while raising knowledge levels regarding the pandemic. Repeat testing is encouraged every six months through campus activations which are held each quarter, which is in line with the national guidelines. No student is encouraged to test twice in the same campaign.

The First Things First Programme has managed to show that incorporating HIV as a chronic disease within the wellness component of providing services helps to remove the stigma attached to the disease, and results in increased HIV testing among young people.

Conclusion

First Things First has grown from 23 campus activations completed in 2011, to 708 campus activations in 2015 alone, spread across every district and province within South Africa. This remarkable success is attributed to the desire, need and requests from students and staff of universities and colleges. A campus activation is an activation which is undertaken over a three to five day forum on a particular campus, where all stakeholders (Department of Health, non governmental organisations, United States Agency For International Development [USAID], Deutsche Gesellschaft für Internationale Zusammenarbeit [GIZ], and Global Fund) supporting the First Things First initiative provide direct service delivery of basic services of HIV, TB and STI prevention, treatment care and support – including other general health and wellness services – on the doorstep of each student and staff member in the post-school sector. The number of First Things First campus activations between 2011 and 2015 is shown in Table 2.

Table 2 Campus activations between 2011 and 2015

Year	2011	2012	2013	2014	2015
Campus Activation	23	91	123	358	708

Source: HEAIDS Annual Review Report, 2014 & 2015[33]

More than a thousand activations were planned for 2016, based on the requests from HEIs and TVETs. HEAIDs, through its First Things First Programme, aims to transform the landscape of the epidemic in the country by educating and providing vital services to young people in an environment that not only sustains hope, but also sustains the dream of a better future. In its future endeavours to sustain and replicate efforts that build knowledge and shift attitudes and behaviour to impact positively on the lives of our youth, HEAIDS aims to:

- bring the First Things First Programme to youth in schools;
- include adolescents aged between the ages of 12 and 15;

- provide stakeholders with information to include the model as a best practice in their prevention efforts;
- reinforce communication to promote behaviour change; and
- effectively coordinate the provision of services by stakeholders to campuses.

HEAIDS aims to strengthen the First Things First Programme at all institutions in South Africa and to develop a sustainability plan to ensure that all young people attending the post-school sector for the first time have access to services, in this way ensuring that young people take care of their health and transition into South Africa's work force after their higher education.

Notes and References

1 Shisana, O., Rehle, T., Simbayi, L.C., Zuma, K. et al., 2014. South African national HIV prevalence, incidence and behaviour survey, 2012. Cape Town: HSRC Press. Also see Mbele, N., et al., 2014. HIV and AIDS related knowledge, attitudes and behaviours of students and staff at South Africa's technical and vocational education and training colleges. HRSC. Pretoria.

2 Ibid.

3 UNAIDS, 2013. AIDS by the numbers. Available at http://heaids.org.za/site/assets/files/1267/unaids_2013.pdf [Accessed 12 November 2015].

4 Ibid.

5 HEAIDS, 2010. HIV/AIDS prevention good practice: Strategies for public higher education institutions (HEIs) in South Africa. Pretoria: Higher Education South Africa.

6 UNAIDS, 2010. Getting to zero, *2011-2015 strategy, Joint United Nations Programme on HIV/AIDS (UNAIDS)*. Available at http://www.unaids.org/sites/default/files/sub_landing/files/JC2034_UNAIDS_Strategy_en.pdf [Accessed November 2015].

7 UNAIDS, 2014. 90–90–90. An ambitious treatment target to help end the AIDS epidemic. Available at http://www.unaids.org/en/resources/documents/2014/90-90-90 [Accessed 12 November 2015].

8 South African National AIDs Council, 2012. The National Strategic Plan on HIV and AIDS, TB and STIs, 2012–2016. Available at http://www.sahivsoc.org/upload/documents/National_Strategic_Plan_2012.pdf [Accessed November 2015].

9 World Health Organization, 2009. Adult mortality and antiretroviral treatment rollout in rural KwaZulu-Natal, South Africa. *Bulletin of the World Health Organization 2009*, 87, pp.754-762.

10 UNAIDS, 2014. Global AIDS response progress reporting 2014. Available at http://www.avert.org/professionals/hiv-social-issues/key-affected-populations/women#sthash.NmEajnf7.dpuf [Accessed 12 November 2015].

11 Bekker, L.G., Johnson, L., Wallace, M. and Hosek, S., 2015. Building our youth for the future. *Journal of International AIDS Society*, Volume 18, Supplement 1, February 2015.

12 Kelly, K., Mkhwanazi, N., Nkhwashu, N., Rapiti, R. and Mashale, R., 2012. HIV prevention situation analysis in KwaZulu-Natal, Mpumalanga and Gauteng provinces, South Africa. USAID Sexual HIV Prevention Programme in South Africa (SHIPP). Available at http://futuresgroup.com/files/publications/Synthesis_of_Research_on_Prevention_of_Sexual_Transmission_of_HIV_in_SA.pdf [Accessed 12 November 2015].

13 Shisana et al., 2014.

14 UNAIDS, 2013.

15 Jewkes, R., Dunkle, K., Nduna, M. and Shai, N., 2010. Intimate partner violence, relationship power inequity, and incidence of HIV infection in young women in South Africa: a cohort study. *The Lancet*, 376(9734), pp.41-48.

16 Mbelle, N., Setswe, G., Sifunda, S., Mabaso, M. and Maduna, V., 2014. HIV and AIDS related knowledge, attitudes and behaviours of students and staff at South Africa's technical and vocational education and training colleges, 2014. Pretoria. Human Sciences Research Council.

17 Ibid.

18 Mchunu, G., Peltzer, K., Tutshana, B. and Seutlwadi, L., 2012. Adolescent pregnancy and associated factors in South African youth. *African Health Sciences*, 12(4), pp.426-434.

19 Reddy, S. P., James, S., Sewpaul, R., Koopman, F. et al., 2010. The South African youth risk behaviour survey 2008. Cape Town: South African Medical Research Council.

20 Mbelle et al., 2014.

21 World Health Organization, 2011. Global status report on alcohol and health. Available at http://www.who.int/substance_abuse/publications/global_alcohol_report/msbgsruprofiles.pdf. [Accessed 12 November 2015].

22 World Health Organization, 2011. Global status report on drugs and alcohol. Available at http://www.who.int/substance_abuse/publications/global_alcohol_report/msbgsruprofiles.pdf [Accessed 12 November 2015].

23 Kagee, A., Donenberg, G., Davids, A., Vermaak, R. et al., 2014. Identifying community risk factors for HIV among South African adolescents with mental health problems: A qualitative study of parental perceptions. *Journal of Child & Adolescent Mental Health*, 26(3), pp.165-176.

24 HEAIDS, 2010. HIV prevalence and related factors – Higher Education sector study, South Africa, 2008–2009. Pretoria: Higher Education South Africa. Available at http://www.dhet.gov.za/Reports%20Doc%20Library/HEAIDS%20Sero%20Prevalence%20Sector%20Report.pdf [Accessed 12 November 2015].

25 Ibid.

26 Mbele, N., et al., 2014. HIV and AIDS related knowledge, attitudes and behaviours of students and staff at South Africa's technical and vocational education and training colleges. HRSC. Pretoria

27 World Health Organization, 2015. HIV/AIDS. Available at http://www.who.int/mediacentre/factsheets/fs360/en/ [Accessed 12 November 2015].

28 Mbelle et al., 2014.

29 Department of Health (South Africa), 2011. National Strategic Plan on HIV, STI and TB 2012-2016. Available at http://www.hst.org.za/publications/national-strategic-plan-hiv-stis-and-tb-2012-2016 [Accessed 12 November 2015].

30 HEAIDS, 2012. First Things First. Available at http://heaids.org.za/programmes/first-things-first/. [Accessed 12 November 2015].

31 Human Sciences Research Council, 2012. Awareness of own HIV status, South Africa 2012. Available at http://www.hsrc.ac.za/en/media-briefs/hiv-aids-stis-and-tb/plenary-session-3-20-june-2013-hiv-aids-in-south-africa-at-last-the-glass-is-half-full [Accessed 12 November 2015].

32 HEAIDS, 2015. HEAIDS Annual Review Report 2015. Available at http://heaids.org.za/site/assets/files/1248/final_heaids_annual_review_report_2015.pdf [Accessed 16 April 2016]

33 Ibid.

Chapter 11

From Data to Insights to Action

Using Data to Fight HIV and AIDS in South Africa

Bernard Katz, John Sargent, Ernest Darkoh, Imeraan Cassiem, and Candice Mitchell

Introduction

The battle to eradicate the human immunodeficiency virus (HIV) and acquired immune deficiency syndrome (AIDS) has been fought on many fronts: in clinics, in communities, in the media and in laboratories. At the same time it has also been fought using data in the world of registers, indicators, graphs, systems, analyses and statistics. The struggle to understand the epidemic, and gain insights into the performance of health facilities and staff, has been a long and difficult one. When Nkosi Johnson delivered his powerful address at the 13th International Aids Conference in Durban, in July 2000, very few operational indicators related to HIV were regularly captured by the National Department of Health (NDoH) in South Africa. Since then, a National Primary Healthcare Clinic (PHC) register system has been developed, improved and standardised. The District Health Information System (DHIS) is at the forefront of HIV operational data collection and monitoring of programme performance. Over 100 different data elements, related to HIV and the connection to tuberculosis (TB), are captured daily in thousands of health facilities nationwide. Furthermore, a sophisticated antiretroviral treatment (ART) management system is in place with over ten years' worth of information of patients who are on antiretrovirals (ARVs). Cutting edge business intelligence and analytics systems are used to analyse, visualise and provide insights into the performance of the health system and the needs of communities.

So how did all of this happen in such a short space of time? In this chapter there is an exploration of the development of the data and analytics environment which supports the fight against HIV, as well as revealing the latest technologies through which new insights are developed daily.

Background to HIV and AIDS Monitoring & Evaluation in South Africa

After the identification of the first cases of AIDS in South Africa, the epidemic progressed through four stages:[1]

- Initial concentrated phase – 1982 to 1987;
- Commencement of the generalised HIV epidemic phase – 1988 to 1994;
- Rapid spread of HIV phase – 1995 to 2000; and
- AIDS mortality phase – post-2000.

Due to the need to strengthen the management of HIV, AIDS and sexually transmitted infections (STIs) in South Africa, the South African Cabinet approved the Comprehensive HIV and AIDS Care, Management and Treatment Operational Plan for South Africa in November 2003.[2] Following a number of discussions and activities, a foundation was laid to support the implementation of the plan which included a Monitoring and Evaluation (M&E) Framework.[3] Through consultation with various stakeholders, the M&E process was based on a logical framework which clearly outlined the information required, with the aim of assessing the causal relationships between the elements of the programme.

Based on this M&E framework, the National Antiretroviral Treatment Guidelines and other related documents, a training manual was developed to capacitate all relevant staff. Capacity building of staff on M&E was required at all levels to ensure proper patient care management and evaluation of the implementation of the plan. To set the scene for the M&E training, the manual provided an overview of HIV and AIDS, the National Antiretroviral Treatment Guidelines, and the Comprehensive Operational Plan for South Africa.

Three indicator sets, representing the 'must know' information, had to be collected and reported by all provinces.

- Indicator Set 1: The M&E framework outlined a primary set of 12 indicators which needed to be reported within six months of commencement of an ART programme.
- Indicator Set 2: Monthly reporting forms were developed for facilities to collect the primary set of 12 indicators and 5 other additional indicators.
- Indicator Set 3: The Division of Revenue Act (DORA) required quarterly reporting on a set of indicators. The first DORA reports were due to be submitted by the 20 July 2005. The primary purpose of the DORA reports was to guide the NDoH in the appropriate allocation of resources to provinces and facilities.

Introduction of District Level Data Collection Systems

The DHIS was implemented in South Africa between 1996 and 1997. This was almost a decade before the first HIV and AIDS Operational Plan for South Africa was introduced in 2003.[4] The DHIS was implemented as the routine data collection system that would allow tracking of public health service delivery performance. It contributes to generating essential data that is then used for health service planning, monitoring and reporting. It is open source software and was adopted as the nationally approved system for the capturing, processing and reporting of routine health data.

The first national minimum data set for PHCs was adopted in 1999,[5] but an essential list of HIV and AIDS programme indicators was only included only in 2006 and 2007 with the roll out of the first agreed National Indicator Data Set (NIDS). The NIDS are reviewed and updated every two years.

Since implementation, the DHIS became the backbone of ensuring the availability of routine data that could be used for health service planning and management, budgeting, and monitoring and reporting, for all levels of the South African health care system. Over the years the DHIS has grown and improved with respect to the amount of data captured, the number of regular users and the relevance of the data.

In 2011, the DHIS contained routine data that represented around 1.4 billion patient encounters. During the periods from 2001 until 2009, the number of data items collected and captured as routine data records in the system increased from 2.5 million to 10.6 million, which was a 400 per cent increase. In addition, the number of DHIS users involved in the capturing or processing of this data increased significantly. In 2001, the number of users was 465, with the number rising to 1 180 in 2009 –an increase of around 250 per cent. Increases in the Data Capturer group accounted for most of the growth in users. The number of highly skilled information officers and managers involved with data processing has, however, remained modest.

Along with the growth in the use of DHIS, there has also been significant progress with regard to the timely capture of the data. In 2003, the average time lapse between the end of a reporting month and the capture of the data into the DHIS was 27 days. In 2010, this gap had been reduced to around 14 days, allowing for much quicker access to the most recent data. Furthermore, over the years there have been critical developments in the DHIS, such as the change from being raw data driven to becoming indicator driven. The use of indicators has a critical role to play in terms of highlighting problems and identifying trends. Furthermore, it contributes to being able to set priorities as well as assisting in policy formulation. Indicators are crucial in assisting with simplifying complex arrays of information.[6] Most of the indicators and related targets currently on DHIS come from priority health programmes of the public health sector.

There have been challenges to implementation and usage of the DHIS. Over the years, the increased demand for routine information revealed weaknesses in the system. One of the key challenges of the DHIS was the limited alignment with the goals and objectives of the health sector, the key indicators of success, and the information system. Furthermore, there was a lack of adequate governance and standardisation of the DHIS. This became evident through the ad-hoc and uncoordinated implementation of new indicator and data sets, as well as the lack of rationalisation of indicators. Added to this was the lack of effective data collection tools to adequately report on the achievement of health sector goals and objectives.[7]

The weaknesses in the DHIS software, and the use of this, contributed to compromised data quality, which in turn led to a lack of confidence in health data.[8] The lack of sufficient and dedicated human resources at health facility level also impacted on the poor quality of data, and this remains a huge challenge in the public health sector. In response to the difficulties experienced, the South African Government developed an official regulatory framework, the District Health Management Information Systems (DHMIS) Policy. To address this critical issue, the NDoH should invest in, and ensure funding for, adequate human resources at facility, sub-district and district levels.

Impact of a Decentralised HIV/AIDS Programme on Data Collection and Reporting

South Africa moved from a doctor-based, hospital centred ART service to decentralised nurse initiated and managed ART (NIMART) during 2010 and 2011.[9] The decentralisation of ART initiation to professional nurses contributed to increased uptake in ART and reduced workload at referral facilities, which meant that the latter could concentrate on complicated cases. From May 2011, the number of patients initiated on ART through NIMART was also captured on the DHIS.[10]

The success of the decentralisation of ART initiation was accompanied by its own challenges, especially with regard to data, since it meant that HIV and AIDS related operational data had to be collected from many more facilities throughout South Africa. Large registers and tally sheets were implemented to collect the programme performance data, which was then captured by DHIS data capturers. This led to significant data quality issues as accountability for data completeness and quality now lay with every facility manager in the country. Furthermore, NDoH staff at PHC and Health District levels gained little value from the data collection activities as a significant volume of data, which was reported up from District to Provincial level, was never reported back down to District level in a usable or actionable format.[11]

Another challenge experienced was the proliferation of in-facility registers. In a study commissioned by the NDoH in 2011 to assess health facility data collection tools, a minimum of 54 registers were identified.[12] The report revealed that data collection from that many registers was time consuming for data collectors and impacted on data quality. Furthermore, the effort and time required for nurses to complete so many registers reduced the time they could have spent with patients. Practically, the number of large registers created space issues, especially in smaller clinics and mobile facilities. Findings from an Auditor-General's audit listed discrepancies between values extracted from registers and values reported on monthly input forms, as one of the contributors to the DoH receiving a qualified audit for 2011/2012.[13]

The implementation of so many registers and other forms of data collection tools at facility level could be attributed to the absence of stringent controls over the demand for programme management information.[14] A key recommendation from the study was to reduce the number of registers to six as of 1 April 2013. The six registers to be implemented were:[15]

- PHC daily tick sheet + reception daily headcount register;
- TIER.Net 2;
- TB register ;
- Theatre register (for PHC facilities performing medical male circumcision (MMC) and termination of pregnancies (TOPs));
- Delivery register; and
- Midnight census for PHC facilities with inpatient facilities (e.g. observation beds, delivery beds).

After an initial pilot project, the scale-up project involved the implementation of the rationalised set of six registers across the nine provinces in South Africa in all PHC facilities. This was due for completion by March 2015, but implementation only commenced during the latter part of 2015, and only in some provinces.[16]

Availability of Cohort Level Data

TIER.Net was developed in response to the inability of the treatment sites in South Africa to cope with the monitoring of large cohorts of patients using only a paper based system. The manual calculation of ART monthly data was proving to be inaccurate and time consuming, with at least a full week required to generate a manual ART cohort report for a low volume treatment site. This added enormous human resource capacity pressures on to the treatment sites. Furthermore, the sites did not have the necessary infrastructure and resources to implement a full electronic medical record (EMR) system. Due to these challenges and constraints, the need was identified for a data collection system that would alleviate the burden. In December 2010 the National Health Council (NHC) adopted the three-TIER strategy and in March 2011 the NDoH released the ART monitoring strategy to standardise ART data collection and reporting across all public health facilities in South Africa.

The three-TIER strategy includes:[17]

- *Paper Register (Tier 1):* Tier 1 is the standardised paper clinical records and folder per patient at the treatment sites. Patients are entered into the register page, according to their ART start date. There is one row per patient and there are six monthly summary columns that allow for the cohort outcome data to be easily tallied. The aggregated monthly and quarterly cohort reports are then extracted from the paper register and sent via fax to the next higher health level.
- *TIER.Net (Tier 2):* Tier 2 is the standardised paper clinical records and folder per patient at the treatment site, but patient information, per visit, is entered electronically into the standalone TIER.Net system. The nationally required aggregated monthly and quarterly cohort reports are built into the system and can be sent from the facility to the next health level either electronically or in hardcopy. Non-aggregated patient level data from the site can be transferred to the next level of the health care system through either the internet or via a memory stick.
- *Electronic Medical Record Software (Tier 3):* Tier 3 is the standardised paper clinical records and folder per patient at the treatment site, but patient information is entered into a full electronic, online medical record software. A central network team as well as a central computer help desk and roving IT support are essential for the successful implementation of this system. The nationally required aggregated monthly and quarterly cohort reports are built into the system and can be accessed centrally.

This three-tier approach allows the NDoH to strategically implement one of the three tiers in each of their ART facilities. The decision of which tier to implement is based on several factors, including the size of the clinic and the resources and infrastructure available in the region.[18] It is, however, important to note that if a country wishes to digitise a national health programme, a two-tier solution is less expensive, can be rolled out more rapidly, and requires less routine support and training.

The implementation of TIER.Net in South Africa involved taking each of the selected facilities through a six-phase process. These phases were developed by BroadReach Healthcare, with funding from USAID through the PEPFAR programme, and were accepted by the NDoH. Phase 0 involves the preparation for TIER.Net, which includes filing, orientation, and process flow. In Phase 1, installation and training takes place. Phase 2 is the process of back capturing, whereby the facility enters the data from the paper registers into TIER.Net. Phase 3 includes back capturing with live capturing, and data cleaning is performed. Phase 4 occurs when the back capturing is complete and only live capturing occurs. Phase 5 consists of the data being signed off by the NDoH at the end of the data cleaning process. The last phase, Phase 6, occurs when the data signoff is complete and the site has gone live. At this point the site is able to produce monthly and quarterly reports at the click of a button and the staff at the site can manage ART patients effectively.

The latest available NDoH TIER.Net implementation summary, as at December 2015, showed that: 86 per cent of all sites were on TIER.Net phase 6, with 9 per cent eligible for TIER.Net rollout and implementation (i.e. on phases 0 – 5), 10 per cent not implementing TIER.Net (including eligible and ineligible), 6 per cent implementing but not eligible, 2 per cent implementing non-standard systems (not TIER.Net); and 0 per cent sites implementing TIER 3.

The TIER.Net system was built to efficiently and effectively capture the minimum data elements and resulting indicators (based on the WHO paper registers) required to monitor HIV and ART services. Monthly and quarterly reports are generated by a 'push of the button'. In addition to these reports, at site level TIER.Net supports the capturing of patients visit details, the tracking of patients through defaulter reports and 'unsuppressed' viral load reports. All of these features enable managers, at all levels of the health system, to effectively manage the ART programme – through effective treatment monitoring, defaulter tracing, treatment adherence monitoring and tracking, viral load completion and suppression rates – in line with the UNAIDS 90-90-90 strategy.

TIER.Net also caters for the capturing of HIV positive patients not yet on ART through the HIV Counselling and Testing (HCT) and Pre-ART modules. These modules have not been well implemented, as the primary focus was on ensuring that all ART patient capturing was up to date. At the time of writing, the TIER.Net TB module was being piloted in some areas of the country. This will ensure that the NDoH has one system for capturing and tracking HIV and TB patients. An integrated information technology (IT) system will allow for testing of evidence based interventions and improved patient management and services. To do this, however, requires extensive human resources to manage the system, but the NDoH has a chronic shortage of data capturing positions in its organogram. The NDoH needs to invest in, and ensure funding for, adequate human resources at facility, sub-district and district level, and cater for routine training and capacity building around data analysis and use. Finally, it is critical to ensure strengthened linkages with Community Health Workers (CHWs) in order to support the tracing of patients, reduce defaulters, and lost to follow up patients.

Through facility assessments, it appeared that TIER.Net data and reports were not being utilised effectively, with data presented in the monthly and quarterly reports mostly being used for reporting rather than to inform and influence decision making on programmatic, facility management, and patient purposes levels. In addition, weak clinical recording in the patient stationary was noted, which has the effect of compromising data quality. The assessments showed that data capturers were accurately capturing the available data from the clinical stationary, but it was the quality, as well as the completeness, of the information recorded on the clinical stationary that was weak. It was also found that problems, in the form of under-reporting, were experienced with patient folder management. A further problem experienced was that Central Chronic Medicine Dispensing and Distribution (CCMDD) patients were not being captured properly in TIER.Net and, therefore, these patients were being classified as unconfirmed 'loss to follow-up' (LTF).[19]

Harnessing the True Power of Data

The growth in the number of data systems and the increase in the amount of available data has created opportunities to better understand the HIV epidemic through the use of analytics. Analytics is the analysis of data, by the use of mathematics, statistics, and computer software.[20] It involves the discovery and communication of meaningful patterns in the data. Data visualisation is often used to communicate the insights generated by analytics.[21] The specific purpose of analytics may vary depending on the specific application. In general terms, however, all analytics are aimed at generating deeper insights from data, which leads to action.

Levels of Analytics

Not all analytics provide the same level of insights. The higher up the analytics ladder one goes, the deeper the insights generated. The analytics levels in Figure 1 illustrate that as you move up the analytics ladder, the types of questions you are able to answer become increasingly complex.

Figure 1 Levels of analytics

Levels of Analytics		Questions Answered
Optimisation	8	How do we do things better?
Predictive Modelling	7	What will happen next?
Forecasting	6	What if these trends continue?
Statistical Analysis	5	Why is this happening?
Alerts	4	What actions are needed?
Query - Drilldown	3	Where exactly is the problem?
Ad hoc Reports	2	How many? How often? Where?
Standard Reports	1	What happened? When?

Source: Business Analytics[22]

The varying levels of data analytics should be viewed as a progression from basic data analysis to advanced data analysis.[23] The basic level is referred to as descriptive analytics. This form of analytics describes or summarises raw data to make it interpretable. Descriptive analytics describes the past and answers the question, 'what has happened?'[24, 25] A simple example of descriptive analytics is the aggregation of data elements from facility level to provincial level, the calculation of an indicator using the data elements, and the comparison of the provincial performance, in that indicator, to a predefined provincial target.

A more advanced level of data analysis is that of predictive analytics. This form of analytics is concerned with understanding the future and has its origins in the ability to predict what might happen. Predictive analytics allows for actionable insights based on calculating probabilities from the data on hand.

Calculations include examining historical data sets to identify patterns, and once patterns have been established, statistical models and algorithms are applied in order to capture relationships between various data sets.[26, 27]

A good example of predictive analytics is presented in Figure 2. The analytics view represents the past, actual performance (Apr 2014 – Mar 2015, dark blue bars) and the future, predicted performance (Apr 2015 – Mar 2016, light blue bars) of LTF in the five sub-districts in a South African health district.[28] (Data is not actual data but only for demonstration purposes).

Figure 2 Analytic view of predictive model (Data is not actual data but only for demonstration purposes)

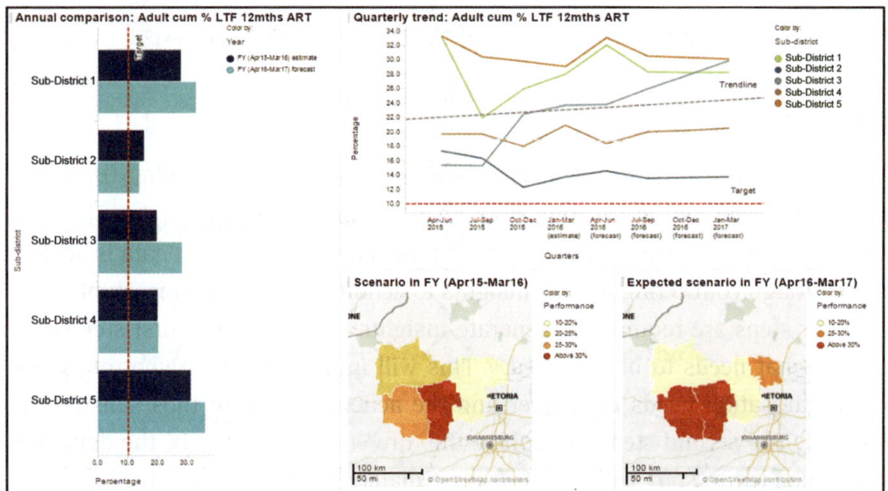

Source: BroadReach Analytics [29]

This analytics view draws on data from most facilities in the health district. Sophisticated statistical analysis is then applied to build the predictive model, and data visualisation tools are used to represent the complex analysis in a simple and clear way. The user is also able to gain insights into why the model is predicting an increase or decrease in the indicator. These insights can then be used to plan interventions in order to prevent a decline in the indicator performance before it actually occurs.

In the case of the sub-district 1, the increase in percentage LTF at 12 months is predicted mainly because there has been a significant increase in early LTF at three months. This now requires concerted effort by the District Health Management Team to address the LTF before the prediction becomes a reality.

A still more advanced level of data analysis is that of prescriptive analytics. This form of analytics is used to advise on a number of possible outcomes and provide guidance towards a solution. Prescriptive analytics attempts to quantify the effect of future decisions, with the final aim of being able to provide advice on possible end results before the decisions are actually made. The use of prescriptive analytics allows for the prediction of multiple futures and, in turn, assists organisations to assess a number of possible outcomes based upon their considered actions. Prescriptive analytics uses a combination of techniques and tools, such as business rules, algorithms, machine learning and computational modelling procedures.[30, 31] For example, prescriptive analytics may be used to address the question of test and treat. The analysis can provide various results related to costs and treatment outcomes based on several different scenarios, one of which may be test and treat.

Data to Insights to Actions

There is often a disconnection between collecting data and making that data actionable. The key is learning how to use data to transform it into insights which can then be used to inform actions. Generating value from data is achievable through connecting data to insights to action, in a fast and repeatable way.

Four steps are required to generate insights from data. The first step is deciding what needs to be achieved.[32] This will involve deciding what questions the organisation needs to answer and the actions you want those answers to support. The second step is to source the 'raw' materials, that is, the data. It is recommended to start with the best immediately available data.[33] It is useful to acquire further datasets over time, but it is recommended to start with the data you have. Data from many relevant sources needs to be aggregated and linked. Often, true insights can only be gained by looking at the whole issue and this requires several different data sources.

The third step is to produce insights quickly. Action that is productive is mainly created through a speedy response.[34] The ability to focus on quick decisions and execution will help to bypass long discussions and will lead to insights that can be used on the front line. It should, however, be a structured output based on repeatable analytical models and automation.[35] The fourth step is to deliver the goods and act.[36] The data needs to be presented in a clear, concise and visually appealing way, often with the assistance of data visualisation tools and techniques. The aim of these simple data visualisations is to present the hidden insights which the analysis has uncovered. The key conditions, which may support the leap from insights to action, include: a level of trust in the reliability and validity of the data and the analysis, a level of understanding of the data visualisations, the forums in which to deliver the insights, and the level of accountability and performance management which exists in the organisation.

The following story illustrates the power of data leading to insights leading to actions. The story begins in a rural district in South Africa mid-2015 with a young man who worked for the district's Department of Health. One of his jobs was to collect data for 25 key indicators related to HIV, TB and various other social development areas. This data was collected from several different government departments in the district. On a quarterly basis, he sent this data to the Office of the Premier where the data from all the districts in the province were analysed. These 25 indicators for each district were presented at a provincial quarterly review session to all stakeholders involved in fighting HIV and TB.

When the analysts first received the data, they developed an index algorithm to determine the ranking of the district by performance across all 25 indicators. In this particular quarter, the young man's district had the poorest performance of all the districts in the province. The analysts created a heat map of the ranking, with the strong performing districts in various shades of green and the poorest performing district in a bright red. When they unpacked the results, they realised the young man's district was not performing poorly because of poor service delivery, but rather because of poor reporting of data. This clearly did not reflect well on the young man, whose job it was to send in the data on a quarterly basis. Approximately two weeks before the quarterly review session, the analysts sent the young man the heat map along with a list of outstanding data. Slowly, but surely, over the two weeks leading up to the quarterly review, the data from the young man's district started to trickle in. This new data was quality checked using an automated data quality assurance module, and once the data was approved it was included in the index. On the day of the review the poorest performing district had shifted to a mid-table rank.

On the morning of the review, while the analysts were setting up the system to show the heat map and other data visualisations to the large, important audience, the young man from the rural district in South Africa approached one of them and asked to see the heat map. He wanted to make sure that his efforts to get the data in before the review was worth it, and that his district was no longer the poorest performer.

While this is a fairly simple example, it illustrates how the aggregation of data from many different sources (several different government departments in different districts), the analysis of data (development of an index algorithm) and the visualisation of the data (presentation in a heat map) led to insights about the reasons for the poor performance of the young man's district (the reason was poor data reporting) and led to action by the young man to address these reasons. Furthermore, presenting a simple visualisation of the analysis in an open forum, such as the quarterly review, ensured – not just the young man – that all who are responsible for the HIV and TB programmes were held accountable for their performance.

Summary of the Data Journey

In conclusion, the journey from the initial collection of basic HIV and AIDS data elements to the use of advanced analytics techniques and systems, has faced many challenges and enjoyed as many successes. Our understanding of South Africa's health system's response to HIV and AIDS has largely been driven by the ongoing improvement to data collection, data processing, advanced analytics and data visualisation. Along the way there were several key milestones and several important lessons (Figure 3).

Figure 3 Key milestones and important lessons

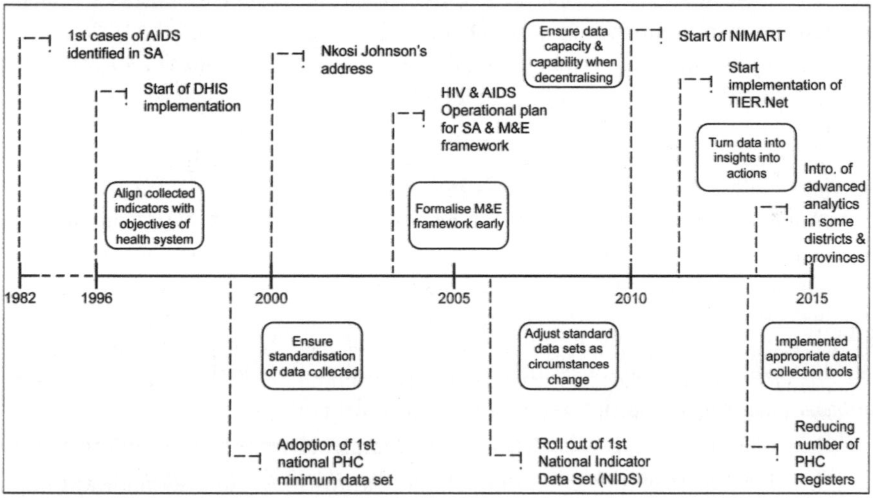

Source: Department of Health, Health System Trust[37, 38, 39, 40, 41]

Today we have access to a significant amount of HIV and AIDS related operational data. The sheer volume of data and the types of reporting currently used, is as much a threat to a manager's ability to use data for planning, operational monitoring and driving accountability as was the lack of data less than 10 years ago. Only through better analytics and better visualisation techniques can we ensure the right information is accessible to the right person at the right time. Only then can better insights be gained and the right actions taken.

Notes and References

1 Karim, S.S.A., Churchyard, G.J., Karim, Q.A. and Lawn, S.D., 2009. HIV infection and tuberculosis in South Africa: an urgent need to escalate the public health response. Lancet, 3749693, pp. 921–933. Available at http://www.thelancet.com/journals/lancet/article/PIIS0140-6736(09)60916-8/fulltext [Accessed 1 December 2015].

2 Department of Health (South Africa), 2003. *Operational plan for comprehensive HIV and AIDS care, management and treatment for South Africa*. Available at http://www.gov.za/af/documents/operational-plan-comprehensive-hiv-and-aids-care-management-and-treatment-south-africa [Accessed 1 December 2015].

3 Department of Health (South Africa), 2004. *Monitoring and evaluation framework for the comprehensive HIV and AIDS care, management and treatment programme for South Africa*. Available at http://www.hst.org.za/sites/default/files/monitorevaluation.pdf [Accessed 1 December 2015].

4 Rohde, J. and Shaw, V., 2003 *South Africa's district health information system*: Case study. Available at http://healthmarketinnovations.org/sites/default/files/South%20Africa%E2%80%99s%20District%20Health%20Information%20System.pdf [Accessed 20 November 2015].

5 Ibid.

6 World Health Organisation. 2002. *Health in sustainable development Planning*: The Role of Indicators. Available at http://www.who.int/mediacentre/events/Indicators-Frontpages.pdf [Accessed 16 June 2016].

7 Department of Health (South Africa), 2011. *District health management information system DHMIS policy*. Available at http://policyresearch.limpopo.gov.za/bitstream/handle/123456789/903/District%20Health%20management%20Information%20System%20Policy.pdf?sequence=1 [Accessed 16 November 2015].

8 Ibid.

9 Elaine, N., Davies, C.G., Homfray, M. and Venables, E.C., 2013. Nurse and manager perceptions of nurse initiated and managed antiretroviral therapy NIMART implementation in South Africa: A qualitative study. *BMJ* (Online) 311. Available at http://bmjopen.bmj.com/content/3/11/e003840.full [Accessed 16 November 2015].

10 Nyasulu, J.C.Y., Muchiri, E., Mazwi, S. and Ratshefola, M., 2013. NIMART rollout to primary healthcare facilities increases access to antiretroviral in Johannesburg: An interrupted time series analysis. SAMJ, (Online) 10314. Available at http://www.samj.org.za/index.php/samj/article/view/6380/4995 [Accessed 16 November 2015].

11 Department of Health (South Africa), 2010. *Clinical guidelines for the management of HIV & AIDS in adults and adolescents*. Available at http://www.sahivsoc.org/upload/documents/Clinical_Guidelines_for_the_Management_of_HIV_AIDS_in_Adults_Adolescents_2010.pdf [Accessed 16 November 2015].

12 Health Systems Trust, 2015. *Rationalisation of Registers RoRs*. Available at http://www.hst.org.za/projects/rationalisation-registers [Accessed 2 December 2015].

13 Ibid.

14 Ibid.

15 Ibid.

16 Ibid.

17 Hennessey, C. (ed.), 2011. *TIER.net user guide* 2011. Available at https://tieredstrategy.files.wordpress.com/2011/10/tier_net_user-guide-v138.pdf [Accessed 27 November 2015].

18 Ibid.

19 Clinton Health Access Initiative. 2015. *ART M&E Facility Assessments Report*. Available at http://www.clintonhealthaccess.org/category/key-chai-documents/ [Accessed 05 December 2016].

20 Analytics, (n.d.). Dictionary.com Unabridged. Random House, Inc. Available at http://dictionary.reference.com/browse/analytics. [Accessed 27 November 2015].

21 Menken, I., 2013. *Social analytics complete certification kit*, Google Books. Available at https://books.google.co.za/books/about/Social_Analytics_Complete_Certification.html?id=kto5mgEACAAJ&redir_esc=y[Accessed 27 November 2015].

22 Business Analytics, 2012. *Developing a BI roadmap*. Available at http://reports4u.co.uk/developing-a-bi-roadmap/ [Accessed 27 November 2015].

23 Optimisation Group, 2015. *The different levels of analytics*. Available at http://blog.optimizationgroup.com/the-different-levels-of-analytics [Accessed 27 November 2015].

24 Ibid.

25 Halo, 2014. *Descriptive, predictive, and prescriptive analytics explained*. Available at https://halobi.com/2014/10/descriptive-predictive-and-prescriptive-analytics-explained/ [Accessed 27 November 2015].

26 Optimisation Group, n.d. *The different levels of analytics*. Available at http://blog.optimizationgroup.com/the-different-levels-of-analytics [Accessed 27 November 2015].

27 Halo, 2014. *Descriptive, predictive, and prescriptive analytics explained*. Available at https://halobi.com/2014/10/descriptive-predictive-and-prescriptive-analytics-explained/ [Accessed 27 November 2015].

28 BroadReach Analytics. 2015. *Analytics Platform*. Available at https://broadreachanalytics.ch/. [Accessed 27 November 2015].

29 Ibid.

30 Optimisation Group 2015.

31 Halo, 2014. *Descriptive, predictive, and prescriptive analytics explained*. Available at https://halobi.com/2014/10/descriptive-predictive-and-prescriptive-analytics-explained/ [Accessed 27 November 2015].

32 Meyer, C., McGuire, T., Masri, M. and Shaikh, A.W., 2013. Four steps to turn big data into action. *Forbes*. Available at http://www.forbes.com/sites/mckinsey/2013/10/22/four-steps-to-turn-big-data-into-action/ [Accessed 28 November 2015].

33 Ibid.

34 Ibid.

35 Ibid.

36 Ibid.

37 Department of Health (South Africa), 2003. *Operational plan for comprehensive HIV and AIDS care, management and treatment for South Africa*. Available at http://www.gov.za/af/documents/operational-plan-comprehensive-hiv-and-aids-care-management-and-treatment-south-africa [Accessed 1 December 2015].

38 Rohde, J. and Shaw, V., 2003 *South Africa's district health information system*: Case study. Available at http://healthmarketinnovations.org/sites/default/files/South%20Africa%E2%80%99s%20District%20Health%20Information%20System.pdf [Accessed 20 November 2015].

39 Ibid.

40 Health Systems Trust, 2015. *Rationalisation of Registers RoRs*. Available at http://www.hst.org.za/projects/rationalisation-registers [Accessed 2 December 2015].

41 Hennessey, C. (ed.), 2011. *TIER.net user guide* 2011. Available at https://tieredstrategy.files.wordpress.com/2011/10/tier_net_user-guide-v138.pdf [Accessed 27 November 2015].

Chapter 12

Bitter Themes and Sugar Daddies

Intergenerational Sex and the Spread of HIV in South Africa

Amy Maphagela

Introduction

The acquired immune deficiency syndrome (AIDS) is ranked as the second cause of death after tuberculosis in South Africa.[1] From a biological point of view, women are more likely to be predisposed to human immunodeficiency virus (HIV) infection than men.[2] Turmen[3] states that the transmission of HIV from male to female is between two and four times more effective than from female to male. Furthermore, female adolescents are particularly prone to HIV infection through sexual intercourse as their immature genital tracts are more likely to sustain tears during sexual activity, resulting in a greater risk of HIV transmission.[4] This chapter argues that younger women in intergenerational, or 'sugar daddy', relationships, are more susceptible to HIV and AIDS. Intergenerational sex is an issue of much concern in the field of HIV and AIDS, as statistics indicate that young women between the ages of 15 and 24, who are most likely to be in relationships with older men, are about three to four times more likely to have been infected with HIV than their male counterparts.[5] Health organisations have created campaigns that caution young women to keep their distance from sugar daddies because they pose a major health concern in the area of HIV and AIDS. This concern has often been branded as 'the sugar daddy syndrome', 'the sugar daddy trap' or 'the sugar daddy phenomenon', in which female adolescents are often most at risk.[6]

The findings in this chapter that support the notion that older men do, indeed, pose a higher health risk to young females when it comes to the spread of HIV and AIDS are based on the study that was conducted in order to investigate how selected black men perceive messaging on intergenerational sexual relationships in selected advertisements from the ZAZI Campaign (the name of the campaign is derived from the Nguni word, *zazi*, which means to know yourself), as well as their general thoughts regarding certain matters pertaining to their sexual relationships with younger females. One of the aims of the ZAZI campaign is to encourage women to know themselves in such ways that they are able to stand up for themselves and take ownership of their choices regarding HIV-related risks. Specific focus has been placed on the views of selected older men who, in these cases, are referred to as sugar daddies, particularly concerning messages of the campaign which warn younger women to avoid intergenerational sexual relationships on the grounds that these present a high risk of HIV infection.

The reason for the higher incidence of infection experienced by these young girls compared to boys of the same age, results from the high incidence of consensual, unsafe, intergenerational sexual relationships that they engage in with older men (five or more years older).[7] Older men have a higher chance of being infected with HIV than teenage boys because they have been sexually active for longer. Therefore, intergenerational relationships are more likely to put young girls at risk of contracting HIV and AIDS, and a large age gap between partners makes it more difficult for younger women to negotiate safer sex.[8] One study estimated that for every year's increase in the age difference between partners, the chances of unprotected sex rose by 28 per cent. Young women are also more likely to become infected with HIV because of sociocultural factors, such as poverty, lack of education, high cultural value of childbearing, low social standing, lack of empowerment, lack of knowledge about the disease, misperception of low vulnerability, and fatalism.[9]

According to Higher Education South Africa (HESA), 'intergenerational sex' refers to sex acts that occur between partners who are usually 20 to 25 years of age whose counterparts are usually 10 years older.[10] In a study conducted by the Human Sciences Research Council (HSRC), it was found that in 2012 about one fifth of all respondents aged 15 to 19 years (19.9%) were involved in age-disparate relationships with a sexual partner who was more than five years older than them.[11] Johns Hopkins Health and Education South Africa,[12] found that amongst those with a partner 10 years or older, only 36 per cent used a condom during their last sexual encounter, and that women of this age group (i.e. 15 to 19 years) were also most likely to engage in sexual activities more frequently than their male counterparts.[13]

Communication to discourage intergenerational sexual relationships has been identified as a key national goal.[14] Interventions that seek to reduce intergenerational relationships have been said to decrease the HIV prevalence among young women, as well as delaying their sexual debut, but, on the other hand, there might be a rise in the HIV prevalence amongst young men.[15] The ZAZI campaign is one that aims to address intergenerational relationships.

Bronwyn Pearce, Deputy Country Director at the USAID/JHU HIV Communication Programme, stated that the main aim of the ZAZI Campaign was to create a movement that encouraged women to stand up and break the silence that allowed the pain in their lives to thrive, as well as for women to define their own values and their own path in life[16] in such a way that they avoid relationships with older men. The stereotypical sugar daddy is an adult male who exchanges money or gifts for sexual favours from a much younger woman. Sugar daddy relationships are associated with both age and economic asymmetries which are believed to limit young women's powers to negotiate safer sexual behaviour.[17]

The decision to focus on men was informed by the common sense ecological observation that, in a media ecology, communication for change that is aimed at women also reaches men – with possible unintended consequences. Other studies relating to sugar daddies that did not seek the views of men regarding communication on intergenerational relationships, include studies conducted by Kriel, Tshibangu-Kalala and Gbalajobi.[18] Specifically, the following questions will be addressed:

1. What do selected men in intergenerational relationships say about intergenerational sexual relationships?
2. What are the views of selected men in intergenerational relationships about the selected campaign messaging on intergenerational sexual relationships as expressed in advertisements of the ZAZI Campaign?
3. What do selected men in intergenerational relationships know about HIV-related risks associated with being in these sexual relationships?

Conceptual Overview

There are a number of reasons why women are more susceptible and prone to acquiring HIV and AIDS than men. Turmen[19] states that, because young women usually marry considerably older men, a power discrepancy forms with regards to experience, authority and control over sexual activity, and resources. Furthermore, these marriages could also mean that girls are unable to further their studies or take employment. Added to this, older men are usually more sexually experienced than their young brides, who are thus at higher risk of acquiring HIV and other sexually transmitted infections (STIs). Turmen[20] and Gupta[21] also mention that in many societies a culture of silence surrounds sex, which also dictates that 'good' women are expected to be unaware about sexual issues and compliant in sexual interactions. This makes it difficult for women to become informed about risk reduction and, even when informed, may struggle to be proactive in negotiating safer sex.[22] Furthermore, Snow[23] states that females are often labelled as 'sluts' or 'loose women' in their attempts to seek information regarding safe sex, or when trying to negotiate safer sexual practices, which may ultimately lead to them being disciplined through violence as such behaviour is frequently condoned by prevailing social norms.

According to Green,[24] Turmen,[25] Luke[26] and Gupta,[27] women's economic dependency increases their exposure to HIV. Research has shown that women are more likely to exchange sex for money or favours when they are economically vulnerable, less likely to succeed in negotiating protection, and even less likely to leave a relationship that they perceive to be risky.[28]

There are a number of cultures that allow and embrace the practice of intergenerational relationships, which means that sugar daddies have become common and widely accepted in Africa, although research has clearly indicated that older men are one of the major contributors to the spread of HIV and AIDS.[29] Young women in rural areas are more directly subjected to traditions that guide relations between generations and between men and women.[30] This means that young women are expected to be dutiful, obedient and respectful towards older men. Leclerc-Madlala[31] goes on to say that these cultural prescriptions have been found to play an important role in undermining young urban women's ability to resist older men's advances and to negotiate safe sex. On the other hand, it has been noted that in urban areas, young women engage in sexual intergenerational relationships as a means of material gain, and for the sake of entertainment and having fun. Some young women have parents who provide them with the necessities of life, which means that engaging in sugar daddy relationships is not about meeting subsistence needs, but about acquiring a 'top-up' that helps boost their status in the eyes of their peers.[32]

Trend analysis of data obtained by the HSRC during surveys conducted in 2005, 2008 and 2012 shows that there was a steady increase in intergenerational sexual relationships among females aged between 15 and 19 years, while this phenomenon barely featured among their male counterparts over the same period.[33] According to Leclerc-Madlala,[34] young women see many benefits when it comes to having a sugar daddy, one of which is marriage, because older men are perceived as being more serious and better potential marriage partners than younger men. Furthermore, across the African continent, young women are encouraged to seek older men as partners and husbands; with families frequently cautioning them about relationships with men their own age as this is believed to increase the risk of marital instability.[35]

Adult men pursue young girls partly because of the pleasure of having a trophy girlfriend, but also because they believe that these girls are uninfected. This has particular significance, as a third of these men may already carry the virus, and most of them believe that sleeping with a virgin will rid them of the infection.[36] According to Smith,[37] married men prefer the pretty, urban, educated young women, seeing them as the most desirable girlfriends who will not only provide sex, but also the opportunity of having more stylish, exciting, and modern sex than what they have with their wives. It has been argued that the main reason why these intergenerational sexual relationships occur is due to the fact that older men tend to be able to provide the younger women with material and other transactional benefits, resulting in what has become known as transactional sex.[38] A study conducted by HESA[39] states that the degree to which transactional sex is acknowledged and spoken about indicates that the general concept of exchanging sex for social and material gain is commonplace.

Men who are regarded as providers in a vast number of cultures, often trade material goods with their partners in exchange for sex. Qualitative data provides evidence that in intergenerational relationships, less direct forms of material transactions are pervasive and carry much greater social acceptance.[40] Older men are sources of social capital that young women may aspire to gain. According to Gauntlett,[41] social capital is the sum of resources, which can be actual or virtual, that accrues to an individual by virtue of possessing a durable network of more or less institutionalised relationships of mutual acquaintance and recognition. Stoebenau et al.,[42] Weckesser,[43] HESA[44] and Defo[45] state that transactional sex is usually associated with scarceness, the effect of Western consumerism, social and political conditions, variances in economic power between men and women and the failure of traditional African marriage customs involving bride wealth.

This suggests that social aspiration, recreation and other non-forced choices may lead young female students into high-risk transactional intergenerational sex. Intergenerational sexual relationships are considered a major behavioural risk factor for HIV infection among young women; hence the urgent need for targeted social and behavioural change communication interventions to raise awareness and reduce high-risk behaviours associated with such relationships. This entails communication aimed at changing widely held community norms that accept and promote these high-risk practices.

Literature on transactional sex, as Luke[46] claims, suggests that gifts are considered a symbol of the young woman's value and the older man's interest; therefore, most young women who do not receive money or gifts in return for engaging in sexual intercourse with a man are most likely to feel offended. This is supported by a study, conducted in Burkina Faso, which found that young women would feel demeaned and insulted if they received nothing in return after sleeping with men, as the exchange of material goods or money for sexual favours was considered unremarkable. The study also concluded that none of these young women associated their transactions with prostitution, which they regarded as being socially unacceptable.[47]

Transactional relationships, sex and prostitution can be regarded as existing on a continuum.[48] At one end of the spectrum, transactional sex bears many resemblances to the practice of prostitution, especially when money is exchanged for sex from one partner to another, or in relationships that are completely based on receiving a material reward for numerous sexual encounters. Thereafter, interpreting the opposite end of the continuum becomes somewhat more problematic in the light of literature which shows that, in many parts of Africa, sex given without material reward is perceived as being demeaning for women.[49]

AIDS educators should continue to investigate how African cultural practices intertwine with the way relationships that bear on HIV and AIDS are perceived and acted upon.[50] After all, traditional cultural practices reflect the values and beliefs held by members of a community, often for periods that span generations. The cultural norms of all social groupings include practices that can be harmful or, at least unhelpful.[51] Intergenerational relationships appear to be traditionally acceptable in African cultures, yet as HESA notes, intergenerational sex is a major vector of the HIV and AIDS epidemic.[52]

Methodology

After verification of the viability of an interview schedule that was established through the application of a pilot study, and informed by an earlier study by Gbalajobi,[53] for this study, ten in-depth interviews were conducted at the University of Johannesburg. These men were identified using the snowball sampling technique following initial contact with men who were introduced to the researcher by informants, who had identified them as people who were willing to discuss their involvement in intergenerational relationships. The ages of this group of participants ranged from 29 to 35 years of age. Findings were analysed for themes using a method of thematic analysis outlined by Boyatzis.[54]

Themes

Four themes were recurrent in my reading of the interview data. These themes are discussed below.

Theme 1: 'We are not sugar daddies'. In this theme, participants perceived intergenerational relationships as those that occurred between a mature female who was above the age of 18, and whose partner was 10 to 15 years older than her. Participants also clearly expressed that intergenerational relationships were acceptable in African cultures. Referring to them as sugar daddies would be incorrect, as that term was a Western concept that was introduced to African people fairly recently, and therefore did not apply to their cultures. It is well known that women tend to age faster than men, providing one of the reasons why these older men pursued younger women, who were also physically more attractive and enjoyed having a good time. Of greater importance, however, was that these older men were able to control the direction and nature of the relationship with their younger partners. This was because younger women did not challenge these men intellectually or otherwise, making it easier for the men to control them.

Theme 2: 'You can't be a sugar daddy and be broke'. Participants defined a sugar daddy as an older man, who was usually married and had a number of resources which he exchanged with his younger partner in order to receive sexual favours from her. Furthermore, participants also mentioned that sugar daddies use their vast resources in order to take advantage of younger women, because they knew that they had the ability to provide these needy or impoverished young women with financial assistance, in exchange for sexual favours.

Theme 3: 'Young women can't be controlled'. In criticising the ZAZI Campaign, participants saw it as containing more flaws than positive health communication strategies, in the sense that they acknowledged that it as a useful initiative, but warned that the actions of the younger women cannot be controlled. Participants pointed out that we live in a materialistic world which is mostly embraced by younger women. Campaigns warning them to stay away from older men could fall on deaf ears because, at the end of the day, these women were going to take whatever steps they deemed necessary to obtain the material goods they sought – even if it meant sleeping with an older, wealthier man. In addition, the campaign was criticised for being misleading as it did not state what the potential dangers of pursuing relationships with older men were, giving the impression that it was acceptable for younger women to engage in promiscuous relationships with age-equivalent males, as they were only cautioned to stay clear of relationships with older men.

Theme 4: 'There's no need to be faithful'. Concerning the health risks associated with intergenerational and sugar daddy relationships, participants suggested that older men do pose a higher health risk to younger women, because their resources and worldly knowledge afford them the ability to engage in multiple sexual relationships. These older men pose a health risk to younger women because they are sexually more active and experienced. This gives rise to the perception that younger women were not extremely sexually active, and therefore would not have any diseases, which meant that the older men could engage in reckless sexual practices with them. A few participants, on the other hand, claimed that the vast worldly experience of older men was precisely the reason why they did not pose a health risk to younger women. By this reasoning, it was through their experience of matters regarding the bedroom and sexual activities that they knew how to practice safer sex.

Discussion

I will now discuss the findings of the research by systematically addressing the research questions that were stated in the introduction, using data from the above identified themes. The purpose of this analysis is to identify whether or not the pre-existing literature relates to the above empirical findings. It will produce new theory by critically combining and interrelating the empirical findings with insights from the broad literature.

Selected men's views regarding intergenerational sex relationships

In response to the research question, 'What do selected men in intergenerational relationships say about intergenerational sexual relationships?' the majority of the interviewed participants acknowledged being in an intergenerational sexual relationship. This was not surprising since, as noted in the methodology section, participants were selected in such a way that they represent individuals in relationships in which the man was 10 to 15 years older than the woman. Participant Nine stated that:

> Scientifically it has been proven that women and men, ok let me just take it more further, let me say I am 70, right, and you are in your fifties, that is a nice match because what happens is, when I'm 75 and you're 73 you're no longer interested in sex anymore, so I would say it's from up there going downwards. So I'm like 30 and she's 20, nice match, nice match! For in case if our relationship lasts long, I'm safe with that.

What is interesting is that the male participants were keen to point out that in their relationships the younger women had reached a stage of maturity that made it unfair to accuse them of taking advantage of their partner's relative youth. In particular, and to illustrate this point, the men were keen to point out the fact that the women they were in relationships with were over the age of legal consent. According to Participant Six:

> It depends on the age group, remember if the age gap is too huge then it is problematic as such... It also depends on the stage of the young female, if she is below 18 then an age gap of more than 10 years is not healthy, but if she is above the age of 25 then an age gap of more than 10 years is good, it is healthy, and then if she is above 30 then an age gap of 15 is not an issue. I think it's a question of not taking advantage of an immature mind so to speak...

The definition which was offered at the start of this research suggests that intergenerational relationships are those in which one partner is young and the other is usually 10 years older (for women 20 to 25 years of age), or if the other partner is considerably older (usually five years older than teenage girls).[55] The views expressed above, however, appear to suggest that a rigid and inflexible definition such as this may not be a fair basis for beginning to think systematically about judgements of how relationships involve or do not involve older men who 'take advantage of younger women'. It may be more useful to consider a view of intergenerational relationships that takes more factors into account. One of those factors includes the distinction between intergenerational relationships and those where the older man is considered a sugar daddy. Participants stated that intergenerational relationships occur between men who are 10 to 15 years older than their partners and women who are mature enough to be in relationships, and that this was common in African cultures which meant that they could not be classified as sugar daddies. Participant One supported this argument by saying that:

> ...If the person is like 20 years older than you and the person is married, it also depends on how old you are, so for example, as a woman, if you are 30 and the guy is 50 or 40 that could be an intergenerational relationship I think, it depends on how you define it. If you are 30 and I am 40 you are old enough, I cannot be said to be a sugar daddy then...

It appears that intergenerational relationships are common and widely accepted in Africa, even though these types of relationships are said to be one of the major contributors to the spread of HIV and AIDS.[56] Participant Five agreed that intergenerational relationships were acceptable in African cultures, adding that labelling men in these types of relationships as sugar daddies was a foreign concept to Africans, since this term was introduced by Westerners to confuse or challenge pre-existing African cultural norms and beliefs. Participant Five made the following remark:

> I think that people are too Western these days so in our culture, if you look at our history as African people, we would even choose a wife before that person is even old enough to be a wife, so we would choose a child while they are still 6 years old or whatever, based on the family background and the values that that family has, so it is nothing taboo for us. It is just Western concepts that are being transferred and they are trying to confuse our people, we are not sugar daddies.

According to Van Dyk,[57] African cultural behaviours should be accepted and respected by Westerners, to whom these practices are unfamiliar, as they do not pose as a major threat to one's health. As it was previously stated, these adult men are keen on dating younger girls as they have the desire of being associated with attractive females within their social circles and, most importantly, these older men believe that young girls are uninfected, while a third of these men may already carry the virus, and most of them believe that sleeping with a virgin will rid them of the infection. According to Participant Eight:

> ...there are *sangomas* (witch doctors/traditional healers) that tell old people to go find young women to cure their HIV, so the sangoma will tell you to sleep with a younger woman so that you can get cured.

In addition to the reasons already mentioned, participants said that they preferred relationships with younger women because they were easier to control as they showed respect for the position of the man by not challenging him. Gender inequity and inequality have been identified as key factors in HIV infection.[58] Issues such as gender inequality and lack of economic independence and information, place girls at higher risk of HIV infection than younger boys and older men. Younger women who find themselves in intergenerational relationships that require them to be submissive are more at risk of contracting STIs and HIV because they are unable to negotiate safer sexual practices. The other reason why older men prefer being in relationships with younger women is due to the fact that men historically control decision making and have a higher status than women, which is a factor that facilitates the spread of HIV.

Janey[59] goes on to say that a worldview can be described as a general design for living and a pattern for interpreting reality. Gender role expectations have been recognised as playing an important role in shaping the worldview of men and women, which emphasises the need for gender awareness and sensitivity. Participant Two illustrated this point by stating the following:

> Well obviously it's because with younger girls it's easier in a sense to deceive them, because when I am older it means that I am more mature and all the stuff, but apart from that they can be easier to handle, for instance you might find that younger girls are not as complicated as old people, like the teenagers, they probably won't be talking about marriage and all that, all they want is just to have fun and that's what we're probably looking for as well. So hence we would probably go for a younger girl than people of your age, who will start talking about marriage, so younger girls are more nicer and more chilled, it's all about fun.

It is known that patriarchy involves both blatant and hidden manifestations of male supremacy, male privilege and the subordination of women; it is not reducible to either one of those.[60] Although it was not mentioned by the participants, their responses in the interviews gave the impression that the role of the younger women was to be submissive, regardless of the fact that they were living in a modern society. These men believed that they could not be challenged by a younger woman because she did not have much worldly experience.

Different cultures may have their own definitions of what it means to be a man, but a cross-cultural model identified three elements of the male role, which include: the protector, who represents the guardian of the family or the country; the provider, who brings in income and material goods; and lastly, the impregnator, who assists with matters of fertility, virility and the prowess of women.[61] Some of the participants expressed that in their culture, their role as a man meant being the provider for his partners, as it was a man's duty to do so.

Participant Six said the following:

> ...It is standard for a man, you have to spend on a woman, especially for us black people. So if you are not prepared to spend on your woman it's like weird for me, but I don't rent a relationship, so if you give a woman money in the way that you're renting a relationship, that is something else, but to surprise your woman and to buy her this or that then, yeah, I've done that.

It can also be said that masculinity is created and expressed both in men's relationships with women, as well as in their relationships with other men. In male dominated social settings such as social clubs, sports bars, sections of the marketplace, and particular bars and eateries, it is common for men to show off their girlfriends and to discuss them with other men. Therefore, male peer groups are one of the significant factors that motivate other men to engage in extramarital relationships.[62] Participant Four concurred with this statement when he said:

> It's actually nice to have a proper woman on your side, like not just a normal woman but a nice woman, a beautiful woman. Like if we can take a look, every man in this world they go for these proper women, the nice ones, the cute ones, the sexy ones, not the boring ones.

The findings from the interviews suggests that a common reason for the older men's preference for pursuing relationships with younger women was the reasoning that women 'age' faster than men. In other words, by dating younger women they ensure that they will still be physically attracted to the women as they age. These men also believe that the younger women they elected to be in relationships with had not engaged in sexual intercourse with many men, and also that these young women would be great to have around because they knew how to have fun. According to Smith,[63] married men preferred the pretty, urban, educated young women who were seen as the most desirable girlfriends, providing not only sex, but also the opportunity, or at least the fantasy, of more stylish, exciting, and modern sex than what they had with their wives. Participant One stated the following:

> ...it would possibly be that the person is more attractive, or is perceived as being more attractive than your wife. So the attractive thing would be how the person looks, and that would attract you to the relationship, but you can love her as long as the person is above 18 because we don't want to be molesting them.

For some men, it is attractive to be in relationships with younger women because in those relationships they feel respected and powerful. Some of this respect and power, as they admitted, flowed from the fact that sugar daddies had financial resources to throw into the relationship that younger women value. Participant Two concurred with these statements by defining sugar daddies in the following way:

> A sugar daddy... well obviously, you can't be a sugar daddy and broke so a sugar daddy has to be a guy that is older, way older but has money as well... Well we can say roughly more than ten to fifteen years or even maybe less than that, but a sugar daddy has to be old enough so that you can see that he is able to adopt that girl or something like that, and obviously that guy must have money. You must be financially well off, you must have resources because as the sugar daddy you must be able to take care of the younger girl that you are dating, so that's a sugar daddy.

Older men spoke of using their financial resources to take advantage of younger women in need – providing a material need or some other form – in order to receive sexual favours from her in return. Participant Ten claimed that:

> A sugar daddy is someone who takes advantage of what they can do for the other person in order to have a relationship with them... Let's say for instance there was some young lady that was poor and she was in need of money and these days there is so much technology and gadgets, that when you have friends that are rich or come from rich families, you feel pressure and the need to have an iPhone and a tablet and this and that, and that's why most young girls get into relationships with older men or people who can maintain them you see, so men take that advantage and say: you know what? I can do this for her because she wants money, I can get into her pants.

It can be argued that the reason why these intergenerational relationships occur is due to the fact that older men have access to social capital; therefore they are able to provide for younger girls. On the other hand, it has been noted that, in urban areas, the leading causes for young women engaging in sexual intergenerational relationships were for material gain, as entertainment, and for fun. Although some young women were not in dire need of financial assistance, they often engaged in such relationships as a means of acquiring a 'top up' that would increase their social status.[64]

Furthermore, some of the participants claimed to have given money or gifts to their partners after having sexual intercourse with them because they knew that she expected something in return for sleeping with them. They also felt as though they had taken something from her, and these perceptions may be the case for most sexual intergenerational relationships. This practice was well illustrated by Participant Two who stated that:

> Ya, no definitely that has to happen, in some sort of a: Yo, look, we had a good time, so obviously she would expect something in return, that's the whole purpose. I mean I have been on dates whereby I know my intentions which is to have fun, which we spoke about, and pleasure which could be sex or entertainment, in the sense that we should be having sexual intercourse but as well as the, my girl who is way younger than me, you do expect something from me and that could be money. So whenever we engage in 'bonking exercises' or activities (sexual intercourse), I'll definitely give you something, just to say: hey thanks, we had fun, it was pleasurable, it was nice, and we enjoyed it, but here you go.

Some participants believed that acts of transactional sex were associated with prostitution in that a man paid for a service rendered by the younger woman. Stoebenau et al.[65] describe this as transactional sex, and note that while it fell outside of formal prostitution or sex work, by the mid-1990s public health researchers regarded sex for gift exchange as an important determinant of HIV transmission, particularly in Africa. As Mark Hunter explained in an article entitled *The materiality of everyday sex*:

> Transactional sex has a number of similarities to prostitution, [but] transactional sex differs in important ways: participants are constructed as "girlfriends" and "boyfriends" ... and the exchange of gifts for sex is part of a broader set of obligations that might not involve a predetermined payment.

Participant Six agreed that giving his partner money after engaging in sexual intercourse with her equated to prostitution, saying:

> No, that's stupid and whoever does that is a stupid guy, you're treating your woman as if she is a prostitute, you never do that. Like if you wanted to buy a prostitute why don't you go and buy a prostitute. You don't treat your woman like a prostitute, like it's demeaning to give woman money after sexual intercourse...

As aforementioned, literature states that transactional relationships, sex and prostitution can be represented as a spectrum of practices. At one end, transactional sex bears many similarities to the practice of prostitution, especially when money is given to the other partner after a single act of sex, or in the case of a relationship that is entirely based on receipt of material reward for multiple sexual encounters. On the other hand, interpreting the spectrum becomes somewhat more difficult in the light of literature that shows that, in many parts of Africa, it is sex given without material reward that is perceived as demeaning for women.[66]

Selected men's views regarding messaging on intergenerational sexual relationships from the ZAZI Campaign

The following research question was posed: 'What are the views of selected men in intergenerational relationships about the selected campaign messaging on intergenerational sexual relationships in selected advertisements of the ZAZI Campaign?'

Participants agreed that the ZAZI Campaign was a useful initiative, but they went on to say that it was not possible to control the choices of another. In this instance, the young women might be warned about the dangers of pursuing older men, but whether they decide to follow the advice could not be determined. This is because the young generation is extremely materialistic and, therefore, they would do just about anything to get the things that they wanted, which usually meant involvement in transactional sexual intergenerational relationships. It has been noted that women's economic dependency increased their vulnerability to HIV. According to Green,[67] Turmen,[68] Luke[69] and Gupta,[70] research shows that the economic vulnerability of women made it more likely that they would exchange sex for money or favours, less likely that they would succeed in negotiating protection, and even less likely that they would leave a relationship that they perceived to be risky. A woman's lower status could leave her more exposed to infection, while men risk infection because of ideals of masculinity associated with risk-taking and sexual conquest. Participant Two made the following comment:

> Well, given the contemporary situation, it's really rare these days where young girls won't fall for these old guys, or sugar daddies, remember that we are living in this modern society where people are so materialistic and they are so attracted to material and wealth and finance and all that, because when we have money, power and status you are the big dog, so normally it is rare when you find that girls won't go for someone that is well established or financially well off. Yes it is true, I saw the video, but it's not really possible in most cases to avoid that, because young girls they want things and they would definitely go for sugar daddies, but morally it is not good because there are those days when you know that with these guys, what they normally do with these young girls, they aren't normally devoted

> to one girl or go out with that one girl, they probably do that with all their young girls of which it is more riskier, so they should stay away from it, but what are the chances that will happen?

According to African popular discourse, researchers and health care workers alike have sounded the alarm over those sugar daddies who say that their main goal is to find young women who they believe might not be infected with HIV. Health organisations have created campaigns that advise young women to stay away from older men because they pose a major health concern in the era of HIV and AIDS, with female adolescents often bearing the higher risk.[71] As a result, the Joint United Nations Programme on HIV/AIDS (UNAIDS) Global Coalition on Women and AIDS advocates the development of effective programmes to educate and empower young women regarding HIV prevention, as well as to increase their economic security.[72] The ZAZI Campaign was also criticised by Participant Six who mentioned that this campaign was misleading as it did not go on to specify what the potential dangers of dating older men were as it did not highlight key issues, such as HIV and AIDS, sexually transmitted diseases (STDs) and forced abortion, to mention a few. The following remarks were made by Participant Six:

> ...but then from the video (ZAZI Campaign) the video seems to be giving the impression that HIV and AIDS and standards are only prevalent and prominent in an intergenerational relationship, that is misleading... it gives the impression that it's prominent and dominant. It's programming the youngsters, it has got a negative impact which has not been well considered, it gives the impression that it is good for youngsters to get into multiple relationships with people of their age, and that they will only get HIV and AIDS and STDs from the older generation or from the sugar daddies. Maybe if they phrased it differently to show other painful encounters and experiences that may come out of intergenerational relationships, like being pregnant for someone who's as old as your father and knowing that your parents will not approve of that then you will be forced to do an abortion. So for me that is not practical right, and not misleading but it gives the real issue, or maybe being exploited because mentally and intellectually you're not there yet and this guy has been around so he can be problematic and controlling, and psychologically he can exploit you, but there are incidences whereby there will be the transfer of HIV and AIDS, but I feel like it kind of misses the point in a way and it gives the blanket statement that

it's cool for them to be promiscuous with men their age as long as it's not intergenerational.

Therefore there is an urgent need to identify the risk perception of young women in intergenerational relationships.[73] This can be achieved by older peers playing a role in encouraging, mentoring and supporting young women on how to successfully resist becoming involved in such relationships. In order to reduce the risk of young girls being infected with HIV, they have to be provided with information regarding the HIV prevalence disaggregated by gender and age groups. In Southern Africa, women are held responsible for sex-related issues, such as reproduction and contraception. Therefore, Dupas[74] states that in addressing intergenerational sex, it should be demanded of older men that they discontinue engaging in potentially exploitative relationships with younger women, and recognise that relationships with younger women constitute an abuse of power and status.

Selected men's views regarding HIV-risks in intergenerational sex relationships

The following research question was put to participants: 'What do selected men in intergenerational relationships know about HIV-related risks associated with being in intergenerational sexual relationships?' Certain participants agreed that younger women who were involved in intergenerational sexual relationships were more at risk of contracting sexually transmitted infections and diseases from their older partners. This is particularly due to the high incidence of consensual, unsafe intergenerational sexual relationships that the young women engage in with men who are five or more years older than them, with the results being a higher rate of infections than is seen in boys of the same age.[75] Older men have a higher chance of being infected with HIV than teenage boys because they have been sexually active for longer and this, therefore, means that young girls in intergenerational relationships are more likely to be at risk of contracting HIV and AIDS. The large age-gap between partners also makes it more difficult for younger women to negotiate safer sex. Studies estimated that for every year's increase in the age difference between partners, the chances of unprotected sex rose by 28 per cent.[76] The following statement was provided by Participant Four:

> Obviously, yes, since us we are older to them which means that we are exposed to many things in life, to many people we have interacted with, with people we have dated and to many things... we have different experiences

> like drugs, some of us have dated many women, some of us we do all these sort of things, not the good ones, so it's a risk for women to go for sugar daddies because sometimes we do mistakes while having pleasure.

The sources in the literature provided sociocultural factors such as scarcity, lack of education and empowerment as some of the reasons why younger women in intergenerational relationships were more likely to be infected with HIV.[77] Participant Seven thought it might be the case that young women were at higher risk due to the fact that the older men might not condomise as much as they should, and – perhaps most importantly – these older men not only had interacted with many different women, but there was a high possibility that they were pursuing sexual relationships with multiple partners. This is illustrated by the following:

> If you look at guys that are much closer to say maybe a first year, or a guy that is in first year, guys in their first years are not as sexually active as guys who are much older or someone that is working. Someone that is working might have a young girl and other girlfriends in other places, so in that sort of relationship where you have an older guy dating a younger girl is more or less dangerous because the older guy is more or less used to having a lot of sexual partners, so you will find that you are most likely to experience reckless sexual behaviour in a relationship where you are dating an older person...

Besides culture, it can be argued that the reason why these intergenerational sexual relationships occur is that older men tend to be in a position to provide younger girls with material and other transactional benefits, leading to what has become known as transactional sex.[78] Reflecting back on the link to HIV, transactional sex is often associated with multiple concurrent partnerships, which are more conducive to the spread of HIV than serial monogamous sexual relationships. One of the reasons why young women are at a high risk of being infected, and are infected with HIV, is that they enter into such relationships with much older, wealthier men as a means to survival.[79]

Conclusion

This chapter has argued that pursuing a sexual relationship with a significantly older partner is one of the major contributing factors to the spread of HIV and AIDS. Statistics indicate that young women between the ages of 15 and 24 are about three to four times more likely to be infected with HIV than their male counterparts. Older men have a higher chance of being infected with HIV than teenage boys because they have been sexually active for longer, and often engage in multiple concurrent relationships. The reason why younger women are more susceptible to HIV and AIDS stems from the fact that intergenerational and sugar daddy relationships are associated with both age and economic asymmetries which are believed to limit young women's powers to negotiate safer sexual behaviour.

Across the African continent, young women are encouraged to seek older men as partners and husbands, as their families believe that relationships with men their own age increases the risk of marital instability. The overall findings indicate that intergenerational relationships are still acceptable in African cultures and that the derogatory term, 'sugar daddies', challenges pre-existing beliefs. Sugar daddies are defined as older men who have access to social capital that they use to entice younger women, with the intention of forming sexual relationships with them. The study indicates that sugar daddies may pursue relationships with younger women on the grounds that these women are seen to be physically more attractive than older women. They are regarded as being sexually more active, more interested and capable of having a 'good time', and more importantly, they are thought to be unlikely to challenge their older male partners, as they have minimal worldly knowledge.

It is important to note that there is an urgent need to identify the risk perception of young women in intergenerational relationships. This can be achieved by older peers playing a role in encouraging, mentoring and supporting young women on how to successfully resist getting involved in such relationships. Campaigns, such as ZAZI, address issues relating to intergenerational relationships by implementing communication for social change, which is a dialogical process in which people from both public and private spheres define who they are, what they need, and how to get what they need, in order to improve their own lives.

This campaign, however, has been criticised for not stating the potential dangers of pursuing older men or detailing what the potential health risks may be in that particular advertisement. The other criticism was that although the campaign has good intentions, these young women cannot be stopped from pursing the relationships that they want to have, more especially since they have something to gain from dating an older man who could provide them with financial security. It was also found that older men do pose a higher health risk to younger women, for the following reasons: they have had many sexual encounters with various women in the past; some of them do not always practise safe sex; and last but not least, these older men have multiple sexual relationships with women, which drastically increases the chances of both parties contracting HIV, STIs or STDs.

Based on the findings of this research, it is recommended that the ZAZI Campaign provide more information on the dangers of pursuing relationships with older men, for example: What constitutes an intergenerational relationship? What health risks are involved when one is in a relationship with an older man? What are the driving forces that encourage and/or lead people into pursuing intergenerational relationships? It would also be recommended that a follow-up study be done on the female (sugar baby) responses to the questions that were answered by the male participants in this research, in order to create new theories and literature based on intergenerational relationships that focus on both the male and female perspectives of the given phenomenon.

HIV and AIDS awareness campaigns have made large investments in protecting and educating students in universities about the disease – as they are the ones who frequently engage in intergenerational relationships – by providing free condoms, educative materials on HIV and AIDS, counselling and free testing, because students are not prohibited from interacting with each other or older men, sexually or otherwise. It is therefore better to provide them with the means to protect themselves sexually, as opposed to being ignorant to the fact that they are partaking in risky forms of sexual relations.

Notes and References

1 Statistics South Africa, 2014. HIV prevalence. Available at http://beta2.statssa.gov.za/publications/P0302/P03022013.pdf [Accessed 04 April 2014].

2 Green, D., 2008. From poverty to power: how active citizens and effective states can change the world. United Kingdom: Oxfam International, p.232; Turmen, T., 2003. Gender and HIV/ AIDS, pp.411-412. Available at http://www.ijgo.org/article/S0020-7292%2803%2900202-9/fulltext [Accessed 18 March 2014].

3 Turmen, 2003, pp.411-412.

4 Ibid.

5 Hasler, T., 2013. HIV and AIDS communication strategies in Northern Uganda: Development workers opinions on what works, p.21. Available at http://krex.k-state.edu/dspace/handle/2097/15784 [Accessed 18 March 2014].

6 Luke, N., 2005. Confronting the 'sugar daddy' stereotype: Age and economic asymmetries and risky sexual behaviour in urban Kenya. *International Family Planning Perspectives*, 31 (1), p.6.

7 Centre for Strategic and International Studies, 2013. The future of the U.S.–South Africa HIV/AIDS partnership: Trip report of the CSIS Delegation to South Africa, January 2013, p.9. Available at http://www.Center for Strategic and International Studies.org/files/publication/130313_Morrison_SouthAfricaHIV_Web.pdf [Accessed 21 January

2014]; Nobelius, A., Kalina, B., Pool, R., Whitworth, J., Chesters, J. and Power, R., 2011. Sexual partner types and related sexual health risk among out-of-school adolescents in rural south-west Uganda. AIDS Care, 23 (2): 252-259; Dupas, P., 2005. Relative risks and the market for sex: Teenagers, sugar daddies and HIV in Kenya, p.2. Available at http://eml.berkeley.edu/~webfac/emiguel/e271_s07/dupas.pdf [Accessed 10 October 2014].

8 Leclerc-Madlala, S., 2008. Age-disparate and intergenerational sex in southern Africa: The dynamics of hyper vulnerability, p.5. Available at http://siteresources.worldbank.org/INTHIVAIDS/Resources/3757981103037153392/AgeDisIntergenAIDS2008.pdf [Accessed 02 April 2014]; HESA, 2010. HIV prevalence and related factors higher education sector study South Africa, p.82. Available at http://www.hesa.org.za/sites/hesa.org.za/files/2010_HEAIDS_HIV%20Prevalence%20and%20Related%20factors_0.pdf [Accessed 04 April 2014]; Snow, R., 2010. The social body: gender and the burden of disease. In Sen, G and Ostlin, P. (eds.), Gender equity in health: the shifting frontiers of evidence and action. New York: Routledge, p.20; Dupas 2005, p.2.

9 Leclerc-Madlala, 2008.; Fiscian, V.S., Obeng, E.K., and Goldstein, K., 2009. Adapting a multifaceted U.S. HIV prevention education program for girls in Ghana. *AIDS Education and Prevention*, 21 (1), pp.67-68.

10 HESA, 2010, p.120.

11 HSRC, 2014. South African national HIV prevalence, incidence and behaviour survey, 2012, p.31. Available at http://www.hsrc.ac.za/uploads/pageContent/4565/SABSSM%20IV%20LEO%20final.pdf [Accessed 04 April 2014]; Pettifor, A.E., Rees, H.V., Kleinschmidt, I., Steffenson, A.E., MacPhail, C., Hlongwa-Madikizela, L., Vermaak, K. and Padian, N.S., 2005. Young people's sexual health in South Africa: HIV prevalence and sexual behaviours from a nationally representative household survey, p.1531. Available at http://scholar.google.co.za/scholar?q=+Young+people%27s+sexual+health+in+South+Africa%3A+HIV+prevalence+and+sexual+behaviors+from+a+nationally+representative+household+surveyandbtnG=andhl=enandas_sdt=0%2C5 [Accessed 10 October 2014].

12 Johns Hopkins Health and Education South Africa. (2014). The third national HIV communication survey, 2012, p.50. Available at http://jhhesa.org/sites/default/files/hiv_survey.pdf [Accessed 04 April 2014].

13 Pettifor et al., 2005, p.1531.

14 HSRC, 2014, p.116.

15 Hallett, T.B., Gregson, S., Lewis, J.J.C., Lopman, B.A. and Garnett, G.P., 2007. Behaviour change in generalised HIV epidemics: Impact of reducing cross-generational sex and delaying age at sexual debut, pp.50-52. Available at http://sti.bmj.com/content/83/suppl_1/i50.full.pdf+html [Accessed 10 October 2014].

16 ZAZI, 2014. New campaign calls on South Africa's women and girls to 'zazi'. Available at http://www.ZAZI.org.za/news/new-campaign-calls-south-africa-s-women-and-girls-ZAZI.html [Accessed 13 January 2014].

17 Fox, A.M., Jackson, S.S., Hansen, N.B., Gasa, N., Crewe, M. and Sikkema, K.J., 2007. In their own voices: A qualitative study of women's risk for intimate partner violence and HIV in South Africa. *Violence Against Women*, 13 (6), p.597; Luke, 2005, p.6; Defo, B.K., 2004. Young people's relationships with sugar daddies and sugar mummies: What do we know and what do we need to know? *African Journal of*

Reproductive Health, 8 (2), p.15; Luke, N. 2003. Age and economic asymmetries in the sexual relationships of adolescent girls in Sub-Saharan Africa. Studies in Family Planning, 34 (2), p.67.

18 Kriel, E., 2011. Exploring sugar-daddy relationship of black female students of the University of Johannesburg, South Africa. Unpublished doctoral dissertation. Johannesburg: University of Johannesburg; Tshibangu-Kalala, F., 2010. Intergenerational sexual relationships and HIV-risk among female adolescent refugees: case studies from targeted programmes in Pretoria. Unpublished masters dissertation. South Africa: University of South Africa; Gbalajobi, A., 2010. Constructing sexual identities with sugar daddy relationships: A case study of sexuality constructs among students at the University of Witwatersrand. Published masters dissertation. Johannesburg: University of Witwatersrand.

19 Turmen 2003, p. 414.

20 Ibid.

21 Gupta, G.R. 2000. Gender, sexuality, and HIV/AIDS: the what, the why, and the how, p.2. Available at http://steppingstonesfeedback.org/resources/10/SS_ICRW_Gupta_Gender_Sexuality_2000.pdf [Accessed 18 March 2014].

22 Turmen, 2003, p.414; Gupta, 2000, p.2.

23 Snow, 2010, p.20.

24 Green, 2008, p.238.

25 Turmen, T. 2003. Gender and HIV/ AIDS, p412. Available at http://www.ijgo.org/article/S0020-7292%2803%2900202-9/fulltext [Accessed 18 March 2014].

26 Luke, 2003, p.74.

27 Gupta, 2000, p.3.

28 Green, 2008, p.238; Turmen, 2003, p.412; Luke, 2003, p.74; Gupta, 2000, p.2.

29 Morrell, R., Epstein, D. and Molestane, R. 2012. Doubts, dilemmas and decisions: towards ethical research on gender and schooling in South Africa. *Qualitative Research*, 12 (6), p.620; Luke, 2005, p.6.

30 Leclerc-Madlala, 2008, p.6.

31 Ibid.

32 Ibid.

33 HSRC, 2014, pp.31-32.

34 Leclerc-Madlala, 2008, p.6.

35 Ibid.

36 Leclerc-Madlala, 2008, p.5; Luke, 2003, p.73.

37 Smith, J. D. 2007. Modern Marriage, Men's Extramarital Sex, and HIV Risk in Southeastern Nigeria. American Journal of Public Health, 97 (6), p.1001.

38 HSRC, 2014, p.116; Zembe, Y.Z., Townsend, L., Thorson, A. and Ekström, A.M., 2013. "Money talks, bullshit walks" interrogating notions of consumption and survival sex among young women engaging in transactional sex in post-apartheid South Africa: A qualitative enquiry. Available at http://www.globalizationandhealth.com/content/pdf/1744-8603-9-28.pdf [Accessed 05 April 2014]; Selikow, T. and Mbulaheni, T., 2013. "I do love him but at the same time I can't eat love": Sugar daddy relationships for conspicuous consumption amongst urban university students in South Africa. Available at http://0-www.tandfonline.com.ujlink.uj.ac.za/doi/pdf/10.1080/10130950.2013.809930 [Accessed 02 April 2014]; Potgieter, C., Strebel, A., Shefer, T.

and Wagner, C., 2012. *Taxi 'sugar daddies' and taxi queens: Male taxi driver attitudes regarding transactional relationships in the Western Cape*, South Africa. Available at http://www.tandfonline.com/doi/pdf/10.1080/17290376.2012.745286 [Accessed 10 October 2014]; Dunkle, K.L., Wingood, G.M., Camp, C.M. and DiClemente, R.J., 2010. *Economically motivated relationships and transactional sex among unmarried African American and white women: Results from a U.S. national telephone survey*. Available at http://www.ncbi.nlm.nih.gov/pmc/articles/PMC2882979/pdf/phr125s40090.pdf [Accessed 02 April 2014]; Hawkinsa, K., Priceb, N., and Mussác, F., 2009. Milking the cow: Young women's construction of identity and risk in age-disparate transactional sexual relationships in Maputo, Mozambique. Available at http://gender.care2share.wikispaces.net/file/view/Hawkins_MilkingtheCow_Mozambique.pdf/67752923/Hawkins_MilkingtheCow_Mozambique.pdf [Accessed 02 April 2014]; Foreman, M., 1998. AIDS and men: taking risks or taking responsibility. London: Panos/Zed Books, p.28.

39 HESA, 2010, p.18.

40 Ibid.

41 Gauntlett, D. 2011. Three approaches to social capital Pierre Bourdieu, p.2. Available at http://www.makingisconnecting.org/gauntlett2011-extract-sc.pdf [Accessed 18 March 2014].

42 Stoebenau, K., Nixon, S., Rubincam, C., Willan, S., Zembe, Y., Tsikoane, T., Tanga, P., Bello, H., Caceres, C., Townsend, L., Rakotoarison, P. and Razafintsalama, V., 2011. More than just talk: The framing of transactional sex and its implications for vulnerability to HIV in Lesotho, Madagascar and South Africa. *Globalization and Health*, 7 (1), p.2.

43 Weckesser, A.M., 2011. Girls, gifts, and gender: An ethnography of the materiality of care in rural Mpumalanga, South Africa, p.56. Available at http://wrap.warwick.ac.uk/45913/1/WRAP_THESIS_Weckesser_2011.pdf [Accessed 18 June 2014].

44 HESA, 2010, p.80.

45 Defo, 2004, p.15.

46 Luke, 2003, p.73.

47 Ibid.

48 Jewkes, R., Morrell, R., Sikweyiya, Y., Dunkle, K. and Penn-Kekana, L., 2012. Transactional relationships and sex with a woman in prostitution: Prevalence and patterns in a representative sample of South African men. *BMC Public Health*. 12 (1), p.2.

49 Jewkes, et al. 2012, p.2.

50 Van Dyk, A.C., 2000. Traditional African beliefs and customs: implications for AIDS education and prevention in Africa, p 64. Available at http://reference.sabinet.co.za/sa_epublication_article/sapsyc_v31_n2_a8 [Accessed 23 February 2014].

51 Maluleke, M.J. 2012. Culture, tradition, custom, law and gender equality. Potchefstroom Electronic Law Journal, 15 (1), p.2.

52 HESA, 2010, p.120.

53 Gbalajobi, 2010.

54 Boyatzis, R.E., 1998. Transforming qualitative information: Thematic analysis and code development. The United States of America: SAGE Publications, Inc.

55 Ott, M.Q., Bärnighausen, T., Tanser, F., Lurie, M.N. and Newell, M., 2011. Age-gaps in sexual partnerships: seeing beyond 'sugar daddies', p.2. Available at http://www.

ncbi.nlm.nih.gov/pmc/articles/PMC3117250/ [Accessed 02 April 2014]; HESA, 2010, p.82.

56 Morrell et al., 2012, p 620; Leclerc-Madlala, 2008, p.5; Luke, 2005, p.6.

57 Van Dyk, 2000, p.64.

58 Hasler, 2013, p.23; Turmen, 2003, p.414.

59 Janey, B.A. (2003). Masculinity Ideology and gender role conflict across cultures: implications for counselling African, Asian, and Hispanic/Latino men, p.5. Available at http://files.eric.ed.gov/fulltext/ED476057.pdf [Accessed 04 April 2014].

60 Edström, J., Das, A. and Dolan, C., (2014). Introduction: undressing patriarchy and masculinities to re-politicise gender. *IDS Bulletin*, 45 (1), p.3.

61 Janey, 2003, p.6.

62 Smith, J. D. 2007. Modern Marriage, Men's Extramarital Sex, and HIV Risk in South eastern Nigeria. *American Journal of Public Health*, 97 (6), p.1001.

63 Smith, 2007, p.1001.

64 Leclerc-Madlala, 2008, p.6.

65 Stoebenau, et al., 2011, p.2.

66 Jewkes, et al. 2012, p.2.

67 Green, 2008, p 238.

68 Turmen, 2003, p.412.

69 Luke, 2003, p.74.

70 Gupta, 2000, p.3.

71 HSRC, 2014, p.116; Luke, 2005, p.6.

72 Fiscian et al., 2009, pp.67-68.

73 Leclerc-Madlala, 2008, p.8.

74 Dupas, 2005, p.3.

75 CSIS, 2013, p.9; Nobelius et al., 2011, p.253; Dupas, 2005, p.2.

76 Leclerc-Madlala, 2008, p. 5; HESA 2010, p. 82; Snow 2010, p. 20; Dupas 2005, p. 2.

77 Leclerc-Madlala 2008, p.6; Fiscian, et al., 2009, pp.67-68.

78 HSRC, 2014, p.116; Zembe et al., 2013, p.2; Selikow and Mbulaheni, 2013, p.87; Potgieter et al., 2012, p.193; Dunkle et al., 2010, p.1; Hawkinsa, et al., 2009, p.171; Luke, 2003, p.73; Foreman, 1998, p.28.

79 Stoebenau et al., 2011, p.2; Weckesser, 2011, p.56.

Chapter 13

Social Representation of HIV and AIDS

Deconstructing AIDS as a Death Sentence to '*Isigulo Sabantu*'

Nompumelelo Zungu

Introduction

It has been suggested that the acquired immune deficiency syndrome (AIDS) epidemic reached South Africa later than other developed and developing countries.[1] Internationally, the few AIDS cases reported were among white men who have sex with men (MSM) and among injecting drug users (IDUs).[2] In South Africa the first recorded cases were reported in the population of MSM, followed by a case of a Malawian migrant miner.[3] These early cases shaped how HIV was socially represented and constructed as a disease of the 'othered' in the country. Once generalised, the human immunodeficiency virus (HIV) epidemic spread quickly and was concentrated among migrant workers in mines, commercial sex workers and truck drivers.[4] AIDS occurred within a morally and sexually conservative environment.[5] In Africa, as elsewhere, AIDS was seen as resulting from the corruptions of culture by modernity, and the desertion of ancestral ways by women and youth.[6] This led many to believe they were protected from HIV as long as they did not belong or associate with 'high risk groups', who were stigmatised and socially represented as carriers of HIV.

The first part of this chapter will provide a brief account of the history of AIDS and stigma. In order to set the context on cultural representations and their link to AIDS and stigma, I will draw data from published and unpublished literature on the subject, using the social representations theory as my framework. The chapter will also utilise data from focus groups collected as part of my previous work among men in the Western Cape.[7] The overall aim of this previous work was to explore social representations of AIDS and narratives of HIV risk among Xhosa men aged between 30 and 60 years. Using this data, I will discuss how those affected and infected are challenging the traditional social representations of AIDS that are associated with death and stigma by deconstructing and reconstructing AIDS as '*isigulo sabantu*'. The term *isigulo sabantu* can be understood as a social representation that attempts to normalise AIDS and reveals how groups deal with the threat of HIV to their identity using certain cultural representations and constructs. The chapter will conclude by reflecting on how 'normalising' AIDS may impact on prevention in the long run, and attempt to propose what can be done to address this challenge.

The Theoretical Lens

In brief, the theory of social representations was developed from Moscovici's work[8] that focused on how people make sense of the world through dialogue and shared codes of communication.[9] Although definitions differ, there is consensus that social representations are characterised by plurality and are shared.[10] According to Moscovici and Marková,[11] 'social representations concern the contents of everyday thinking and the stock of ideas that gives coherence to our religious beliefs, political ideas and the connections we create as spontaneously as we breathe'. They make it possible to 'classify persons and objects, to compare and explain behaviours and to objectify them as parts of our social setting ... all behaviour appears at the same time as a given and a product of our way of representing it'.

The social representations theory offers a systematic tool to examine social knowledge, especially the relationship between the group, science and common sense.[12] According to Moscovici,[13] there are three processes that underpin the generation of social representations, namely: the transformation of expert ideas into lay thinking; the imposition of past ideas on new events; and the saturation of a new event using interpretations that exist in culture.

The theory posits that individuals acquire representations through social communication and interactions in a cultural context,[14] and that these representations have a 'mobile and circulating character'.[15] Thus, the social group is critical for their development, maintenance and transformation.[16] Social representations 'reflect an intellectual process at a cultural level and on a historical time scale'[17] and 'permit the elucidation of the link between knowledge and context'.[18] Social representations, however, are not static, and the group can change them over time to 're-represent history, context and identity'.[19] These 'local representational systems' are sources of insight into cultural symbols, codes and practices.[20]

The local perspectives contained in social representations are key for understanding social and cultural realities, psychosocial phenomena and behaviour.[21] Furthermore, Campbell and Jovchelovitch,[22] suggest that local systems are unique systems of knowledge that do not reflect ignorance, distortion and error. Instead, these co-existing systems reflect community identity and life that is involved in the generation of social representations.[23] Social representations theory 'makes an important contribution by providing a form of analysis which deals with the social aspects of the activity and the effects of social phenomena on individual activities'.[24]

Culture, AIDS and Stigma

The HIV epidemic, in particular, has been shaped not only by cognitive and biological forces, but by behavioural, social, and cultural factors as well. In psychology, two cultural paradigms have been the most researched and they focus on two overlapping conceptual distinctions, namely: the distinction between independent and interdependent self-concept;[25] and the distinction between individualism and collectivism.[26] In recent years, there have been strong advocates for the incorporation of culture and cultural meaning into the HIV infection and prevention discourse.[27] Airihihenbuwa[28] posits that African theory and practice, particularly within the context of health, must be rooted in African culture; and that cultural codes and meanings should be seen as central to public health.

Culture has been described as a set of shared practices, values, norms and forms of social interaction, accepted by particular communities at particular times according to their worldviews and historical experiences.[29] Culture is important for understanding how different groups construct health and illness; a view supported by Brandt,[30] who states that 'the way a society responds to disease reveals its deepest cultural, social and moral values'. Critical health psychology places the person's experience and the meaning that they adopt as the core of health and illness, and recognises the importance of consciousness and the ability to reflect on behaviour in the attempt to make meaning.[31] Culture cannot be separated from how AIDS is socially constructed.

Culture gives meaning to, and shapes, communication about AIDS. Often groups use shared metaphors, cultural codes and symbols to construct their realities and meaning. In the past, without effective treatment for infection with HIV, AIDS became a death sentence and groups used new and old epistemologies to explain AIDS and its 'exceptionalism'. Even the word used in isiXhosa for AIDS, *uGawulayo*, is a metaphoric construction and is derived from the word *ukugawula*, which means to cut down, and which speaks to this association of HIV with death. Thus, AIDS is constructed metaphorically as an axe cutting down members of the group.[32] Understanding the use of coded language and the meaning embedded in the social representation of HIV and AIDS is critical for the development of relevant and context-based knowledge systems; hence, the importance of incorporating shared knowledge and culture in the study of the social construction of HIV and AIDS.

Scholarship on HIV and AIDS related stigma and AIDS conspiracies has illustrated a commonality in the construction of AIDS as a death sentence, a disease of the immoral, across different ethnic groups, languages and geographical locations throughout southern Africa.[33] Furthermore, terms that are used for HIV and AIDS tend to be coded language. For example, in the Western Cape and Limpopo Provinces, HIV and AIDS are referred to as *amagama amathathu* – 'a three-letter plague'.[34] Other coded terms for AIDS include *uwine ilotto* (you have won the lotto),[35] which refers to a lifestyle of gambling with fate and getting the winning number, which is HIV and AIDS. This social representation of AIDS speaks to the life of sexual excess, where individuals who live certain lifestyles are seen as playing with fate or 'asking to be infected'.[36] Indeed the association of AIDS with immorality and sexual perversion has led to the stigmatisation of those who are affected by it.

Even religious symbols and metaphors are commonly used to represent and code HIV and AIDS; for example, in Limpopo, participants in a Human Sciences Research Council (HSRC) and Penn State Stigma Project, used the term *koloyi ya Elijah* (Elijah's chariot) to refer to a person who had died of AIDS. The metaphor speaks to the silence and the suddenness of death that AIDS entails; like Elijah's chariot, AIDS suddenly takes a person.[37] Groups tend naturally to use both old and new symbols and metaphors to construct and represent new concepts, including new diseases.[38]

The media, too, has played a significant role in early representations of AIDS. It has been suggested that early media reporting perpetuated the idea that 'AIDS was a '*moffie*'[39] disease contracted through sex with foreigners'.[40] Globally, pictorial images of the disease circulated during the 1980s 'parallels depictions of the syphilitic in pictures produced from the 14th to the 19th centuries that emphasize visual stigmata, degeneracy, sexual transgression, pollution, plague, isolation, suffering, and victimization'.[41] Fear tactics, accompanied by images of tombstones, emaciated bodies of gay men dying of AIDS and the 'Grim Reaper', were also common.[42] Similarly in South Africa, early reports borrowed from the global representations of AIDS which constructed it as a death sentence. Pictures of emaciated bodies of people living with HIV were often shown together with coffins, as a reminder of what befalls a person with AIDS. Headlines signalling doom and gloom were common, as shown in Figure 1 below.

Figure 1: AIDS reporting in the media

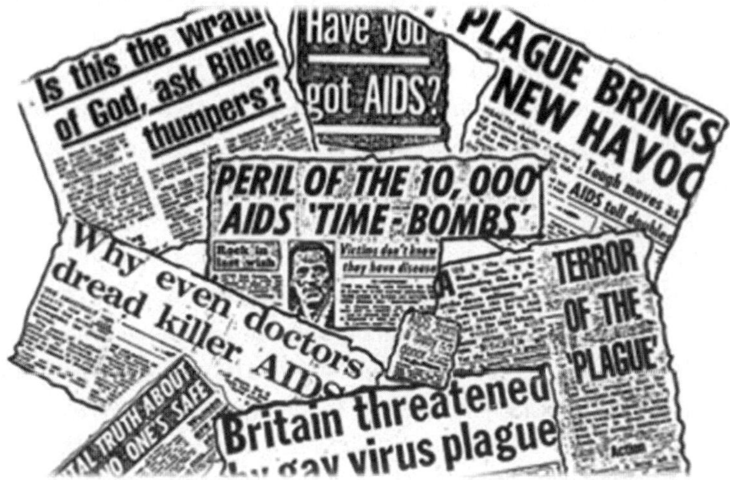

Source: Van Rooyen[43]

Challenging and Deconstructing the Bio-medical Representations of AIDS: Socio-cultural Representations of AIDS

> I see it [AIDS] from other people. People talk and say that a person with AIDS has *isigulo sabantu.* What can they do? Others say a person with it has brought it on themselves and things like that... (Ronnie: Gugulethu Group 1)

In the context of fear tactics and stigma, an HIV diagnosis spelt death and rejection for many. It has been suggested that cultures all over the world have evolved illness representations that can accommodate not only new diseases, but also new epistemologies for explaining disease.[43] In the study conducted among men in the Western Cape, AIDS was re-represented as *isigulo sabantu.*[44] For clarity, I will start by defining the meaning of *isigulo sabantu* and later discuss sub-themes that emerged with regard to the various meanings and uses of this social representation in different contexts.

Participants provided several meanings or versions of the definition of *isigulo sabantu.* The first definition suggests that AIDS is a disease that affects or is common among African people. The second version suggests that AIDS is a disease of humans because it can only be contracted from other human beings, not animals. The third version of the definition suggests that there is a type of AIDS that afflicts Africans and has its root in the African supernatural realm. Within this context, AIDS as *isigulo sabantu* is conceptualised as an African traditional disease (sexually transmitted diseases caused by polluted states of women) that shares symptoms with AIDS but is not AIDS (as it is understood bio-medically). For example, Thami explained:

> [Some] say it is a sickness of humans' *sisifo sabantu*. They say it is a Black man's disease. (Gugulethu, Group 4)

Analysing the different versions of the meaning of *isigulo sabantu,* it emerged from the data that this social representation of AIDS was used to suit different contexts. It could be utilised interchangeably, depending on the needs of the individual or group making use of it. As the data showed, some men used *isigulo sabantu* to deal with AIDS-related deaths and destruction – in this instance, it was used to normalise AIDS by suggesting that it affects mostly Africans – but all of the above versions were equally prevalent in the group. In another instance, it was used to portray bravado, or being untouched, as displayed in rhetorical questions such as:

> Really, who was it [AIDS] created for, if it is not for people? (Ronnie: Gugulethu Group 1)

This version was prevalent among younger men. Here the emphasis was placed on the source of HIV being human, not animals. Used this way, the *isigulo sabantu* social representation attempts to de-stigmatise AIDS by constructing it as a normal, chronic disease that is prevalent among Africans, instead of a severe and uncontrollable disease only found in othered groups and foreigners. It also constructs AIDS as a chronic condition rather than a death sentence; indeed, advances made in treating and managing AIDS have made this possible. In social representations theory these are given the term 'polemical representations',[45] that is, those social representations that are generated to normalise phenomena or are generated in the course of social and political conflict or controversy in society,[46] as is demonstrated in the following quotes:

> Mzi: In the township AIDS is . . . regarded as *isigulo sabantu* (an African disease). People do not go like worrying too much about it anymore. If you say *ubani no bani* (so and so) has it, they say it [AIDS] is known, *sisigulo sabantu* (a disease of Africans). Many people are saying: 'Hey, this thing is there, you will only know when you are sick.' Because we know *sisigulo sabantu,* you would not be the first person to have it, because AIDS is something that is common. (Gugulethu Group 1)

> Ronnie: I also want to add to that point. Really, who was it created for if it is not for people? It is like any other disease, like TB and cancer …. (Gugulethu Group 1)

In one context, *sisigulo sabantu,* or a variation *sisifo sabantu,*[47] was used to socially represent AIDS as a disease that affects Africans or *abantu* (humans), and it was this version that was prevalent. Implicit in the presentation is the idea that:

> … there is no shame in being infected with HIV because AIDS does not affect animals, it affects humans, and it is a disease of humans. (Mtho: Gugulethu Group 1)

This social representation contains a suggestion that AIDS was created for humans (or men). Similar rhetorical questions were reported among Owambo men in Namibia: 'AIDS did not come to Africa for dogs'.[48]

Explored in the context of stigma, the social representation is understood as an attempt to dissociate the spread of HIV from what has been referred to by Joffe[49] as a 'sin cocktail'. The sin cocktail suggested that HIV spread because of sinful behaviour. It makes an association between AIDS and animals, expressed through theories of origin that traced the spread of HIV to green monkeys, bestiality and blood-ingesting rituals in Africa.[50] Participants demonstrated that the *isigulo sabantu* social representation recognises that it is humans who are affected and infected by HIV and AIDS. The social representations of AIDS as a disease afflicting humans, or as an African disease, are an attempt to challenge the dominant negative community narratives and social representations of AIDS in the townships. Therefore, *isigula sabantu* provides a positive alternative representation of AIDS.

This finding supports earlier work on social representations of AIDS, showing that, although the core of social representations is held over time, they can be challenged and reshaped.[51] For example, *isigulo sabantu* reflects voices of those who live at the frontline of the epidemic and are affected by it. It mirrors the process whereby organisations of people living with HIV and AIDS have challenged its association with death by placing emphasis on positive living. *Isigulo* or *sisifo sabantu* representations construct AIDS more positively compared to social representations that have been reported in stigma scholarship.[52] This can be seen in the following exchange:

> Researcher: When you say '*sisifo sabantu',* is it a way of normalising it?
>
> Welile: This term '*sisifo sabantu*', it is something that started this way: When K has HIV, I will still take K as *uMntu* [a person]; I must accept him and not see him as someone I cannot sit close to or by his side. (Gugulethu group 1)

This social representation seems to also have an important function when dealing with stigma and in identity work.[53] On one hand, it seems to illustrate an 'internalisation of the international pervasive link between AIDS and the African'.[54] According to Baker,[55] because HIV was identified in Africa, it became descriptively imbued as 'African AIDS' during the mid-1980s.

Therefore, at one level, the *isigulo sabantu* representation may assist the group to shrug off 'courtesy stigma',[56] 'secondary stigma'[57] or 'stigma by association'.[58] Courtesy stigma and secondary stigma can be described as stigma by association; they are a type of stigma that is directed at groups associated with AIDS, those with the highest HIV-prevalence, or those considered to be at high risk of HIV.[59]

The finding on *isigulo sabantu* is important for understanding how groups respond to the threat of HIV-related stigma. It supports previous findings that illustrated that the response to risk is not limited to 'not me, not my group', as described by Joffe.[60] The current paper contributes to the theory of risk response by illustrating that not all in-group members respond by othering; instead, some members will identify with those that are stigmatised and respond by challenging and reshaping bio-medical representations that are used to explain the cause of AIDS using cultural representations such as 'witchcraft'.

The Role of Cultural Representations in the Deconstruction and the Social Re-representations of AIDS

The role of culture in social representations of AIDS emerged prominently in the men's narratives, a link which the next section will explore in detail. The idea that AIDS is a disease that afflicts Africans and has supernatural roots is contained in the definition of *isigulo sabantu,* as illustrated in the quotes below:

> Musa: There are even people who think AIDS is through witchcraft, so the people tell themselves I have a strong *muti* [African medicine]. They are always strengthening themselves with *muti.* They say I will not be bewitched

> with AIDS, because they use *muti* for protection. That is the reason they do not believe in being infected [with HIV through sex]. (Langa Group 5)
>
> Roro: Yes, they are taking *mutis* [African medicine] that they believe in it for prevention [of HIV]. (Gugulethu group 5)

As observed above, AIDS was socially constructed using cultural explanations that tap into the supernatural realm which involves *muti* and witchcraft. The findings illustrate that the meaning of AIDS cannot be separated from the culture of the groups affected by it:

> Researcher: I want to go to this thing that you were saying that HIV is *sisifo sabantu*; what does that mean?
>
> Themba: We take it that way that it is for *abantu* [Africans], *sisifo sabantu* [African death/disease/traditional disease]. (Gugulethu Group 1)

This social representation of AIDS as being caused by witchcraft was very prevalent, but was expressed, as seen previously, through phrases such as 'other people believe', suggesting an attempt to distance the narrators from the social representations held by the group. Participants indicated that some community members used cultural representations of AIDS to explain how it is contracted. They said that there were people who believed that AIDS was caused by witchcraft or spiritual forces, a finding that was not unique to this study.[61]

To understand the meaning of *isigulo sabantu* in the context of culture, an exploration of relevant literature is introduced, namely, the scholarship of Ngubane,[62] Bührmann[63] and Hammond-Tooke,[64] among others. The decision to do this was motivated by an attempt to contextualise the findings and illustrate that *isigulo sabantu* is another version of an existing cultural social representation tied to African groups; and an historical analysis of the aetiological explanation was deemed to be valuable. In researching the meaning and function of *isigulo sabantu,* its meaning was found to be nuanced and context-dependent.

As illustrated above with reference to stigma, it was used to question and debunk social representations of AIDS that construct it as an abnormal disease affecting foreign identities. Cultural representations were used to frame AIDS within the African traditional disease paradigm. *Isigulo sabantu* gives meaning to AIDS within the African knowledge system by highlighting a spiritual dimension to illness and health. It also introduces the idea that AIDS is not a new disease, but a traditional disease that has existed in the past, as suggested in the quote below:

> This sickness [AIDS] ... if we can speak the truth ... this sickness did not come with our children ... This sickness was there in the olden days but did not have the same name and was not as strong as this sickness we have now. We people of the olden days know it ... truly this AIDS was just seen in our children, but it was among our fathers. (Xoli: Gugulethu Group 2)

In line with the idea that AIDS can be explained culturally, the various narratives were analysed and it was deduced that *isigulo* or *sisifo sabantu* is an isiXhosa version of a more familiar isiZulu term, *ukufa kwabantu* (sickness of the people or death of the people).[65] *Ukufa kwabantu* is used to explain illness and its sources among Africans. Another familiar isiZulu term is *isifo sabantu* (singular) or *izifo zabantu* (plural),[66] or a variation *izinto zabantu* (African things). *Izinto zabantu* is used to describe misfortunes or ill health, the source of which is believed to have supernatural origin (ancestors) or other human beings using sorcery or witchcraft (*ubuthakathi*).[67] *Izinto zabantu* describes illnesses believed to originate from ancestors, pollution (such as the polluted state of a woman) and spirit possession (often associated with a calling by ancestors to become a traditional healer and attend initiation to become *ithwasa* – an initiate).[68]

There is abundant evidence showing that in Africa, 'illness representations are commonly constructed to put an emphasis on external and uncontrollable supernatural factors'.[69] The importance of recognising cultural belief systems and practices in dealing with AIDS has been highlighted,[70] and is supported by findings in this study. In the Xhosa culture (and in most African cultures) a core belief is that diseases are due to a violation of cultural taboos or to witchcraft.[71] It has been pointed out that there is a 'distinct symbolic resonance between AIDS, witchcraft, poison and pollution'.[72]

Indeed, African aetiological explanations for AIDS tend to tap into indigenous knowledge and cultural and spiritual beliefs,[73] as illustrated in the last quote. These explanations go beyond the answers provided by the bio-medical aetiological models[74] by looking for 'ultimate causes'[75] to explain AIDS. *Ukuthwasa* (the process or training to become a traditional healer) and witchcraft[76] are examples of cultural causes used by Africans to explain symptoms related to AIDS. Ashforth[77] calls it 'an AIDS induced epidemic of witchcraft in the post-apartheid era'.

To understand *isigulo sabantu* further, previous unpublished research, conducted in the same population by the HSRC, was reviewed, and it was found that the notion that there is an AIDS that can be classified as part of *izigulo zabantu* [plural for diseases that afflict Africans] was prevalent and supported the current finding.[78] This previous research conducted in the Western Cape in 2003 found that participants referred to *iAIDS yesi Xhosa* (Xhosa AIDS) or *iAIDS yeSintu* (African AIDS). This is an isiXhosa term used to describe AIDS attributed to spiritual or African witchcraft and sorcery. How *iAIDS yesi Xhosa* is used is similar to the way men in the present Western Cape study used *sisifo sabantu* (a Black man's disease).

This AIDS is different from the bio-medically constructed AIDS, referred to as the 'Western AIDS' by those who hold such beliefs. The association between AIDS and witchcraft has been reported nationally.[79] AIDS represented as *sisifo sabantu* is believed to afflict Africans exclusively and can only be cured by African traditional healers. To support the notion that there is an AIDS that is *isifo sabantu*, it was reported that it was now common for those living with AIDS to visit traditional healers for treatment.[80] Others were reported to wear *white beads* and go through a process of *intwaso* (a calling to train as a traditional healer) to become *ithwasa* (an initiate). Cases of *intwaso* were also reported to be common among people living with HIV and AIDS in Soweto.[81] The role of witchcraft and traditional healing has often been explored in the context of AIDS;[82] however, scholars tend to use a lens of denialism to explore cultural representations of AIDS. Below I argue for a more nuanced understanding of the role of witchcraft and traditional healing within the context of AIDS.

Social Representations, Identity Work and Stigma

Having established that there are variations in the use of *isigulo* and *isifo sabantu* social representations, I will now explore AIDS related stigma and the role of these social representations in the construction and protection of identity. This is what has been termed 'identity work' by Joffe,[83] referring to the process of re/construction and defence of identity. Goffman[84] defines stigma as 'an attribute that is deeply discrediting, [reducing the bearer] from a whole and usual person to a tainted, discounted one'. From the data collected in the Western Cape, it emerged that *isigulo sabantu* plays a significant role in protecting group identity against stigma. A close exploration of data shows that cultural representations of AIDS are examples of the process of anchoring.[85] The process allows people living with HIV and AIDS to be categorised within what is familiar culturally, namely, to be socially represented as either 'bewitched or as *amathwasa* [plural]'.

Studies showing a link between AIDS and a belief in witchcraft abound, but the role of witchcraft and *ukuthwasa* in the construction and defending of identity, and their relevance in mitigating stigma, has not been explored extensively in South Africa. The data from my previous work in the Western Cape suggests that the social representations of AIDS as *intwaso* and witchcraft are adopted in an attempt to distance the self and the group from the AIDS identity, and simultaneously to protect the identity of the individual and the group from AIDS-related stigma. Constructing the identities of people living with AIDS (PLWA) using *intwaso* and witchcraft is legitimised by drawing similarities between AIDS, being bewitched and a call to *ukuthwasa*.

To elaborate, all those affected by the above feel powerless. The similarity to *ukuthwasa* is very strong, as this state entails being 'entered' by *idlozi* (an ancestor who acts as spiritual guide to the initiate)[86] and not having agency to refuse the call. Those who are bewitched are also socially represented as victims of evil spirits, sent to enter them and make them ill.[87] Similarly, HIV also enters the blood stream 'silently', attacks the immune system and renders the victim powerless to resist the virus. These similarities assist in further concretising the social representations of PLWA as suffering from *isigulo sabantu*, as describe in the quote below:

> Sometimes other people when they have AIDS they become sick, they go *bathwase* (train to become healers). They wear *intsimbi* (African beads) ... They say they have *intwaso* (they have a calling from the ancestors). They slaughter goats and perform other rituals to the ancestors ... while it is AIDS that they have ... Others say they have been bewitched and they visit traditional healers for treatment. (Lethu: Langa Group 1)

> Yes that thing he is talking about is very common here in the township, people blame witchcraft. They say they have been bewitched with AIDS ... Some people who are living with AIDS are now wearing white and red African beads around their hands and ankles as a sign that *bayathwasa* (training to become healers) or *banobizo* (they have a calling). They wear these beads all the time as a sign of *intwaso* (calling). You see when you have that thing *yentwaso* you become sick and lose weight, so you look like you have AIDS, but it is not AIDS, you have *intwaso.* You must go to another traditional healer to be trained. If you refuse to go and become *ithwasa* your ancestors will turn away from you, and you will become worse. (Lungisa: Group 1)

Social representations that attribute the cause of AIDS to nature and the supernatural should be understood within a wider South African narrative that tended to de-emphasise the role of sex in the spread of HIV and its association with African people.[88] Historically, Africans have been constructed as the 'inherently diseased and sexual other in both colonial and post-colonial times'.[89] It cannot be denied that representations of AIDS in Africa located AIDS within 'African sex'. African sex was described as risky[90] and was constructed as 'inherently pathological'.[91] It has been highlighted that the association of AIDS with race was seen in early AIDS literature.[92] In the early scholarship on AIDS the label 'African AIDS' was used and indexed under separate typology, projected as an antithesis to 'Western AIDS'.[93] Even the spread of HIV in Africa was associated with risky sexual practices that were reported as inherently African, such as a preference for dry sex, douching with baboon urine and other drying substances, wife sharing and widow cleansing.[94] Using research selectively, Africa in general was constructed as a 'continent that is prone to AIDS due to promiscuity and endemic amorality'.[95]

Arguably, the association between African sex and HIV is the reason why AIDS is stigmatised. African sex, in particular, tends to be represented as a 'different and unique sex that is forbidden, often painful, an agonizing act that is both irresistible and coercive'.[96] As a result, resisting certain narratives about the spread of HIV and minimising the role of sex and HIV in the progression to AIDS, has been a common response in South Africa.[97] The mainstream scholarship has interpreted this as a form of denialism.[98] Denialism was portrayed prominently in former President Mbeki's argument that 'AIDS is not caused by HIV'.[99]

Mbali[100] has argued that the government AIDS denialism response 'is a response to a history of racist understanding of African sexuality'. In some quarters Mbeki's AIDS theory is now understood as an attempt to defend an African identity, among other things.[101] Moscovici,[102] posits that social representations 'are bound up with identity and they emerge precisely in response to danger to the collective identity of the group'.[103] Furthermore, the 'central purpose of representations is to defend against feeling threatened'.[104]

An analysis of the national narrative shows that it was aimed at directing attention away from sexual behaviour of Africans as a driver of HIV infections.[105] Undeniably, 'the notion of a unique essentialised African sexuality'[106] that is "othered" has existed in the West for centuries'.[107] The political narrative, like the supernatural narrative outlined above, positioned the groups most affected as passive victims lacking agency and afflicted by forces greater than the self. The rapid spread of HIV in South Africa was perceived as a 'direct threat to national identity and the newly constructed collective that linked good physical health and good political health'.[108] In this context, AIDS become a visible symbol of an unhealthy nation as South Africa gained the status of being the country with the highest number of people living with HIV and AIDS globally.[109]

The theme of collective national identity also began to emerge in prevention campaigns launched by the South African National AIDS Council (SANAC) and the Department of Health. In the 2009 World AIDS Day campaign, the message was, 'I am responsible, we are responsible, South Africa is taking responsibility'.[110] Hence, the failure of individuals to prevent HIV infection was constructed as collective failure. This put pressure on the group to uphold the identity of a healthy nation, especially in the face of a disease that cannot be hidden, and which exposes those living with it to scrutiny. Consequently, the group needed to reconstruct AIDS as *isigulo sabantu* to explain the associated symptoms and to mitigate stigma:

> You see by the loss of weight, but they say, they have *intwaso* and they are wearing *intsimbi;* but you can see when a person has lost weight something is wrong and you want to know what happened, because this person was not this weight, so what happened to them? ... They say *intwaso*, but in this case it gets worse ... You can see it is this thing [HIV], but they will not tell you, they just say it is *intwaso* (the calling) that is making them sick. (Olwethu: Langa Group 4)

> You can see if this person is 'clean' [HIV negative] from the way they look; even if you are seeing them for the first time, even when they wearing these things they like wearing [white and red beads], it is how they look that tells you it is HIV. A person who is sick, you can see there is something that is wrong with that person; they are not in good health, you can just see it. (Scelo: Langa Group 2 – emphasis by participant)

As seen above, cultural representations of AIDS and the wearing of beads are an attempt to deal with the outward displays of the disease. Without a doubt, AIDS is a stigmatising condition.[111] By representing the person living with AIDS as a *thwasa,* the person is 'not alone, but part of a community, they have a social place, and their problem is understood through their connection to other'.[112] *Intwaso*, as a way of positively representing AIDS using culture, is a development that has been noted by participants as common in the township. *Intwaso* plays an important role in the social representations of those living with AIDS and in the reconstruction of a 'spoiled identity'.[113] Culture provides alternative social representations for coping with AIDS, as noted in reports of people living with HIV and AIDS wearing *intsimbi* (African beads worn by *thwasa* initiates) as a symbol of being called by ancestors, thus differentiating themselves from those living with AIDS and socially representing themselves as people living with a special gift (*intwaso*). Wearing beads is a way that individuals silently explain outward symptoms that are observed by others, as seen in the quote below:

> You look at how the person is looking. When that thing [HIV] starts, if you know a person, you can see it and many people will go to traditional healers for answers. Their families will take them everywhere to see different traditional healers and when they come back they will be wearing these beads and telling everyone they have *ubizo* (a calling from ancestors). So you wonder but have to accept it because that is what people who go to traditional healers will tell you, so you also believe it. (Mandla: Group 5 Langa)

One of the stigmas identified by Goffman[114] is the 'stigma of the body', characterised by physical deformity or defects. AIDS, in its symptomatic stage, deforms the body and opens it to speculation due to the signs and symptoms that cannot be hidden.[115] Thus, the AIDS body is represented as a 'repulsive and ugly [object that is] highly stigmatised'.[116] To mitigate the stigma of the body and the crisis of identity, the fear of being discriminated against and the associated anxiety,[117] some people living with HIV and AIDS anchor their experience of living with the disease by turning to culture.

The use of African beads, as seen above, provides people living with HIV and AIDS with an opportunity to reconstruct their identity and address stigma of the body. African beads appear to be a non-verbal social representation language, pregnant with cultural meaning and symbolism, that the wearer uses to communicate to the larger group. The beads contain a coded message and are in contrast to the red ribbon worn as a symbol of solidarity with those affected by HIV and AIDS. The beads are a symbolic rejection of an AIDS identity and adoption of *ithwasa* identity. It has been observed that *intwaso* provides an opportunity for the person to be 'reborn and break away [from the past]'.[118]

Intwaso assists those infected to redeem their pre-AIDS identity and deal with 'spoiled identity'.[119] 'The adoption of the "*ithwasa*" identity marks a distinct change in the individual's social status, and identity, and is a way of not only coping with a health problem but of coping with marginalisation and low status'.[120] Bührmann's[121] work among Xhosas found that *ukuthwasa* entailed an 'emergence of a new aspect of personality and social influences'. *Intwaso* is an example of how culture and social representations intersect to mitigate stigma, protect group identity and reconstruct the identity of people living with HIV and AIDS. This social representation reflects community identity and life that is involved in the generation of social representations.[122] The section below will explore the role of socio-cultural representations in health-seeking behaviour.

The Influence of Socio-cultural Representations of AIDS on Health-seeking Behaviour

Wight[123] observed that young men's perceptions of risk are shaped, in part, by the cultural meanings associated with their lifestyle and friendship groups. This scholar concluded that recognising the role of cultural factors in the response of lay people to a new health threat has implications for health promotion, conceptualisation and management of risk. When AIDS is culturally represented as illustrated above, it is believed that only traditional healers (not Western-trained doctors), can prevent, treat and cure it.[124] Furthermore, the symptoms are expected to improve when a person visits a traditional healer for treatment (in the case of witchcraft), or answer 'the call' (in the case of *ukuthwasa*).[125] This is in contrast to AIDS that is understood bio-medically, which is understood to be incurable.[126] The quotes below make an indirect association between a disease of foreign identities (which AIDS continues to be, to some extent), and the othered foreigners who sell 'things that prevent HIV and cure AIDS':

> There are people who use other things, *imithi* [traditional medicines], herbalist medicines, things that are sold at train stations. Things sold by *amakwirikwiri* (foreigners), things that prevent HIV that are sold out there; things that say they can cure AIDS mostly sold by *amakwirikwiri*. (Daniel: Langa Group. 1)

> [For protection] I would drink *izifo zonke* (herbal mix for all conditions). (Sipho: Langa Group. 4)

> Others use *umagogotha* (another herbal mix used for HIV related conditions). (Musa: Langa Group. 4)

> Yes *umagogotha* is something that cleans the blood. (Zuko: Langa Group. 4)

Participants reported that people who hold cultural social representations and act on them are: '... always visiting traditional healers and herbalists for *mutis* used for protection [HIV prevention] and treatment for AIDS' (Madoda: Gugulethu

Group 4). In such instances, condoms and antiretroviral therapy may not feature in the treatment modalities offered by healers, as observed in the extracts above.

This raises an important question about the role of holding cultural social representations of AIDS in the rejection of HIV prevention methods, delayed health-seeking and poor uptake of ARVs, or their rejection in favour of traditional forms of interventions. Belief in the supernatural as a cause of illness has been associated with low self-efficacy, and impacts negatively on health-seeking behaviour, informs fatalistic belief systems and risky sexual behaviour.[127] The use of *isigulo sabantu* to normalise AIDS is a positive development; however, this social representation underpins fatalistic beliefs about HIV. These beliefs were observed in the apparent bravado of men who spoke in cavalier terms about their sexual behaviour, as in: 'Even if I become infected it does not matter, HIV is *sisigulo sabantu,* or, I am not the first person to be infected with HIV'.

In high-risk situations,[128] premature deaths are perceived as a given, with the only area of indeterminacy being how the person will die. In the context of the study, it was reported that some men think in terms of '... we are going to die anyway' (Phelo: Gugulethu Group 4). Another participant echoed these sentiments: 'They say we are all going to die, so we cannot die not having experienced sex' (Zuki: Gugulethu Group 4). Cusick and Rhodes[129] refer to these rhetorical questions as 'flouting the basic premise of scientific rationality by questioning the worth of death avoidance'.

Evidence abounds which shows that holding fatalistic health beliefs has a negative impact on adoption of preventative methods.[130] In a context of high rates of poverty and faced with a plethora of everyday risks, some men may experience paralysis in deciding how to act in view of the risks in the future (such as being infected with HIV). Beck[131] posits that awareness of risk can provoke such alarm that it creates an atmosphere of powerlessness and paralysis as people find themselves in a 'risk trap'.

Indeed, where HIV-prevalence is high and 'everyone' seems to be dying of AIDS, the fear associated with 'social death'[132] may diminish as people socially represent AIDS as a common disease that 'came for humans not dogs'. Another observation that emerged from the data is that the social representation of AIDS as *isigulo sabantu* may affect prevention practices negatively. Some men among the participants reported that they engaged in risky sexual behaviour because they did not believe that testing HIV positive would have a negative impact on their identity or sexuality.

This thinking led some men, as reported in the examples below, to knowingly engage in unprotected sex with partners whose HIV status they did not know.

One of the participants admitted to having had unprotected sex with a partner he suspected of being HIV positive:

> I slept with this woman [extra-marital partner] ... and I suspected this woman is infected [with HIV], but I was weak and I slept with her. I said I will talk about it. I will accept it ... What I can do is just to continue getting busy [having sex] with that infected one ... (Jakes: Gugulethu Group 2)

This narrative illustrates the complexities of how individuals respond to risk. The risky sexual behaviour reported above should be understood, in part, as informed by social representations of *isigulo* or *sisifo sabantu* and the acceptance of AIDS as a 'normal' disease. Although not explicitly mentioned in the study, the results of *isigulo sabantu* and the normalisation of AIDS may be pointing towards the role of antiretroviral treatment (ART) in normalising infection with HIV and living with AIDS. The availability of ART makes it possible for AIDS to become a 'normal' chronic disease. Indeed, research among men living with AIDS suggests that treatment enables positive social and economic participation, and affects masculinity positively by allowing users of ARVs to begin to reconstruct their shattered sense of social value.[133]

Nevertheless, Campbell et al.[134] point out that, even within this context of the provision of antiretrovirals (ARVs), 'stigma remains strong, and antiretroviral treatment users remain mired in conflictual symbolic relationships between the HIV/AIDS positive people and the untested'. They also highlight that 'to date, the restoration of users' own sense of self-worth through treatment has not reduced fear and sexual embarrassment in framing community responses to people living with HIV/AIDS',[135] which, to some extent, challenges the idea that risky behaviour can be explained by the normalisation of AIDS alone.

Conclusion

This chapter presented data on how conventional social representations of AIDS as a death sentence are being deconstructed and re-represented as *isigulo sabantu,* a disease that is normal and is common among Africans. I have also illustrated how this social representation of AIDS plays a role in protecting the group and the individual's identity from stigma, by redeeming them from 'spoiled identity' using cultural representations. Using data collected among African men in the Western Cape, I pointed to how the group neither refutes nor rejects these cultural representations, but perpetuates them through shared knowledge, and which, I argued, is a way of counteracting AIDS related stigma and protecting the individual and the group's identity. I also explored how *isigulo sabantu* representations may inform health-seeking and risky sexual behaviour, and concluded that holding certain cultural representations of AIDS may be a barrier to early diagnosis and treatment. This may happen through seeking of more traditional interventions that are in line with cultural representations and rejecting the conventional interventions, such as condoms and ART.

I also demonstrated that the representation of *isigulo sabantu* may also assist to normalise AIDS, which we are already seeing in South Africa. The evidence suggesting that holding this representation may also encourage an adoption of fatalistic beliefs that encourages risky sexual behaviour is, however, of concern. This was observed when individuals questioned the worth of death avoidance in a context of high HIV prevalence, and where everyone around them seemed to be infected and would die of the disease anyway. Therefore, while the representation of *isigulo sabantu* is an attempt to normalise AIDS and is a positive development, it should also be questioned in contexts were it impacts negatively on health-seeking behaviour and is used to justify risky sexual behaviour. Fatalistic beliefs and their association with risky sexual behaviour, have been reported previously; however, not enough research is being undertaken within the South African context to understand their nature, what informs them, and their impact on protective behaviour. There is a need for socio-behavioural interventions that are aimed at risk reduction and counteracting the impact of fatalistic beliefs on populations that are at high risk for HIV infection.

The chapter also illustrated the challenge of interfacing people's culture and beliefs within accepted bio-medical interventions. Although there was some recognition that a large number of Africans still sought traditional healing before consulting bio-medical doctors, there were no formal partnership programmes in place to routinely refer or screen patients of traditional healers for HIV and AIDS. This is despite knowledge that some of these patients have HIV and AIDS as underlying reasons for the consultation. While some strides have been made to link traditional circumcision[136] to medical screening in the Western and Eastern Cape, this has not extended to other health-related conditions and initiations (such as *ukuthwasa*). This is despite the evidence that some people living with AIDS, and who consulted traditional healers due to AIDS-related symptoms, are likely to be 'diagnosed' as being bewitched or having *intwaso*. The weakness in HIV screening mechanisms may be contributing to delays in health-seeking by patients of traditional healers. Therefore, while South Africa has made strides to combat the epidemic, there is evidence to suggest that the response is not tackling complex cultural and structural issues that continue to drive new infections and delay health seeking. As illustrated in this chapter, there is a need for a more nuanced approach, not only in our understanding of the drivers of the epidemic, but in our response going forward.

Notes and References

1 Abdool Karim, S., 2005a. Introduction. In Adbool Karim, S.S. and Abdool Karim, Q. (eds.*), HIV/AIDS in South Africa,* pp.31-36. Cape Town: Cambridge University Press; Zungu, N., n.d. Social representations of AIDS and narratives of risk among Xhosa men. University of Cape Town.

2 Shisana, O., Zungu, N. and Simbayi L., 2014. South Africa's response to the HIV and AIDS epidemics. In Meyiwa, T., Nkondo, M., Chutiga-Mabungu, M., Sithole, M. and Nyamnjoh, F. State of the Nation South Africa 1994–2014: A twenty-year review of freedom and democracy, pp.347-378. Cape Town: HSRC Press; Reddy, V., Sandfort, T. and Rispel, L., 2009. From social silence to social science: Same-sex sexuality, HIV and AIDS and gender in South Africa. Cape Town: HSRC Press.

3 Gouws, E. and Abdool Karim, G., 2005. HIV infection in South Africa: The evolving epidemic. In Adbool Karim, S.S. and Abdool Karim, Q. (eds.), HIV/AIDS in South Africa, pp.49-78. Cape Town: Cambridge University Press; Shisana, O., Zungu, N. and Simbayi, L., 2014. South Africa's response to the HIV and AIDS epidemics. In Meyiwa, T., Nkondo, M., Chutiga-Mabungu, M., Sithole, M. and Nyamnjoh, F. State of the Nation: South Africa 1994-2014: A twenty-year review of freedom and democracy, pp.347-378. Cape Town: HSRC Press.

4 Marks, S., 2002. An epidemic waiting to happen? The spread of HIV/AIDS in South Africa, a social and historical perspective. *Africa Studies*, 6(1), pp.13-26.; Shisana et al., 2014, pp.347-378.

5 Van Rooyen, H., 2015. Reimagining HIV counselling and testing in an evolving epidemic. Paper presented at the HSRC World AIDS Day Commemoration, 1 December 2015, Pretoria.

6 Delius, P. and Glaser, C., 2002. Sexual socialisation in South Africa: A historical perspective. *African Studies* 61(1), pp.27-54; Marks, 2002, pp.13-26; Posel, D., 2004. Sex, death and embodiment life and death in a time of AIDS: The Southern African experience. Johannesburg: WISER.

7 See Zungu, N., n.d. Social representations of AIDS and narratives of risk among Xhosa men. University of Cape Town.

8 Moscovici, S., 1976. La psychanalyse, son image et son public, *2*nd ed. Paris: Presses Universitaires de France.

9 Moscovici, S., 1984a. Social representations: Explorations in social psychology. Oxford: Polity Press. Moscovici, S., 1984b. The phenomenon of social representations. In Farr, R.M. and Moscovici, S. (eds.), Social representations, pp.3-70. Cambridge UK: Cambridge University Press.

10 Hammond, S., 1993. The descriptive analyses of shared representations. In Breakwell, G. M. and Canter, D.V. (eds.), Empirical approaches to social representations, pp.205-222. New York: Oxford University Press.

11 Moscovici, S. and Marková, I., 1998. Presenting social representations: A conversation. *Culture & Psychology,* 4, pp.371-410.

12 Moscovici, 1984a; Moscovici, S. 1988. Notes towards a description of social representation. *Journal of Social Psychology*, 18, pp.211-250; Farr, R., 1993. Theory and methods in the study of social representations. In Breakwell, G. M. and Canter, D.V. (eds.), *Empirical approaches to social representations,* pp.15-38. New York: Oxford University Press; Farr, R. and Moscovici, S., 1984. Social representations. Cambridge: University Press.

13 13 Moscovicci, 1984b, pp.3-70.

14 Moscovici, 1984a; Moscovici, 1988, pp.211-250.

15 Moscovici, 1984a, p.18.

16 Ibid.

17 Emler, N. and Ohana, J., 1993. In Howarth, C. 2001. Towards a social psychology of community. *Journal of the Theory of Social Behaviour*, 31(2), pp.223-238.

18 Jovchelovitch, S., 2007. Knowledge, community and culture. New York: Routledge, p.15.

19 Jovchelovitch, S., 2007, p.163.

20 Ibid.

21 Campbell, C. and Jovchelovitch, S., 2000. Health, community, and development: Towards a social psychology of participation. *Journal of Community & Applied Social Psychology,* 10, pp.255-270; Guareschi, P. A. and Jovchelovitch, S., 2004. Health and the development of community resources in Southern Brazil. *Journal of Health Psychology*, 9 (2), pp.311-322; Jovchelovitch, S., 2007. Knowledge, community and culture. New York: Routledge.

22 Campbell and Jovchelovitch, 2000.

23 Ibid.

24 McKinlay, A., Potter, J. and Wetherell, M., 1993. Discourse analysis and social representations. In Breakwell, G. and Canter, D. (eds.), Empirical approaches to social representations, pp.134-156. Oxford: Oxford University Press, p.134.

25 Markus, H. R., and Kitayama, S., 1991. Culture and self: Implications for cognition, emotions, and motivation. *Psychology Reviews*, 98, pp.224-253.

26 Triandis, H.C., 1989. The self and social behaviour in differing cultural contexts. *Psychology Reviews*, 96, pp.506-520.

27 Aggleton, P., 1996. Global priorities for HIV/AIDS intervention research. *International Journal of STDs and AIDS,* 7, pp.13-16; Airihihenbuwa, C. O., 1995. Health and Culture: Beyond the Western paradigm. California: Sage Publications; Airihihenbuwa, C.O. and Obregon, R., 2000. A critical assessment of theories/model used in health communication for HIV/AIDS. *Journal of Health Communication*, 5, pp.5-15.

28 Airihihenbuwa, 1995.

29 Lehman, D. R., Chiu, C. and Schaller, M., 2004. Psychology and culture. *Annual Reviews in Psychology*, 55, pp.698-714.

30 Brandt, A., 1988. AIDS and metaphor: Towards the social meaning of epidemic disease. *Social Research*, 55(3), pp.413-432.

31 Crossley, M.L., 2000. Narrative psychology: Self, trauma and construction of meaning. UK: Open University Press; MacLachlan, M., 2004. Culture, empowerment and health. In Murray, M. (ed.), Criteria health and psychology, pp.101-117. New York: Palgrave Macmillan.

32 Selikow, T., 2004. We have our own special language. Language, sexuality and HIV/AIDS: a case study of youth in an urban township in South Africa. *African Health Sciences*, 4(2), pp.102-108.

33 Joffe, H., 1996a. The shock of the new: A psychodynamic extension of social representations theory. *Journal of the Theory of Social Behaviour*, 26(2), pp.197-219; Joffe, H. 1999. Risk and the 'other'. United Kingdom: Cambridge University Press; Joffe, H. and Bettega, N., 2003. Social representations of AIDS among Zambian adolescents. *Journal of Health Psychology*, 8, pp.616-631; Mogensen, H.O., 1997. The narratives of AIDS among the Tonga of Zambia. *Social Science & Medicine*, 44(4), pp.431-439; Niehaus, I., 2007. Death before dying: Understanding AIDS stigma in the South Africa Lowveld. *Journal of South African Studies*, 33(4), pp.845-860; Uys, L., Chirwa, M., Dlamini, P., Greeff, M. et al., 2005. Eating plastic, winning the lotto, joining the WWW: descriptions of HIV/AIDS in Africa. *Journal of the Association of Nurses in AIDS Care*, 16(3), pp.11-21.

34 Steinberg, J., 2008. Three-Letter Plague. Johannesburg: Jonathan Ball.

35 Uys et al., 2005, pp.11-21.

36 Ibid.

37 HSRC and Penn State, [2002-2008]. Unpublished data; Airhihenbuwa, C., Okoror, T., Shefer, T., Brown, D. et al., 2009. Stigma, culture, and HIV and AIDS in the Western Cape, South Africa: An application of the PEN-3 cultural model for community-based research. *Journal of Black Psychology*, 35(4), pp.407-432.

38 Joffe, H., 1996b. AIDS research and prevention: A social representational approach. *British Journal of Medical Psychology*, 69, pp.169-190; Joffe, 1999.

39 'Moffie' is a derogatory Afrikaans word for a gay man. Hodes, R., 2014. Broadcasting the pandemic. A history of HIV on South Africa Television. Cape Town: HSRC Press, p.40.

40 Hodes 2014, p. 40.

41 Gilman, S. L., 1988. Disease and representation: Images of illness from madness to AIDS. Ithaca, NY: Cornell University Press; Schoeneman, T., Schoeneman-Morris, K., Obradovic, J. and Beecher-Flad, L., 2010. Social representations of AIDS: Pictures in abnormal psychology books, 1984-2005. *Journal of Applied Social Psychology*, 40(1), p.14.

42 Hodes, 2014, p.40.

43 Van Rooyen, 2015.

44 Liddell, C., Barrett, L. and Bydawell, M., 2005. Indigenous representations of illness and AIDS in Sub-Saharan Africa. *Social Science & Medicine*, 60, pp.691-700.

44 Zungu, n.d.

45 Moscovici, 1988, pp. 211-250.

46 Howarth, C., 2001. Towards a social psychology of community. *Journal of the Theory of Social Behaviour*, 31(2), pp.223-238.

47 The term *isigulo* refers to sickness, while *isifo* (singular) is derived from the word for death and is used to refer to a disease (Ngubane, 1977). *Sabantu* is derived by combining a prefix, *Sa-*, and *bantu; Sa-* denotes ownership and *bantu* refers to humans in general and can also be used to identify something as African.

48 Brown, J., Sorrell, J. and Raffaelli, M., 2005. An exploratory study of constructions of masculinity, sexuality and HIV/AIDS in Namibia, Southern Africa. *Culture, Health & Sexuality*, 7(6), pp.585–598.

49 Joffe, 1999, pp.40.

50 51 Farmer, P., 1992. AIDS and accusation. University of California: Berkeley; Joffe, 1999.

51 Joffe, 1999; Voelklein, C. and Howarth, C., 2005. A review of controversies about social representations theory - A British debate. *Culture & Psychology*, 11(4), pp.431-454.

52 Campbell, C.A., Foulis, C., Maimane, F.S. and Sibiya, Z., 2005. I have an evil child at my house: Stigma and HIV/AIDS management in a South African community. *American Journal of Public Health*, 95, pp.808-815; Gilbert, L. and Walker, L., 2010. 'My biggest fear was that people would reject me once they knew my status': Stigma as experienced by patients in an HIV/AIDS Clinic, Johannesburg, South Africa. *Health and Social Care in the Community*, 18(2), pp.139-146; Morgan, J., 2003. The disease that has no cure. AIDS and Society Unit: Centre for Social Science Research. Cape Town: University of Cape Town; Reid, G. and Walker, L., 2003. Secrecy, stigma and HIV/AIDS: An introduction. *African Journal of AIDS Research*, 2(2), pp.85-88; Uys et al., 2005, pp.11-21.

53 Joffe, 1999.

54 Ibid, p. 46.

55 Baker, H.D., 2005. Negotiating power and profitability of HIV/ AIDS in South Africa, (Unpublished M.A. thesis). Brown University, US., pp.25.

56 Goffman, E., 1963. Stigma: Notes on management of spoiled identity. Englewood Cliffs, NJ: Prentice Hall.

57 Uys et al., 2005, pp.11-21.

58 Walker, L., 2007. HIV/AIDS: Challenging stigma by association. In Burke, P. and Parker, J. (eds.), Social work and disadvantage, pp.79-96. London: Jessica Kingsley Publishers.

59 Petros, G., Airihihenbuwa, C., Simbayi, L., Ramlagan, S. and Brown, B., 2006. HIV/ AIDS and 'othering' in South Africa: The blame goes on. *Culture, Health & Sexuality*, 8(1), pp.67-77.

60 Joffe, 1999.

61 Mfecane, S., 2010. Exploring masculinities in the context of ARV use: A study of men living with HIV in a South African village. Unpublished doctoral thesis. University of Witwatersrand, Johannesburg; Posel, D., Kahn, K. and Walker, L., 2007. Living with death in a time of AIDS: A rural South African case study. *Scandinavian Journal of Public Health*, 69, pp.138-146.

62 Ngubane, H., 1977. Body and mind in Zulu medicine: An ethnography of health and disease in Nyuswa-Zulu thought and practice. London, New York: Academic Press.

63 Bührmann, M.V., 1984. Living in two worlds: Communication between a white healer and her black counterparts. Cape Town: Human & Rousseau.

64 Hammond-Tooke, W.D., 1989. The Bantu speaking people of Southern Africa. London: George Routledge/Kenyan Paul.

65 Ngubane, 1977.

66 Ibid.

67 Bührmann, 1984; Hammond-Tooke, 1989; Ngubane, 1977.

68 Bührmann, 1984; Ngubane, 1977; Swartz, L., 1986. Trans-cultural psychiatry in South Africa part 1. *Transcultural Psychiatric Research Review*, 23, pp.273-303.

69 Bogart, L. M., Galvan, F. H., Wagner, G. J. and Klein, D. J., 2011. Longitudinal association of HIV conspiracy beliefs with sexual risk among Black males living with HIV. *AIDS & Behaviour*, 15(6), pp.1180-1186.

70 Posel et al., 2007, pp.138-146.

71 Ngubane, 1977; Posel et al., 2007, pp.138-146; Urbasch, M., 2002. Representations and restitutions of African traditional healing systems. In Faure, V. (ed.), Bodies and politics, pp.5-24. Johannesburg: French Institute of South Africa.

72 Stadler, J. J., 2003. 'The young, the rich, and the beautiful: secrecy, suspicion and discourses of AIDS in the South African Lowveld', *African Journal of AIDS Research*, 2,(2), pp.127-39; McNeill, F.G. 2009. Condoms cause AIDS: Poison, prevention & denial in Venda, South African. *African Affairs*, 10 (432), p.355.

73 Campbell, C., Nair, Y., Maimane, S. and Nicholson, J., 2007. Dying twice: A multilevel model of the roots of AIDS stigma in two South African communities. *Journal of Health Psychology*, 12(2007), pp.403-416; Kalichman, S. C. and Simbayi, L., 2004. Traditional beliefs about the cause of AIDS and AIDS-related stigma in South Africa. *AIDS Care*, 16, pp.572-580; Liddell, C., Barrett, L., and Bydawell, M., 2005. Indigenous representations of illness and AIDS in sub-Saharan Africa. *Social Science & Medicine*, 60(4), pp.691-700.

74 Furnham, A., Akande, D. and Baguma, P., 1999. Beliefs about health and illness in three countries: Britain, South Africa and Uganda. *Psychology, Health & Medicine*, 4(2), pp.189-201; Urbasch, 2002, pp.5-24.

75 Jali, M.N., 2009. Collaboration of indigenous African, Western and European medicine: Policy guidelines. Unpublished doctoral dissertation. University of Limpopo, Limpopo; Mfecane 2010; Wreford, J., 2005. Missing each other: Problems and potential for collaborative efforts between biomedicine and traditional healers in South Africa in the time of HIV/AIDS. *Social Dynamics*, 31(2), pp.55-89.

76 Posel et al., 2007, pp.138-146.

77 Ashforth, A., 2005. Witchcraft, Violence and Democracy in South Africa. Chicago, IL and London: University of Chicago Press.

78 Capacity Building for Research on AIDS in South Africa, Pennsylvania State University, Human Sciences Research Council, University of the Western Cape, University of Limpopo, Fellowship Programme 2003-2008. Unpublished data. Pretoria: HSRC.

79 Shisana, O. and Simbayi, L., 2002. Nelson Mandela/HSRC study of HIV/AIDS: South African National HIV prevalence, behavioural risk and mass media household survey, 2002. Cape Town: HSRC Press; Shisana, O., Rehle, T., Simbayi, L.C., Parker, W., Zuma, K. and Bhana, A. 2005. South African national HIV prevalence, HIV incidence, behaviour and communication survey, 2005. Cape Town: HSRC Press.

80 See Zungu, n.d.

81 Mabuza, G., 2009. HIV and AIDS Stigma: Experiences from an HIV and AIDS awareness intervention in Soweto. Paper presented at the HSRC and Penn State stigma capacity building programme colloquium, 15th and 16th of October 2009, Soweto, South Africa.

82 Campbell et al., 2007, pp.403-416; Niehaus, I. and Jonsson, G. 2005. Dr. Wouter Basson, Americans, and wild beats: Men's conspiracy theories of HIV/AIDS in the South African Lowveld. *Medical Anthropology*, 24(2), pp.179-208.

83 Joffe, 1999.

84 Goffman, E., 1963. Stigma: Notes on management of spoiled identity. Englewood Cliffs, NJ: Prentice Hall, p.3.

85 Anchoring is a 'mechanism that is used to anchor new ideas and reduce them to ordinary categories and images that make them familiar'; Moscovici, 1984b, p.29.

86 Ngubane, 1977.

87 Ibid.

88 Mbeki, T., 2001. Address of the President of South Africa, at the Third African Renaissance Festival. Held in Durban on the 31st of March 2001. Available at http://www.unisa.ac.za/ [Accessed 03 April 2016]

89 Mbali, M., 2004. AIDS discourse and South African State: Government denialism and post-apartheid AIDS policy-making. *Transformation*, 54, p.105.

90 Baker, 2005, p. 30.

91 Mbali, 2004, p.104.

92 Sontag, 1977 cited, in Baker, 2005.

93 Sontag, 1977 and Chirimuuta, 1985, cited in Baker, 2005, p.30; Vaughan, M., 1991. Curing their ills: Colonial power and African illness. Cambridge and Oxford: Polity Press, p.205.

94 Baker, 2005; Mbali 2004; Natrass, N. 2004. The moral economy of AIDS in Southern Africa. Cambridge Africa collection. Cambridge: Cambridge University Press.

95 Mbeki, 2001, p.7.

96 Baker, 2005, p.30.

97 Cameron, E., 2005. Witness to AIDS. Cape Town: Tafelberg; Fassin, D. and Schneider, H. 2003. The politics of AIDS in South Africa: Beyond the controversies. *British Medical Journal,* 326(7387), pp.495-497; Gumede, W., 2005. Thabo Mbeki and the battle for the soul of the ANC. Johannesburg: Struik Publishers, Zebra Press.

98 Natrass, N., 2007. Mortal combat. AIDS denialism and the struggle for anti-retrovirals in South Africa. Scottsville: University of KwaZulu-Natal Press; Natrass, N. and Kalichman, S., 2010. The politics and psychology of AIDS denialism. In Rohleder, P., Swartz, L., Kalichman, S.C. and Simbayi, L. C. (eds.), HIV/AIDS in South Africa 25 years on: Psychosocial perspectives, pp.123-134. New York: Springer; Posel, D., 2005. Democracy in a time of AIDS: Interventions. *The International Journal of Postcolonial Studies*, 7(3), pp.310-315.

99 Gevisser, M. 2008. *The dream deferred.* Cape Town: Jonathan Ball Publishers; Natrass, 2007; Natrass and Kalichman, 2010, pp.123-134.

100 Mbali, 2004, p.115.

101 Gevisser, 2008; Mbali, 2004, pp.104-122.

102 Moscovici, 1976.

103 Cited in Joffe, 1999, p.100.

104 Joffe, 1999, p.10.

105 Gumede, 2005; Nattrass, 2007; Posel, 2005.

106 Baker, 2005, p.32.

107 McFadden, P., 2001. Cultural practices as gendered exclusion: Experiences from Southern Africa. In Sisask, A. (ed.), Discussing women's empowerment – Theory and practice, pp.58-72. *Sida Studies No. 3.* Stockholm: Sida.
108 Faure, V., 2002. Bodies and politics: Healing rituals in the democratic South Africa. Johannesburg: South African French Institute of South Africa, p.1.
109 UNAIDS, 2006. 2006 report on the global AIDS epidemic: 6th global report. Geneva: UNAIDS.
110 SANAC, 2009. SANAC press release: South Africans urged to take responsibility for their health as world AIDS day turns 21. Available at http://www.sanac.org.za/ [Accessed 11 June 2011].
111 Kalichman and Simbayi 2004a, pp.572-580; Petros et al., 2006, pp.67-77.
112 Nathan, cited in Urbasch, 2002, p.17.
113 Goffman, 1963.
114 Ibid.
115 Ibid.; Herek, G.M., Capitanio, J.P. and Widaman, K.F., 2002. HIV-related stigma and knowledge in the United States: Prevalence and trends, 1991-1999. *American Journal of Public Health*, 92(3), pp.371-377; Mfecane, 2010; Simbayi, L.C., Kalichman, S. Strebel, A., Cloete, A., Henda, N. and Mqeketo, A., 2007. Internalized stigma, discrimination, and depression among men and women living with HIV/AIDS in Cape Town, South Africa. *Social Science & Medicine*, 64, pp.1823-1831.
116 Gilbert and Walker, 2010, p.140.
117 Simbayi et al., 2007, pp.1823-1831.
118 Chang, Y.K., 2002. Zulu divining rituals and the politics of embodiment. In Faure, V. (ed.), *Bodies and politics: Healing rituals in the democratic South Africa,* p.41. Johannesburg: South African French Institute of South Africa.
119 Goffman, 1963.
120 Chang, 2002, p.43.
121 Bührmann, 1984, p.26.
122 Campbell and Jovchelovitch, 2000, pp.255-270.
123 Wight, D., 1999. Cultural factors in young heterosexual men's perception of HIV risk. *Sociology of Health & Illness*, 21(6), pp.735-758.
124 Mfecane, 2010.
125 Campbell, C., Skovdal, M., Madanhire, C., Mugurungi, O., Gregson, S. and Nyamukapa, C., 2011. 'We, the AIDS people. . .': How antiretroviral therapy enables Zimbabweans living with HIV/AIDS to cope with stigma. *American Journal of Public Health*, 101(6), pp.1004-1010.
126 Posel et al., 2007, pp.138-146.
127 Bogart et al., 2011, pp.1180-1186; Liddell et al., 2005, pp.691-700.
128 Zwi, A.B. and Cabral, A.J., 1991. Identifying 'high risk situations' for preventing AIDS. *British Medical Journal*, 303(14), pp.1527-1529.
129 Cusick, L. and Rhodes, T., 2000. Sustaining sexual safety in relationships: HIV-positive people and their sexual partners. *Culture, Health & Sexuality*, 2(4), pp.473-487, p.474.
130 Bogart et al., 2011, pp.1180-1186.

131 Beck, U., 2000. Risk society revisited: Theory, politics and research programmes. In Adam, B., Beck, U. and Van Loon, J. (eds.), Risk society and beyond: Critical issues for social theory, pp.211-229. London: Sage Publications Ltd.

132 Ashforth, A. and Nattrass, N., 2005. Ambiguities of 'culture' and the antiretroviral rollout in South Africa. *Social Dynamics*, 31, pp.285-303; Oxlund, B., 2009. Love in Limpopo: Becoming a man in a South African university campus. Unpublished doctoral dissertation. University of Copenhagen, Copenhagen.

133 Campbell et al., 2011, pp.1004-1010; Mfecane, 2010.

134 Campbell et al., 2011, pp.1004-1010.

135 Ibid, p.1004.

136 In response to a large number of initiates who were dying due to HIV and AIDS-related complications, it was recommended that before attending traditional initiation, initiates are required to visit a medical doctor and produce a certificate indicating they are in good health – it is expected that they will also be screening for HIV. Available at https://www.westerncape.gov.za/news/western-cape-government-ready-upcoming-initiation-season. [Accessed 11 June 2011].

Chapter 14

Using the HEAIDS First Things First Model to Improve Early Community HIV Counselling and Testing Trends amongst Young People

Ramneek Ahluwalia and Ravikanthi Rapiti

Introduction

Young people aged 15 to 24 are amongst those most affected by the human immunodeficiency syndrome (HIV) pandemic, with this group accounting for an estimated 11.8 million young people living with HIV, and almost 40 per cent of all new infections.[1] The Joint United Nations Programme on HIV and AIDS (UNAIDS) reported that, in 2012, young people needed to be at the centre of preventing the progression of the HIV and acquired immune deficiency syndrome (AIDS) pandemic, estimating that they comprised 42 per cent of new HIV infections.[2] In Southern Africa, the HIV prevalence was at 7.2 per cent for this age group.[3] In spite of this, many young people did not know their status and HIV testing amongst them was low.[4] Research shows that only 25 per cent of females and 15 per cent of males between the ages of 15 and 24 years reported having had an HIV test.[5] In 2007, the World Health Organization (WHO) recommended routine HIV testing, and it was then that South Africa undertook a massive HIV testing initiative – in the form of the HIV Counselling and Testing (HCT) Campaign[6] – to test as many people as possible so that they would know their status. Although this increased testing among the population, testing amongst young people still remained low and many did not know their status.[7]

Research evidence indicated that HIV testing may be successful in identifying HIV-infected youth in the primary clinic setting; however, monitoring trends indicated that HCT amongst young people in this setting did not reveal an uptake of HCT services.[8] Other research evidence has shown that young people tend to be sexually active, but with low condom usage,[9] which makes testing for HIV and knowing one's status imperative.[10] Specific research undertaken with young people at higher education institutions found that two thirds (65 per cent) of students were sexually active and reported using condoms only in their later sexual encounters (after one or numerous unprotected sexual encounters), and that 54 per cent of these students had never had an HIV test.[11] In addition, the research found that fear of stigma and rejection, and a lack of understanding about living positively with HIV, contributed to the low levels of HIV testing.[12] Pertaining to the availability of services, only 16 per cent of students said that HCT services were available on campus.[13] It is against this platform that the First Things First programme, under the auspices of the Higher Education Training of HIV and AIDS Programme (HEAIDS), undertook to bring HCT service provision to young people through post-school institutions in South Africa. This chapter reflects on the design of the HCT service implementation in the post-schooling sector, and its outcomes.

First Things First

HEAIDS is the flagship HIV prevention programme of the South African Department of Higher Education and Training. HEAIDS uses the First Things First model to bring the sexual and reproductive health (SRH) and wellness services to the post-schooling sector. This programme is conducted in partnership with a range of public and private sector role players. One of the aims of the model is to bring HCT to the youth, and this service provision is embedded in components of the programme aimed at:

- HIV, tuberculosis (TB) and sexually transmitted infections (STIs);
- men's health and empowerment;
- women's health and empowerment;
- alcohol and drug abuse prevention; and
- lesbian, gay, bisexual, transgender/transsexual and intersex (LGBTI) people.

The First Things First (FTF) HIV Testing Services campaign model was created and funded under a private-public partnership between Innovative Medicines South Africa (IMSA) and the Foundation for Professional Development (FPD), with support from USAID/PEPFAR, in 2011. The project was implemented in partnership with the South African National AIDS Council (SANAC), National Department of Health (NDOH), and Higher Education South Africa (HESA). After IMSA funding ceased, FPD received funding from USAID/PEPFAR to support the Higher Education Sector to continue the project that was designed to provide HIV counselling and testing on tertiary education campuses in South Africa from 2012 to 2014.

The HEAIDS First Things First Programme was implemented in 2011 and was designed to address the HIV prevention focus of the South African National Strategic Plan on HIV, STIs and TB 2012 to 2016,[14] as well as to encourage health-seeking behaviour and enhance the quality of life for young people. The programme is implemented at institutions in the post-school sector which includes Technical Vocational Education and Training Colleges (TVETs) and Higher Education Institutions in South Africa. Figure 1 provides a map which illustrates the vast breadth of coverage of the programme.

Figure 1: The landscape of the implementation of First Things First programme at TVETs and HEIs in South Africa

HEAIDS Presentation at ICASA 2015[15]

The programme implements a strategy called 'campus activations' which mobilises young people within the post-school sector to access HCT services and to learn their HIV status. By learning their status, young people would be in a position to seek the services they require – this speaks to the United Nations vision and target of 90-90-90.

So, what is a campus activation?

Campus Activation

A campus activation is a campaign that takes place at a pre-arranged post-school sector institution over two or three days. Over this period, HEAIDS together with relevant stakeholders, coordinates the provision of direct service delivery of basic services of HIV prevention, care and support, including general health and wellness, on the doorstep of each student and staff in the post-school institution. Stakeholders include the South African National Department of Health, local non-governmental organisations (NGOs), the United States Agency for International Development (USAID) with funding from the President's Emergency Plan for AIDS Relief (PEPFAR), the German Government for International Development (GIZ) and partners of the Global Fund. Prior to every planned activation, HEAIDS conducts active social mobilisation of young people, educating them about the services that will be provided. The HEAIDS peer education programme was implemented in the post-school sector before campus activations in order to raise awareness and knowledge levels, and for capacity development of volunteers. Campus activations encourage HCT and the general wellness of young people through the rendering of the following services:

- HIV, TB and STI education, screening and referral;
- hypertension, diabetes and/or cardiovascular risk factors education, screening and referral;
- cancer education, screening and referral;
- sexual reproductive health services;
- condom promotion programme; and
- medical male circumcision.

The Trends

Using the HEAIDS Integrated Online Reporting System (HIORS), which is a robust monitoring and reporting tool developed especially for HEAIDS, data is entered and reports are generated campus wide at institutional and national level. HEAIDS used the HIORS to provide a microscopic lens on the HCT trends from 2013 to 2015 in the post-school sector.

HCT service provision

The HEAIDS First Things First Programme's focus on HCT between 2013 and 2015 has brought about noteworthy results. The data shows that in 2013, 41 373 students tested for HIV; however, as the programme grew, 174 026 young people tested for HIV in 2015. Figure 2 provides an illustration of the HCT services provided in 2013, 2014 and 2015.

Figure 2: HCT services from 2013 to 2015

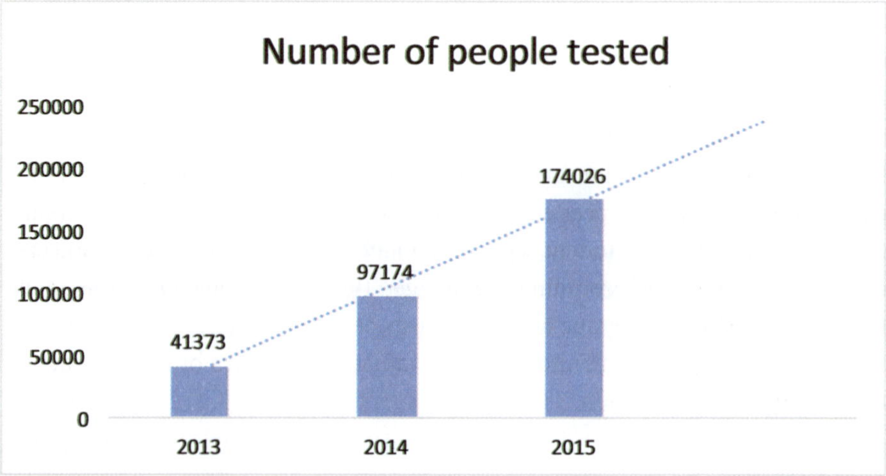

Number of people tested

250000
200000
150000
100000
50000
0

41373
97174
174026

2013
2014
2015

HEAIDS Annual Review Report, 2015[16]

HCT Services between 2014 and 2015

The coverage during 2014 and 2015 showed a significant increase in HCT in each province. As shown in Figure 3, the Eastern Cape (15 per cent), Mpumalanga (23 per cent) and the Western Cape (19 per cent) contributed to high levels of HCT coverage.

Figure 3: HCT coverage – comparison by province amongst TVETs

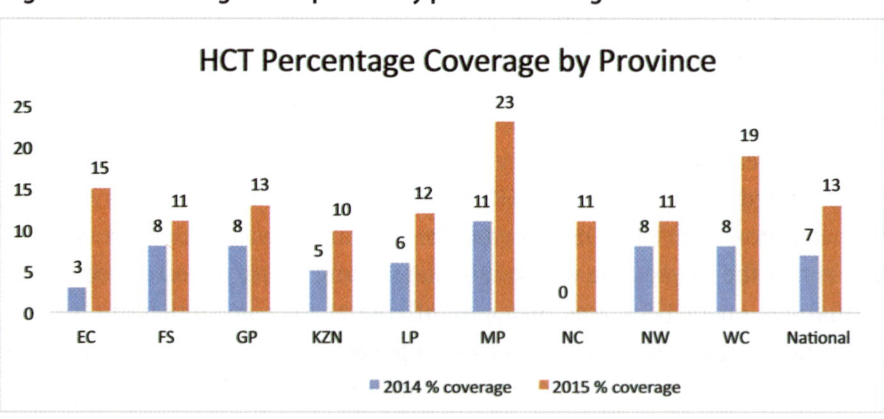

Source: Annual Review Report, 2015[17]

Of particular note was the national coverage of 13 per cent, which was a significant increase from the reported seven per cent reported for. This increase in testing was attributed to the increase in the capacity development of the HEAIDS Peer Educators and their subsequent role in mobilising young people on the campuses on which they operated. In addition, HEAIDS provincial coordinators that were employed full-time and who were stationed in each of the provinces facilitated the programme (peer educator programme) through peer mentors (such as life orientation staff, student services managers, and student services officers) on every campus. Each coordinator managed the First Things First programme implementation at an average of 30 campuses per province and was also responsible for overseeing the monitoring and evaluation activities of the programme in the relevant province.

Potential Evidence for Early Testing Amongst Young People

HEAIDS undertook several health systems strengthening initiatives to mobilise young people to access HCT. These initiatives were based on the premise that it was vital to reach young people and encourage them to test for HIV. Contributing elements to the increase in HCT could be attributed to the increase in the number of young people trained as peer educators, the increase in the number of campus activations, young people accessing HCT services at mass campaigns, and the use of radio and social media as a channel to reach young people.

Increase in peer educator enrolment

Figure 4 shows the number of young people trained as peer educators from 2013 to 2015.

The increase in the number of young people testing for HIV could potentially be attributed to them receiving HCT service provision messages delivered by peer educators. The HEAIDS peer educator programme was established in 2013. The aim of the programme was to capacitate young people at post-school sector institutions on HCT services that were offered at their institution. In 2014, 2 162 young people were part of the peer educator programme, and in 2015 this increased to 4 895 who participated in mobilising young people to seek HCT services.

Figure 4: The increase in developing young people as peer educators

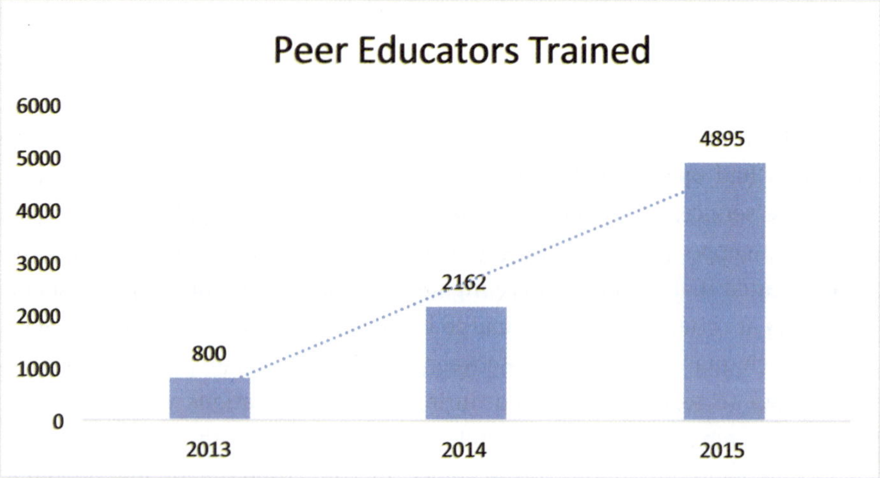

Peer Educators Trained
6000
5000
4000
3000
2000
1000
0
800
2162
4895
2013
2014
2015

Source: HEAIDS Annual Review Report[18]

Demand of services

The campus activations served as the mass campaigns in which the First Things First programme brought services to the 'doorstep' of young people.

Figure 5: Trends in the number of campus activations between 2013 and 2015

800
700
600
500
400
300
200
100
0
15
238
396
488
2013
2014
2015
Target 2016
Universities
TVET Colleges

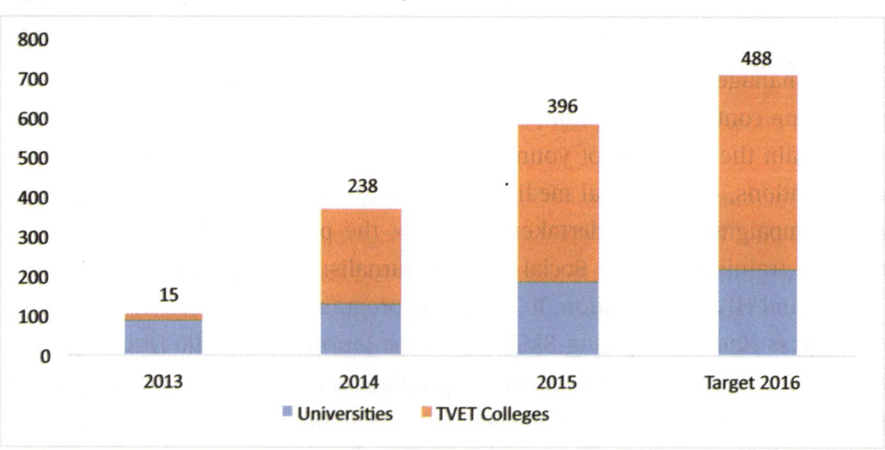

Source: HEAIDS Annual Review Report[19]

In 2013, 103 campus activations were conducted. In 2014, HEAIDS conducted 370 campus activations and in 2015, a total of 586 activations were completed, signifying that there was an increase in activations undertaken of more than 50 per cent across the entire post-school sector. This is indicative of the demand for services by young people, and this marked rise signified that the higher education sector had opened its doors, increasing partnerships and coordination of health care services to students and staff. This, therefore, denoted an increased buy-in and support of the health services in the sector. The schedule of activations indicated that, because of the high demand and high number of students, activations at certain institutions had to be planned – at the minimum – at least twice in each quarter of the year. Between 2013 and 2015, 95 per cent of young people aged 16 to 24 years tested during campus activations where the First Things First campaign took place, while only five per cent went through for routine testing using the campus health clinics. By comparing the number of young people that routinely tested with those that tested during the First Things First campaigns, the data reveals that young people responded to the youth-focussed campus interventions, and that youth-targeted campaigns are a feasible option for improved testing rates amongst young people. It is anticipated that in 2016, HEAIDS will complete 708 campus activations due to the demand of services.

Mass communication

Future Beats, a radio and social media component of the First Things First programme, aimed at capacitating social media journalists, radio presenters and station managers at campus radio stations so that they could air relevant HIV prevention content. In addition, content needed to be presented in a format that would gain the attention of young people who accessed campus or community radio stations, or the social media pages of institutions where the First Things First campaigns were undertaken. In 2014, the programme focused on three types of training, that is: Social Media; Journalism and Ethics; and Train the Trainer and HIV Sensitisation. In 2015, the programme expanded its training to encompass Radio Presenting Skills, In-house Journalism, Radio Drama as well as HIV Sensitisation. Figure 6 provides an illustration of the numbers of participants trained to use the radio and social media channels to reach young people. The capacitation of the staff ensured that HIV-related content was aired regularly to students through a medium that they accessed regularly – that is, the campus or community radio station and its social media pages.

Figure 6: Capacity building activities undertaken in 2014 and 2015

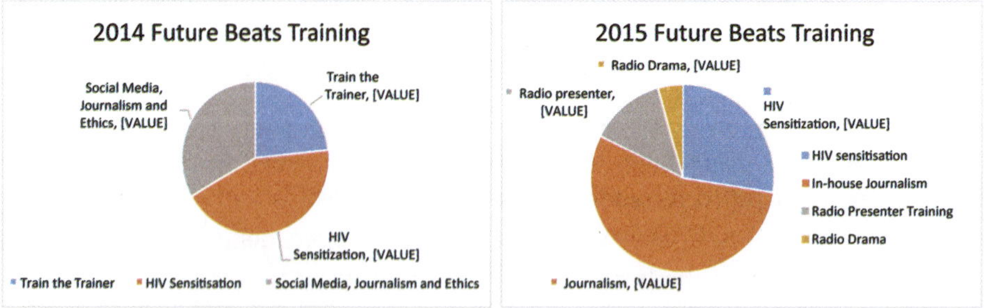

Source: HEAIDS Annual Review Report[20]

Conclusion

Now in its fourth year, the First Things First campaign encourages students to take responsibility for knowing their HIV status by providing HCT services. This is a necessary step towards treatment, care and support, and preventing new infections. The programme has enjoyed tremendous success with the uptake of HCT. This could be attributed to various elements discussed in this chapter, such as the campus activations, the strong partnerships established, coordination of various stakeholders, mobilisation by peer educators, demand creation and mass communication. By creating the vision of building a culture where our youth screen and become educated in order to detect the virus early, young people are initiated on treatment and are educated on living positively. Using campus activations as a platform to test and take care of their health has been successful, as can be seen through the large number of students who accessed HCT as a result of the initiative. The increase in the training of peer educators served as an instrumental tool to mobilise young people to seek out HCT services. Capacitating campus and radio staff to conduct mass communication activities around HIV prevention contributed to the demand creation of HCT among young people, and this was evident in the increase in the number of staff that attended the HEAIDS Future Beats training. The comparison of the data, especially between 2014 and 2015, is indicative of the huge success of HEAIDS with regard to HCT. The HEAIDS First Things First programme set its sights on increasing testing nationally to 26 per cent in 2016, and with its focussed targeted activities can contribute to the reduction of new infections and to the UNAIDS target of 90-90-90.

Notes and References

1 United Nations, 2012. HIV prevalence among population aged 15-24 years. Available at http://mdgs.un.org/unsd/mi/wiki/6-1-HIV-prevalence-among-population-aged-15-24-years.ashx [Accessed January 2016].

2 UNAIDS, 2014. *The Gap Report*. Available at http://www.unaids.org/sites/default/files/en/media/unaids/contentassets/documents/unaidspublication/2014/UNAIDS_Gap_report_en.pdf [Accessed January 2016].

3 Shisana, O., Rehle, T., Simbayi, L.C., Zuma, K., Jooste, S., Zungu, N., Labadarios, D., Onoya, D. et al., 2014. South African National HIV Prevalence, Incidence and Behaviour Survey, 2012. Cape Town: HSRC Press.

4 Black, S., Wallace, M., Middelkoop, K., Robbertze, D., Bennie, T, Wood, R. and Bekker, L.G., 2014. Improving HIV testing amongst adolescents through an integrated Youth Centre rewards program: Insights from South Africa. *Children and Youth Service Review*, 45, pp.98-105. Available at http://dx.doi.org/10.1016/j.childyouth.2014.03.025

5 Pettifor, A.E., Rees, H.V., Kleinschmidt, I., Steffenson, A.E., MacPhail, C., et al., 2005. Young people's sexual health in South Africa: HIV prevalence and sexual behaviors from a nationally representative household survey. *AIDS*, 19, pp.1525-1534. doi: 10.1097/01.aids.0000183129.16830.06.

6 South African National AIDS Council, 2010. The national HIV counselling and testing strategy. Available at http://www.capegateway.gov.za/other/2010/6/hct_campaign_strategy_2_3_10_final.pdf [Accessed November 2015].

7 Maluleke, T.X., 2010. Sexual risk behaviour amongst young people in the Vhembe district of the Limpopo province, South Africa. *Health SA Gesondheid*, 15 (1), Art, p.505.

8 MacPhail, C., Pettifor, A., Moyo, W. and Rees, H., 2009. Factors associated with HIV testing among sexually active South African youth aged 15-24 years. *AIDS Care*, 21, pp.456-467. doi: 10.1080/09540120802282586; Ramirez-Avila, L., Nixon, K., Noubary, F., Giddy, J., Losina, E., et al., 2012. Routine HIV testing in adolescents and young adults presenting to an outpatient clinic in Durban, South Africa. *PLoS ONE*, 7 (9), e45507. doi:10.1371/journal.pone.0045507.

9 Chimbindi, N.Z., McGrath, N., Herbst, K., Tint, K.S. and Newell, M.L., 2010. Sociodemographic determinants of condom use among sexually active young adults in rural KwaZulu-Natal, South Africa. *Open AIDS Journal*, 4, pp.88–95. doi: 10.2174/1874613601004010088.

10 South African National AIDS Council, 2010. HIV counselling and testing (HCT) policy guidelines. Available at http://sanac.org.za/wp-content/uploads/2015/12/Dept-of-Health-HCT-Policy-Guidelines.pdf [Accessed February 2016].

11 HEAIDS, 2010. HIV prevalence and related factors – Higher education sector study, South Africa, 2008-2009. Pretoria: Higher Education South Africa. Available at http://www.dhet.gov.za/Reports%20Doc%20Library/HEAIDS%20Sero%20Prevalence%20Sector%20Report.pdf [Accessed November 2015].

12 Ibid.

13 HEAIDS, 2014. The HEAIDS study on knowledge attitude and behaviour (KAB) survey of the technical and vocational education and training colleges (TVETs). Available at http://heaids.org.za/site/assets/files/1229/4936_hesa_hiv_and_aids_in_the_higher_education_sector.pdf [Accessed January 2016].

14 South African National AIDs Council, 2012. The National Strategic Plan on HIV and AIDS, TB and STIs, 2012-2016. Available at http://www.sahivsoc.org/upload/documents/National_Strategic_Plan_2012.pdf [Accessed November 2015].

15 Alhuwalia, R., 2015. Role of Higher Education in Mitigating HIV and TB in Africa. Presented at ICASA 2015, Harare, Zimbabwe. Available at http://heaids.org.za/resources/speeches-presentations/[Accessed January 2016].

16 HEAIDS, 2015. HEAIDS Annual Review Report, 2015. Available at http://heaids.org.za/site/assets/files/1248/final_heaids_annual_review_report_2015.pdf. [Accessed April 2016].

17 Ibid.

18 Ibid.

19 Ibid.

20 Ibid.

PART II

STRENGTHING THE MULTI-SECTORAL RESPONSE TO HIV AND AIDS

SECTORAL PERSPECTIVES AND EXPERIENCES

Chapter 15

Our Journey Together

The History of UNAIDS' Contribution to the AIDS Response in South Africa

Erasmus Morah, Natalie Ridgard and Nancy Fee

Introduction

This chapter presents the history of the Joint United Nations Programme on HIV and AIDS (UNAIDS) in South Africa,[1] and the contribution that UNAIDS has made to the national acquired immune deficiency syndrome (AIDS) response. The second part of the chapter looks at the early years of the epidemic, when UNAIDS was established globally and, in 1996, an Inter-Country Team for eastern and southern Africa was set up. This includes the period up to 1999, when Thabo Mbeki became the second president of South Africa. Part three focuses on the period during which the UNAIDS Country Office in South Africa was set up and became operational in 2001. UNAIDS thus began a relationship, which was fraught with difficulty and frustration, with the government led by President Thabo Mbeki. Using an approach of 'quiet diplomacy', UNAIDS managed, nevertheless, to score a few notable achievements during this period.

Part four traces the change in the leadership of South Africa in 2008, and then again shortly thereafter in 2009. This was a time when the mutual relationship flourished and a lot of behind-the-scenes work took place between UNAIDS and its South African partners, both at a global and country level. In part five, the focus is on the six short years between then and now (2009 to early 2016), chronicling South Africa's transformation, with the help of UNAIDS, from laggard to continental leader. In part six, we take a look beyond the mountain top to what lies ahead in efforts to end the AIDS epidemic as a public health threat by 2030.

Throughout, and in part seven, there is a focus on how the UNAIDS Executive Director, Michel Sidibé, took a great interest in South Africa from the beginning of his term in January 2009. This was especially the case in the period from 2009 to 2011, when so much catalytic work was needed. The past three decades illustrates the truth of Sidibé's belief that 'if you get the politics of the response right, the government and the people would do the rest'. 'We have inspired and kept South Africa company in the AIDS response', noted Sidibé.[2]

The Beginning of the AIDS Epidemic and Early Institutional Response in South Africa, 1981-1999

The Government of South Africa and the United Nations system were among those who responded early to the HIV epidemic. The world's first reporting of what became known as AIDS was from Los Angeles in 1981. By the end of 1981 and early 1982, the first AIDS deaths were officially recorded in South Africa.

The first International AIDS Conference was held in Atlanta in 1985. In an historic move two years later, in 1987, the United Nations (UN) General Assembly discussed the threat posed by HIV to global health and human security. This resulted in the mandating of the World Health Organization (WHO) to take the lead in coordinating a global response. In the same year, WHO created its Global AIDS Programme, often referred to as the GPA, under the visionary leadership of Jonathan Mann. One of the early actions of GPA to raise global awareness on the new pandemic was to declare, in 1988, 1 December as 'World AIDS Day'. Following Jonathan Mann's resignation over a dispute on the right global strategy to fight the epidemic, Michael Merson was appointed as the new Director of the GPA in 1990.

In 1988, the South African government quickly created an AIDS Unit within the National Department of Health (NDoH) to coordinate policy and action. By 1991, epidemiological evidence emerged to show that the number of HIV infections generated through heterosexual and homosexual transmission were equal. This finding coincided with the creation of the National AIDS Committee of South Africa (NACOSA) in 1992, in an attempt by civil society groups to broaden consultation on the response and to involve more stakeholders.

The year 1994 was like no other in the history of South Africa. It saw the end of the brutal and oppressive race-based system of apartheid, and ushered in the new government of South Africa, led by President Nelson Mandela. The new leadership of a democratic and free South Africa made combatting HIV one of its 22 lead projects. Nkosazana Dlamini-Zuma became South Africa's first health minister. The same year, NACOSA developed its first strategy on AIDS, which was subsequently endorsed by government as the National AIDS Plan for South Africa. Also, in 1994, the National Association of People Living with HIV (NAPWA) was founded under the leadership of Pieter Bussi.

In 1996, UNAIDS was established in Geneva, building on aspects of the WHO GPA. Under its diligent scientist-leader, Peter Piot, UNAIDS was mandated to champion and drive a global UN inter-agency and multi-sectoral response to the epidemic. It was felt that the HIV challenge was so complex, and its threats so exceptional, that only a multi-sectoral, multi-stakeholder response would be adequate. Operational flexibility to manage such a complex behaviour-change oriented response, and a holistic multi-sectoral response that encompasses both state and non-state actors, could only be achieved outside the traditional public health sector management paradigm. The first challenge UNAIDS and, later, National AIDS Councils (NACs) faced was the 'authority to coordinate' across agencies and to work with a range of government sectors.

In 1996, UNAIDS immediately set up an Inter-Country Team for East and Southern Africa in Pretoria, headed by Elhaj As Sy, a well-known African figure from the environmental movement. The South African government formed the Inter-Ministerial Committee (IMC) on AIDS in 1997, and appointed Deputy President Thabo Mbeki as its Chairperson. The establishment, in 1998, of the World Bank Multi-Country AIDS Programme (MAP), cemented the adoption of the multi-sectoral response approach to the epidemic across countries, especially in sub-Saharan African countries. Developing countries that did not adopt a multi-sectoral approach and set up standalone or quasi autonomous NACs, often under the highest office in the land, found it difficult to obtain access to AIDS grants or soft loans from the World Bank. As a middle-income country, South Africa did not qualify to receive soft loans from the World Bank. MAP still, however, created an added pressure, together with UNAIDS advocacy, towards the eventual creation of the South African National AIDS Council (SANAC) in 2000.

Three developments in the late 1990s proved noteworthy for the South African AIDS response. The Treatment Action Campaign (TAC) was launched in 1998, under the leadership of Zackie Achmat. TAC changed forever the landscape and tempo of the interaction between civil society and the government and their engagement with AIDS. Supported by the AIDS Law Project (set up in 1993 by Judge Edwin Cameron), under the leadership of Mark Heywood, TAC was able to use the progressive post-1994 South African Constitution and laws to force government to improve conditions, protection and treatment for people living with HIV. In the same year, 1998, NAPWA member and AIDS activist, Gugu Dlamini, was stoned and stabbed to death by a group of men for publicly disclosing her positive HIV status on World AIDS Day. This ultimate sacrifice by Gugu Dlamini continues to be commemorated by the government and people of South Africa.

Thabo Mbeki became the President of South Africa in 1999, sending the AIDS discourse in the country into a different direction. A great many lives and opportunities – and substantial energy on unhelpful debates on AIDS – was lost during this presidency.

The Early Difficult Years of the South African AIDS Response, 2000-2008

The years between 2000 and 2008 were a difficult period for the South African AIDS response, dominated as they were by President Mbeki's embrace of 'AIDS-causes-HIV denialism'. AIDS denialism was a global phenomenon based on the belief among some dissident, or pseudo-, scientists that HIV did not cause AIDS. Some of these pseudoscientists went so far as to completely reject the existence of HIV. Others viewed HIV as merely a harmless passenger-virus that could be leveraged by other adverse socio-political circumstances or behavioural factors. These beliefs were scientifically, and conclusively, discredited; however, they also featured alongside another global debate that portrayed conventional HIV discourse as 'inherently racist', by typifying Africans or black people as unable to control their 'insatiable sexual drives'. All of these discussions were in the context of a post-apartheid medicine discourse, and larger continental debates marked by Afro-pessimism and doubts about the feasibility of AIDS treatment among the African group. The overall viability and sustainability of the African states and societies were seen to be under a systematic external attack. These larger contexts may explain, in part, why the 'AIDS-causes-HIV denialism' gained a strong foothold – and had such a significant political impact – in South Africa under the presidency of Mbeki.

Embracing the belief that HIV did not cause AIDS, and that antiretrovirals (ARVs) were 'unsafe and toxic', President Mbeki asserted that poverty and malnutrition were the cause of AIDS deaths, as 'a virus could not cause a syndrome'. His views were supported by a cadre of loyal cabinet members and, most vociferously, by his Minister of Health, Manto Tshabalala-Msimang. President Mbeki was also supported by a handful of dissident scientists, some of whom were members of the Presidential Advisory Panel on AIDS, which he established in 2000.

President Mbeki was correct in his understanding that unemployment, food security, access to clean drinking water, sanitation and many other conditions of poverty exacerbate people's vulnerability to HIV infection, including their difficulty in maintaining a strong immune system. He was also proven correct to have been suspicious of the global pharmaceutical corporations and their profiteering tendencies, at a time when thousands of (South) Africans were dying of AIDS. In 2001, the Pharmaceutical Manufacturer's Association of South Africa (representing 39 drug companies) was forced to withdraw an action against the government over a law that allowed the government to import cheaper generic drugs, including those for HIV.

President Mbeki, however, used his position on AIDS denialism and in government to block access to life-saving antiretroviral treatment (ART) for ordinary South Africans for a long time. This included blocking the use of Nevirapine for the prevention of mother-to-child transmission (PMTCT) of HIV, even though this was offered to the government for free for a limited period by the manufacturer. These actions had catastrophic results for the country, with hundreds of thousands of lives lost and missed opportunities to prevent a larger epidemic.

The XIII International AIDS Conference (AIDS2000) was held for the first time on African soil in July 2000 in Durban, South Africa. Five thousand of the most respected HIV scientists in the world signed the Durban Declaration, a reaction to President Mbeki's subscription to AIDS denialism. AIDS2000 was characterised by conflict between politics and science, and vocal activism for access to universal HIV treatment. Peter Piot, then UNAIDS Executive Director, added his voice to the call of activists and scientists (including those of the late 12-year old, Nkosi Johnson, and Judge Edwin Cameron) for President Mbeki to affirm the link between HIV and AIDS, and to demand treatment action and an end to the AIDS denialism. During these difficult years, Piot also personally met with and engaged President Mbeki, but without success.

At the national level, under the leadership of the UNAIDS Team Leader for the Inter-Country Team Office, Bunmi Makinwa (2000-2003), UNAIDS succeeded through 'quiet diplomacy' to broker notable achievements with the South African government. UNAIDS was able to negotiate a 'deal' with President Mbeki to say nothing more on AIDS publicly – the next best thing to no agreement. This strategy worked for a number of years, peppered with occasional statements from President Mbeki, which caused public outcry. For instance, in an interview with the Washington Post in September 2003, Mbeki said, 'Personally, I don't know anybody who has died of AIDS'.[3] Over the years, President Mbeki increasingly withdrew from the public debate on AIDS.

UNAIDS was able to advocate successfully for Minister Tshabalala-Msimang to meet with people who held different views from hers. TAC was among the groups she met. She also hosted an official dinner for Piot and presented him with a bouquet of flowers, signalling a change in Piot's unofficial status as an undesirable person in South Africa, to a global figure accepted by the South African government. During these years, UNAIDS managed to achieve modest progress through cooperation with the African National Congress (ANC), the ruling party. The official position of the ANC on ARVs was at variance with that of President Mbeki, and such an opportunity allowed the HIV programme to make considerable progress. At the end of his term in 2008, Piot visited South Africa and received a formal, and very warm, reception at Luthuli House, the ANC headquarters in Johannesburg.

Towards the end of 2000, South Africa's presidency challenged Stellenbosch University to develop a programme for education, research and community service related to HIV management in the workplace. As a result, in January 2003, the Africa Centre for HIV and AIDS Management was established under the leadership of Professor Jan Bosman du Toit. In 2001, at the Abuja summit, African leaders pledged to accord the three diseases of HIV, tuberculosis (TB) and malaria top priority, and committed themselves to dedicating a target of 15 per cent of their national budgets to health. The South African government supported the Abuja Declaration. AIDS Watch Africa (AWA), made up of a group of committed African leaders, was also created at the Abuja summit to stimulate action, mobilise resources and spearhead efforts and accountability to address these three diseases. President Mbeki was a member of this group of African leaders.

The UNAIDS Country Office in South Africa was established in 2001, headed by: Ivan Lloyd (2001); Bernard Nywati (2002); and Mbulawa Mugabe (late 2002–mid 2008). The country office continued to work behind the scenes to broker understanding with the government of South Africa. At the end of 2001, South Africa became a signatory to the first Political Declaration on HIV and AIDS of the UN General Assembly Special Session on HIV and AIDS, which clearly defined targets for tracking the global AIDS response.

On the ground, UNAIDS continued to work with officials in government departments, primarily the Departments of Health and Social Development, to ensure that the AIDS response made progress, albeit slow. This included providing technical support for the generation of epidemiological estimates and acting as the Secretariat for the Donor Co-ordination Forum of the Department of Health. UNAIDS also funded a number of interventions. These included civil society efforts to ensure the greater involvement of people living with HIV (GIPA) in the response efforts. In 2002, the UN Secretary General called for a Global Fund to finance a multi-sectoral AIDS response, and thus the Global Fund to Fight AIDS, TB and Malaria was born. UNAIDS supported South Africa with its first proposal to the international financing body.

In January 2003, President George Bush announced an initiative to combat HIV and AIDS worldwide that would come to be known as the President's Emergency Plan for AIDS Relief or PEPFAR. Following the adoption by South Africa's cabinet of a policy endorsing ART in 2003, Project Phidisa – supported by the South Africa National Defence Force and the United States (US) National

Institute of Health – began enrolling military family members with HIV on ART. By 2004, PEPFAR were funding ART for people living with HIV (PLHIV) across South Africa, working with non-governmental organisations (NGOs) and the South Africa health system. This was the era of initial scale-up of HIV treatment when patients would arrive at a treatment facility incapacitated and near death and, weeks later, would walk out to return to their families and their lives. The programmes supported by PEPFAR in these early days proved that President George Bush was right, that it was possible to scale-up successful HIV treatment. PEPFAR helped South Africa to launch the era of HIV treatment that continues to this day.

By the time the WHO and UNAIDS launched targets to place three million people on treatment by 2005 (3×5) in 2003, the groundwork for the modest domestic financing of HIV in the country had been laid. South Africa was ready to fully acquiesce to the universal roll out of HIV treatment. The national PMTCT roll out had begun the previous year following a Constitutional Court order (as a result of an action brought by TAC, supported by the AIDS Law Project). The Universal ARV treatment plan, brought to life under the leadership of Deputy President Jacob Zuma as Chairperson of SANAC, began a slow roll out in Gauteng in April 2004. It would be a good two years later, in 2006, that UNAIDS adopted the UNAIDS Commitments of Scaling up towards Universal Access to treatment in Brazzaville.

In 2004, UNAIDS adopted the global 'Three Ones' principles for the coordination of national AIDS responses: one agreed AIDS framework; one national AIDS co-ordinating body; and one agreed country-level monitoring and evaluation system. At the country level, the UN Joint Team on AIDS was established to better coordinate UN support to the national response. The UNAIDS Country Office was strengthened with additional technical staff. Support for the fledgling AIDS response in South Africa was growing.

South Africa leveraged the UNAIDS 'Three Ones' principles to shape the ground breaking South Africa National Strategic Plan (NSP) on HIV and AIDS and STI, 2007–2011. Along with civil society and others, UNAIDS worked with government partners to develop the first widely agreed-upon multi-sectoral plan for HIV in South Africa. The NSP was spearheaded by Phumzile Mlambo-Ngcuka, Deputy President of South Africa, and Nosizwe Madlala-Routledge, Deputy Minister of Health, who was acting while Minister Tshabalala-Msimang was hospitalised for an illness. Madlala-Routledge represented one of the few voices of reason in government during these difficult days. She was fired from her position in 2007, ostensibly for attending a conference without permission, but many believe it was because of her views on AIDS which were contrary to those of the Health Minister and President Mbeki.

To his credit, President Mbeki had substantially 'removed himself' from the HIV discourse since 2002. In a more positive approach, he also mentioned AIDS a few times in his State of the Nation Address in February 2005, stating, 'With regards to AIDS in particular, the government's plan, which is among the best in the world, combining awareness, treatment and home-based care is being implemented with vigour'.[4]

During the many years of South Africa's tumultuous response to the epidemic, UNAIDS succeeded in distinguishing itself as a behind-the-scenes political engineer. Under the overall guidance of the UNAIDS Executive Director, Michel Sidibé (2009 to present), the UNAIDS Country Office began the process of systematically repairing and repositioning the organisation's severely damaged relationship with the South African government at the highest level. Mark Stirling was the Director of UNAIDS Regional Support Team (2003-2009), based in Johannesburg at the time, and he also contributed valuable programmatic leadership support to the country office.

This approach by UNAIDS differed markedly from the approach taken by the UN Special Envoy on AIDS, Stephen Lewis. Focusing on 'speaking truth to power', Lewis, from the early days, aligned himself openly with TAC and other activists. He capitalised on the Toronto International AIDS Conference in 2006 to drive home his stinging criticism of the South African government. South Africa, he declared, "is the unkindest cut of all. It is the only country in Africa, amongst all the countries I have traversed in the last five years, whose government is still obtuse, dilatory and negligent about rolling treatment. It is the only country in Africa whose government continues to propound theories more worthy of a lunatic fringe than of a concerned and compassion state. Between six and eight thousand people a day die of AIDS in South Africa. The government has a lot to atone for. I'm of the opinion that they can never achieve redemption".[5] While slow to rollout treatment, the government was criticised for persisting in promoting unhelpful nutritional diets such as lemons, beetroot, garlic and African (sweet) potatoes.

The UNAIDS Country Office and Sidibé were on hand to play midwives to, and witness, the beginning of the transformation in the South African AIDS response. In late 2008, Kgalema Motlanthe replaced Mbeki as President. On his first day in office, he appointed Barbara Hogan as Minister of Health. On her appointment, Minister Hogan stated, 'The age of denialism is completely over in South Africa'.[6] Thus, with a short and simple statement, Minister Hogan signalled the dawn of a new leadership on HIV in South Africa, changing the lives of millions of South Africans forever.

The Dawn of a New National AIDS Response: South Africa Takes Responsibility, 2009-2010

'Know your epidemic, know your response and act on its politics',[7] the Executive Director of UNAIDS, Michel Sidibé, told his Country Directors. At the time of his appointment as UNAIDS Executive Director in January 2009, South Africa was among the worst performers on HIV issues in Africa. Sidibé promptly set out to woo the newly-appointed South African Minister of Health, Aaron Motsoaledi. His first aim was to convince the energetic and passionate Minister, who was nevertheless understandably nervous, that South Africa should lead the continent in responding to the HIV epidemic. His second aim was, together with Minister Motsoaledi, to convince newly-elected President Jacob Zuma to distinguish his leadership and administration by turning around the South African AIDS response.

In June 2009, during his first State of the Nation Address, President Zuma directly referred to HIV prevention and treatment. This was a marked contrast to previous State of the Nation addresses in which HIV was mentioned a few times, but not accorded the prominence it deserved. This was a sign of things to come. In October 2009, President Zuma delivered a speech which dealt the final blow to high-level political AIDS denialism in South Africa. He acknowledged HIV as one of South Africa's most serious problems, saying that '... all South Africans need to know their HIV status, and be informed of the treatment options available to them'.[8]

During the World AIDS Day commemoration on 1 December 2009, at which Sidibé joined President Zuma and Minister Motsoaledi, President Zuma launched the 'I am responsible; we are responsible; South Africa is taking responsibility' campaign. This signalled a new era of individual, collective and political action for the HIV response. President Zuma also announced important high-level policy shifts, which cemented the change in political leadership on HIV and TB. These included a massive HIV counselling and testing campaign linked to an accelerated treatment and care programme, which was launched in 2010.

Reading the dramatic change in the political climate, Sidibé channelled massive resources into the UNAIDS Country Office in South Africa, making it the largest country office in the world. The focus of the new fit-for-purpose office was to build the capacity of a decentralised HIV and TB response. Catherine Sozi became the UNAIDS Country Director, January 2009-2014. Sheila Tlou (2010-present), became Director of the UNAIDS Regional Support Team in Johannesburg. During this period, UNAIDS substantially deepened its relationship with the first CEO of SANAC, Nono Simelela, Minister Motsoaledi and President Zuma. This would prove critical for the quality and nature of UNAIDS collaboration with the government.

In April 2010, Sidibé returned to South Africa to witness the launch of the HIV Counselling and Testing campaign. Over these two years (2009 and 2010), Sidibé visited South Africa an astonishing ten times, firmly demonstrated UNAIDS's high-level commitment to see the country through a remarkable transition on the approach to AIDS. Said Minister Motsoaledi, 'UNAIDS Executive Director Michel Sidibe visited us regularly during President Zuma's first year in office. He worked to convince the President that by scaling up domestic resources and implementing the world's largest response, we would irrevocable change the course of South Africa's future and serve as model for the region'.[9]

The HIV counselling and testing campaign in South Africa was the largest and most ambitious campaign in Africa. To launch the campaign, President Zuma, along with Sidibé, Minister Motsoaledi and others, publicly tested for HIV. For a country gripped by the fear and ignorance of AIDS denialism for so many years, this act was significant. Over a period of 15 months, 15 million people were offered HIV counselling and testing, 13.2 million were tested, and 8 million were screened for TB. The testing campaign kick-started the lacklustre HIV treatment programme. Of the 2.2 million who tested HIV positive over the 15-month period, 400 000 were initiated on HIV treatment. This increased by 50 per cent the number of people on HIV treatment since roll out started six years earlier. Treatment expansion was accompanied by many innovations. Task-shifting through a nurse-initiated management of antiretroviral therapy enabled many more people to be put on treatment. Eighty per cent of South African health facilities became accredited antiretroviral therapy sites.

In 2010, South Africa began major domestic investment in its AIDS response. This was ground breaking and went far beyond the initiatives of every other country in Africa. In terms of the public purse, 'the AIDS response has become one of our top political priorities,' said Minister Motsoaledi.[10] Continuing its behind-the-scenes high-level advocacy, UNAIDS brokered a meeting between the Minister, WHO, the Clinton Health Access Initiative (CHAI), PEPFAR and other partners, to develop a new tender strategy for the procurement of antiretrovirals. This strategy led to a 53 per cent reduction in cost, with savings of R250-R350 million annually. In addition, the Global Fund to Fight AIDS, Malaria and TB awarded South Africa a R310 million grant, primarily aimed at treatment scale-up. UNAIDS played a critical role in both grant proposal development and oversight functions within the Global Fund Country Co-ordinating Mechanism (CCM).

South Africa has always been home to world-renowned HIV scientists and researchers. Led by Professor Salim Abdool Karim, the Centre for the AIDS Programme of Research in South Africa (CAPRISA) – a UNAIDS collaborating centre[11] – released, in 2010, the results of the transformative CAPRISA 004 trial at global AIDS conference in Vienna (AIDS2010). Funded by PEPFAR through the U.S. Agency for International Development (USAID), this study showed that a microbicide containing 1 per cent tenofovir was 30 per cent effective in reducing women's risk of acquiring HIV infection during intercourse and 51 per cent effective in preventing genital herpes infections among women participating in the trial. This home grown, cutting-edge research bolstered the country's global image as a leader in AIDS science and research.

In two short years, the groundwork was laid for South Africa to transform from international HIV pariah, to a model country of the global AIDS response by 2016. Sidibé's vision – to understand the HIV epidemic and response and to act on its politics – became a defining factor for South Africa's AIDS response in the years that followed.

The Laggard Becomes the Continental Leader, 2011-2015

In his State of the Nation Address of February 2014, President Zuma said, 'The HIV and AIDS turnaround is one of the biggest achievements of this administration and we are used as a model country by UNAIDS'.[12] By early 2011, the national AIDS response was well established in South Africa. Led by President Zuma and Minister Motsoaledi, evidence-based policies were being approved, and interventions were being scaled up. From 2011 to 2015, the national response expanded massively. This programme expansion had a major impact on the epidemic. In a range of interventions, South Africa moved from being a laggard to becoming the African leader in its national AIDS response.

The third National Strategic Plan (NSP) on HIV, STIs and TB, 2012-2016, was developed with substantial UNAIDS technical and strategic information support. The NSP was a world-class integrated NSP: a truly multi-sectoral plan, mobilising all of South Africa to respond to the massive AIDS epidemic. The NSP also combined the AIDS response with that of sexually transmitted infections (STIs) and TB, assigning responsibilities to a wide range of government departments.

Civil society was a key stakeholder in the NSP. PLHIV networks, community-based organisations, faith-based groups, women and youth groups and the business sector, were all identified as key implementers of the NSP. Building on the

NSP, SANAC worked to re-organise the civil society structures working on the AIDS response, recognising some 18 sectors. UNAIDS supported this important reform agenda, and collaborated closely with the SANAC Deputy-Chair, Steve Letsike, to set up and operationalise the SANAC Civil Society Partnership Forum.

President Zuma launched the third NSP on World AIDS Day in 2011 – showing his continued commitment to the response in South Africa. The NSP also led to a massive increase in overall government funding of the response. Across Africa, the South African NSP was highlighted as a continental 'best practice'.

From 2013, there were increasing efforts to evaluate and document innovative provincial and district AIDS responses, particularly those working to promote a multi-sectoral response. As the epicentre of the AIDS epidemic within South Africa, the KwaZulu-Natal province (KZN) developed 'Operation Sukuma Sakhe' (OSS), its version of the national 'war on poverty' concept developed by President Mbeki. Championed by the Premier of KZN, this community-based service delivery model supported communities to identify needs, and to hold local government accountable to responding to these needs.

At the 2013 SANAC Plenary, then Deputy President and Chairperson of SANAC, Kgalema Motlanthe, called for all provinces to adopt the OSS approach. With the support of UNAIDS, the KZN province prepared a best practice documentation of OSS. This was launched early in 2014 by Deputy President Motlanthe, Premier Mchunu, Minister Motsoaledi and Sidibé in KZN.

During this period, South Africa rapidly became the largest domestic financier of a national response on the continent. The government increased domestic funding for AIDS by nearly 700 per cent between the 2006/7 and 2015/16 financial years. This represented an increase from R2.1 billion to almost R15.3 billion over this period. By 2015, the South African government provided over 80 per cent of total domestic AIDS resources. The 'AIDS Conditional Grant' was established with national resources directed towards provinces, and 'ring fenced' for specific funding of HIV activities. In a financial analysis of the global AIDS response, UNAIDS congratulated South Africa for this level of support, one of the highest for a country that was not part of the Organisation for Economic Co-operation and Development (OECD).

In 2015, South Africa increasingly focused on ensuring the financial sustainability of the AIDS response. The government committed to putting 6.4 million people on HIV treatment. With UNAIDS, PEPFAR and other development partners' support, the government undertook an 'Investment Case Study on the HIV and TB Response', to ensure the most financially sustainable way of funding the AIDS response. The Investment Case study was a scientific review of the most effective and affordable prevention and treatment interventions. The results of the

Investment Case have been used in NDoH budget discussions with the National Treasury, and to add TB to the 'ring fenced' AIDS Conditional Grant to Provinces.

By 2015, South Africa was receiving about US$413 million a year in US government funds (over US$5 billion since 2004) through the PEPFAR programme. UNAIDS was strongly engaged in advocating for continued PEPFAR support for South Africa, including the development of the PEPFAR 'Country Operation Plans', re-focusing of targets across districts based on the burden of the disease, emphasising the prevention agenda and supporting engagement of civil society organisations (CSOs).

Using the results of the Investment Case, the South African CCM, ably led by SANAC Chief Executive Officer (CEO), Fareed Abdullah, prepared a high quality concept note for continued Global Fund grants to South Africa, and succeeded in obtaining US$304 million for HIV and TB programmes over three years. UNAIDS is an active member of the CCM, and co-ordinated the UN Joint Team on AIDS to provide technical support in the development of the concept note. UNAIDS continues to liaise with the Global Fund Technical Review Panel and other groups to support and justify the South African grant. In 2015, UNAIDS played a critical role in expanding the inclusiveness and accountability of the CCM to integrate NDoH and WHO as voting members.

From 2013, an increasing number of development partners withdrew from South Africa, after deciding to focus their financial support on lower income countries. Many large and small AIDS CSOs in South Africa depended on funding from external development partners, and were strongly impacted by this withdrawal. In consultation with the Presidency, NDoH and SANAC, UNAIDS responded to this CSO financial crisis, in particular to networks of people living with HIV (specifically NAPWA and TAC) by seeking emergency funding, and supporting a study on the strategic role of CSOs to ensure financial sustainability.

At the 2014 global AIDS conference (AIDS2014) in Melbourne, Australia, UNAIDS announced the 90-90-90 targets: that by 2020, 90 per cent of all people living with HIV would know their HIV status; 90 per cent of all people diagnosed with HIV infection would receive sustained antiretroviral therapy; and 90 per cent of all people receiving antiretroviral therapy would have viral suppression. Within 48 hours of returning from AIDS2014, Minister Motsoaledi succeeded in defending the new targets before Parliament and secured the needed budgetary commitments. Thus, South Africa was not only the first country to adopt these targets, but also the first to extend them to TB, and the first to implement them nationwide, through the innovative 'District Implementation Plan' (DIP) approach.

The DIP process, spearheaded by Yogan Pillay, Deputy-Director General of Strategic Health Programmes in NDoH, works from the bottom up to establish local targets and to identify the causes of poor performance against agreed indicators. This process builds on the 'three feet' idea, of focusing on local plans and action (as opposed to a high-level aerial view from, for example, 30 000 feet). With the support of UNAIDS, PEPFAR and other partners, DIP was rapidly rolled out to all 52 districts in South Africa in 2015. DIP plans take into account all available resources, both from the government and development partners. The DIP approach is also being reviewed by the National Health Insurance (NHI) planning teams as a possible 'best practice' for the expansion of all health planning at district level.

In late 2014, changes in the UN Country Team also provided new leadership opportunities on HIV to the UN system in South Africa. Gana Fofang was appointed as the UN Resident Coordinator, and Erasmus Morah was appointed UNAIDS Country Director, following a period of interim UNAIDS directorship by Fritz Leherisson and Benjamin Alli. Appointed as the highest ranking UNAIDS Country Director in Africa and globally, Morah was challenged by Sidibé to deliver on three key agenda items: support the roll out and realisation of the 90-90-90 targets on the ground; substantially strengthen UNAIDS engagement with CSOs without compromising UNAIDS' excellent relationships with the government (an extremely difficult balancing act to achieve); and, with an eye on the global AIDS conference in Durban (AIDS2016), document and tell the South African success story on AIDS.

With the rapid expansion of the treatment programme, South Africa has worked to improve the effectiveness and efficiency of the programme. This has included the adoption of WHO treatment guidelines. In 2013, a single fixed-dose combination ARV pill replaced a multi-pill regimen, making it more convenient for patients and less expensive for the government. South Africa also began implementing WHO's Option B+ guidelines for PMTCT.

Continually on the lookout for the latest innovation, South Africa has become the global price trendsetter for ARVs, and has promoted the use of economies of scale among developing countries. In 2014, South Africa led a breakthrough negotiation, in partnership with UNAIDS, CHAI and Roche, to significantly reduce the price of viral load tests for some 70 low-income countries (e.g. to less than US$10 from as high as US$65 per test).

In 2015, KZN commemorated putting one million people on HIV treatment. UNAIDS worked with the KZN Office of the Premier to finalise a documentary of this treatment achievement, which was to be disseminated at the Durban AIDS2016 Conference. Deputy President Cyril Ramaphosa, accompanied by

Minister Motsoaledi, addressed the commemoration of World TB Day and launched a massive nationwide National TB Screening Campaign. UNAIDS continues to be a strong advocate and technical contributor to the NDoH for the better integration of HIV and TB services.

South Africa still has the highest number of new HIV infections a year globally. The results of the Human Sciences Research Council (HRSC) population-based study showed continued increases in risky sexual behaviour and reduced condom use. This led South Africa to seek innovative approaches to comprehensive prevention, especially for young women and adolescent girls. In his 2015 budget speech, Minister Motsoaledi highlighted the need to intensify prevention efforts. These include a revitalised behaviour change communication programme; increased HIV testing, including targeting of those most likely to be infected; expanding voluntary medical male circumcision, especially among young adult men; working on the elimination of mother-to-child transmission (eMTCT) of HIV; and ensuring larger numbers were on ARVs, to expand 'treatment as prevention'.

Many of those newly infected with HIV in South Africa were young women and adolescent girls. For a range of biological and sociological reasons, young women are especially vulnerable to HIV transmission. A government of South Africa and UNAIDS analysis showed that in South Africa in 2015, nearly 2 000 adolescent girls and young women were newly infected with HIV every week. In response to this, a government, PEPFAR and UNAIDS team developed the 'DREAMS' (Determined, Resilient, Empowered, AIDS-free, Mentored and Safe women) project proposal on comprehensive prevention and empowerment of young women and adolescent girls. This was funded by PEPFAR for US$67 million over two years in five districts of two provinces. The South African proposal received the bulk of PEPFAR funds available for DREAMS in 10 countries, and the PEPFAR Ambassador, Deborah Birx, personally attended the launch of the DREAMS initiative on 17 November 2015. At the launch, the United States Ambassador in South Africa, Patrick Gaspard, said: 'The DREAMS initiative will create opportunities for entrepreneurship, micro-financing, education, and awareness, resulting not only in an AIDS-free generation, but a generation ready to lead South Africa, the continent, and the world'.[13]

On 24 June 2016, Deputy President, Cyril Ramaphosa launched an ambitious, three-year mass nationwide HIV prevention campaign targeting young women and girls. This campaign, costing R3 billion from PEPFAR, Global Fund, the German government and government departments, will be used to substantively broaden and expand the DREAMS approach to all districts of the country. It will seek to reduce the interlinked problems of HIV, school dropout, teenage pregnancy and gender-based violence and to maximise health, education and economic opportunities for young women and adolescent girls. UNAIDS and UNFPA partnered with the government and other actors to provide the technical support for the development and launch of the campaign.

The South African Constitution is admired globally for the full recognition of human rights. South Africa, therefore, aims to ensure a human rights-based approach to HIV, especially in addressing stigma and discrimination against people living with HIV. Following the UNAIDS supported pilot project in the Eastern Cape, a large scale stigma index survey was undertaken on a national basis, involving over 10 000 PLHIV. Deputy President, Cyril Ramaphosa, launched South Africa's first National Stigma Index Survey, undertaken by SANAC, in partnership with PLHIV and NAPWA. The results were shared at the South African AIDS Conference in Durban in 2015.

The impact of South Africa's HIV policies and programmes is now evident in the numbers. In South Africa there was a 40 per cent reduction in new HIV infections in adults between 2010 and 2014, and a drop in new infections from 550 000 in 2010 to 330 000 in 2014. By 2014, PMTCT coverage was more than 95 per cent of pregnant women. There was an 85 per cent decline in new infections among children under the age of 15, from 60 000 a year in 2010 to 9 200 in 2014. The HIV transmission rate among children at 18 months of age was estimated at less than 5 per cent at the time of writing. This makes South Africa eligible to apply for 'pre-elimination' of mother-to-child-transmission status in recognition of high burden countries which have achieved significant success and are on the path to elimination. Most significantly, there was a massive scale-up of the treatment programme, from 784 000 people on treatment in 2004 to over 2.9 million people in 2014 – an increase of 373 per cent. These efforts resulted in a massive reduction of 58 per cent in AIDS related deaths from 2005 to 2014, with the bulk of this reduction occurring between 2010 and 2014.

In five short years, between 2011 and 2015, South Africa has become the continental leader of the AIDS response, rising to the challenge of AIDS activists and the United Nations. South Africa has successfully built on the leadership of President Zuma and Minister Motsoaledi to establish an effective, evidence-based AIDS response. South Africa has shown how to embrace the evidence and global targets to respond to the largest AIDS epidemic in the world.

Beyond the Mountain Top – What Lies Ahead to End AIDS in South Africa

The District Implementation Plans for HIV and TB have transformed the UNAIDS 90-90-90 targets from a global concept to a meaningful planning and implementation process in South Africa, which cuts across all levels, from national to district to a local level. DIP has led to the better utilisation of the provincial conditional grant for HIV and TB (estimated in excess US$1 billion annually), which will in turn lead to better use and accountability for funds.

In partnership with UNAIDS, PEPFAR and others, the government is in the early stages of taking the DIPs beyond health indicators. This process will engage other key government departments, such as Social Development and Basic Education, and build their capacity to plan for results, which will ensure that ending AIDS as a public health threat is achievable, while leaving no one behind. The tracer indicators for the DIP+ plans, as they are being called, address many of the social determinants of health that need to be taken into account for a comprehensive and robust multi-sectoral response to HIV and TB. During this process, it will be important to engage civil society in the planning and implementation process, as without the partnership of civil society the great programmes that South Africa has built up will have limited success.

The DIPs aim to better utilise the government HIV funding at local level, and are therefore one element of the effort to ensure sustainable financing for HIV and TB. More than ever, South Africa and its development partners cannot afford to take their foot off the financing pedal. The country needs to build strong investment cases for HIV and TB (including at lower levels in the districts), in order to maintain key donors for the long haul. Donors such as PEPFAR and the Global Fund, which have been with South Africa since the beginning, need to stay the course until the trajectory of the epidemic is well and truly broken.

At the heart of sustainable financing is the question of who pays for what and how. UNAIDS recently supported a study that examined different options for the diversification of current domestic HIV and TB funding models. This study suggested different scenarios for integrating HIV into the broader health financing agenda. These may include options for National Health Insurance, which is Minister Motsoaledi's ambitious goal for achieving equity and access to South Africa's health system.

Civil society organisations are under increasing financial pressure, and many are at the brink of closure. UNAIDS was able to find emergency funding for TAC and Section 27 (the successor to the AIDS Law Project) to avoid their closure. The longest established network of people living with HIV in South Africa, NAPWA, is also experiencing a severe crisis and faces closure. UNAIDS contributes financial resources and works together with the South African Presidency and NDoH to provide technical support to help NAPWA and its current leader, Mluleki Zazini, become more relevant and sustainable in responding to the evolving epidemic.

There is a critical need to identify options for a sustainable financing framework for the future of CSOs in South Africa. These options should focus on ensuring the financial viability, sustainability and good management of local South African AIDS CSOs, in order to continue their contribution to the South African AIDS response. CSOs also need to look inwards, to reflect and ensure that they are fit-for-purpose in light of the changing AIDS response in South Africa.

South Africa is walking the last mile towards the pre-certification of the eMTCT. To get there, it is critical to continue the high-level political leadership provided by President Zuma, Minister Motsoaledi, and the many passionate and committed staff in the NDoH. An even stronger multi-sectoral response is needed to reach eMTCT. This can be achieved by absorbing the 70 000 volunteer community caregivers into the Departments of Health and Social Development. Using these community caregivers for the 'three feet' approach of implementing interventions with scale and quality at the family and household level, will enable South Africa to achieve this historic goal.

South Africa continues to provide bold leadership for breakthrough results. It has proven time and again that it is possible to implement game changing innovations through a 'learning by doing' approach – the HIV counselling and testing campaign, task shifting, and mobile platforms such as MomConnect and B-Wise are evidence of this. The country was scheduled to provide pre-exposure prophylaxis (PrEP) in June 2016, initially to sex workers and possibly for men who have sex with men, and for other key populations at a later date. Another bold policy innovation is the Universal HIV Test and Treat Offer among the general population, announced by Minister Motsoaledi to commence in September 2016. Combined, these game-changer decisions and interventions aim to fast-track the AIDS response in South Africa over the next five years.

South Africa needs to continue to tell the 'good news' story of the national AIDS response. It is up to UNAIDS and other partners to help keep the political leadership engaged, donors sympathetic, and the people of South Africa energised, so that all are moving together towards the shared goal of ending AIDS. When the world came to Durban in 2000 for the international AIDS conference, only a handful of South Africans were known to be on ART, most of these through private insurance schemes. Today, as the world returns to Durban in July 2016 for the 21st International AIDS Conference, South Africa boasts more than 3.4 million people on the life-saving antiretroviral therapy.

Some Concluding Remarks and Discussion – Getting the Science and Politics of the Response Right

It always seems impossible until it is done.

Nelson Rolihlahla Mandela

South Africa's AIDS journey has all the elements of an epic tale – and UNAIDS was an important part of this journey. The 1990s saw the dawning of democracy in the country. The ANC-led government had its hands full with the project of reconciliation and reparation. As President Nelson Mandela would later acknowledge, not enough was done on AIDS in those early days. In the 2000s, there was a misguided debate, catalysed by President Thabo Mbeki, on whether HIV caused AIDS, and questioned the value of ART. Valuable time was lost, and the epidemic grew. The stage was set, and the country became the epicentre of the global AIDS epidemic. President Mbeki was unable to embrace mainstream science on AIDS and to respond boldly to the epidemic. The impact on South Africa was increasingly devastating, with almost every family and community losing loved ones to AIDS.

Finally, in 2009, there was redemption. A new administration – headed by President Jacob Zuma and his Health Minister, Motsoaledi – turned it all around for South Africa. The country was led from despair to hope. There are many other personalities and important contributors not mentioned in this story – among these, people living with HIV, activists, scientists, researchers and public health professionals. They all left their mark on the AIDS response in South Africa.

From 2009, South Africa's leadership honestly confronted the reality of AIDS, and implemented a large-scale national AIDS response that has become an example to the world. UNAIDS supported the government throughout this journey, and worked to bridge the science and the politics of AIDS in South Africa. Piot had noted, 'You need politics and science to work together. Politics without science can be dangerous. However, science without politics is powerless'. Looking back on UNAIDS engagement in South Africa, Piot concluded that 'Whenever we made progress on AIDS, it was because of good politics. Whenever there was no progress, it was because of bad politics'.[14] UNAIDS repeatedly confronted the South African government on their de facto policy of AIDS denialism. It also worked with South African AIDS activists to highlight the impact of the government's AIDS denialism on the people of South Africa, and to eventually break the silence on AIDS in the country.

As UNAIDS Executive Director, Michel Sidibé expressed his conviction that, 'In the end, it's all down to politics. Get the politics right and the government and people of South Africa would do the rest'.[15] Sidibé worked with President

Mothlante and, later, President Zuma and Minister Motsoaledi, to reframe the South African AIDS response. This was done through a close and respectful relationship. Sidibé engaged deeply with South African leaders on his 26 visits to South Africa between January 2009 and April 2016. This included work with strategic allies such as First Lady Tobeka Madiba Zuma, the newly appointed UNAIDS Special Advocate for the Health of Women, Children and Youth. As Minister Motsoaledi publicly stated at the World AIDS Day commemoration in 2015, Sidibé and UNAIDS succeeded to 'inspire us and the rest of the world to believe that we can bring an end to AIDS. UNAIDS jointly walked the AIDS response with us and kept us company'.[16]

Sidibé and UNAIDS inspired and motivated South Africa with a global vision on how to respond to the world's largest AIDS epidemic. This vision included the goals of the 'three zeroes', '90-90-90 targets', 'fast track' and 'Ending AIDS by 2030'. The South African government has adopted these ambitious targets. They have developed roadmaps to achieve these targets, and made the necessary funding available.

UNAIDS supported South African leaders in keeping HIV high on the national political agenda, and to fund the response. UNAIDS has driven the dialogue on smart investments and sustainable financing, and supported South Africa in strengthening the overall policy and national AIDS co-ordination mechanism and processes. UNAIDS has increasingly invested in the strengthening of civil society engagement, including a sharp focus on the voice of networks of people living with HIV.

Through its family of co-sponsoring agencies (WHO, UNICEF, UNFPA, UNODC, UN Women, ILO, World Bank, UNDP, UNESCO, UNHCR and WFP),[17] UNAIDS has continued to advocate for, and provide technical guidance on, bold programmatic initiatives and innovations. These have included the Elimination of Mother to Child Transmission of HIV, HIV Counselling and Testing campaigns, new WHO treatment guidelines, promotion of medical male circumcision, PrEP and Universal Test and Treat, key population interventions, social protection measures for orphans and vulnerable children (OVC), and a critical focus on the needs of young women and adolescent girls.

South Africa has come from a dark place into the light. It remains the epicentre of the global AIDS epidemic, with many challenges to overcome. According to 2015 UNAIDS estimates, it still accounts for the world's largest number of new infections annually (380 000); 180 000 still die each year because of AIDS; and only half of the 6.9 million South Africans living with HIV are receiving ARVs. Programme and operational challenges include drug stock-outs and loss to follow-up of people enrolled on treatment. Many of these are due to weaknesses in an overburdened health system, and arising from the massive rapid scale-up of what is already the world's largest treatment programme. These challenges should be expected and must be tackled.

UNAIDS will continue to provide leadership to South Africa and, indeed, the global community to promote a multi-sectoral response to HIV and TB, and infuse scientific evidence, global targets and norms into the work that South Africa is doing at a country level.

Journeying together over the past 20 years, South Africa and UNAIDS initially opposed each other, but eventually came together to respond boldly to one of the largest epidemics the world has ever known. The pace of the journey has, at varying times, been a walk, a jog or a run. It is now a sprint to achieve 90-90-90 targets by 2020, and to end AIDS as a public health threat by 2030. UNAIDS is proud and privileged to journey together with this remarkable country.

Notes and References

1 While the authors are grateful to a number of reviewers – Bunmi Makinwa, Tabita Ntuli, Kerry Cullinan, Amakobe Sande, Eva Kiwango, Kerry Pelzman and two others who preferred not to be named – the views and opinions expressed are entirely those of the authors, and do not represent the official policy, endorsement or account of UNAIDS, or any of its co-sponsoring UN agencies.

2 Senior author's interview and discussions with the subject.

3 Interview, Washington Post, 27 September 2003.

4 President Mbeki, South African State of the Union address, February 2005.

5 Remarks by Stephen Lewis, UN Special Envoy for HIV/AIDS for the Closing Session of the XVI International AIDS Conference, Toronto, Canada, 2006.

6 Dugger, Celia 2008, "Study Cites Toll of AIDS Policy in South Africa", New York Times, New York.

7 Senior author's interview and discussions with the subject.

8 Address by the President of the Republic of South Africa, HE Mr Jacob Zuma, to the National Council of Provinces (NCOP), NCOP Chamber, 29 October 2009, Cape Town.

9 UNAIDS (2015), How AIDS Changed Everything; MDG 6: 15 Years, 15 Lessons of Hope from the AIDS Epidemic, Geneva, p. 227.

10 UNAIDS (2015), How AIDS Changed Everything; MDG 6: 15 Years, 15 Lessons of Hope from the AIDS Epidemic, Geneva, p. 227.

11 CAPRISA was created in 2001 and formally established in 2002, under the U.S. National Institutes of Health (NIH)-funded Comprehensive International Program of Research on AIDS (CIPRA), by five partner institutions: University of KwaZulu-Natal, University of Cape Town, University of Western Cape, National Institute for Communicable Diseases, and Columbia University in New York.

12 President Zuma, South African State of the Union address, February 2014.

13 USA Embassy, Pretoria: Press Release: "DREAMS Program to Help Fight HIV/AIDS Infection among Young Girls", 17 November 2015.

14 Daily Maverick (June 2012), "Peter Piot: A Life on the virus frontier, South Africa.
15 Senior author's interview and discussions with the subject.
16 South African World AIDS Day Commemoration, 1st December 2015 (statements made by the Minister prior to introducing the Deputy President Ramaphosa to speak at the event).
17 United Nations Children's Fund (UNICEF), United Nations Fund for Population Activities (UNFPA), United Nations Office on Drugs and Crime (UNODC), United Nations Entity for Gender Equality and the Empowerment of Women (UN Women), International Labour Organisation (ILO), United Nations Development Programme (UNDP), United Nations Educational, Scientific and Cultural Organisation (UNESCO), United Nations High Commissioner for Refugees (UNHCR), and World Food Programme (WFP).

Chapter 16

Community-led Integrated Service Delivery 'War Rooms' and the Fight Against HIV, AIDS and TB in KwaZulu-Natal Province, South Africa

Tom Zhuwau, Nonhlanhla Ndlovu, Veni Naidu, Tryphinah Ngwenya and Senzeni Mkhize

Introduction

The 1978 World Health Assembly's Alma Ata Declaration ushered in primary health care as a global approach to improve health service delivery and health outcomes. This was more so in low and middle income countries with limited health resources. The primary health care approach also witnessed a remarkable rise in the use of lay health workers in the delivery of basic health services.[1] The advent of the human immunodeficiency virus (HIV) and acquired immune deficiency syndrome (AIDS) and the marked rise in tuberculosis (TB) infections from the early 1980s to the mid-2000s, gave additional impetus to the increased use of lay health workers and community-based structures to fight these twin epidemics in settings with limited resources.

The fight against poverty, inequality and disease remains central to the 2015 Sustainable Development Goals (SDGs), the goals that followed the Millennium Development Goals (MDGs). The 17 SDGs address issues of poverty, inequality, disease and sustainable development.[2] The first SDG deals with ending poverty in all its forms, and everywhere. It is necessary to mobilise a wide range of community structures, as agents of change, to provide the means of achieving the goals.

This chapter explores the experiences of KwaZulu-Natal in rolling out community-led structures and the provision of service delivery 'War Rooms' to fight the TB, HIV and AIDS epidemics. The chapter highlights how lay health workers, paid a nominal monthly stipend, are at the forefront of pushing back epidemics which, a few years back, were destroying the province. The lay health workers, commonly known as community caregivers (CCGs), have become a symbol of hope in the delivery of primary health care in poor and under-served communities of KwaZulu-Natal.

Background

Poverty, inequality, disease and lack of economic opportunities remain a challenge for South Africa. The National Development Plan prioritised the eradication of poverty and the creation of economic opportunities as a sustainable response to these challenges. In November 2014 the Deputy President of South Africa, Mr Cyril Ramaphosa, implored the country to adopt and use home-grown strategies and best practices to address poor service delivery and fight social ills. He cited successful lessons learnt from the Operation Sukuma Sakhe (OSS) model of the KwaZulu-Natal province. OSS is an integrated service delivery model using the concept of community-led 'service delivery War Rooms' as a one-stop shop for addressing community and household issues. The concept was derived from observing how the street and village development committees of Tanzania dealt with local development needs.

The OSS concept is rooted in development theory which recognises that people must play a key and participative role in their development.[3] Participative development theory argues that mainstream development approaches are often prescriptive, top-down, 'experts' driven, and alienating. They do not give voice to communities and individuals. To counter the orthodoxy approach to development, participative development approaches argue that people are the greatest asset to any development. It is further argued that development practitioners need to recognise that people are surrounded by assets which give them agency: social, environmental, cultural, economic, infrastructural, and relational. According to Kretzmann and McKnight,[4] participative development, therefore, focuses on:

- community assets and strengths rather than problems and needs;
- it identifies and mobilises individual and community assets, skills and passions;
- it is community driven – 'building communities from the inside out'; and
- it is relationship driven.

KwaZulu-Natal is South Africa's second largest province and is home to 10.2 million people (20 per cent of the country's population).[5] Approximately 5.7 per cent of the population of KwaZulu-Natal is illiterate, 2.9 per cent is without access to safe water, and 25.2 per cent is unemployed. In 2012 KwaZulu-Natal had the highest HIV prevalence level among pregnant women at 37.4 per cent.[6] The adult HIV prevalence for the province in 2012 was 27.9 per cent,[7] although a 2012 population based survey conducted by the Human Sciences Research Council (HSRC) put this figure at 16.9 per cent.[8]

In 2014, the average life expectancy at birth for KwaZulu-Natal was 59 years for females and 54 years for males,[9] compared to 82.5 years for Japanese females and 80 for males.[10] By addressing the burden of disease in communities through targeted prevention activities, KwaZulu-Natal will be set to meet the 2030 SDG targets and improve life expectancy.

The provision of primary health care in wards and through the War Rooms is the key vehicle to improving health outcomes. The number of clinic visits grew steadily from 26 million in 2009/2010 to 31.9 million in 2013/2014. Since 2011 a total of 6.5 million people had been tested for HIV in the province, which translated to 64 per cent of the total population. In 2014, 44 per cent of the 1.7 million people living with HIV in the province were on antiretroviral treatment (ART) – a 22 per cent increase in the number of people accessing ART from 2011/2012 to 2013/2014. Approximately 56 per cent of pregnant women made their first antenatal visit before 20 weeks in KwaZulu-Natal in 2013/2014, a 15 per cent increase over 2011/2012 of women booking health services in their early pregnancies.[11]

More than 69 per cent of KwaZulu-Natal's citizens lived below the poverty line in 2006.[12] Poverty and poor health are inextricably linked,[13] with poverty both a cause and a consequence of poor health. Poverty increases the likelihood of poor health outcomes because it forces people to live in poor conditions, without decent shelter, poor nutrition, overcrowding, lack of safe clean water and sanitation.[14] Poverty also creates illiteracy, leaving people ill-informed and disempowered about their health. Overcrowded and poor living conditions contribute to the spread of airborne diseases, such as TB, and respiratory infections, such as pneumonia. Poverty reduces access to health services.

The four leading causes of 'years of life lost' (YLL) in South Africa in 2013 were HIV-related conditions, TB, pneumonia and diarrhoeal diseases.[15] The YLL is due to premature mortality as compared to a normative standard. It represents a mortality gap. The burden of disease is reflected in terms of premature mortality based on the age at death and, therefore, highlights the causes of death that should be targeted for prevention activities. The top five leading causes of YLL in KwaZulu-Natal are HIV and AIDS, TB, diarrhoeal diseases, lower respiratory infections, and cerebrovascular disease.[16]

The socio-economic determinants such as overcrowding, unemployment, low income and poverty negatively impact health outcomes, especially HIV and AIDS, TB and maternal and child mortality. Poor health, in turn, traps people in poverty, reducing not only the productivity of the individual, but also that of the family as family members take off work to care for the sick. Often families have to dispose of assets to pay for health care and treatment. Health care expenses and transportation costs to access care also contribute to creating the poverty trap.

In October 2014, the Ministers of Health from Brazil, Russia, India, China and South Africa (BRICS) adopted the 90-90-90 strategy on HIV and TB, which aims to achieve the following by 2030:[17]

- 90 per cent of all people with HIV to be diagnosed;
- 90 per cent of people diagnosed with HIV to receive ART;
- 90 per cent of those on ART to have a suppressed viral load;
- 90 per cent of vulnerable groups screened for TB;
- 90 per cent diagnosed and started on TB treatment; and
- 90 per cent TB treatment success.

Integrated Service Delivery Approaches and Poverty Reduction Models

Integrated service delivery refers to a number of service agencies working together to collaborate and co-ordinate their support, services and interventions under one roof.[18] The model targets specific client groups with complex needs that require services from a number of agencies. These agencies co-ordinate themselves in such a manner that they are able to provide support on an ongoing basis until the desired needs or the desired outcome is met.

Integrated service delivery approaches are designed to improve outcomes for the clients. How this is achieved depends on a number of factors, such as the capacity and capabilities of the agencies providing services, the quantity and quality of client needs, the governance structures supporting the delivery of services to clients, and the involvement of clients and their participation in their own development. Important aspects to consider during integration include:[19]

- Communication between service agencies to ensure that clients' needs, progress and changes are recorded;
- Adequate and appropriate responses designed to meet clients' needs;
- Areas of duplication clarified and each service agency knowing what they will be contributing to the client;
- One plan developed for the client which includes the work done by all service agencies. This should include actions the clients themselves agreed to take;
- Building understanding and knowledge sharing among service agencies so they can work together more effectively;
- Building funding streams and budgets to support each other in service delivery;

- Joint identification of systematic issues that create problems in service delivery;
- Development of streamlined processes which can provide seamless services to clients;
- Identify where service agency gaps exist and jointly invite other agencies to join the service delivery team and provide resources;
- Identify cases that require integrated case management so that a team approach be taken to co-ordinate various services through a cohesive plan; and
- Identify and agree on the use of standardised reporting tools that feed into a single monitoring and evaluation system.

Conditional Cash Transfer (CCT) programmes are common in Latin America to fight poverty, inequality, unemployment and diseases. Mexico's *Progresa* and *Oportunidades* programmes consisted of cash rewards in exchange for people's investment in education, health or food. *Progresa* was one of the first CCT programmes in the world. Its goal was to help parents in rural areas invest in their children's future (education) through investment in their good health, especially by fighting diseases and malnutrition. This was based on the premise that rural areas have less access to health care, and poor health leads to inter-generational poverty. At the time, the programme targeted households with children under the age of five, achieving a 30 per cent drop in diarrhoea infections in the first year of operation.

Progresa resulted in a country-wide programme called Oportunidades. It has been shown that it is essential to intervene as early as possible to protect children's health, because early disease is a major factor in lifelong bad health, with the associated increase in poverty that accompanies poor health.[20] Brazil, following the example of Mexico's CCT programme, introduced the *Bolsa Familia* programme.

The sharp decline in Brazil's income inequality occurred as a result of cash transfers created to reduce poverty. *Bolsa Familia* provided incentives to households to invest in their children's education, health and nutrition, targeting households with an income of less than US$828 per annum. The government paid these households between US$132 and US$1248 a year if they met certain conditions: children under the age of 17 had to regularly attend school; pregnant women had to visit clinics for prenatal and antenatal care; and parents needed to make sure their children were fully immunised by the age of five and received growth check-ups until the age of six. It also provided a small allocation to extremely poor households without any conditions. By 2010, *Bolsa Familia* had grown into one of the world's largest CCT programmes, providing approximately US$24 billion to nearly 50 million people – about a quarter of Brazil's population.

These cash transfers not only reduced poverty in real time, but kept the next generation from poverty. This, together with better hourly wages for low-skilled labour, led to declines in inequality in Brazil.[21]

The Tunisian War on Poverty programme was founded on the principle of non-governmental organisations (NGOs) providing developmental support in communities, as well as specific government funded programmes to help needy children with social services and deprived families with direct assistance to meet their most basic needs.[22]

Poverty programmes find expression in cash transfers to prevent citizens from developing poor health and to incentivise them to access health care as part of their own development. In many developing countries there are critical shortages of health care professionals, as there are with professionals in other social services in South Africa. Governments, therefore, rely on the support of NGOs.

NGOs make available community fieldworkers, who have a limited amount of training, supplies and support, to provide essential primary health care and social services to hard-to-reach populations. Programmes involving community health workers (CHWs) in China, Brazil, Iran and Bangladesh, have demonstrated that utilising such workers helps improve health outcomes for large populations in under-served areas.

One such model in South Africa is the Municipal Ward-Based Primary Health Care Outreach Team (WBPHCOT). In 2010 the National Health Council adopted the Primary Health Care (PHC) Re-engineering model for national implementation; one of the three streams being the WBPHCOT.[23] WBPHCOTs engage with communities and provide services to vulnerable populations in deep rural, rural, peri-urban, and informal urban settlements, in close association with facility-based health services, other government departments, NGOs and other community-based structures and local communities.

The WBPHCOT initiative aims to contribute significantly towards increasing life expectancy, decreasing maternal and child mortality, combating HIV and AIDS, decreasing the burden of disease from TB, and strengthening health system effectiveness. Strengthened primary care at district level is also essential for the smooth implementation of National Health Insurance. The limitation of this model is that it is focused on health care service delivery while making referrals to other government departments.

Currently WBPHCOTs have limited community participation or community empowerment through alignment with existing community structures. Central to their work is the co-ordination of services and linkages to referrals to the War Rooms – where War Rooms exist. Both entities can work synergistically to achieve the health goals set for the community.

There are currently more than 72 000 lay people delivering community-based care in a wide range of health and social programmes. The participation of community fieldworkers in War Rooms helps to reach poor households in need. They are employed by NGOs funded by government departments to perform HIV support work, TB directly observed treatment short course (DOTS), home-based care and psychosocial support.

There are also several regional programmes put in place by large districts in alliance with universities and other health care organisations working within their districts. One such example is the Tshwane model created by the Tshwane District Office of the Gauteng Department of Health and Social Development, in alliance with the Departments of Family Medicine at the Universities of Limpopo and Pretoria. In 2010 the Departments of Family Medicine at the Universities of Pretoria and Limpopo, together with the Tshwane District Office of the Gauteng Department of Health and Social Development, developed a conceptual framework for implementing Community-Oriented Primary Care (COPC) through health posts in Tshwane. The health post is developed as a service unit that is physically located in a community and serves the population in a defined geographic area within a specific municipal ward. It has been conceptualised as a 'nerve centre' that drives and co-ordinates all primary care interventions in the community.

Each health post serves between 2 000 and 3 000 households in a defined geographic area within a municipal ward. On initiation, the geophysical area served by the health post is identified and mapped using ward-based maps to define the boundaries of health post activity. Each CHW is assigned between 150 and 200 households, although the ideal ratio of households per CHW has yet to be tested in practice for feasibility and impact.

There are some similarities between the health post and the War Room concept used in KwaZulu-Natal. A point of difference is that the health post is used almost exclusively for primary healthcare interventions, whereas in KwaZulu-Natal the War Room has political and oversight functions designed to integrate service delivery from all government departments. The health post concept holds promise in the delivery of primary health care services, as evidenced by some innovative work done in the Sedibeng District, Gauteng.

Sedibeng District has pioneered a complementary 'health post' approach in Emfuleni sub-district. Physical structures, called health posts, have been established in six communities of Ward 25 in Boipatong. These health posts are led by a nurse team leader, who supervises an outreach team of up to 10 CHWs and health promoters who visit households daily. The structures that house the activities range from converted containers to portable huts, and are where: CHWs can meet daily; the nurse team leaders can provide support and training to the

CHWs; as well as conduct basic health screening, attend to minor ailments, control chronic diseases, offer family planning, mother and child care, and referral to the main clinic where necessary.

It would appear that there are two key advantages of the OSS service delivery model employed in KwaZulu-Natal:

- The emphasis on insisting on the involvement of communities and government at all levels in the delivery of services, coupled with oversight at every level along the political spectrum; and
- Integration of all services that impact on the health and well-being of communities; i.e. it addresses the social determinants of health in communities.

Integrated Service Delivery Models (ISDM) in South Africa

Integrated Service Delivery Models (ISDM) are seen as the best possible way of bringing together fragmented services offered to individuals, families and communities.[24] Integration, co-ordination, collaboration and collocation are at the heart of ISDM, which work through community-based partnerships to rebuild the fabric of society. These models view an individual, a household and a community as an inter-connected system, working to promote human values, fight poverty, crime, diseases, deprivation and social ills. They recognise that, in order to ensure maximum development, an individual's basic needs must be met, including their physical, social, economic and spiritual needs. ISDMs are systemic and holistic.

These models, born out of the War on Poverty campaign, contain the following key elements:

- Community partnerships and a community-driven approach (active citizenry);
- Integration of all community-based fieldworkers, be they from government, civil society or business;
- The integration of community structures through the War Room, including the Ward AIDS Councils and Ward Committees;
- A single well-defined basket of services; and
- A well-defined monitoring, evaluation and reporting system with the ability to analyse data, produce reports and make informed decisions based on multiple data sources and factors.

The primary focus of ISDMs is to bring together communities that need help, with those who provide help, in a mutually sustainable manner. Having an integrated approach means that all spheres of government (national, provincial and local) play a clearly defined role. It ensures that the different government departments work together in a cohesive manner and that an integrated planning tool is used. Co-ordination does not end merely with the provision of services from service providers. Communities are engaged to ensure that they contribute to their own development and that they are able to stay out of the poverty trap when they exit the system.

The ISDM is an innovative approach to service delivery which requires careful change management amongst all stakeholders so that they fully understand the approach, their roles and responsibilities, and their commitment to making it a success. Integrated service delivery models are co-ordinated at various levels, including the ward, local municipality, district municipality and provincial level.

Some of the well-known ISDMs in South Africa emanating from the War on Poverty campaign, and which have War Rooms as the service delivery engine, are Operation Masiphathisane in the Eastern Cape, Operation Hlasela in the Free State, Ntirhisano in Gauteng, OSS in KwaZulu-Natal, Operation Vuka Sisebente in Mpumalanga, and Operation Balelapa in the Northern Cape.

Operation Sukuma Sakhe

Since 1994, the South African government has embraced a pro-poor policymaking agenda with the aim of poverty eradication. In 2008, when former President Mbeki announced the nationwide campaign against poverty, the War on Poverty campaign was embraced and launched in three deprived wards in Msinga. After 2008, KwaZulu-Natal hosted various mass campaigns called 'Operation Mbo'. The campaign approach used joint departmental planning and the provision of integrated services to contribute to poverty eradication.

In 2009, the KwaZulu-Natal provincial government launched the Flagship Programme to give priority to the War on Poverty campaign to eradicate poverty and other social problems affecting local communities, such as food security, TB, HIV and AIDS, gender inequality and violence. The approach then evolved from a government-led model to a community-led model. This led to the launch of OSS in April 2011. OSS was positioned so that communities could stand up to fight social ills and rebuild the fabric of society, in partnership with community and local government stakeholders working together in a multi-sectoral service delivery approach.

From inception, District Task Teams (DTTs) were established in all 11 Districts and Local Task Teams (LTTs) in 52 local municipalities, with over 800 War Rooms set up across KwaZulu-Natal. War Rooms interact with existing structures, such as the Ward AIDS Committees and the Ward Committees. The Premier (overall champion), in coordination with Members of the Executive Council (MECs) and Heads of Departments (HODs) – who championed the various districts – took the lead in securing buy-in and support from all existing structures, and assisted in establishing the governance structures for OSS at each level. The Premier, MECs, Mayors and Ward Councillors champion service delivery and are responsible for reducing the impact of HIV in their communities.

The Provincial Task Team (PTT) provides strategic and implementation direction on OSS, orientates all stakeholders on OSS through marketing and communication, monitors and reports on progress against OSS objectives, and mentors districts to achieve OSS goals. The DTT provides implementation direction on OSS, mobilises resources, provides human capacity development and mentors LTTs. The LTTs attend to escalated issues from the War Room and mentor Ward Task Teams (WTT). The WTT profile households, resolve cases, escalate unresolved cases to government departments, co-ordinate the activities of the community fieldworkers, and ensure reporting and alignment is done amongst all community structures.

Community-driven War Rooms as Change Agents

At the centre of the OSS model is the War Room, which is the service delivery engine set up at ward level so that the different stakeholders can deliver a fully co-ordinated and integrated basket of services. War Rooms are generally situated in community buildings, such as community halls and churches. Collectively, community leaders, government departments, civil society organisations, community fieldworkers and members from community structures come together to effectively and efficiently respond to HIV and AIDS, poverty and social ills, such as crime, gender-based violence, stigma and discrimination, family disintegration and substance abuse. War Rooms are open five days a week and one War Room is established per ward. Key elements to a community-driven approach listed below.

- *Community participation*
  The active involvement of community members is facilitated so that they can identify the issues that affect their health and well-being, make decisions about how to address these issues, and develop and implement the community-based interventions required to achieve change.

- *Community empowerment*
  Communities gain the understanding and authority required to ensure that appropriate action is taken in addressing the issues that affect their health and well-being.
- *Community accountability*
  Community members are considered as their own 'agents of change' and not as passive recipients of government services.
- *Inter-sectoral collaboration*
  - Communities jointly plan with all community based structures and sectors to deliver services in an integrated manner.
  - Community structures are strengthened to ensure more effective participation in sustainable community development.
- *Transparency*
  All structures should function in an open and transparent manner.
- *Government accountability*
  - All individuals within the health system will remain answerable to the communities they serve.
  - All individuals within the health system will work together with communities to improve the health and well-being of the communities they serve.

Through OSS, community structures effectively interact with the community and with each other through the War Room (see Figure 1). Community structures provide services to people in the ward and bring other referrals to the War Room. As such they are strategic partners and change agents in the War Room. The War Room co-ordinates activities targeted to the needs of its beneficiaries, whether those be HIV testing campaigns; behavioural changes to address drivers of the HIV, AIDS and TB epidemic; empowerment of youth and women addressing the needs of the most vulnerable affected by HIV and AIDS; addressing food and nutritional security; health promotion campaigns; or provision of other services, for example, access to social grants or vital registration.

Community fieldworkers are representatives of government departments working at community level and reporting through the War Room. These are the community change agents; they are the link between government, other community service providers and local communities. They lead the change by working directly with beneficiaries in communities and are at the front line of implementation of OSS. Community fieldworkers are catalysts for change, because they work within an environment where communities want to change. They embody the following characteristics of change agents:

Figure 1: Community Structures Found in a War Room

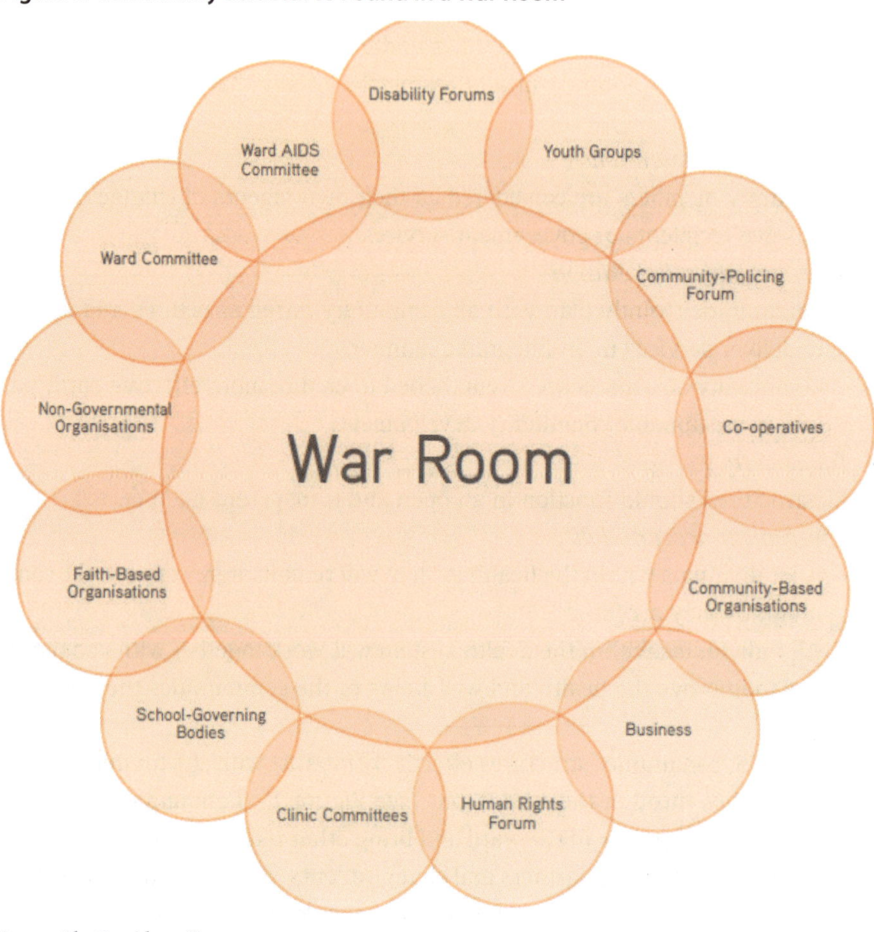

Source: The Presidency[25]

- Clear vision – They have a common vision of working with community members to alleviate poverty. They have all been capacitated on the OSS model.
- Patient yet persistent – They ensure that households are moving closer to their goal of exiting poverty.
- Ask tough questions – By asking the right questions they empower community members to become accountable for their health and well-being.
- Knowledgeable and lead by example – They are accepted in the communities for their knowledge on the subject matter in the area they represent, and are trusted for the information they impart.
- Strong relationships built on trust – They establish trustworthy relationships with households and key stakeholders within the community.

There are currently approximately 19 250 community fieldworkers, appointed directly by various government departments, in KwaZulu-Natal. Examples of community fieldworkers are Community Development Workers (CDWs), CCGs, Assistant Extension Officers (AEOs), Sport and Recreation Coordinators (SRCs) and Social Crime Prevention Volunteers (SCPVs). They bring community needs to the War Room and integrate the delivery of services to households within the community.

There are approximately 12 000 CCGs in KwaZulu-Natal. CCGs provide health information to empower communities to participate and take accountability for their own health, while providing health services to those in need. Through engagement with communities and community structures, community members can be enabled to become actively involved in issues that affect their health and well-being and jointly develop community-based interventions to achieve better health outcomes.[26]

War Rooms were established to respond to community needs. Community needs are assessed through household and community profiling, through community structures and through community fieldworkers. Identified needs are either resolved immediately or brought into the War Room for prioritisation. Needs that are not resolved in the War Room are escalated to the next level: the LTT, to co-ordinate with various government departments. A co-ordinated response is put together from government's basket of services. All needs, from the time they enter the War Room, are recorded and progress is followed through until closure through a paper-based monitoring and evaluation system. There is a move towards the establishment of a central command centre that captures data from the War Room, and then automatically aggregates the information to produce a district and provincial report.

The War Room acts as a one-stop shop for a variety of services for a variety of beneficiaries in need. Services offered by the War Room range from screening and referring clients for TB, HIV, PMTCT, pregnancy testing, immunisation and malnutrition, to DOTS support, adherence clubs and the provision of ART drugs.

Community mobilisation is central to the successful delivery of services in Operation Sukuma Sakhe. It raises the awareness of community members to development initiatives affecting them and embraces their full participation. Communities are mobilised to participate in service delivery events such as the Premier's Members of the Executive Council OSS Days, the MEC's Izimbizo, Operation Mbo and Public Service Volunteer Week (PSVW). These occasions are also used as platforms for community members to engage leaders on the social issues affecting them, such as crime, and to plan responses on the issues raised. The approach to mobilising communities to fight social ills is non-confrontational and focuses on problem-solving. It is one which encourages communities to help come up with solutions.

Results from War Rooms

Health facilities are located in wards that are linked to War Rooms. The provision of PHC in wards, and through the War Rooms, is the key vehicle to improving health outcomes. The number of clinic visits has grown steadily from 26 million in 2009/2010 to 31.9 million in 2013/2014 (District Health Information System). HIV and AIDS, sexually transmitted infections (STIs) and TB remain a key challenge for the province, and are therefore amongst the critical focus areas of OSS. Some of the achievements in health are (PCA data 2011 to 2014):

- The early identification of an individual's HIV status assisted in linking them to appropriate care and treatment to achieve better health outcomes. A total of 6.5 million people were tested for HIV in the province since 2011, which translates to 64 per cent of the total population.
- ART provided an effective means of medical care and illness management for people living with HIV. Out of an estimated 1.7 million people living with HIV in the province, including children, 44 per cent were on ART in 2013/2014. There was an increase of 22 per cent in people accessing ART from 2011/2012 to 2013/2014.
- A polymerase chain reaction (PCR) test, conducted six weeks after birth to determine the HIV status of all babies who are born to HIV-positive mothers, ensures that, should the baby test positive, the linkage to ART services is made as early as possible. Mother-to-child transmission (MTCT) was reduced to two per cent or below in all districts. HIV transmission around 18 months was below three per cent for all districts in 2013/2014, with the exception of eThekwini (3.6 per cent) and Harry Gwala Districts (4.2 per cent).
- Education and awareness campaigns targeted people aged 15 to 49 years, and were important to ensure communities were informed and equipped with information about their health, social ills and the health and social services available to them. A total of 1.4 million people were reached with anti-gender based violence information in the province between 2011/2012 and 2013/2014; this translates to 25 per cent coverage of the population aged 15 to 49 years.
- Medical male circumcision (MMC) recently emerged as a critical intervention in reducing HIV transmission between discordant couples (where one partner is HIV-infected and the other partner is HIV-negative). The uptake of MMC

showed a 19 per cent increase between 2011/2012 and 2013/2014, translating to 15 per cent coverage of males in the province.

- Booking early for antenatal care services (ANC) ensured that pregnant women received interventions as early as possible for optimum health for themselves and the child. Approximately 56 per cent of pregnant women made their first antenatal visit before 20 weeks in KwaZulu-Natal in 2013/2014, showing a 15 per cent increase in pregnant women booking early from 2011/2012.
- The number of underweight children under five years declined from 44 per 1 000 in 2010, to less than 14 in 2014;
- The mortality rate in facilities of children under one declined from 10.8 per cent in 2010 to 7.3 per cent in 2014; and
- A maternal mortality in-facility ratio of 138/100 000 live births was achieved, a decrease from 195/100 000 recorded in 2010. Many deaths occur in communities that go unnoticed and unrecorded.

In an effort to address poverty and decrease the chances of one in 20 children dying before their fifth birthday, the government of KwaZulu-Natal launched the Phila Mntwana in 2013 as a community-based initiative. Phila Mntwana aims to create a nurturing environment for children, promoting access to education, health, safety and healthy living conditions. By 2014, 1 125 Phila Mntwana centres were established in the province, of which 185 were based at War Rooms and 288 in Early Childhood Development (ECD) centres. Since inception in 2014 to 2015, approximately 168 429 children were attended to at Phila Mntwana centres and the following services were offered:

- Children were identified and referred to their nearest health facility for moderate acute malnutrition (2 011), severe malnutrition (292), diarrhoea (3 072), feeding difficulties (2 384), immunisation (9 864), provider initiative counselling and testing (1 932), TB investigation (3 864), developmental difficulties (1 298), and deworming (44 158);
- Vitamin A supplementation was provided to 87 989 children over 12 months at the Phila Mntwana centres; and
- Children were also identified and referred to other government departments for appropriate services such as birth registration (1 164), ECD services (2 890), orphans and vulnerable children (OVC) services (397), and other referrals for social services and grants (2 890).

Dr Sibongile Zungu, then HOD for Health in the province in 2014/2015 attributed the success of these health outcomes to Community Caregivers, saying:

> It is without a shadow of doubt that the successes we have seen in the last few years with regard to HIV and AIDS, prevention of Mother-To-Child Transmission as well as the TB cure rate, have been impacted positively by the Operation Sukuma Sakhe model and the role played by Community Caregivers.

War Rooms as Game Changers

Operation Sukuma Sakhe has shown that integrated service delivery models at community level work on condition that they receive the commitment from political, administrative and community leaders, at all levels, to work together. It requires senior level leadership at each level. At the provincial level the Premier is the champion, supported by the Ministers of the Executive Council, who are each allocated a specific district to which they provide mentorship. HODs from the provincial level are also allocated specific districts to provide technical support and resources.

Success also requires that communities take the lead in their own development, identify their needs, resolve their own issues, and escalate issues that they require assistance with. It requires stakeholders from various community structures to participate in the War Room. At the heart of the War Room, community fieldworkers employed by government and non-government organisations provide services at household level. Community fieldworkers who reside within the communities they serve are better placed to understand the needs of the communities, and have easier access to community members to identify and provide services. Their services are co-ordinated and integrated by the War Room. There is improved coverage with appropriate allocation of community fieldworkers across wards.

Members of the AIDS Councils are integrated in the War Room, providing reports to the South African National AIDS Council (SANAC) via the Provincial AIDS Councils. While AIDS Councils have their own mandate and are advocates for HIV and AIDS interventions, the War Room stakeholders are implementers and community mobilisers.

Evidence has shown that community responses to HIV are effective and sustainable. Communities are better able to mobilise themselves to demand services, deliver services, support health systems, and work with vulnerable populations that formal systems cannot reach. They also give a 'voice' to those in need of services, provide feedback on which policies and programmes are working and suggest ways to improve them. There is evidence that suggests that community-based service delivery has better health outcomes and can lead to radical scale-up of interventions through demand creation.

Operation Sukuma Sakhe is one of the best possible solutions to ending the AIDS epidemic by bringing together fragmented services offered to individuals, families and communities. ISDMs work through multi-sectoral partnerships based in communities that come together under one roof to co-ordinate services and track service delivery to the most vulnerable.

Conclusion

War Rooms deal with complex and multiple issues that require multiple interventions. The model, therefore, begins with integrated planning, the integration of community structures, the integration of services and the integration of community fieldworkers to respond in an integrated manner. It has shown that multiple stakeholders, working together under 'one roof' – the War Room – results in communities benefitting through improved health and well-being. The model allows for communities to participate in their own development providing ownership and empowerment.

The successes of Operation Sukuma Sakhe in KwaZulu-Natal seem to provide much needed answers to the critical question of how to encourage people to be involved in their own local development. The critical issue of ward-based planning and how it cascades into the Integrated Development Plan (IDP) of local government, is adequately addressed by the establishment of War Rooms at ward level to ensure effective service delivery and response to people's development issues within local government. It should be noted that the structures established in KZN through OSS were further supported through resources mobilised by the national government, such as the HIV Conditional Grants, and other development partner assistance, such as that provided through the U.S. President's Emergency Plan for AIDS Relief (PEPFAR) and its implementing partners.

The lessons learned from Operation Sukuma Sakhe should be used to reinforce the call for meaningful public participation as expressed in Section 152(1) of the Constitution of the Republic of South Africa 1996 as well as in the Municipal Systems Act 32 of 2000, Section 4(2). The White Paper on Local Government calls for the implementation of a developmental local government as part of the realisation of a developmental state. The existing public participation programmes of government need to be informed by a policy framework. The integrative nature of Operation Sukuma Sakhe in dealing with community development provides empirical evidence on how the public participation framework is translated into practice.

The paper therefore recommends that government uses the OSS Model as one of its key programmes in its toolkit on community development, integrated planning and public participation. The fight against epidemics such as HIV/AIDS and TB require an integrated approach that puts people at the forefront of pushing back the frontiers of these epidemics. The rural province of KwaZulu-Natal amply demonstrated that ordinary volunteer caregivers, receiving a nominal stipend from government, have pushed back HIV and TB using their passion for their communities and basic health tools and aids.

Notes and References

1 Lewin, S.A., Babigumira, S.M, Bosch-Capblanch, X., Aja, G., Zwarenstein, M., Daniels K., 2006. Lay health workers in primary and community health care: A systematic review of trials. Geneva: World Health Organisation.

2 International Council for Science and International Social Science Council, 2015. Review of the Sustainable Development Goals: The science perspective. Paris: International Council for Science (ICSU).

3 Kretzmann, J.P., 2010. Asset-based strategies for building resilient communities. In Reich, J.W., Zautra, A., and Hall, J.S. (eds.), Handbook of adult resilience. New York: Guildford Press; Mathie, A. and Cunningham, G., 2003. From clients to citizens: Asset-based community development as a strategy for community-driven development. *Development in Practice*, 13(5), pp.474-486; Sen, A., 1999. Development as freedom. Oxford: Oxford University Press; Kretzmann, J.P. and McKnight, J.L., 1993. Building communities from the inside out: A path toward finding and mobilizing a community's assets. Evanston, Ill.: Center for Urban Affairs and Policy Research, Northwestern University.

4 Kretzmann and McKnight, 1993.

5 Statistics South Africa, 2014. Mid-Year Population Estimates 2014. Pretoria: Statistics South Africa.

6 KwaZulu-Natal Department of Health, 2014 Annual Report. Pietermaritzburg: KwaZulu-Natal Provincial Government.

7 Ibid.

8 Shisana, O., Rehle, T., Simbayi, L.C., Zuma, K., Jooste, S., Zungu, N., Labadarios,D., and Onoya, D. 2014. South African National HIV Prevalence, Incidence and Behaviour Survey, 2012. Pretoria: Human Sciences Research Council.

9 Statistics South Africa, 2014. Mid-Year Population Estimates 2014. Pretoria: Statistics South Africa.

10 Health Systems Trust, 201. District Health Barometer 2015. Durban: Health Systems Trust.

11 Ibid.

12 Statistics South Africa, 2014. Mid-Year Population Estimates 2014. Pretoria: Stats SA.

13 Health Poverty Action Group,2015. Key Facts: Poverty and Poor Health. Available at http://www.healthpovertyaction.org/info-and-resources/the-cycle-of-poverty-and-poor-health/key-facts/ [Accessed 09 November 2015].

14 World Bank, 2001. Dying for change. Poor people's experience of health and ill-health. Washington DC: World Bank. Available at http://siteresources.worldbank.org/INTPAH/Resources/Publications/Dying-for-Change/dyifull2.pdf. [Accessed 09 November 2015].

15 HST, 2015.

16 Ibid.

17 Ibid.

18 Queensland Council of Social Services, 2013. A guide to integrated service delivery to clients. For Community Service Organisations. Australia: Queensland Council of Social Services.

19 Ibid.

20 Skoufias, E. and Di Maro, V., 2008. Conditional cash transfers, adult work incentives, and poverty. *Journal of Development Studies*, 44(7), pp.935-960.

21 Ozler, B., 2014. Lesson's from Brazil's war on poverty. Available at http://fivethirtyeight.com/features/lessons-from-brazils-war-on-poverty/ [Accessed 14 November 2015].

22 United Nations Development Programme, 2000. Statement by the Republic of Tunisia to the World Summit for Social Development Copenhagen, Denmark Tuesday, March 7, 1995 Available at http://www.un.org/documents/ga/conf166/gov/950310143402.htm [Accessed 10 November 2015].

23 Pillay, Y. and Barron, P., 2011. The implementation of PHC re-engineering in South Africa. Available at https://www.phasa.org.za/the-implementation-of-phc-re-engineering-in-south-africa/ [Accessed 18 November 2015].

24 RICHARDSON, D. and PATANA, P. 2012. Integrating service delivery: why, for who and when. Available at http://www.oecd.org/els/soc/richardson_patana%20 integrating%20service%20delivery%20why%20for%20who%20and%20how.pdf. [Accessed 16 November 2015].

25 The Presidency, 2015. Best Practice Guidelines for the Implementation of an Integrated Service Delivery Model. Pretoria: The Presidency.

26 Couros, G., 2015. The innovator's mindset: Empower learning, unleash talent, and lead a culture of creativity. USA: Dave Burgess Consulting, Inc.

Chapter 17

The Story of HIV, AIDS and TB in the Mining Industry in Southern Africa

Thuthula Balfour-Kaipa, Vanessa Govender and Khanyile Baloyi

Introduction

The South African mining industry (SAMI) is one of the sectors hardest hit by the human immunodeficiency virus (HIV), acquired immune deficiency syndrome (AIDS) and tuberculosis (TB). Consequently, the sector has had to respond in the most decisive and unprecedented manner. From this response, there is a compelling narrative that has to be shared: a story that was once one of despair, but is now a story of hope and promise.

TB was, from the beginning of the 20th century, recognised as a major public health threat in the mining industry. In the single sex hostels and the peri-mining communities that catered for the mineworkers' social life, a new epidemic, HIV, reared its ugly head in the 1990s. This conferred upon the mineworkers an additional health risk, which itself increased the risk of developing active TB.

There was thus the transmission and subsequent spread of two diseases nearly 100 years apart: TB following the discovery of gold in 1886 and HIV in the early 1990s, which resulted in the emergence of an HIV-TB co-epidemic in the 1990s.

This story meanders through a paradigm shift in the mining industry from an era of hopelessness, without lifesaving drugs for treating HIV; and from focusing on offering *only* HIV counselling and testing, *only* for employees, to an era of intensified awareness, education and prevention; and finally through to the current era of promise for both employees and communities. Early diagnosis, treatment, rehabilitation and eradication are the buzz. Screening, not just for HIV, but for TB as well as risk factors for chronic diseases of lifestyle, have become the norm. Eradication of the virus, and ending stigma and discrimination, form a paradigm shift in thinking in the mining industry, as is the shift from siloed programmes to more integrated health programmes.

A Mine Medical Officer's Story

I recall so vividly a cold winter's night in June 2000, as a mine medical officer in Carletonville. At about midnight I was summoned to attend to a patient, 'gasping for breath' as the nurses often reported someone who was in respiratory distress. As it turned out the patient, a young 28-year old migrant worker from Mozambique, was suffering from the opportunistic infection *Pneumocystis Carinii Pneumoniae* and newly diagnosed as HIV positive, with a CD4 count of 4. As was often the case in those days, patients were diagnosed very late. They tested late as they knew there was no hope in accessing ARVs.

In big bold letters on the top of his medical record were the letters 'DNR', meaning 'do not resuscitate'.

There was no access to the precious lifesaving, costly ARVs. This patient had no choice. I too had no choice, I ordered that the patient be transferred into the side ward, made comfortable with oxygen and to draw the curtains around him. Of course there were no family members at his side and as we did in those days, when 'DNR' was written all over the files, we all quickly rose to the occasion and became the family member, the loved one, the chaplain, and the caring friend praying for his speedy, pain free death. [1]

A lot has happened since those dark days of the 1990s: politically, in leadership and policy development, in epidemiological research, in addressing stigma and discrimination, in testing for HIV and in accessing antiretroviral drugs. Today nobody writes 'DNR'. We have what it takes to prolong life, for healthy lives, and productive ones.

HIV, TB and Silicosis in the SAMI

The year 1886 heralded the discovery of gold on the Witwatersrand. Since then, mining has been a significant contributor to the South African economy. With the discovery of gold came the influx of Black migrant workers, who were recruited from rural labour-sending communities in South Africa (internal migrants), and also from the neighbouring countries of Lesotho, Swaziland, Botswana, Mozambique and Zimbabwe, for short duration contracts in hazardous working conditions. Soon thereafter, TB was recognised as an important health hazard, characterised by high morbidity and mortality rates amongst the Black miners. Overcrowding, migrant labour, poor nutrition and dusty working conditions were some of the risk factors identified as contributing to the scourge of TB. Ailing mineworkers were often repatriated home without adequate treatment.

The gold mines, in particular, with ore bodies high in crystalline silica content, exposed mineworkers to this invisible dust that is a strong and lifelong risk factor for acquiring, not only silicosis, but TB as well.

The SAMI started HIV testing in 1985 and in 1986 the first miners tested positive. From 1990 to 1998, the HIV status of a randomly selected cohort of employees from one company was followed up annually. During the life of the study, the HIV prevalence in the cohort of 2292 employees increased from one per cent to 26 per cent. From 1998 to 2000, a community study in the Carletonville area (Mothusimpilo Study) organised by the Centre for Scientific and industrial Research and the South African Institute for Medical Research, illustrated that for each of the three years, the prevalence of HIV increased from 28 per cent to 30 per cent.[2]

Driven by the HIV epidemic, TB rates in the industry, particularly in the gold mines, rose precipitously to rates of around 3 000 to 7 000 cases per 100 000 population. Additional risk factors were noted as increased duration of exposure to silica dust, diagnosis of silicosis and age.[3]

At about the same time, Corbett et al researched the risks of silicosis and HIV infection, and found that they combine multiplicatively in increasing the risk of TB infection. They stated that 'TB remains as much a silica-related occupational disease in HIV-positive as well as in HIV-negative miners'. They also noted that, 'HIV-positive silicotics have considerably higher TB incidence rates than those reported from other HIV-positive Africans. The increasing impact of HIV over time may indicate epidemic TB transmission with rapid disease development in HIV-infected miners'.[4]

Tuberculosis, silicosis and HIV/AIDS have thus always been the 'toxic trio' in the industry, and one cannot address one without the other.

Figure 1 and Table 1 illustrate the number of TB cases in the industry from 2003 to 2014. TB rates in the mining industry have, over the years, declined from very high levels in 2003, 8 000 per 100 000 of the population to 3 500 per 100 000 of the population. This is 3.7 times the South African national TB rate of 948 cases per 100 000 of the population.

Figure 1: Pulmonary TB cases in the SAMI, by commodity

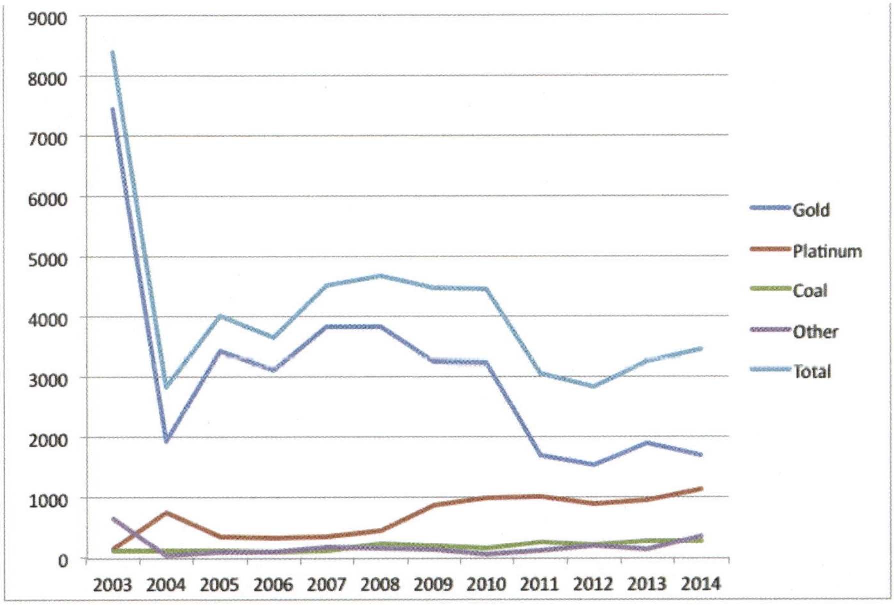

Source: Department of Mineral Resources[5]

Table 1: Pulmonary TB cases in the SAMI, by commodity

	2003	2004	2005	2006	2007	2008	2009	2010	2011	2012	2013	2014
Gold	7461	1926	3442	3115	3846	3829	3266	3243	1696	1529	1900	1697
Plati-num	157	745	355	338	358	453	873	993	1005	895	949	1134
Coal	123	117	121	88	127	241	207	162	249	212	269	279
Other	659	39	97	107	185	158	133	54	112	202	137	350
Total	8400	2827	4015	3648	4516	4681	4479	4452	3062	2838	3255	3460

Source: Department of Mineral Resources[6]

The response by the SAMI can be categorised into three levels: the tripartite level, employers collectively through the Chamber of Mines, and interventions at company level. These are dealt with below.

The Tripartite Story

In 1991, the Leon Commission of Inquiry was established to investigate the spate of illnesses and injuries in South African mines. These robust deliberations, coupled with constitutional rights to an environment that is healthy and safe, led to the promulgation of the Mine Health and Safety Act (Act No. 29 of 1996) (MHSA). The MHSA included comprehensive provisions on the responsibilities of employers and workers regarding health and safety in mines, and provided for the inclusion and participation of all stakeholders in the establishment of health and safety in mines. The Mine Health and Safety Council (MHSC) was a ground-breaking tripartism that heralded a new era in which government, employer organisations and trade unions worked collaboratively in respect of health and safety in mines, and were held accountable, reporting back at a summit at least once every two years.

The MHSC comprises a tripartite board represented by state, employer, and labour members under the chairmanship of the Chief Inspector of Mines. With its overarching vision as 'Every mineworker returning from work unharmed every day. Striving for Zero Harm', its main task was to advise the Minister of Mineral Resources on occupational health and safety legislation and research outcomes. Over the years, this tripartite council has been proactive in steering, and placing firmly on the agenda of top leadership, the importance of embracing and achieving the health milestones. In 2003, the industry milestones were set for the elimination of silicosis and noise induced hearing loss, but by 2011 these milestones included objectives and a robust action plan for HIV, AIDS and TB.

Table 2 is an illustration of the various initiatives that were undertaken from the Leon Commission in 1993 until 2014.

Table 2: Illustration of milestones for Health and Safety and HIV/AIDS and TB

	Health and Safety	HIV/AIDS and TB
1993	Leon Commission of enquiry into Health and Safety on the Mines	
1995		Labour Relations Act
1996	Introduction of the Mine Health and Safety Act (MHSA)	Anglo American HIV Prevalence Survey = 0,02%
1997	MHSA proclaimed by former State President Dr N.R. Mandela	
1998	Established the MHSC and MQA	Employment Equity Act and Code of Good Practice for HIV/AIDS

	Health and Safety	HIV/AIDS and TB
2000		South African Business Coalition on HIV and AIDS established case law: Hoffmann vs SAA HIV prevalence in SAMI = 25%
2002		Peak of government-led AIDS denialism Constitutional Court ruling: Antiretrovirals (ARVs) to pregnant mothers during birth Anglo American starts providing ARVs
2003	MHSC Summit: Agreed Targets and Milestones on Health (elimination of noise-induced hearing loss and silicosis) and Safety	Declaration of Intent HIV/AIDS
2004		SA Government launched 'Operational Plan for Comprehensive HIV and AIDS Care, Management and Treatment'
2006	MHSC Summit: Review and report back on 2003 milestones	HIV/AIDS Mining Summit Campaign: Zero new infections; Zero deaths from HIV; Zero mother to child transmission; Zero stigma and discrimination
2008	Presidential Health and Safety Audit	
2008	Developed Tripartite Action Plan to achieve and fast track the 2003 milestones; Mining Industry Occupational Safety and Health (MOSH)	
2010	Included Health and Safety in Revised Mining Charter	DMR commissioned review of HIV/AIDS and TB in SA mining industry
2011	Approved Culture Transformation Framework	HIV/AIDS and TB Summit and Action Plan
2012	Ministerial Health and Safety Audit	SADC Declaration on TB in Mines; DMR 164 reporting on HIV/AIDS and TB DoH National Strategic Plan for HIV/AIDS, STIs and TB (2012-2016)
2014	MHSC Tripartite Summit, feedback on the action plan	HIV/AIDS and TB milestones included within the MHSC Summit Action plans for Occupational Health and Safety First DMR 164 comparative report

Source: Author[7]

The 2003 MHSC summit was heralded as an important inflection point in the history of health and safety in the SAMI. The tripartite stakeholders, at that summit, formulated milestones for health and safety, and entered into a historic tripartite agreement towards achieving these milestones for the elimination of silicosis and noise-induced hearing loss and the prevention of fatalities.

At the same time, in a parallel initiative, the inaugural Mining HIV/AIDS Summit was convened which resulted in the 'Declaration of Intent' being signed on the 30 April 2003. The principals represented government, employers and labour. The declaration highlighted ten commitments compelling the industry to institute HIV and AIDS policies and workplace programmes in every workplace by the end of 2004. The programmes would focus on the promotion of reducing stigma, discrimination and prejudice against employees affected and infected by HIV/AIDS.[8]

The tripartite group reaffirmed its commitment to implement and review the 5-year National Strategic Plan (NSP) on HIV/AIDS and sexually transmitted infections (STIs), to share experiences and best practices, and to strengthen partnerships between government, business and labour. Importantly, that Declaration of Intent noted that the 'mining sector (inclusive of employers, unions and communities) has played a pioneering role in establishing proactive, comprehensive, multi-stakeholder response to the management of HIV/AIDS'. The Declaration of Intent also noted, and recognised, that HIV/AIDS exacerbated the TB epidemic and had the potential to reverse the gains made in TB management, placing on record the importance of integrating programmes to address these twin epidemics.

The parties committed to strengthen healthcare infrastructure and to introduce HIV policies and programmes at every workplace that addressed prevention, treatment, care and support, stigma and discrimination against those infected and affected by HIV. In addition to committing to transform living conditions, alleviating poverty and providing good nutrition were identified as key to effective programmes and long-term positive outcomes. The parties agreed that the Tripartite HIV/AIDS Committee should bring to bear the vision of no new HIV infections, through the execution of an effective plan with specific targets and timelines.

The tripartite declaration on HIV/AIDS in 2003 outlined four pillars of response, as illustrated in Figure 2.

The 2006 summit reflected on the commitments made in 2003 and acknowledged that HIV/AIDS was a multidimensional social problem that no one sector could take responsibility for, yet the mining sector was the only one that had demonstrated a collective response to the HIV/AIDS challenge – as evidenced by the tripartite declaration, follow-up summits and numerous workplace initiatives. Alignment to the NSP for HIV/AIDS and STIs was critical, and the summit further reflected and focussed on what had been done since 2003 to identify the gaps, challenges and opportunities to enhance the progress made. By this time, corporates joined the zero policy of the National Department of Health (DoH) for:

- zero new HIV infections;
- zero AIDS deaths;
- zero discrimination; and
- zero mother to child transmission.

Figure 2: Four pillars of response

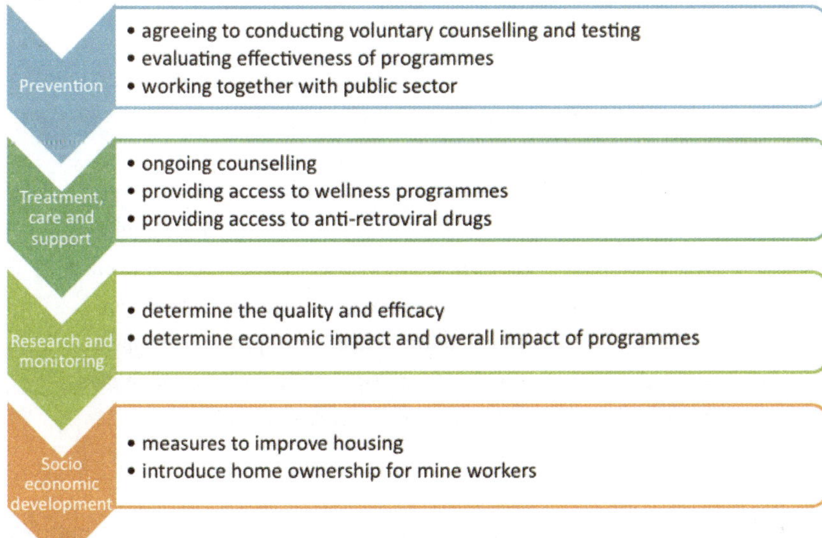

Source: Declaration of Intent – Mining HIV/AIDS Summit 2003[9]

At the same time, the Zero TB strategy was evolving as well, with many mining corporates expanding HIV testing to include TB and wellness screening tests for non-communicable diseases, further destigmatising and demystifying the HIV and TB diseases. Much of this was made possible by increasing civil activism and international support. The role played by The Global Fund to Fight AIDS, Tuberculosis and Malaria (The Global Fund), the United States President's Emergency Program for AIDS Relief (PEPFAR), and the United States Agency for International Development (USAID) cannot go unmentioned.

The 2011 MHSC summit was heralded as a historical event in the Health and HIV calendar in the industry, not just mining; not just in South Africa, but across the continent, if not globally. On 18 November 2011, the Principals representing State, Employers and Organised Labour agreed to set actions and commitments as outlined in the MHSC HIV/AIDS and TB action plan to reduce and prevent HIV/AIDS and TB at mines.[10] These commitments on the Summit action plan for Occupational Health and Safety, to include HIV, AIDS and TB targets was a major breakthrough. The mining industry will go down in the history books as being the first to set industry targets for HIV and TB. Prior to 2011, health targets in the SAMI existed only for silica dust and noise control.

In addition, the stakeholders at this 2011 Summit collectively agreed and committed to significant social reform in the sector by introducing the Culture Transformation Framework.

It was appropriate that the theme for the Summit was 'Zero Harm through Action'. In the words of David Msiza,[11] Chairperson of the MHSC, it meant "the time for talking is over".

Dr Lindiwe Ndelu, Chief Director Occupational Health in the Department of Mineral Resources (DMR), explained,

> "In 2011, for the first time we set targets for HIV/AIDS; some of the projects, and there were 22, were very ambitious. The ILO 200 further contextualised the workplace programmes to integrate HIV/TB initiatives. The DMR commissioned a study by the National Institute of Occupational Health to document the status quo of HIV in the mining industry and provide recommendations which subsequently were incorporated into the Summit Action Plan in 2011. This was a tremendous achievement for the mining industry".[12]

Dr Lindiwe Ndelu further explained that the aims of the plan were to improve the situation of HIV/AIDS and TB in the SAMI, and to significantly improve the lifestyle of mineworkers, which would lead to focused action in the fight against HIV and TB. A key commitment was to develop an integrated policy and guidelines for implementation of HIV/AIDS, TB and silicosis programmes, and develop audit tools and a reporting framework.

At the 10th tripartite summit in 2014, stakeholders reaffirmed and built upon the 2003 milestones and the tripartite commitments of 2011. In support of the National Development Plan of South Africa, the following commitments and action plans were developed to – once again – prioritise and place these key issues high on the agenda:

- Occupational safety – reduction of fatalities;
- Occupational health – elimination of occupational lung diseases and noise induced hearing loss;
- HIV/AIDS and TB – reduction and prevention;
- Culture transformation – implementation of approved framework; and
- Centre of excellence implementation.

It is noteworthy that the milestones for HIV/AIDS and TB were finally included in the Occupational Health and Safety Summit Action Plans, acknowledging the burden of these diseases on the industry. These milestones set the tone for holistically accelerating the journey to zero harm and ensuring that every mineworker returned from work unharmed, every day.

The 2014 milestones reflected what was already happening in the mining industry, but it was now formalised into a tripartite agreement that:

> By December 2024 the TB incidence rate should be at, or below, the National TB incidence rate; and 100 per cent of employees should be offered HIV counselling and testing (HCT) annually, with all eligible employees linked to an antiretroviral treatment (ART) programme as per the NSP.[13]

Reporting on HIV, AIDS and TB in the SAMI

One of the 2011 summit commitments was to develop a reporting tool on TB and HIV and AIDS. This was realised in 2012. Known as the DMR 164, it was implemented in 2013, compelling the industry to report on HIV and TB input indicators.

In 2014, mining houses implemented this integrated and collective reporting for the first time. In 2015, in its 2014/15 Annual Report, the Mine Health and Safety Inspectorate, documented that compliance of reporting of HIV and TB increased by 49.2 per cent, from 233 mines (423 032 employees) in 2013 to 459 (465 923 employees) in 2014.[14] This, in itself, was a significant accomplishment. Prior to the DMR 164 instruction from the Chief Inspector of Mines, each mine operated in a silo fashion, with little sharing of data and even less analysing of data from an industry perspective. The DMR 164 HIV and TB reporting mechanism was a significant step forward in the SAMI, as it began to illustrate the collective impact that had been made, and publicly demonstrated what it had been doing for years. It is envisaged that as the industry progresses on this journey, there will be greater emphasis on output indicators, such as cure rates and treatment successes that can be further analysed for impact.

The data comparison between 2013 and 2014 demonstrated how the industry had evolved in its approach and response to the twin epidemics of HIV and TB. As illustrated in Table 3, the total number of employees diagnosed with TB was 4 461 in 2014, compared to 3 593 in 2013. Of note is that only 1.2 per cent of those who were screened for TB were diagnosed with the disease. MDR-TB cases increased from 149 in 2013 to 190 in 2014, and XDR-TB cases increased from 11 to 18. Small improvements in reporting have been noted, such as the number of employees screened for TB improving by 7.9 per cent. The industry remains hopeful of achieving its target of screening 100 per cent of employees for HIV and TB annually.

Screening for TB in an HIV positive individual, and similarly screening all TB patients for HIV, is a common leading practice in workplace programmes in the SAMI. Continuous improvement to build efficiencies to ensure follow-up care, treatment and support for both HIV and TB, is key to enhancing workplace programmes.

The SAMI has realised that this collective reporting on distinct indicators is only the beginning of evolving into more elaborate and impactful data collection and analysis.

Table 3: HIV/TB Data Comparison between 2013 and 2014

	2013		**2014**	
	Number	**%**	**Number**	**%**
Total labour force	423 032	100	465 923	100
HIV				
Counselled for HIV	229 151	54.2	259 297	55.7
Tested for HIV	192 557	84.0	183 202	70.7
HIV positive	17 384	9.0	19 084	10.4
Co-infected with TB and HIV	2 905	80.8	2 820	63.2
Living with HIV and on ART in 2014	28 887		24 740	
TB				
Screened for TB	308 403	72.9	376 718	80.8
Diagnosed with TB	3 593	1.2	4 461	1.2
On TB treatment	3 483	96.9	3 999	89.6
Diagnosed with MDR-TB	149	4.1	190	4.3
On MDR-TB treatment	172	4.8	197	2.03
Diagnosed with XDR-TB	11	0.3	18	0.4

Source: Mine Health and Safety Inspectorate[15]

A Response from the Chamber of Mines

The Chamber of Mines of South Africa has been an integral part of this incredible journey of HIV/AIDS and TB in the mining industry. Working in close collaboration with various ministries, including the DoH and DMR, and contributing to multi-stakeholder platforms – including the MHSC, South African National AIDS Council (SANAC) and the Southern African Development Community (SADC) Regional TB in Mining Initiative – much progress has been made in responding to HIV/AIDS and TB in the mining industry.

The approach of the Chamber of Mines to improving the control of TB, HIV and silicosis, was to focus on primordial prevention of these diseases through eliminating the predisposing conditions. Great strides have been made by the industry in improving the housing and living conditions of mineworkers and in controlling dust.

The Chamber of Mines established the Mining Industry Occupational Safety and Health (MOSH) Learning Hub in 2008, with a specific team on the promotion of leading practices in dust control. Over the years, various practices have been promoted and adopted by companies, and substantial gains in dust control have been achieved.

The medical interventions on TB, HIV and silicosis were led by the Chamber of Mine's Health Policy Committee (HPC). As a result of concerns around the control of TB in the mining industry, HPC established a TB Task Team in March 2009. Some of the strategies identified by the Task Team to improve TB control were: collation of data on TB, conducting annual audits of TB programmes using the TB Review Tool, utilising TEBA Bank to support completion of TB treatment, improving dialogue with the DoH, and sharing of leading practices in the industry.

The TB Review Tool was developed by the MHSC to review TB programmes. The Chamber of Mines adopted the tool and conducted TB reviews from 2010 until 2013, when the reviews were taken over by the MHSC. Results of reviews were shared with decision makers, such as the Chamber Council and the Ministers of Health and Mineral Resources, and formed the basis for recommendations to improve TB programmes. Improvements to programmes were observed during the duration the reviews were conducted.

An example of how the reviews led to policy change is the management of contractors. The challenge of uneven services provided to contractors was identified by the TB Reviews. Taking steps to address this particular challenge, in 2014 the Council of the Chamber of Mines adopted a position that stated that contractors should be managed similarly to permanent employees, and TB services should thus be uniform across all employees. The Chamber of Mines continues to promote and monitor this position among its members.

In 2015, the Chamber of Mines, together with the DoH, the DMR, and the mining unions, launched Masoyise iTB, a major TB and HIV screening campaign in South Africa's mining sector. The Masoyise iTB initiative will run over three years and forms part of the broader national campaign announced by Deputy President, Cyril Ramaphosa, on World TB Day 2015.

The companies affiliated to the Chamber of Mines have agreed to play their part in this campaign by ensuring that every employee is screened and tested for TB and HIV each year from 2016 to 2018. Most companies already have comprehensive TB screening, testing, treatment and contact tracing in place, which are aligned with World Health Organization (WHO) practices. In fulfilling this obligation, the Chamber of Mines works through a multi-stakeholder Steering Committee, with the objective of ensuring testing in the whole mining industry. The project will be used to improve contact tracing beyond the mine, to increase access to diagnostics and promote the involvement of small mines in TB and HIV screening. Through the project, an impact will be made on decreasing the prevalence of TB and HIV.

The Chamber of Mines also supports improvements to compensation for occupational lung diseases, including TB and silicosis. The Ex-Mineworker Project is a tripartite project between the Chamber of Mines, the DoH and the National Union of Mineworkers (NUM) and it aims to increase access for ex-mineworkers to benefit medical examinations (BME) that are essential for compensation purposes.

The project supported the strengthening of occupational health services within the DoH to enable them to provide BMEs. BME sites were established in Nongoma in KwaZulu-Natal and Mthatha in the Eastern Cape, and four hospitals each in the Free State and North West were provided with additional equipment. A One Stop Service Centre was later set up in Carletonville in Gauteng, providing a comprehensive clinic for ex-mineworkers. The project also supported improvements to the administrative processes of the Compensation Commissioner for Occupational Diseases with the aim of speeding up payments for compensation. This has led to more people being compensated.

Workplace Programmes

In April 2014, the ILO launched its ground-breaking, evidence-based research report, *Effective responses to HIV and AIDS at work: A multi-country study in Africa*,[16] that took cognisance of the results achieved in ten countries to better understand what responses worked well; and how, where and why they did so. The ILO noted that 'intensified prevention, treatment, care and support efforts – many in workplaces – have begun to turn the tide against HIV and AIDS worldwide'. The SAMI can be applauded on leading the charge with regards to workplace programmes and 'turning the tide'. At the same time, however, the Joint United Nations Programme on HIV and AIDS (UNAIDS) Gap Report (2014) Gap Report[17] also talked about the 12 'populations left behind', amongst those being people living with HIV, migrants, sex workers, gay men and other men who have sex with men, the most vulnerable and most affected people. The SAMI, having thrived due to easy access to a vibrant and cheap source of labour in migrants, is thus a 'population left behind'.

Over the years, the SAMI recognised that mineworkers (as migrants), separated from their spouses, families and familiar social and cultural norms, often experience language barriers, substandard living conditions, exploitative working conditions and a lack of social protection, such as health insurance and other social security benefits. The resulting isolation and stress may lead migrant workers to engage in risky behaviours, such as unsafe sex or drug use, and they may face sexual violence and other human rights abuses. Migration can place people in situations of heightened vulnerability to HIV and has been identified – in certain regions – as an independent risk factor for HIV. The increased HIV risk and vulnerability are exacerbated by inadequate access to HIV prevention, treatment and care services and the fear of being stigmatised.

The workplace is an important entry point into HIV and AIDS programmes and policies, and the International Labour Organization (ILO) Recommendation No 200[18] reflects the need to strengthen workplace efforts, to ensure universal access to prevention, treatment, care and support, for persons living with and/or affected by HIV and AIDS, whilst also reaching out to the community.

> It [the recommendation] calls for the design and implementation of national tripartite workplace policies and programmes on HIV and AIDS to be integrated into overall national policies and strategies on HIV and AIDS and on development and social protection.

In 2012, the South African Cabinet noted the recommendation by the ILO concerning HIV and AIDS and the World of Work, and then revised the South African Code of Good Practice on HIV and AIDS and the World of Work, 2012 (HIV Code), including its Technical Assistance Guidelines.

Over the years, the SAMI developed elaborate and comprehensive health services. These ranged from in-house managed care facilities, emergency and primary care as a minimum at medical stations situated close to the shafts and hostel dwellings, to secondary care hospitals. In some instances, mining houses have completely outsourced these health services as a non-core service. Regardless of the choice of service delivery mechanism, according to the MHSA, it is incumbent upon the owner of the mine to provide emergency medical care and occupational health services for all employees, including contractors.

A significant thrust of the early programmes was, and remains, encouraging workers to undergo voluntary and confidential HIV counselling and testing as early as possible. Intense education and awareness programmes were developed for employees at all levels, using innovative communication modalities, to build an environment that was free from stigma and discrimination on the basis of real or perceived HIV status. Where possible, mining houses encouraged and offered testing for spouses and partners, realising that improved access to HIV education, information, and support would contribute to curbing the crisis. Over the years, workplace initiatives matured at various levels – developing novel policies, protocols, instituting employee assistance programmes, providing self-funded treatment (antiretroviral drugs), care and support to employees, spouses and sometimes the entire family. Worth noting, was the innovative arrangements made with TEBA Bank, a regional recruitment agency for the SAMI. Through TEBA Bank, home-based care and support programmes for the SAMI, former mineworkers were able to access rehabilitation care and compensation assistance at regional bases, set up in the neighbouring labour-sending countries. This partnership demonstrates how the SAMI extends its ethical and social obligations into the communities.

HIV and AIDS workplace programmes in South Africa were developed and implemented as far back as the 1990s, long before the tripartite summits and declarations of intent. There was, however, a real temptation to exclude potential employees from the formal workforce if they tested HIV positive. As companies developed their own customised and individual policies, key principles began to emerge, such as ensuring respect for the fundamental human rights of all workers and including the right to be free from compulsory testing and disclosure of HIV status.

There are many sections of the Constitution that relate to HIV in the workplace. It was, however, the case of Hoffmann v SAA,[19] which illustrated how a complaint of discrimination on the basis of HIV and AIDS was likely to be dealt with in constitutional terms. The case was concerned with pre-employment testing and discrimination and, worth noting, was that it occurred prior to the

Employment Equity Act. Mr Hoffmann was refused a position as a flight attendant based on a positive HIV test. The case shows the importance of not only ensuring that medically relevant factors are considered, but that blanket exclusions of groups of people, such as all HIV-positive persons, are a travesty of human dignity and justice.

In addition to this case law that made many senior mining executives sit up and take notice, the promulgation of the Labour Relations Act (No. 66 of 1995) and Employment Equity Act (No. 55 of 1998) saw a set of legal provisions for employers that clearly outlined non-discrimination, voluntary counselling and how employers' should proactively manage HIV at work. The National Economic Development and Labour Council (NEDLAC) and other stakeholders further established the Code of Good Practice on Key Aspects of HIV and AIDS and Employment,[20] which set the foundation for companies on which to base their individual policies and programmes. Sectors, such as mining, manufacturing, automotive, banking and transport, pioneered leading initiatives, including conducting research to document prevalence rates and to analyse the impact of the epidemic on business and the economy.

These large corporations soon realised that to demonstrate impact and to effectively advocate for HIV and AIDS programmes, they needed a structure to make the voice of business heard. In the year 2000, several large corporates, some of them mining houses, organised themselves as founding members of the South African Business Coalition on HIV and AIDS (SABCOHA). In its flagship report (2004-2012), SABCOHA highlighted the role it played in the business sector, specifically capacitating and supporting small and medium businesses operating in the vicinity of large mining houses. Many mining houses depended upon the deep technical expertise of SABCOHA to expedite their own HIV and TB programmes by accessing funding and support from PEPFAR, Centres for Disease Control and Prevention (CDC) and The Global Fund, and other development partners. These public private partnerships were an important mechanism that enhanced workplace programmes, and still continue to feature as an important workplace enhancing strategy. In 2012, following strategic consultation with its member base, SABCOHA became the South African Business Coalition on Health and AIDS, acknowledging that business could no longer focus on HIV only, but that the business response required a new, mature evolution towards a 'health' focus.

Anglo American Workplace Case Study

An example of a proactive and bold response to HIV was the Anglo American workplace case study. As early as 1986, the big international mining houses were acutely aware of the dire HIV/AIDS situation in the country. Dr Brian Brink, former Chief Medical Officer at Anglo American narrated,

> We [Anglo American] carried out an HIV prevalence survey in the mining industry in 1986, using the newly discovered HIV antibody testing technology. Out of 18 450 specimens from South African mineworkers tested for HIV, there were only 4 (0.02%) that were positive. Out of 3165 specimens from Malawian mineworkers there were 119 (3.76%) that were HIV positive. That was a crisis.[21]

But there was a greater humanitarian crisis looming.

> ...And then came the unintended consequence – the South African government of the day, despite all our efforts to persuade them otherwise, decided to prohibit entry to South Africa for any Malawian mineworker who did not have an HIV test and for any mineworker who tested HIV positive. That was a case of grossly unfair discrimination, which led to the suspension of all Malawian labour on South African mines. And that was when I first realised the profound importance of human rights in shaping our response to AIDS and for that matter, to any disease.[22]

Dr Brink recalls,

> Anglo American was grappling with the consequences of AIDS on the business and whether there was any way that treatment could be made available to a sickening and dying workforce. Without doubt, the most defining moment in my career was the decision by Anglo American, on the 6th of August 2002, to provide free antiretroviral therapy to all employees in need of AIDS treatment. There were many people involved in making that decision, but it took unusual and inspired leadership as well as great courage for such a large company to take such a public stance...

The impact of these bold efforts is reflected in the statistics that tell a poignant story as illustrated in Table 4: that new HIV infection rates can decrease with sustained effort; that the percentage of employees on ART can increase year on year; and that employee voluntary counselling and testing campaigns can attain up to 94 per cent participation rates.

Table 4: Anglo American Key Indicators 2008 to 2013[23]

Anglo American Key Indicators 2008 to 2013						
	2008	2009	2010	2011	2012	2013
Number of employees	81450	66661	73129	77075	70720	68881
Best estimate of HIV prevalence	18%	18%	16.5%	16.7%	16.8%	16.3%
Estimated number of HIV positive employees	14 444	12 057	12 066	12 864	11 884	11 243
Number of employees participating in VCT	63 817	54 662	68 741	70 909	57 847	51 594
Number of contractors participating in VCT			32 176	38 659	37 397	40 814
Percentage employee VCT uptake	78%	82%	94%	92%	82%	75%
New HIV infections				902	527	529
Crude HIV incidence				1.17%	0.75%	0.77
Number of HIV positive employees enrolled in HIV wellness programmes	7 361	6 116	7105	7 846	8 361	8 407
% HIV wellness programme enrolment	51%	51%	60%	61%	70%	75%
Number of employees taking ART	3 072	3 211	3 971	473	5 332	5 237
% of HIV positive employees taking ART	21%	27%	33%	37%	45%	47%

Many companies, such as Anglo Gold Ashanti and Gold Fields, and other non-mining enterprises, followed quickly, intensifying the HIV, counselling and testing to enrol individuals onto treatment. Many companies in many sectors funded the entire programme, from prevention through to testing and treating, at their own expense. At the same time, a renewed energy saw efforts around education, training, awareness raising, support for employees affected and infected, and innovation around available resources, both financial and human resources, gaining momentum.

The Powerful Role of Peer Educators

A vital resource in achieving good outcomes at the workplace are peer educators. The peer educators approach works because it makes 'ongoing HIV and AIDS awareness activities feasible, accessible and sustainable'. The ILO took cognisance of the results achieved in ten countries to better understand the factors external to the workplace that have an impact on good workplace outcomes.[24] One such example is increasing knowledge on HIV and AIDS, which is critical to achieving other good outcomes, such as reduction of risky behaviours. The study found that peer educators are 'powerful catalysts for reducing stigma and discrimination' and that their 'effectiveness is largely due to them delivering information in a manner that is accessible to their peers'.

Mr Erick Gcilitshana, National Health and Safety Secretary of NUM says,

> The NUM embraced peer educators. They are the people that know the conditions of co-workers. They stay together in the same hostels and residential areas and know each other's lifestyle. Other workers thus find it easier to open up to peer educators. We also encouraged shop stewards to be peer educators as they are the workers' leaders and again this proved to be successful. Workers are still scared of being victimised by management should they be found to have HIV, and peer educators thus fulfil a vital role.

Peer education in South Africa has its roots in the mining industry at a time when prevalence rates were soaring at 33 per cent, government was indecisive, drugs were too costly and available only to the privileged few, and where prevention was key. It found its roots in workplaces and organisations, in communities, in health and safety structures, and even in management. International donors saw the merits of peer education, invested in these training programmes and entrusted the rollout to SABCOHA and other non-governmental organisations, not only in South Africa, but throughout the African continent.

Business collaborated and agreed that peer educators needed the right communication tools that translate complex health issues into an easily understandable format in different languages. In addition to training peer educators, many mining houses devised innovative means to address and transcend cultural and language barriers through illustrative comics, industrial theatre, and social media. It was vital that the mining houses drove the right messages at work that could be taken home, and vice versa. In some organisations, chief executive officers stood in the frontline to test first, or joined the queue to 'see what it felt like', visibly displaying healthy leadership.

Peer educators engage in formal activities, educating co-workers and members of the community on HIV/AIDS and other health issues. As a valuable resource in the community, they stimulate participation and encourage people to think about the implications of HIV/AIDS and other chronic diseases of lifestyle – for themselves and others in their work teams and at home. As one peer educator shared, 'often there will be no questions at the meeting, but once I get to my desk the phone rings and doesn't stop ringing for all sorts of issues'. The real talks, however, between peer educators, co-workers and community often take place informally, as and when opportunities arise.

Peer Education: A Case Study – Sibanye Gold

Realising that much more needed to be done to provide support and education that would inspire new behaviours, specifically positive health-seeking behaviours, and reduce risky behaviours, companies invested in peer educator training. Sibanye Gold was one of these, many years ago, encouraging employees at all levels in the organisation to get involved and become active in peer educator training.

Sibanye Gold TB and HIV Ambassador

Dr James Malemela, Vice President of Health and Wellness at Sibanye Gold, shares the story of John 'Chief' Motone, who hails from Khutsong near Carletonville.[25] John joined Sibanye Gold in 2008 as an underground employee. In June 2010, he was diagnosed with pleural TB. After two weeks of hospitalisation, he was discharged and complied diligently with his TB treatment from June 2010 to May 2011.

Whilst on treatment, he joined the company's Driefontein operations wellness team as a peer educator. In 2013, he decided to go public with his illness in a bid to encourage fellow employees who had contracted any illness to comply with prescribed treatment. In addition, as a keen athlete, he took up the cause of promoting healthy living to employees and communities around the company's operations. Chief participated in TB and HIV events, and gave motivational talks on adherence to TB and HIV treatment.

His determination was seen beyond his job: he participated in many national marathons and has completed the Comrades Marathon three times.

He represents the story of about 2 000 employees who have started Highly Active Antiretroviral Treatment (HAART) between 1999 and 2011, and who remain employed and productive in the organisation. The average sick leave days of employees on long term HAART are three days per year.

Figure 3: Data warehouse showing sick leave of employees on HAART[26]

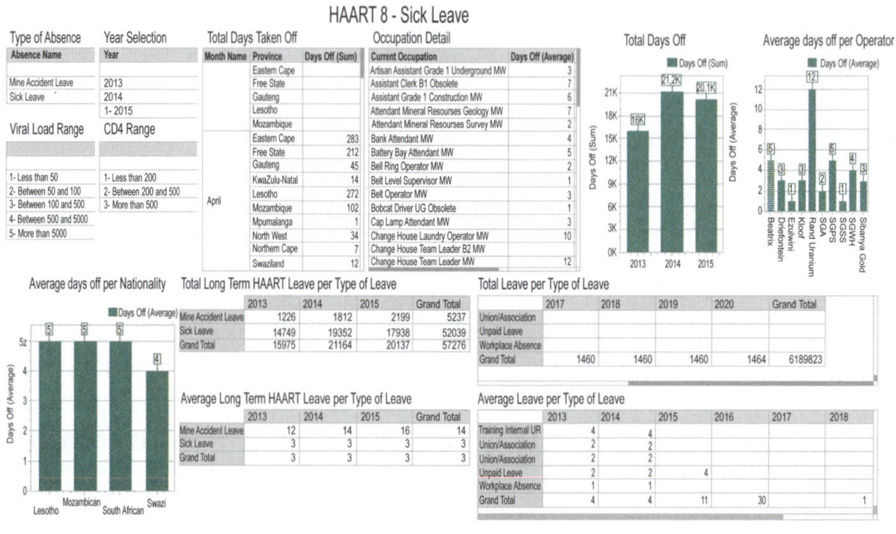

Absence Name
Mine Accident Leave
Sick Leave

Year
2013
2014
1- 2015

Viral Load Range
1- Less than 50
2- Between 50 and 100
3- Between 100 and 500
4- Between 500 and 5000
5- More than 5000

CD4 Range
1- Less than 200
2- Between 200 and 500
3- More than 500

Month Name	Province	Days Off (Sum)
	Eastern Cape	
	Free State	
	Gauteng	
	Lesotho	
	Mozambique	
April	Eastern Cape	283
	Free State	212
	Gauteng	45
	KwaZulu-Natal	14
	Lesotho	272
	Mozambique	102
	Mpumalanga	1
	North West	34
	Northern Cape	7
	Swaziland	12

Current Occupation	Days Off (Average)
Artisan Assistant Grade 1 Underground MW	3
Assistant Clerk B1 Obsolete	7
Assistant Grade 1 Construction MW	6
Attendant Mineral Resourses Geology MW	7
Attendant Mineral Resourses Survey MW	2
Bank Attendant MW	4
Battery Bay Attendant MW	5
Bell Ring Operator MW	2
Belt Level Supervisor MW	1
Belt Operator MW	3
Bobcat Driver UG Obsolete	1
Cap Lamp Attendant MW	3
Change House Laundry Operator MW	10
Change House Team Leader B2 MW	
Change House Team Leader MW	12

	2013	2014	2015	Grand Total
Mine Accident Leave	1226	1812	2199	5237
Sick Leave	14749	19352	17938	52039
Grand Total	15975	21164	20137	57276

	2017	2018	2019	2020	Grand Total
Union/Association					
Unpaid Leave					
Workplace Absence					
Grand Total	1460	1460	1460	1464	6189823

	2013	2014	2015	Grand Total
Mine Accident Leave	12	14	16	14
Sick Leave	3	3	3	3
Grand Total	3	3	3	3

	2013	2014	2015	2016	2017	2018
Training Internal UR	4	4				
Union/Association	2	2				
Union/Association	2	2				
Unpaid Leave	2	2	4			
Workplace Absence	1	1				
Grand Total	4	4	11	30		1

Figure 4: Picture of Chief at the 90th comrades' marathon[27]

Figure 5: Peer educators congratulated by Gauteng Principal Inspector of Mines[28]

From Hopelessness to Hope

The South African mining industry has carried a particularly high burden of HIV, AIDS, TB and MDR-TB, otherwise known as multi-drug-resistant TB. Along with exposure to respiratory crystalline silica dust, TB rates soared to the unenviable status of being the highest in the world. In response, in the past two decades, the SAMI has set industry milestones, the Chamber of Mines undertook a number of initiatives, and workplace programmes have been transformed to be more integrated and comprehensive.

At a regional level, South Africa played a lead role when, in August 2012, SADC heads of state signed the SADC Declaration on TB in the Mines, renewing efforts by all stakeholders in managing and controlling TB, HIV and silicosis across the region. At a national level, South Africa strengthened its HIV and TB responses by exercising diligence and commitment in restructuring the South African National AIDS Council, that now operates in a more integrative and collaborative manner.

As the district health and primary health programmes are being reengineered towards a National Health Insurance, workplace programmes have thrived as they strive to partner more effectively with the public health facilities to improve access to care, optimise referral systems and ensure continuity of care.

Today, the SAMI along with South Africa's National strategies for HIV and TB, are amongst the best in the region, if not the world. Today, South Africa has the largest HIV treatment programme in the world and TB case detection rates and treatment success rates have increased steadily.[29]

The Health and HIV journey for the SAMI between 2011 and 2014, cannot go by unnoticed. As this story illustrated, it was during this time that the industry further pledged its commitment to fight against HIV/AIDS and TB in a tripartite agreement. This journey should be heralded as an important national, regional and certainly a global milestone.

In SA and in the SAMI, 'DNR' has thankfully become a long forgotten practice; however, there still remains much to be done by the mining houses in terms of rapid, urgent scaling up on HIV and TB testing and treating, Thanks to political will, employers' advocacy, workers activism, civil activism and an international community that never, ever, gave up, 'ending the AIDS epidemic' is a reality and will be a journey full of hope and promise. The destination will be one where no-one is left behind, especially those who are most vulnerable, like the mineworkers.

> "If part of the success we have seen comes from 'what gets counted gets done', then it is time for everyone to be counted and reached. Increasingly we are seeing multiple epidemics in countries. Never has it been more important to focus on location and population – to be at the right place for the right people... Working together, ending the AIDS epidemic is possible, and it will take leaving no one behind".[30]

Notes and References

1 Govender, VG, a former medical officer at Gold Fields, a mining company based in Johannesburg, South Africa.

2 Dr Thuthula Balfour-Kaipa, 2016. Head of Health, Chamber of Mines of South Africa. Archives, Version 6 - February 2003.

3 Department of Health, 2007. Tuberculosis strategic plan for South Africa, 2007-2011. Republic of South Africa. Available at http://www.tbfacts.org/wp-content/uploads/2016/02/tbstratplan_0.pdf [Accessed 18 August 2016].

4 Corbett EL1, Churchyard GJ, Clayton TC, Williams BG, Mulder D, Hayes RJ, De Cock KM. HIV infection and silicosis: the impact of two potent risk factors on the incidence of mycobacterial disease in South African miners. AIDS. 2000 Dec 1;14(17):2759-68. Available at http://www.ncbi.nlm.nih.gov/pubmed/11125895 [Accessed 22 August 2016].

5 Department of Mineral Resources, 2015. Mine health and safety inspectorate Annual Report 2014/2015. ISBN: 978-0-621-44065-2. Not available online.

6 Ibid.

7 Govender, VG. Author's own notes.

8 Mining Industry Tripartite HIV/AIDS Summit. Declaration of Intent, 2003. Available at http://www.gov.za/sites/www.gov.za/files/aidsmining_1.pdf [Accessed 18 August 2016]

9 Declaration of Intent – Mining HIV/AIDS Summit 2003.

10 MHSC, 2011.MHSC Summit HIV/AIDS and TB Action Plan. Available at http://www.mhsc.org.za/sites/default/files/HIV-AIDS-Action-Plan1.pdf [Accessed 18 August 2016].

11 MHSC Annual Report 2011-2012. Available at http://www.mhsc.org.za/sites/default/files/MHSC%20Annual%20Report%202011%20-%202012.pdf [Accessed 18 August 2016].

12 Ndelu,L. Chief Director Occupational Health, Department of Mineral Resources, Pretoria, South Africa. Interview with Govender, VG.

13 MHSC. 2014 Occupational Health and Safety Summit milestones. Available at http://www.chamberofmines.org.za/industry news/media releases/2014/send/11-2014/41-2014-occupational-health-safety-summit-m. [Accessed 18 August 2016].

14 Department of Mineral Resources, 2015.

15 Mine Health and Safety Inspectorate. 2014/2015 Annual report.

16 International Labour Organisation, 2015. 'Effective Responses to HIV and AIDS at work: a Multi-country study in Africa. Available at http://www.ilo.org/aids/Publications/WCMS_358170/lang--en/index.htm [Accessed 22 August 2016].

17 UNAIDS, 2014. Gap Report 2014. Available at http://www.unaids.org/sites/default/files/media_asset/UNAIDS_Gap_report_en.pdf [Accessed 28 November 2015].

18 ILO, 2010. Recommendation 200: Recommendation concerning HIV and AIDS and the world of work. Available at http://www.ilo.org/dyn/normlex/en/f?p=NORMLEXPUB:12100:0::NO::P12100_INSTRUMENT_ID:2551501 [Accessed 18 August 2016].

19 Hoffmann v South African Airways 2000 (2) SA 628; 2001 (10) BHRC 571; (2000) 3 CHRLD 146. Available at http://www.saflii.org/za/cases/ZACC/2000/17.html [Accessed 27 November 2015].

20 Department Of Labour. Employment Equity Act, Act No. 55 of 1998. Republic of South Africa. Code of Good Practice on Key Aspects of HIV/AIDS and Employment Available at http://www.labour.gov.za/DOL/legislation/codes-of-good-ractise/employment-equity/code-of-good-practice-on-key-aspects-of-hiv-aids-and-employment [Accessed 18 August 2016]

21 Brink, B. Former Chief Medical Officer, Anglo American, Johannesburg, South Africa.19 November 2015. Interview with Govender, VG.

22 Brink, B. 2014. Honorary Doctorate Address to the Health Sciences Graduation, 11 December 2014, University of Witwatersrand, Johannesburg, South Africa.

23 Brink, B. Former Chief Medical Officer, Anglo American, Johannesburg, South Africa.19 November 2015. Interview with Govender, VG.

24 International Labour Organisation, 2015. 'Effective Responses to HIV and AIDS at work: a Multi-country study in Africa. Available at http://www.ilo.org/aids/Publications/WCMS_358170/lang--en/index.htm [Accessed 22 August 2016].

25 Malemela, J, Vice President of Health and Wellness at Sibanye Gold. "Sibanye Gold TB and HIV Ambassador", email communication, 8 December 2015.

26 Ibid.

27 Ibid.

28 Ibid.

29 National Department of Health, 2014. Joint review of HIV, TB and PMTCT programmes in South Africa. Available at http://www.health.gov.za/index.php/shortcodes/2015-03-29-10-42-47/2015-04-30-08-18-10/2015-04-30-08-23-21?download=578:who-final-report-of-joint-hiv-tb-pmtct-review-main-report. [Accessed 18 August 2016].

30 Sedibe, M. UNAIDS, 2014. Foreword in UNAIDS Gap Report 2014. Available at http://www.unaids.org/sites/default/files/media_asset/UNAIDS_Gap_report_en.pdf [Accessed 18 August 2016].

Chapter 18

The South African Private Sector Response to the AIDS Epidemic

Brad Mears

Introduction

The South African private sector's response to the HIV epidemic varies greatly between sectors and has changed in profile over time. During the early stages of the epidemic, the private sector was very vocal on the national human immunodeficiency virus (HIV), tuberculosis (TB) and sexually transmitted infection (STI) response. More recently, however, there is much less focus on advocacy as the acquired immune deficiency syndrome (AIDS) responses have become part of ongoing corporate health and wellness programmes. During the late 1990s and early 2000s there was a high degree of activity in many sectors, driven by the:

- early recognition of the imminent economic threat posed by HIV;
- response to pressure from shareholders and activists;
- response by some leaders in acknowledging the moral imperative to proactively address HIV; and
- private sector leadership which, in the context of a muted public sector response, filled a vacuum and added to the calls for an intensified fight against the epidemic.

In comparison to how companies responded to health issues in general, HIV received a significantly higher level of attention. Initially this was due to the unknown impact that the epidemic could have had on a company's profitability. Following that, the high degree of social activism and focus by the international community on HIV, drove company leaders to focus proportionally more on HIV, and giving it more attention than they would normally have paid to health in general. Companies with labour intensive operations, and high levels of HIV prevalence, paid particular attention to the threat posed by HIV. In the absence of HIV, most companies would have continued to discount the importance of health (specifically in the workplace and health in the surrounding community), not only as a key element to economic growth, but as a part of strengthening the resilience of our society.

Recognising the need for a private sector response, the South African Business Coalition on HIV/AIDS (SABCOHA) was constituted by a group of strategic business representatives and registered as a non-profit company in 2001. The main objective of the organisation was to mobilise business leaders from all sectors of industry to take effective action on HIV and AIDS by expanding on, or implementing, sustainable responses. The aim was to gather and spread information, knowledge, skills and material resources in collaboration with local and international bodies with similar objectives. In 2013, SABCOHA revised its name to the South African Business Coalition on Health and AIDS with the objective of covering the whole spectrum of health and wellness, and with a new vision of 'healthy workplaces shaping healthy communities'.

Initially there was a highly committed, but small group of business leaders who took bold steps in spearheading the business sector's response. Overall private sector unity could, however, have been stronger, and government should have been lobbied more effectively.

Sectors, such as the mining, automotive, manufacturing, banking, and transport industries, were able to develop pioneering programmes in the 1990s. Initial strategies included the provision of prevention education programmes, education materials and comprehensive wellness services.

Companies in the banking mining and automotive sectors took bold steps in responding to HIV, including providing self-funded anti-retroviral programmes to employees, spouses, and in some cases, the entire family. By 2006, 90 000 patients in the private sector were on treatment, and by 2008, this had increased to 120 000 (around 21 per cent of the patients treated at the time).[1]

By 2005 many companies had begun to widen their focus, contextualising HIV within an even broader wellness response. To lower stigma and avoid HIV exceptionalism, companies began to focus on behaviour change communication and the management of a broader range of conditions, including tuberculosis, hypertension, diabetes, obesity and mental health.

In contrast, sectors such as the agriculture, retail and security sectors were less able to respond to the epidemic. The reasons for this inability to respond may have been attributed to affordability. With the presence of a committed leadership, however, and through engagement with government, some of the barriers to treatment could have been removed.

After 2009 the business sector had largely integrated HIV into workplace wellness programmes, but companies had limited capacity to invest more resources due to the financial crisis. Engagement with government and other social partners became fragmented because of fatigue, poor structural arrangements and an overall lack of trust.

There were few public-private partnerships (PPPs) with government, but those that existed were often very successful. Those, such as the condom distribution programme with South African Breweries (SAB) – which witnessed the distribution of over 60 million condoms to 6 000 taverns – proved the power of PPPs. The testing of 45 195 members of the community by EOH, Aveng Group, Standard Bank, AngloGold Ashanti and other providers in support of the government's 2011 HIV counselling and testing (HCT) Campaign, and Operation Sukuma Sakhe in KwaZulu-Natal (KZN), set the benchmark on how companies could become an extension of the government's public health mandate. Although there was a paucity in PPPs, the instances where government and business collaborated proved that there was ample opportunity to extend public health services through the private sector and the workplace. The important role played by donors needs to be highlighted with respect to encouraging PPPs.

In 2006, the business sector, through SABCOHA, and in partnership with the South African National Standards Agency, developed the South African National Standard 16001 (SANS) on the development, implementation, monitoring and evaluation of workplace HIV programmes. Underpinned by a philosophy of continuous improvement, and based on the APIME model – assess, plan, implement, monitor and evaluate – businesses were able to measure the internal progress of their workplace programmes. In 2013, the South African Bureau of Standards (SABS) developed a second edition to cover wellness and disease management, including HIV and AIDS. Although the SANS standard was extensively promoted, and provided an enabling framework within which companies could measure the success of their programmes, uptake by companies was poor.

Effective monitoring and evaluation remains a challenge, not only for the private sector, but for the entire national response. One of the problems encountered was due to the initial reluctance of companies to release company prevalence data, because of the possible negative repercussions. Vital data could have been shared, which would have informed a more comprehensive national response. Regrettably, this reluctance by companies to share data led to increase in suspicion and a poorer understanding of the dynamics of the epidemic. An opportunity exists for closer collaboration between government and businesses in the development of a powerful monitoring and evaluation system.

In 2014, an HIV data reporting framework group was set up between the South African National AIDS Council (SANAC), the Department of Health and a number of private sector companies. One of the first tasks for this group was to develop a reporting tool on the private sector contribution to HIV, TB, and STIs.

An account of the private sector's response is as much about those opportunities that were seized upon by forward looking companies, as it was about missed opportunities. Throughout the late 1990s and early 2000s, individual companies consistently pioneered some remarkable programmes, but the private sector simultaneously failed to reach out to government to respond to the epidemic in a united fashion. While some sub-sector leaders exhibited insight and bold leadership, other sector leaders remained aloof from the crisis, and responses were consequently fragmented and sub-optimal.

By 2012, SABCOHA had raised approximately US$21 million from donors to fund the programmes referred to in this article. Over the same period, however, the private sector contributed just over US$2 million to the response of the business sectors to HIV. Government contributed less than R1 million towards the private sector's response to HIV. These figures reveal an interesting truth about the response of the business sector. I guess the donors need to be thanked for their support.

Setting the Legislative and Policy Framework

The work which unfolded in the 1990s included activities like:

- scenario planning;
- prevention of workplace discrimination;
- the Code of Good Practice on Key Aspects of HIV/Aids and Employment;
- the promulgation of the Labour Relations Act, and the Employment Equity Act;
- the ABC strategy; and
- the establishment of SABCOHA, which this chapter discusses in detail.

During the 1990s companies began to better understand the threat that HIV posed to their operations. With the development of legislation and case law on how employers should respond appropriately, companies began to take firm steps towards implementing comprehensive awareness, training and prevention programmes in workplaces. Through scenario planning initiatives such as Vision 20/20, sponsored by the Metropolitan Health Group, the understanding of how HIV would impact the sustainability of a business grew, and leadership began to place HIV higher up on the agenda in boardroom meetings. This occurred simultaneously with leaders becoming better informed and overcoming their own internal stigma and prejudices relating to the virus. Although HIV was spoken about more openly in the boardroom, levels of stigma in the workplace remained high. Despite voluntary counselling and testing being offered in the late 1990s, uptake of testing by workers in many workplaces was slow, mainly due to fear of discrimination and possible dismissal. Where company leaders demonstrated visible, genuine leadership and empathy towards workers, trust improved and workplace HIV programmes became more effective. High levels of discrimination continued in the workplace, however, in spite of the leadership shown by executives. Extensive training of senior and middle management still needed to occur before employer-sponsored services became more fully utilised by workers, and access to testing improved.

In the late 1990s, the provision of antiretroviral therapy (ART) was not yet publicly available to South Africans. Most employers who dealt with HIV would focus on the ABC message – abstinence, being faithful and condom use. Although testing became more readily available in the late 1990s, employers were left with the vexed question of whether or not to treat. This was at a time when ART was still very expensive and employees who tested positive could not yet access antiretroviral (ARV) drugs through public facilities. Only those companies with health insurance, or self-funded healthcare facilities, could consider treating their employees.

Companies were better able to shape internal policies relating to HIV issues once labour legislation was passed regarding the rights of workers who were either infected, or perceived to be infected with HIV. The case of *Hoffmann v South African Airways 2001 (1) SA 1 (CC)*, clearly spelt out how employers should conduct themselves in relation to the prevention of discrimination; and stated that employees infected with HIV could not be unfairly dismissed.

The Labour Relations Act (No. 66 of 1995) as amended and the Employment Equity Act, No. 55 of 1998, as amended by Act 47 of 2013, set out legal provisions to prevent employers from discrimination, allowed them to provide voluntary testing for HIV, and provided guidelines for their proactive management of the impact of HIV in the workplace. Through the National Economic Development and Labour Council (NEDLAC) and in consultation with employers, employees and government, a Code of Good Practice on Key Aspects of HIV/AIDS and Employment was developed.

This period also witnessed the establishment of the SABCOHA. This was the first step towards co-ordinating the business sector's response with the establishment of a national structure aimed at empowering business to do more in the response to HIV. A combination of donor funding and private sector money enabled the development of workplace best practices, national and provincial co-ordination, and provided a focal point through which government could be more effectively lobbied by business.

Introducing Workplace Treatment Programmes

This work, which gained real traction in the mid-2000s, involved:

- researching and quantifying the size of the HIV threat – higher prevalence in labour intensive mobile workforces, counting the cost and the impact on skills;
- ARVs and the decision by employers to treat; and
- the Millennium Development Goals and Global Compact which committed the private sector to get involved.

As shown in the research done by Stellenbosch's Bureau for Economic Research (BER) conducted on behalf of the SABCOHA, most companies in the mining, automotive, manufacturing, retail, construction and transport sectors had well-developed internal policies and prevention programmes in place by 2005. Anonymous seroprevalence surveys conducted by epidemiologists began to quantify the risk posed to the business sector. Based upon a risk analysis, by either conducting an actuarial or a seroprevalence study, companies implemented prevention programmes, awareness and communication programmes, and provided voluntary counselling and testing.[2]

With up to 20 per cent of companies in the mining and construction sector reporting acute impacts on productivity, and sharp increases in employee costs and benefits in the financial services sector, a significant burden was placed upon company leadership to act. This was demonstrated when Anglo American took the lead in 2003 and made the decision to provide ART to its HIV positive mine workers. Similar steps were taken by South African Breweries, Standard Bank, and even smaller businesses, across the sectors. Companies did not have the expertise to manage the treatment of HIV internally and so disease management providers were established.

Multinational companies, who had head offices in the United States of America (US) or Europe, placed a premium upon ensuring that the South African operating entities were both empowered and required to implement policies and programmes that were commensurate with the threat posed by HIV. International commitments to the Millennium Development Goals and the principles of a Global Compact dictated that multinationals respond appropriately. Corporate image, perceptions by shareholders, and the media focus upon AIDS in Africa, ensured multinationals led by example in the development of corporate best practices. In addition, the impact of the activist community cannot be ignored, and the positive role they played in obtaining commitments from companies to do more in the response to HIV must be acknowledged.

Although the prevalence of HIV was high amongst semi-skilled workers, the biggest threat to most employers was the potential loss of skills amongst the skilled workforce. Prevalence amongst workers in South African companies varied between 10 per cent in retail, to 14 per cent in manufacturing, 23 per cent in the mining sector and up to 39 per cent in the commercial agricultural sector of the Limpopo and Mpumalanga Provinces.[3] Although companies felt threatened by the impact of HIV, research by the BER showed that employers were managing to contain the associated costs, without passing the impact onto their clients. Notwithstanding the high prevalence of HIV in some sectors, less than 20 per cent of employers considered mechanisation as an option to avoid the impact of HIV.[4]

By 2005, 70 per cent to 100 per cent of companies in the mining, manufacturing and financial services sectors were already providing ART to employees. The provision of these services to employees in the retail, communications and storage sectors varied between 20 per cent and 50 per cent. The construction, security and cleaning sectors were unable to cost effectively provide ART to workers.[5] The fear of discrimination by workers remained a barrier, however, and therefore uptake of treatment was low.

Managing HIV in the SMME Sector

Perhaps the most ambitious of the private sector responses, managing HIV in the small, medium and micro-sized enterprises (SMME) sector entailed:

- the development of the SMME Workplace HIV Toolkit;
- partnering with the donor community in addressing vulnerable sectors;
- supply chain development programmes – 500 SMME's trained; and
- the threat posed to the informal sector – 55 566 micro-enterprises trained.

A different picture emerges when you study how well SMMEs have performed, as well as those companies operating in the informal sector. These companies have not been able to respond comprehensively due to competing priorities, lack of resources, and difficult economic circumstances. SMMEs in South Africa have not responded as well to the threat of HIV, with the private sector response primarily limited to larger companies.

In South Africa at least 55 per cent of the formal economy was employed by SMMEs, yet only about 25 per cent of these smaller companies were estimated to have established any workplace programmes. This is despite the fact that, potentially, HIV could have had a more significant impact on SMMEs than on larger companies. The World Economic Forum developed a private sector response to HIV for SMMEs – from which the big brother approach in the automotive industry is derived – where original equipment manufacturers (OEMs) make resources available to suppliers in order to implement effective workplace programmes.

In partnership with Eskom, and with funding from the United Kingdom (UK) Department for International Development (DfID), over 500 SMMEs were trained by SABCOHA. This HIV supply chain development programme was the first of its kind. Similar programmes were subsequently adopted by Volkswagen SA, Mercedes Benz, the Siyakhana SME project, and the Durban Automotive Cluster.

In partnership with the Border Kei Chamber of Commerce, the Siyakhana Programme continues to be East London's flagship programme responding to the primary health care needs of small and medium sized enterprises. During 2012, Siyakhana Programme targeted 3 448 employees of 32 companies with a comprehensive set of interventions ranging from health awareness and education to counselling, screening and treatment. Of the 2 244 workers who received health education and counselling, 1 855 were tested for HIV. A total of 2 082 of those workers were also screened for hypertension, diabetes, poor vision and TB, among other ailments.

An important stakeholder in the Nelson Mandela Bay and Sarah Baartmann Districts is the Automotive Industry Development Centre Eastern Cape (AIDC EC) in cooperation with the Deutsche Gesellschaft für Internationale Zusammenarbeit (GIZ), targeting the workforce of the automotive industry from 2009, and the commercial agricultural sector from 2013. Since inception, a total of 7 469 employees had access to wellness interventions. A total of 5 890 employees were offered on-site wellness days during which 4 965 participated in a comprehensive Health Risk Assessment, and 4 645 of those took an HIV test.

The research, conducted by the Bureau for Economic Research, clearly showed the vulnerability of small and medium sized enterprises, however, the threat was often mitigated through the replacement of labour. Companies that found themselves within a cluster or supply chain development programme would have received the benefit of a HIV workplace intervention. Those that found themselves outside of a protective environment of this nature may have accessed programmes through a Chamber of Commerce. Although many small and medium sized companies would have an established policy on HIV, and perhaps a prevention programme, steps beyond this would have been cost-prohibitive.

The Informal Sector

The informal sector is a rapidly expanding sector and forms a fundamental and vibrant component of the South African economy. The death of a business owner who operates an informal business would result in spouses and children being without income and security. Due to this, SABCOHA, in partnership with the International Executive Services Corp (IESC), provided capacity building to 55 566 micro-enterprises throughout South Africa to mitigate the impact of HIV in the informal sector. The BizAIDS programme provided training on health risk, financial and legal management for small and micro business owners.

Workplace Treatment

The introduction of workplace treatment programmes was made possible by employer self-funded programmes, health insurance schemes and the extension of treatment beyond employees. Workplace treatment programmes also focused on fighting stigma and HIV exceptionalism, and evolved into general workplace wellness programmes.

There is very little research that analyses the self-funded schemes data separate from the medical aid scheme data. Private sector prevalence statistics have shown a high proportion of employees who are HIV-positive and not on medical aid. This is linked to a higher prevalence in the lower income groups within companies who could not afford medical aid.

According to the AIDS Law Project and Treatment Action Campaign (2006), by the end of 2006, the estimated number of patients in the private sector on ART was approximately 90 000. This number includes employees treated through workplace hospitals and clinics, as well as outsourced disease management programmes.

By the middle of 2008, 568 000 adults and children were receiving ART in South Africa, with the public health sector accounting for 79 per cent of this total. Coverage in 2008 varied between provinces, from 25.8 per cent in the Free State to 71.7 per cent in the Western Cape. Twenty-one per cent of the patients treated were in the private sector, equating to approximately 120 000 individuals.[6]

Of significance was the increased support received from donors for treatment to be provided to workers from vulnerable industries, especially those working in small, medium and micro-enterprises. The pivotal role played by The Global Fund to Fight Aids, Tuberculosis and Malaria (The Global Fund), the United States President's Emergency Plan for AIDS Relief (PEPFAR) and the United States Agency for International Development (USAID), and the Centres for Disease Control and Prevention in providing funding for programmes in vulnerable sectors, such as transport, mining, agriculture, and micro-enterprises, cannot go unmentioned.

As the concept of workplace treatment programmes began to evolve, so the question of who the employer should provide treatment to, needed to be answered. Based upon both actuarial studies and anonymous prevalence testing, employers determined operational risk. With the threat of infection by a spouse and the possibility of parents raising children who were HIV positive, employers needed to decide if they would treat the spouse and the children in addition to the employee. Although little consistency was achieved in the private sector in this regard, the extent to which private sector treatment could alleviate the burden on public health facilities was proven.

Endeavours to address the spread of HIV among truck drivers and related communities also commenced in the middle 2000s. The North Star Alliance established clinics or Roadside Wellness Centres, which were converted shipping containers designed to meet the standards of the World Health Organization. In 2007, North Star Alliance had received 5 000 visitors. By 2013, there were 280 000 visitors, with centres in 13 African countries.

Similarly, in partnership between the Bargaining Council for the Road Freight Industry, the Department of Transport and Mercedes Benz SA, Trucking Wellness established 22 roadside clinics in South Africa, as well as mobile units to reach not only drivers, but communities adjacent to truck stops – including sex workers. The partnership between employers in the trucking industry, government and the bargaining council presented a unique model through which truck drivers – and the adjacent community – could be reached, tested and treated.

A Call for Co-ordination

The four zeros policy, national co-ordination and business support for the development of the National Strategic Plan (NSP) and the development of seven provincial private sector strategies, are essentially practical expressions and experience of a call for greater co-ordination to increase the efficacy of AIDS prevention and treatment programmes in the private sector.

A private sector policy on HIV – The Four Zeros

In 2006, the private sector, through SABCOHA, developed a private sector policy on HIV: Stop HIV/AIDS Now – The Four Zeros. The need for the private sector to clearly delineate its principle position was identified. All energies of business could be more efficiently directed if there was a clear set of principles upon which the private sector could base its actions. The development of the Four Zeros Policy document gave rise to robust debate within the private sector and with other social partners. This policy was presented to and accepted by Business Unity South Africa (BUSA).

The business sector believed that HIV could be stopped and based the policy on the following principles:

- human rights framework;
- outcomes based scientific knowledge and research;
- culture of health seeking behaviour;
- universal applicability of the policy; and
- partnerships across sectors and communities being essential for the realisation of the goal.

The Four Zero Policy

- Zero new HIV infections;
- Zero people getting sick or dying from AIDS;
- Zero mother-to-child transmissions of HIV; and
- Zero tolerance for discrimination

Although the business sector was an integral part of the first NSP, the call for a co-ordinated response by all sectors was made by the national government. Sensing that government was going to shift its policies on HIV, the business sector, through SABCOHA began the process of establishing provincial structures for business.

Provincial structures

In 2009, in support of the NSP on HIV, STIs and TB 2007-2011, SABCOHA embarked upon a process of strengthening businesses responses in the provinces. This was evidenced by the establishment of private sector provincial structures in the Northern and Western Cape during 2009 and 2010. A revised implementation plan for the Northern Cape was launched in Kimberley, which extended the Private Sector Provincial Plan from 2012 until 2016. These initiatives were entirely sponsored by BHP Billiton and Metropolitan respectively.

In 2009, SABCOHA also embarked upon a process of simultaneously establishing five provincial structures in the Eastern Cape, KZN, North West, Limpopo and Free State. The strategy for this re-organisation was launched in conjunction with the appointment of representatives of the private sector on provincial structures, which were subject to extensive stakeholder engagement.

Each strategy delineated what interventions would be undertaken by the private sector in a province. Interventions were placed into three categories:

1. company level interventions;
2. sectorial interventions; and
3. multi-sectorial interventions.

The purpose of the provincialisation programme was to create the platform for business and government to engage at a provincial level, and for companies to receive more operational support from local government

National co-ordination

With the announcement of a revised SANAC structure in June 2012, SABCOHA assisted BUSA with the identification of five representatives from the business sector. The present list of members includes Dr Brian Chicksen from AngloGoldAshanti, Dr Thuthula Balfour-Kaipa from the Chamber of Mines, Dr Elize Strydom from AgriSA and Mr Louis Hollander from the Road Freight Association. With sponsorship from SABCOHA, the foundations for the current NSP 2012–2016 were laid. An envisioning process was conducted in mid-2011.

The 2011 HCT Campaign

In support of the government's HCT campaign conducted between 2010 and 2011, SABCOHA developed a comprehensive HCT strategy document for the private sector to use, support and endorse.

With a revised SANAC, and strengthened political will, it was hoped that the inclusion of the private sector would result in a more harmonised and strengthened response to HIV.

Increasing Monitoring and Evaluation

A critical gap in the private sector's response to HIV was the absence of effective monitoring and evaluation systems. This meant that businesses were unable to:

- assess the efficacy of workplace programmes;
- determine gaps in responses where they existed; and
- determine the quality and impacts of employer programmes.

In 2009, SABCOHA made extensive efforts to establish a Monitoring and Evaluation (M&E) Unit for the private sector. SABCOHA also received SANAC support for the unit. SABCOHA then established a web-based M&E facility, called Bizwell.

Bizwell HCT Statistics 2010–2015	
	Number of people
Counselled:	367 101
Tested:	341 185
Tested positive:	33 969
Screened for TB:	157 614
Screened for TB & referred:	3 218

SABCOHA developed mechanisms to collect HCT data from the private sector and the first report was submitted to SANAC at the end of 2011. SABCOHA viewed the development of Bizwell as a medium term investment, whereby the indicators for which information would be collected could be gradually extended, based upon the funding received. Through the submission of regular reports to SANAC, the Bizwell data began to outline the scale of the testing campaigns conducted by business. Reporting in the mining sector contributed the most data to the system at 70 per cent, followed by manufacturing at 11 per cent, while other sectors each contributed less than 10 per cent of the data loaded on the Bizwell system.

Although the need for Bizwell was well-founded, the lack of resources – and inability of the business sector to submit high quantities of data – severely hampered its value to the overall AIDS response.

Public-Private Partnerships

There is also a case for increasing public-private partnership to improve co-ordination, leverage resources and increase the impact of interventions.

PPPs are cooperative efforts between sectors resulting in a unique and effective partnership. The potential success of such partnerships can be demonstrated by the following examples:

- The Trucking Wellness Programme brought together the Bargaining Council for the Road Freight Industry, the Department of Transport, and Mercedes Benz SA to establish twenty-five truck stops across South Africa.
- The distribution of 67 483 600 million condoms to 6 000 taverns (Project Promote) thanks to South African Breweries' logistics capacity in partnership with the National Department of Health and the Bargaining Council for the Contract Cleaning Industry.
- Funded by the Global Fund and co-ordinated by SABCOHA, a partnership between EOH Health, Standard Bank, Aveng Group and testing providers,

resulted in businesses supporting the government's 2011 HCT campaign by testing 44 000 people in the community. Those who were positive were immediately linked to treatment. Phase II of the programme rolled out health screening in the informal business sector and Phase III was still in progress at the time of writing this chapter.

- With funding from the Centre for Disease Control and Prevention, and with sponsorship from BMW SA, Dow Chemical, Edcon, Mercedes Benz SA, SASOL, Unilever SA, Woolworths and Xstrata, SABCOHA conducted a school holiday programme. Working with dance4life, loveLife, Soul City, Play Soccer, Operation HOPE and SA Rugby Legends, over 1 400 children were protected and educated during the 2010 FIFA World Cup.
- Metropolitan Health Risk Management's partnership with the Centre for HIV/AIDS Prevention Studies (CHAPS), a PEPFAR-funded South African non-governmental organisation (NGO) which implemented and disseminated evidence-based approaches to prevent the spread of HIV in Southern Africa, aiming to train over 415 general practitioners (GPs) for medical male circumcision (MMC) work to reach over 32 000 men in South Africa for high quality MMC.
- Through a survey conducted in 2009, SABCOHA identified the need for peer educators in the workplace to be supported in order for them to contribute effectively and efficiently over the long term. Besides telephonic support, the need for ongoing training for peer educators, where face-to-face interaction is the preferred medium, is addressed by companies providing venues for capacity building and motivational workshops to take place.

In proportion to the size of the epidemic, the number of PPPs was too low. The lack of political will from both government and the private sector led to a failure for the two sectors to co-operate. Lack of political will and leadership resulted in inadequate resources being allocated in tackling the disease.

Conclusion

Much can be learned from both limited successes and many failures when studying South Africa's response to the AIDS epidemic. With the absence of resolute leadership in government and the private sector at the beginning, our response began on shaky ground. Coupled with this was the poor allocation of resources, and a failure to measure outcomes. Both government and business could not communicate with one another, and in many cases were unable to transcend the ideological differences that kept the two sectors apart. Perhaps it was the very thing that makes business what it is – that is, business is fiercely competitive – that prevented business from uniting, trusting itself, and being able to trust government. Perhaps business had to overcome its own prejudices and fears, and maybe some of those prejudices still exist today.

With the learnings of the past, SANAC, with funding from the GIZ, developed a Private Sector Engagement Strategy. The strategy lays the platform upon which the private sector, government and the other social partners can engage much more constructively.

Afterthought

Some concluding questions and answers:

- Did the business sector do enough in the response to HIV?
  Certainly not. Some South African businesses stand out as world leaders in what they have achieved, whilst others have not even recognised the need to take action yet. In light of current HIV data there still a lot of room for improvement, especially in the field of prevention.
- Were there some pioneering programmes and bold steps taken by companies?
  Absolutely!
- Was there adequate leadership?
  In the beginning there was a small, but powerful, group of committed company leaders who invested both personal and organisational time and resources into the fight against HIV. Overall sectoral leadership was not realised, and by 2012 business leaders were no longer invested in HIV.
- Did government support businesses efforts in the fight against HIV?
  No. This was mainly due to mistrust and a general failure by business and government to reconcile ideological differences and achieve common interests. Many opportunities were missed, where workplaces and the business sector could have advanced governments mandate of public health. Due to the social distance between government and business, the leadership of both sectors were difficult to reach. There has been little by way of mutual acknowledgement by either sector for both the remarkable achievements made, or for their respective failures.
- Have we learnt anything from the challenges posed by HIV?
  Most definitely. Our only hope is that we can learn from our mistakes, and what little we have that has united us in the fight against HIV, can be built upon and strengthened.

Notes and References

1 Adam, M.A. and Johnson, L.F., 2009. Estimation of adult antiretroviral treatment coverage in South Africa. *South African Medical Journal* 2009, 99(9), p.661.

2 Ellis, L. and Terwin, J., 2005. The Impact of HIV/AIDS on selected business sectors in South Africa. Bureau for Economic Research, Stellenbosch University.

3 International Organization for Migration, Integrated Biological and Behavioural Surveillance Survey, 2010.

4 Ibid.

5 Connelly, P. and Rosen, S., 2005. Treatment of HIV/AIDS at South Africa's largest employers: Myth and reality. Health and Development Discussion Paper No. 5, June, 2005. Available at http://www.bu.edu/cghd/files/2011/11/HDDP-No-5.-June-2005.-Connelly-Rosen.pdf [Accessed 4 August 2016].

6 Adam and Johnson, 2009, p.661.

Chapter 19

The Evolution of HIV Financing since 'Durban 2000' and its Impact on South Africa's Response to the Epidemic

Fareed Abdullah

Introduction

Outside the walls of the Durban 2000 AIDS Conference, the epidemic was raging out of control. In South Africa alone, it was estimated that 4.2 million people were living with the human immunodeficiency virus (HIV), or one in five people between the ages of 15 and 49. Communities were to witness a quarter of a million deaths in that year alone.[1] The predictions were that this number of deaths was going to get even worse in the years to come and that life expectancy was dropping precipitously. No doubt there was a sense of panic, fear and disbelief about the scale of the tidal wave that had come crashing through our front door.

The health system was just coming out of its first administrative reform, and once the 1996 Growth, Employment and Redistribution (GEAR) strategy had been adopted by government, there was concern about the increase in disability and foster care grants and additional investments in health care and education. We had not factored in the additional cost burden of a major epidemic that was sweeping across the country. We knew treatment was available but also knew that it was unlikely to be within our financial reach on any large scale.

When the International AIDS Conference opened in Durban 16 years ago, only one man was on antiretroviral treatment (ART).[2] Edwin Cameron, a High Court judge who was steeped in the human rights traditions of South Africa's mass democratic movement, was unable to countenance the glaring contradiction between his new lease on life and the bleak future of the thousands of others suffering from the acquired immune deficiency syndrome (AIDS).

Triple combination therapy had been shown to be effective in suppressing plasma viral load at the Vancouver AIDS Conference in 1996, and by the time the conference came to Africa in 2000, it was widely in use in North America, Europe and elsewhere by those few who could afford treatment. Cameron found it unpalatable that he was on ART only because he could afford the US$400 each month. When the AIDS Conference organisers asked Cameron to be a guest speaker at the first Plenary Session in 2000, he emphasised how wrong it was that even though a treatment for AIDS was available, the majority who needed it would be denied life.

> In this I exist as a living embodiment of the iniquity of drug availability and access in Africa. This is not because, in an epidemic in which the heaviest burden of infection and disease are borne by women, I am male; nor because, on a continent in which the virus transmission has been heterosexual, I am proudly gay; nor even because, in a history fraught with racial injustice, I was born white. My presence here embodies the injustices of AIDS in Africa because, on a continent in which 290 million Africans survive on less than one US dollar a day, I can afford monthly medication costs of approximately US$400 per month.
>
> Amidst the poverty of Africa, I stand before you because I am able to purchase health and vigour. I am here because I can pay for life itself.[3]

While the unaffordable cost of treatment was a major obstacle in 2000, there were other forces in motion in South Africa that would prove to be as challenging as the cost of ART.

Though Durban 2000 is remembered for Cameron's speech and the rise of South African treatment activism, many will also recall it as the stage on which then President of South Africa, Thabo Mbeki, expressed his doubts about the science of AIDS and the virtues of ART. Although he was roundly rebuked by Nkosi Johnson, an 11-year old boy, at the opening ceremony and a clearly concerned Nelson Mandela at the closing ceremony, it wasn't enough to prevent AIDS denialism from gaining traction.

Yet the issue of costs remained unresolved, and what should have been a rational discussion about where to find the money became a budget discussion that was drawn into the boggy mire of the fight between the denialists and their detractors of the sane and rational school. This can only be characterised as a wholly unnecessary internecine war between erstwhile comrades that both claimed to be acting in the interests of our fledgling democracy.

However, funding was constantly being found for treatment. At every stage of the growth of the treatment agenda, more and more funding was found. This article tries to look beyond the surface of the issues and explains that there was a coalescence of public outrage skilfully reported by the media, extreme mortality and morbidity in the health care system, and legal forces that continuously placed the need to budget for treatment or to raise the funds from donors. These external factors helped a democratic, modern and rational system of resource allocation to always factor in a major epidemic into its planning processes. This is where Mbeki came up against the logic of his own democratic administration.

Sixteen years later, South Africa has more than 3 million people on lifelong ART and spends R23 billion[4] per annum responding to the HIV epidemic. These funds come mainly from domestic, but also international sources. Much has been written about the history of AIDS in South Africa and the unfolding of events on the political and policy fronts, but it remains an enigma how the South African government came to fund eighty per cent of the country's response to HIV while squeezed between a controversial policy and a constrained fiscal environment.

Is there resilience in the factors that led to this funding success story? Can we conclude that the same conditions exist today as they did 16 years ago? What are the prospects for funding the rest of the journey over the next 16 years so that we reach the goal of an AIDS-free generation as envisaged by the National Development Plan?

The Trajectory of Domestic Financing

As the country with the largest epidemic in the world, HIV was always going to be a big expenditure item on South Africa's public sector account. Since 1994, most provinces had budgeted for condoms, HIV education and training services through the AIDS Training and Information Centres, but there was no systematic budgeting for the prevention of mother-to-child transmission of HIV (PMTCT) or ART, as these were seen as unaffordable, unavailable and difficult to implement. In the case of PMTCT, early initiation of Zidovudine (AZT) monotherapy[5] was shown to be effective as far back as 1994, and triple combination therapy (HAART), only came into widespread use when results were presented to the Vancouver AIDS Conference in 1996.

When it was possible to provide short course AZT for PMTCT,[6] the Western Cape government made the first budgetary provision for this intervention. This was in March 1998 and, at that stage, there were no overt signs of the great controversy on the horizon.

Even though, at the national level, South Africa's policy was frustratingly equivocal on ART, there was widespread recognition in the National Treasury (Treasury) – and in the provinces where the epidemic was extracting its financial toll on the health services – for the need to cater for the additional costs related to AIDS care in primary health care clinics and hospitals. As far back as 2000, the Treasury put together a task team to look at ways of adjusting budgetary allocations for health services in provinces to cater for the additional burden of AIDS. This task team recommended the creation of a conditional grant for AIDS which has become the single most important AIDS funding stream since 2000 (see Figure 1).[7]

Figure 1 AIDS Conditional Grant allocations 2000/2001 through 2017/18

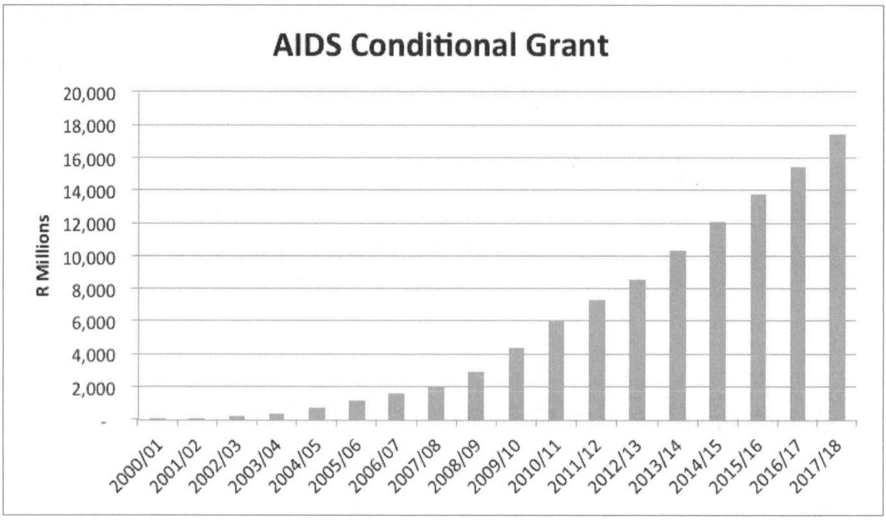

Source: Results for Development[8]

The creation of the HIV conditional grant had perhaps more to do with designing an equitable method of allocating central fiscal resources to the provinces for health care. For decades under apartheid there did not appear to have been any rational planning or allocation of resources for health across the provinces. The Treasury, under the Mandela administration, moved rapidly to determine an equitable method for allocating resources to the nine provinces. Per capita equity was a good starting point, but provinces were so different, and adjustments needed to be made for neglected infrastructure in some provinces, expensive tertiary hospitals that serviced multiple provinces, and the unequal burden of AIDS across provinces. Conditional grants were created to effect these adjustments.

The Academic Complexes and National Tertiary Education conditional grant compensated provinces for the additional costs of academic complexes. The Health Infrastructure Grant compensated previously neglected regions of the country with massive backlogs in infrastructure, and the AIDS conditional grant provided sorely needed funding to provinces for the additional burden of AIDS health care costs. Unlike the base formula of per capita allocations in the underlying health allocation, the AIDS conditional grant was split according to the burden of HIV disease.

With time, each conditional grant was assessed independently as to its expenditure and impact, and future allocations were based on estimates of need. Unlike other conditional grants, the HIV conditional grant was doing well in terms of its expenditure history. Provinces were spending AIDS funds and, where they were not, they were able to book other health care expenditures to the AIDS conditional grant as the burden of disease was very high in all provinces. Impact was easier to measure, and when ART was included in the conditional grant each patient enrolled was counted as a life saved. Future estimates of expenditure had more credibility than other conditional grants, given the effective modelling tools that had been developed locally and internationally to predict the number of patients that would need ART in future years.

It is still the case that the expenditure rate of the AIDS conditional grant is very high (consistently almost 100 per cent in most provinces) and that the impact of ART and PMTCT on adult, child and infant mortality is one of the most successful outcomes of the current administration. Life expectancy in South Africa has increased from 53 years in 2003 to 61 years in 2015,[9] earning the ART programme the reputation as one of the most effective investments the country has made. Future planning for the AIDS response is of high quality and the Treasury relies heavily on cost estimates from financial modelling undertaken by researchers, many of whom are funded by the United States President's Emergency Plan for AIDS Relief (PEPFAR), linked to the National Department of Health (NDoH) and the South African National AIDS Council (SANAC).

The conditional grant only provided an instrument for dedicated AIDS funding. There were numerous other factors that spurred growth in HIV funding over the last 16 years. The pressure from the public, especially AIDS activists of the Treatment Action Campaign (TAC), clinicians in the public sector, all sorts of civil society and non-governmental organisation (NGO) formations and networks, opposition parties and the media, was becoming more powerful with each passing month. For the first time, the highly regarded ANC government was being called names and was treated as an uncaring pariah in the face of a tragedy. The TAC was extremely smart and well organised. They used a combination of mass mobilisation tactics that South Africans had assimilated from street protest lore in the eighties, and highly skilled strategy in the South African courts, precipitating a key judgement of the Constitutional Court that ruled against the sole authority of the Executive to make policy in the historic Nevirapine judgement.

In 2001, government announced pilot sites for single dose Nevirapine. There were to be two pilot sites per province and these had to be budgeted for. The conditional grant was an easy mechanism to fund these pilots. While allowing funds to flow to provinces, it required national oversight of these funds. This was followed by the Constitutional Court decision forcing government to roll-out the single dose Nevirapine programme. This was another stimulus for the growth of the HIV conditional grant, even though the pressure for funding it was external. Instead of blocking the allocation of funds for PMTCT, the Health Department and National Treasury officials facilitated it. Those officials opposed to funding PMTCT could not effectively block it. Many were also feeling the heat of the public outcry and the pressure from the provincial counterparts especially in the Western Cape, KwaZulu-Natal and Gauteng.

More protest action and a well organised policy reform exercise within government, led by the Cabinet Committee formed to review the provision of ART, forced the hand of the government. The cabinet decision to provide ART that followed in 2004 led to yet another major spike in funding.

The decision came a few months after United States (US) President George Bush used his State of Union Address to announce the US Leadership Against HIV/AIDS, Tuberculosis and Malaria Act of 2003[10] (Public Law 108-25 is otherwise known as the PEPFAR Act). This legislation, signed in May 2003, authorised up to US$15 billion over five years and created the Office of the Global AIDS Coordinator to coordinate US-supported HIV programmes world-wide. South Africa was designated as one of fourteen original PEPFAR focus countries.

The agreement between the activists and government to implement the 2007–2011 National Strategic Plan (NSP) was another event that led to a spike in funding, and the appointment of Ministers Barbara Hogan (in 2008) and Aaron Motsoaledi (in 2009) bolstered the support of the National Health Department and the rationalists within it for the ART intervention. The Motsoaledi era saw rapid movement to decrease the threshold for treatment. In 2009, the Health Minister announced that the CD4 treatment threshold would rise to 350, and that all pregnant women, tuberculosis (TB) patients and children with HIV, would start lifelong ART. The policies were shaping up, but more importantly the mood had changed dramatically. After a decade of controversy, government was now ahead of the curve on all major policy issues. Motsoaledi has been consistent with his strict adherence to the evidence and the latest science. This has been borne out by his recent decision to adopt the World Health Organization (WHO) Guidelines for test-and-treat and Pre-Exposure Prophylaxis (PrEP) for high risk key populations.

The Global Fund to Fight AIDS, TB and Malaria

In November 2010 the Global Fund had approved a new grant for South Africa. This US$300 million grant was the largest yet and would help the further expansion of the South African ART programme. The donor world had noticed the change in stance by the South African government and began to believe in the turnaround.

The Global Fund had reason to be sceptical about South Africa. Its first experience with the country was in 2001, when it approved a grant for the Kwa-Zulu Natal province that included a small component for ART. National government did everything to obstruct the flow of funds and prevent implementation of planned programmes. Two years later the Global Fund approved a US$65 million grant for the Western Cape Province that provided funds for the comprehensive rollout of the ART programme in that province. In this second instance, politicians did not intervene and allowed officials to embark on the first public sector ART programme. The programme proved highly successful, with the province testing all aspects of ways and means of implementing treatment. By 2004, the province was well on its way to comprehensive coverage for both PMTCT and ART. The lessons learnt in the Western Cape proved crucial to the national rollout that was to come following the change in national policy in 2004.

The establishment of the Global Fund to Fight AIDS, TB and Malaria is usually accredited to Kofi Annan, then Secretary General of the United Nations, who made the call in 2000 for a financing institution that would support countries in rolling back the tide against three diseases that were spiralling out of control. It is widely acknowledged, however, that the real originator of the concept was Jeffrey Sachs, and that it was tied to his work as chair of the WHO Global Task Team on Financing Health and his work on motivating for the Millennium Development Goals. It rapidly mobilised funds from the US and European governments and began funding the national rollout of treatment in almost every country in Southern Africa. In countries such as Zambia, Namibia, Tanzania and Malawi, the Global Fund contributed up to 90 per cent of the cost of treatment, yet South Africa remained a difficult destination for the Fund.

The Global Fund remains an important investor in South Africa. In its last round of funding approved in 2014, the Global Fund earmarked funding for key populations, such as sex workers, prison inmates and men who have sex with men (MSM). More recently, in 2016, the Global Fund committed funds to reduce new infections in young women between the ages of 15 and 24.

PEPFAR and the Global Fund are important investors in South Africa's national response. Current funding from PEPFAR for 2016 and 2017 exceeds US$410 million per year and that from the Global Fund is US$325 million over the 2016 to 2018 timeframe. Both PEPFAR and the Global Fund support the national programme in many ways. Global Fund resources are tactical with earmarked funds for key populations, such as sex workers, prison inmates and MSM. PEPFAR funds complement these interventions, as well as supporting technical assistance in support of more than three million on ART, scaling up prevention programming, and orphans and vulnerable children (OVC) programmes. More recently, following on the focus on the PEPFAR DREAMS initiative (which seeks to ensure that adolescent girls and young women lead determined, resilient, empowered, AIDS-free, mentored and safe lives), and the development of South Africa's national campaign for girls and young women, the Global Fund has also committed funds to reduce new infections in young women between the ages of 15 and 24.

The revitalisation of the SANAC Secretariat and its oversight of the GF portfolio of grants have led to a higher level of utilisation of GF funds in South Africa. The GF only contributes five per cent of total expenditure on HIV in South Africa but due to a closer collaboration its investments are strategic and determined by the needs of the country. Though a case can be made for increasing the contributions of the GF to South Africa the country has benefitted from the weakening of the rand against the dollar.

Figure 2 Global Fund annual disbursements to South Africa[11]

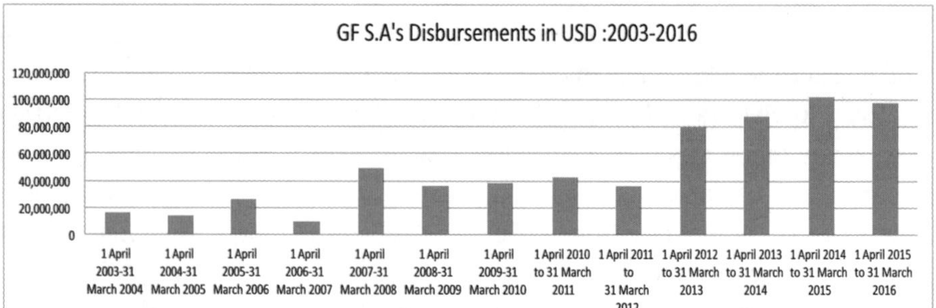

Source: Authors

The US remains the largest contributor to the Global Fund. PEPFAR funding differed from the Global Fund in that it focussed almost all of its investments in 15 high priority countries. PEPFAR was launched in 2004, and even though this was at a time in which the national government policy was being reluctantly revised, the two governments could not find common ground and all of PEPFAR funding was channelled to NGOs. In hindsight, this did not prove to be a bad thing. It led to the massive expansion of a large number of NGO programmes that complemented the rollout of ART in all nine provinces. Armed with resources at clinic and hospital levels, South African clinicians moved mountains to reach large numbers of patients in need of treatment throughout the country.

PEPFAR funded more than half of the 13 million HIV test kits used in the national HIV Counselling and Testing (HCT) campaign in 2010 and 2011 and funded almost all of the Nurse Initiated Management of ART (NIMART) training of nurses – this being one of the most important steps that limit the rate of the national ART expansion. By 2016, PEPFAR reported that it was supporting (in one form or another) 2.9 million patients who were on ART.

Table 1 PEPFAR planned funding in South Africa, 2004–2015 (US$ in Millions)[12]

2004	2005	2006	2007	2008	2009	2010	2011	2012	2013	2014	2015
93	144	221	397	590	551	560	548	523	484	459	413

Source: PEPFAR

South Africa was an extremely important destination for PEPFAR, as the country with the highest number of PLHIV, and an essential partner in the effort to meet ambitious global targets. Almost one third of all PEPFAR funding was allocated to South Africa and the desired impact was achieved for both countries.

In 2012, the US and South African governments signed the PEPFAR Partnership Framework Implementation Plan (PFIP) in support of South Africa's NSP 2012-2016. The agreement proposed a reduction of up to 50 per cent of PEPFAR funding to South Africa over five years. The planned PEPFAR funding reduction reflected South Africa's prioritisation of its national HIV response and own funding increases. The South African government asserted its ownership of the response, particularly related to care and treatment, and agreed to PEPFAR's transition from provision of direct service delivery to a more technical assistance focused mode of operation. In actuality, PEPFAR's annual funding to South Africa has not been reduced as quickly as proposed in 2012. Rather than the intended US$350 million in Country Operational Plan 2016 (COP16) under the PFIP, PEPFAR COP16 funding is US$410 million, plus (a) an additional US$24 million for expanding male circumcision to cover 80 per cent of all targeted males in the 27 focus districts, (b) US$18 million to accelerate ART, and (c) additional funds for DREAMS.

In 2015 PEPFAR agreed with the South African government to refocus on the 27 highest HIV burdened districts representing 80 per cent of the estimated people living with HIV (PLHIV) burden. During 2015, PEPFAR completed a co-ordinated transition with the National and Provincial Departments of Health from the other

25 districts. In addition, PEPFAR launched the DREAMS programme in 2015, dedicating more than US$66 million to five districts over two years (2015/16, and 2016/17). The Global Fund is also supporting programmes focused on adolescent girls and young women (AGYW) in ten districts, while GIZ supports AGYW activities in one district. As a result of these focused interventions, a national AGYW focused campaign was launched, leveraging the development assistance, and national, provincial and districts departments' AGYW interventions, in all nine provinces and 52 districts. These programmes have also been the catalyst for significant civil society and private sector organisation engagement.

South Africa also received significant support from other countries and private foundations over the last decade. Funding from the United Kingdom's Department for International Development (DfID) programme, German Development Funding, as well as Scandinavian and other countries, have had a considerable impact, as have contributions from private foundations, such as Atlantic Philanthropies and the Bill and Melinda Gates Foundation. In addition, the role of both South African and international business and foundations should not go unmentioned.

Reducing the Cost of Treatment

A major factor in the successful expansion of the ART programme has been the dramatic reduction in the cost of treatment – including drugs, labs and human resources. When Justice Edwin Cameron bemoaned the high monthly cost of his own treatment, he could not have dreamed that the cost of antiretroviral drugs would be reduced to less than US$100 per year per person, or about two per cent of what he was paying in 2000. The international effort to promote the manufacture of quality generics, and the impact of increasing volumes, made the biggest difference in driving costs down. In addition, South Africa's role in negotiating substantial reductions in the prices of antiretrovirals is now legendary, with the price reductions realised in South Africa having a global impact.

Another significant factor was the decision by the national government to implement task shifting or NIMART. In direct contrast to the high thresholds set by Health Minister Tshabalala-Msimang for the accreditation of treatment sites in the 2004-2006 period, the current Health Minister argued for treatment initiation to be done by NIMART-trained nurses. Staff costs now make up a larger share of input costs for the ART programme, and the task shifting decision dramatically reduced these costs and allowed treatment to be provided at clinics where there are no doctors in attendance.

Prospects for Future Investments

HIV has a special place in the hearts of South African policymakers, activists and government officials. This should not come as a surprise given the huge burden of disease in South Africa. More than 6 million South Africans are living with HIV and a few million have already died from the disease. Every community and every family has been affected. In health care, AIDS still stands out as the most important priority to tackle. Its correlation with mortality rates and life expectancy is so gripping that it will continue to receive attention from decision makers and the holders of the purse strings.

Though there is more talk these days of addressing other pressing needs, such as chronic diseases, the AIDS imperative has shifted to the need to make investments in prevention. Now that there are more than 3 million South Africans on treatment and the likelihood of doubling that number over the next few years is a very real prospect, the case for preventing new infections has become all the more compelling. South Africa will not be able to afford a continually expanding treatment programme and generating a few hundred thousand new infections each year becomes untenable.

There are effective prevention interventions available and many more are proving to be good investments. Our own estimates (National Department of Health and SANAC), in a study called the Investment Case Study,[12] predicts that the country will need to spend approximately R600 billion over the next twenty years to address both treatment and prevention.

The current fiscal position does not allow for this level of investment and yet the choice of stopping the train halfway down the track does not really exist. This means turning our attention to optimising our investments, finding efficiencies and, most importantly, generating new revenues through innovative financing options.

Conclusion

How it became possible for South Africa to make initial investments in the treatment of AIDS in the context of an obtrusive government policy, was somewhat miraculous. The fact that government was able to sustain continuously growing investments in HIV under difficult fiscal conditions, reflects the premium that the Treasury places on the HIV investment.

This short history of the resourcing of the AIDS response points to the organic democracy of allocating resources in South Africa. While ultimately the decision makers in government sign budgets into existence, there is no doubt that the social power of activists, the severity of the epidemic and the public desire for government to control AIDS impacted the decisions that led to where South Africa is today.

The AIDS movement in South Africa makes a compelling case for further investment from the government. The social, political and economic forces that propelled the growth of AIDS funding over the last sixteen years are still poised to propel the response further towards the achievement of the goals agreed at the United Nations High Level Meeting in June 2016 and the goals of the National Development Plan. This does not mean we should underestimate the difficulty of raising the additional resources. The failure of the economy to grow and the likelihood that we will not experience higher levels of economic growth for a while to come, pose the greatest challenge. The weakening of the rand will also impact on the use of available funds. HIV will always stand out as the first amongst priorities as the same societal forces will continue to exist for as long as the epidemic continues to dominate South Africa's burden of disease profile, and for as long as we do not control the high levels of incidence, morbidity and mortality from this well-known scourge. There is always the robust competition for resources between AIDS programming and the broader health sector, with increasing opinions emerging from important quarters that the overall health response should acquire primacy over disease specific funding. The integration of HIV as a chronic condition with other diseases is also under intense scrutiny as is its integration with programmes that address its social and structural drivers such as poverty, gender based violence, intergenerational and transactional sex, alcohol and substance abuse, lack of schooling and risky sexual behaviours.

Notes and References

1 UNAIDS, 2000. Global epidemic report, 2000. Geneva: UNAIDS. Available at http://data.unaids.org/pub/Report/2000/2000_gr_en.pdf [Accessed 4 July 2016].

2 To say that there was only one man on treatment in South African is, of course, a very liberal use of the author's literary licence. In fact, there were at least a few thousand patients on triple combination therapy or HAART in the year 2000, mainly in the private sector through programmes such as AID for AIDS and through research sites, such as the HIV Clinic at Somerset Hospital in Cape Town, run by Professor Robin Wood.

3 Cameron, E., 2000. Plenary Address to the Durban AIDS Conference 2000. International AIDS Society. Available at www.tac.org.za/Documents/Speeches/edwin.htm [Accessed 4 July 2016].

4 National Department of Health and SANAC, 2015. Investment Case Report. 22 March 2016. Available at www.sanac.org.za [Accessed 4 July 2016].

5 Please see https://aidsinfo.nih.gov/news/101/actg-076-questions-and-answers [Accessed 4 July 2016].

6 Short-Course Regimen of AZT Proven Effective in Reducing Perinatal HIV Transmission. Available at https://www.cdc.gov/media/pressrel/r980210.htm [Accessed 4 July 2016].

7 Guthrie T., Ryckman, S.S. and Hecht, R., 2015. Consolidated Spending on HIV and TB in South Africa (2011/12 – 2013/14). *Results for Development*, November 2015.

8 Ibid.

9 Dorrington, R.E., Bradshaw, D., Laubscher, R. and Nannan, N., 2015. Rapid mortality surveillance report 2014. Cape Town: South African Medical Research Council.

10 Pepfar Act 2003. https://www.gpo.gov/fdsys/pkg/PLAW-108publ25/pdf/PLAW-108publ25.pdf [Accessed 5 October 2016].

11 Compiled by the South African National AIDS Council using disbursement data sourced from the Global Fund Country Team responsible for South Africa.

12 PEPFAR 2015 Annual Report to Congress. Available at www.pepfar.gov/documents/organization/239006.pdf [Accessed 4 July 2016].

13 Department of Health, South Africa, and South African National AIDS Council: South African HIV and TB Investment Case - Summary Report Phase 1. March 2016 available at http://sanac.org.za/category/publications/reports [Accessed 5 August 2016].

PART III

LEVERAGING SOCIAL AGENCY

PERSPECTIVES FROM ACTIVISTS AND PRACTITIONERS

Chapter 20

The Intersectionality of HIV, AIDS and Disability in South Africa

Hendrietta Bogopane-Zulu

Introduction

South Africa is said to have one of the highest prevalences of the human immunodeficiency virus (HIV) in the world.[1] When South Africa undertook to deal with the scourge of HIV and the challenges it posed, people with disabilities were not considered, as they were often perceived to be sexually inactive and thus not at risk of HIV infection.

According to Hanass-Hancock,[2] disability and HIV are more interrelated in Eastern and Southern Africa (ESA) than anywhere in the world. The ESA region is known as the epicentre of the global HIV epidemic. It is estimated that 68 per cent of all people living with HIV reside in sub-Saharan Africa, which includes ESA. What was still to be determined was the empirical evidence that the latter was linked to high disability prevalence rates, until a 2011 World Health Organisation study conducted across countries, which suggested that disability prevalence in the ESA region ranges between 14 per cent and 36 per cent.[3]

When the South African National AIDS Council (SANAC) was first launched, disabled people were not represented on the body as a sector. After it was relaunched in 2007, SANAC, the highest national multi-sectoral partnership body working and advising government on matters related to HIV and acquired immune deficiency syndrome (AIDS), included the representatives of people with disabilities – both in the national and in some of the nine Provincial AIDS Councils. Subsequently, Cabinet adopted the National Strategic Plan (NSP) 2007-2011.[4] Through the efforts of the Disabled People South Africa (DPSA), people with disabilities were recognised as a vulnerable group to HIV and AIDS, thereby setting the ground for resource mobilisation for disability as a sector and placing more impetus thereon in the national AIDS response.

This move entrenched the sector's slogan of 'Nothing about us, without us', which calls for disabled people to be actively involved in matters affecting them, but also calls on all South Africans to take heed of the rights of disabled people.

The United Nations Convention on the Rights of Persons with Disabilities (UNCRPD) provides a global policy framework to promote equal rights to health for persons with disabilities, including sexual and reproductive health, on a par with those without disabilities. The framework is also intended to enable policies to implement AIDS programming for persons with disabilities and programmes to fight against stigma, discrimination and other barriers faced by persons living with HIV.[5]

The UNCRPD does not, however, explicitly refer to HIV and AIDS in the definition of disability. Be that as it may, State Parties are required to recognise that where persons living with HIV (asymptomatic or symptomatic) have impairments which, in interaction with environment, result in stigma, discrimination or other barriers to their participation, they can fall under the protection of the Convention.

State Parties to the Convention, of which South Africa is a signatory, are required to ensure that national legislation complies with this understanding of disability. Some countries have afforded protection to people living with HIV under national disability legislation, while others have adopted anti-discrimination laws and other measures that explicitly cover discrimination on the basis of HIV and AIDS.[6]

Intersectionality of HIV and AIDS and Disability: Myth or Reality?

The growing relationship between HIV, AIDS and disability is an emerging and growing cause for concern, as persons with disabilities are at higher risk of exposure to HIV due to risk factors such as poverty, lack of access to information, poor access to health care services and risk of sexual abuse, to which women and girls with disabilities are more vulnerable. Nonetheless, there is an increasing realisation and understanding that persons living with HIV and AIDS are also at risk of becoming disabled on a permanent or periodic basis as a result of their condition, or from their treatment in instances of toxicity or poor absorption of the drugs used for antiretroviral therapy (ART).[7]

The information on the intersectionality of HIV, AIDS and disability throughout the world is largely based on the experiences of persons with disabilities, but much more research needs to be done around the link between them. Despite the lack of extensive research worldwide on the relationship between HIV, AIDS and disability, the existing evidence drawn from experiences of people with disabilities and people living with HIV and AIDS about the link between the two, and the growing research in this field, also suggest the interrelation between the two.

The Intersectionality of HIV, AIDS and Disability: Its Unintended Consequences

In South Africa, the link between HIV, AIDS and disability brought to the fore another unintended consequence – that of people who became disabled as a result of living with HIV – which gave rise to the debate about whether these people should receive the disability social grant. During the period 2001 to 2003, a series of workshops and focus group discussions were held with the disability sector to engage on HIV, AIDS and disability. The objectives of these workshops were:

- to educate disabled people around HIV and AIDS, as well as HIV, AIDS and disability;
- to educate care givers, sign language interpreters and mentors within the sector to enable them to give similar training throughout the country for their respective organisations and sectors; and
- lastly, to foster discussion within the sector about HIV, AIDS and disability.

These training workshops covered both theoretical and practical aspects, including issues around what HIV is, research around the world and South Africa, how disabled people are affected by HIV, and practical exercises, such as how to use condoms. For example, training a blind person how to identify a condom that has a faulty package, how to open a condom without damaging it, how to insert and use it, and so on. Many of the exercises were customised for respective disabilities.

The workshops were held in partnership with diverse structures (jointly and separately), namely: the Department of Health, SANAC, the United States Agency for International Development (USAID), Policy Project, and the Joint United Nations Programme on HIV and AIDS (UNAIDS). Throughout these workshops and focus groups, a common thread surfaced with regards to the issue of whether people who are living with HIV and those who become disabled as a result of living with HIV should receive the disability social grant or not. There was general concern that this would lead to competition for the scarce resources of the disability grant. Some of the studies conducted around this matter reflected that:

> There has been anecdotal evidence of the likelihood of 'pervasive incentives' where HIV positive people on ARVs may avoid taking ARV medication in order for their CD4 counts to drop to a level where they are considered sick enough to access the disability grant.[8]

Another unforeseen consequence of the link between HIV and Disability arose when concerns over the possible drug interaction between antiretrovirals (ARVs) and medication for chronic illnesses were highlighted. The likelihood of adverse effects of ARVs on disabled people with certain sensory and cognitive disabilities were highlighted. (This matter will be discussed in detail later in this chapter.)

Disability Rights Movement and HIV and AIDS in South Africa

South Africa has a proud disability rights struggle history. Examples of a few scenarios are given below.

- In 1985, disabled activists gathered under the banner of DPSA to fight against the racial oppression in the country at the time, as well as for the right to speak for themselves on matters affecting them. At this stage very little, if anything, was known about HIV and AIDS by the people of this sector. The main focus of the struggle, at this time, was liberation from racial oppression.
- In 1994, the first ever democratically elected Parliament included a disabled Member of Parliament.
- In 2006, over 3 500 disabled people held a week-long DPSA congress in Durban and elicited extensive inputs on HIV and AIDS, which formed part of the draft NSP 2007-2011. Furthermore, in 2007 the disability sector ran a series of workshops to develop a sector operational plan aligned to the NSP 2007-2011 and the accompanying Monitoring and Evaluation Framework.
- The representation of disabled people on SANAC grew from one person in 2000 to five representatives in 2009.

Figure 1 shows the timeline of the increased involvement of disabled people in the national AIDS response in South Africa.

Figure 1: Timeline of the increased involvement of disabled people in the national AIDS response in South Africa[9]

Protection of Rights and Legal Framework

People with disabilities have the same rights as all other South Africans, as enshrined in the Constitution of the country. Specific mention is made of the rights of disabled people in the Bill of Rights.

> The State may not unfairly discriminate directly or indirectly against anyone on one or more grounds including race, gender, sex, pregnancy, marital status, ethnic or social origin, colour, sexual orientation, age, disability religion, conscience, belief, culture, language, and birth. [10]

The DPSA has, in addition, developed its own disability rights charter which further explains and highlights the basic Constitutional Rights.

These are all interlinked with the UNCRPD that South Africa ratified together with other treaties and conventions protecting the rights of women and children, among others. An array of legislation protects the rights of disabled people over a wide spectrum of living, employment, benefits, and protection from discrimination.

Despite this legal and constitutional protection, disabled people were still lagging behind in the fight against HIV and AIDS. They still faced discrimination, especially in relation to service delivery at health institutions.

Factors that Compound the Impact of HIV, AIDS and Disability

One of the challenges around the impact of HIV, AIDS and disability is that the voices of those affected have not yet been properly documented and there is still a lack of research in this regard, as discussed in the previous section.

To discuss the relationship between HIV, AIDS and disability, it becomes imperative to go beyond the debate of whether HIV can cause disability or not, and look at the factors that compound the impact of HIV and AIDS on disabled people. Once a person living with HIV becomes disabled as a result thereof, then they have to contend with the realities of being both HIV positive and disabled. Below are some of the factors that reflect this relationship.

Stigma, denial, exclusion and discrimination

A report published by SANAC states that HIV and AIDS were among the most stigmatised medical conditions in the world.[11] Disabled people also still contend with stigma, denial, exclusion and discrimination, despite the legal framework that exists in the country and through the UNCRPD. Given that both sectors have to deal with some form of stigmatisation and discrimination, the report further points out that being both HIV positive and disabled would result in being 'doubly stigmatised'.

Figure 2: Case study featuring discrimination faced by people who are living with HIV and are disabled[12]

HELEN'S STORY

Helen Ndamase was diagnosed HIV positive in 1993, when she was 19 years old. When she went for voluntary counselling and testing (VCT) at the Chris Hani Hospital, she learned of her HIV status from a nurse who was showing a colleague a glove on which was written, 'This one is HIV positive'.

In 2004, Helen fell ill and was hospitalised. She subsequently started ART. Around this time she started experiencing problems with her vision. A visit to St Johns Eye Hospital revealed that she was infected with Cytomegalovirus, which predisposes HIV positive people to blindness.

> 'To this day, I do not know whether my blindness was a result of ARV side effects or was caused by Cytomegalovirus infection.' (Helen Ndamase, HIV positive and blind)

Helen did not receive proper counselling to help her adjust to her HIV status or newly acquired blindness. Both doctors and nurses were very unsupportive and ill-equipped to deal with her situation. Being blind and HIV positive, Helen needed additional care and support for herself and additional help with her baby. She experienced additional discrimination, in that she was often ignored by health professionals who would rather talk to the person accompanying her as if her blindness and HIV status had affected the functioning of her brain or hearing.

The community that Helen came from was, like the health personnel, 'ill-equipped' to deal with her situation. Helen is worried about her son's wellbeing. He is continuously teased by his friends about his mother's condition.

Helen's story not only highlights the extent of the discrimination faced by people who are living with HIV and are disabled, but also reflects the unpreparedness, bad attitudes or lack of capacity of the health profession in giving the required support to disabled people who are HIV positive. During some of the focus groups and workshops conducted with disabled people, many reflected how they experienced discrimination from health professionals because of the assumption that people with disabilities did not have sex. This means that the health professionals do not pay attention when giving them relevant information on HIV treatment and prevention, and this limits access to proper health care services.

Poverty

Much has been written and documented about disability and poverty, both locally and internationally. Many researchers and experts have asserted that poverty causes disability and, furthermore, can lead to secondary disabilities for those individuals who are already disabled as a result of poor living conditions, health endangering employment, malnutrition, and poor access to health care and education opportunities.[13]

Situations of poverty often contribute to risky sexual and other behaviours, in order to secure an income. Some of the female respondents at workshops conducted with disabled people indicated that: 'They take what they can get when someone wants them. Women are sometimes tricked into sex, by a man promising to be with her and marry her – but after sex he leaves'.

Cost of disability

On the heels of poverty is the cost of disability to disabled people, their families and the economy of the country. An unpublished study by the Department of Social Development states that:

> A critical aspect of the poverty trap is the disability-related out-of-pocket costs persons with disabilities and their families incur, such as sign language interpreters, additional transport costs, personal assistance and assistive devices. There is also the opportunity cost of family members foregoing work opportunities in order to take care of a family member.[14]

In addition, the study states that exclusion, and lack of reasonable accommodation and support, place an unfair burden on persons with disabilities and their families who have to bear the associated costs.

This study has sought to address the key elements of disability-related economic vulnerability in the following ways:

- estimate opportunity cost related to disability in key life areas (education and employment) and loss of income considering disability type and degree;
- estimate out-of-pocket cost related to disability in key life areas (education, employment and health);
- describe economic effects of a disability grant and tax rebates;
- identify disability-related costs that are currently borne by households of persons with disabilities that should be borne by the state; and
- determine types and range of services to reduce economic vulnerability.

These are but some of the economic realities people living with HIV and who are disabled have to contend with.

Information/knowledge barriers

Lack of information presents a serious and pertinent problem to people with disabilities. Lack of information in Braille for blind people, or sign language interpretation for deaf or hearing impaired people, or programmes for people with intellectual and communication impairment, will be the realities that HIV positive people who become disabled will have to adapt to. The same applies to those who need to use wheelchairs or crutches, and for whom navigating physical and environmental barriers will prove to be another challenge.

The story below of John Meletse (Figure 3) is another example of the double discrimination and marginalisation faced by HIV positive disabled people. The story, however, also reflects how appropriate assistance and support of traditional health services can respond to the needs of HIV positive disabled people.

Figure 3: Case study featuring the double discrimination and marginalisation faced by HIV positive disabled people[1]

JOHN MELETSE'S STORY

John Meletse was born deaf. He was diagnosed with HIV in 2002. He works for the Gay and Lesbian Association (GALA) and focuses on documenting the life stories of deaf, gay and lesbian people.

On the day John went for VCT, he was met with the same inhumane treatment at the clinic that he had been exposed to as a deaf person over the previous years, even before he contracted HIV. When he introduced himself, indicated that he was deaf and his reason for visiting the clinic, the reaction of the nurses at the clinic was a combination of shock, guilt and pity. Interestingly, there was a sign language poster on the wall, yet none of the nurses knew sign language. After being passed from one nurse to another several times, one took his blood sample without pre-counselling, and he was told to wait 15 minutes for his results. After a while, he was called into a consulting room where the doctor informed him by writing on a piece of paper that he was HIV positive and then dismissed him. Yet again, there was no post testing and counselling. The cold experience at the clinic continued when John went to seek treatment.

'You are given a beautiful cocktail of tablets and no one explains what they are for and how they could help you.' (John Meletse, deaf, gay and HIV positive)

This was the pattern for John until he went to the clinic with a sign language interpreter, Ruth. Ruth's help improved John's understanding of his condition and the treatment he was receiving.

His HIV status and sexual orientation exposed him to more discrimination, as many support groups do not welcome homosexual people, let alone disabled people. John therefore started a support group for deaf and gay men.

Challenges

There still remain many challenges in ensuring that the prevalence of disabled people acquiring HIV, and people living with HIV who become disabled as a result of their condition or treatment is reduced. The factors given above as compounding aspects that increase the prevalence of the link between HIV, AIDS and disability need to be addressed with the same vigour and momentum as when the country undertook to deal with the scourge of HIV and AIDS.

Poverty remains one of the critical factors that require attention in reducing the prevalence of HIV infections among disabled people. The economic emancipation of disabled people, beyond being merely grant recipients, will contribute significantly towards their being able to make decisions for themselves and not rely on those who support them.

Dealing with stigma and discrimination at service delivery points will go a long way towards ensuring that disabled people are encouraged to go to these points, first and foremost, and not opt to stay at home to avoid ill-treatment.

Access to treatment and information is important in ensuring that disabled people learn more about HIV, AIDS and disability in a format or language that they can understand. Secondly, ensuring that people at frontline service points are taught how to interact with diverse disabilities will also ensure that disabled people can visit these points, confident that they can express themselves and knowing that they will be heard and attended to properly.

Cultural practices and societal beliefs – such as that having sex with a person with albinism, or with a virgin, will heal HIV – should be addressed. Disabled girls, in particular, are more at risk of sexual abuse as a result of such beliefs.

Achievements

Despite the challenges highlighted above, there are several meaningful achievements that have been recorded over the past two decades. This section will only highlight a few of those. These achievements reflect the following common threads:

- upholding the slogan: 'Nothing about us, without us';
- mainstreaming disability throughout structures and activities in society; and
- documenting people's experiences that they have shared to enhance already existing information and data, albeit very little.

ZAZI – Know Your Strength

'Zazi – Know Your Strength', is a campaign aimed at empowering and mobilising young women between the ages of 16 and 24 in the fight against HIV and AIDS. This campaign is in response to the Africa Accelerated Agenda for Women and Girls in the fights against HIV and AIDS.

The conceptualisation of the campaign, its brand identity and communication elements were informed by young women who participated in workshops and focus group sessions. This campaign carries the aspirations of young women of the type of society they envisage for all young women in South Africa. Young women across the country from rural, peri-urban and urban settings were brought together in workshops and focus group sessions to engage on issues affecting them as young women, including: intergenerational sex, dual protection, gender-based violence, self-esteem, resisting peer pressure, knowing yourself and your status.

The key on the logo (Figure 4) symbolises power, opening and closing doors, and dreams. The colour green speaks to a new beginning, birth, a new season, a better future, and is likened to the green in the South African flag. It is also a colour for protection of women and children internationally.

Figure 4: ZAZI logo

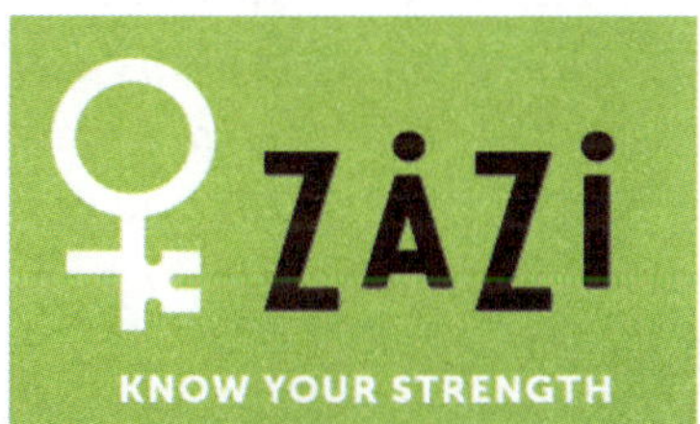

Key elements that made this campaign attractive to young women were its youthfulness and depiction of innocence, strength, decisiveness and remaining true to oneself. The campaign was popularised through a song by a well-known artist which was part of a marketing campaign that was launched in 2014.

The roll-out of the campaign included:

- conducting capacity building workshops with communities, public and private radio stations;
- developing a Sexual and Reproductive Health Toolkit;

- engaging health promoters, care givers and youth ambassadors through dialogues and door-to-door campaigns;
- engaging community leaders; and
- media campaigns.

This campaign involved the active participation of young girls with disabilities. The television advertisement also shows deaf young girls in the group. This approach is significant in ensuring that there is integration and dispelling of myths about people with disabilities, and showing that disability and HIV are everyone's responsibility and not just the responsibility of disabled people. The former Department of Women, Children and People with Disabilities was also one of the partners in this campaign. It ensured that issues of accessibility were taken into account.

Investigative and training workshops on HIV as a cause of disability

The previous sections made reference to the intersectionality of HIV and disability, highlighting the insufficient research on the subject and the need for extensive studies in this regard.

The former Department of Women, Children and People with Disabilities in partnership with UNAIDS, SANAC and the Disability Sector held a series of workshops to explore, engage with and highlight the disabling effect of HIV on those living with the virus. These workshops started with the relationship between HIV and blindness, with further workshops to be held focusing on HIV and deafness and HIV and cancer, amongst others. In addition to the above workshops, further engagements on this subject were held with SANAC.

Many of the participants at these workshops were HIV positive and were developing some form of a disability, but had no knowledge of the possible relationship of their disability to their HIV status. Some of the health professionals present at these workshops also had no information on the subject matter. The workshops were held in collaboration with both international and local academics and experts on the matter.

Conclusion

South Africa has made, and continues to record, considerable progress in responding to the special needs of people with disabilities in the context of the HIV epidemic. The country launched the largest HIV counselling and testing campaign in the world, which resulted in more than 13 million people receiving counselling and being tested for HIV over a period of a year, and this included people with disabilities. Not only is the HIV treatment programme the largest in the world, but the country was lauded internationally for resourcing the fight against AIDS largely from domestic sources. Disabled people were among those who benefitted from this massive resource mobilisation against the scourge, even though there is agreement that much more still needs to be done for the disability sector in this regard.

Stigma and discrimination towards sexuality and sexual rights of people with disabilities still remain a challenge that threatens universal access to HIV prevention, treatment and care programmes and services.

This chapter is a reflection of what can be done when disabled people work with government and other sectors of society, both locally and internationally, to ensure the protection of the rights of disabled people and their self-representation in addressing any societal challenge.

Notes and References

1 Nothing About Us Without Us! HIV, AIDS and Disability in South Africa, 2010. SANAC.

2 Disability and HIV: What drives this relationship in Eastern and Southern Africa, *African Journal of Disability,* 2(1). Hanass-Hancock, J. Regondi, I. Naidoo, K., 2013.

3 Ibid.

4 National Strategic Plan (NSP) 2007-2011.

5 Disability and HIV. UN Enable. Available at http://www.un.org/disabilities [Accessed 12 March 2015].

6 DISABILITY AND HIV Policy Brief, 2009. UNAIDS/WHO/OHCHR: http://data.unaids.org/pub/Manual/2009

7 HIV/AIDS and Disability: Final Report of the 4th International Policy Dialogue. March 11-13, 2009. Health Canada.

8 Nothing About Us Without Us! HIV, AIDS and Disability in South Africa, 2008. SANAC.

9 SANAC/DPSA/SA GOVERNMENT/ UN JOINT PROGRAMME ON HIV and AIDS: Nothing About Us...Without Us: HIV, AIDS and Disability in South Africa.

10 Bill of Rights, Constitution of the Republic of South Africa, 1996, Section 9.3.

11 Nothing About Us Without Us! HIV, AIDS and Disability in South Africa, 2008. SANAC.

12 SANAC, 2008. HIV, AIDS and Disability Training Report.

13 Disability and Development: Poverty and Disability, 2010. World Bank. Available at http://web.worldbank.org/WBSITE/EXTERNAL/TOCS/EXTSOCIALPROTECTION/EXTDISABILITY [Accessed 12 March 2015].

14 Research Report on Cost of Disability, 2015. Department of Social Development.

15 SANAC, 2008. HIV, AIDS and Disability Training Report.

Chapter 21

Civil Society's Perspective – South Africa National AIDS Council's Governance Framework and the Coordination Dilemma of HIV Response

What Works and What Lies Beneath?

Mmapaseka Steve Letsike

Introduction

Over the past decade South Africa has made significant progress in the fight against the human immunodeficiency virus (HIV), tuberculosis (TB) and sexually transmitted infections (STIs), but has also experienced notable obstacles. The Human Sciences Research Council (HSRC) estimated that in 2015 there were 6.4 million South Africans living with HIV.[1] The year 2015 saw remarkable progress in antiretroviral treatment (ART) with more than three million patients receiving the treatment. The 2015 Millennium Development Goals report recorded South Africa as the region with the highest decline in the number of new infections in the world, with 98 000 less infections in 2013 in comparison to 2010.[2] This was largely due to the collaborative efforts of the South African government and civil society, with the support of development partners. The largest contribution of these efforts was, however, carried by the civil society movement, a movement that proposed a rights-based approach to a governing party, health officials and politicians that were all in denial.[3]

Historical Background

Civil society emerged in the 1980s when a number of civil society organisations (CSOs) united to overthrew the apartheid state. The year 1994 marked victory for CSOs as South Africa became a democratic state. The key challenge for the government was to transform the fragmented public health system and to redress the inequalities of apartheid. There was low political will to tackle HIV and the acquired immune deficiency syndrome (AIDS), and focus was placed mainly on HIV prevention. During this period, the National AIDS Council was established in 2000, adopting a multi-sectoral response to HIV and, furthermore, as a result of this work a National Strategic framework was later developed. It was not, however, to prove that easy as large numbers of HIV-infected South Africans died, many of them because they had no access to treatment or services. It was during this trial and error period of denial that various shortcomings – weakness in the political line, the weakness in leadership to prioritise and preserve lives, and most importantly the weakness to protect, promote and fulfil the constitutional right to life, and certainly the right to health – became apparent. It was against this backdrop that the Treatment Action Campaign (TAC) was formed in 1998 with an initial focus on improving awareness of HIV treatment, the reduction of medicine prices, and the right to access antiretroviral drugs.[4] The TAC lobbied for access to antiretroviral treatment through a combination of high-level protests, social mobilisation, civil disobedience campaigns, and legal action (including against pharmaceutical companies).

Many organisations, however, existed long before the TAC, such as the National Association of People Living with HIV, Networking HIV and AIDS Community of South Africa (NACOSA) and the Positive Women's Network, and were established in the early 1990s as formations of support groups. Many of these organisations were also led by people living with HIV, as well as those affected by HIV, and were services oriented – ensuring and providing services to people living with HIV and their families. Several of these organisations involved people who founded the TAC, many of whom are still alive, leading a healthy lifestyle, while other lives were lost.

The South African narrative, however, does not end here, but continues to take note of the successes, and the work towards milestones which is a growing positive phenomenon, with increased commitment for change that recognises shared responsibility. Taking government to court proved to be a good approach by the TAC as the outcome of the court case secured a better future for many South Africans and, most importantly, the judgement forced the South African government to adhere to its constitutional obligations. During this period, we not only saw the rise and collective efforts of people living with HIV and AIDS (PLHIV), and solidarity with civil society working locally and internationally in the HIV sphere, but also saw the attention paid by the Government Department of Health to the health needs of communities rise far more slowly than expected, particularly in providing access to treatment. This became an ongoing struggle for the TAC and many other organisations and activist groups.

Subsequently, the South African National AIDS Council (SANAC), a multi-sectoral body, was established in 2000 by the South African government. Although the structure was established by government, civil society played a significant role in the struggle against HIV and, most importantly, in the formation and articulation of how SANAC would function. SANAC's mandate included the co-ordination of the HIV, TB and STI response in South Africa. Through SANAC, the country saw a high level of political commitment to tackling HIV, TB and STI using a multi-sectoral approach.

The commitment of this political leadership was demonstrated by and led by the Deputy President of the Republic of South Africa, who is the chairperson of SANAC and deputised by Steve Letsike who also chairs the National Civil Society Forum. The two leaders lead SANAC and champion collective efforts on the HIV response, which is conducted alongside – and together with – the custodian of health in the country, the Minister of Health, as well as other Ministers on the Inter-ministerial Committee (IMC) and sector leaders of the CSF.

Governance and Accountability in the HIV Response

SANAC was the driving force behind the transformation observed in this country's response to HIV over the last ten years. The invigoration of SANAC in 2007 through the agreement reached in the SANAC plenary meetings in those heady days of change, is perhaps the main reason that we can claim the world's largest national antiretroviral treatment programme and a true decline in HIV-related mortality.

Whereas the National Strategic Plan (NSP) for the years 2007 to 2011 was aimed at addressing the urgent need to scale up treatment, the current NSP (2012-2016) focuses on the prevention of new infections. The current NSP tackles the structural drivers of the epidemic over a 20-year period and calls for a major investment in prevention programmes to roll back the epidemic where the majority of new infections are generated, that is: in young women; most at risk and marginalised populations; multiple concurrent partnerships; alcohol and substance abuse; informal settlements; road networks; and in prisons. It also highlights human rights and access to justice as key ingredients to a successful response. Crucially, it explains that TB and HIV are so inter-related that the two diseases cannot be dealt with separately.

The current NSP states that the South African response to HIV and TB will be all-encompassing and multi-sectoral in nature. This does not diminish the increasingly complex task of increasing the number of people on antiretroviral treatment to more than 3 million by 2016 – a mark that was reached in 2015.

The current NSP (as described in broad terms above) has direct implications for the governance of SANAC. It was imperative that the SANAC Plenary, its various committees, the Provincial and District Councils on AIDS and the Secretariats at National, Provincial, District and Local levels are reformed in a way that facilitates the work of implementing the new NSP in an unfettered way.

This general finding (the need to improve and align the SANAC structures to the requirements of the new NSP), was well documented in the mid-term review (MTR) of the previous NSP. The MTR dealt extensively with the need to make SANAC more efficient and fit-for-purpose, and also identified the need to significantly strengthen the SANAC Secretariat as a well-functioning independent institution that could fulfil its mandate arising out of the SANAC Plenary and its committees. Understandably so, the MTR should be a process that determines the progress of the NSP, and makes recommendations on what still needs to be done. Similarly, during 2011 the MTR further explored the need to expand the work of SANAC to provincial and district levels where true implementation of the SANAC programme is taking place.

SANAC Secretariat and UNAIDS conducted sector audits in order to access the landscape of the multi-sectoral approach, and the progress and capacity thereof. The reports, however, revealed the weaknesses of civil society sectors. The report brought into public display the serious challenges in the SANAC sectors, with no more than three of the nineteen sectors passing muster. Whilst the sectors were critical in helping build consensus in a country divided by HIV, it was abundantly clear that new forms of civil society formation needed to take place in the SANAC space. Whilst the civil society sectors had made a sterling contribution to the work of SANAC, the findings indicated that some key actors were not linked to the SANAC project. With the notion of 'No one will be left behind', some actors remain secondary and tertiary to the SANAC project.

In the course of crafting the NSPs, one of the stated objectives was the reform of the governance arrangements of SANAC and the strengthening of the Secretariat. With this in mind, the Deputy President appointed an ad hoc governance task team of experienced advisors to make recommendations in this important area. The recommendations of the ad hoc committee focused on governance and accountability, which included leadership, political, structural and reporting mechanisms; while the NSP thematic areas covered resources, evidence, leadership, political, structural, programmatic, and human rights. All these issues required a strong element of co-ordination and committed individuals to help steer the country in the right direction. Further, as a result of these issues the SANAC Secretariat was brought into existence and was appointed by the SANAC Trust.

A 2008 review of the institutional arrangements for National AIDS Council (NACs) in Sub-Saharan Africa[5] suggested that the following factors were important for the development of an effective National AIDS Commission or Council.

1. Senior level commitment and drive within the NAC Secretariat, complemented by high level political connections of the Chair of the Board, as well as the relationships between the senior level management of the NAC and the President's office;
2. Having a legal framework that clearly defines the authority and mandate of the NAC was critical. Where this was absent in other countries, the Secretariat's ability to manage and co-ordinate the response was severely hampered; and
3. The capacity to plan, manage and co-ordinate the AIDS response at decentralised levels remained key. This was a weak point in many countries, where people with the necessary skills were often absent or over-stretched.

Prior to 2010, SANAC only managed to have the elements of the first point in place – in the form of senior level commitment and good political relationships. It did not, however, have a legal framework, nor was the structure able to produce the coherent effort needed to work with and improve capacity at decentralised levels.

There was an urgent need for this to change if the SANAC Secretariat and its members were to have any hope of fulfilling their mandate. The SANAC Secretariat needed to be fully staffed to have the capacity and capability of fulfilling the following leadership and coordination functions[6]:

1. Co-ordinate the multi-sectoral response to HIV and AIDS, ensuring good inter-sectoral collaboration for achievement of NSP goals;
2. Facilitate the co-ordination of, and capacity building for, NSP implementation at decentralised levels (provinces, districts, municipalities and wards) in conjunction with Provincial Councils on AIDS;
3. Prepare annual implementation plans that reflect planning from ward level upwards, with activities linked to NSP objectives and indicators;
4. Facilitate and co-ordinate all communications, campaign and advocacy work related to HIV and AIDS, ensuring that activities are aligned with NSP objectives and targets;
5. Co-ordinate the activities of Technical Task Teams (TTT), ensuring appropriate membership and dissemination of TTT outputs;
6. Maintain a database of NSP costs and resourcing (government and donor), and mobilise resources to meet funding gaps;
7. Lead the preparation of progress reports and annual reviews of NSP implementation, including compiling and synthesising progress reports from each sector;
8. Ensure sectoral and donor co-ordination; and
9. Ensure regular reporting to SANAC governance structures.

After 2009, SANAC demonstrated, to a large extent, great effort in mandating and coordinating HIV/ AIDS in a collective and comprehensive way. It was evident that collective effort was required when the President of the Republic, Jacob Zuma, launched the biggest HIV Counselling and Testing (HCT) campaign South Africa had seen. Through cooperative effort between government and civil society – with the support of development partners – targets were reached, and the SANAC End Term Review 2012 estimated that 20 million South Africans were tested within a period of 18 months.

In 2012, SANAC established the SANAC Civil Society Forum (CSF) – an advisory body to eighteen diverse sectors in response to HIV, TB and STIs in South Africa – that seemed to be accepted as a best practice model globally.[7] Government and civil society engaged vigorously on issues that hindered the reduction of HIV, TB and STIs, and worked to preserve the lives of people living with HIV and TB. The formal setting of the structure was intended to enhance the voice of communities within SANAC, thus ensuring representation and that contributions to the HIV response made by community groups were well supported and recognised. What the AIDS epidemic highlighted was the need to strengthen civil society and the art of doing this. Legitimacy, accountability, transparency, credibility and representation were all cross-cutting themes to address in strengthening the sector. It was essential that legitimacy became a fundamental concern to ensure that CSOs acted effectively with integrity for the public good. As civil society becomes more visible in the public sphere and its input and services increase, its credibility can no longer be taken for granted. Civil society adopted these basic roles: health and welfare service delivery, advocacy, and the watchdog role. What this meant was that, at the most fundamental level, CSOs could provide the necessary institutional base for service delivery when questions about the effectiveness of the State arose.

Whilst the civil society sectors made a sterling contribution to the work of SANAC, much emphasis was placed on addressing the weakness in good governance as a priority for the CSF. Good governance includes considerations of leadership, accountability, transparency, monitoring and evaluation. It is fair to state that the governance and accountability issues were deliberated intensely within the SANAC governance structures across all levels of government and with the outgoing group of civil society representatives. This was approved in 2012 at a high level meeting with then SANAC chairperson and former president Kgalema Motlanthe, and later in 2015 at the SANAC Lekgotla, chaired by SANAC current chairperson and Deputy President Cyril Ramaphosa. Although there have been positive outcomes around increased awareness of accountability, responsiveness and transparency, there was, however, still much that needed to be done in order for the CSF to be a fully effective advisory body. There were constraints that hindered development of a healthy civil society. There were wider governance issues that related to the relationship between the broader community and the state, and the trust between the SANAC Secretariat and civil society.

By early 2010, it was widely accepted that SANAC had experienced a number of operational challenges and constraints while implementing the NSP on HIV, STIs and TB 2007-2011. The NSP aimed to inform national, provincial, district and community-level stakeholders on strategic directions to be taken into consideration when developing implementation plans. The absence of a functioning monitoring and evaluation system resulted in SANAC being unable to maintain a comprehensive oversight of all NSP objectives.

The CSF had the mandate to strengthen civil society sectors, share resources and information, and represented the collective voice of the CSOs to influence policy, programmes and decision making processes. By strengthening the partnerships between government, CSOs and the private sector for an integrated and expanded national response to HIV, STIs and TB in South Africa, the CSF ensures that the needs of those affected by HIV and TB are addressed.

At the time of writing, the forum was fully functional and playing a vital role in the response to HIV, AIDS and TB. The CSF wants to be part of prevention programmes and planning processes in relevant HIV and AIDS initiatives, and have an impact on policies. CSF works mainly with community groups at grassroots level and is therefore aware of the needs of target groups in the HIV and AIDS response. Civil society provides a space for the public voice, for the practice of citizenship and for the building of social unity.[8] Eighteen civil society sector constituencies exist, which include the youth sector, women's sector, LGBTI (lesbian, gay, bisexual, transgender/transsexual and intersexed) sector, men's sector, sex workers, research sector and PLHIV. Each sector has a role to play in the response to HIV and AIDS, TB and STIs, and each has a plan aimed at dealing with these conditions in line with the NSP on HIV, STIs and TB 2012-2016.

The establishment of the CSF made allowance for 'streamlining' the sectors and for greater accountability amongst them. This approach was fit for purpose and clearly demonstrated the need for a paradigm shift in SANAC to allow an independent CSF, supported by adequate resources.

The CSF also includes the Provincial AIDS Council's (PCA) Co-Chair, similar to the national structure of shared responsibility. The PCA Co-chairs, representing civil society, have seats on the SANAC CSF to represent the Provincial[9] Civil Society Forum and champion provincial implementation priorities within the national structures. Central to this is a structured form of governance regime that underpins the response. This needs to comprise multiple actors with different and often competing interests, to develop approaches accountable to people living with and affected by HIV and AIDS, and those with other health and social problems.

The SANAC Secretariat is also mandated to provide financial and logistical support to the CSF. The Chief Executive Officer (CEO) of SANAC was to ensure that the secretariat was aligned with the priorities identified in the NSP, and that structures were supported appropriately. This has not been achieved, particularly with regard to the monitoring and support of the civil society strategy. In fact, a strengths and weaknesses analysis highlighted a number of important areas that need further work at SANAC.

Although the governance framework reflected a relationship between the national and provincial structures, coordination in this regard was not optimal. There were weak and compromised relationships between the SANAC Secretariat, CSF, Department of Health, and many other stakeholders.

The implementation of the Governance and Accountability Framework, approved in 2012, required a better co-ordination and collaboration across all three spheres of government and sectors, including civil society, labour and the private sector.[10] Some of the Provincial AIDS Councils (PCAs) did not receive dedicated funding from their respective provincial governments and this affected their ability to co-ordinate their district and local councils. There was a lack of proper co-ordination across the various government departments in all three spheres of government, and this needed to be addressed.

There were also challenges with the co-ordination of civil society sectors, partly due to inadequate resources for this function within civil society. Civil society structures require more support to ensure that co-ordination is strengthened.[11]

Although the new Governance and Accountability Framework seeks to address weaknesses within SANAC and to improve efficiency, some challenges still remain, including the clarification of roles and responsibilities across the various structures.

These challenges, and lack of support, led to the council's downfall, which saw the CSF addressing a public 'motion of no confidence' to the SANAC CEO in 2013. As the letter was addressed to the Deputy President Motlanthe in his capacity as the chairperson of the Council, he referred the matter to the SANAC Trust. The lack of attention to the myriad issues raised by the CSOs, and remedies to resolve these issues, had demonstrated a dysfunctional SANAC that lacked effectiveness, as the SANAC Trust had – in many areas – failed to hold the Secretariat to account. SANAC should be able to address issues experienced by its members and provide a meaningful and clear process of remedial action. Accountability, as a tool of governance, determines who is to be held responsible, looks at which actors appear not to be answerable and why, and what gaps exist in measuring accountability. Problems with accountability and participation are central to the agenda of international organisations, governments, and donors within the HIV and AIDS response, but in practice these concepts are often understood too narrowly and applied unequally. All these bodies demand structures to ensure accountability and the participation of those working in the field of HIV and AIDS, and those affected by the disease, but they may fail to reciprocate such levels of accountability and participation.

Without critical reflection, accountability gaps remained and SANAC continued to be challenged by questions around its meaningful involvement and support for each stakeholder. Challenges persisted on the question of co-ordination, and monitoring of the implementation of the NSP. Both the SANAC Secretariat and the government sector through the Department of Public Service and Administration (DPSA) developed their respective monitoring frameworks, but there were still challenges with the flow of information for reporting purposes. There was no clear co-ordination of programmes and integration within government, and this resulted in poor reporting. There also needed to be clarity on the specific monitoring roles of the DPSA and Department of Planning, Monitoring and evaluation (DPME) in relation to government programmes, as well as the roles of the national and provincial secretariats of SANAC.

The poor reporting on the part of Government was reflected in that of the CSOs. Many CSOs received funding from development partners, and thus their accountability was to those funders that supported their work. The failure to co-ordinate and collect data from CSOs means weak evidence of civil society's contributions to the HIV response, and weaknesses in how it is articulated in relevant reports. It was clear that the data collected often came from service provision CSOs, and those civil society groups that provided social and structural support were, however, often ignored. Since their work remained undocumented, it was challenging to measure the impact thereof. Despite capacity issues, investment in community groups remains critical for the success of the NSP, and the success to the global targets of 90-90-90[12] set by the Joint United Nations Programme on HIV and AIDS (UNAIDS) strategy.

The NSP is used by SANAC as a framework for the co-ordination and monitoring of the implementation of HIV, TB and STIs programmes by sectors, with operational plans at the level of provinces, districts and municipalities. It is a five-year costed strategy that should be used by all stakeholders involved. It is imperative that the SANAC Plenary meetings and its various committees are fit for the purpose of incorporating good governance, accountability and effective use of resources into all its activities. All this can be achieved only if there are standard operational procedures, in this context referred to as procedural guidelines, which capture both the composition and the roles and responsibilities of the national structures of SANAC and its members. The challenge that confronted SANAC in 2015, however, was that it operated without procedural guidelines as there was a conflict between the legally updated and approved 2008 Procedural Guidelines, and the more recent adoption of the Governance and Accountability framework. It remains critical that SANAC Plenary reviews the Procedural Guidelines and align them to the Governance framework. Indicators of integrity at organisational level could be: the appropriate mobilisation of people and resources for common and agreed-upon goals; institutional stewardship which fosters appropriate individual and institutional behaviours; and congruence, as measured by appropriate and agreed-upon rules which govern institutional culture, and the acting out and respect of these rules by individuals and the particular organisation.

There needs to be internal consistency in an institution's functioning, and external consistency in its relationships with the world around it, based on agreed values which benefit all, managed by a system which is fair and reflexive. Achieving this requires a society that is underpinned by notions of integrity and social justice. A key component of integrity is ethical leadership, which is a function of individual integrity, institutions of integrity and the integrity of institutions.

In order to support the 2012-2016 NSP, the Deputy President appointed an ad hoc Governance Task Team of wise and experienced advisors to make recommendations in the area of governance and co-ordination. The general finding (the need to improve and align the SANAC structures to the requirements of the new NSP) was well documented in the MTR, and thus the Accountability framework was developed in 2012. The primary issue, though, is that while representation is attended to and becomes uniform, a problem still remains with co-ordination[13] that is not aligned at national and provincial level, or even at the local level. The SANAC Trust, therefore, failed to facilitate this role according to what was expected to be achieved as prescribed in the NSP.

The NSPs of 2000-2005 and 2007-2011 on HIV and AIDS gave rise to the establishment of AIDS councils within municipalities. All provinces set up PACs with the intention of linking with government departments, non-governmental organisations (NGOs) as well as with district and local AIDS Councils. The PACs help mobilise resources and ensure that government and donor funding gets to the places where it is most needed. All provinces established District AIDS Councils (DACs) and Local AIDS Councils (LACs) with the aim of leading, planning, co-ordinating and monitoring HIV and AIDS response in the districts and municipalities. Leadership and governance of the PCAs, DACs and LACs is with the elected government and civil society (and other constituencies) representatives.

There is no clear link between the SANAC Secretariat and the PCA Secretariat. In theory, the PCA Secretariat works from the Office of the Premier in each Province, however, some provinces still house the PCA Secretariats within the Department of Health. There is a need to clarify and redefine the standard or modes of operating by SANAC in order to provide provinces with guidelines and assist them with the monitoring process.

Conclusion

Provincially, there needs to be greater representation and ownership of PCA co-ordination. Ideally this should be extended to DCA co-ordination. Representation in SANAC governance structures at national and provincial levels come from both government and civil society. It should also be emphasised that implementation of the NSP occurs at the local level, which means that should this level be compromised, SANAC stands to achieve less than intended and as planned.

Ultimately, the SANAC Plenary has to be the driving force behind providing leadership and overall oversight of the implementation of the NSP. This Plenary is the highest body that advises government on all HIV, TB and STI related policies and policy issues. The decisions of SANAC are taken at the Plenary. This is where consensus on overall policy is developed, and guidance is provided for the high level strategy to address the country's response to tackling HIV, TB and STIs. It approves and makes recommendations to the Inter-Ministerial Committee on overall policy and national strategic interventions necessary to tackle HIV, TB and STIs.

Many challenges remain regarding co-ordination and governance in the CSF structure.[14] The CSF's problems regarding lack of support and finances will need to be urgently resolved, thus it remains critical that civil society institutionalises. Institutionalisation can be achieved by taking initiative to strengthen the governance and co-ordination which will ultimately further the impact CSF has on the HIV response in South Africa. There is a need to improve collaboration and co-ordination between the government departments and CSOs in the provinces, while there is a great need to bolster the integration of civil society in the response. It is noted that most LACs are not functioning fully and that Premiers should budget adequately, and that there should be contributions from various departments and other avenues from which to generate resources.

There is a need for accountability of both government and civil society for implementation at the local level. There is a greater need to hold the domestic and international funders accountable for the support of interventions identified and agreed upon by the community groups, and not to dictate the agenda of programme.

There is a serious need for sectors to be aligned, financed and to be held accountable in order to meaningfully document civil society's contribution, and to facilitate impact evaluation. There is a need to mend the links between the secretariats and civil society, building trust and good working relationships, and in a similar manner to facilitate relationships between CSFs.

The approach will require a well thought-out process that will lead SANAC to determine the real structure that is fit for purpose. The effort will require collective commitment and should have an outcome that is documented and tracked for follow-up. The SANAC should ensure meaningful empowerment and involve representatives of the diverse CSOs in the design, delivery and monitoring of relevant interventions to ensure that community's realities, risks and needs are adequately reflected, and that practical solutions are collectively developed.

SANAC should therefore apply an equal and supportive approach to elected leaders and sectors at all levels, clearly articulating roles and rights, while respecting the diversity and contributions they bring. Incorporation of local level resources (for example, existing community structures and positive networks) to leverage local knowledge in order to design and deliver better targeted, more accessible social and health interventions with high coverage quotients. The goodwill of SANAC members exists, however, accountability and good governance remains critical for the execution of the NSP. Shared responsibility needs to be strengthened and recognised for the success of SANAC and ultimately to benefit the end user.

Notes and References

1 The Human Science Research Council, 2014. South African national HIV prevalence, incidence and behaviour survey, 2012. Cape Town: HSRC Press.

2 United Nations, 2015. Millennium Development Goals Report: New York: United Nations.

3 Simelele, N.P. and Venter, W.D.F., 2014. A brief history of South Africa's response to AIDS. *SAMJ: South African Medical Journal*, 104(3), pp.249-251.

4 Heywood, M. 2009. South Africa's treatment action campaign: combining law and social mobilization to realize the right to health. *Journal of Human Rights Practice*, 1(1), pp.14-36.

5 Dickinson, C., Mundy, J and Whitelaw Jones, J., 2007. A Synthesis of Institutional Arrangements of National AIDS Commissions in Seven African Countries. London: HLSP Institute.

6 'The South African National AIDS Council, 2008. Procedural Guidelines 2008. Available at http://www.justice.gov.za/vg/hiv/docs/2008_SANAC%20procedural%20guidelines%2027%20May%202008.pdf [Accessed 6 July 2016].

7 A sector is defined as a 'group of organisations that democratically represents a defined constituency and is appropriately representative around a common them aligned to the over-arching subject of strategy for HIV, TB and STIs'. Avialable at http://sanac.org.za/category/civil-society-sectors/> [Accessed 06 July 2016].

8 The National Development Agency and The Community Agency for Social Enquiry, Planact and Africa Skills Development, 2008. Review of the State of the Civil Society Organisations in South Africa. Available at http://www.nda.org.za/home/43/files/Research%20Reports/Review-of-the-State-of-CSOs-in-SA-NDA-Audit-of-CSOs.pdf [Accessed 29 July 2016].

9 SANAC's Civil Society Forum 2013 resolutions.

10 SANAC's 2015 Lekgotla resolutions.

11 SANAC Civil Society Forum's 2015 Discussion Document (2015).

12 United Nations, 2014. Joint AIDS programmes 90/90/90 Strategy 2014. Available at www.unaids.org/sites/default/files/media_asset/90-90-90_en_0.pd> [Accessed 6 July 2016].

13 Access Chapter 2, 2015. Capacity for Transformation Report. Available at www.ac2.org.za. [Accessed 4 August 2016].

14 Ibid.

Chapter 22

The Impact of 'Widow Sex Cleansing' in HIV Prevention

A Reflection

Pholokgolo Ramothwala

Introduction

South Africa is a multicultural country with over eleven recognised ethnic groups, each with its own cultural practices. Within ethnic groups, cultural practices may vary. For example, the Bapedi includes the Balobedu, Bapedi ba-ga Sekhukhune and others, each expressing cultural practices and customs in different ways – even though they fall in the same group and the underlying principles are the same.

Many of these cultural and traditional practices have been in existence for many years and will remain for generations to come. The official definition of tradition is the transmission of customs or beliefs from generation to generation. A custom can be described as a traditional and widely accepted way of behaving or doing something that is specific to a particular society or community.

In many instances there is no clear distinction between the culture and tradition. At times they are used to refer to the same thing. In this chapter both words will be used to argue a point that certain cultural practices in the twenty-first century continue to impact negatively on the prevention of the human immunodeficiency virus (HIV) and wellness of people who have HIV.

It is almost impossible not to find traditional practices in any community in South Africa. Around the world, different ethnic groups follow some kind of tradition. They vary only to the degree that the traditions are still being practised, or how they are influenced by modernisation and advancements in the rule of law. In some communities tradition has evolved and new traditional practices have emerged.

This often happens in response to certain developments, either by the courts or the community. South Africa has been a shining example of this type of development. Post-apartheid many old cultural practices were adjusted or changed to align with social development goals and constitutional obligations.

The emergence of HIV in South Africa also brought new challenges to the way certain cultural and traditional practices were being performed. From the beginning, HIV was associated with many issues (right or wrong) that have delayed the integration of cultural practices by the way the epidemic was dealt with.

Great strides have been made in the use of the law to protect the vulnerable. As a result of applicable laws, many people have potentially been protected from exposure to HIV through the protection of their rights. The challenge arises in the practical application of legal successes in the context of HIV and cultural practices, and not much has been achieved so far. This is because the issue is very complex and needs to be addressed at different levels.

It is important to look at the importance of customary law in relation to customs and traditional practices, and how the previous and current gains have brought opportunities, but why some of those opportunities are difficult to be realised. In *Human rights and African Customary Law under South Africa Constitution*, T.W. Bennett[1] argues that there are three types of customary law: the official code, ethnographic texts, and living law 'which is still by and large waiting to be discovered'. This is experienced every day in people's lives. This chapter uses these differentiations to argue why the 'living law' is the most powerful one and condemns many people with HIV to lives they do not want.

In the Supreme Court appeal case of *Moropane v Southon*[2] appeal Judge Bosielo on when does a customary marriage entered into after the commencement of the Recognition of Customary Marriages Act 120 of 1998 (the Act) become valid highlighted the issue of customery law that '[I]t is now generally accepted that there are three forms of indigenous law: (a) that is practised in the community; (b) that found in statues, case law or text books on indigenous law (official); and (c) academic law that is used for teaching purposes.' Further during the *Nonkululeko Letta Bhe and others versus President of the Republic of South Africa and Minister for Justice and Constitutional Development* judgement,[3]

Justice Langa, argued that all of these laws differ, and that this difference makes it difficult to identify the true indigenous law. Thus the evolving nature of indigenous law only compounds the difficulty of identifying the living indigenous law.

The questions on the definition of customary or indigenous law make it difficult to tell where to draw its boundaries. Who really actually has the authority to draw the limits of this law? A question that could be asked is whether the constitution has the power to set the limits, and the answer is: yes, it does. It could be argued that the same determination can be made with the boundaries of culture. In the Bhe case, the judiciary had to intervene to make sure that tradition did not infringe on the rights of other citizens. It was found that people's rights were infringed and that customary law was applied incorrectly.[4]

Sustaining Culture in the Context of HIV: Are We Getting it Right?

In most rural areas tribal authorities are in charge and customary law seems to be applied more frequently. In turn, the dominance of this law in rural settings makes it difficult for people to challenge it in a formal court of law. An individual has to consider the consequences of such a challenge before he or she acts or practises differently. The courts will not be able to prevent the difficulties that complainants face when they challenge tradition or certain cultural practices. The level of literacy about how legal systems work also prevents many people from challenging some of the traditional practices.

**Tsakane Ngobeni,[5] a 33-year-old woman from Agincourt in Mpumalanga, shared her own personal experience in the way a 'cultural practice' affected her. Her husband died from acquired immune deficiency syndrome (AIDS), and neither her family nor her in-laws knew what caused his death. As a couple, they had decided not to tell their family about their HIV status. They were afraid their family would 'not understand'. After his death, Tsakane chose not to disclose her HIV status, explaining that her family cursed people who had AIDS. She said if she told them that she had HIV, her in-laws would chase her out and she needed a place to stay.

In her culture, twelve months after her husband's death, a male relative from her husband's family had to take over the responsibility of looking after her. In her case, there was talk of them getting married. The man had already been chosen for her by 'the elders' with her participating in the decision-making process. She did not want the man, as she had no intention of marrying him. She explained why, 'It will be difficult for me to marry him because I don't love him. Besides, how do I tell him I have HIV? What if I infect him?'

She then found a way to delay the marriage by requesting an extension of another year before she married him. She knew that she would have to marry him when that extension ended unless her circumstances changed. Her in-laws and her family believed the new man would provide for her as she was unemployed. She saw it differently. 'At the moment I am looking for a job. If I am working I can afford to pay for my own accommodation and buy food,' she said. She planned to run away from home if she got a job, and to 'start a new life'. If she did not get that job, it might just push her to accept the marriage she did not want.

Tsakane had an option to get an interdict against her in-laws who, she said, were pushing her to marry the man. She was also aware, however, that going the legal route would not be in her best interests. She would be discriminated against by her family and, more importantly, she would lose her only source of income. She preferred to find a way within her own culture's limits to negotiate her way out of the situation. It was unlikely that she would get out of the arrangement without having to defy her in-laws and the tradition they believed in. In this case, she saw the practised customary law and tradition being more powerful than the legal system, even though it infringed on her rights, and this kind of practice continues in the twenty-first century.

Besides having the courts as the defenders of the vulnerable, South Africa's National Strategic Plan on HIV (NSP) identified the role that culture plays in new HIV infections and the violation of human rights in its section on 'Cultural Attitudes and Practices: The missing link'.[6]

The NSP raised a number of concerns on cultural practices. It recognised that the relationship between culture and HIV was under-researched. There was, however, some evidence that cultural attitudes and practices expose South Africans to HIV infections. The two main issues that arose were:

1. Gender inequalities inherent in most patriarchal cultures where women are accorded a lower status than men, impact significantly on the choices that women can make in their lives, especially with regard to when, with whom and how sexual intercourse takes place. Such decisions are frequently constrained by coercion and violence in the women's relationship with men.
2. There are several sex-related cultural beliefs and behavioural practices, such as rites of passage to adulthood, especially among male youth, rites of marriage, premarital sex, virginity testing, fertility and virility testing, early or arranged marriages, fertility obligations, polygamy, prohibition of past-partum sex and also during breastfeeding, and rites related to death, such as levirate and sororate (a widower or sometimes a husband of a barren woman marries his wife's sister), which are also believed to spread HIV infection.

Even though the NSP identified several cultural practices as barriers against the fight on HIV and AIDS, cleansing of a widow or widower through sexual intercourse after the partner's death is not identified as a contributing factor to the spread of HIV and AIDS. This is despite many testimonies attesting to this practice.

The link of this practice to HIV is completely unresearched in South Africa, and it continues formally and informally. In the mid-2000s, an organisation called Rural AIDS and Development Action Research Programme (RADAR), which was part of Wits University's School of Public Health, investigated the issue of sexual cleansing.[7] Its then director, Dr Mosa Moshabela, raised his concern on the practice of this particular type of cleansing in the Bushbuckridge area. He argued for the modification of the practice in recognition of the existence of HIV and AIDS. He was not the only one who was concerned about the practice. A senior nurse, working at Tintswalo hospital in the same area worked closely with support groups of people living with HIV. She was also concerned that most people performing the cleansing were at risk of HIV infection because some of her patients who participated in the practice already had HIV. She believed that this form of cleansing fuelled the spread of HIV and AIDS in the area. To make it worse, those who practised the cleansing saw nothing wrong with it.

The 2005 South African National HIV prevalence, HIV Incidence, Behaviour and Communication Survey found that there was a high HIV prevalence amongst widows. Though it was not proven, in her report, Dr Olive Shisana, then Chief Executive Officer (CEO) of the Human Sciences Research Council (HSRC), commented that the researchers were surprised by this unexplained high prevalence. Yet no research has, to date, been done on sex cleansing as one of the possible contributors for this.

The Relevance of (Sex) Cleansing in South Africa's Failure to Reduce new HIV Infections

Most South African ethnic groups have their own name for cleansing. It is usually performed after a death in a family, but some people practise this when something bad happened to them or their family. In this chapter we look at the practice in the Tsonga speaking communities where cleansing is called 'Ku Basisa', while in Zulu communities it is called 'inhlambululo'. Whichever language is used, they refer to the same thing: cleansing.

It is important to acknowledge that, whether people agree or not, cleansing happens in many forms, which may mean being prayed for at church, or visiting a traditional healer, and in some instances performing some sort of ceremony. The end result of the activity is to allow a person to move on without worrying about getting 'bad luck', and if it makes people feel better, then they should be allowed to practise it.

With cleansing, the belief is that being cleansed not only helps to get rid of bad fortune, but also helps people to move on with their lives. It is also a formal way of accepting a widow or widower back into society as they move on with life. The challenge here is presented by a specific form of cleansing which includes sexual intercourse. As far back as the mid-2000s, the Health Systems Trust (HST) issued a report titled *Dose of reality*[8] which included sex cleansing, raising the same concerns as the countries of Uganda, Tanzania and Kenya. The report identified a direct link between the spread of HIV and AIDS and sexual cleansing. Although in African culture cleansing is common and acceptable, the sexual form seems to add pressure to those who do not want to participate in the practice and who do not see any benefits for the grieving person.

The Women's Leadership Centre in Namibia also sounded the alarm when they issued a statement, raising their concerns about 'harmful cultural practices and beliefs' that affect women.[9] One of the main issues in their statement was on 'sexual cleansing rituals which are enforced in some communities' in Namibia'. Their statement confirmed the same practice, as seen in some communities in South Africa, of cleansing a widow after the death of her husband through sexual intercourse with a man chosen by the family. Though this chapter is focused more on the Tsonga and partly on Zulu-speaking communities, there is anecdotal evidence that the practice is widespread in many other communities across the continent.

Justice Langa said, on the question of primogeniture (in the Bhe judgment):

> 'What is more, [referring to abuse of customary law], abuses of indigenous law/tradition are at times construed as a true reflection of indigenous law, and these abuses tend to distort the law and undermine its value. The difficulty is one of identifying the living indigenous law and separating it from its distorted version.[10]

Even though cleansing is commonly accepted in many South African families, it should not be practised in a way that a person might feel harmed in the process. Cleansing of a person through sexual intercourse seems to be harmful to those who do not want to go through with it. The question that arises is: should the people who practise it be concerned about the risk that a person might be infected with HIV or another sexually transmitted infection (STI), or about whether it could lead to an unwanted pregnancy?

Namibia's Women's Leadership Centre also raised these concerns, that is, that women were falling pregnant and becoming infected with HIV during the cleansing.[11] In South Africa, activists in some of the affected communities raised alarm bells concerning this practice.[12]

The custom has its supporters, with some traditionalist believers looking forward to the opportunity of practising it. While there are those who look forward to it, there are many who are agonised by the thought of being sexually cleansed. Unfortunately the women who refuse to be cleansed are accused of bringing bad luck to the family. This type of burden has forced them to participate in the practice against their will. In some cases women have fallen pregnant while others have contracted HIV, and some fear that they might infect their sex partner, as in the case of Tsakane Ngobeni cited earlier.

This chapter focuses mostly on Bohlabela, parts of the Vhembe and the Mopane districts, which is where most of the interviews were conducted. Zulu- and Sotho-speaking people, based in parts of Gauteng, North West and KwaZulu-Natal, were interviewed in order to get a broader understanding of the practice. During the interviews it became clear that Sotho-speaking communities were not familiar with the practice.

How Sex Cleansing Works

Those who practise it believe that a person who has lost their partner must abstain from sex for a period of between six months and a year. This period of celibacy is regarded as part of the 'mourning period'. The end of the mourning period is marked by an official ceremony, which can sometimes be delayed by months depending on the readiness of the family.

As part of the cleansing process, the grieving person is expected to find a man or a woman to have sex with for seven consecutive days. This person can either be a relative, an old lover, or a stranger (referred to as the cleanser). During the seven days, the two are not supposed to skip a single day without having sex, but this requirement is variable. In some communities the grieving person is only expected to have sex once. After the cleansing day or days, 'elders' gather at the house to mark the end of the mourning with a celebration. There are rules that must be adhered to if the process is to be deemed to have been done properly.

Several people interviewed in the Bohlabela, Mopani and Vhembe districts shared their experiences and thoughts about 'sex cleansing' in the era of HIV. Some were concerned about its benefits and questioned its relevance in the twenty-first century.

Mrs Manzini is a 67-year-old pensioner experienced in performing cleansing ceremonies around Agincourt village where she lives. She explained the process and a list of rules for the 'sex cleansing'. First, the two participants had to have sex for the full seven days. They were not to skip a single day or else they would not have done it properly. No condom or any form of protection could be used 'because their fluids must mix' – she referred to this as an important part of the process. Finally, there was to be no relationship between the two after the process had been completed.

Despite her son dying from AIDS-related illness, she did not 'think' using condoms or people getting tested before being cleansed was important. According to her, if a person did not go through the process, he or she would have bad luck and possibly would get sick. She said that in some cases a person might become mentally retarded or their children might die. When it came to HIV, she did not believe that this traditional practice should be changed, and she was not the only one who thought this way. This belief was very strong in her community as many still practised sex cleansing. Groups that supported the practice and those who disagreed with the practice were in agreement on one thing, though: that 'something is likely to happen' if you did not cleanse. They only differed on what the cleansing should include.

Who are the Cleansers?

In a formal cleansing process, a suitable cleanser is chosen by the family elders. Informal cleansing processes have, however, been reported where the widow or widower was instructed by his or her family to go out and cleanse themselves before other cleansing processes were completed. In this case, the participant was allowed to choose his or her partner. This informal sex cleansing process was reported to be dominant in the Zulu-speaking communities.

There are those who want to find their own partner, but regardless of who chooses the partner, a suitable person cannot always be found with whom to do the cleansing. In such instances, a cleanser can be hired.

Sipho, from the Bohlabela district, is known to perform sex cleansing for a fee. At the age of twenty nine, he has provided his services for several women who needed to be cleansed. His fee is between five hundred and a thousand rand, sometimes more. He does not know his HIV status and believes it is not necessary for him to test because 'he does not have HIV'.

In one instance, he was 'hired' to do a cleansing for a woman in his area. Before the cleansing was completed there was a disagreement between Sipho and the woman, and the local tribal council had to intervene after his parents complained to them. The woman who was being cleansed did not want to complete the process. When the traditional authorities intervened, the woman was found guilty of wanting to break tradition and was fined a goat for her decision to stop the process. Sipho continues to be available to do cleansings on request. He thinks cleansing should continue as long as people support it.

Thembi Matokane was a community liaison officer for RADAR at Tintswalo hospital at the time of the study. Part of her job was to regularly liaise with people with HIV or AIDS in the surrounding areas about positive living with HIV. She participated in a study which looked at the role of the cleanser. She has interacted with these people and described them as businessmen who only wanted to make money from cleansing. There were both male and female cleansers, but she felt it was more likely to find male than female cleansers. She saw women as being more vulnerable in this process than men.

There was no obligation placed on the cleanser after performing the ceremony. If the grieving person became infected with HIV or any other STI, nothing could be done. The same belief was held by some community members in Majozi, Vhembe district. It was said that should a woman fall pregnant in the process, she could do nothing about it.

The case study of Sipho, and those that follow of Mercy, Priscilla, Hazel and Yvonne's aunt, shed light on the positive impact that HIV education and community response has made on the few who chose to break the long-standing tradition and to protect themselves.

Opinions on Sexual Cleansing

Mercy Mhlongo's story

Mercy lost her husband in the late 1990s to an undisclosed illness. At the time she did not know much about HIV. She later became an active member of her community, educating people about HIV through the Treatment Action Campaign (TAC). Though she was not sure when she got infected, she only found out that she was HIV positive after her husband died. Today she openly lives with HIV.

After her husband's death, it was never in question whether she would participate in the cleansing process. She knew that after the funeral she had to be cleansed and was fully aware of the meaning of the process, including the sexual aspect. As she put it, 'I did not mind to do it [sex cleansing] because it is important in my culture. If I had not done it, maybe I would be dead or sick by now'. She believes people were affected in different ways if they did not do the process, claiming to have heard of people who became sick after they had failed to do the cleansing properly.

She maintained that, at the time her husband died, she did not know her HIV status, which was why she did the cleansing. Had she known more about HIV at the time, she would not have gone through the process. After being through the TAC education programmes, she knew more about HIV, but also understood her rights. She had information that helped her to decide what she wanted to do with her life. Though she was educating people about HIV, her views about cleansing remained the same. In her opinion, there were many people in the Agincourt area alone who had done sexual cleansing and were proud of it.

Priscilla Ndlovu's story

Priscilla's husband died in 2006 and she was due to undergo cleansing mid-2007. She knew that he had died from AIDS and that she was HIV positive. She was also aware of her tradition's expectations of her and the consequences that might arise if she did not go through with the practice. Her HIV status meant, however, that by participating in the process she might infect the other person. Entertaining the idea not to do the cleansing did not mean that she did not believe in it, but only that she was caught between two different issues that were 'equally important' to her, struggling to find the right choice in her case.

As a mother of seven children, she was concerned that if she did not perform the cleansing, it would bring 'bad' fortune to her family and that her decision might possibly 'affect' her children's future. She did not want to take the risk of passively waiting without enquiry. She consulted with other people who advised her to 'cheat the process'. From other women who found themselves in a similar situation, she was advised that the solution was to negotiate the use of a condom with the man helping with the cleansing. They would then take their fluid and place it on the cloth they were given to wipe as proof that they had sex. In that way, no one would ever know what they had done and it would remain their secret. Priscilla's story shows just how important the power of the family's, or even society's, expectations are in forcing a person to act against their will.

**Yvonne's aunt story

Majozi is about 300 kilometres from Agincourt in the Vhembe district. This was where a lady, who identified herself as Yvonne's aunt, lived. She was a widow who knew that she needed to be 'cleansed' after the mourning period following her husband's death. She did not have a problem with this as she believed that by going through the cleansing, she would be protecting her children from 'bad things'.

She also believed people who performed sexual cleansing were not to use condoms if they were to do it properly. Her cleansing occurred in one day – as she put it 'it happened in just a few minutes' – as in her 'culture', she only needed to have sex once with the person.

When she did the process, she found a stranger to assist her, and she was not worried about HIV or falling pregnant. According to her, if she had slept with a relative and fell pregnant, that person would be expected to look after the child even though they might not have a relationship. If the person was a stranger to her and she fell pregnant during the cleansing, there was 'nothing' she could do. There was no obligation on the man to take responsibility for the child or her.

Testimonies of these stories and many uncaptured ones make a case that the practice of sex cleansing exists and is possibly prevalent in some communities. Nkoankoa held a position between Majozi and Agincourt in the way that the sex cleansing was practised. People in these districts believe in the same cleansing practices; that sex cleansing was necessary to prevent bad fortune; that the cleansing should be done for seven days; and, as in Agincourt, in the absence of someone willing to assist, it was commonly acceptable to hire a person like Sipho to do the cleansing.

Hazel Manzini's story

Hazel Manzini had a different view on sex cleansing. She agreed with Priscilla that the process of sexual cleansing could be 'cheated' by using a condom, but she also held the belief that 'if you don't want to do it you don't have to'. She lived near Priscilla, and lost her husband a few years previously, but because of her religious convictions she refused to go through the cleansing process. Instead, she followed the Christian beliefs which stated that 'people do not have to be cleansed either sexually or with anything else'. She related an incident where she was told that if she did not do the cleansing she would have bad luck and might become ill, but she stuck to her beliefs and 'nothing happened' to her. She believed that 'bad luck will only happen if you believe it will happen'.

Responding to the Issues Raised

There are many people and organisations that have raised the alarm on this practice. As far back as the early 2000s, the practice was seen as a potential problem. Dr Mosa Moshabela, a RADAR Director at the time, shared his concerns in an interview.[13] Part of his duties was the management of one of the biggest antiretroviral (ARV) clinics in Bohlabela district. He had organised a workshop on cleansing, raising his concerns about the risks that accompanied sex cleansing. He argued that the practice could, and should, be modified to prevent new HIV infections through this custom.

According to him, many women – including nurses in the hospital he worked in – had done this cleansing. Some of the nurses he had spoken to had lost their husbands and were compelled to undergo the cleansing process. He said they were still traumatised years after the event.

Matron Mnisi worked at Tintswalo hospital for many years. She was part of the HIV and AIDS unit in the hospital. Her Christian beliefs and interaction with patients who were infected with the virus provided a very interesting perspective on sex cleansing and vulnerability of women in and around Arconhoek. She did not believe that men and women should go through sex cleansing at all. In her opinion, this kind of cleansing should be abolished.

She also believed that because of the socio-economic status of most women in rural areas, cleansing affected women a great deal more than men. In her opinion, women were often made to agree to the cleansing by their in-laws, because they would not have anywhere to go if they refused. Many of them were unemployed and relied on their husbands for survival. Thus, if they refused to be cleansed 'they might be thrown out of their houses'. In most cases these women lived with their husbands in the same house as their in-laws. She added that 'poverty should not force people to be cleansed'. Circumstances in families often make it difficult for the woman to offer a legal challenge once her husband dies.

In some situations the woman may be so illiterate that she is unaware of her rights, making it easy for the in-laws to take advantage of her. As a professional nurse, Matron Mnisi was worried about the potential HIV and STIs risk that the sexual cleansing practice brought to a community that already had almost a 20 per cent HIV infection rate.

She added that rural communities should be a priority, not only because of the key negative role that illiteracy plays, but also because any information takes a long time to reach them. In her religion, people were not allowed to be cleansed. She said that after death anyone was allowed to mourn the loved one, but cleansing was just 'wrong'.

Thembi Matokane worked for Tintswalo hospital as project manager. She also ancetodally looked at the issue, saying that she was shocked that some of the people who complained about the cleansing had HIV. Most of them had not disclosed their HIV status to their families, and because of the rules that are applied during the cleansing of a person, the practice makes it difficult for those who have been quiet about their status. Though she did not have any evidence of this, she thought that some people might have completed the cleansing despite knowing their status.

Same Ethnic Group, a Different Practice

In Giyani, people used to perform the same practice as discussed above; however, currently the cleansing seems to be conducted in a different way. During the interviews, Mamaila Chabalala and Yuza Baloyi[14] explained that the practices that used to happen 'in the olden days ... now it doesn't happen'. Although they believe certain cultural practices were – and are – still important, they acknowledge that the world was changing and some cultural practices were fading away.

In the Giyani area, in the past it was expected that when someone died the grieving person had to be cleansed. Included in the cleansing would be sex with another person, as was the practice in the other villages. They had the same belief that a person who was not cleansed might get sick – a person was likely to get ill with chest infections and then 'they get AIDS' – or they might die, and to prevent that, he or she had to be cleansed.

For some unknown reason that has changed and 'young people are doing as they want'. Chabalala and Baloyi blamed young people for defying tradition and believed that the government was being complacent in driving culture underground. They believed the affording of rights through the constitution had affected the current way of life in a manner with which they did not agree.

It was a shock to them that someone was even trying to find out about sex cleansing. For them, it was forbidden to discuss certain cultural practices. In the end, their belief on sexual cleansing was changing because of the new influences of the law. Those who still practised it, did so quietly in their homes because they did not want others to know about it. This was in sharp contrast to the same beliefs that dominated communities across parts of KwaZulu-Natal, Limpopo and outside the borders of South Africa.

Conclusion

South Africa has achieved a great deal when it comes to using the law to protect the rights of the vulnerable. As the constitutional court judgement in the Bhe case puts it:

> It should however not be inferred ... that customary law can never change and that it cannot be amended or adjusted by legislation. In the first place, customary law is subject to the Constitution. Adjustments and development to bring its provisions in line with the Constitution or to accord with the spirit, purport and objects of the Bill of Rights are mandated. Secondly, the legislative authority of the Republic vests in parliament. Thirdly, the constitution envisages a role for national legislation in operation, implementation and changes to customary law.[15]

Constitutional Court's judgement of *Alexkor Ltd and Another v Richtersveld Community and Others* also warned of the limits of indigenous and customary law when it said:

> In applying indigenous law, it is important to bear in mind that, unlike the common law, indigenous law is not written. It is a system of law that was known to community, practised and passed on from generation to generation. It is a system of law that has its own values and norms. Throughout its history it has evolved and developed to meet the changing needs of the community. And it will continue to evolve within the context of its values and norms consistently with the constitution.[16]

Clearly more education is needed at community level where this practice is still a concern to people. As recently as November 2015, the women's sector of the South African National AIDS Council raised this practice as a violation of women's rights and potential contributor to the rising numbers of new HIV infections in certain communities in Limpopo.[17]

We are now in the twenty-first century. While recognition of culture is important, things have changed and the constitution is now the supreme law of the country. Recognition of human rights has become too important for certain cultural practices to remain as if the times had not changed. In order for everyone to enjoy the gains that South Africa has made in fighting HIV, it is necessary to review some of the cultural practices because of their impact on the AIDS epidemic in South Africa. That kind of change will not, however, be achieved by the constitution alone. A lot more collaboration between different stakeholders in communities and government is important. There is a need for leadership by traditional leaders. Marius Pieterse argues as follows in his paper 'Killing it softly: Customary law in the new constitutional order':

> The institution of traditional leadership is usually mentioned in the same breath as customary law. The two are indeed interdependent. Leaders of indigenous communities enjoy high status and significant support among their people. They are regarded as the custodians of African culture and customary law and perform a variety of important executive and judicial functions.[18]

In the case of Sipho, the cleanser, the woman who decided that she did not wish to continue with her cleansing was punished for her decision by the tribal authority. What does that say about the 'custodians of African culture'? Should the same respect and status still be given to them? It would be safe to argue that while some traditional leaders recognise the impact of HIV and AIDS in their communities, there is more work to be done. More dialogue and more formal discussions still need to take place between advocates of this practice and affected communities.

Creating a law that prohibits this practice from continuing might be one solution, but just as the Children's Act made it illegal for females under the age of 18 to be subjected to virginity testing,[19] having a piece of law will not resolve the problem. Communities must also play a role in educating those who advocate for this harmful practice. If that does not happen, the alternative will be that the practice will continue, while those who are affected keep quite, fearing victimisation and ostracism.

Notes and References

1 See Bennett, T. W., 1995. *Human Rights and African Customary Law under South Africa Constitution*, Cape Town: Juta and Company.
2 Moropane v Southon (755/12) [2014] ZASCA 76 (29 May 2014).
3 *Bhe and Others v The Magistrate, Khayelitsha and Others* Case CCT 49/03.
4 *Bhe and Others v The Magistrate, Khayelitsha and Others* Case CCT 49/03.
5 Date March 2007, Agincourt Mpumalanga **identity protected.
6 See the National Strategic Plan on HIV, AIDS and TB 2009-2016 produced by the SA National AIDS Council, p. 27.
7 Source: Interview with Dr Mosa Moshabela, then RADAR director, March 2008.
8 Please see http://www.hst.org.za/news/dose-reality.
9 Cultural practices, women's rights, HIV and Aids. A case study of the Caprivi Region in Namibia in OPENSPACE, Open Society Initiative for Southern Africa, 2 (5), October 2009.
10 *Bhe and Others v The Magistrate, Khayelitsha and Others* Case CCT 49/03.
11 Cultural practices, women's rights, HIV and Aids. A case study of the Caprivi Region in Namibia in OPENSPACE, Open Society Initiative for Southern Africa, 2 (5), October 2009.
12 Treatment Action Campaign Support Group, Agincourt, December 2007.
13 Interview with Dr Mosa Moshabela, Then RADAR director, March 2008.
14 Interview, Giyani local elders section F, April 2008.
15 *Bhe and Others v The Magistrate, Khayelitsha and Others* Case CCT 49/03.
16 Alexkor Ltd and Another v Richtersveld Community and Others (CCT19/03) [2003] ZACC 18; 2004 (5) SA 460 (CC); 2003 (12) BCLR 1301 (CC) (14 October 2003).
17 Report by Limpopo delegates at SANAC Women's sector summit, November 2015.
18 Pieterse M "Killing it softly: customary law in the new constitutional order" 2000 De Jure 35-53.
19 Children's act 38 of 2005, section 12.4.

Chapter 23

Transiting from Traditional Initiation to Medical Male Circumcision as a Prevention Strategy

Is Anyone Listening?

Nkululeko Nxesi

Introduction

South Africa is still faced with a human immunodeficiency virus (HIV) and acquired immune deficiency syndrome (AIDS) pandemic. While the country has taken positive strides towards fighting the spread of HIV and the impact of AIDS, new infections are the order of the day and people are still dying of AIDS-related diseases. In response to this the South African government, through the National Department of Health (DoH) and its partners, is intensifying its programmes to reduce new HIV infections. Although the South African government has made enormous strides in the provision of life-saving drugs following the 2000 AIDS conference held in Durban, everyone agrees that prevention is still key in achieving an AIDS-free society.

Since the 2000 AIDS conference that took place on our shores, the South African government, in partnership with the private and civic society sectors, has developed and scaled up a number of HIV prevention strategies and programmes. One of these is the Medical Male Circumcision (MMC) programme. The MMC programme has been projected as one of the key and impactful biomedical HIV prevention strategies to help South Africa reduce new HIV infections in the country.

Scientific evidence shows that men who have undergone MMC have a 60 per cent chance of not contracting HIV. Based on this, the South African government has rolled out its MMC programme throughout the country. Some non-governmental organisations (NGOs) have been contracted to provide MMC services throughout the country with the aim of assisting the government to meet its target. In response to the call for the implementation of MMC as set out in the National Strategic Plan (NSP),[1] the DoH developed the Strategic Plan for the Scale up of Medical Male Circumcision in South Africa, 2012-2016. This strategic plan provides a framework for the scale up of the current MMC programme in South Africa, setting the target at 4.3 million circumcisions by the end of 2016.

As of today, more than 1 million men have been circumcised through the MMC programme, mostly in the urban areas and KwaZulu-Natal (KZN). The MMC programme has been relatively well received in urban and other areas where traditional initiation is not practised. One of the contributing success factors of MMC is the fact that this service is offered free of charge at government public health care facilities and by those NGOs contracted by, or in partnership with, the South African government.

MMC is viewed as a safe medical practice as there are no recorded deaths of people who have undergone the procedure. As a result, MMC is said to have other benefits apart from that of reducing the chances of HIV infection. These other benefits include:

- the promotion of men's health; and
- a potential alternative to traditional initiation, which has a high incidence of botched circumcisions.

These advantages mean that it makes logical sense for MMC to be supported by those in South Africa who are not only concerned about continuing HIV infections, but also about the increasing traditional initiation-related mortality rate from botched traditional circumcisions and illegal initiations.

While the MMC programme has been praised for its safety and for providing protection from HIV, it is important to note that it has been experiencing challenges with acceptance in areas that observe and practise traditional initiation. This resistance is higher in the Eastern Cape, Limpopo and Mpumalanga provinces, as well as from Black African churches that practise traditional initiation.

It is important to briefly list these challenges.

Low Uptake of MMC

One of the biggest challenges of MMC is the low uptake of its services in areas where traditional initiation is observed. Provinces like the Eastern Cape have struggled to provide MMC reports because communities in this province largely practise traditional initiation.

Reasons for the low uptake of MMC services include the social stigma for those who have undergone MMC. There have been reports of young men who have undergone MMC and who have subsequently been re-circumcised at a traditional initiation. This was more prevalent in areas like the Alfred Nzo and OR Tambo district municipalities in the Eastern Cape. This occurs because in these communities the young men are not recognised as being enough of a man through MMC services. To escape daily peer pressure and insults, many of the young boys who have undergone MMC succumb to cultural pressure and submit to participating in traditional initiations. Many are aged between 11 and 15, and because of this they often attend illegal initiation schools where they are subjected to unprofessional traditional surgeons and traditional nurses. For them to qualify as 'real men' who have undergone the full traditional initiation process, they are re-circumcised. This results, in most cases, in penile complications and a few amputations. While MMC is a safe medical procedure, it has, however, contributed to the injuries and deaths of initiates and innocent boys who made use of the MMC services before attending traditional initiation schools where they were re-circumcised or badly treated.

The Eastern Cape Province's Application of Health Standards in Traditional Circumcision Act of 2001 states that only boys that are 18 years and above are eligible to attend traditional initiation schools. The province has, however, seen an increase in under-age initiates. This increase can, amongst other factors, be attributed to the fact that young boys who are unable to wait until they are age compliant undergo MMC and then flood traditional initiation schools. This increases the number of under-age initiates and illegal initiation schools. It also increases negative attitudes towards MMC from those involved in ensuring safe traditional initiation practice, which includes traditional initiation forums, traditional practitioners and traditional leaders.

At the time of writing, there were growing allegations that those NGOs involved in MMC services in the Eastern Cape were colluding with certain health officials, illegal traditional surgeons and traditional nurses to 'dump' young boys who had been medically circumcised into traditional initiation schools. The rumour was that: '...this NGO collect young boys and circumcised them and come traditional initiation season the very same NGO [mobilises] them and dump them in one or two traditional initiation schools in that area'.[2] When these boys arrive at the traditional initiation schools they are, however, ill-treated and re-circumcised as described above. This places a negative aspect on MMC, and is part of the reason for its continued low uptake in communities practising traditional initiation.

Linked to the above is the growing tendency of certain government male nurses, entrusted to register potential traditional initiates, who manipulate the boys and their families into agreeing to an actual circumcision. According to the 2001 Application of Health Standards in Traditional Circumcision Act, boys need to have a medical assessment and obtain a health clearance at a health facility before attending a traditional initiation school. It has been reported that, in some areas, boys were forced to use the health officials for a MMC, failing which they would not be given a medical clearance to attend traditional initiation school. If this is true, a few problems arise. The first of these is that any boy who arrived at a traditional initiation school already circumcised would not be recognised as a man – even if he spent the whole duration of the initiation period with the other initiates. In fact, it was precisely those initiates that were with him at the initiation school – his peers – who would be the first to publicly stigmatise him as half a man. The second problem arises from the provision of MMC policy that only medical doctors are allowed to perform MMC, but in this case in the Eastern Cape, male nurses are also performing the procedure. The third issue is that while the services of MMC are supposed to be free, some of these male nurses charged the families of prospective initiates for performing the procedure while making use of government time and resources illegally.

During the 2015 December initiation season, a certain male nurse who was deployed by the Department of Health as a designated medical officer (DMO) in a traditional initiation in Mount Frere, established his own traditional initiation school with initiates that he had circumcised using government resources at the hospital.[3] He charged all of them for the medical procedure and, on top of that, charged their parents for the initiation school in his capacity as the initiation school principal. This constitutes serious fraud which was interpreted by traditional practitioners and traditional leaders as direct competition between MMC and the traditional initiation practice. To protect themselves against this, traditional practitioners become uncooperative with the DoH and the monitoring teams, hiding initiates during monitoring and medical assessments. This had the disastrous consequences of increased injuries and deaths of initiates.

The law dictates that parents must consent to any operation to be performed on a minor. This principle applies to all other services that are provided to a minor, including school enrolments. It has been reported that in certain parts of South Africa (specifically the Eastern Cape and Gauteng), young boys are taken by their schools to hospitals and NGO MMC service centres to be circumcised. In 2013, 36 children in Mount Ayliff returned from school circumcised without their parent's knowledge and consent. It was alleged that these boys were taken from the school under the pretext that they were to be vaccinated through a DoH and Department of Basic Education partnership programme called the Integrated School Health Programme. This angered parents who feared that their children would be subjected to social stigma for the rest of their lives. The parents had no recourse for this wrong doing, which was widely publicised in the media. Given the publicity, one would have thought that this kind of practice would stop, but because the MMC service providers were chasing targets, they did not care about parental consent or the sensitivity around the matter and continued taking boys from schools. Using bakkies and other vehicles, criss-crossing the countryside between villages, boys were also collected to be circumcised without parental consent or the knowledge by traditional and community leaders.

In certain areas, some parents who knew about this reluctantly gave their consent to the MMC, seeing it as a means of saving their children from potentially botched traditional circumcisions and death. Those areas that have MMC services were, however, struggling with increasingly high volumes of underage and illegal initiation schools as young boys attempted to complete their rites of passage into manhood. This process became more dangerous and complicated once they arrived at the initiation schools as, at that point, their parents were not there to protect them. Anecdotal evidence points to the fact that boys that were targeted were mainly from single parent households (female headed families).

The taking of young boys without parental consent is a clear human rights violation. Those NGOs that provided services in this way undermined the rights of the indigenous communities and incorrectly used their financial muscle to achieve their own agenda, operating as if they were an undercover agency. In one village it was reported that an NGO stole boys from their parents at night. This conduct was no different from that of the illegal traditional practitioners who abducted young boys to attend illegal traditional initiation schools. The only difference was that they were taken to health care MMC services while the traditional practitioners took them to illegal initiation schools. From a human rights point of view, the MMC service providers in communities observing traditional initiation need to be held accountable for their actions.

South Africa is known for its strong human rights approach on issues of HIV and AIDS. The South African government is said to have the best and most liberal constitution in the world, one that respects and promotes human rights. Human rights are about allowing people to make informed decisions about their lives. For people to make informed decisions, the service provider must give them accurate information, including details of the advantages and disadvantages of the service to be rendered. In the case of MMC services in the areas practising traditional initiation, people were generally not given enough information to make correct and informed decisions. In their efforts to meet targets in the time frames allocated, the NGOs disrespect people by disparaging their judgement and undermining their basic right to choose between MMC and traditional initiation for their children.

The South African National Strategic Plan on HIV, STI and TB (NSP) has a human rights component to it. The NSP promotes a human rights approach to protect vulnerable populations. Even HIV counselling and testing (HCT), which represents a fundamental shift from voluntary counselling and testing (VCT), allows the patient to have the final say as to whether they want to take the HIV test or not. The difference between VCT and HCT is that with the former only the patient could ask for the testing, while the latter allows the health care provider to offer HIV counselling and testing. At the inception of the HCT programme, there was a huge misunderstanding from some quarters about what it meant. Some health officials thought that HCT meant mandatory HIV testing and, fearing a backlash from NGOs and human rights organisations in the wake of the policy shift from VCT to HCT, focused on informing the public about the importance of consent of people who wanted to be tested for HIV. Even life-saving treatment, such as antiretroviral (ARV) drugs, is not compulsory for those who need them. Rather it is all about people making their own decisions and taking the treatments voluntarily. The state, and its partners in the form of NGOs, working in the space of HIV and AIDS does, however, have a responsibility to give information about the importance of taking ARV treatment. This helps people to make good, correct and informed decisions based on an understanding of the benefits of the treatments, so that they can voluntarily enrol in the ARV treatment programme. Unfortunately, the MMC services in areas practising traditional initiation have been denuded of this sensible and respectful approach to working with people.

Dehumanisation of African Culture

One of the challenges facing MMC programmes in areas practising traditional initiation arises from the way it was publicised. From public platforms, MMC proponents attacked and dehumanised traditional initiation practices as barbaric, outdated and something that was killing young men. This approach – of advancing MMC by attacking traditional initiation practices – is unhelpful as it only serves to increase the tension and widens the gap between the two different approaches. In one village in the Eastern Cape, community members who were against MMC and the way an NGO attacked traditional initiation practices in schools, blocked vehicles of the NGO and sub-merged them in a ditch. This particular NGO was guilty of publicly ridiculing those who had participated in traditional initiation practices, further insulting them by doing this in front of women and girls.

In another incident, a male nurse[4] was assigned to a Community Development Foundation of South Africa (CODEFSA) rescue centre in Zalu, Palmerton in Lusikisiki. Addressing more than 200 initiates who had been rescued by initiation forums and their traditional nurses, he told them that they had brought complications upon themselves by choosing to use traditional surgeons instead of MMC services. His statements were not taken kindly and were seen as a direct insult and as undermining their identity and culture. This male nurse was banned from the rescue centre as initiates wanted nothing to do with him, vowing not to allow themselves to be medically checked by a person who was opposed to their African culture. CODEFSA and the initiation forum, understanding the negative consequences of the incident, requested a replacement from the hospital in the form of another male nurse who respected traditional initiation. When the hospital refused to do this, CODEFSA found a private medical doctor – who had undergone the traditional initiation – to provide medical care, and so secured the cooperation of all initiates. The point here is that the failure of one person to understand the beliefs and culture of others and demonstrate sensitivity around the issues, nearly had the same potentially disastrous consequences that would have followed if many initiates had refused medical attention. The lesson from this case is that health care professionals can provide medical care to traditional initiates without insulting them, but by respecting and embracing the same culture.

Another incident involved a boy from a village in Lusikisiki who was circumcised by a MMC NGO, and was left on a soccer field to find his own way home. Once at home, the grandmother did not know what to do as they shared a one-roomed mud hut. Members of the community, in the form of the traditional initiation forum, were called in to assist. This was one of many cases that, for the most part, go unnoticed and unreported. This was an example of unethical conduct on the part of the NGOs responsible for the MMC services in the community.

Government, shockingly, remains silent and seems in denial of the problem. In spite of widespread publicity and the circulation of horrific pictures of re-circumcised penises to those in authority, and with the MMC programme in the Eastern Cape having contributed towards the most horrible and worst cases of botched traditional circumcisions, the silence and unwillingness of health officials to address the issues are incomprehensible.

People report having been paid money for bringing boys to be medically circumcised. Some community care volunteers under the DoH in the Eastern Cape confessed that they are given around R500 to bring boys to public health facilities for medical circumcision by the NGO entrusted with the MMC programme. Some went so far as to complain that they were forced to focus on one issue – that is, promoting MMC services and touting boys to use MMC services – instead of doing other community work, such as conducting awareness campaigns and educating people to promote safe traditional initiation. In addition, they claimed that they had put their lives at risk, as they were confronted by men from the communities who accused them of working with foreign entities to destroy their African culture, specifically traditional initiation.

Looking at this from another angle, young boys (as young as 12 and 13 years old) have been kidnapped to attend illegal traditional initiation schools. There is a notorious route along which this was known to take place, with the exchange point of the trafficked children at a place called Phakade (an off ramp of the N1 from Kokstad to Mthatha). It is here that people would be paid money for bringing boys from Pondoland and KZN to be illegally delivered to initiation schools in Mount Frere, Mount Ayliff or Matatiele. Traditional leaders and communities involved in safe traditional initiation have fought against this nefarious practice. Ironically, the actions of certain NGOs providing MMC services in the Eastern Cape are exactly the same as those illegal traditional practitioners who are involved in the abduction and trafficking of young boys. The question is, does this make it right because it is not done by traditional initiation practitioners? I will leave that to you, the reader.

A Comment on Under-age and Illegal Initiates

Another serious negative consequence of MMC in areas practising traditional initiation is that some parents took their boys to traditional initiation at very young ages. They did this in order to avoid their children being taken by the MMC service providers. This did not, however, solve the problem. The 2015 summer traditional initiation season saw an upsurge of young boys in traditional initiation schools, with the youngest being only 11 years old. When asked why they had come to traditional initiation so young, they responded – without fear – that their parents had encouraged them to do this to avoid the stigma of being taken by the NGO conducting MMC in their area.

One has to acknowledge that MMC is a new and powerful HIV prevention strategy that emerged after the international AIDS conference held in Durban in 2000. The research shows that MMC reduces one's chances of contracting HIV by 60 per cent. Without a doubt, this prevention strategy, combined with other interventions, will assist in the eradication of new HIV infections in South Africa and, by extension, throughout the world. Given the challenges discussed, however, it is important for both policymakers and decision makers to ensure that MMC is implemented in a manner that is culturally sensitive and respectful of human rights. The fact that MMC is a powerful biomedical HIV prevention method does not give liberty to its implementers to undermine people's culture, violate human rights, and leave broken families and communities. Given the fact that the unethical behaviours of NGOs implementing MMC are not government policy, government needs to come forward to condemn and act against them. Currently these NGOs seem to be running erratically without observation of human rights.

The following are the suggested solutions for these challenges:

- Government should have meetings with traditional leaders to properly introduce MMC and explain its role in the fight against HIV and AIDS in this country;
- Research should be conducted on the social and medical impact of MMC in communities practising traditional initiation;
- The conduct of unethical behaviour by MMC service providers in communities practising traditional initiation needs to be investigated;
- Create an honest dialogue between government and traditional practitioners with the view of collaboration and integration of MMC within traditional initiation practice; and
- Ensure that MMC does not compete with traditional initiation practices.

In conclusion, MMC has the potential to contribute to the reduction of new HIV infections. However, while it has benefits it is important that its application takes into account all socio-cultural aspects. Failure to do so could mean that the programme will have adverse effects that would haunt our societies long after this country has achieved an AIDS-free society.

Based on the challenges listed above, time will tell if MMC is a relevant HIV prevention strategy in communities practising traditional initiation.

I would like to acknowledge that there is not much literature on this subject and a great deal of the information contained here is personal encounters from the years of working in the Eastern Cape promoting safe traditional initiation. Unless expressly stated, identities of people are withheld in order to protect them and their families or the young men who had encounters with them.

Notes and References

1 See National Strategic Plan on HIV, AIDS and TB 2012-2016 produced by the SA National AIDS Council in 2012.

2 This was a rumour making rounds in the Eastern Cape which couldn't be officially attributed to a single person or organisation.

3 Identity of the doctor withheld due to confidentiality and consent considerations.

4 Identity of the nurse withheld due to confidentiality and consent considerations.

Chapter 24

Fighting Stigma and Winning the Struggle against HIV

Sithembiso Radebe

Introduction

At the time of my diagnosis I was 26 years old,[1] freshly graduated from the University of Limpopo in South Africa. It had only been five months since I was admitted as an attorney and I was in the prime of my life.

I was pregnant for the first time, and even though I was not married I took comfort from the fact that I was old enough and would be in a position to financially care for my child. I was in a relationship for over a year before I fell pregnant. I did not want a baby at the time, and I should have known better and used protection. Most of us tend to stop using protection a few months into a relationship because we feel that trust has developed. The pregnancy was not planned and my relationship with the father of my child turned sour and ended after finding out about the pregnancy. How I wish I had made different choices.

Five months into my pregnancy I found myself at a clinic one morning for a check-up. I had been having monthly check-ups by a medical doctor, but it had never crossed my mind to get tested, because the human immunodeficiency virus (HIV) – according to me – was simply not on my plate.

There were several pregnant women queuing to get in, and the nurse assistant said that all those coming for the first time should come to test for HIV, if they wanted to. I was the first to stand up because I was so confident that the test would be negative. I tested positive, though, and for a moment I could not see; it suddenly became dark. In disbelief I left to seek a second opinion. My mother and sister drove the 35 km from home with me sitting quietly in the back. It was the longest trip I have ever taken.

My sister waited in the car while my mother and I went inside, but when it was my turn to see the doctor, I left my mother in the waiting room. The results were confirmed. With tears in my eyes, I sat down and told my mother right there in the doctor's waiting room. Even today I can still see my mother's face. She looked at me, her face turned red and tears filled her eyes, but she tried to hold them back and she said, 'At least now we know and we can protect the child. Don't cry, let's go home'.

What follows is story of, as the title of this book suggests, triumph. I have chosen to look at it as triumph because looking at it differently would be tantamount to submission, to defeat. I have chosen life, not submission.

Disclosing to my Family

The following day my mother entered my room and I could see that this was too heavy for her. Obviously she needed support and a shoulder to cry on. I gave her permission to disclose my status to my stepfather and on the same day I told my siblings. Fortunately for me, everyone in my family was supportive even though their concern was more for the unborn child, but that was enough for me. It remained a secret between my siblings, my parents and myself for many years. I was put on antiretrovirals (ARVs) and four months later I gave birth to a healthy baby girl.

Reality and trauma hitting me

After giving birth I felt that my family was not as supportive as they were during my pregnancy, and I guess everybody simply went back to living their lives. Three weeks after giving birth I went back to work, but I was no longer the same person. I was devastated, felt dirty and was suicidal. On numerous occasions I attempted to take my own life; life was useless and meaningless.

I began to fear for my family's acceptance in the society and for their wellbeing, especially for my child, who was still a toddler at the time. My personality and character changed, my dreams died and all that I had cared about did not matter anymore. I cursed God for not protecting me and blamed the man who I thought had infected me with the virus. The horror of my childhood began to flash back and I was convinced that I didn't have much time to live.

I could not give love or create a bond with my child because I did not want her to miss me when I died. I stopped dreaming and planning, convincing myself that I lived each day as it came as I did not know if tomorrow would come.

Alcohol and other drugs

The secret was weighing heavily on me, I was suffocating in my own skin and the death I had been waiting for was not coming. Night after night I sat up, unable to sleep. I started drinking in an attempt to drown my sorrows and partied like my life depended on it. I smoked a pack of cigarettes a day and I drank each and every day. I did not care what people said about me or what they thought.

My family were the last people I wanted to hear from because I wanted them to hate me so that my death would not affect them.

Facing death

In the year 2013 I came face to face with death and guess who was there for me? My family. I was ill the whole of that year and it was only then that I realised how scared I was of dying and that I was actually not ready for death. I realised that I had a life that was dependent on me, that my family loved me and I had so much to live for. When I got better and started to walk again, it was like waking up from a nightmare.

From that day on my life changed. Even though I did not disclose my status to the extended family and to the public, I was a different person: happy and healthy, the person that I am today.

The HIV Struggle as I See It

Post-apartheid South Africa was marked by a number of celebrations and other historical achievements, both socio-economical and political. No sooner had the people of South Africa won one of the biggest battles over racial lines – after defeating slavery and colonialism – than another enemy entered the fray; this one was a silent killer who entered through the back window when everyone was busy kicking the evil of apartheid through the main door. Very little was known about this killer which suddenly became a household name, a topic of media debates and a real concern to the first democratic regime. Today, the infamous HIV has become the definition of South Africa as a nation, being at the top of the world's list in terms of prevalence.

Looking at the statistics, one may understand that, so far, the fight against this vicious killer has not been easy. From so little public knowledge of the virus, through denialism to every form of stigmatisation, we still have a long way to go before we can confidently say that we have unleashed a fully-fledged war on HIV and acquired immune deficiency syndrome (AIDS).

Presently we are facing a new struggle after that of anti-apartheid, a struggle which will not be defeated by mere chanting. It is also not a war which requires guerrilla warfare. This war – on the virus that infects and affects everybody, and which needs the input of the entire citizenry of South Africa, irrespective of race, colour, creed, faith or political affiliation – requires action; it is a war which can only be won by the unity and cohesion of all sectors of society.

Part of the previous denialist theses was that HIV was only contracted by poor, rural and illiterate people. It turns out that this enemy knows no class, race, age or profession, and I am the living proof of that. I do not classify myself as being poor, and is also a fact that I am not illiterate, but I live with the virus. HIV and AIDS infections also do not stop at the front of state portals. According to survey results of the year 2000 study conducted by the Centre for the Study of Aids, University of Pretoria, approximately 100 000 (10 per cent) of all government servants were infected, and deaths from the disease were estimated to rise to 250 000 by 2012.[2] Besides this, a number of professionals in various fields were equally affected, making it a national crisis and a global concern. This means that as much as we may talk about development, and talk about economic upliftment, the fight against HIV should remain a priority as our life as a nation depends on it.

Quoting the Freedom Charter and the SA Constitution, former President Nelson Mandela emphasised that South Africa belongs to all those who live in it, black and white. This means that an assault on one should be viewed as an assault on all. Do we, for example, manage other cases of infected people who are not South African citizens? Do statistics show accurate data when it comes to the real number of infections?

If we cannot manage to count everyone who lives in the country, we will be unable to accurately issue statistics which are precise and, as a result, we will lose the fight against HIV. For instance, imagine that we were of the view that we faced 10 enemy soldiers as a country, when in actual fact we were fighting 50. The government would retaliate with enough soldiers and weapons to fight against an army of 10, and the end result would surely be defeat.

How much support do the grassroots activists give to the many campaigns undertaken by the state and stakeholders? Do we use such programmes as mere campaigns to score points, or are they inclusive and results-oriented tools, able and bound to make changes?

It is, therefore, the responsibility of each and every inhabitant of this land to become involved, no matter how small the change may be. This goes to show that HIV and AIDS should be a concern for everybody, because the virus is spreading like bush fire. As Africans say: 'You cannot fold your arms when your neighbour's house is on fire; for soon it will reach your own house too'.

The truth remains that HIV may not infect everyone at this present moment, but it surely does affect the majority of our populace. There are many policies, projections and predictions related to the socio-economic growth within the country over the years to come. Fair enough, but are the analysts taking HIV and AIDS into consideration and the amount of damage this is causing to our human capital? If we do take the latter into consideration, we will have no doubt that our priority, right now in South Africa, should be the fight and subsequent victory over HIV. Without being an analyst and even less a scientist, I can confidently guarantee that some of the people who are making predictions without viewing the HIV war as a top priority, may find themselves agreeing with my statement a little too late.

Fact: HIV affects our economy, our education system, our socio-economic life – in short it affects all spheres of our lives in South Africa. I sat and thought, will I live to see the age of fifty? In me alone the country may lose another skilled professional and a mother, which might leave another orphan: what a sad reality.

Effects of HIV on Society

The effects of HIV and AIDS on families in South Africa is devastating. The majority of people infected by the virus are young adults, like myself. I was 26 years old when I first tested positive. Many children are forced to grow up without their parents because of HIV and AIDS.

- HIV and AIDS affect all spheres of our lives including family life, employment, income, and education. When parents die, the surviving children are forced to care for their younger siblings; children, in search of a better future and for survival, enter into relationships with older people; and this results in a vicious circle of infection.
- Children are raised by relatives who do not care for them and suffer a gross amount of abuse. A child raised in a loveless household may not be able to love themselves, or give love to others, because they never experienced love and protection during their childhood.

Reflections on stigma

First let me acknowledge the two different types of stigma in our society today.

Internal stigma: This is the type of stigma which is created within the mind of the person living with the HIV virus and is based on what he or she perceives as people's thoughts and thinking around his or her condition. For instance, I thought I was a disappointment to my family and to my profession. I felt unworthy of being loved by anyone, that I was not as beautiful as I used to be, and that no man would ever want to marry me. I thought I was going to die in a short space of time to the extent that I saw my coffin each time I closed my eyes. Eventually I died inside. The respectful, caring, intelligent and goal-oriented young woman was no more, and as a result an uncaring, unmotivated and drunkard human being was born.

This is the biggest and most dangerous form of stigma, as only the infected individual can halt it. Positive thinking and forgiveness, as well as living positively with the virus, are the best cures for this type of stigma.

External stigma: These are perceptions that people have about HIV and AIDS and are mostly ideas and thoughts, usually erroneously formed by mere speculation or ignorance on HIV and AIDS and about people living with the virus. This type of stigma is inflated by a sheer lack of knowledge on the subject. Some of it simply arises from the human failings of selfishness and wickedness.

Although we have educated society against the stigma of HIV and AIDS, more often than not HIV positive people still suffer inequalities and discrimination.

The impact of HIV and AIDS on the economy

Considering its impact on the economy, HIV and AIDS have become one of the critical priorities for the budget of the South African government as well as for the business community.

According to Daimler Chrysler South Africa, the 2002 expenses related to HIV and AIDS were equivalent to four per cent of all its salaries in the country. A study conducted in 2000 by South Africa's second largest company, Sasol, indicated that 15 per cent of its local workforce was HIV positive, of which 11 per cent had AIDS. According to the Chief Executive Officer (CEO) of South Africa's largest company, SAB Miller, the cost of HIV and AIDS included costs associated with increased absenteeism, reduced productivity, decreased turnover, and increased healthcare costs.

Before I took ill in 2013 I had managed my own law firm practice, I had employees and I was a tax payer, contributing to the country's economy, no matter how small my contribution was. When I became ill my employees lost their jobs. This proves that even if you're not infected you are somehow affected.

What Drives the HIV Pandemic in our Communities?

The socio-cultural factors

Culture is still a hindering factor in the battle against HIV and AIDS in the sense that we still do not find it easy to talk openly about sex, and avoid any frank dialogue or debate around HIV and AIDS. Superficial debates in local media, based solely on speculation – and sometimes on more rhetorical, than practical, principles – are not shedding enough light on the topic.

Let us go through some of the daily life factors which are still hampering this battle.

Polygamy and promiscuity

The ideal of 'one partner' has long been promoted, but fails to be a reality. Most people see nothing wrong with having multiple sexual partners and, in fact, in some of our cultures it is a sign of virility and sometimes wealth. The legal system, while trying to undo the injustices of the past, perpetuated polygamy with the introduction of the Customary Marriages Act 120 of 1998 which legalised and permitted multiple partners. This is a practice not seen only amongst the black African communities. Muslim law also allows a man to marry up to four wives, however, it is an undeniable fact that across all racial boundaries black Africans are the most infected and affected by the virus.

I will not overlook the intergenerational relationships, too, where older men date younger girls who could be their daughters or granddaughters, and vice versa. This practice is perpetuated by poverty and lack of employment, especially in rural areas.

Legislation on family

The family is the smallest unit of any society. This means that if family is given a push in the right direction, then slowly we will start creating a successful society. Most of us are used to a family structure with an absent father, the result being a family without a head. We are slowly becoming animals, which is why we see murderers, rapists and robbers. I define an animal as a species that when it is born it sees only the mother, but not the father. For instance, a dog never sees the father when it is born because the father is busy scrubbing through the rubbish bins and a lion does not see the father when it is born because the father is busy hunting.

We feel the need to have a CEO for enterprises and directors for public offices, but as a nation we do not yearn for a head of the family as much. It is my subjective opinion that a household with a responsible and present father ensures the safety and the security of the entire family. There are rules and regulations and therefore there will be none or less incidences of child delinquency, which usually result in abuse of substances leading to promiscuity and then possible HIV infection.

Strict laws governing the family would be of the essence in order to preserve this unit, which is a building block of our nation. Our legislation does not include enough respect and protection for families. Laws for the purpose of breaking up families are way too easily accessible and the process is not costly. The Regional Courts have jurisdiction over divorce matters and individuals can even approach the courts without legal representation.

A spouse who commits adultery is not punishable by law and there is no legal punishment against third parties who are involved in sexual relationships with married partners. The Constitutional Court, in the case of DE v RH 182 and 14 was of the opinion that love and respect are foundations of a solid marriage and not legal rules. I appreciate the developments in our legal system, especially the laws related to inequality and discrimination.

Let us respect the law but most importantly let us not forget the good part of our culture as black Africans - The culture that needed a man to provide for and protect his family, the one in which a woman was caring for her family, the one where the young respected the elders and the one where each family had a leader. The Southern African Development Community (SADC) countries have forgotten their roots and culture – no wonder we are leading the world in terms of HIV and AIDS infections.

One may argue, however, that adultery laws are outdated, sexist and an infringement of human rights as the courts should not be regulating adult consensual behavior that occurs in private. The nation must stop misusing the legal system.

Alcohol and drug abuse

It is probable that after the scourge of HIV and AIDS, the next problem we will face is that of drug and alcohol abuse, especially among the youth.

I have observed that every Sunday most liquor stores are closed. It is ironic because as from Monday morning they are wide open till late, until the next Sunday. The amount of alcohol and drugs available to our youth is simply huge, and this plays a big role in their careless sexual behaviour.

The drug problem in our townships and cities is another factor contributing to the spread of HIV. Communities and law enforcement agencies have to increase the fight against drug cartels and dealing.

Religious and spiritual beliefs

The church, especially the so-called prophets, play a significant role in the number of deaths due to HIV and AIDS. People are vulnerable and they trust their religious leaders. However, some of them take advantage and undermine the trust placed upon them by the members of the public. For a person to know that they are HIV positive, a medical test would have had to be conducted, not a spiritual test.

As much as I cannot deny that a miracle may happen and one might be HIV negative after a prayer, people should continue taking their medication until such a case is medically proven. After I was prayed for by a number of prophets, I was made to believe that I was healed from the virus. I stopped taking my ARV medication for over a year. When I stopped my CD4 count was 800, and it was sad for me to test a year later and found that I was still HIV positive and my CD4 count was 316.

HIV positive people who spread the virus

I fail to understand a person who knowingly spreads the virus in the name of anger and revenge. There are no circumstances or situations which are so compelling that a person knowingly infects another. That is just pure evil.

Yes, it is true that after finding out about one's status all sorts of unkind and inhuman emotions can arise. I acknowledge that such a person needs support and attention, but we must guard against self-pity and wickedness. What motivated me was a dream of seeing an HIV and AIDS-free generation for my daughter to grow up in.

What do you gain after infecting other people? Rather close the door, and sulk and cry all you want, instead of contributing to killing the nation. This is a harsh truth. That is why I love talking about the topic of healing and forgiveness.

Looking Into the Future

As early chapters of this book have shown, South Africa currently has the largest antiretroviral treatment programme globally, and these efforts have been largely financed from its own domestic resources; I applaud the government for this achievement. The country now invests more than US$1 billion annually to run its HIV and AIDS programmes.

The South African government has demonstrated the will and courage to tackle this deadly pandemic and though more still needs to be done, there is undeniable proof of the effort made by the leadership. As highlighted by the

Deputy President of the country at the opening of the seventh South African AIDS Conference in June 2015, 'We have the right policies in place and the political will to see them implemented. South Africa has the biggest HIV treatment programme in the world, with more than three million people on life-saving antiretroviral, moving on to five million.' He added, 'Thanks to the progress we have made, thanks to partnerships we have forged, thanks to the resources we have mobilised, we now know that the fight against AIDS and TB can be won.' As much as the Deputy President stated facts, it is also a fact that we are still faced with numerous challenges, such as new infections annually and very limited resources available to back up this ferocious fight.

Even with the progress made in the decrease of mother-to-child infection, we should know that we could do better if all pregnant women were to be tested on time. The biggest challenge in this regard is due to denial, with most women wasting time in getting tested and so are too late to be put on medication. A compulsory testing policy would save a lot of innocent children as their mothers could be put on medication to avoid mother-to-child infections. It also serves as 'one stone killing two birds', as the mother may also get treatment on time.

The development in the medication for HIV and AIDS is also noticed. The introduction of the one pill, as well as the Tribuss and Truvada pills, gives me hope that someday a cure will be discovered.

Conclusion

The people of South Africa, together with government, have come up with a number of initiatives to fight the scourge of HIV, and most of these programmes have proved to be successful and effective. However, there is still more to be done. There is no limit to the amount of programmes needed in this regard. A constant quest for new effective initiatives should be encouraged, especially among the demographic masses of infected and affected groups.

More efforts should be put into prevention measures, such as advertisements, awareness campaigns and the continuous education of masses on the topic. I took a drive around the streets of the big city of Johannesburg looking up at the bill boards, seeing not even a single one on awareness about HIV. All of them were about alcohol, food, clothes and upcoming social events. Is that all we are good for as a nation?

People infected with HIV should be put in key positions in organisations such as the South African National AIDS Council (SANAC) and other projects, as they bring first-hand experience to the way issues are handled. A lot can be achieved if the infected work hand-in-hand with medical doctors and politicians.

Let the infected not only be used for study and research purposes to further other people's careers. In all endeavours and programmes pertaining to HIV, how many HIV-infected people are involved? There is an adage that anything done for us without us, is against us. These are the people who live with the virus. They understand the dynamics which may go unnoticed by someone who is not infected. They therefore may be more proactive on certain issues and at a certain level as far as HIV is concerned. The struggle against apartheid was intensive because it was fought by people who were affected by it, so the same approach must be used going forward.

We cannot wait for the 1 December to raise awareness on the topic. It is an everyday issue and a national crisis. I tried to get radio interviews in an attempt to spread awareness and, surprisingly, I would be very lucky if I was given more than ten minutes on air while celebrity gossips and issues of no use to the nation were prioritised. The broadcasting and publishing agencies should come on board full force.

The Deputy President was correct in saying we need a massive HIV prevention campaign that begins with the promotion of condom use and the reduction of multiple concurrent partnerships, but that also addresses sexual coercion, transactional sex, intergenerational sex, risky sex linked to the use of alcohol and drugs, lack of access to work for young women, ignorance, powerlessness and poverty.

As HIV and AIDS concern everyone, those in leadership should lead by example. Normally any campaign should have a starting point in the public office. As we saw when the 'Know your status' campaign was introduced, some of the political and administrative leaders took a public test. Surprisingly, none of them has ever been found positive. This gives those who are positive the impression that the disease is only for the poor and uneducated. On numerous occasions a person has only revealed their HIV positive status on their death bed. At that point there is not much that the revelation can do, other than to increase fear in the masses.

If a famous or influential person can come out while still energised, he or she can make a difference. They could be an encouragement to those living with the virus and his or her words of warning might be taken seriously. We need to see more people in positions of power and influence coming out, and lending their hand in making a difference.

We cannot keep fighting an enemy that we are afraid to denounce. The topic of HIV and AIDS has been made a legal and social taboo. Even when discussed, there are limits to the things to be said and done, because more often than not we are afraid to offend people living with it.

We should be open and face the reality instead of ducking and diving in the name of human rights and rights to privacy. In fact, the more we shy away from openly speaking about HIV and AIDS, the more we increase the stigma around the topic, and so we create a society of guilt and victimisation.

Increasing the campaign of knowing one's status will give all stakeholders clear figures with which to gauge the strength of the enemy. We should encourage voluntary testing so as to have accurate statistics. It will be a waste of time if we solely rely on non-accurate statistics as this will lead us into underestimating the enemy we are facing.

As a country we are already doing well in terms of the roll out of the treatment. Medication alone is not effective, however, if a decent diet is not combined with the treatment. A follow-up dietetic treatment should follow the medical treatment in order to support a better treatment for the indigents and those unable to cater for themselves. It is common knowledge that medication without a balanced diet becomes toxic, more especially in the case of strong drugs, such as ARV.

In a possible case scenario, the erection of public gyms in certain places would also encourage more infected people who cannot afford gym memberships to get their routine exercises every day.

It would be a plus if the government could continue to invest in local research programmes trying to find a cure. We should, however, also be involved in exchange programmes with stakeholders from other countries which have won the battle already, with the view of exchanging information and experience regarding the matter.

As said earlier, this issue concerns everyone and only through unity and speaking with one voice can we win this vicious battle. I would like everyone to contribute, no matter how small the change may be in their own vicinity.

This paper is dedicated to all those who are living positively with the virus and to those who, just like myself, want to see a positive difference in this regard.

A *luta continua!* But at some point the struggle has to end. Together, let us put a halt to the spread of HIV and AIDS.

Notes and References

1 It should be noted that this personal account will at times sound subjective and judgemental. That is done purposely in order to fully encapsulate my feelings about the subject I am writing about. It may not sound scientific but I believe many scientific researches will identify with some of the experiences expressed herein. If not, this is a challenge to researchers to study this further.

2 Please see the 2004 Southern Africa Report by the SA Institute of Race Relations.

PART IV

CHANGING THE COURSE OF HISTORY

SELECTED SPEECHES THAT SHAPED THE GLOBAL AIDS AGENDA SINCE 2000

Closing address by Nelson Mandela at the 13th International Aids Conference, Durban

14 July 2000

To have been asked to deliver the closing address at this conference which in a very literal sense concerns itself with matters of life and death, weighs heavily upon me for the gravity of the responsibility placed on one.

No disrespect is intended towards the many other occasions where one has been privileged to speak, if I say that this is the one event where every word uttered, every gesture made, had to be measured against the effect it can and will have on the lives of millions of concrete, real human beings all over this continent and planet. This is not an academic conference. This is, as I understand it, a gathering of human beings concerned about turning around one of the greatest threats humankind has faced, and certainly the greatest after the end of the great wars of the previous century.

It is never my custom to use words lightly. If twenty-seven years in prison have done anything to us, it was to use the silence of solitude to make us understand how precious words are and how real speech is in its impact upon the way people live or die.

If by way of introduction I stress the importance of the way we speak, it is also because so much unnecessary attention around this conference had been directed towards a dispute that is unintentionally distracting from the real life and death issues we are confronted with as a country, a region, a continent and a world.

I do not know nearly enough about science and its methodologies or about the politics of science and scientific practice to even wish to start contributing to the debate that has been raging on the perimeters of this conference.

I am, however, old enough and have gone through sufficient conflicts and disputes in my life-time to know that in all disputes a point is arrived at where no party, no matter how right or wrong it might have been at the start of that dispute, will any longer be totally in the right or totally in the wrong. Such a point, I believe, has been reached in this debate.

The President of this country is a man of great intellect who takes scientific thinking very seriously and he leads a government that I know to be committed to those principles of science and reason.

The scientific community of this country, I also know, holds dearly to the principle of freedom of scientific enquiry, unencumbered by undue political interference in and direction of science.

Now, however, the ordinary people of the continent and the world - and particularly the poor who on our continent, will again carry a disproportionate burden of this scourge - would, if anybody cared to ask their opinions, wish that the dispute about the primacy of politics or science be put on the backburner and that we proceed to address the needs and concerns of those suffering and dying. And this can only be done in partnership.

I come from a long tradition of collective leadership, consultative decision-making and joint action towards the common good. We have overcome much that many thought insurmountable through an adherence to those practices. In the face of the grave threat posed by HIV/AIDS, we have to rise above our differences and combine our efforts to save our people. History will judge us harshly if we fail to do so now, and right now.

Let us not equivocate: a tragedy of unprecedented proportions is unfolding in Africa. AIDS today in Africa is claiming more lives than the sum total of all wars, famines and floods, and the ravages of such deadly diseases as malaria. It is devastating families and communities; overwhelming and depleting health care services; and robbing schools of both students and teachers.

Business has suffered, or will suffer, losses of personnel, productivity and profits; economic growth is being undermined and scarce development resources have to be diverted to deal with the consequences of the pandemic.

HIV/AIDS is having a devastating impact on families, communities, societies and economies. Decades have been chopped from life expectancy and young child mortality is expected to more than double in the most severely affected countries of Africa. AIDS is clearly a disaster, effectively wiping out the development gains of the past decades and sabotaging the future.

Earlier this week we were shocked to learn that within South Africa 1 in 2, that is half, of our young people will die of AIDS. The most frightening thing is that all of these infections which statistics tell us about, and the attendant human suffering, could have been, can be, prevented.

Something must be done as a matter of the greatest urgency. And with nearly two decades of dealing with the epidemic, we now do have some experience of what works.

The experience in a number of countries has taught that HIV infection can be prevented through investing in information and life skills development for young people. Promoting abstinence, safe sex and the use of condoms and ensuring the early treatment of sexually transmitted diseases are some of the steps needed and about which there can be no dispute. Ensuring that people especially the young, have access to voluntary and confidential HIV counselling and testing services and introducing measures to reduce mother-to-child transmission have been proven to be essential in the fight against AIDS. We have recognised the importance of addressing the stigmatisation and discrimination, and of providing safe and supportive environments for people affected by HIV/AIDS.

The experiences of Uganda, Senegal and Thailand have shown that serious investments in and mobilisation around these actions make a real difference. Stigma and discrimination can be stopped; new infections can be prevented; and the capacity of families and communities to care for people living with HIV and AIDS can be enhanced.

It is not, I must add, as if the South African government has not moved significantly on many of these areas. It was the first deputy president in my government that oversaw and drove the initiatives in this regard, and as President continues to place this issue on top of the national and continental agenda. He will with me be the first to concede that much more remains to be done. I do not doubt for one moment that he will proceed to tackle this task with the resolve and dedication he is known for.

The challenge is to move from rhetoric to action, and action at an unprecedented intensity and scale. There is a need for us to focus on what we know works.

- We need to break the silence, banish stigma and discrimination, and ensure total inclusiveness within the struggle against AIDS;
- We need bold initiatives to prevent new infections among young people, and large-scale actions to prevent mother-to-child transmission, and at the same time we need to continue the international effort of searching for appropriate vaccines;
- We need to aggressively treat opportunistic infections; and
- We need to work with families and communities to care for children and young people to protect them from violence and abuse, and to ensure that they grow up in a safe and supportive environment.

For this there is need for us to be focused, to be strategic, and to mobilise all of our resources and alliances, and to sustain the effort until this war is won.

We need, and there is increasing evidence of, African resolve to fight this war. Others will not save us if we do not primarily commit ourselves. Let us, however, not underestimate the resources required to conduct this battle. Partnership with the international community is vital. A constant theme in all our messages has been that in this inter-dependent and globalised world, we have indeed again become the keepers of our brother and sister. That cannot be more graphically the case than in the common fight against HIV/AIDS.

As one small contribution to the great combined effort that is required, I have instructed my Foundation to explore in consultation with others the best way in which we can be involved in the battle against this terrible scourge ravaging our continent and world.

I thank all of you most sincerely for your involvement in that struggle. Let us combine our efforts to ensure a future for our children. The challenge is no less.

I thank you.

Source: Nelson Mandela Foundation

Speech given at the Opening ceremony of the 13th International AIDS Conference in Durban, July, 2000

Nkosi Johnson

"Hi, my name is Nkosi Johnson. I live in Melville, Johannesburg, South Africa. I am 11 years old and I have full-blown AIDS. I was born HIV-positive.

When I was two years old, I was living in a care centre for HIV / AIDS-infected people. My mommy was obviously also infected and could not afford to keep me because she was very scared that the community she lived in would find out that we were both infected and chase us away.

I know she loved me very much and would visit me when she could. And then the care centre had to close down because they didn't have any funds. So my foster mother, Gail Johnson, who was a director of the care center and had taken me home for weekends, said at a board meeting she would take me home. She took me home with her and I have been living with her for eight years now. She has taught me all about being infected and how I must be careful with my blood. If I fall and cut myself and bleed, then I must make sure that I cover my own wound and go to an adult to help me clean it and put a plaster on it.

I know that my blood is only dangerous to other people if they also have an open wound and my blood goes into it. That is the only time that people need to be careful when touching me.

In 1997 mommy Gail went to the school, Melpark Primary, and she had to fill in a form for my admission and it said does your child suffer from anything so she said yes: AIDS.

My mommy Gail and I have always been open about me having AIDS. And then my mommy Gail was waiting to hear if I was admitted to school. Then she phoned the school, who said we will call you and then they had a meeting about me. Of the parents and the teachers at the meeting 50 per cent said yes and 50 per cent said no. And then on the day of my big brother's wedding, the media found out that there was a problem about me going to school.

No one seemed to know what to do with me because I am infected. The AIDS workshops were done at the school for parents and teachers to teach them not to be scared of a child with AIDS. I am very proud to say that there is now a policy for all HIV-infected children to be allowed to go into schools and not be discriminated against.

And in the same year, just before I started school, my mommy Daphne died. She went on holiday to Newcastle- she died in her sleep. And mommy Gail got a phone call and I answered and my aunty said please can I speak to Gail? Mommy Gail told me almost immediately my mommy had died and I burst into tears. My mommy Gail took me to my Mommy's funeral. I saw my mommy in the coffin and I saw her eyes were closed and then I saw them lowering it into the ground and then they covered her up. My granny was very sad that her daughter had died.

Then I saw my father for the first time and I never knew I had a father. He was very upset but I thought to myself, why did he leave my mother and me? And then the other people asked mommy Gail about my sister and who would look after her and then mommy Gail said ask the father.

Ever since the funeral, I have been missing my mommy lots and I wish she was with me, but I know she is in heaven. And she is on my shoulder watching over me and in my heart.

I hate having AIDS because I get very sick and I get very sad when I think of all the other children and babies that are sick with AIDS. I just wish that the government can start giving AZT to pregnant HIV mothers to help stop the virus being passed on to their babies.

Babies are dying very quickly and I know one little abandoned baby who came to stay with us and his name was Micky. He couldn't breathe, he couldn't eat and he was so sick and Mommy Gail had to phone welfare to have him admitted to a hospital and he died. But he was such a cute little baby and I think the government must start doing it because I don't want babies to die.

Because I was separated from my mother at an early age, because we were both HIV positive, my mommy Gail and I have always wanted to start a care centre for HIV / AIDS mothers and their children. I am very happy and proud to say that the first Nkosi's Haven was opened last year. And we look after 10 mommies and 15 children.

My mommy Gail and I want to open five Nkosi's Havens by

the end of next year because I want more infected mothers to stay together with their children- they mustn't be separated from their children so they can be together and live longer with the love that they need.

When I grow up, I want to lecture to more and more people about AIDS- and if mommy Gail will let me, around the whole country.

I want people to understand about AIDS- to be careful and respect AIDS- you can't get AIDS if you touch, hug, kiss, hold hands with someone who is infected.

Care for us and accept us- we are all human beings.

We are normal. We have hands. We have feet. We can walk, we can talk, we have needs just like everyone else- don't be afraid of us- we are all the same!"

Nkosi Johnson, July, 2000

Opening Assembly Special Session on Aids, Secretary-General Sees 'Turning Point – Aids Can No Longer Do Its Work in Dark'

GENERAL ASSEMBLY, 5 June 2001

Festus Mogae

FESTUS MOGAE, President of Botswana: The HIV/AIDS pandemic is severely limiting development prospects in affected countries through the loss of skilled human resources, decline in productivity and reallocation of budgetary and human resources from development activities towards actions to address the disease. The unchecked spread of the pandemic poses a serious threat to the goal of reducing global poverty by half by the year 2015. In today's global village, no country is safe from the ravages of the pandemic. "It is therefore in the interest of each and every one of us to ensure that we do everything in our power to eliminate the spread of HIV/AIDS in the quickest possible time and in the most effective way."

The international community must support strengthened HIV/AIDS prevention strategies and provide assistance to develop and extend social support systems to deal with the consequences of HIV/AIDS. There must be improved access to anti-retroviral drugs for the poor and for the most affected countries, while drugs must be made available at affordable prices on a sustained basis. Traditional, cultural and religious beliefs, as well as practices that inhibit the fight against the pandemic, must also be dealt with decisively. Most importantly, it must be ensured that the fight against HIV/AIDS is not waged at the expense of sustainable development and improved living standards for developing nations.

In Botswana, the National HIV/AIDS Strategic Plan embodies a multi-sectoral approach and a close working relationship among the public and private sectors as well as non-governmental organizations (NGOs). The implementation of the Plan is overseen by committed leadership across the broad spectrum of my country's society. "Our key prevention strategies include: house-to-house counselling, behaviour change, voluntary counselling and testing as well as prevention of mother-to-child transmission programmes."

A combination of hospitalization and community home-based approaches is the cornerstone of care for AIDS patients and support to orphans, vulnerable children and affected families in my country. Treatment strategies include pain management and symptomatic treatment as well as prevention and treatment of opportunistic infections. "We shall shortly introduce retroviral treatment in our public health facilities to complement all these activities.

Needless to say, substantial resources are necessary to mount an effective fight against the disease. Botswana fully supports the proposal to establish a Global Fund for HIV/AIDS. It is important, however, that such a Fund embraces the criteria to ensure that its resources are used to meet the needs of the countries most seriously affected by the pandemic, such as Botswana. "It would be unjust to exclude countries like my own on account of per capita income."

Message on World AIDS Day 2002

Kofi Annan

The worldwide HIV epidemic has created a terrible burden for millions of individuals, families and communities around the world. Relieving it requires improved healthcare, better access to treatments, more vigorous prevention efforts, more effective social outreach, and support for those most vulnerable – particularly orphans.

But there is another terrible burden imposed by AIDS, which each and every one of us has the capacity to relieve: the burden of HIV-related stigma.

Some people with AIDS are being denied basic rights such as food or shelter, and dismissed from jobs they are perfectly fit to perform. They may be shunned by their community, or most tragic of all, by their own family.

The fear of stigma leads to silence, and when it comes to fighting AIDS, silence is death. It suppresses public discussion about AIDS, and deters people from finding out whether they are infected. It can cause people -- whether a mother breastfeeding her child or a sexual partner reluctant to disclose their HIV status -- to risk transmitting HIV rather than attract suspicion that they might be infected.

But the walls of stigma and silence are weakening. There is evidence of progress on every continent. Leaders are speaking out at the highest level. The rights of people living with HIV/AIDS are being defended through the courts. Standards are being set in the workplace. Schools, the media and youth education programmes are helping to create a generation better equipped to live in the world of AIDS. And last year, at a Special Session of the General Assembly, all the Member States of the United Nations unanimously adopted a Declaration of Commitment on HIV/AIDS which sent a clear message around the world. They pledged to enact or enforce legislation outlawing discrimination against people living with HIV and members of vulnerable groups.

But whatever laws and regulations are adopted, the most powerful weapons against stigma and silence are the voices of the world's people speaking up about AIDS. By adopting the slogan "Live and Let Live," this year's World AIDS Campaign challenges us to ensure that all people, with or without HIV, can realize their human rights and live in dignity. On this World AIDS Day, let us resolve to replace stigma with support, fear with hope, silence with solidarity. Let us act on the understanding that this work begins with each and every one of us.

President Jacob Zuma on the Occasion of World Aids Day, Pretoria Showgrounds, 1 December 2009

Today we join millions of people across the globe to mark World AIDS Day.

We join multitudes who have determined that this epidemic cannot be overcome without a concerted and co-ordinated effort.

We join millions who understand that the epidemic is not merely a health challenge. It is a challenge with profound social, cultural and economic consequences. It is an epidemic that affects entire nations. Yet it touches on matters that are intensely personal and private.

Unlike many others, HIV and AIDS cannot be overcome simply by improving the quality of drinking water, or eradicating mosquitoes, or mass immunisation.

It can only be overcome by individuals taking responsibility for their own lives and the lives of those around them.

Fellow South Africans, as a country, we have done much to tackle HIV and AIDS. In every sector of society, there are individuals and groups who have worked tirelessly to educate, advocate, care, treat, prevent and to break the stigma that still surrounds the epidemic. Today, we wish to acknowledge their dedicated efforts.

As government we are ready to play our role of leadership, building on the foundation that has been laid over the past 15 years. Under the leadership of Presidents Nelson Mandela, Thabo Mbeki and Kgalema Motlanthe, the democratic government has put in place various strategies to comprehensively deal with HIV and AIDS, tuberculosis and sexually transmitted infections. Working with other sectors through the South African National AIDS Council, we have managed to harness unity in confronting this scourge. The amount of resources dedicated to prevention, treatment and care has increased with each successive year. But it is not enough. Much more needs to be done. We need extraordinary measures to reverse the trends we are seeing in the health profile of our people.

We know that the situation is serious. We have seen the statistics. We know that the average life expectancy of South Africans has been falling, and that South Africans are dying at a young age. We have seen the child-headed and granny-headed households, and have witnessed the pain and displacement of orphans and vulnerable children. These facts are undeniable. We should not be tempted to downplay the statistics and impact or to deny the reality that we face.

At the same time, the epidemic is not about statistics. It is about people, about families, and communities. It is about our loved ones. For many families, it is a burden that they have to bear alone, fearful of discrimination and stigma.

Dear Compatriots, now is not the time to lament. It is the time to act decisively, and to act together. Our message is simple. We have to stop the spread of HIV. We must reduce the rate of new infections. Prevention is our most powerful weapon against the epidemic. All South Africans should take steps to ensure that they do not become infected, that they do not infect others and that they know their status. Each individual must take responsibility for protection against HIV. To the youth, the future belongs to you. Be responsible and do not expose yourself to risks. Parents and heads of households, let us be open with our children and educate them about HIV and how to prevent it.

Ladies and gentlemen, we are still marking the 16 days of activism against violence on women and children. During this period, it is important that we also remember to uphold the rights of women and children, including their right to protection from infection with HIV. Many women are unable to negotiate for protection due to unequal power relations in relationships.

As we mark the International Day of Persons with Disabilities on Thursday, the 3rd of December, let us remember the impact of HIV on persons with disability. We have to tailor government programmes and messages to also speak to the needs of this sector.

Fellow South Africans, to take our response a step forward, we are launching a massive campaign to mobilise all South Africans to get tested for HIV. Every South African should know his or her HIV status. To prepare for a continuous voluntary testing campaign, we would like to announce a few new measures, to expand our response. All children under one year of age will get treatment if they test positive. Initiating treatment will therefore not be determined by the level of CD cells. This decision will contribute significantly towards the reduction of infant mortality over time.

All patients with both tuberculosis (TB) and HIV will get treatment with antiretrovirals if their CD4 count is 350 or less. At present treatment is available when the CD4 count is less than 200. TB and HIV/AIDS will now be treated under one roof. This policy change will address early reported deaths arising from undetected TB infection among those who are infected with HIV. We have taken this step, particularly on learning that approximately one per cent of our population has TB and that the co-infection between TB and HIV is 73 per cent.

All pregnant HIV positive women with a CD4 count of 350, or with symptoms regardless of CD4 count, will have access to treatment. At present HIV positive pregnant women are eligible for treatment if their CD4 count is less than 200. All other pregnant women not falling into this category, but who are HIV positive, will be put on treatment at fourteen weeks of pregnancy to protect the baby. In the past this was only started during the last term of pregnancy.

In order to meet the need for testing and treatment, we will work to ensure that all the health institutions in the country are ready to receive and assist patients and not just a few accredited ARV centres. Any citizen should be able to move into any health centre and ask for counselling, testing and even treatment if needed. The implementation of all these announcements is effective from April 2010. Institutions are hard at work to ensure that systems are in place by the 31st of March.

What does this all mean? It means that we will be treating significantly larger numbers of HIV positive patients. It means that people will live longer and more fulfilling lives. What does it NOT mean? It does not mean that we should be irresponsible in our sexual practices. It does not mean that people do not have to practise safer sex. It does not mean that people should not use condoms consistently and correctly during every sexual encounter. We can eliminate the scourge of HIV if all South Africans take responsibility for their actions.

I need to re-emphasise, at this point, that we must intensify our prevention efforts if we are to turn off the tap of new HIV and TB infections. Prevention is our most powerful and effective weapon. We have to overcome HIV the same way that it spreads – one individual at a time. We have to really show that all of us are responsible.

The HIV tests are voluntary and they are confidential. We know that it is not easy. It is a difficult decision to take. But it is a decision that must be taken by people from all walks of life, of all races, all social classes, all positions in society. HIV does not discriminate. I am making arrangements for my own test. I have taken HIV tests before, and I know my status. I will do another test soon, as part of this new campaign. I urge you to start planning for your own tests.

Ladies and gentlemen, we are also mindful of the social impact of the epidemic, and continue to provide psycho-social support and home-based care, through the Home Community-Based Care and child care programmes of government.

Let me use this opportunity to salute all our caregivers including those neighbours who assist and support families in distress. We also thank our international partners, who continue to provide material support to our campaign against AIDS.

On this day, our hearts go out to all South Africans who are in distress as a result of this epidemic. To families looking after sick relatives, we wish you strength. We understand what you are going through. To those who have lost their loved ones to the epidemic we share your pain, and extend our deepest condolences.

Fellow South Africans, at another moment in our history, in another context, the liberation movement observed that the time comes in the life of any nation when there remains only two choices: submit or fight. That time has now come in our struggle to overcome AIDS. Let us declare now, as we declared then, that we shall not submit. We have no choice but to deploy every effort, mobilise every resource, and utilise every skill that our nation possesses, to ensure that we prevail in this struggle for the health and prosperity of our nation.

History has demonstrated the strength of a nation united and determined. We are a capable, innovative and motivated people. Together we fought and defeated a system so corrupt and reviled that it was described as a crime against humanity. Together we can overcome this challenge.

Let today be the dawn of a new era. Let there be no more shame, no more blame, no more discrimination and no more stigma. Let the politicisation and endless debates about HIV and AIDS stop. Let this be the start of an era of openness, of taking personal responsibility, and of working together in unity to prevent HIV infections and to deal with its impact.

Working together, we can achieve these goals!

I thank you.

Issued by: The Presidency
1 December 2009

Address at AIDS 2012, Keynote Address International AIDS Conference, July 23, 2012

Elton John

Thank you, Luiz, and good afternoon to you all.

I'm extremely honoured to be here.

I'd like to begin with a story.

It's the story of a young man coming to terms with his sexuality.

A young man who got mixed up in drugs and drink.

He took chances with unprotected sex, and he was at very high risk of contracting HIV.

This young man hit absolute rock bottom.

His life was a mess.

He was self-destructive.

He was angry.

He was spiraling out of control.

He should have died, to be honest. And he almost did.

But then, something amazing happened.

People showed him compassion and love.

People showed him respect and understanding.

People offered him a hand and a chance to get better.

And he DID get better. He turned everything around.

He has a wonderful life, a loving partner, and a beautiful son.

He's been sober for 22 years.

Now, he's standing in front of you giving this speech.

Ladies and gentlemen, by all rights, I shouldn't be here.

I should be dead. Six feet under, in a wood box.

I should have contracted HIV in the 1980s and died in the 1990s.

Just like Freddie Mercury.

Just like Rock Hudson.

Just like so many friends and loved ones of yours and mine.

Every day, I wonder: how did I survive?

I don't know the answer, and I never will.

But I do know WHY I'm here.

I'm here to deliver to you, and to anyone who will listen, the message that saved my life...

...the message that can save millions of lives if we put it to practice:

No matter who you are, or who you love...

No matter where you live, or how you live...

No matter what you have or haven't done...

Everyone deserves compassion.

Everyone deserves dignity.

Everyone, everyone, everyone deserves love.

Why am I telling you this?

Because the AIDS disease is caused by a virus, but the AIDS epidemic is not.

The AIDS epidemic is fueled by stigma. By hate. By misinformation. By ignorance. By indifference.

There's much talk now about the end of AIDS. And rightly so.

We can end AIDS, thanks to you. You have made it possible.

Because of your research and your advocacy, we have lifesaving treatment and prevention.

But that's not good enough.

It isn't good enough to beat this disease once and for all.

You know it, and I know it.

We need more than medicine. We need more than money.

We need love.

If that word makes you uncomfortable, if it makes you a bit uneasy, let's pick another.

Compassion. Kindness. Understanding. Empathy.

Call it whatever you'd like, but the idea is the same:

We need more humanity — more love — if we're going to end AIDS.

I've just been to the unfolding of the AIDS Memorial Quilt, where I saw so much love for the dead.

What we need now is more love for the living.

Cynics might say, how can a sentiment possibly beat a virus?

That's an easy question to answer — especially for the people in this room who have dedicated their lives to ending AIDS.

It's been three decades of this epidemic, and we've seen how human beings react when those around them become HIV-positive.

There are some people who look at the sick and search for reasons to blame them.

She's got HIV? It must be her fault. It's because she's a drug user, or a prostitute.

He has AIDS? It's because he's gay. Because he's poor.

They must deserve it, these people.

They live immoral lives.

They deserve to be sick and to die, because they've brought it on themselves.

And then there are people who look at the sick and think of reasons to love them.

You're ill? I'll be ill one day, too.

You have personal struggles? So do I.

You're dying? There will come a time when I am also dying.

How can I help you? How can I love you?

After thirty-one years and thirty million people gone, we have seen both responses, you and I.

We've seen hate in Uganda. Stigma in the Ukraine. Indifference in America.

We've seen gay people targeted, discriminated against, and even killed.

We've seen people living with HIV ostracized by their families and stigmatized by their communities.

We've seen AIDS orphans abandoned in the streets, children raped and abused.

It makes me sick, all of this fear — all of this ignorance and hate.

But we've also seen love, haven't we?

We've seen monks working with drug addicts in Thailand.

Social workers helping HIV-positive prisoners.

Corporations putting lives ahead of profits.

We've seen Catholic nuns and priests helping sex workers in India…and I know that Jesus is smiling down on them despite what the Vatican may say!

We've seen George W. Bush and conservative American politicians pledge tens of billions to save the lives of Africans with HIV.

Think of all the love. Think of where we'd be without it.

Nowhere, that's where. We'd be nowhere at all.

Thanks to all of this compassion, thanks to all of this love, more than 8 million people are on treatment.

Thanks to people who have chosen to care, and to act, we can see an end to this epidemic on the horizon.

It's not a mirage. It's real. It's very, very real.

But it's going to take a lot more compassion to get us there.

A hell of a lot more.

How exactly can compassion get us to our destination, some may ask?

Let me tell you.

Do you want to end new infections among injection drug users?

Well, you're not going to do it by locking them up or leaving them to die of addiction or AIDS.

That only spreads the disease and the suffering.

We need to give these people support, clean needles, and treatment.

Instead of judging them, let's help them.

Instead of despising them, we need to love them.

Do you want to curb new infections among MSM in Africa?

You're not going to do it by stoning gay men and passing laws against homosexuality.

For Christ's sake, this is the 21st century, not the 12th century!

Show compassion to ALL of your people, like President Joyce Banda of Malawi does.

If you show compassion, no one will be forced into the shadows.

If you show compassion, no one will be afraid to seek treatment.

Do you want to stop the epidemic in South Africa?

Then show compassion by telling those living with HIV to be proud of knowing their status.

That's what the South African government is beginning to do — and it's working.

We need to put our arms around people who are HIV-positive. Celebrate the actions of individual change. Celebrate people who are willing to get tested.

That's the compassion that will help get everyone tested and on treatment.

Do you want to end the epidemic in America?

Then show compassion to those who can't afford treatment and are on waiting lists to receive it.

Show compassion for HIV-positive people in Washington, DC, most of whom are poor and black and forgotten, even though they live in the capital of the richest and most powerful nation on earth.

America has shown so much love for those living with HIV in the developing world. If this country wanted to end new infections at home it could do so in a heartbeat.

All it takes is a bit more funding — a bit more understanding.

All it takes is dialogue and the power of words to change actions.

All it takes is the compassion that my friends Elizabeth Glaser and Elizabeth Taylor and Larry Kramer and Ryan White taught us about decades ago.

Maybe you think I'm naive. Maybe you think I'm off my rocker.

Here I am, telling an audience of 7 000 global health experts that we can end AIDS with love.

I know we need more than that.

We need prevention programs to be funded.

We need treatment programs to be expanded.

We need critical research to continue.

We need a vaccine to be discovered.

Everyone at this conference is united by the dream of universal treatment, prevention, and a vaccine.

We dream about it every day, you and I.

And God bless everyone who is working to make that dream a reality.

But even if our dream came true — even if we had a vaccine — it wouldn't be enough.

A vaccine won't end stigma in Eastern Europe.

A vaccine won't end homophobia in Uganda.

A vaccine won't end rapes in South Africa.

A vaccine won't help poor people who can't afford it in Asia.

A vaccine won't change laws in America that criminalize those with HIV.

Science can stop the disease, but science alone can't end the plague.

Yes, we now have accurate and inexpensive at-home tests for HIV.

But we can't convince people to get tested if they feel that nobody cares about them.

Why would you bother if you're told by society that your life doesn't count?

Yes, we now have miraculous treatments that double as prevention.

But we can't get those living with HIV on treatment if they're afraid to disclose their status because of stigma or homophobia.

Yes, I hope and pray that we will discover a vaccine. We all do.

But we won't get that vaccine to those in need if governments shun their most marginalized citizens.

THAT is why compassion is critical.

THAT is why love is the cure.

Millions of people around the world feel ashamed because of who they are, because of their HIV-positive status, because of their sexuality, because of their poverty.

They are ashamed because they feel they've done something wrong by how they live, or the disease they have, or who they love.

They feel subhuman, worthless, like they don't matter at all.

Shame and stigma prevent them from getting help, from getting treatment, from protecting themselves in the first place.

I've felt that shame before.

It almost killed me.

It's killing people all around the world, right now.

We have to stop it.

We have to replace the shame with love.

We have to replace the stigma with compassion.

No one gets left behind.

That is how we will end this plague.

In 1995, I released a song called "Believe."

In one verse, I sing:

I believe in love, it's all we've got

Love has no boundaries, no borders to cross

Love is simple, hate breeds

Those who think difference is the child of disease

I truly believe that love is the most powerful force in the world.

I know that from experience.

During the darkest days of my recovery from addiction, I was shown extraordinary compassion by people I didn't even know.

People whose names I never even learned.

Nurses who worked at the clinic where I was receiving treatment.

Other patients who didn't know me as Elton the rock star, only as Elton the addict.

Everyone around me was kind, everyone was compassionate, everyone was forgiving.

Their love changed my life. It saved my life.

The gift of love from a community of people who believe in you and support you — it's the most remarkable gift you could ever receive.

It costs nothing at all, but it's the most precious thing in the world.

Everyone deserves it.

Not nearly enough people receive it.

But we can do something about that, you and I.

We MUST do something about that.

And when we do, I promise you:

We will wake up from this 31-year nightmare into a brand new day.

Thank you.

World Aids Day, 1 December 2015

Edwin Cameron

Twenty nine years ago, I tested positive for HIV. The death toll from Aids across the world was rising each day – and on that day the bells of imminent debilitation and death rang out loud as I sat stunned in my home in South Africa. But here I am, on World AIDS Day 2015, nearly three decades later, feeling very much alive, vigorous and healthy.

World AIDS Day offers an opportunity for people worldwide to unite in the fight against the effects of HIV, to show their support for people living with it and to commemorate those who have died. For me, perhaps most pertinently, the day reminds us that HIV is still all too present, for all too many people.

I have been receiving successful HIV treatment for more than 18 years. Antiretroviral (ARV) treatment saved my life. At the end of 1997, I was seriously ill when, with a feeling of total joy, I realised the treatment had lifted me off my deathbed.

But I was one of the lucky ones. I started on ARVs at a time when the treatment was available only for those who could afford it. I was using a third of my judge's salary to pay for medication. Today, treatment is affordable. The main challenges to its availability and accessibility are infrastructural and social – chiefly, stigma.

South Africa introduced free ARV medication more than 10 years ago. This came at a heavy cost – including a lengthy battle with former president Thabo Mbeki and his AIDS denial policies. Although today treatment is available, and although more than 3 million South Africans now access it, the number of new infections is still distressingly high. Almost 200,000 people a year in my country are still dying of AIDS today.

Stigma remains a central problem – fear of the disease, fear of people with the disease, rejection, ostracism and discrimination. Add to this our attitudes about masculinity in South Africa and many other parts of the world: men's belief that they are invincible, that they have a right to sex and should have access to women's bodies, that sex with protection is not real sex, that they are no longer "real men" if they become HIV-positive, that they'll be seen as weak if they seek medical attention. It is the behaviour of men, and groups of men, that drives the epidemic.

Not enough is done to ensure men have access to HIV services. Women usually access health facilities during their reproductive years for antenatal and child health services. Men have far fewer opportunities to access health services. Surprisingly, little is done even to engage the men whose partners participate in prevention of mother-to-child transmission programmes. It's a critical missed opportunity that needs to be addressed urgently.

What impelled me to speak openly about my HIV status, in 1999, was the murder of Gugu Dlamini. She was a young woman living in a poor part of Durban who was stoned to death in the street after she spoke openly on radio about the fact that she was HIV-positive. Her death drove me – a man who was living with protection that she never had – to try to combat stigma.

Today, stigma is undoubtedly declining. This is partly because people are talking about being on treatment. The massive drives in my country to get people tested have also helped; many more people know their HIV status, and many more know someone living with HIV. But the insidious effects of stigma and harmful ideas about manhood continue.

In September, UN member states ratified the sustainable development goals, a framework for global development policy over the next 15 years. The targets include ending the AIDS epidemic by 2030.

If we are to end the HIV pandemic, we need strategies that target all the actors. We have to understand how HIV spreads, and AIDS kills, in a broader field of gendered power and inequality, and unequal access to health services. This means that we must continue to implement strategies to empower women and advance their human rights. It also means that we must engage men and boys to increase their proactive support for gender equality, and we must do a better job of reaching men with critical HIV services.

In theory, if we could find every person with HIV – every last person today in our country – that's nearly 6 million people out of our populace of more than 50 million – and reach them and say, "start on treatment immediately", we could stop this epidemic in its tracks.

On World AIDS Day, an imperative focus must be to get men to come forward for testing and treatment. HIV can be beaten in the human body, and in our country, if we combat stigma and change our ideas about manhood, expand testing and treatment, and proffer practicable prevention strategies to everyone.

Remarks by President Barack Obama on World AIDS Day, 2 December 2013[1]

South Court Auditorium, Eisenhower Executive Office Building

Thank you, everybody. Everybody, please have a seat. Well, thank you, Grant, for your outstanding leadership of the Office of National AIDS Policy. And thanks to all of you for being here. This is a pretty distinguished crowd, I have to say, and it is wonderful to be here.

I should say, actually, welcome back, because many of you have joined us before as we've marked new milestones in our fight against HIV and AIDS. And I'm honored that you could join us in commemorating World AIDS Day, which was yesterday. And this is a time for remembering the friends and loved ones that we've lost, celebrating the extraordinary progress – thanks to some people in this room – that we've been able to make, and most importantly, recommitting ourselves to the mission that we share, which is achieving an AIDS-free generation.

I especially want to welcome ministers from our partner countries; members of my administration, including Secretary Sebelius, Secretary John Kerry; Congresswoman Barbara Lee; Mark Dybul from the Global Fund to Fight AIDS, Tuberculosis and Malaria. And we've also got here Francis Collins from the National Institutes of Health; Michel Sidibe from UNAIDS; Deborah von Zinkernagel, who's carrying on the great work of Eric Goosby as our Acting Global AIDS Coordinator; and our many friends from the philanthropic world, including Bill Gates. So thank you all for joining us here today.

Every year, this is a moment to reflect on how far we've come since the early days of the AIDS epidemic. And those of you who lived through it remember all too well the fear and the stigma, and how hard people with HIV had to fight to be seen, or heard, or to be treated with basic compassion. And you remember how little we knew about how to prevent AIDS, or how to treat it. What we did know was the devastation that it inflicted – striking down vibrant men and women in the prime of their lives and spreading from city to city and country to country seemingly overnight.

Today, that picture is transformed. Thanks to the courage and love of so many of you in this room and around the world, awareness has soared; research has surged. Prevention, treatment and care are now saving millions of lives not only in the world's richest countries but in some of the world's poorest countries as well. And for many, with testing and access to the right treatment, the disease that was once a death sentence now comes with a good chance at a healthy and productive life. And that's an extraordinary achievement.

As President, I've told you that in this fight, you'll have a partner in me. And I said that if the United States wanted to be the global leader in combating this disease, then we needed to act like it – by doing our part and by leading the world to do more together. And that's what we've done, in partnership with so many of you. We created the first comprehensive National HIV/AIDS Strategy, rooted in a simple vision that every person should get access to life-extending care, regardless of age or gender, race or ethnicity, sexual orientation, gender identity or socio-economic status.

We've continued to support the Ryan White CARE Act to help underserved communities, and we lifted the entry ban so that people with HIV are no longer barred from the United States – which led to the International AIDS Conference being held here last year for the very first time in over 20 years.

This summer, I issued an executive order creating the HIV Care Continuum Initiative to boost our federal efforts to prevent and treat HIV. Last month, I signed the HIV Organ Policy Equity Act, to finally allow research into organ donations between people with HIV – a step achieved with bipartisan support.

And thanks to the Affordable Care Act, millions of insured Americans will be able to get tested free of charge. Americans who were uninsured will now be able to have access to affordable health care coverage, and beginning in January, no American will be again denied health insurance because of their HIV status.

On World AIDS Day two years ago, I announced an additional $35 million for the AIDS Drug Assistance Program, which helps people pay for lifesaving medications. At one time, the need was so great that over 9,000 people were on the waitlist. We vowed to get those numbers down. And I'm proud to announce that, as of last week, we have cleared that waitlist. We are down to zero. And we're going to keep working to keep it down.

So we're making progress. But we're all here today because we know how much work remains to be done. Here in the United States, we need to keep focusing on investments to communities that are still being hit hardest, including gay and bisexual men, African Americans and Latinos. We need to keep up the fight in our cities – including Washington, D.C., which in recent years has reduced diagnosed infections by nearly half.

And we're going to keep pursuing scientific breakthroughs. Today I'm pleased to announce a new initiative at the National Institutes of Health to advance research into an HIV cure. We're going to redirect $100 million into this project to develop a new generation of therapies. Because the United States should be at the forefront of new discoveries into how to put HIV into long-term remission without requiring lifelong therapies – or, better yet, eliminate it completely.

And of course, this fight extends far beyond our borders. When I became President, I inherited President Bush's phenomenal program, PEPFAR, which has helped millions around the world receive lifesaving treatment. And we haven't just sustained those efforts, we've expanded them – reaching and serving even more people, especially mothers and children. Earlier this year, PEPFAR reached a wonderful milestone – the one millionth baby born without HIV. And that alongside the rapid decline in new HIV infections and deaths from AIDS in sub-Saharan Africa.

On my visit to South Africa this year, I visited a clinic run by Bishop Desmond Tutu and had the honor of spending time with some of their extraordinary young patients and counselors and outreach workers and doctors. Every day, they are doing extraordinary work. And when you visit this facility, you cannot help but be inspired by what they do each and every day, in part thanks to the support of the United States of America. They're saving lives and they're changing the way their country, and the world, approaches this disease. And that's work that we have to continue to advance.

On World AIDS Day two years ago, I set new prevention and treatment targets for PEPFAR, like increasing the number of mothers we reach so that we prevent their children from becoming infected, and helping 6 million people get treatment by the end of 2013. Today, I'm proud to announce that we've not only reached our goal, we've exceeded our treatment target. So we've helped 6.7 million people receive lifesaving treatment. And we're going to keep at it. Which is why, after I leave here today, I'll be proud to sign the PEPFAR Stewardship and Oversight Act, to keep this program going strong. Count on the legislator to applaud legislation.

Looking ahead, it's time for the world to come together to set new goals. Right now we're working hard to get a permanent leader in place at PEPFAR, and once we do, one of our first items of business will be convening a meeting early next year, so the United States and our partners worldwide – including governments, the Global Fund, UNAIDS, and civil society – can sit around one table and develop joint HIV prevention and treatment goals for the countries where we and the Global Fund do business. We'll hold each other accountable, and we'll continue to work to turn the tide of this epidemic together.

And that includes keeping up our support for the Global Fund. Its success speaks for itself. It's helping over 6 million people in over 140 countries receive antiretroviral therapy. And now it's time to replenish the Fund. The United States will contribute $1 for every $2 pledged by other donors over the next three years, up to $5 billion total from the United States. And the United Kingdom has made a similar promise.

So today I want to urge all those who are attending the Global Fund's replenishment meetings both today and tomorrow to take up this commitment. Don't leave our money on the table. It's been inspiring to see the countries most affected by this disease vastly increase their own contributions to this fight – in some cases, providing more than donor countries do. And that ought to inspire all of us to give more, to do more, so we can save more lives.

After all, none of the progress we've made against AIDS could have been achieved by a single government or foundation or corporation working alone. It's the result of countless people – including so many of you – working together from countries large and small, philanthropies, universities, media, civil society, activists. More than anything, I think it's thanks to the courageous people living with HIV around the world who've shared their stories; you've lent your strength, demanded your dignity be recognized, and led the fight to spare others the anguish of this disease.

We can't change the past or undo its wrenching pain. But what we can do – and what we have to do – is to chart a different future, guided by our love for those we couldn't save. That allows us to do everything we can, everything in our power to save those that we can. And that's my commitment to you as President.

The United States of America will remain the global leader in the fight against HIV and AIDS. We will stand with you every step of this journey until we reach the day that we know is possible, when all men and women can protect themselves from infection; a day when all people with HIV have access to the treatments that extend their lives; the day when there are no babies being born with HIV or AIDS, and when we achieve, at long last, what was once hard to imagine – and that's an AIDS-free generation.

That's the world I want for my daughters. That's the world that all of us want for our families. And if we stay focused, if we keep fighting, and if we honor the memory of those that we've lost, if we summon the same courage that they displayed, by insisting on whatever it takes, however long it takes, I believe we're going to win this fight. And I'm confident that we'll do so together.

So thank you very much for your extraordinary efforts. Appreciate it. God bless you. Thank you. Thank you. Good work.

Notes and References

1 Reprinted here as delivered and as it appear in the White House website. For the purposes of this book, only modification was deletion of words in parentheses which were included in the transcribed version of the speech, i.e. words denoting appeases, pauses and laughter.

President Bush Announces Five-Year, $30 Billion HIV/AIDS Plan

Rose Garden

THE PRESIDENT: Thank you all for coming. Welcome to the Rose Garden. Today, I'm joined by some very determined people who are battling one of the worst epidemics of modern times: the spread of HIV/AIDS.

I want to thank you all for being here. I'm honored to be in your presence, and I want to thank others who are joining us in this important cause, as well, starting with Ambassador Mark Dybul, who is the U.S. Global AIDS Coordinator. He runs our PEPFAR initiative. Mark, thank you for being here, as well as Rajat Gupta, who is the Chairman of the Board of the Global Fund to Fight AIDS, Tuberculosis, and Malaria. Rajat, we're proud you're here.

He's told me something very interesting. Actually, he and I attended the same graduate school, and he said, "It's important for people who have been successful in the business world to contribute something back to society." And Rajat, thank you for that spirit, and thank you for that compassion and concern.

Secretary Mike Leavitt is with us, Department of Health and Human Services; Ambassador John Negroponte, Deputy Secretary of State. I'm about to make an important initiative. I appreciate my – members of my administration for joining us to hear this initiative.

The U.S. and our citizens have tackled HIV/AIDS aggressively. Many HIV-positive Americans are able to lead productive lives. The story has been quite different elsewhere, especially in sub-Saharan Africa.

When I took office, an HIV diagnosis in Africa's poorest communities was usually a death sentence. Parents watched their babies die needlessly because local clinics lacked effective treatments. The story of a mother of Kenya affected me deeply when she couldn't afford drugs, except for one person in her family. So she forgave [sic] her own treatment to save her son.

Despairing families who had lost everything to AIDS started to believe that they had been cursed by the Almighty God. This modern-day plague robbed Africa and other countries of the hope of progress, and threatened to push many communities toward chaos.

The United States has responded vigorously to this crisis. In 2003, I asked Congress to approve an emergency plan for AIDS relief. Our nation pledged $15 billion over five years for HIV/AIDS prevention, treatment and care in many of the poorest nations on Earth. In the years since, thanks to the support of the United States Congress and the American people, our country has met this pledge. This level of assistance is unprecedented, and the largest commitment by any nation to combat a single disease in human history.

This investment has yielded the best possible return: saved lives. To date, the emergency plan has supported treatment for 1.1 million people infected with HIV. This is a promising start, yet without further action, the legislation that funded this emergency plan is set to expire in 2008. Today I ask Congress to demonstrate America's continuing commitment to fighting the scourge of HIV/AIDS by reauthorizing this legislation now. I ask Congress to double our initial commitment and approve an additional $30 billion for HIV/AIDS prevention, for care, and for treatment over the next five years.

This money will be spent wisely through the establishment of partnership compacts with host nations. These compacts would ensure that U.S. funds support programs that have the greatest possible impact and are sustainable for the future. America will work with governments, the private sector, and faith- and community-based organizations around the world to meet measurable goals: to support treatment for nearly 2.5 million people, to prevent more than 12 million new infections, and to support care for 12 million people, including more than 5 million orphans and vulnerable children.

To help assess the progress we have made to date, Laura, the First Lady, is going to go to Africa next month. She's going to meet with community leaders and visit with participants in HIV/AIDS programs during her trip to Zambia, Senegal, Mali, and Mozambique. And she's going to come back with her findings. I really thank her for her concern about HIV/AIDS. She and I share a passion. We believe strongly that to whom much is given, much is required. Much has been given to the United States of America. Therefore, I believe strongly, as does she, that much is required of us in helping solve this problem.

The statistics and dollar amounts I've cited in the fight against HIV/AIDS are significant. But the scale of this effort is not measured in numbers. This is really a story of the human spirit and the goodness of human hearts. Once again, the generosity of the American people is one of the great untold stories of our time. Our citizens are offering comfort to millions who suffer, and restoring hope to those who feel forsaken.

You know, one good example of this good work is supported by – that the U.S. supports is called the Coptic Hope Center in Nairobi, Kenya. Three years ago, the center had a staff of four people, and resources to treat no more than five HIV/AIDS patients a day. Today, the staff consists of 40 people and 10 volunteers who provide care and treatment services to over 6,000 people. I want to thank the

Director of the Hope Center, Bishop Paul, who's with us today. I want to thank you for being here. I want to thank you for your leadership and for your care for your fellow human beings.

Dr. Bill Pape is with us, as well. Dr. Pape is an expert on infectious diseases and founded in Haiti a leading HIV treatment program, which is a major PEPFAR partner. Dr. Pape has shown that even in the most difficult circumstances, dedicated and caring people can make great progress in fighting HIV/AIDS. We're sure proud you're here, doc. Thanks for coming.

Also with us is Kunene Tantoh. Kunene is HIV-positive. She coordinates a mentoring program supported by U.S. funds for other mothers with HIV in Cape Town, South Africa. Kunene is proof that people with HIV can live productive lives and make a significant difference in the lives of others. Kunene, I want to thank you for joining us. Thank you for bringing Baron. Baron is four years old, and he's letting us know. (Laughter.) We appreciate you all coming. Thank you for the example you have set.

Similar success stories are playing out all across the African continent where victims of HIV/AIDS are finding new reservoirs of strength and support. Villages in Africa now talk of the Lazarus effect, dying communities being brought back to life, thanks to the compassion of the American people. This is the impact that has made our emergency plan and the modern-day good Samaritans who are implementing it so effective. It's important that we continue the work we have begun.

I'm honored that you were here today. I'm honored to be representing a nation that cares deeply about the suffering of others. I look forward to working with Congress on this great and noble effort.

May God bless you all. May God continue to bless the United States.

END 1:22 P.M. EDT

http://georgewbush-whitehouse.archives.gov/news/releases/2007/05/20070530-6.html

Index

E

M

Q